Digital Ethics Lab Yearbook

Series Editors

The Digital Ethics Lab Yearbook is an annual publication covering the ethical challenges posed by digital innovation. It provides an overview of the research from the Digital Ethics Lab at the Oxford Internet Institute. Volumes in the series aim to identify the benefits and enhance the positive opportunities of digital innovation as a force for good, and avoid or mitigate its risks and shortcomings. The volumes build on Oxford's world leading expertise in conceptual design, horizon scanning, foresight analysis, and translational research on ethics, governance, and policy making.

More information about this series at http://www.springer.com/series/16214

Christopher Burr • Silvia Milano
Editors

The 2019 Yearbook of the Digital Ethics Lab

Springer

Editors
Christopher Burr
Digital Ethics Lab
Oxford Internet Institute,
University of Oxford
Oxford, UK

Silvia Milano
Digital Ethics Lab
Oxford Internet Institute,
University of Oxford
Oxford, UK

ISSN 2524-7719 ISSN 2524-7727 (electronic)
Digital Ethics Lab Yearbook
ISBN 978-3-030-29144-0 ISBN 978-3-030-29145-7 (eBook)
https://doi.org/10.1007/978-3-030-29145-7

This Springer imprint is published by the registered company Springer Nature Switzerland AG.
The registered company address is: Gewerbestrasse 11, 6330 Cham, Switzerland

Acknowledgements

We would like to acknowledge the entire community of the Oxford Internet Institute. It is a remarkable department and truly one of the best places where to conduct the inherently interdisciplinary research with which all the contributors to this volume are engaged.

In addition, the seminars run by the Digital Ethics Lab (DELab) provide a stimulating and supportive environment to test research ideas at an early stage. We would like to acknowledge the ongoing support from all the DELab's members, past and present, and not just the contributors to the current collection. The DELab is fortunate to be able to invite many fascinating speakers to the seminars, and the academic year 2018–2019 has been no exception. We would like to thank Ivana Bartoletti, Nigel Crook, Natalia Efremova, Paul Galwas, Omar Guerrero, Tony Hart, Funmi Olorunnipa, Thomas Philbeck, Paul Timmers, and Genevieve Vanderstichele, all of whom had delivered thought-provoking talks and contributions.

On a personal note, we would like to thank Carl Öhman and David Watson. As the Editors of the previous volume, their advice and insights were very helpful. We would also like to thank Danuta Farah for all her support and for keeping the DELab running so smoothly.

We would like to acknowledge the funders of the DELab—The Alan Turing Institute, Facebook, Google, Oxford's John Fell Fund, Microsoft, and Engineering and Physical Sciences Research Council (EPSRC)—and thank them for supporting our research unconditionally. We are also deeply grateful to Springer Nature for publishing the yearbook and in particular to Ties Nijssen for his interest in the DELab and support during the process that led to the publication of this volume.

Finally, our thanks to Luciano Floridi and Mariarosaria Taddeo. As Director and Deputy Director of the DELab, respectively, their ongoing advice, encouragement, and tireless efforts to ensure the DELab remains a world-leading group in Digital Ethics are greatly appreciated by all.

We look forward to seeing what 2019–2020 holds in store.

The Editors
Christopher Burr and Silvia Milano

Contents

Contributors

Nikita Aggarwal Faculty of Law, University of Oxford, Oxford, UK
Oxford Internet Institute, University of Oxford, Oxford, UK

Christopher Burr Digital Ethics Lab, Oxford Internet Institute, University of Oxford, Oxford, UK

Josh Cowls Oxford Internet Institute, University of Oxford, Oxford, UK
The Alan Turing Institute, London, UK

Luciano Floridi Oxford Internet Institute, University of Oxford, Oxford, UK
The Alan Turing Institute, London, UK

Robert Gorwa Department of Politics and International Relations, University of Oxford, Oxford, UK

Silvia Milano Digital Ethics Lab, Oxford Internet Institute, University of Oxford, Oxford, UK

Jessica Morley Oxford Internet Institute, University of Oxford, Oxford, UK

Carl Öhman Oxford Internet Institute, University of Oxford, Oxford, UK

Julia Slupska Oxford Internet Institute, University of Oxford, Oxford, UK

Mariarosaria Taddeo Oxford Internet Institute, University of Oxford, Oxford, UK
The Alan Turing Institute, London, UK

David Watson Oxford Internet Institute, University of Oxford, Oxford, UK
The Alan Turing Institute, London, UK

Chapter 1
Introduction to the 2019 Yearbook of the Digital Ethics Lab

Christopher Burr and Silvia Milano

Abstract Digital technologies, like artificial intelligence (AI), continue to reshape our lives in profound ways. If we are to maximise the associated opportunities while minimising the potential risks, it is vital that we first have a clear understanding of the myriad ways that technologies can alter patterns of human activity. The chapters of the 2019 Yearbook of the Digital Ethics Lab aim at advancing such an understanding by contributing to ongoing discussions and research. This chapter provides a contextual introduction for the Yearbook and a brief summary of each of the subsequent chapters.

Keywords 2019 Yearbook · Digital Ethics Lab · Data Ethics · Ethics of technology · Conceptual engineering

1.1 Introduction

Digital technologies, like artificial intelligence (AI), continue to reshape our lives in profound ways. For example, they have furthered our understanding and delivery of healthcare by offering new ways to treat mental health issues (Lucas et al. 2017), and intergovernmental organisations are exploring how AI can help achieve sustainable development goals across the globe (Chui et al. 2019). However, at the same time, concerns remain over the use of machine learning technologies to disrupt online platforms through misuse of targeted advertising and real-time bidding (ICO 2019). If we are to maximise the opportunities of these novel technologies, while minimising the potential risks, it is vital that we first have a clear understanding of the myriad ways that technologies can alter existing patterns of human activity, both

C. Burr (✉) · S. Milano
Digital Ethics Lab, Oxford Internet Institute, University of Oxford, Oxford, UK
e-mail: christopher.burr@oii.ox.ac.uk; silvia.milano@oii.ox.ac.uk

C. Burr, S. Milano (eds.), *The 2019 Yearbook of the Digital Ethics Lab*,
Digital Ethics Lab Yearbook, https://doi.org/10.1007/978-3-030-29145-7_1

at the individual and social level and also directly (e.g. by influencing choice behaviour via personalised and targeted recommendations) or indirectly (e.g. by mediating our relationship to the natural environment through ubiquitous sensors and big data streams). The chapters in this collection all aim at advancing such an understanding by contributing to ongoing discussions and research.

Each year, the Digital Ethics Lab (DELab) Yearbook aims to showcase the research of the lab's members, focusing on salient and timely themes that capture a snapshot of the ongoing debates. Although the lab's members work on a wide range of topics, across many disciplines, their research is interwoven through a shared focus on some of the most pressing ethical questions that we face as citizens of increasingly digital societies. The chapters of this second volume of the DELab Yearbook follow this trend and continue to express a shared and unifying interest in digital ethics.

This year, by way of an introduction, we have chosen to emphasise another recurring theme that is present in many of the chapters: the implicit belief that if we wish to understand how technology is reshaping our lives, it is vital that we first attend to the concepts we employ to frame and regulate our discussions. The following two sections offer a theoretical perspective that can support this belief and an illustrative example of the ethical significance that concepts can have in our study of digital technologies. We then close by offering a brief summary of the following chapters.

1.2 Representing Ourselves, Others, and Our Environment

Philosophers and cognitive scientists often treat concepts as mental representations: the constituents of thought that allow us to perceive and interact with the world, as well as engaging in other cognitive processes such as learning, categorisation, judgement, imagination, and decision-making. For example, in development psychology, concepts are considered by many to play a central role in explaining our ability to learn and categorise objects, e.g. acquiring the concept CAT allows children to learn about many different cats by providing a superordinate category that groups them together based upon shared characteristics, while also allowing them to differentiate cats from dogs (Carey 2009).[1]

In recent years, theoretical and empirical developments in the cognitive sciences have cast new light on the role that our concepts play in influencing our perception (both of the external world and our internal states) (Clark 2016), our emotions (Seth 2013), our decision-making (Burr 2017), and our actions (Adams et al. 2013). Known collectively as 'predictive processing', this research programme maintains that the brain combines prior knowledge with incoming sensory evidence to yield a representation that reflects the brain's best guess concerning the most likely state of

[1] We adopt the common practice found in the literature on concepts of using small caps to differentiate the concept (e.g. CAT) from the object it signifies (e.g. cat).

the world. According to this account, our brains continuously generate predictions about the state of the world, across a variety of spatiotemporal scales, and incoming sensory information acts as an error signal to inform the brain which of its predictions are accurate, and which require refining and updating. The descending predictions thus represent what the brain already "knows" about the world and the current context, and incoming sensory information continually keeps this "knowledge" in check.

Underlying this research is the claim that high-level concepts (or, mental representations) should be treated as top-down constraints on this process of predictive inference about the perceptual states we expect to encounter (both in the world and within our bodies), conditional upon the actions that we take. For example, possession of the concept CUP will constrain and shape actions in the world (e.g. reaching and grabbing), as well as the possible perceptual states we experience (e.g. expecting to see a cup on your desk; being sad when there is no coffee in the cup).[2] Some of this research has begun to show how the very words (or, linguistic concepts) we employ influence the way we perceive states of the world (Lupyan and Clark 2015), extending the role that language plays in both cognition and perception (Boroditsky 2010; Casasanto 2008). As Lupyan and Clark (2015, p. 282, emphasis added) note, "[l]anguage not only functions as a means of communicating our thoughts but plays an *active role in shaping them*. Rather than passively reflecting the joints of nature, words and larger constructions help carve joints into nature."

This shaping can occur indirectly by co-opting our affective systems and in turn altering our emotional judgements and engagement with certain objects, (e.g. approaching an encounter with a colleague under the expectation of hostile intentions that colour the way we interpret their actions and statement Barrett and Bar 2009). Alternatively, this influence can occur more directly by influencing our attentional processes such that we assign greater importance to particular states of the world and, therefore, reorient ourselves towards these states over others, (e.g. orienting our visual gaze towards the lip movements of a conversational partner when in a noisy environment that impacts our ability to hear what they are saying Hohwy 2012).

What do the above developments have to do with digital ethics? The short answer is that findings from the behavioural and cognitive sciences play an important role in teaching us about ourselves (e.g. how we reason, decide, and act) and, therefore, may prove to be consequential in helping us form a clearer understanding of how technology is reshaping our lives and society. The aforementioned developments are no exception. It is possible that they may offer us a theoretical foundation to support the claim that the choices we make about which concepts to employ are not merely semantic quibbles but consequential decisions that can profoundly impact the way we live our lives and structure our societies. More specifically, they provide the means for considering how the concepts we employ may alter the way we per-

[2] This is a very brief overview of an interesting but complex account. For an accessible overview, see Clark (2016).

ceive, evaluate, attend, and act in relation to digital technologies. From this basis, we can consider whether certain choices have ethical significance.

To give an illustrative example, consider the following. You purchase the latest personal tracking device, which monitors your daily behaviours in order to learn about your habits and activities, with the overall aim of steering you towards outcomes that are expected to be more conducive to your overall well-being (e.g. daily meditation practice, more frequent exercise, better time management). Let's also assume that, in order to achieve this goal, the smart device measures relevant biometric signals (e.g. heart-rate variability, skin conductance, etc.) in order to monitor your overall level of attention and emotional engagement in a particular task.[3] In order to provide meaningful feedback from which you can learn, the smart device will need to (re)present this information back to you. It could do this through a quantitative scale (e.g. a 0–10 scale that represents your emotional engagement), a qualitative scale (e.g. 'very distracted' to 'highly attentive'), or even some imagistic representation (e.g. emoticons that depict a happy or sad individual).

From the perspective of predictive processing, these digital representations may be in partial competition with the internal concepts that our brains have evolved to rely upon. That is, both seek to represent an individual's affective state, but on the basis of very different sources of information. Typically, when we form predictions that pertain to our own emotional states and associated concepts (e.g. HAPPINESS or SADNESS), they are refined and updated according to the error signals that originate from within our bodies or, in the case of another person, their perceived bodily expressions (e.g. a red face signifying anger). However, personal trackers aim to bypass this process—known as 'interoception'—and instead monitor our emotions through a variety of techniques that rely on the external measurement of biometric signals.[4] In addition to ongoing questions regarding the accuracy and validity of these measurement procedures, there is the further concern about how this information is stored and presented to the user. For instance, unlike digital representations, our inner emotional states are not perpetually recorded in discrete forms in silico. Rather, our emotions are typically appraisals of our current context, and assumed to provide salient information about how to act in the current environment (Frijda et al. 1989). They have an immediacy and embeddedness that connects us to the present in ways that permanently stored digital representations do not.

It remains an open question how the use of digital technologies that seek to (re) conceptualise the process of emotional understanding and engagement will alter the way we seek to represent ourselves, others, and our wider environment. For the present purpose, it suffices to note that this may be just one of many examples of

[3] In case these ideas seems outlandish, see the following article that discusses the use of attention-monitoring technologies being tested in classrooms (Mehta 2019), and the following handbook of the ways in which technologies can measure emotional states (Calvo et al. 2015).

[4] See Calvo et al. (2015) for an introduction to current techniques in affective computing and Burr and Cristianini (2019) for an overview of the digital footprints that can be used to infer psychological characteristics of users.

how digital technologies could disrupt patterns of perception, cognition, and action, by seeking to alter the way we conceptualise our world.

1.3 Predicting, Persuading, and Supporting Ourselves and Others

The previous section highlights the importance of conceptual engineering from a theoretical standpoint. In this section, we briefly illustrate how this applies to new digital technologies with an example taken from the field of personalisation and recommendation systems.

One of the most prominent current applications of machine learning (ML) is in personalisation and recommendation systems (Zanker et al. 2019). Leveraging vast amounts of user data, these systems structure the digital environments in which we operate (e.g. serving us targeted advertisements or curating our news feeds) and can have profound impacts on our preferences and sense of identity. A typical way to frame the technical task of a recommender system is "finding good items" (Jannach and Adomavicius 2016) for the user, that is items that are relevant, beneficial, or match the user's preferences, depending on the context. As noted by Jannach and Adomavicius, much of the earlier research on recommender systems has been concerned with a specific formulation of the problem—recommending items on the basis of datasets containing user ratings—and with the main focus on improving the accuracy with which then system predicts user ratings.[5] In other words, the problem formulation that has been standardly adopted in the recommender system community has focused the attention on modelling individual users, in order to serve them recommendations that will generate predictable behaviour (such as rating film, clicking through a link, or purchasing a recommended item). This individualistic, behavioural conceptual framing of the recommendation problem has a natural theoretical background in the microeconomic theory of revealed preferences, sharing some of its shortcomings.

The first, relatively obvious, shortcoming of this user-centred, individualistic conceptualisation of the recommendation problem is that it obscures how recommendations affect other stakeholders, giving a social dimension to the problem. The interests of service providers, for instance, can be very directly affected by the recommendation algorithm. In the absence of an explicit recognition of this feature of recommendation, the interests of other stakeholders are often accommodated as a

[5] The famed Netflix Prize, a $1 million award that was announced in 2006 for the algorithm that could improve the accuracy of Netflix's own system for predicting user ratings of films by at least 10%, was probably instrumental in fixing the standard problem for recommender systems research as that of predicting user ratings. Interestingly, Netflix did not implement the winning algorithm into its recommender system, due to efficiency issues, as the increase in accuracy was offset by increased computational complexity, but the teams who worked on the Netflix dataset produced technical breakthroughs that had wide influence in the field.

second thought, introducing a bias in the recommendation algorithm (Jameson et al. 2015; Paraschakis 2018), or indirectly by picking a specific proxy to infer the user's preference for recommended items, for example using purchase or click-through rates, which match the providers' or the system's interests. This has only recently come under the attention of researchers (Milano et al. 2019), leading to a recent re-conceptualisation of recommender systems as multi-stakeholder environments (Abdollahpouri et al. 2017; Burke and Abdollahpouri 2017; Jannach and Adomavicius 2016; Zheng 2017). The recognition of the social dimension of recommender systems highlights how the way we conceptualise the task of any algorithmic system is not neutral. The choice of which measures to optimise, and how to evaluate the system's performance, is always a normative one. Ideally, this should respond to the interests of all the stakeholders. In practice, however, this is very difficult to achieve.

The second issue with the user-centred, individualistic conceptualisation of the recommendation problem is that it assumes or presupposes a fixed set of underlying user attitudes. The focus on accuracy measures, in particular, is indicative of this concern. Recommendations, however, can be used to nudge and to persuade, with the effect to modify user preferences (Jameson et al. 2015; Tintarev and Masthoff 2011), or function as 'traps', exploiting features of the user's psychology in order to influence their behaviour (Seaver 2018). In some contexts, users can also approach recommender systems explicitly with the purpose of learning about their preferences and be able to modify them, as has been observed in a study of a popular music recommender system by Karakayali et al. (2018).

The third issue concerns the conception of personal identity that underlies recommender systems. Within these systems, users are typically categorised on the basis of the available demographic data and past recorded interactions with the system. This representation is essentially synchronic, reflecting the totality of the information available to the system, and is not directly accessible to the user. But personal identity is in important respects something that is under construction, malleable, that changes over time reflecting the trajectories and plans in our lives. It is also treated by certain ethical frameworks as a core right of individuals to self-determine and choose their own identities and pursue a life of flourishing (Sen 2010). These trajectories and plans are shaped by personal choices, but are also constrained by the opportunities afforded by our environments (de Vries 2010). This identity-shaping aspect of recommendations needs to be better conceptualised and integrated in the design of recommender systems.

The conceptualisation of identity has also significant implications for in the for how we approach the issue of algorithmic fairness in the context of recommendation. One of the issues that are often discussed in relation to algorithmic decision making, especially in social domains, is their tendency to reproduce or further entrench social biases, and perpetuating discrimination (Chakraborty et al. 2019; Edizel et al. 2019; Zhu et al. 2018). Technical approaches to the issue of fairness-aware recommendation focus on defining relevant sets of protected characteristics, and devising recommendation algorithms that minimise measures of unfairness relative to the groups determined by these characteristics. One issue that this approach faces, however, is that the selection of protected categories can itself be sensitive to social biases, as well as to considerations of intersectionality. For example, how will the recommender treat a user who belongs to a protected category with respect to race, but not with respect to gender? Conceptualising recommender systems as multi-stakeholder platforms goes some way to help us address these issues in greater clarity (Abdollahpouri et al. 2019).

1.4 Summary of Chapters

The issues raised and discussed in each of the chapters have myriad implications for how we think about and frame the impact of digital technologies on society. While there is no clear division between the chapters that would necessitate grouping them into distinct sections, we have tried to order the contributions to this volume according to shared themes. This is most evident in the first two chapters that focus on cybersecurity.

In Chap. 2, Slupska and Taddeo argue that policy-makers involved in cybersecurity governance need to pay closer attention to the "generative metaphors" they use to describe and understand new technologies. As we have argued in this introduction, the concepts we deploy have the potential to shape how we perceive and interact with the world. Slupska and Taddeo demonstrate the significance of this point by focusing on the metaphor of 'cyber war', and arguing that it diminishes possibilities for international collaboration in a number of key ways. Instead, they suggest alternative metaphors designed to provide a more collaborative conceptual frame for cybersecurity governance.

Taddeo continues the focus on cybersecurity in Chap. 3, where she offers a theory of cyber deterrence and outlines the regulatory and strategic implications for state actors. Her discussion takes as a starting point the observation that the current understanding of cyber conflicts is based on an analogy with more traditional domains of kinetic violence, which is too restrictive.

In Chap. 4, Watson takes a broader perspective and investigates the tendency towards anthropomorphism when conceptualising AI. He surveys a range of learning techniques, including neural network algorithms, in order to assess their "anthropomorphic credentials". While technical in nature, the purpose of this discussion is to highlight the practical implications of adopting the wrong conceptual metaphors. Most notably, Watson argues that by inappropriately anthropomorphizing a statistical model, we may risk granting it a degree of agency that overstates its own abilities, while robbing us of our own. The ethical implications of this issue are most starkly noticed in sensitive social domains such as financial or criminal risk assessment and medicine.

In Chap. 5, Burr and Morley critique the concept of 'empowerment' in digital health technologies. Similar research that critiques the use of empowerment exists (Morley and Floridi 2019), but in this chapter the authors focus on the topic of mental health specifically. Because of the particular challenges that mental health issues raise, both for the individuals who are suffering and the healthcare system more generally, over-use of the concept 'empowerment' can prevent designers, policymakers, and other stakeholders from recognising the additional barriers that prevent individuals from accessing the help that they need. As such, Burr and Morley argue that we should focus on how to design and govern to promote *engagement*, prior to empowerment, and use the framework of biomedical ethics to structure their analysis and recommendations.

In Chap. 6, Aggarwal and Floridi take an in-depth look at the risks involved with publishing country of origin information (COI) reports, such as the potential harms to subjects of the reports and/or those involved in their development. COI reports are routinely developed and used to support decision-making in the asylum process, and are used both by governmental agencies, asylum seekers, and their legal advisers, for a variety of reasons that the authors discuss. Alongside other contributions, the article primarily focuses on the question of 'how to publish COI reports in an ethical manner'.

In Chap. 7, Cowls draws on the work of Max Weber to explore the present democratic deficit of AI, which, as he highlights through its power to "rationalise", is changing the relationship between individuals and the state. His discussion highlights the importance of formulating the right questions to frame the discussion on the features of AI that matter most for democratic institutions.

In Chap. 8, Öhman et al. explore the phenomenon of so-called *Islamic Prayer Apps*—applications which automatically post Islamic prayers from their users' social media accounts. The authors argue that, despite being accountable for millions of tweets daily, religious motivations for online social automation have gone under the radar of mainstream researchers. Moreover, as the profiles from which the prayers are tweeted are not purely bots, but authentic users who have merely automated an aspect of their social life, the phenomenon put into question the current discourse on online automation, placing tension on the *conceptual assumption* that 'bots' and 'not bots' exist as distinct categories that can be easily separated. This reveals an opportunity to broaden the scope of the current research agenda on online automation. As such, the chapter calls for conceptual engineering that goes beyond the bot/user dichotomy.

Finally, Chap. 9, contributed by DELab director Luciano Floridi, provides a perfect bookend to this year's collection by asking what the future of AI could be. The discussion of the likely future directions of AI research follow two threads: (i) the shift from historical to synthetic data, and (ii) the translation of what Floridi calls 'difficult tasks' (that is, tasks that typically require complex sensory-motor abilities) into what he calls 'complex tasks' (which are computationally demanding, but require only minimal abilities to complete). Both trends highlight the need for careful consideration of conceptual framing in identifying the relevant features that permit us to generate safe and representative synthetic data and translate difficult tasks into complex ones.

References

Abdollahpouri, H., R. Burke, and B. Mobasher. 2017. Recommender Systems as Multistakeholder Environments. In *Proceedings of the 25th Conference on User Modeling, Adaptation and Personalization – UMAP'17*, 347–348. https://doi.org/10.1145/3079628.3079657.

Abdollahpouri, H., G. Adomavicius, R. Burke, I. Guy, D. Jannach, T. Kamishima, … L. Pizzato. 2019. Beyond Personalization: Research Directions in Multistakeholder Recommendation. *ArXiv*: 1905.01986 [Cs]. Retrieved from http://arxiv.org/abs/1905.01986.

Adams, R.A., S. Shipp, and K.J. Friston. 2013. Predictions Not Commands: Active Inference in the Motor System. *Brain Structure and Function* 218 (3): 611–643. https://doi.org/10.1007/s00429-012-0475-5.

Barrett, L.F., and M. Bar. 2009. See It with Feeling: Affective Predictions During Object Perception. *Philosophical Transactions of the Royal Society B: Biological Sciences* 364 (1521): 1325–1334. https://doi.org/10.1098/rstb.2008.0312.

Boroditsky, L. 2010. How the Languages we Speak Shape the Ways We Think: The FAQs. In *The Cambridge Handbook of Psycholinguistics*, ed. M.J. Spivey, K. McRae, and M. Joanisse, 615–632. New York: Cambridge University Press.

Burke, R., and H. Abdollahpouri. 2017. Patterns of Multistakeholder Recommendation. *ArXiv*: 1707.09258 [Cs]. Retrieved from http://arxiv.org/abs/1707.09258.

Burr, C.D. 2017. Embodied Decisions and the Predictive Brain. *Philosophy and Predictive Processing*. https://doi.org/10.15502/9783958573086.

Burr, C., and N. Cristianini. 2019. Can Machines Read Our Minds? *Minds and Machines*. https://doi.org/10.1007/s11023-019-09497-4.

Calvo, R.A., S. D'Mello, J. Gratch, and A. Kappas. 2015. *The Oxford Handbook of Affective Computing*, Oxford Library of Psychology. New York: Oxford University Press.

Carey, S. 2009. *The origin of concepts*. New York: Oxford University Press.

Casasanto, D. 2008. Who's Afraid of the Big Bad Whorf? Crosslinguistic Differences in Temporal Language and Thought. *Language Learning* 58: 63–79.

Chakraborty, A., G.K. Patro, N. Ganguly, K.P. Gummadi, and P. Loiseau. 2019. Equality of Voice: Towards Fair Representation in Crowdsourced Top-K Recommendations. *FAT*. https://doi.org/10.1145/3287560.3287570.

Chui, M., R. Chung, and A. van Heteren. 2019. *Using AI to Help Achieve Sustainable Development Goals*. Retrieved 28 June 2019, from UNDP website: https://www.undp.org/content/undp/en/home/blog/2019/Using_AI_to_help_achieve_Sustainable_Development_Goals.html.

Clark, A. 2016. *Surfing Uncertainty: Prediction, Action and the Embodied Mind*. New York: Oxford University Press.

de Vries, K. 2010. Identity, Profiling Algorithms and a World of Ambient Intelligence. *Ethics and Information Technology* 12 (1): 71–85. https://doi.org/10.1007/s10676-009-9215-9.

Edizel, B., F. Bonchi, S. Hajian, A. Panisson, and T. Tassa. 2019. FaiRecSys: Mitigating Algorithmic Bias in Recommender systems. *International Journal of Data Science and Analytics*: 1–17. https://doi.org/10.1007/s41060-019-00181-5.

Frijda, N.H., P. Kuipers, and E. Ter Schure. 1989. Relations Among Emotion, Appraisal, and Emotional Action Readiness. *Journal of Personality and Social Psychology* 57 (2): 212.

Hohwy, J. 2012. Attention and Conscious Perception in the Hypothesis Testing Brain. *Frontiers in Psychology* 3. https://doi.org/10.3389/fpsyg.2012.00096.

ICO. 2019. *Update Report into ADTECH and Real Time Bidding*. Retrieved from Information Commissioner's Office Website: https://ico.org.uk/media/about-the-ico/documents/2615156/adtech-real-time-bidding-report-201906.pdf.

Jameson, A., M.C. Willemsen, A. Felfernig, M. de Gemmis, P. Lops, G. Semeraro, and L. Chen. 2015. Human Decision Making and Recommender Systems. In *Recommender Systems Handbook*, ed. F. Ricci, L. Rokach, and B. Shapira, 611–648. https://doi.org/10.1007/978-1-4899-7637-6_18.

Jannach, D., and G. Adomavicius. 2016. Recommendations with a Purpose. In *Proceedings of the 10th ACM Conference on Recommender Systems – RecSys'16*, 7–10. https://doi.org/10.1145/2959100.2959186.

Karakayali, N., B. Kostem, and I. Galip. 2018. Recommendation Systems as Technologies of the self: Algorithmic Control and the Formation of Music Taste. *Theory, Culture & Society* 35 (2): 3–24. https://doi.org/10.1177/0263276417722391.

Lucas, G.M., A. Rizzo, J. Gratch, S. Scherer, G. Stratou, J. Boberg, and L.-P. Morency. 2017. Reporting Mental Health Symptoms: Breaking Down Barriers to Care with Virtual Human Interviewers. *Frontiers in Robotics and AI* 4. https://doi.org/10.3389/frobt.2017.00051.

Lupyan, G., and A. Clark. 2015. Words and the World: Predictive Coding and the Language-Perception-Cognition Interface. *Current Directions in Psychological Science* 24 (4): 279–284. https://doi.org/10.1177/0963721415570732.

Mehta, I. 2019. *China Is Reportedly Trialing Attention-Detecting Bands in Schools*. Retrieved 29 May, 2019, from The Next Web website: https://thenextweb.com/plugged/2019/04/05/china-is-reportedly-trialling-attention-detecting-bands-in-schools/.

Milano, S., M. Taddeo, and L. Floridi. 2019. Recommender Systems and Their Ethical Challenges. *SSRN Electronic Journal*. https://doi.org/10.2139/ssrn.3378581.

Morley, J., and L. Floridi. 2019. *The Limits of Empowerment: How to Reframe the Role of mHealth Tools in the Healthcare Ecosystem*, 25. https://doi.org/10.1007/s11948-019-00115-1.

Paraschakis, D. 2018. *Algorithmic and Ethical Aspects of Recommender Systems in E-Commerce*. PhD thesis, Malmö. Retrieved from http://muep.mau.se/bitstream/handle/2043/24268/2043_24268 Paraschakis.pdf?sequence=3&isAllowed=y.

Seaver, N. 2018. Captivating Algorithms: Recommender Systems as Traps. *Journal of Material Culture*: 1359183518820366. https://doi.org/10.1177/1359183518820366.

Sen, A. 2010. *The Idea of Justice*. London: Penguin.

Seth, A.K. 2013. Interoceptive Inference, Emotion, and the Embodied Self. *Trends in Cognitive Sciences* 17 (11): 565–573. https://doi.org/10.1016/j.tics.2013.09.007.

Tintarev, N., and J. Masthoff. 2011. Designing and Evaluating Explanations for Recommender Systems. In *Recommender Systems Handbook*, ed. F. Ricci, L. Rokach, B. Shapira, and P.B. Kantor, 479–510. https://doi.org/10.1007/978-0-387-85820-3_15.

Zanker, M., L. Rook, and D. Jannach. 2019. Measuring the Impact of Online Personalisation: Past, Present and Future. *International Journal of Human-Computer Studies*. https://doi.org/10.1016/j.ijhcs.2019.06.006.

Zheng, Y. 2017. Multi-stakeholder Recommendation: Applications and Challenges. *ArXiv*: 1707.08913 [Cs]. Retrieved from http://arxiv.org/abs/1707.08913.

Zhu, Z., X. Hu, and J. Caverlee. 2018. Fairness-Aware Tensor-Based Recommendation. *CIKM*. https://doi.org/10.1145/3269206.3271795.

Christopher Burr is a philosopher of cognitive science and artificial intelligence. His research explores philosophical and ethical issues related to the opportunities and risks that digital technologies pose for mental health and well-being.

He has held previous posts at the University of Bristol, where he explored the ethical and epistemological impact of big data and artificial intelligence and completed his PhD in 2017.

Research Interests: Philosophy of Cognitive Science and Artificial Intelligence, Ethics of Artificial Intelligence, Philosophy of Technology, Decision Theory, and Philosophy of Mind.

Silvia Milano is a Postdoctoral Researcher at the Digital Ethics Lab. Her research focuses on the ethics of AI and looks in particular at the ethical challenges posed by recommender systems.

Silvia completed a PhD in Philosophy at the London School of Economics and Political Science.

Research interests: Philosophy and Ethics of AI, Recommender Systems, Formal Epistemology.

Chapter 2
Generative Metaphors in Cybersecurity Governance

Julia Slupska and Mariarosaria Taddeo

Abstract Policy-makers involved in cybersecurity governance should pay close attention to the "generative metaphors" they use to describe and understand new technologies. Generative metaphors structure our understanding of policy problems by imposing mental models of both the problem and possible solutions. As a result, they can also constrain ethical reasoning about new technologies, by uncritically carrying over assumptions about moral roles and obligations from an existing domain. The discussion of global governance of cybersecurity problems has to date been dominated by the metaphor of "cyber war". In this chapter, we argue that this metaphor diminishes possibilities for international collaboration in this area by limiting states to reactive policies of naming and shaming rather than proactive actions to address systemic features of cyberspace. We suggest that alternative metaphors—such as health, ecosystem, and architecture—can help expose the dominance of the war metaphor and provide a more collaborative and conceptually accurate frame for negotiations.

Keywords Cyber norms · Cybersecurity · Governance · Conceptual metaphors · Generative metaphors · Cyber war

J. Slupska (✉)
Oxford Internet Institute, University of Oxford, Oxford, UK
e-mail: Julia.slupska@cybersecurity.ox.ac.uk

M. Taddeo
Oxford Internet Institute, University of Oxford, Oxford, UK

The Alan Turing Institute, London, UK
e-mail: mariarosaria.taddeo@oii.ox.ac.uk

C. Burr, S. Milano (eds.), *The 2019 Yearbook of the Digital Ethics Lab*,
Digital Ethics Lab Yearbook, https://doi.org/10.1007/978-3-030-29145-7_2

2.1 Introduction

The debate on the regulation of international "cyber warfare" is a negotiation over the assignment of moral obligations. Consider the example of the WannaCry ransomware attack, which affected more than 200,000 computers across 150 countries, with total damages estimated at billions of dollars (Berr 2017). In this case, a hacking group—attributed by the US and UK governments to North Korea—targeted a vulnerability in the Microsoft Windows operating system. The vulnerability had been discovered by the US National Security Agency (NSA) but not disclosed to the public (Collier 2018). A hacking group named the Shadow Brokers stole the vulnerability from the NSA and released it online, making the WannaCry attack possible. In this complex web of actors and cyber intrusions, whom do we blame for the billions of dollars of damage and impaired functionality in crucial services like hospitals? Is it just the hacking group behind the attack? Or the US government, which did not disclose a potentially dangerous vulnerability? Or Microsoft, for creating software with vulnerabilities? Or the hundreds of organisations—including hospitals—and users who did not update their systems with the patch that Microsoft released to address the problem? These are pressing questions, as their answers point to which actors carry the responsibility for ensuring global cybersecurity. Existing attempts to address them by developing norms of conduct for cyber conflict—such as the United Nations Governmental Group of Experts (UN GGE) or the *Tallinn Manual*—have largely stalled and left them unresolved (Grigsby 2017).

Imagine a new group of national negotiators coming together to address risks posed by information and communication technologies (ICTs). Such a group would need to make several critical decisions before formal negotiations began. These might include the venue (UN GGE or elsewhere?), number of states (small circle of like-minded states or broad inclusiveness?), and the nature of stakeholders (private sectors and or NGOs representatives?). However, this group should also consider an underlying and often overlooked question: which metaphors will structure the negotiating process? In this chapter, we focus on the generative power of metaphors and their impact in policy-making. "Generative metaphors" prescribe new solutions to policy problems through a process of reconceptualization (Schön 1979). In particular we address the case of cyber security and analyse the impact, limits, and advantages of four metaphors in this area, namely: war, health, ecosystem and infrastructure.

Metaphors constrain ethical reasoning, leaving us to assume, sometimes uncritically, a certain framework to define the moral scenario and ascribe responsibilities (Thibodeau and Boroditsky 2011). When this happens, applying an alternative metaphor can open up space for new thinking. To date, efforts to create norms for international cybersecurity have been dominated by the metaphor of war. While this metaphor may be suitable to address some malicious uses of ICTs, it is not optimal to frame and understand them in all circumstances. As we argue in this chapter, the metaphor diminishes possibilities for international collaboration in this area by limiting states to reactive policies of naming and shaming rather than proactive actions to address systemic features of cyberspace.

In this chapter, we distinguish between "metaphors" and "analogies" and outline relevant existing literature on their role in cognition and ethical reasoning. We then analyse extant literature on metaphors in cybersecurity policy and argue that they fail to incorporate insights from cognitive linguistics. Lastly, we compare four metaphors in this policy area and develop a technique for exploring clashing metaphors to foster innovative thinking on policy problems posed by ICTs.

2.2 Metaphors and Analogies

Metaphors are often defined as either *describing* or *understanding* one thing in terms of another. This difference hints at a complex debate regarding the role of metaphor in thought. Until the 1970s, metaphors were commonly seen as a matter of poetry or rhetoric (Lakoff and Johnson 1980). In this view, metaphors are essentially epiphenomenal: they merely *describe* beliefs that exist prior to the speaker's use of metaphor but do not *influence* the speaker's thinking. In contrast, proponents of conceptual metaphor theory (CMT) argue that metaphors are central to human cognition and have a *causal role* in partially determining an agent's judgements or choice behaviour (Lakoff and Johnson 1980).

According to CMT, metaphorical expressions are "surface realisations" of underlying cognitive processes in which the *source* domain "structures" the *target* domain. For example, Lakoff and Johnson posit that our understanding of ideas (*target*) is metaphorically structured by food (*source*). As evidence for this structure, they provide dozens of "linguistic" metaphors, such as "He's a voracious reader" or "We don't need to spoon-feed our students" (1980: 47–48).

The extent to which linguistic metaphors reflect underlying conceptual structures is still disputed. As Black (1993) points out, this disagreement is exacerbated by the fact that opponents tend to pick relatively trivial metaphors. Following Black, we focus on metaphors that are commonly in use, "rich" in background implication, and "strong" in the sense that they create a more powerful link than a mere comparison. In Black's account, strong metaphors lead us to "see" *A* as *B*; for example asserting seriously that "The internet is a drug!" is (at least) to think of the internet as a drug. Strong metaphors are therefore *constitutive*, as they create mental models for what they describe.

This understanding informs our proposed distinction between metaphor and analogy. An analogy is a *comparison* between two objects, concepts, or phenomena. As an ideal-type, an analogy is carefully elaborated to note both similarities and dissimilarities between source and target to further understanding. Metaphors are based on analogies, but they go further by asserting that *A* is *B*.

Constitutive metaphors are useful to understand new phenomena, like cyber conflicts. Lakoff and Johnson (1980) argue that to name and make sense of intangible or unprecedented experiences, we categorise the world through metaphors. Johnson

(1993) maintains that a similar process of 'moral imagination' underlies moral reasoning: we use metaphors to apply existing ethics to new situations. Because of their constitutive power, metaphors carry over associations and assumptions about roles and obligations from one realm to another.

The same process occurs when considering legal approaches to new technologies, as legal precedent works through analogy (Gill 2017). For example, the legal metaphors of text, speech and machine for computer code each suggest a different legal regime for regulating code (Vee 2012). When faced with problems posed by new technologies, the first response is to "explain why the new technology can be treated identically to an earlier technology" (Froomkin 1995, cited in Wolff 2014:2). Consequently, Wolff (2014) argues that the field of internet law is particularly adept at assessing metaphors and understanding their deterministic role.

2.3 Metaphors in Cybersecurity Policy

In contrast, existing research on cybersecurity metaphors tends to approach metaphors disparagingly: they often identify cybersecurity metaphors, analyse their strengths and limitations, and then implore the reader to use metaphors carefully, if at all. Lapointe identifies 'ecosystem,' 'public health', 'battlefield', 'global commons', and 'domain' and then states: "substantive discussion of the way ahead depends on our ability to leaven our literal discourse with a dash of metaphor rather than the other way around" (2011:18). Betz and Stevens (2013) "interrogate" metaphors of 'space' and 'health', which "channel us into a winner-takes-all modality", and suggest that we should avoid the dominant metaphors and seek out "positive-sum formulations." Wolff discusses the metaphors of the 'burglar', 'war', and 'health' and concludes that it is "far too late … to try to rein in the metaphorical language surrounding computer security issues"; however it is "possible that the most productive ways of discussing them are […] those most resistant to metaphoric thinking" (2014: 14).

These approaches share three limitations. They pick illustrative examples of metaphors in political speech or suggest hypothetical ones, but do not systematically assess actual policies or policy proposals. They warn against metaphors and call for more literal language, without offering any suggestions for language which might replace the metaphors that they complain of. Sauter's analysis (2015) offers a partial exception, as she considers policy documents on internet regulation and suggests an alternative metaphor of 'global commons', although she does not elaborate the implications of using this metaphor in internet regulation. All these analyses are further limited by the lack of a precise explanation of metaphors. This ambiguity can lead theorists to understate their importance. For example, Shimko's (1994) paper on metaphor in foreign policy decision-making states that analogies "offer concrete policy guidance" while metaphors "provide an underlying intellectual construct for framing the situation" but do not have "direct implications in terms of formulating and selecting foreign policies" (1994:665).

In contrast, Schön's (1979) work on "generative metaphors" highlights the interdependence between framing and formulating policy. Such metaphors generate new solutions to problems through reconceptualising them. Schön uses the memorable example of a group of engineers attempting to design a synthetic brush who are flummoxed by the uneven, "gloppy" strokes of their designs. Suddenly, one of them exclaims "You know, a paintbrush is a kind of pump!" This metaphor calls the engineers' attention to the spaces in between the bristles, through which paint flows, resulting in a far more successful design.

Schön (1979) argues that metaphors play a similar role in prescribing policy. Policy analysis is often understood as a form of problem-solving, where the problems themselves are assumed to be given. However, problems are not given, but "constructed by human beings in their attempts to make sense of complex and troubling situations." For example, understanding low-income neighbourhoods as a "disease" versus a "natural" community has direct implications for policy choice in the issue of housing, as each of these metaphors carry a normative judgement about what is "wrong" and what needs fixing (Schön 1979).

Schön proposes that policy is better understood as a matter of "problem-setting." Many conflicting policy solutions are traceable to this process of problem-setting, which encompasses the metaphors underpinning the problem framing. These metaphors are generative and define a mental model of the problem that makes certain policy solutions appear natural or appropriate.

With this expanded conceptual toolkit, we can now return to the subject of cyber security. The rise of 'cyber' neologisms stems from the need to find words to describe new socio-technical phenomena. Most, if not all, cyber-words have a metaphorical element, as they assign new phenomena to existing conceptual categories. This is a crucial aspect to consider in discussions of "cyber war". For the choice of the topics to debate, the trades-off to define, the space of possible solutions, and the posture of the actors involved in the discussion are determined by the "war'" metaphor.

2.4 Cyber War: Description or Mere Metaphor?

One of the most prominent articles on cyber war denies its existence:

> Cyber war has never happened in the past. Cyber war does not take place in the present. And it is highly unlikely that cyber war will occur in the future. (Rid 2012)

Referencing military theorist von Clausewitz, Rid suggests that for an offensive act to qualify as an act of war, it must meet three necessary conditions: "it has to have the potential to be lethal; it has to be instrumental; and it has to be political" (2012:8). Following an analysis of offensive acts that are sometimes described as cyber war—like the 2007 DDoS attacks on Estonia or the 2010 Stuxnet attack on Iranian centrifuges—Rid argues that no cyberattacks to date have fulfilled these conditions. He concludes that the "'war' in 'cyber war' has more in common with the 'war' on obesity than with World War II—it has more metaphoric than descriptive value" (2012:9).

Rid proposes a "more nuanced terminology" as an alternative (Rid 2012). Past and present cyberattacks are "merely sophisticated versions of three activities that are as old as warfare itself", namely: subversion, espionage, and sabotage. He argues that using these terms will allow policy makers and theorists to gain greater clarity in discussions of cyberattacks.

However, the distinction that Rid makes between "descriptive" and "merely metaphorical" is confusing, as metaphors *are* descriptive. As we outlined in Sect. 2.1, (strong) metaphors generate mental models that carry over associations from one domain to another. Discussions of cyber war also include cyber weapons, bot armies, and virtual arsenals. In describing cyber conflicts as a war, these metaphors extend the conceptual category of 'war' to encompass meaningfully cyber operations and define a set of 'obvious' solutions (Schön 1979). Indeed, to date, the conceptual framework of war has shaped almost all initiatives seeking to create international cybersecurity policy.

The UN Governmental Group of Experts (GGE) process, which lasted from 2005 to 2016, started as a "cyber arms control" treaty within the UN General Assembly 'First Committee' for disarmament and 'politico-military' security (Maurer 2011). Although the arms control approach was never realised, the later stage of negotiations sought to apply solutions from another branch of the laws of war, namely international humanitarian law (IHL), which sets out 'taboo' targets such as non-combatants or prisoners of war (Grigsby 2017; Nye 2017). Similarly, the more recent "Digital Geneva Convention" suggested by Microsoft adopts IHL principles and proposes a neutral verification body similar to the "role played by the International Atomic Energy Agency in the field of nuclear non-proliferation" (Smith 2017a). In the same vein, *The Tallinn Manual*—commissioned by NATO—explicitly applies existing laws of war to cyber conflict by interpreting the legal thresholds of "use of force" and "armed attack" used in the UN Charter (Dev 2015). All these solutions draw on regulatory frameworks developed for conventional kinetic (i.e. violent) war, because cyber conflict is conceptualised as a kind of war.

Rid's paper seeks to counter cyber war's constitutive effect through criteria and precise language. Yet, conceptual categories are rarely defined by the kind of rigid criteria that Rid imposes on the concept of 'war.' Studies in cognitive linguistics show that categories operate by *prototypes* rather than *necessary and sufficient criteria* (see Lakoff (1987) for a review). When categorising a phenomenon, we assess its similarity to the prototype through gradations of 'fit' rather than clear criteria. The prototypical 'war'—in the Western imagination—is a lethal confrontation between armies directed by nation states, complete with explosions, blood, and guts.[1] The war on obesity is far removed from the prototypical war as it involves neither clashing nation-states nor armies; while World War II fits the concept of war

[1] It is useful to note that the concept of war emerged later than we might think; ancient Romans spoke of 'conquest' rather than war (van der Dennen 1995).

perfectly. It is only by ignoring wars like the Cold War, the War on Terror, or trade wars that Rid's paper manages to present war as a category with clear boundaries.

As we explained in the previous section, cyber-words have a metaphorical element, as they assign new phenomena to existing conceptual categories. Dismissing the use of 'cyber war' as "merely metaphorical" is also dismissing the ubiquity and necessity of this categorization. Perhaps the best evidence for this is the fact that the nuanced terminology, like "cyber espionage", that Rid suggests as an alternative to "cyber war" is also metaphorical.

In his history of the terminology used by US intelligence officials for state-sponsored hacking, Jones (2017) points out that the doctrinal category of Computer Network Exploitation (CNE) only emerged in 1996:

> With this new category, "enabling" was hived off from ***offensive warfare***, to clarify that exploiting a machine—hacking in and stealing data—was not an attack [...]. The new category of CNE subdued the protean activity of hacking and put it into an older legal box—that of espionage. (2017:15)

Espionage, unlike warfare, is necessary, ubiquitous, and—crucially—entirely unregulated by international law. Therefore, the unregulated legal status of government hacking relies on the metaphor of espionage. Jones criticises this "disanalogy with espionage": state-sponsored hacking is significantly different from traditional espionage, as the ease and scale of information exfiltration, as well as the fact that the techniques of cyber espionage and cyberattack are often identical (Brown and Metcalf 1998:117, cited in Jones 2017:15).

The fact that state-sponsored hacking does not fit easily within the conceptual category of espionage suggests that Rid's suggested use of cyber espionage must also be understood as metaphorical. The disanalogy of cyber espionage also illustrates a critical point: conceptual categories are not 'fixed' but socially constructed, sometimes with strategic intent.

One way in which these categories are constructed is when foreign policy analysts assert the relevance of a certain metaphor because it is in the same "general realm of experience"—to use Shimko's (1994) phrase. A powerful example is an edited volume titled *Understanding Cyber Conflict: 14 Analogies*. The volume "explores how lessons from several wars since the early nineteenth century, including the World Wars, could apply—or not—to cyber conflict in the twenty-first century" in fourteen chapters grouped around questions like: "What Are Cyber Weapons Like?" and "What Might Cyber Wars Be Like?". Following the distinction we make in section two, these chapters use *analogies* as explicit comparisons between the domain of cyber conflict and the domain of kinetic warfare. However, none of the fourteen chapters looks to conflicts outside the realm of war, ignoring, for example, conflictual dynamics existing in trade or environmental negotiations. This both stems from and reinforced the underlying constitutive metaphor which leads researchers and policy-maker to see cyber conflict as a kind of war.

Consequently, although Rid's article clearly articulates the inaccuracies of describing cyber conflict as a war, his proposed solution has two problems. Firstly, it understates, and therefore underestimates, the constitutive effect metaphors have in generating entire mental models. Secondly, it fails to consider that the proposed, supposedly clean and analytical language, is also metaphorical, and therefore carries over its own assumptions about roles, responsibilities, and regulatory models. The question of whether we can ever escape metaphorical language is hotly contested in the philosophy of language (see Eco and Paci 1983), and largely outside of the scope of this paper.

However as Gill (2017) and others point out, as information is formless, metaphorical language is particularly common in law and policy related to the digital environment. Therefore, precise language is insufficient to address metaphorical reasoning, particularly as it is likely that new expressions will also be metaphorical. New concepts—such as Kello's (2017) use of 'unpeace' to describe the ambiguous, constant conflict below the threshold of war—offer one way to address this conceptual puzzle. However, if we use 'unpeace' instead of 'war', but still think in terms of arms control, armies, and laws of war, the underlying war metaphor will still structure our thinking. Instead, we should seek out ways to expose how deeply our thinking on cyber conflict is entrenched in the conceptual category of 'war'. This in turn will allow us to identify more constructive metaphors for analysing cyber conflict.

In the following section, we elaborate a method for policy-makers and researchers to critically assess policy metaphors: first, identify metaphors which structure the regulation of new technologies, particularly cases where this structure is problematic; second, seek out other metaphors which might be applied to the same policy area; third, by contrasting these competing metaphors, generate a wider variety of potentially useful policies and regulatory approaches.[2]

2.5 Comparing Metaphors

To illustrate how metaphors shape ethical reasoning, the following sections will discuss the roles and obligations suggested by four metaphors in cybersecurity governance, these are the metaphors of war, health, ecosystem, and infrastructure.

2.5.1 War

As we outlined in the previous section, most existing norm initiatives—including the UN GGE, the Tallinn Manual, and the Digital Geneva Convention—have relied on the conceptual framework of war. The war metaphor is appealing both because the laws of war are one of the most developed and well respected international regulatory regimes and because cyber conflict holds many similarities to war (Schmitt and Vihul 2014). However, the inevitable focus on attributing attacks and punishing wrong-doers steers foreign policy on a reactive cycle of 'naming and shaming',

[2]This approach is inspired by Luke's (2010) guide to "metaphor-hacking".

which is further complicated by the politics and uncertainties of attribution. War also implies a zero-sum politics in which states are solely responsible to their own citizens, which ignores systemic and structural causes of cyber conflict, such as the worldwide spread of insecure "Internet of Things" (IoT) devices which can be co-opted for DDoS attacks.

Problems with the regulatory model of war can be divided into *conceptual* and *practical* ones. The conceptual difficulties have been described in depth elsewhere (Rid 2012; Taddeo 2016, 2017), and so they will be only briefly summarised here. Most cyber operations, such as DDoS attacks, cause temporary losses of functionality rather than permanent destruction. The existing laws of war are built on the tenet of 'war as a last resort'. In contrast, cyber-attacks are ubiquitous and (mostly) non-violent (non-kinetic). Therefore, approaches to the regulation of state-run cyberattacks that rely on International Humanitarian Laws (IHL)—like for example the *Tallinn Manual's* -leaves unaddressed the vast majority of existing and potential incidents—which do not cause physical destruction (Taddeo 2016).

Furthermore, cyber conflicts involve a variety of state and non-state actors in often ambiguous relationships of dependency and antagonism. This poses a problem as the conceptual framework of war relies on clearly defined state antagonists. Ambiguity around actors and motives involved in cyberattacks complicates the problems of attribution and proportionality (Taddeo 2017; Taddeo and Floridi 2018). Even in cases where an attack is traced to a particular national territory, the precise nature of a state's involvement—whether it coordinated, facilitated, or merely turned a blind eye to an attack by "patriotic hackers—often remains obscure. This makes it difficult to calculate what a "proportional" response should be.

These conceptual shortcomings underlie a set of practical problems created using the metaphor of war. The adversarial framing has complicated international negotiations. This is evident in the break-down of the UN GGE negotiations, the longest running effort to create norms for cyber conflict. The widely acknowledged cause for this rupture was the opposition by Russia, China, and Cuba to the U.S./U.K. insistence on confirming the applicability of the right to self-defence and IHL to cyberspace (Grigsby 2017; Korzak 2017; Lotrionte 2017). The opposing nations argued the right to self-defence would link cyber conflict to kinetic conflict in a way that favours the stronger military powers. As the Cuban expert declaration explains, the application of IHL "would legitimize a scenario of war and military actions in the context of ICT" (Rodríguez 2017).

The language of war, which continually reintroduces the largely incompatible Anglosphere and SCO state understandings of "information warfare", likely exacerbated this worry. In the Anglosphere, both 'cybersecurity' and 'information security' are technical terms referring to the "preservation of the confidentiality, availability and integrity of information in cyberspace" (Giles and Hagestad 2013). However, within the framework of the Shanghai Cooperation Organisation (SCO), China and Russia among others have solidified a contrasting regional understanding based on the notion of an "information space", which includes information in human minds. Intrusions such as psychological operations or "information weapons" aimed at "mass psychologic brainwashing to destabilise society and the state" may threaten a state's information security (SCO 2009:209). This is evident in Cuba's GGE submissions, which repeatedly denounce the "aggressive escalation" of the U.S.'s "radio and television war against Cuba" alongside other hostile uses of telecommunications (UNGA 2015, 2016, 2017).

This contrasting use of spatial metaphors—global "cyberspace" vs. national "information space"—lies at the heart of the UN GGE disagreement. Western states wished to focus on information *architecture* rather than *content,* and feared that Russia's new treaty could be used to limit free speech under the guise of increasing information security (Maurer 2011; McKune 2015; 1027026 2018).

The *Tallinn Manual* and the UN GGE limited themselves by approaching cybersecurity as a matter of war—both explicitly, in trying to apply IHL, and implicitly, by negotiating within fora for arms control and focusing on taboos for targets. Underlying both the conceptual and practical difficulties outlined in this section is a set of ethical assumptions reinforced by the war metaphor. War implies a zero-sum mentality for states, in which their primary responsibility is to punish attackers and defend their own security and that of their own citizens. Wider or more cooperative notions of responsibility are easily overshadowed.

Conflict in the cyber domain is also like kinetic conflicts in many ways, and we are not arguing that borrowing concepts or thinking in terms of conventional war will never be useful for regulating cyber conflict. Rather, by compiling these shortcomings we seek to highlight that this metaphorical framing should not be the only, or even the primary, framework for negotiating international cybersecurity. Metaphors based on the health of systems offer, for example, an alternative to the one of war.

2.5.2 Public Health

The Cyber Green Institute—a non-profit stemming from the Asia Pacific CERT community—works to improve cybersecurity through monitoring what they describe as the "health of the global cyber ecosystem" (CyberGreen 2014). CyberGreen argues that "traditional approaches to cybersecurity from a national security or law enforcement perspective" are limited because they rely on the decision-making of nation states rather than the "variety of key stakeholders comprising the cyber ecosystem". These approaches also take a *reactive* posture to threats and often overlook proactive measures to improve underlying conditions:

> Such approaches are analogous to treating a case of malaria through medicine, while leaving the nearby mosquito swamp untouched or developing cancer treatment technology while paying little attention to the population's tobacco use (CyberGreen 2014)

In contrast, CyberGreen takes direct inspiration from the "public health model" for cybersecurity, and particularly organisations such as the World Health Organisation (WHO). This is a clear example of a generative metaphor, which is often alluded to in CyberGreen's website, blog, and training materials (see Fig. 2.1).

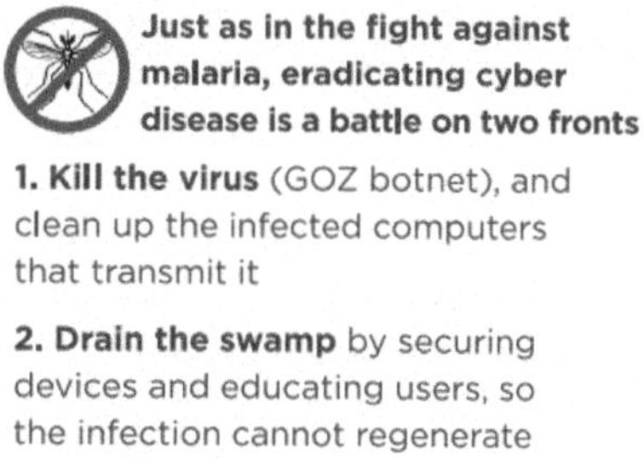

Fig. 2.1 Screenshot from 'Improving Global Cyber Health' infographic (CyberGreen 2016b)

Fig. 2.2 CyberGreen data visualisation indicating nodes that could be used to participate in a DDoS attack

The metaphor is not limited to a general approach, as the public health model generates specific policies such as producing global statistics on health risk factors akin to the WHO's Indicator and Measurement Registry (IMR). CyberGreen treats the IMR as a blueprint for statistical methods and data collection techniques to ensure harmonised "cross-comparable" statistics which can be used by national CERTs (CyberGreen 2014). Like public health officials tracking obesity, CyberGreen runs its own proprietary internet scans to detect the use of services such as Open recursive DNS or Open NTP, which can be vulnerable to amplifying distributed denial of service (DDoS) attacks.[3] Such attacks are difficult to mitigate once they are launched due to massive traffic volume. However, it is possible to reduce the number of servers or botnets that can be used to increase traffic volume (UC-CERT 2016). CyberGreen publishes these metrics and compiles them into persuasive visualisations (see Fig. 2.2).

[3] In amplification attacks, attackers try to exhaust a victim's bandwidth by abusing the fact that protocols such as DNS or NTP allow spoofing of sender IP addresses (see US-CERT 2016).

These metrics help CyberGreen to convince and motivate national stakeholders to "clean up their own cyber environments" without "naming and shaming" (CyberGreen 2014). Recent studies show that metrics collected by third parties, such as Transparency International's Corruption Perceptions Index, are a powerful and increasingly common governance mechanism (Cooley and Snyder 2015). Such mechanisms regulate state behaviour indirectly, through the social pressure created by quantification and rankings.

A similar set of norms—which are not explicitly endorsed by CyberGreen—encourage companies and individual users to practice good cybersecurity or "cyber hygiene". For example, good cyber hygiene might involve patching software and changing passwords frequently. Although such practices are widely recommended by the cybersecurity community, the metaphor of hygiene may shift partial responsibility on to the user, implying they may be blamed for a cyberattack if they did not take the recommended cyber security measures. Negative obligations are noticeably absent within the conceptual framework of public health.

This is an interesting example of how metaphors shape ethical reasoning; as biological viruses do not have moral agency, they cannot be held responsible for their actions. Therefore, the public health model removes focus from banning bad behaviour.

2.5.3 *Ecosystem*

Cybersecurity practitioners use the phrase "cyber ecosystem" frequently. For example, it appears fifteen times in the new U.S. Cybersecurity Strategy (DHS 2018). Yet, this use of "ecosystem" rarely carries the connotation of a "biological community of interacting organisms" (OED). In the words of Lakoff and Johnson, it is a "dead metaphor"—one that has largely stopped carrying over metaphorical association.

The metaphor of cyberspace as an ecosystem is particularly useful when considering the extent to which cyberspace has become a constitutive part of the reality in which we live. As Chehadé (2018) quips: "cyberspace as a distinct space is dead—all space is now cyber." Floridi (2014) argues ICTs are creating "a new informational environment in which future generations will live most of their time" and calls for an "e-environmental ethics." The ecosystem metaphor reflects the interdependence of various interacting organisms and their informational environment—"inforgs" in the "infosphere" in Floridi's terms (Floridi 2014). Ecological metaphors also reflect the way interconnected systems support multiple (positive and negative) feedback loops; concepts from ecology have been applied to explain developments in offensive cyber policies (Fairclough 2018).

Norm entrepreneurs who took the metaphor of a "cyber ecosystem" seriously might aim for a Cyber Paris Agreement rather than a Digital Geneva Convention. The 2016 Paris Agreement aims, in the long term, to hold global temperatures "well below 2 °C above pre-industrial levels" (Falkner 2016). Under the Paris Agreement states submit voluntary pledges called "nationally determined contributions" (NDCs). State progress towards NDCs will be reviewed regularly against an international system for monitoring emissions and financial contributions (Peters et al. 2017). Unlike previous climate change agreements, which attempted to impose targets for states, the Paris Agreement relies on mobilising 'bottom-up' civil society and domestic pressure to stimulate more ambitious pledges and mitigation efforts (Falkner 2016).

Cybersecurity negotiators following an ecosystem model would start with the notion of a shared responsibility for a global ecosystem. Rather than defining an "armed attack" or a taboo victim, negotiators would attempt to define the conditions necessary for a healthy ecosystem, akin to the 2 °C limit. They would then identify specific, measurable actions—for example, botnet reduction—which states can undertake to improve the cyber ecosystem. States could voluntarily set NDCs, and an international body and civil society could use data collection efforts such as CyberGreen's metrics to verify compliance with NDCs. The notion of a "healthy ecosystem" here indicates a concept of environmental health rather than public health. Although the metaphors of "cyber health" and "cyber ecosystem" have a lot in common (such as a systemic approach to responsibility), they draw from different realms and carry slightly different implications for responsibility. Most importantly, while diseases such as malaria have no agency, problems like pollution are a direct result of human decisions.

A possible objection may point out that the notion of a healthy ecosystem implies a level of consensus that does not exist among states engaging in cyber conflict. Environmental pollution is generally a by-product of achieving other goals, such as prosperity. In environmental negotiations, states seek to limit these by-products because they recognise all states benefit from a healthy global ecosystem. Furthermore, state's competing visions for the future of the internet might make it challenging to define a healthy ecosystem: for example, some countries would prefer more government control, while others would see openness as a sign of health.

With these objections in mind, there are two important reasons why working within the environmental framework might be more constructive. First, discussions on defining a healthy cyberspace would help negotiators identify both high consensus areas, such as structural risk mitigation measures which would benefit all states, and which states agree on these issues. In contrast, international collaboration on structural risk mitigation simply was not prioritised in international initiatives following the war model. Focusing on structural risk mitigation may be useful as international collaboration to reduce botnets or take other actions that would make attacks less effective might help build trust before addressing more controversial issues.

Second, although climate change is now more widely accepted, environmental policy has decades of experience in addressing robust disagreement. Therefore, it provides mechanisms such as NDCs that prioritise flexibility: sceptical states can set low targets, while states that are more ambitious are rewarded for setting higher targets by comparison. This mechanism could be applied to a highly controversial aspect of cyber conflict: vulnerabilities disclosure.

Buchanan (2017) argues that one of the most effective actions states could take to mitigate mistrust and cyber conflict would be unilaterally disclosing zero-day vulnerabilities—i.e. vulnerabilities which have not yet been disclosed to the public or to software vendors. Like global warming, vulnerabilities are a threat to collective security. If a state wants to keep a vulnerability secret, it must accept that other threat actors may discover the vulnerability and target the state's own citizens (as happened in WannaCry). A state that discloses vulnerabilities may lose the ability to infiltrate certain systems, but it ensures that all users are more secure from threat actors exploiting the vulnerability. Unilaterally disclosing vulnerabilities therefore signals a state's desire for stability.

This led Microsoft's Brad Smith to call for vulnerabilities to be treated "like weapons in the physical world" (Smith 2017b). However, as Buchanan (2017) points out, an arms control approach in which states promise not to stockpile vulnerabilities is hard to verify without intruding into a state's networks. Positive acts (such as instances of disclosure) are easier to verify than the absence of negative acts (such as keeping vulnerabilities secret) because they are public and can be confirmed by the software vendor.

Existing processes for state disclosure of vulnerabilities, such as the U.S. Vulnerability Equities Process, have been criticised for the low incentives states have to disclose vulnerabilities to the public (Ambastha 2019). Rather than relying solely on individual state's desire for stability (which might easily be outweighed by their interests in intelligence gains), a Cyber Paris Agreement could create pressure for states to commit to measurable goals for responsibly disclosing more vulnerabilities. Due to the market for purchasing vulnerabilities, several mechanisms such as the Common Vulnerability Scoring System (CVSS) exist for assessing the value of vulnerabilities (Ablon et al. 2014; Sasha Romanosky 2019). These scoring systems could be translated into a metric for state commitments. The mechanism of measurable commitments would enable flexibility (some states may not commit to any disclosures) while creating greater incentives for action.[4] In the words of Yurie Ito, CyberGreen's founder, "what gets measured, gets done" (CyberGreen 2016a).

The metaphor-sceptic might object that policy-makers could adapt environmental policy mechanisms to cybersecurity without seeing cyberspace as an ecosystem. However, the notion of a shared ecosystem elicits the concept of shared responsibility. Environmental activists have been highly successful in convincing international audiences of the existence of a shared threat (Gough and Shackley 2001). Drawing on an environmental metaphor allows us to take advantage of the generative effect of the metaphor and transfer existing understandings about roles and responsibilities towards the global ecosystem to a new domain.

[4] Of course, states might choose to only give up vulnerabilities in cases where they have a second vulnerability which guarantees their ability to exploit the same systems. However, even such seemingly useless disclosures will make most users safer, as third parties will be less able to exploit these vulnerabilities when they are disclosed.

The ecosystem metaphor also allows for a far more holistic ethical approach than one of war, which reduces the complex dynamics of cyber conflict to a focus purely on adversarial states and therefore takes away attention from the roles and responsibilities of relevant actors like CERTs or companies. Rather than thinking simply in terms of protecting one's own systems, the cyber ecosystem suggests a *relational* responsibility for a shared ecosystem. National actors—both CERTs and governments—should address the risks computers in their networks pose to others.

Even if aspects of the proposed environmental model fail—for example, if no amount of regulatory innovation or civil society activism convinces states to commit to specific numbers of disclosures—simply imagining how negotiators might apply the ecosystem framework to cybersecurity ipso facto is useful, as it exposes the constitutive effect of cyber war. This metaphor leads us to focus narrowly on conflict (and deterring conflict) in the first place, rather than more broadly on proactive, holistic international cybersecurity policy. This cannot be addressed merely by avoiding words like cyber war, as omissions do not provide an alternative framework. However, applying another strong metaphor to the same issues shows that the war framework is an option rather than an obvious consequence of the way things are.

2.5.4 *Infrastructure*

Cyber security can also be considered with respect to the stability of the cyberspace as an infrastructure. For example, the first major norm proposed by the Global Commission on the Stability of Cyberspace (GCSC) states that:

> Without prejudice to their rights and obligations, state and non-state actors should not conduct or knowingly allow activity that intentionally and substantially damages the general availability or integrity of the *public core* of the Internet, and therefore the stability of cyberspace (GCSC 2017, added emphasis).

The GCSC defines the "public core" to include packet routing and forwarding, naming and numbering systems, the cryptographic mechanisms of security and identity, and physical transmission media. Attacks on any of the activities, one could deduce, would be considered attacks to the public core of the infrastructure and, therefore, should be forbidden.

The GCSC is an international, multi-stakeholder effort launched in 2017. The GCSC has consciously moved away from the language of cyber war and security, which is particularly evident in the GCSC's motto: "Promoting stability in cyberspace to build peace and prosperity."Although the ban on attacking the "public core" norm follows a similar logic to the taboos set by IHL on certain targets, by banning attacks on certain kinds of *infrastructure*, the GCSC cleverly avoids many of the pitfalls of distinguishing between civilian and military targets.

The metaphors of online "infrastructures" may be better for emphasising ethical *design* rather than conservation. Under this framework, the designers of digital environments have a strong obligation to build infrastructure carefully and safely, and governments may have an additional obligation to regulate companies within their territory to ensure that they do so. The regulation of large-scale infrastructure may therefore be a generative source for policy. However, humans have never previously built infrastructures so vast that they were shared by citizens from all over the planet. As large infrastructure projects are usually regulated *nationally*, it is not clear whether and how framing the problem of cyber security in terms of infrastructure can provide a framework for international governance.

2.6 Conclusion

When designing international governance for cybersecurity, should we negotiate over a war, health policy, or an ecosystem? Each metaphor identifies a different problem to be solved and expresses a different set of arguments about responsibility. Therefore, theorists and policy-makers should evaluate the metaphorical framing of negotiations and regulatory approaches. Metaphors do not just suggest a general approach, as many policy analysts suggest. On the contrary, they prescribe specific policies: policy-makers in a cyber war must protect their population, avoid attacks on 'taboo' targets, and punish and deter wrong doers. In contrast, policy-makers in a cyber ecosystem must commit to mitigating systemic risks that threaten this shared environment.

Table 2.1 summarises the obligations suggested by the four metaphorical frameworks outlined in this essay.[5] How do we compare and evaluate between these approaches? Should we look for how developed and well-accepted various normative regimes are? Or should we instead prioritise analytical clarity or how well the metaphor "fits"? Or should we perhaps think instead of mundane and inescapable political realities, and ask which metaphor is the most persuasive? Which one will be accepted by the powers that be?

In this chapter we have argued that assuming uncritically a certain metaphor bypasses explicit consideration of these problems, by matching the new problem of cyber conflict to an existing problem with set roles and responsibilities. In particular, the metaphor of war introduces a reductionist notion of state responsibility, which obscures the possibility for cooperation on improving structural features of cyber conflict. The interdependence of digital infrastructures—as illustrated by the complexity of campaigns like WannaCry—renders a focus on securing one's border against outsiders seem outdated.

Through exploring these metaphors, we also elaborate a method for policy-makers and researchers to critically assess policy metaphors: first, identify metaphors which structure the regulation of new technologies, particularly cases where

[5] This is an indicative list of proposed obligations for states within each conceptual framework – obligations for private actors are italicised. The norm initiatives do not necessarily advocate all of the norms in their category.

Table 2.1 Map of metaphors and obligations

Metaphor	Norm initiatives	Positive obligations	Negative obligations
War (strict)	Wassenaar arrangement Tallinn manual	Set up an arms control regime	No attacks above "armed attack" threshold (unless in self-defence)
War (loose)	UN GGE Digital Geneva convention	Protect your citizens Attribute attacks/punish malicious foreign states Create a body for attribution	No attacks on private actors/civilians Stop stockpiling weapons Companies—do not aid attacks on civilians
Health	Cyber green initiative	Clean up your ecosystem/ swamp (i.e. minimise botnets/weak protocols) Individuals—practice cyber hygiene	?
Ecosystem	n/a	Clean up your ecosystem (similarly to above) Proactively disclose vulnerabilities	?
Infrastructure	Global commission on stability of cyberspace	Regulate companies to build safe environment Companies—build safe environments	No attacks on the public core

this structure is problematic; second, seek out other metaphors which might be applied to the same policy area; third, by contrasting these competing metaphors, generate a wider variety of potentially useful policies and regulatory approaches.

Problems posed by new technologies require both imagination and analytic rigour. Analysing policy at the level of metaphor allows both for more creative solutions and a more systematic analysis of imagination itself. It also serves as a useful reminder that war in new domains is not the inevitable result of geopolitics or technological development. We can and should construct a more collaborative system for international cyber-politics.

References

Ablon, L., M.C. Libicki, and A.A. Golay. 2014. Markets for Cybercrime Tools and Stolen Data: Hackers' Bazaar. *Rand*. https://doi.org/10.7249/j.ctt6wq7z6.

Ambastha, M. 2019. Taking a Hard Look at the Vulnerabilities Equities Process and Its National Security Implications. *Berkeley Tech Law Journal*. http://btlj.org/2019/04/taking-a-hard-look-at-the-vulnerable-equities-process-in-national-security/.

Berr, J. 2017. 'WannaCry' Ransomware Attack Losses Could Reach $4 Billion. *CBS News*, May 2017.

Betz, D.J., and T. Stevens. 2013. Analogical Reasoning and Cyber Security. *Security Dialogue* 44 (2): 147–164. https://doi.org/10.1177/0967010613478323.

Black, Max. 1993. More about metaphor. In *Metaphor and thought*, vol. 31, 19–41. https://doi.org/10.1111/j.1746-8361.1977.tb01296.x.

Brown, Gary D., and Andrew O. Metcalf. 1998. *Easier said than done: Legal reviews of cyber weapons*. Journal of National Security Law and Policy.

Buchanan, B. 2017. *The Cybersecurity Dilemma: Hacking, Trust and Fear Between Nations*. Oxford Scholarship Online 2017. https://doi.org/10.1093/acprof.

Chehadé, F. 2018. *Joseph Nye and Fadi Chehadé – Norms to Promote Stability and Avoid Conflict in Cyberspace|Blavatnik School of Government*. Blavatnik School of Government. https://www.bsg.ox.ac.uk/multimedia/video/joseph-nye-and-fadi-chehade-norms-promote-stability-and-avoid-conflict-cyberspace.

Collier, J. 2018. Cyber Security Assemblages: A Framework for Understanding the Dynamic and Contested Nature of Security Provision. *Politics and Governance* 6 (2): 13–21. https://www.cogitatiopress.com/politicsandgovernance/article/view/1324/1324.

Cooley, A., and J. Snyder. 2015. *Ranking the World: Grading States as a Tool of Global Governance*. https://doi.org/10.1017/CBO9781316161555.

CyberGreen. 2014. *The Cyber Green Initiative: Concept Paper Improving Health Through Measurement and Mitigation*.

———. 2016a. *Cyber Security Agency of Singapore Becomes Cornerstone Sponsor for CyberGreen*. https://www.cybergreen.net/2016/10/11/Cyber-Security-Agency-of-Singapore-Becomes-Cornerstone-Sponsor-for-CyberGreen/.

———. 2016b. *Improving Global Cyber Health*. https://www.cybergreen.net/img/medialibrary/CG-infographic-2016-web.pdf.

Dev, P. 2015. 'Use of Force' and 'Armed Attack' Thresholds in Cyber Conflict: The Looming Definitional Gaps and the Growing Need for Formal U.N. Response. *Texas International Law Journal* 50: 381–402.

DHS. 2018. U.S. Department of Homeland Security Cybersecurity Strategy. https://www.dhs.gov/sites/default/files/publications/DHS-Cybersecurity-Strategy_1.pdf.

Eco, U., and C. Paci. 1983. The Scandal of Metaphor: Metaphorology and Semiotics. *Poetics Today* 4: 21. https://www.jstor.org/stable/1772287?seq=1#metadata_info_tab_contents.

Fairclough, G. 2018. *Offensive Cyber, Ecology and the Competition for Security in Cyberspace: The UK's Approach*. http://podcasts.ox.ac.uk/offensive-cyber-ecology-and-competition-security-cyberspace-uks-approach.

Falkner, R. 2016. The Paris Agreement and the New Logic of International Climate Politics. *International Affairs*. https://doi.org/10.1111/1468-2346.12708.

Froomkin, A. M, and others. 1995. Anonymity and its enmities. J. Online L. Art.

Floridi, L. 2014. *The 4th Revolution: How the Infosphere Is Reshaping Human Reality*. 1st ed. Oxford: Oxford University Press. https://global.oup.com/academic/product/the-fourth-revolution-9780199606726?cc=gb&lang=en&.

GCSC. 2017. *Call to Protect the Public Core of the Internet*. New Delhi: . https://cyberstability.org/news/global-commission-proposes-definition-of-the-public-core-of-the-internet/.

Giles, K., and W. Hagestad II. 2013. Divided by a Common Language: Cyber Definitions in Chinese, Russian and English. *5th International Conference on Cyber Conflict*, 1–17.

Gill, L. 2017. Law, Metaphor and the Encrypted Machine. *Osgoode Hall Law Journal* 13: 16. https://ssrn.com/abstract=3138684.

Gough, C., and S. Shackley. 2001. The Respectable Politics of Climate Change: The Epistemic Communities and NGOs. *International Affairs*. https://doi.org/10.1111/1468-2346.00195.

Grigsby, A. 2017. The End of Cyber Norms. *Survival* 59 (6): 109–122. https://doi.org/10.1080/00396338.2017.1399730.

Johnson, M. 1993. *Moral Imagination: Implications of Cognitive Science for Ethics*. Chicago: University of Chicago Press.

Jones, M.L. 2017. The Spy Who Pwned Me. *Limn*, 8. https://limn.it/issues/hacks-leaks-and-breaches/.

Kello, Lucas. 2017. *The virtual weapon and international order*. Yale University Press.

Korzak, E. 2017. UN GGE on Cybersecurity: The End of an Era? *The Diplomat*. https://thediplomat.com/2017/07/un-gge-on-cybersecurity-have-china-and-russia-just-made-cyberspace-less-safe/.

Lakoff, G. 1987. Categorization. In *Women, Fire and Dangerous Things*.

Lakoff, George, and Mark Johnson. 1980. *Metaphors we live by*. 1st ed. Chicago: University of Chicago Press.

Lapointe, A. 2011. *When Good Metaphors Go Bad: The Metaphoric 'Branding' of Cyperspace*. Center for Strategic & International Studies. http://csis.org/publication/when-good-metaphors-go-bad-metaphoric-branding-cyberspace.

Lotrionte, C. 2017. Geopolitics Eclipses International Law at the UN. *The Cipher Brief*, 6 Aug 2017. https://www.thecipherbrief.com/geopolitics-eclipses-international-law-un-1092.

Lukes, D. 2010. *Hacking a Metaphor in Five Steps*. Metaphor Hacker. http://metaphorhacker.net/2010/07/hacking-a-metaphor-in-five-steps/.

Maurer, T. 2011. Cyber Norm Emergence at the United Nations. *International Relations*, no. September, 1–69. http://belfercenter.hks.harvard.edu/files/maurer-cyber-norm-dp-2011-11-final.pdf.

McKune, S. 2015. An Analysis of the International Code of Conduct for Information Security. https://citizenlab.ca/2015/09/international-code-of-conduct/.

Nye, J. 2017. A Normative Approach to Preventing Cyberwarfare. *Project Syndicate*, 13 Mar 2017. https://www.project-syndicate.org/commentary/global-norms-to-prevent-cyberwarfare-by-joseph-s%2D%2Dnye-2017-03?barrier=accesspaylog.

Peters, G.P., R.M. Andrew, J.G. Canadell, S. Fuss, R.B. Jackson, J.I. Korsbakken, C. Le Quéré, and N. Nakicenovic. 2017. Key Indicators to Track Current Progress and Future Ambition of the Paris Agreement. *Nature Climate Change*. https://doi.org/10.1038/nclimate3202.

Rid, T. 2012. Cyber War Will Not Take Place. *Journal of Strategic Studies* 35 (1): 5–32.

Rodríguez, M. 2017. Declaration by Miguel Rodríguez, Representative of Cuba, at the Final Session of Group of Governmental Experts on Developments in the Field of Information and Telecommunications in the Context of International Security.

Romanosky, S. 2019. Developing an Objective, Repeatable Scoring System for a Vulnerability Equities Process. *Lawfare*. https://www.lawfareblog.com/developing-objective-repeatable-scoring-system-vulnerability-equities-process.

Sauter, Molly. 2015. Show me on the map where they hacked you: Cyberwar and the geospatial internet doctrine. *Case Western Reserve Journal of International Law* 47: 63.

Schmitt, M.N., and L. Vihul. 2014. The Nature of International Law Cyber Norms. *The Tallinn Papers* 5: 1–31. https://doi.org/10.2307/1952804.

Schön, D.A. 1979. Generative Metaphor: A Perspective on Problem-Setting in Social Policy. *Metaphor and Thought*. https://doi.org/10.1017/CBO9781139173865.

SCO. 2009. Annex 1 to the Agreement Between the Governments of the Member States of the SCO in the Field of International Information Security.

Shimko, K.L. 1994. Metaphors and Foreign Policy Decision Making. *Political Psychology* 15 (4): 655. https://doi.org/10.2307/3791625.

Smith, B. 2017a. *The Need for a Digital Geneva Convention – Microsoft on the Issues*. Microsoft on the Issues. https://blogs.microsoft.com/on-the-issues/2017/02/14/need-digital-geneva-convention/.

———. 2017b. The Need for Urgent Collective Action to Keep People Safe Online: Lessons from Last Week's Cyberattack – Microsoft on the Issues. Microsoft one the Issues. https://blogs.microsoft.com/on-the-issues/2017/05/14/need-urgent-collective-action-keep-people-safe-online-lessons-last-weeks-cyberattack/#sm.000bi5yyf12twdrz104kfp70qrzfk.

Taddeo, M. 2016. On the Risks of Relying on Analogies to Understand Cyber Conflicts. *Minds and Machines*. https://doi.org/10.1007/s11023-016-9408-z.

———. 2017. The Limits of Deterrence Theory in Cyberspace. *Philosophy & Technology*: 1–17. https://doi.org/10.1007/s13347-017-0290-2.

Taddeo, Mariarosaria, and Luciano Floridi. 2018. Regulate artificial intelligence to avert cyber arms race comment. *Nature*. https://doi.org/10.1038/d41586-018-04602-6.

Thibodeau, P.H., and L. Boroditsky. 2011. Metaphors We Think with: The Role of Metaphor in Reasoning. *PLoS One*. https://doi.org/10.1371/journal.pone.0016782.

UC-CERT. 2016. DNS Amplification Attacks|US-CERT. US-CERT. https://www.us-cert.gov/ncas/alerts/TA13-088A.
UNGA. 2015. Report of the Secretary General: Developments in the Field of Information and Telecommunications in the Context of International Security.
———. 2016. Report of the Secretary-General Developments in the Field of Information and Telecommunications in the Context of International Security.
———. 2017. Report of the Secretary-General Developments in the Field of Information and Telecommunications in the Context of International Security.
van der Dennen, J.M.G. 1995. *The Origin of War*. Groningen: University of Groningen.
Vee, A. 2012. Text, Speech, Machine: Metaphors for Computer Code in the Law. *Computational Culture*: A Journal of Software Studies 2:12
Wolff, J. 2014. Cybersecurity as Metaphor: Policy and Defense Implications of Computer Security metaphors. *2014 TPRC Conference Paper*, 1–16. http://scholar.google.com/scholar?hl=en&btng=search&q=intitle:cybersecurity+as+metaphor:+policy+and+defense+implications+of+computer+security+metaphors+josephine#0.

Julia Slupska is a doctoral student at the Centre for Doctoral Training in Cybersecurity. Her research focuses on the ethical implications of conceptual models of cybersecurity. Currently, she is studying cybersecurity in the context of intimate partner violence and the use of simulations in political decision-making. Previously, she completed the MSc in Social Science of the Internet on the role of metaphors in international cybersecurity policy. Before joining the OII, Julia worked on an LSE Law project on comparative regional integration and coordinated course on Economics in Foreign Policy for the Foreign and Commonwealth Office. She also works as a freelance photographer.

Research Interests: cybersecurity governance, conceptual models, foreign policy, feminist approaches to cybersecurity, simulations, metaphors.

Mariarosaria Taddeo is a Research Fellow at the Oxford Internet Institute, where she co- leads (with Luciano Floridi) the Privacy and Trust Stream (social lead) of the PETRAS research hub on IoT. She is also Junior Research Fellow at St Cross College and Faculty Fellow at the Alan Turing Institute. Her recent work focuses mainly on the ethical analysis of cyber security practices, cyber conflicts, and ethics of data science. Her area of expertise is Philosophy and Ethics of Information, although she has worked on issues concerning Epistemology, Logic, and Philosophy of AI.

In 2010, she was awarded The Simon Award for Outstanding Research in Computing and Philosophy in recognition of the scholarly significance of her two articles: An Information-Based Solution for the Puzzle of Testimony and Trust (Social Epistemology, Springer) and Modelling Trust in Artificial Agents, a First Step toward the Analysis of e- Trust (Minds & Machines, Springer). In 2013, she received the World Technology Award for Ethics acknowledging the originality and her research on the ethics of cyber conflicts, and the social impact of the work that she developed in this area.

Research interests: information and computer ethics, philosophy of information, philosophy of technology, ethics of cyber-conflicts and cyber-security, applied ethics.

Chapter 3
Norms and Strategies for Stability in Cyberspace

Mariarosaria Taddeo

Abstract Cyber attacks are escalating in frequency, impact, and sophistication. For this reason, it is crucial to identify and define *regulations* for state behaviour and *strategies* to deploy countering measures that would avoid escalation and disproportionate use of cyber means, while protecting and fostering the stability of our societies. To this end, strategies to deter cyber attacks and norms regulating state behaviour in cyberspace are both necessary; unfortunately neither is available at the moment. In this chapter, I offer a theory of cyber deterrence and a set of policy recommendations to fill this vacuum.

Keywords Artificial intelligence · Cyber attacks · Cyber conflicts · Deterrence · Ethics of AI · Regulation · Stability · State

3.1 Introduction

Cyber attacks are becoming more frequent and impactful. Each day in 2017, the United States suffered, on average, more than 4000 ransomware attacks, which encrypt computer files until the owner pays to release them. In 2015, the daily average was just 1000. In May 2017, when the WannaCry virus crippled hundreds of IT systems across the UK National Health Service, more than 19,000 appointments were cancelled. A month later, the NotPetya ransomware cost pharmaceutical giant Merck, shipping firm Maersk, and logistics company FedEx around US$300 million each. Estimates show that global damages from cyber attacks may reach $6 trillion a year by 2021 (Cybersecurity Ventures 2017).

M. Taddeo (✉)
Oxford Internet Institute, University of Oxford, Oxford, UK

The Alan Turing Institute, London, UK
e-mail: mariarosaria.taddeo@oii.ox.ac.uk

C. Burr, S. Milano (eds.), *The 2019 Yearbook of the Digital Ethics Lab*, Digital Ethics Lab Yearbook, https://doi.org/10.1007/978-3-030-29145-7_3

The fast-pace escalation of cyber attacks occurred during the past decade has prompted a mounting concern about international stability and the security of our societies. To address this concern, in April 2017, the foreign ministers of the G7 countries approved a 'Declaration on Responsible States Behaviour in Cyberspace' (G7 Declaration 2017). In the opening statement, the G7 ministers stress their concern

> [...] about the risk of escalation and retaliation in cyberspace [...]. Such activities could have a destabilizing effect on international peace and security. We stress that the risk of interstate conflict as a result of ICT incidents has emerged as a pressing issue for consideration. [...], (G7 Declaration 2017, 1).

Paradoxically, state actors often play a central role in the escalation of cyber attacks. State-run cyber attacks have been launched for espionage and sabotage purposes since 2003. Well-known examples include Titan Rain (2003), the Russian attack against Estonia (2006) and Georgia (2008), Red October targeting mostly Russia and Eastern European Countries (2007), Stuxnet and Operation Olympic Game against Iran (2006–2012). In 2016, a new wave of state-run (or state-sponsored) cyber attacks ranged from the Russian attack against a Ukraine power plant,[1] to the Chinese and Russian infiltrations of US Federal Offices,[2] to the Shamoon/Greenbag attacks on government infrastructures in Saudi Arabia.[3] WannaCry has been attributed to North Korea and NotPetya to Russia in 2017. Russia has also been linked to a series of cyber attacks targeting US critical national infrastructures disclosed in 2018 (Taddeo and Floridi 2018a).

This trend will continue. The relatively low entry-cost and the high chances of success, e.g. attacks breaching a system, mean that states will keep developing, relying on, and deploying cyber attacks. At the same time, the Artificial Intelligence (AI) leap of cyber capabilities—the use of AI technologies for cyber offence and defence—indicates that cyber attacks will escalate in frequency, impact, and sophistication (Taddeo and Floridi 2018a).

Cyber attacks contribute to shape political relations, national, and international equilibria of our societies and are becoming a structural element of their power dynamics. For this reason, it is crucial to identify and define *regulations* for state behaviour and *strategies* to deploy countering measures that would avoid escalation and disproportionate use of cyber means, while protecting and fostering the stability of our societies.

Regulations and strategies will only be effective insofar as they will rest on a deep understanding of the nature of these attacks, of their differences from violent (kinetic) ones, as well as on a clear understanding of the moral principles that should shape state behaviour in cyberspace. In the first part of this chapter, I will analyse

---

[1] https://www.wired.com/2016/03/inside-cunning-unprecedented-hack-ukraines-power-grid/, accessed on the 20.06.2019.

[2] https://www.nytimes.com/2016/12/13/us/politics/russia-hack-election-dnc.html?_r=0, accessed on the 20.06.2019.

[3] https://www.symantec.com/connect/blogs/greenbug-cyberespionage-group-targeting-middle-east-possible-links-shamoon, accessed on the 20.06.2019.

existing approaches to the regulation of state behaviour in cyberspace and to the specification of deterrence strategies as countering strategies. This analysis will provide the groundwork for the theory of cyber deterrence and for the policy recommendations that I offer in the second part of the chapter.

3.2 Analogies and Regulation

Efforts to regulate state-run (or sponsored) cyber attacks—and cyber conflicts understood as attack-and-response dynamics—rose to prominence almost a decade ago, when the risks for national and international security and stability arising from the cyber domain became clear.[4] As I argued elsewhere (Taddeo 2014a, b), these efforts often rely on an *analogy-based approach*, according to which the regulatory problems concerning cyber attacks are only apparent, insofar as these are not radically different from other kinetic attacks. Those endorsing this approach claim that the existing legal framework governing inter-state, kinetic attacks is sufficient to regulate cyber attacks, and by extension cyber conflicts. All that is needed is an in-depth analysis of such laws and an adequate interpretation of the phenomena, as

> a thick web of international law norms suffuses cyber-space. These norms both outlaw many malevolent cyber-operations and allow states to mount robust responses (Schmitt 2013, 177).

According to this view, interpretations often highlight that existing norms raise substantial barriers to the use of cyber weapons and to the use of force to defend cyberspace; and international law contains coercive means of permitting lawful responses to cyber provocations and threats of any kind. The legal framework that is referred to encompasses the four Geneva Conventions and their first two Additional Protocols, the international customary law and general principle of law, the Convention restricting or prohibiting the use of certain conventional weapons, and judicial decisions. Arms control treaties, such as the Nuclear Non-Proliferation Treaty and the Chemical Weapons Convention, are often mentioned as providing guidance for action in the case of kinetic cyber attacks (Schmitt 2013). At the same time, coercive measures addressing economic violations are generally considered legitimate in the case of cyber attacks that do not cause physical damage (Lin 2012; O'Connell 2012).

Others maintain that the problem at stake is not whether cyber attacks and cyber conflicts can be interpreted in such a way as to fit the parameters of kinetic conflicts, economic transgressions, and conventional warfare, and hence whether they fall within the domain of international humanitarian law, as we know it. The problem rests at a deeper level and questions the very normative and conceptual framework of international humanitarian law and its ability to address *satisfactorily* and *fairly*

[4] http://www.nato.int/docu/review/2013/cyber/timeline/EN/index.htm, accessed on the 20.06.2019.

the changes prompted by cyber conflicts (Dipert 2010; Floridi and Taddeo 2014a, b; Taddeo 2014a).

Consider for example inter-state cyber conflicts. Regulation of these conflicts need to be developed consistently to (a) Just War Theory, (b) human rights, and (c) international humanitarian laws. However, applying (a)–(c) to the case of cyber conflicts proves to be problematic given the changes in military affairs that they prompted (Dipert 2010; Taddeo 2012a; Floridi and Taddeo 2014a, b). When compared to kinetic ones, cyber conflicts show fundamental differences: their domain ranges from the virtual to the physical; the nature of their actors and targets involves artificial and virtual entities alongside human beings and physical objects; and their level of violence may range from non-violent to potentially highly violent phenomena. These differences are redefining our understanding of key concepts such as harm, violence, target, combatants, weapons, and attack, and pose serious challenges to any attempt to regulate conflicts in cyberspace (Dipert 2010; Taddeo 2012b, 2014a, b; Floridi and Taddeo 2014a, b).

Things are not less problematic when considering ethical issues. Cyber conflicts bring about three sets of problems, concerning risks, rights, and responsibilities (3R problems) (Taddeo 2012a). The more contemporary societies are dependent on digital stechnologies, the more the 3R problems become pressing and undermine ethically blind attempts to regulate cyber conflicts. Consider the risks of escalation. Estimates indicate that the cyber security market will grow from US$106 billion in 2015 to US$170 billion by 2020, posing the risk of a progressive weaponization and militarisation of cyberspace (Taddeo and Floridi 2018a). At the same time, the reliance on malware for state-run cyber operations (like Titan Rain, Red October, and Stuxnet) risks sparking a cyber arms race and competition for digital supremacy, hence increasing the possibility of escalation and conflicts (MarketsandMarkets 2015). Regulations of cyber conflicts need to address and reduce this risk by encompassing principles to foster cyber stability, trust, and transparency among states (Arquilla and Borer 2007; Steinhoff 2007; European Union 2015; Taddeo Forthcoming).

At the same time, cyber threats are pervasive. They can target, but can also be launched through, civilian infrastructures, e.g. civilian computers and websites. This may (and in some cases already has) initiate policies of higher levels of control, enforced by governments in order to detect and deter possible threats. In these circumstances, individual rights, such as privacy and anonymity may come under sharp, devaluating pressure (Arquilla 1999; Denning 2007; Taddeo 2013).

Ascribing responsibilities also prove to be problematic when considering cyber attacks. Cyberspace affords a certain level of anonymity, often exploited by states or state-sponsored groups and non-state actors. Difficulties in attributing attacks allow perpetrators to deny responsibility, and pose an escalatory risk in cases of erroneous attribution. The international community faced this risk in 2014, when malware initially assessed as capable of destroying the content of the entire stock exchange was discovered on Nasdaq's central servers and allegations were made of a Russian origin for the software.[5]

In the medium- and long-term, regulations need to be defined to ensure security and stability of societies, and avoid risks of escalation. To achieve this end, efforts to regulate state-run cyber attacks will have to rely on an in-depth understanding of this new phenomenon; identify the changes brought about by cyber warfare and the information revolution (Floridi 2014; Taddeo and Buchanan 2015; Floridi and Taddeo 2016); and define a set of shared values that will guide the different actors operating in the international arena. The alternative is developing unsatisfactory, short-sighted approaches and facing the risk of a cyber backlash: a deceleration of the digitization process imposed by governments and international institutions to prevent this kind of conflicts to erode both the trust in economy and in political institutions. For this reason, it is necessary to seize the limits of the analogy-based approach, and to move past it. As Betz and Stevens (2013) put it:

> It is little wonder that we attempt to classify [...] the unfamiliar present and unknowable future in terms of a more familiar past, but we should remain mindful of the limitations of analogical reasoning in cyber security.

Analogies can be powerful, for they inform the way in which we think and constrain ideas and reasoning within a conceptual space (Wittgenstein 2009). However, if the conceptual space is not the right one, analogies become misleading and detrimental for any attempt to develop innovative and in-depth understanding of new phenomena, and they should be abandoned altogether. When the conceptual space is the right one, analogies are at best a step on Wittgenstein's ladder and need to be disregarded once they have taken us to the next level of the analysis. This is the case of the analogies between kinetic and cyber conflicts.

Cyberspace and cyber conflicts are now *relatively* new phenomena. Over the past two decades, possible uses, misuses, risks, and affordances of both have become clearer. As societies, we now know the successes, the failures, and the lessons learned necessary to start analysing and understanding the nature of cyberspace and cyber conflicts and to regulate appropriately both the environment and the actions in it to avoid risks of escalation and instability.

3.3 The Strategic Nature of Cyberspace

Escalation follows from the nature of cyber attacks and the dynamics of cyberspace (Floridi and Taddeo 2014a, b; Taddeo 2014a, 2016, 2017). Non-kinetic cyber attacks—aggressive uses of information and communications technologies that do not cause destruction or casualties, e.g. Distributed Denial of Service (DDoS) attacks—cost little in terms of resources and risks to the attackers, while having

[5] http://arstechnica.com/security/2014/07/how-elite-hackers-almost-stole-the-nasdaq/, accessed on the 20.06.2019.

high chances to be successful, e.g. impairing the services of targeted server or website. At the same time, cyber defence is porous by its own nature (Morgan 2012): every system has bugs in the program (vulnerabilities), identifying and exploiting them is just a matter of time, means, and determination. This makes even the most sophisticated cyber defence mechanisms ephemeral and, thus, limits their potential to deter new attacks.

Even when successful, cyber defence does not lead to strategic advantages, insofar as dismounting a cyber attack, may bring tactical success, but very rarely leads to the ultimate defeating of an adversary (Taddeo 2017). This creates an environment of *persistent offence* (Harknett and Goldman 2016), where attacking is tactically and strategically more advantageous than defending. As Haknett and Goldman argue, in an offence-persistent environment, defence can achieve tactical and operational success in the short term if it can adjust constantly to the means of attack, but it cannot win strategically. Offence will persist and the interactions with the enemy will remain constant. This is why inter-state cyber defence have shifted from reactive (defending) towards an *active* (countering) defence strategies.

In this scenario, state actors make policy decisions to protect their abilities to launch cyber attacks. *Strategic ambiguity* is one of these decisions. According to this policy, states decide neither to define nor to inform the international community about their *red lines*—thresholds that once crossed would trigger state response—for non-kinetic cyber attacks (Mariarosaria Taddeo 2011). This approach leaves de facto unregulated cyber attacks that remain below the threshold of an armed attack.

Strategic ambiguity has often been presented as a way to confuse the opponents about the consequences of their cyber attacks. As the US National Intelligence Officer for Cyber Issues officer put it:

> Currently most countries, including ours, don't want to be incredibly specific about the red lines for two reasons: You don't want to invite people to do anything they want below that red line thinking they'll be able to do it with impunity, and secondly, you don't want to back yourself into a strategic corner where you have to respond if they do something above that red line or else lose credibility in a geopolitical sense.[6]

By fostering ambiguity, state actors also leave open for themselves a wider room for manoeuvring. Strategic ambiguity allows state actors to deploy cyber attacks for military, espionage, sabotage, and surveillance purposes without being constrained by their own policies or international red lines. This makes ambiguity a dangerous choice, one that is strategically risky and politically misleading.

The risks come with the cascade effect following the absence of clear thresholds for cyber attacks. The lack of thresholds facilitates a proliferation of offensive strategies. This, in turn, favours an international cyber arms race and the weaponization of cyberspace, which ultimately spurs the escalation of cyber attacks. This is why strategic ambiguity is a policy hazard that fuels, rather than arrests, escalation of interstate cyber attacks. Cyber attacks would be deterred more effectively by a regime of international norms (defining proportionality criteria for responses, set-

[6] http://www.c4isrnet.com/articles/cyber-red-lines-ambiguous-by-necessity, accessed on the 20.06.2019.

ting red lines, and procedure for accountability, and for capability building) that makes attacks politically costly to the point of being disadvantageous for the state actors who launch them.

As I mention in Sect. 3.1, stability of cyberspace hinges on both regulations and strategies. Having considered the limits of the existing approaches to the regulation of state behaviour in cyberspace, I shall now focus on existing view for the designing deterrence strategies for cyber attacks.

3.4 Conventional Deterrence Theory

Concerned by the risks of escalation, international organisations such as NATO, the UN Institute for Disarmament Research (UNIDIR), and national governments, like the UK and US have started to consider whether, and how to, deploy deterrence to foster stability of cyberspace.

However, deploying cyber deterrence strategies is challenging. For conventional deterrence theory (hereafter: deterrence theory) does not work in cyberspace, as it does not address the global reach, anonymity, or the distributed and interconnected nature of this domain. Deterrence theory has three core elements: attribution of attacks, defence, and retaliation as types of deterring strategies; and the capability of the defender to signal credible threats (see Fig. 3.1). None of these elements is attainable in cyberspace.

Consider attribution first. Prompt, positive attribution is crucial to deterrence: the less immediate is attribution, the less severe will be the defender's response. The less positive the attribution, the more time will be necessary to respond. In cyberspace, attribution is at best problematic, if not impossible. Cyber attacks are often launched in different stages and involve globally distributed networks of machines, as well as pieces of code that combine different elements provided (or stolen) by a number of actors. In this scenario, identifying the malware, the network of infected machines, or even the country of origin of the attack is not sufficient for attribution, as attackers can design and route their operations through third-party machines and countries with the goal of obscuring or misdirecting attribution. The limits of attribution in cyberspace pose serious obstacles to the deployment of effective deter-

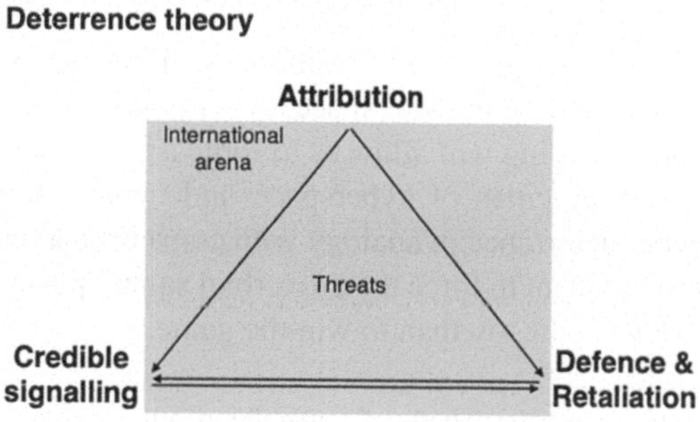

Fig. 3.1 The core elements of deterrence theory and their dependences. (This figure was published in M. Taddeo. "The Limits of Deterrence Theory in Cyberspace." *Philosophy & Technology*, 2017)

rence. Recalling Fig. 3.1, without attribution defence and retaliation, as well as signalling, are left without a target and are undermined by the inability of the defender to identify the attacker.

Signalling credible threats is also problematic in cyberspace. This element hinges on state's reputation. In kinetic scenarios, reputation is gained by showcasing military capabilities and by showing ability to resolve (to deter or defeat the opponent) over time. To some extent, the same also holds true in cyberspace, where a state's reputation also refers to a state's past interactions in this domain, its known cyber capabilities to defend and offend, as well as its overall reputation in resolving conflicts. However, state's reputation in cyberspace may not necessarily correspond to actual capabilities in this domain, as states are reluctant to circulate information about the attacks that they receive, especially those that they could not avert. This makes signalling less credible and, thus, more problematic than in other domains of warfare.

Also conventional deterrence strategies, defence and retaliation, are problematic in cyberspace. Every system has its security vulnerabilities and identifying and exploiting them is simply a matter of time, means, and determination. This makes vulnerable even the most sophisticated defence mechanisms, thus limiting their potential to deter new attacks by defence. Unlike deterrence by defence, deterrence by retaliation may be effective in cyberspace. However, this strategy is coupled with serious risk of escalation. This is because the means to retaliate, i.e. cyber weapons, are *malleable* and difficult to control. Cyber weapons can be accessed, stored, combined, repurposed, and redeployed much more easily than it was ever possible with other kinds of military capability. This was the case, for example, of Stuxnet. Despite being designed to target specific configuration requirements of Siemens software installed on Iranian nuclear centrifuges, the worm was eventually released on the Internet and infected systems in Azerbaijan, Indonesia, India, Pakistan, and the US (Farwell and Rohozinski 2011).

Clearly, classic deterrence theory faces severe limitations when applied in cyberspace. But it would be a mistake to conclude that as classic deterrence theory does not work in cyberspace, then deterrence is unattainable in this domain. As USN Commander Bebber stated:

> History suggests that applying the wrong operational framework to an emerging strategic environment is a recipe for failure. During the World War I, both sides failed to realize that large scale artillery barrages followed by massed infantry assaults were hopeless on a battlefield that strongly favored well-entrenched defense supported by machine gun technology. […] The failure to adapt had disastrous consequences.[7]

We need to adapt. And adapting will be successful only if it rests on an in-depth understanding of cyberspace, cyber conflicts, their nature, and their dynamics. This understanding will allow us to forge a new theory of deterrence, one able to address the specificities of cyberspace and cyber conflicts. The alternative—developing cyber deterrence in analogy with conventional deterrence—is a recipe for failure. It is equivalent to force the proverbial square peg in the round hole, we are more likely to smash the toy than to win the game.

[7] https://www.thecipherbrief.com/column_article/no-thing-cyber-deterrence-please-stop, accessed on the 20.06.2019.

3.5 Cyber Deterrence Theory

Cyber attacks and defence evolve with digital technology. As the latter becomes more autonomous and smart, leveraging the potential of AI, so do cyber attacks and cyber defence strategies. Both the public and private sectors are already testing AI systems in autonomous war games. The 2016, DARPA Cyber Grand Challenge was a landmark in this respect.[8] The Challenge was the first, fully autonomous competition in which AI capabilities for defence were successfully tested. Seven AI systems, developed by teams from the United States and Switzerland, fought against each other to identify and patch their own vulnerabilities, while probing and exploiting those of other systems. The Challenge showed that AI will have a major impact on the waging of cyber conflicts, it will provide new capabilities for defence, shape new strategies, but also pose new risks. Autonomous AI systems, with capacity to improve their own strategies and launch increasingly aggressive counter-attacks with each iteration, may lead to violation of the principle of proportionality and escalation of responses, which could, in turn, trigger kinetic conflicts. In this scenario, cyber deterrence is ever more necessary.

Elsewhere (Taddeo 2018), I argued that cyber deterrence rests on three core elements: target identification, retaliation, and demonstration (Fig. 3.2).

Target identification is essential for deterrence. It allows the defendant to isolate (and counter-attack) enemy systems independently from the identification of the actors behind them, thus side-stepping the attribution problem, while identifying a justifiable target for retaliation, i.e. a system the system used for the attack in the first place. Identifying the attacking system and retaliating is a feasible task, which AI systems for defence can already achieve. The 2016, DARPA Cyber Grand Challenge showed, for example, that system can counter (retaliate) attacks originating from opponents by identifying a vulnerabilities and exploiting them to slow down their operations. As shown in Fig. 3.2, cyber deterrence does not encompass defence among its possible strategies. This is due to the offence persistent

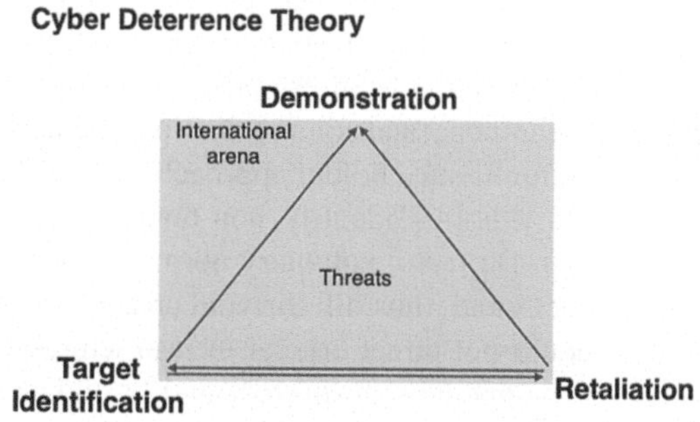

Fig. 3.2 The three elements of Cyber Deterrence Theory and their dependencies. "How to Deter in Cyberspace", (Taddeo 2018)

[8] https://www.darpa.mil/program/cyber-grand-challenge, accessed on the 20.06.2019.

nature of cyberspace, which makes retaliation more effective than defence both tactically and strategically.

Cyber deterrence uses target identification and retaliation for demonstrative purposes. According to this theory, deterrence in cyberspace works if it can demonstrate the defendant's capability to retaliate a current attack by harming the source system. While not being able to deter an incoming cyber attack, retaliation will deter the *next* round of attacks coming from the same opponent. This is because the mere threat of retaliation will not be sufficient to change the opponent's intentions to attacks. The chances of success and the likelihood that the attack will remain unattributed remain too high for any proportionate threat to be effective. Thus, to be successful, cyber deterrence needs to shift from threatening to prevailing.

3.6 A Regime of Norms

Cyber deterrence alone is not a cure for all problems. Indeed, it is insufficient to ensure stability of cyberspace. This is true especially when considering how the rising distribution and automation, multiple interactions, and fast-pace performance of cyber attacks make control progressively less effective, while increasing the risks for unforeseen consequences, proportionality breaches, and escalation of responses (Yang et al. 2018). An international regime of norms regulating state behaviour in cyberspace is necessary to complement cyber deterrence strategies and foster stability.

Over the past twenty years, the UN, the Organisation for Cyber Security and Co-operation in Europe (OSCE), and the ASEAN Regional Forum (ARF) and several national governments (G7 and G20) have convened consensus to define such a regime. The G7 Declaration is the latest of a series of successful transnational initiatives made in this direction before the failure of the UN Group of Government Experts (UN GGE) on 'Developments in the field of information and telecommunications in the context of international security'.[9]

The G7 Declaration identifies two main instruments: confidence building measures (CBMs) and voluntary norms. CBMs foster trust and transparency among states. In doing so, they favour co-operations and measures to limit the risk of escalation. CBMs range from establishing contact points, shared definitions of cyber-related phenomena, and communication channels to reduce the risk of misperception, and foster multi-stakeholder approach.

Voluntary norms identify non-binding principles that shape state conduct in cyberspace. De facto, voluntary norms identify red lines for state-run, non-kinetic cyber attacks and, thus, fill the void created by strategic ambiguity. They stress that states should not target critical infrastructures and critical information infrastructures of the opponent (norms 6, 8, and 11 of the G7 Declaration); should avoid using

[9] https://www.justsecurity.org/42768/international-cyber-law-politicized-gges-failure-advance-cyber-norms/, accessed on the 20.06.2019.

cyber attacks to violate intellectual property (norm 12 of the G7 Declaration); and remark the responsibility of state actors to disclose cyber vulnerabilities (norms 9 and 10 of the G7 Declaration).

CBMs and (in part) voluntary norms have been then included in the 2017 cyber security framework launched by the European Commission. The framework is one of the most comprehensive regulatory frameworks for state conduct in cyberspace so far. Yet it does not go far enough. The EU treats cyber defence as a case of cybersecurity, to be improved passively by making member states' information systems more resilient. It disregards active uses of cyber defence and does not include AI.

This was a missed opportunity. The EU could have begun defining red lines, harm assessment, proportionate responses in its latest rethink. For example, the 2016 EU directive on 'Security of Network and Information Systems' provides criteria for identifying crucial national infrastructures, such as health systems or key energy and water supplies that should be protected. The same criteria could be used to define illegitimate targets of state-sponsored cyber attacks.

The EU cyber security framework remains a step in the right direction, but more work needs to be done. After the failure of the UN GGE, it is crucial that discussion on the regulation of state behaviour resume. Regional forums, such as NATO and the EU, may be a good starting point for more fruitful discussions. When considering state-run cyber defence, it is crucial that the following three steps are taken into consideration to avoid serious imminent attacks on state infrastructures, and to maintain international stability. These are:

- **Define 'red lines'** distinguishing legitimate and illegitimate targets and definitions of proportionate responses for cyber defence strategies.
- **Building alliances** by mandating 'sparring' exercises between allies to test AI-based defence capabilities and the disclosure of fatal vulnerabilities of key systems and crucial infrastructures among allies.
- **Monitor and enforce rules at international level** by defining procedures to audit and oversee AI-based state cyber defence operations, alerting and remedy mechanisms to address mistakes and unintended consequences. A third-party authority with teeth, such as the UN Security Council, should rule on whether red lines, proportionality, responsible deployment or disclosure norms have been breached.

3.7 Conclusions

"Those who live by the digit may die by the digit" (Floridi 2014). Indeed, if the threats coming or targeting cyberspace pose serious risks to the stability and security of our societies is because we live in societies that are increasingly more dependent on digital technologies. As Ericcson and Giacomiello put it:

> In 1962, Arnold Wolfers wrote that national security is the absence of threat to a society's core values. If modern, economically developed countries are increasingly becoming information societies, then, [...] threats to information can be seen as threats to the core of these societies, (Eriksson and Giacomello 2006, 222).

A relation of mutual influence exists between the way conflicts are waged and the societies waging them. As Clausewitz remarked, more than an art or a science, conflicts are a social activity. And much like other social activities, conflicts mirror the values of societies while relying on their technological and scientific developments. In turn, the principles endorsed to regulate conflicts play a crucial role in shaping societies.

Think about the design, deployment, and regulation of weapons of mass destruction (WMDs). During World War II, WMDs were made possible by scientific breakthroughs in nuclear physics, which was a central area of research in the years leading to the War. Yet, their deployment proved to be destructive and violent beyond what the post-war world was willing to accept. The Cold War that followed, and the nuclear treaties that ended it, defined the modes in which nuclear technologies and WMDs could be used, drawing a line between conflicts and atrocities. In doing so, treaties and regulations for the use of WMDs contributed to shape contemporary societies as societies rejecting the belligerent rhetoric of the early twentieth century and to striving for peace and stability.

The same mutual relation exists between information societies and cyber conflicts, making the regulation of the latter a crucial aspect, which does and will contribute to shape current and future societies. In the short term, regulations are needed to avoid a digital wild west, as remarked by Harold Hongju Koh, the former Legal Advisor U.S. Department of State. In the long term, regulations are needed to ensure that cyber conflicts will not threaten the development of open, pluralistic, and tolerant information societies (Taddeo and Floridi 2018b).

The only way to ensure this outcome is to develop new domain-specific, conceptual, normative, and strategic frameworks. Analogies with kinetic conflicts, strategies to deter them, and existing normative frameworks should be abandoned altogether, as they are misleading and detrimental for any attempt to develop innovative and in-depth understanding of cyberspace, cyber conflicts, deterrence, and ensure stability. The effort is complex, but also necessary.

References

Arquilla. 1999. Ethics and Information Warfare. In *Strategic Appraisal: The Changing Role of Information in Warfare*, ed. Zalmay Khalilzad and John Patrick White, 379–401. Santa Monica: RAND.

Arquilla, J., and Douglas A. Borer. 2007. *Information Strategy and Warfare: A Guide to Theory and Practice*. New York: Routledge.

Betz, D.J., and T. Stevens. 2013. Analogical Reasoning and Cyber Security. *Security Dialogue* 44 (2): 147–164. https://doi.org/10.1177/0967010613478323.

Cybersecurity Ventures. 2017. *2017 Cybercrime Report*. https://cybersecurityventures.com/2015-wp/wp-content/uploads/2017/10/2017-Cybercrime-Report.pdf.

Denning, D.E. 2007. The Ethics of Cyber Conflict. In *Information and Computer Ethics*. Hoboken: Wiley.

Dipert, R. 2010. The Ethics of Cyberwarfare. *Journal of Military Ethics* 9 (4): 384–410.

Eriksson, Johan, and Giampiero Giacomello. 2006. The Information Revolution, Security, and International Relations: (IR)Relevant Theory? *International Political Science Review* 27 (3): 221–244. https://doi.org/10.1177/0192512106064462.

European Union. 2015. *Cyber Diplomacy: Confidence-Building Measures – Think Tank*. Brussels. http://www.europarl.europa.eu/thinktank/en/document.html?reference=EPRS_BRI(2015)571302.

Farwell, James P., and Rafal Rohozinski. 2011. Stuxnet and the Future of Cyber War. *Survival* 53 (1): 23–40. https://doi.org/10.1080/00396338.2011.555586.

Floridi, L. 2014. *The Fourth Revolution, How the Infosphere Is Reshaping Human Reality*. Oxford: Oxford University Press.

Floridi, Luciano, and Mariarosaria Taddeo, eds. 2014a. *The Ethics of Information Warfare*. New York: Springer.

———, eds. 2014b. *The Ethics of Information Warfare*, Law, Governance and Technology Series. Vol. 14. Heidelberg: Springer.

———. 2016. What Is Data Ethics? *Philosophical Transactions of the Royal Society A: Mathematical, Physical and Engineering Sciences* 374 (2083). https://doi.org/10.1098/rsta.2016.0360.

G7 Declaration. 2017. *G7 Declaration on Responsible State Behavior in cybeRspace*. Lucca. http://www.mofa.go.jp/files/000246367.pdf.

Harknett, Richard J., and O. Emily Goldman. 2016. The Search for Cyber Fundamental. *Journal of Information Warfare* 15 (2): 81–88.

Lin, Herbert. 2012. Cyber Conflict and International Humanitarian Law. *International Review of the Red Cross* 94 (886): 515–531. https://doi.org/10.1017/S1816383112000811.

Markets and Markets. 2015. Cyber Security Market by Solutions & Services – 2020. http://www.marketsandmarkets.com/Market-Reports/cyber-security-market-505.html?gclid=CNb6w7mt8MgCFQoEwwodZVQD-g.

Morgan, Patrick M. 2012. The State of Deterrence in International Politics Today. *Contemporary Security Policy* 33 (1): 85–107. https://doi.org/10.1080/13523260.2012.659589.

O'Connell, M.E. 2012. Cyber Security Without Cyber War. *Journal of Conflict and Security Law* 17 (2): 187–209. https://doi.org/10.1093/jcsl/krs017.

Schmitt, M. 2013. Cyberspace and International Law: The Penumbral Mist of Uncertainty. *Harvard* 126 (176): 176–180.

Steinhoff, Uwe. 2007. *On the Ethics of War and Terrorism*. Oxford/New York: Oxford University Press.

Taddeo, Mariarosaria. 2011. Information Warfare: A Philosophical Perspective. *Philosophy & Technology* 25 (1): 105–120. https://doi.org/10.1007/s13347-011-0040-9.

———. 2012a. An Analysis for a Just Cyber Warfare. In *2012 4th International Conference on Cyber Conflict (CYCON 2012)*, 1–10. NATO CCD COE and IEEE Publication.

———. 2012b. Information Warfare: A Philosophical Perspective. *Philosophy and Technology* 25 (1): 105–120.

———. 2013. Cyber Security and Individual Rights, Striking the Right Balance. *Philosophy & Technology* 26 (4): 353–356. https://doi.org/10.1007/s13347-013-0140-9.

———. 2014a. Just Information Warfare. *Topoi*, April, 1–12. https://doi.org/10.1007/s11245-014-9245-8.

———. 2014b. The Struggle Between Liberties and Authorities in the Information Age. *Science and Engineering Ethics*. https://doi.org/10.1007/s11948-014-9586-0.

———. 2016. On the Risks of Relying on Analogies to Understand Cyber Conflicts. *Minds and Machines* 26 (4): 317–321. https://doi.org/10.1007/s11023-016-9408-z.

———. 2017. Cyber Conflicts and Political Power in Information Societies. *Minds and Machines* 27 (2): 265–268. https://doi.org/10.1007/s11023-017-9436-3.

———. 2018. How to Deter in Cyberspace. *The European Centre of Excellence for Countering Hybrid Threats* 2018 (6): 1–10.

Taddeo, Mariarosaria, and Elizabeth Buchanan. 2015. Information Societies, Ethical Enquiries. *Philosophy & Technology* 28 (1): 5–10. https://doi.org/10.1007/s13347-015-0193-z.

Taddeo, Mariarosaria, and Luciano Floridi. 2018a. Regulate Artificial Intelligence to Avert Cyber Arms Race. *Nature* 556 (7701): 296–298. https://doi.org/10.1038/d41586-018-04602-6.

———. 2018b. How AI Can Be a Force for Good. *Science* 361 (6404): 751–752. https://doi.org/10.1126/science.aat5991.

Wittgenstein, Ludwig. 2009. *Philosophical Investigations*, Rev. 4th edn. Chichester/Malden: Wiley-Blackwell.

Yang, Guang-Zhong, Pierre E. Jim Bellingham, Peer Fischer Dupont, Luciano Floridi, Robert Full, Neil Jacobstein, et al. 2018. The Grand Challenges of Science Robotics. *Science Robotics* 3 (14): eaar7650. https://doi.org/10.1126/scirobotics.aar7650.

Mariarosaria Taddeo is a Research Fellow at the Oxford Internet Institute, where she co- leads (with Luciano Floridi) the Privacy and Trust Stream (social lead) of the PETRAS research hub on IoT. She is also Junior Research Fellow at St Cross College and Faculty Fellow at the Alan Turing Institute. Her recent work focuses mainly on the ethical analysis of cyber security practices, cyber conflicts, and ethics of data science. Her area of expertise is Philosophy and Ethics of Information, although she has worked on issues concerning Epistemology, Logic, and Philosophy of AI.

In 2010, she was awarded The Simon Award for Outstanding Research in Computing and Philosophy in recognition of the scholarly significance of her two articles: An Information-Based Solution for the Puzzle of Testimony and Trust (Social Epistemology, Springer) and Modelling Trust in Artificial Agents, a First Step toward the Analysis of e- Trust (Minds & Machines, Springer). In 2013, she received the World Technology Award for Ethics acknowledging the originality and her research on the ethics of cyber conflicts, and the social impact of the work that she developed in this area.

Research interests: information and computer ethics, philosophy of information, philosophy of technology, ethics of cyber-conflicts and cyber-security, applied ethics.

Chapter 4
The Rhetoric and Reality of Anthropomorphism in Artificial Intelligence

David Watson

Abstract Artificial intelligence (AI) has historically been conceptualized in anthropomorphic terms. Some algorithms deploy biomimetic designs in a deliberate attempt to effect a sort of digital isomorphism of the human brain. Others leverage more general learning strategies that happen to coincide with popular theories of cognitive science and social epistemology. In this chapter, I challenge the anthropomorphic credentials of the neural network algorithm, whose similarities to human cognition I argue are vastly overstated. I submit that three alternative supervised learning methods – namely lasso penalties, bagging, and boosting – offer subtler, more interesting analogies to human reasoning as both an individual and a social phenomenon. Despite the temptation to fall back on anthropomorphic tropes when discussing AI, however, I conclude that such rhetoric is at best misleading and at worst downright dangerous. The impulse to humanize algorithms is an obstacle to properly conceptualizing the ethical challenges posed by emerging technologies.

Keywords Artificial intelligence · Machine learning · Epistemology · Social epistemology · Cognitive science · Digital ethics

4.1 Introduction

Ever since the seminal work of Turing (1950) if not before, experts and laypeople alike have tended to frame computational achievements in explicitly epistemological terms. We speak of machines that *think*, *learn*, and *infer*. The name of the discipline itself – *artificial intelligence* – practically dares us to compare our biological

---

D. Watson (✉)
Oxford Internet Institute, University of Oxford, Oxford, UK

The Alan Turing Institute, London, UK
e-mail: david.watson@oii.ox.ac.uk

C. Burr, S. Milano (eds.), *The 2019 Yearbook of the Digital Ethics Lab*, Digital Ethics Lab Yearbook, https://doi.org/10.1007/978-3-030-29145-7_4

modes of reasoning with the behavior of algorithms. It is not always clear whether such language is meant to be literal or metaphorical.

In this chapter, I attempt to move beyond the platitudes and critically examine specific examples of algorithms that employ learning strategies found in cognitive science and social epistemology. I argue that the best-known instance of such an algorithm, namely neural networks, are at best a loose approximation of one idealized neuroscientific model. More illuminating analogies can be found in other areas of computational statistics, notably three cases I shall explore in considerable depth: lasso penalties, bagging, and boosting. These three methods are extremely general and widely used in data science, although they are for the most part unfamiliar to audiences beyond this domain. I will explain the basic ideas behind each, with a focus on their epistemological motivations and implications. Finally, I shall argue that while the connections between machine learning algorithms and human cognition may be intriguing and suggestive, the rhetoric of anthropomorphism can do more harm than good when it comes to conceptualizing the important ethical challenges posed by emerging technologies.

The rest of this chapter is structured as follows. In Sect. 4.2, I briefly review some background terminology that will be essential to the proceeding analysis. In Sect. 4.3, I examine the neuroscientific inspiration behind the neural network algorithm and underscore three important differences between human cognition and so-called "deep learning". In Sects. 4.4, 4.5 and 4.6, I introduce lasso penalties, bagging, and boosting, respectively. I show how each resembles or builds upon popular theories of cognitive science and social epistemology, providing informative and unexpected examples of interdisciplinary convergence. Though it is easy and tempting to speak of algorithms in anthropomorphic terms, I caution against such rhetoric in Sect. 4.7. I conclude in Sect. 4.8 with a summary.

4.2 Terminology

All algorithms reviewed in this chapter are instances of *supervised learning*. The typical supervised learning setup involves a matrix of features X (a.k.a. predictors, independent variables, etc.) and a vector of outcomes Y (a.k.a. the response, dependent variable, etc.) that together form some fixed but unknown joint distribution $P(X, Y)$. The goal is to infer a function f that predicts Y based on X. If Y is continuous, then f is a regression function; if Y is categorical, then f is a classifier. For a good textbook introduction to statistical learning, see Hastie et al. (2009).

The performance of a supervised learner f is measured by a *loss function*, which quantifies the model's error. For instance, a classifier may record a loss of 0 for correct predictions and 1 for misclassifications. Loss can be decomposed into *bias* and *variance*, roughly akin to the concepts of accuracy and precision. A low-bias, high-variance model is one that both overshoots and undershoots the mark, occasionally by large margins but in roughly equal proportions. A high-bias, low-variance model is more consistent in its outputs – but consistently wrong. See Fig. 4.1 for an

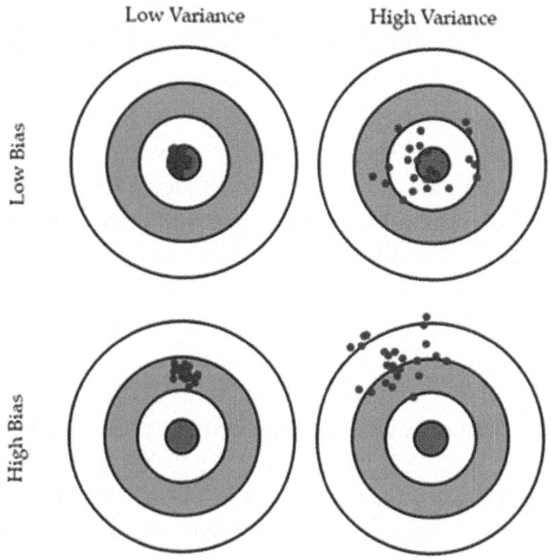

Fig. 4.1 Visual depiction of bias and variance, key concepts in evaluating supervised learning algorithms

illustration. There is an inherent bias-variance trade-off in all supervised learning algorithms.

Predictions from multiple models can be combined in a process known as *ensemble learning*. A learning ensemble consists of many individual *base learners* or *basis functions*, whose outputs are typically pooled either by summation or averaging. This strategy can be especially advantageous with low-bias, high-variance models such as decision or regression trees, which are often referred to as *weak learners*. Two popular forms of ensemble learning are introduced and reviewed in Sects. 4.5 and 4.6.

A model f is judged by its ability to *generalize*, i.e. to successfully predict outcomes on data that were not included in its training set. If f performs well on training samples but poorly on test samples, then we say that f is *overfit* – it has learned the properties of some particular observations, but not the underlying distribution from which they were drawn, $P(X, Y)$. Overfitting may be mitigated by a number of clever strategies collectively referred to as *regularization*. Specific examples of regularization will be detailed in Sects. 4.4, 4.5, and 4.6.

To guard against overfitting, models are typically evaluated not based on their in-sample performance, but on their out-of-sample performance. Ideally, this would be done by training on one dataset and testing on another sampled from the same population. However, data scarcity can make this strategy inefficient in practice. The typical solution is to implement a resampling procedure that divides the data in some systematic way. The most popular example of such a method is *cross-validation*. To cross-validate an algorithm, we split the data into k subsets (or *folds*) of roughly equal size. We then train k separate models, with each fold held out once for testing. The average generalization error across the k trials is reported.

Another common resampling procedure is based on *bootstrapping*. Bootstrapping was originally proposed as a nonparametric technique for estimating the variance of a statistic (Efron 1979). The idea is simple. Say we have observed the height of n individuals. Our goal is to compute not just the mean of this sample, but also the corresponding standard error. (Of course, we could do so analytically under minimal parametric assumptions, but the following method applies more generally.) We create a *bootstrap sample* by drawing n observations *with replacement* from the original data. The replacement step ensures a degree of variation across bootstrap samples, as some observations will appear multiple times in a single bootstrap, and others not at all. By recording the mean of each bootstrap sample and repeating the procedure some large number of times B, we get an unbiased estimate of the sampling distribution of the mean. The standard deviation of this distribution is a plug-in estimator for the standard error.

Note that a little over one third of observations will tend to be excluded from any given bootstrap sample. Specifically, each observation has an exclusion probability of $e^{-1} \approx 0.368$, which is extremely useful for model evaluation, since these unsampled cases – the so-called out-of-bag (OOB) observations – form a natural test set. This will be especially important when we examine bagging in Sect. 4.5.

Having reviewed this background material, we may now apply the relevant concepts with formal clarity to a number of machine learning algorithms.

4.3 Neural Networks

Research in neural networks began in 1958 with Frank Rosenblatt's perceptron model (Rosenblatt 1958). Rosenblatt was a US Navy psychologist, and the perceptron algorithm he developed was explicitly inspired by a mathematical idealization of the neuron, the brain's most basic information processing unit. Biological neurons are connected by synapses that enable communication through electrical or chemical signals. Building on this basic idea, Rosenblatt proposed a model architecture in which input features are mapped to outputs through an intermediate layer of neurons (see Fig. 4.2). The weights connecting these components are analogous to the synaptic strength of incoming and outgoing channels. At the output layer, values are passed through a nonlinear activator function to mimic the thresholding effect of biological neurons, which respond to stimuli by either firing or not firing.

Neural networks have evolved considerably since Rosenblatt first published his perceptron model. Modern variants of the algorithm tend to include many more layers – thence the name *deep* neural networks (DNNs) – an approach inspired at least in part by anatomical research. In their influential study of the cat visual cortex, Hubel and Wiesel (1962) differentiated between so-called "simple" cells, which detect edges and curves, and "complex" cells, which combine simple cells to identify larger shapes with greater spatial invariance. The authors hypothesized that a hierarchy of neural layers could enable increasingly complex cognition, allowing the brain to operate at higher levels of abstraction. DNNs implement this theory at scale. Employing complex convolutional architectures (Krizhevsky et al. 2012),

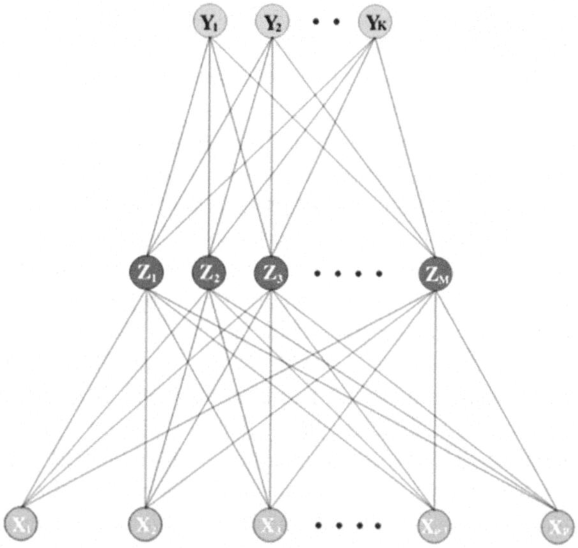

Fig. 4.2 Schematic depiction of a single-layered neural network. Input features X are combined at each neuron Z, which in turn combine to produce predictions Y. (From Hastie et al. 2009, p. 393)

clever activation functions (Glorot et al. 2011), and sophisticated backpropagation methods (Goodfellow et al. 2016), DNNs have led the latest wave of excitement about and funding for AI research. Descendants of the perceptron algorithm now power translation services for Google (Wu et al. 2016), facial recognition software for Facebook (Taigman et al. 2014), and virtual assistants like Apple's Siri (Siri Team 2017).

The biomimetic approach to AI has always inspired the popular imagination. Writing about Rosenblatt's perceptron, the *New York Times* declared in 1958 that "The Navy has revealed the embryo of an electronic computer today that it expects will be able to walk, talk, see, write, reproduce itself and be conscious of its existence" (*New York Times* 1958). The exuberance has only been somewhat tempered by the intervening decades. The same newspaper recently published a piece on DeepMind's AlphaZero, a DNN that is the reigning world champion of chess, shogi, and Go (Silver et al. 2018). In the essay, Steve Strogatz describes the algorithm in almost breathless language:

> Most unnerving was that AlphaZero seemed to express insight. It played like no computer ever has, intuitively and beautifully, with a romantic, attacking style. It played gambits and took risks....AlphaZero had the finesse of a virtuoso and the power of a machine. It was humankind's first glimpse of an awesome new kind of intelligence. (Strogatz 2018)

Excitement about DNNs is hardly limited to the popular press. Some leading researchers in deep learning have suggested that the anthropomorphic connection in fact runs both ways, proposing that "neural networks from AI can be used as plausible simulacra of biological brains, potentially providing detailed explanations of the computations occurring therein" (Hassabis et al. 2017). At least one philosopher has argued that DNNs instantiate a mode of "transformational abstraction" that resolves longstanding epistemological debates between rationalists and empiricists (Buckner 2018).

There is no denying that the achievements of AlphaZero and other top performing DNNs are impressive. But a large strain of literature in computational statistics has recently emphasized the limitations of these algorithms, which deviate from human modes of learning in several fundamental and alarming ways.

A complete list of the differences between DNNs and biological neural networks would be too long to enumerate here. See Marcus (2018) for a good overview. Instead I will highlight three especially noteworthy dissimilarities that underscore the shortcomings of this paradigm, which I argue has been vastly overhyped since DNNs first attained state of the art performance in speech recognition (Dahl et al. 2012; Mohamed et al. 2012; Raina et al. 2009) and image classification tasks (Krizhevsky et al. 2012; Lecun et al. 1998, 2015). These results notwithstanding, numerous studies have shown that compared to human brains, DNNs are *brittle*, *inefficient*, and *myopic* in specific senses to be explained below.

DNNs tend to break down in the face of minor attacks. In a landmark paper, Goodfellow et al. (2014) introduced *generative adversarial networks* (GANs), a new class of DNNs designed to fool other DNNs through slight perturbations of the input features. For instance, by adding just a small amount of noise to the pixels of a photograph, Goodfellow et al. (2015) were able to trick the high-performing ImageNet classifier into mislabeling a panda as a gibbon, even though differences between the two images are imperceptible to the human eye (see Fig. 4.3).

Others have fooled DNNs into misclassifying zebras as horses (Zhu et al. 2017), bananas as toasters (Brown et al. 2017), and many other absurd combinations. While GANs were originally viewed as something of a curiosity in the deep learning community, they have since been widely recognized as a profound challenge that severely undermines the applicability of DNNs to sensitive areas such as clinical medicine (Finlayson et al. 2019). It has also spawned an entire literature of its own, with many researchers identifying creative new uses for GANs (e.g., Elgammal et al. 2017; Odena et al. 2017; Radford et al. 2015). Needless to say, humans are much more resilient to minor perturbations of our sensory stimuli. This disconnect

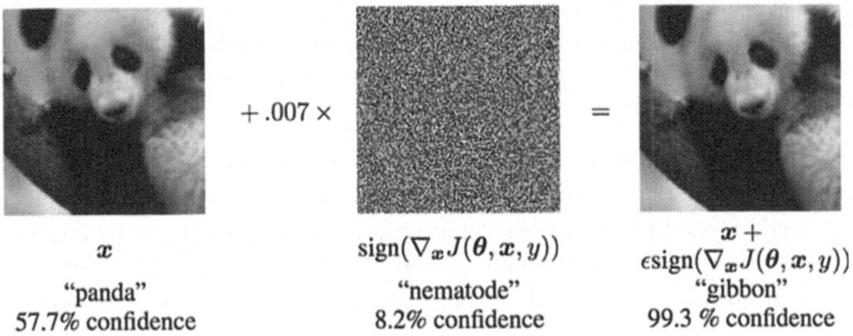

Fig. 4.3 Example of an adversarial perturbation from Goodfellow et al. (2015, p. 3)

between biological and artificial neural networks suggests that the latter lack some crucial component essential to navigating the real world.

Another important flaw with DNNs is that they are woefully data inefficient. High-performing models typically need millions of examples to learn distinctions that would strike a human as immediately obvious. Geoffrey Hinton, one of the pioneers of DNNs and a recent recipient of the ACM's prestigious Turing Award for excellence in computing, has raised the issue himself in interviews. "For a child to learn to recognize a cow," he remarked, "it's not like their mother needs to say 'cow' 10,000 times" (Waldrop 2019). This limitation is especially frustrating in cases where abundant, high-quality data are prohibitively expensive or difficult to collect. Gathering large volumes of labelled photographs is not especially challenging, but comparable datasets for genetics or particle physics are another matter altogether. Reinforcement learning arguably poses a clever workaround to this problem, in which synthetic data are generated as part of the training process (Sutton and Barto 2018). However, this approach is constrained by our ability to simulate realistic data for the target system.

A final important difference between human cognition and deep learning is that the latter has proven itself to be strangely myopic. The problem is most evident in the case of image classification. Careful analysis of the intermediate layers of convolutional DNNs reveals that whereas the lowest level neurons deal in pixels, higher level neurons operate on more meaningful features like eyes and ears, just as Hubel & Wiesel hypothesized (Olah et al. 2018). Yet even top performing models can learn to discriminate between objects while completely failing to grasp their interrelationships. For instance, rearranging Kim Kardashian's mouth and eye in Fig. 4.4 actually improved the DNN's prediction, indicating something deeply wrong with the underlying model, which performs well on out-of-sample data (Bourdakos 2017). A new kind of DNN called *capsule networks* was recently proposed to try and overcome these deficiencies (Hinton et al. 2018; Sabour et al. 2017), but the technology is still in its infancy.

The problems of algorithmic brittleness, inefficiency, and myopia are not necessarily unique to DNNs, although they are perhaps the worst offenders on all fronts. What these flaws do establish, however, is that cutting-edge AI models do not process information in anything like the way we humans do, despite Rosenblatt's stated intentions and best efforts. There can be no denying that deep learning represents a

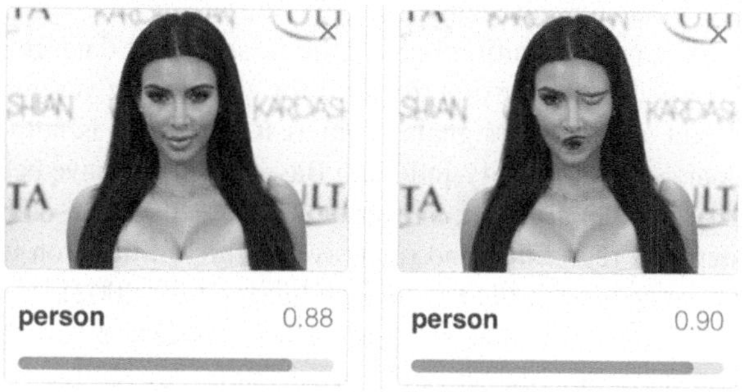

Fig. 4.4 Predictions from a convolutional DNN on two images of Kim Kardashian. Alarmingly, rearranging her facial features does not adversely affect the model's prediction. (From Bourdakos 2017)

major advance in AI research. Yet it would be a mistake to say that these algorithms *recreate* human intelligence. Instead they introduce some other mode of inference that outperforms us in some ways and falls far short in others.

Often lost in the excitement surrounding DNNs is the fact that other approaches to machine learning exist, many with considerable advantages over neural networks on a wide range of tasks. The next three sections are devoted to several such methods, with an emphasis on their epistemological underpinnings and anthropomorphic connections.

4.4 Lasso Penalties

Lasso penalties are a popular form of regularization in machine learning. They are designed for modelling *sparse* datasets, i.e. those in which at least some of our recorded variables are uninformative with respect to the response. For instance, biological knowledge tells us that only a small percentage of genes are likely to be involved in any given clinical outcome. However, high-throughput technologies allow scientists to test thousands or even millions of genetic associations in a single experiment. The lasso provides a fast, principled method for selecting top features in such settings.

Originally introduced by Tibshirani (1996), lasso penalties impose a cost not just on predictive errors – that is the role of the loss function – but on the model parameters themselves, preventing them from growing too large in absolute value. For instance, a linear regression with a lasso penalty solves the following optimization problem:

$$\min_{\beta\in\mathbb{R}^p} \frac{1}{n} y - \mathbf{X}\beta_2^2 + \lambda\beta_1$$

The first summand corresponds to the mean square error, the typical loss function in regression tasks. The second summand puts a data-adaptive weight λ on the L_1-norm (i.e., the sum of absolute values) of the coefficient vector β. This term effectively shrinks all model parameters toward 0. At the optimal value of the lasso penalty λ, usually selected via cross-validation, this algorithm will tend to remove uninformative predictors altogether (see Fig. 4.5).

The basic intuition behind the lasso is that datasets are often intolerably noisy. We need some sensible method for eliminating variables that hinder our ability to detect and exploit signals of interest. The lasso is not the only way to achieve this goal. Several sparsity-inducing Bayesian priors have been proposed to similar effect (Carvalho et al. 2010; Ishwaran and Rao 2005). So-called "greedy" algorithms like stepwise regression and recursive feature elimination iteratively remove predictors by comparing nested models (Guyon et al. 2002). Projection techniques such as principal component analysis (Jolliffe 2002) and t-stochastic neighborhood embedding (van der Maaten and Hinton 2008) are designed to recover latent variables,

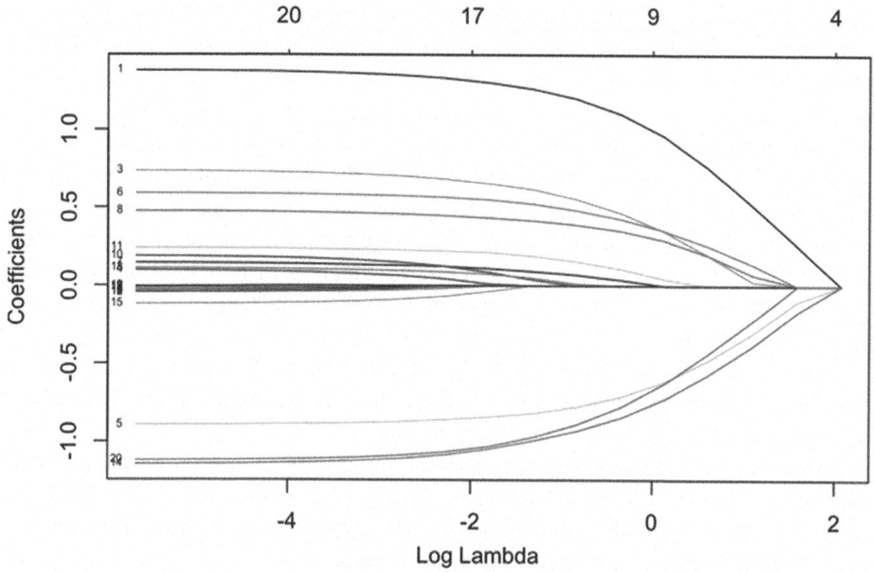

Fig. 4.5 Example of the "lasso path" of model coefficients in a linear regression. All weights converge toward zero as the penalty parameter increases

low-dimensional data projections that preserve as much information as possible from the original high-dimensional feature space.

The lasso is unique, however, in its combination of speed and interpretability. Recursive refitting can be prohibitively slow with large datasets, and stepwise regression is inapplicable when features outnumber samples. Bayesian methods are notorious for their computational overhead. By contrast, fast optimization algorithms exist for computing complete lasso paths in generalized linear models (Friedman et al. 2010) and estimating sparse inverse covariance matrices (Friedman et al. 2007) without any dimensionality constraints. Whereas projection techniques require complex, potentially nonlinear combinations of the original inputs, a fitted lasso regression is no more difficult to understand than an ordinary linear model, with nonzero coefficients on just a subset of the original features. These practical advantages help explain why lasso penalties have become so widespread in contemporary statistics and machine learning, as they enable the analysis of high-dimensional datasets that are challenging or impossible to model using traditional regression and classification techniques (Bühlmann and van de Geer 2011).

Lasso penalties bear a striking resemblance to a process psychologists call *sensory gating*, i.e. the suppression of irrelevant stimuli in one's immediate phenomenal experience. Sensory gating prevents flooding of the higher cortical centers, which can make it difficult for agents to efficiently process information. Research has shown that sensory gating is a fundamental aspect of early childhood development (Kisley et al. 2003). Gating deficiencies are associated with a wide range of psychiatric conditions, including epilepsy (Boutros et al. 2006), Alzheimer's

Disease (Jessen et al. 2001), and schizophrenia (Bramon et al. 2004). Experiments conducted on animal and human subjects have revealed complex physiological underpinnings of gating behavior, which has been observed in single neurons as well as sensory, motor, and limbic subregions of the brain (Cromwell et al. 2008).

Lasso penalties have the same inhibitory effect on noisy variables that gating has on uninformative sensory inputs. Both methods thrive in complex systems where attention must be selectively apportioned. Just as a model that puts too much weight on irrelevant features will perform poorly on new datasets, so an individual who does not screen sensory data will struggle to function in new environments. Of course, there are major differences between the two. For instance, the lasso imposes a global penalty that simultaneously drives all parameters toward zero, while sensory gating is more selective in its screening mechanism. In this respect, sparsity-inducing Bayesian methods are perhaps more directly analogous to sensory gating. However, the overall effect is similar in any case.

To the best of my knowledge, no research in lasso penalties has been explicitly motivated by connections to the cognitive process of sensory gating. Yet the success of this statistical technique can be at least partly explained by the fact that it implements a strategy that is essential to human intelligence.

4.5 Bagging

"Bagging" is a portmanteau of "bootstrap aggregating". The term was coined by Leo Breiman (1996), whose seminal contributions to statistical learning include the original classification and regression tree (CART) algorithm (Breiman et al. 1984) as well as random forests (Breiman 2001). Bagging is a prime example of ensemble learning, defined in Sect. 4.2 above. The method is completely general and can be used in conjunction with any base learner.

To bag the estimates of some base learner f, we simply average results across a large number of bootstrap samples. The generalization error of a bagged prediction can be easily estimated using the OOB samples randomly excluded from the individual draws. Recall from Sect. 4.2 that when bootstrapping, each observation has an approximately 36.8% exclusion probability. Thus, to calculate the error for a single data point, we restrict our attention to the $B^* \approx B/e$ bootstrap samples in which it was not selected.

Bagging is most widely used with CART or some other tree-based algorithm as the base learner. One reason for this is that decision trees are unstable predictors – they are low-bias, high-variance models that benefit from bagging since overestimates and underestimates tend to cancel out over a sufficiently large number of bootstrap replicates. Bagging also smooths out the jagged decision boundaries and regression surfaces induced by recursive partitioning – the basis of all tree-based algorithms – which naturally produces step functions (see Fig. 4.6). As a practical note, bagging can take advantage of parallel processing power by distributing base

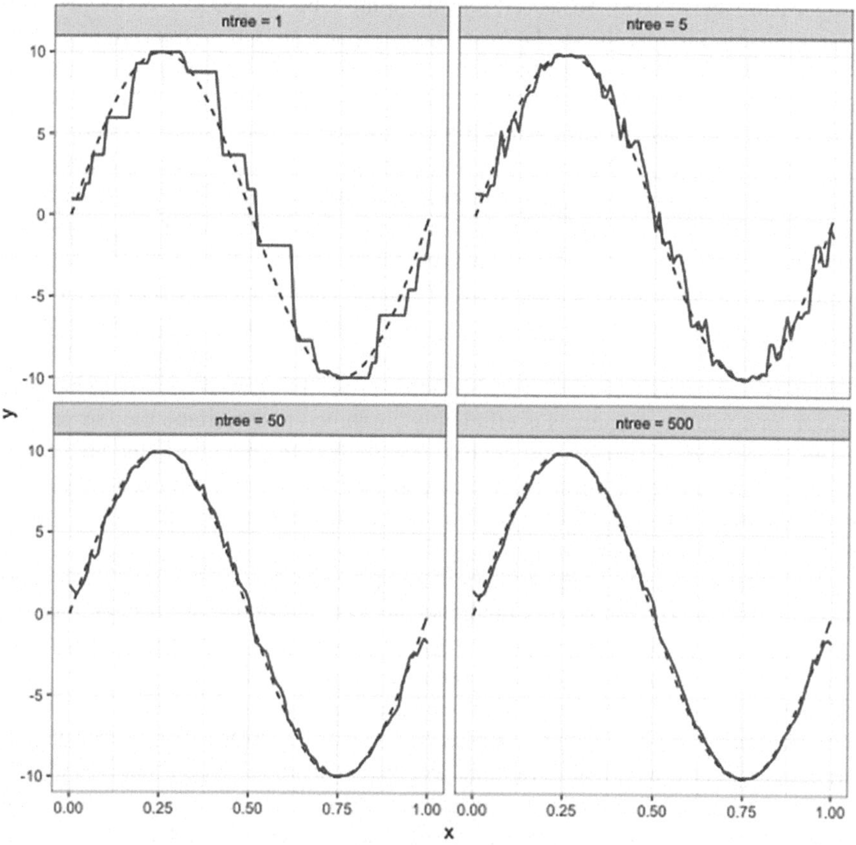

Fig. 4.6 Bagged estimates converging on a sine function as the number of trees in the ensemble increases

learners across multiple cores, dramatically decreasing run time on modern machines.

Bagging is the key statistical innovation behind the random forest algorithm, one of the most popular techniques in all of supervised learning. Random forests have generated state of the art results in a number of quantitative disciplines, including genomics (Chen and Ishwaran 2012), econometrics (Mullainathan and Spiess 2017), and computational linguistics (Kontonatsios et al. 2014). The statistical theory underlying random forests and other bagged estimators has proven surprisingly difficult to develop, mostly due to tricky problems arising from the bootstrapping procedure. In fact, it is common for statisticians to prove theorems about a slightly modified version of the algorithm in which base learners are trained not on bootstrap samples, but rather on data subsamples – i.e., observations drawn randomly *without* replacement – which are more theoretically tractable (Scornet et al. 2015;

Wager and Athey 2018). However, bootstrapping tends to produce better results in practice, which is why the method remains popular among data scientists.

The success and broad applicability of bagging should come as no surprise to anyone familiar with the so-called "wisdom of crowds". Despite the resurgence of interest in aggregated decision-making due to web-enabled mass communication (Kittur and Kraut 2008), the basic concept at work here is in fact quite old. Condorcet's jury theorem (1785) states that any verdict reached by a set of independent and better than random jurors is more likely to be correct than the judgment of any individual juror. Moreover, the probability of a correct majority judgment approaches 1 as the jury size increases. Francis Galton famously reported in 1907 that observers at a county fair accurately guessed the weight of an ox – not individually, but in aggregate, when their estimates were averaged (Galton 1907). Faith in humanity's collective wisdom arguably undergirds all free markets, where information from a variety of sources is efficiently combined to determine the fair price of assets (Fama 1965). Crowdsourcing has recently become popular in the natural sciences, where online enthusiasts have helped map the neural circuitry of the mammalian retina (Kim et al. 2014) and discover new astronomical objects (Cardamone et al. 2009; Watson and Floridi 2018).

Just as lasso penalties mirror the process of sensory gating, bagging implements a computational version of this fundamental principle of social epistemology. By pooling the estimates of many better than random models (i.e., weak learners) we can create a single high-performing ensemble capable of modelling extremely complex systems with irregular decision boundaries and regression surfaces. In his book *The Wisdom of Crowds* (2004), James Surowiecki identifies five criteria that he argues distinguish wise from irrational groups: (1) diversity of opinion; (2) independence; (3) decentralization; (4) aggregation; and (5) trust. Bagging meets all four criteria that are relevant in statistical applications. (It is hard to imagine how a base learner could "trust" the ensemble to be fair?) The random perturbations induced by bootstrapping ensure diversity across the submodels. Each sample is treated independently of all the rest, to the extent that base learners are often trained in parallel. The system is completely decentralized, with no global parameters governing the ensemble. Finally, aggregation is simple – voting in the case of classification and averaging in the case of regression.

4.6 Boosting

Boosting is another ensemble method, similar in some respects to bagging. However, whereas base learners in bagged models are fit independently of one another, boosting is a sequential procedure in which each model builds upon the last. Thus f_2 attempts to correct what f_1 got wrong, f_3 focuses on the errors of f_2, and so on. Much like bagging, boosting is a completely general approach that can work in principle with any combination of base learners. In practice, it is most often used with decision or regression trees.

Boosted predictions are made by summing across the individual basis functions. Stochastic gradient boosting, the most popular modern form of the algorithm, operates on bootstraps or subsamples of the original data to train each base learner, thereby enabling fast OOB estimation of the overall generalization error.

The first successful boosting algorithm was implemented by Freund and Schapire (1995). Their pioneering AdaBoost algorithm earned them the 2003 Gödel Prize, one of theoretical computer science's highest honors. Subsequent improvements by Friedman (2001, 2002) and more recently Chen and Guestrin (2016) have rendered boosting one of the most powerful methods in all of machine learning. The latter authors introduced XGBoost, an especially fast and scalable version that has gone on to dominate in a number of public data science competitions (Gorman 2017). Bayesian versions of boosting have also been developed (Chipman et al. 2010) with extensions to causal inference (Hahn et al. 2017; Hill 2011), survival analysis (Sparapani et al. 2016), and high-dimensional modeling (Linero 2018; Linero and Yang 2018).

The statistical properties of boosting have been difficult to establish, although solid progress has been made in the last decade, especially with regards to the original AdaBoost algorithm (Schapire and Freund 2012). Researchers in this area tend to follow a similar strategy to those who study bagging, relying on slight idealizations to derive convergence rates and other relevant theorems (Buhlmann and Hothorn 2007; Bühlmann and Yu 2003; Ehrlinger and Ishwaran 2012).

Boosting requires the careful calibration of several hyperparameters, which makes it somewhat less user-friendly than bagging. For instance, whereas bagged estimates do not degrade as the number of bootstraps B grows large, boosting is much more susceptible to overfitting. To offset against this, a shrinkage coefficient ν is used to moderate the learning rate. The XGBoost algorithm includes a number of additional parameters that control everything from the overarching architecture of the model to the recursive partitioning subroutine (Chen et al. 2019). Bayesian methods introduce a number of extra parameters to define prior distributions, although sensible defaults have been shown to work well in a wide variety of settings (Chipman et al. 2010). Cross-validating the optimal values for all these parameters can be time-consuming, but the extra effort is often worth it. Hastie et al. (2009) observe that boosting tends to dominate bagging in most applications.

The sequential nature of boosting bears some striking similarities to a process cognitive scientists call *predictive coding* (Rao and Ballard 1999). According to this theory, human perception is a dynamic inference problem in which the brain is constantly attempting to classify the objects of phenomenal experience and updating predictions based on new sensory information. The process is often formalized along Bayesian lines, with current predictions serving as a prior distribution and new data providing a likelihood for dynamic updating (Friston 2009; Friston and Kiebel 2009). The theory has also been extended to sensorimotor functions (Körding and Wolpert 2007) and mirror neuronal systems to account for our ability to interpret the behavior of others in intentional terms (Kilner et al. 2007). Another way to model the same process is as a boosting procedure in which basis functions are iteratively fit to environmental stimuli based on the best available prediction and resulting residual feedback.

Boosting has some practical advantages over Bayesian inference as a formal model for predictive coding. First, the former makes no parametric assumptions, which are often necessary to ensure the mathematical tractability of complex Bayesian updating procedures. Second, boosting with weak learners is more computationally efficient than integrating over high-dimensional distributions, an essential and time-consuming step for Bayesian inference with multiple input channels. Finally, boosting naturally strikes a data-adaptive balance between individual basis functions, whereas Bayesian posteriors require a prior distribution to be defined upfront.

None of this is to say that the human brain in fact implements a boosting procedure when engaged in predictive coding. However, I argue the prospect is at least as plausible as the Bayesian alternative, which is currently popular in computational neuroscience (Doya et al. 2007). I suspect the two models would render similar results in most cases, especially as data continues to accrue and the likelihood gradually overwhelms the prior. The success of Bayesian boosting algorithms suggests that the two choices may not even be mutually exclusive. In any event, it is remarkable that statistical methods developed on independent grounds appear to have converged on formal procedures for modeling how the human brain processes sensory information.

4.7 Ethical Considerations

We have now reviewed a number of supervised learning algorithms that either deliberately or coincidentally mirror certain aspects of human cognition to varying degrees. In a sense, this is only to be expected. For better or worse, we are our own best source of inspiration when it comes to modelling intelligence. There is nothing especially remarkable or problematic about this.

However, issues arise when we begin to take these metaphors and analogies too literally. Recent years have seen AI deployed in a number of socially sensitive contexts, such as credit scoring, criminal justice, and military operations (Mittelstadt et al. 2016). These domains frequently involve high-stakes decisions with significant impact on the lives of those involved. Public and private institutions have traditionally relied upon human experts to adjudicate on matters of such extreme risk. This makes sense for at least three reasons. First, and most obviously, it is exceedingly important that we get these risky decisions right. Experts are presumably those in the best position to minimize error. A second, closely related point is that we want to trust the reasoning that goes into important decisions. This amounts to an emphasis on process over product, a desire to ensure that there are no weak links in the inferential chain connecting inputs and outputs. Finally, experts are an appropriate locus of moral responsibility. They are accountable agents worthy of praise or blame depending on the outcome of their actions.

To summarize, high risk decisions should ideally be made by (i) accurate, (ii) trustworthy, and (iii) responsible agents. Of these three desiderata, AI can most plausibly be said to meet the first. Of course, the extent to which AI does in fact match or surpass human performance is an empirical question that must be handled on a case by case basis. With desideratum (ii), however, we quickly run into fundamental limits on our ability to trace the inductive reasoning of complex learning machines. Modern algorithms routinely contain millions of parameters describing subtle, nonlinear interactions. A frantic torrent of research in the last few years has sought to establish general-purpose tools for explainable AI (for recent surveys, see, e.g., Adadi and Berrada 2018; Guidotti et al. 2018), but several commentators have observed that the target of such investigations remains fundamentally underdetermined (Doshi-Velez and Kim 2017; Lipton 2016). As we found in Sect. 4.3, trust cannot be guaranteed by mere accuracy alone, as high-performance models often fail in surprising ways. I am most pessimistic about AI's chances of meeting desideratum (iii). Algorithms may be causally responsible for any number of significant outcomes, but *moral* responsibility remains well beyond the ambit of even the most advanced machine learning program.

Perhaps we may relax these desiderata somewhat to accommodate new modes of trust and agency. For instance, Floridi & Sanders argue that ethical discourse has been "unduly constrained by its anthropocentric conception of agenthood" (2004, p. 350). They note that artificial agents (AAs) can be interactive, autonomous, and adaptable. Yet they readily concede that "it would be ridiculous to praise or blame an AA for its behaviour or charge it with a moral accusation" (p. 366), going on to clarify that AAs instantiate a form of "aresponsible morality" (p. 364). In a similar vein, Taddeo (2010) argues that AAs can earn one another's *e-trust*, an emergent second-order property arising in distributed digital systems with certain first-order relational properties. This phenomenon is not to be confused with old-fashioned human trust, a considerably messier affair that cannot be adequately modelled by neat mathematical functions or the formal apparatus of rational choice theory. These views are consonant with my remarks above that DNNs exhibit a novel kind of intelligence, similar in some respects but far from identical to the human original.

However, I am skeptical that these modified notions of agency and trust are sufficient to upgrade AI to the level required for high-stakes decision making, or indeed that many of the algorithms currently in use even meet these watered-down desiderata. I submit that our willingness to cede ever more authority to AAs derives primarily from their accuracy, and collaterally from our anthropomorphic impulse to conflate desiderata (i)–(iii). Humans with an impressive track record of accurate judgments in some particular domain generally tend to be trustworthy and responsible as well, at least with respect to their given area of expertise. Thus we falsely impute these latter values to the machine when it outperforms human experts. This is just another example of the well-documented cleaving power of the digital (Floridi 2017), which regularly decouples features of the world that have always been indivisible, such as location and presence, or law and territoriality. Just because accurate decisions are typically made by trustworthy, responsible humans does not necessarily entail any inherent link between these traits.

The proliferation of highly accurate yet untrustworthy and aresponsible algorithms demonstrates how the rhetoric of anthropomorphism has vastly outpaced the reality of contemporary AI. Algorithms are not "just like us" and the temptation to pretend they are can have profound ethical consequences when they are deployed in sensitive domains like finance (Eubanks 2018) and clinical medicine (Watson et al. 2019). By anthropomorphizing a statistical model, we implicitly grant it a degree of agency that not only overstates its true abilities, but robs us of our own autonomy.

Algorithms can only exercise their (artificial) agency as a result of a socially constructed context in which we have deliberately outsourced some task to the machine. This may be more or less reasonable in different situations. Software for filtering spam emails is probably unobjectionable; automated systems for criminal sentencing, on the other hand, raise legitimate concerns about the nature and meaning of justice in an information society. In any event, the central point – one as obvious as it is frequently overlooked – is that it is always *humans* who choose whether or not to abdicate this authority, to empower some piece of technology to intervene on our behalf. It would be a mistake to presume that this transfer of authority involves a simultaneous absolution of responsibility. It does not. The rhetoric of anthropomorphism in AI may be helpful when explaining complex models to audiences with minimal background in statistics and computer science. It is misleading and potentially dangerous, however, when used to guide (or cloud) our ethical judgment.

A more thoughtful and comprehensive approach to conceptualizing the ethical challenges posed by AI requires a proper understanding not just of how these algorithms work – their strengths and weaknesses, their capabilities and limits – but of how they fit into a larger sociotechnical framework. The anthropomorphic impulse, so pervasive in the discourse on AI, is decidedly unhelpful in this regard.

4.8 Conclusion

Anthropomorphism is a powerful force in AI research. Some of the most innovative achievements in contemporary machine learning are directly or indirectly inspired by prominent theories of neuroscience, cognitive psychology, and social epistemology. Experts and laypeople alike actively promote the notion that these technologies are humanlike in their ability to find and exploit patterns in data.

I have argued that the extent to which such algorithms do indeed mimic human intelligence is overstated in at least one prominent instance, but also underappreciated in other less familiar cases. Anthropomorphic analogies can help frame learning strategies and even inspire novel approaches to AI research.

However, we must be cautious in our rhetoric. Algorithms are not people, and the temptation to grant them decision-making authority in socially sensitive applications threatens to undermine our ability to hold powerful individuals and groups accountable for their technologically-mediated actions. Supervised learning provides society with some of its most powerful tools – and like all tools, they can be used either to help or to harm. The choice, as ever, is ours.

References

Adadi, A., and M. Berrada. 2018. Peeking Inside the Black-Box: A Survey on Explainable Artificial Intelligence (XAI). *IEEE Access* 6: 52138–52160.

Bourdakos, N. 2017. Capsule Networks Are Shaking Up AI. Retrieved 3 April, 2019, from https://hackernoon.com/capsule-networks-are-shaking-up-ai-heres-how-to-use-them-c233a0971952.

Boutros, N.N., P. Trautner, O. Korzyukov, T. Grunwald, S. Burroughs, C.E. Elger, et al. 2006. Mid-Latency Auditory-Evoked Responses and Sensory Gating in Focal Epilepsy: A Preliminary Exploration. *The Journal of Neuropsychiatry and Clinical Neurosciences* 18 (3): 409–416.

Bramon, E., S. Rabe-Hesketh, P. Sham, R.M. Murray, and S. Frangou. 2004. Meta-Analysis of the P300 and P50 Waveforms in Schizophrenia. *Schizophrenia Research* 70 (2): 315–329.

Breiman, L. 1996. Bagging Predictors. *Machine Learning* 24 (2): 123–140.

———. 2001. Random Forests. *Machine Learning* 45 (1): 1–33.

Breiman, L., J. Friedman, C.J. Stone, and R.A. Olshen. 1984. *Classification and Regression Trees*. Boca Raton: Taylor & Francis.

Brown, T.B., D. Mané, A. Roy, M. Abadi, and J. Gilmer. 2017. Adversarial Patch. *arXiv* preprint, 1712.09665.

Buckner, C. 2018. Empiricism Without Magic: Transformational Abstraction in Deep Convolutional Neural Networks. *Synthese* 195 (12): 5339–5372.

Buhlmann, P., and T. Hothorn. 2007. Boosting Algorithms: Regularization, Prediction and Model Fitting. *Statistical Science* 22 (4): 477–505.

Bühlmann, P., and S. van de Geer. 2011. *Statistics for High-Dimensional Data: Methods, Theory and Applications*. Berlin: Springer.

Bühlmann, P., and B. Yu. 2003. Boosting with the L_2 Loss: Regression and Classification. *Journal of the American Statistical Association* 98 (462): 324–339.

Cardamone, C., K. Schawinski, M. Sarzi, S.P. Bamford, N. Bennert, C.M. Urry, et al. 2009. Galaxy Zoo Green Peas: Discovery of a Class of Compact Extremely star-Forming Galaxies∗. *Monthly Notices of the Royal Astronomical Society* 399 (3): 1191–1205.

Carvalho, C.M., N.G. Polson, and J.G. Scott. 2010. The Horseshoe Estimator for Sparse Signals. *Biometrika* 97 (2): 465–480.

Chen, T., and C. Guestrin. 2016. XGBoost. In *Proceedings of the 22nd ACM SIGKDD International Conference on Knowledge Discovery and Data Mining – KDD'16*. ACM Press.

Chen, X., and H. Ishwaran. 2012. Random Forests for Genomic Data Analysis. *Genomics* 99 (6): 323–329.

Chen, T., T. He, M. Benesty, V. Khotilovich, Y. Tang, H. Cho, … Y. Li. 2019. *xgboost: Extreme Gradient Boosting*. CRAN. https://cran.r-project.org/web/packages/xgboost/index.html.

Chipman, H.A., E.I. George, and R.E. McCulloch. 2010. BART: Bayesian Additive Regression Trees. *The Annals of Applied Statistics* 4 (1): 266–298.

Condorcet, N. 1785. *Essai sur l'application de l'analyse à la probabilité des décisions rendues à la pluralité des voix*. Paris: Imprimerie Royale.

Cromwell, H.C., R.P. Mears, L. Wan, and N.N. Boutros. 2008. Sensory Gating: A Translational Effort from Basic to Clinical Science. *Clinical EEG and Neuroscience* 39 (2): 69–72.

Dahl, G.E., D. Yu, L. Deng, and A. Acero. 2012. Context-Dependent Pre-trained Deep Neural Networks for Large-Vocabulary Speech Recognition. *IEEE Transactions on Audio, Speech, and Language Processing* 20 (1): 30–42.

Doshi-Velez, F., and B. Kim. 2017. Towards a Rigorous Science of Interpretable Machine Learning. *arXiv* Preprint: 1702.08608.

Doya, K., S. Ishii, A. Pouget, and R. Rao, eds. 2007. *Bayesian Brain: Probabilistic Approaches to Neural Coding*. Cambridge: MIT Press.

Efron, B. 1979. Bootstrap Methods: Another Look at the Jackknife. *Annals of Statistics* 7 (1): 1–26.

Ehrlinger, J., and H. Ishwaran. 2012. Characterizing L2-Boosting. *Annals of Statistics* 40 (2): 1074–1101.

Elgammal, A.M., B. Liu, M. Elhoseiny, and M. Mazzone. 2017. CAN: Creative Adversarial Networks, Generating "Art" by Learning About Styles and Deviating from Style Norms. In *ICCC*.

Eubanks, V. 2018. *Automating Inequality: How High-Tech Tools Profile, Police, and Punish the Poor*. New York: St. Martin's Press.

Fama, E.F. 1965. The Behavior of Stock-Market Prices. *The Journal of Business* 38 (1): 34–105.

Finlayson, S.G., J.D. Bowers, J. Ito, J.L. Zittrain, A.L. Beam, and I.S. Kohane. 2019. Adversarial Attacks on Medical Machine Learning. *Science* 363 (6433): 1287 LP–1281289.

Floridi, L. 2017. Digital's Cleaving Power and Its Consequences. *Philosophy & Technology* 30 (2): 123–129.

Floridi, L., and J.W. Sanders. 2004. On the Morality of Artificial Agents. *Minds and Machines* 14 (3): 349–379.

Freund, Y., and R.E. Schapire. 1995. A Decision-Theoretic Generalization of On-line Learning and an Application to Boosting BT – Computational Learning Theory. In *EuroCOLT*, ed. P. Vitányi, 23–37. Berlin/Heidelberg: Springer.

Friedman, J.H. 2001. Greedy Function Approximation: A Gradient Boosting Machine. *The Annals of Statistics* 29 (5): 1189–1232.

———. 2002. Stochastic Gradient Boosting. *Computational Statistics & Data Analysis* 38 (4): 367–378.

Friedman, J., T. Hastie, and R. Tibshirani. 2007. Sparse Inverse Covariance Estimation with the Graphical Lasso. *Biostatistics* 9 (3): 432–441.

———. 2010. Regularization Paths for Generalized Linear Models via Coordinate Descent. *Journal of Statistical Software* 33 (1): 1–41.

Friston, K. 2009. The Free-Energy Principle: A Rough Guide to the Brain? *Trends in Cognitive Sciences* 13 (7): 293–301.

Friston, K., and S. Kiebel. 2009. Predictive Coding Under the Free-Energy Principle. *Philosophical Transactions of the Royal Society B: Biological Sciences* 364 (1521): 1211–1221.

Galton, F. 1907. Vox populi. *Nature* 75 (1949): 450–451.

Glorot, X., A. Bordes, and Y. Bengio. 2011. Deep Sparse Rectifier Neural Networks. In *Proceedings of the Fourteenth International Conference on Artificial Intelligence and Statistics*, ed. G. Gordon, D. Dunson, and M. Dudík, 315–323. PMLR.

Goodfellow, I., J. Pouget-Abadie, M. Mirza, B. Xu, D. Warde-Farley, S. Ozair, et al. 2014. Generative Adversarial Nets. In *Advances in Neural Information Processing Systems 27*, ed. Z. Ghahramani, M. Welling, C. Cortes, N.D. Lawrence, and K.Q. Weinberger, 2672–2680. Red Hook: Curran Associates Inc.

Goodfellow, I., J. Shlens, and C. Szegedy. 2015. Explaining and Harnessing Adversarial Examples. In *ICLR*. San Diego. Retrieved from http://arxiv.org/abs/1412.6572.

Goodfellow, I., Y. Bengio, and A. Courville. 2016. *Deep Learning*. Cambridge: MIT Press.

Gorman, B. 2017. *A Kaggle Master Explains Gradient Boosting*. Retrieved 4 April, 2019, from http://blog.kaggle.com/2017/01/23/a-kaggle-master-explains-gradient-boosting/.

Guidotti, R., A. Monreale, S. Ruggieri, F. Turini, F. Giannotti, and D. Pedreschi. 2018. A Survey of Methods for Explaining Black Box Models. *ACM Computing Surveys* 51 (5): 1–42.

Guyon, I., J. Weston, S. Barnhill, and V. Vapnik. 2002. Gene Selection for Cancer Classification Using Support Vector Machines. *Machine Learning* 46 (1): 389–422.

Hahn, R.P., J.S. Murray, and C.M. Carvalho. 2017. Bayesian Regression tree Models for Causal Inference: Regularization, Confounding, and Heterogeneous Effects. *arXiv* Preprint: 1706.09523.

Hassabis, D., D. Kumaran, C. Summerfield, and M. Botvinick. 2017. Neuroscience-Inspired Artificial Intelligence. *Neuron* 95 (2): 245–258.
Hastie, T., R. Tibshirani, and J. Friedman. 2009. *The Elements of Statistical Learning: Data Mining, Inference, and Prediction*. New York: Springer.
Hill, J.L. 2011. Bayesian Nonparametric Modeling for Causal Inference. *Journal of Computational and Graphical Statistics* 20 (1): 217–240.
Hinton, G.E., S. Sabour, and N. Frosst. (2018). Matrix Capsules with EM Routing. In *International Conference on Learning Representations*. Retrieved from https://openreview.net/forum?id=HJWLfGWRb.
Hubel, D., and T. Wiesel. 1962. Receptive Fields, Binocular Interaction and Functional Architecture in the Cat's Visual Cortex. *The Journal of Physiology* 160 (1): 106–154.
Ishwaran, H., and J.S. Rao. 2005. Spike and Slab Variable Selection: Frequentist and Bayesian Strategies. *The Annals of Statistics* 33 (2): 730–773.
Jessen, F., C. Kucharski, T. Fries, A. Papassotiropoulos, K. Hoenig, W. Maier, and R. Heun. 2001. Sensory Gating Deficit Expressed by a Disturbed Suppression of the P50 Event-Related Potential in Patients with Alzheimer's Disease. *American Journal of Psychiatry* 158 (8): 1319–1321.
Jolliffe, I.T. 2002. *Principal Component Analysis*. New York: Springer.
Kilner, J.M., K.J. Friston, and C.D. Frith. 2007. Predictive Coding: An Account of the Mirror Neuron System. *Cognitive Processing* 8 (3): 159–166.
Kim, J.S., M.J. Greene, A. Zlateski, K. Lee, M. Richardson, S.C. Turaga, et al. 2014. Space–Time Wiring Specificity Supports Direction Selectivity in the Retina. *Nature* 509: 331.
Kisley, M.A., S.D. Polk, R.G. Ross, P.M. Levisohn, and R. Freedman. 2003. Early Postnatal Development of Sensory Gating. *Neuroreport* 14 (5): 693–697.
Kittur, A., and R.E. Kraut. 2008. Harnessing the Wisdom of Crowds in Wikipedia: Quality Through Coordination. In *Proceedings of the 2008 ACM Conference on Computer Supported Cooperative Work*, 37–46. New York: ACM.
Kontonatsios, G., I. Korkontzelos, J. Tsujii, and S. Ananiadou. 2014. Using a Random Forest Classifier to Compile Bilingual Dictionaries of Technical Terms from Comparable Corpora. In *Proceedings of the 14th Conference of the European Chapter of the Association for Computational Linguistics*, vol. 2. Short Papers, 111–116.
Körding, K., and D. Wolpert. 2007. Bayesian Statistics and Utility Functions in Sensorimotor Control. In *Bayesian Brain: Probabilistic Approaches to Neural Coding*, ed. K. Doya, S. Ishii, A. Pouget, and R. Rao, 299–320. Cambridge: MIT Press.
Krizhevsky, A., I. Sutskever, and G.E. Hinton. 2012. ImageNet Classification with Deep Convolutional Neural Networks. In *Proceedings of the 25th International Conference on Neural Information Processing Systems*, vol. 1, 1097–1105. Curran Associates Inc.
Lecun, Y., L. Bottou, Y. Bengio, and P. Haffner. 1998. Gradient-Based Learning Applied to Document Recognition. *Proceedings of the IEEE* 86 (11): 2278–2324.
LeCun, Y., Y. Bengio, and G. Hinton. 2015. Deep Learning. *Nature* 521 (7553): 436–444.
Linero, A.R. 2018. Bayesian Regression Trees for High-Dimensional Prediction and Variable Selection. *Journal of the American Statistical Association* 113 (522): 626–636.
Linero, A.R., and Y. Yang. 2018. Bayesian Regression Tree Ensembles That Adapt to Smoothness and Sparsity. *Journal of the Royal Statistical Society: Series B (Statistical Methodology)* 80 (5): 1087–1110.
Lipton, Z.C. 2016. The Mythos of Model Interpretability. *arXiv* Preprint: 1606.03490.
Marcus, G. 2018. Deep learning: A Critical Appraisal. *arXiv* Preprint: 1801.00631.
Mittelstadt, B.D., P. Allo, M. Taddeo, S. Wachter, and L. Floridi. 2016. The Ethics of Algorithms: Mapping the Debate. *Big Data & Society* 3 (2): 1–21.
Mohamed, A., G.E. Dahl, and G. Hinton. 2012. Acoustic Modeling Using Deep Belief Networks. *Transactions on Audio, Speech and Language Processing* 20 (1): 14–22.
Mullainathan, S., and J. Spiess. 2017. Machine Learning: An Applied Econometric Approach. *Journal of Economic Perspectives* 31 (2): 87–106.

New Navy Device Learns by Doing. 1958. *New York Times*, 25.
Odena, A., C. Olah, and J. Shlens. 2017. Conditional Image Synthesis with Auxiliary Classifier {GAN}s. In *Proceedings of the 34th International Conference on Machine Learning*, ed. D. Precup and Y.W. Teh, vol. 70, 2642–2651. Sydney: International Convention Centre, PMLR.
Olah, C., A. Satyanarayan, I. Johnson, S. Carter, L. Schubert, K. Ye, and A. Mordvintsev. 2018. The Building Blocks of Interpretability. *Distill*. https://doi.org/10.23915/distill.00010.
Radford, A., L. Metz, and S. Chintala. 2015. Unsupervised Representation Learning with Deep Convolutional Generative Adversarial Networks. *arXiv* Preprint: 1511.06434.
Raina, R., A. Madhavan, and A.Y. Ng. 2009. Large-Scale Deep Unsupervised Learning Using Graphics Processors. In *Proceedings of the 26th Annual International Conference on Machine Learning*, 873–880. New York: ACM.
Rao, R.P.N., and D.H. Ballard. 1999. Predictive Coding in the Visual Cortex: A Functional Interpretation of Some Extra-Classical Receptive-Field Effects. *Nature Neuroscience* 2 (1): 79–87.
Rosenblatt, F. 1958. The Perceptron: A Probabilistic Model for Information Storage and Organization in the Brain. *Psychological Review* 65: 386–408. American Psychological Association.
Sabour, S., N. Frosst, and G.E. Hinton. 2017. Dynamic Routing Between Capsules. In *Advances in Neural Information Processing Systems*, ed. I. Guyon, U.V. Luxburg, S. Bengio, H. Wallach, R. Fergus, S. Vishwanathan, and R. Garnett, vol. 30, 3856–3866. Red Hook: Curran Associates, Inc.
Schapire, R.E., and Y. Freund. 2012. *Boosting: Foundations and Algorithms*. Cambridge: MIT Press.
Scornet, E., G. Biau, and J.P. Vert. 2015. Consistency of Random Forests. *Annals of Statistics* 43 (4): 1716–1741.
Silver, D., T. Hubert, J. Schrittwieser, I. Antonoglou, M. Lai, A. Guez, et al. 2018. A General Reinforcement Learning Algorithm That Masters Chess, Shogi, and Go Through Self-Play. *Science* 362 (6419): 1140 LP–1141144.
Sparapani, R.A., B.R. Logan, R.E. McCulloch, and P.W. Laud. 2016. Nonparametric Survival Analysis Using Bayesian Additive Regression Trees (BART). *Statistics in Medicine* 35 (16): 2741–2753.
Strogatz, S. 2018. One Giant Step for a Chess-Playing Machine. *New York Times*. Retrieved from https://www.nytimes.com/2018/12/26/science/chess-artificial-intelligence.html?rref=collection%2Ftimestopic%2FArtificial Intelligence.
Surowiecki, J. 2004. *The Wisdom of Crowds*. New York: Doubleday.
Sutton, R., and A. Barto. 2018. *Reinforcement Learning: An Introduction*. 2nd ed. Cambridge: MIT Press.
Taddeo, M. 2010. Modelling Trust in Artificial Agents, a First Step Toward the Analysis of e-Trust. *Minds and Machines* 20 (2): 243–257.
Taigman, Y., M. Yang, M. Ranzato, and L. Wolf. 2014. DeepFace: Closing the Gap to Human-Level Performance in Face Verification. In *2014 IEEE Conference on Computer Vision and Pattern Recognition*, 1701–1708.
Team, S. 2017. Hey Siri: An On-device DNN-Powered Voice Trigger for Apple's Personal Assistant. *Apple Machine Learning Journal* 1 (6). Retrieved from: https://machinelearning.apple.com/2017/10/01/hey-siri.html.
Tibshirani, R. 1996. Regression Shrinkage and Selection via the Lasso. *Journal of the Royal Statistical Society Series B (Methodological)* 58 (1): 267–288.
Turing, A. 1950. Computing Machinery and Intelligence. *Mind* LIX (236): 433–460.
van der Maaten, L., and G. Hinton. 2008. Visualizing Data Using t-SNE. *Journal of Machine Learning Research* 9: 2579–2605.
Wager, S., and S. Athey. 2018. Estimation and Inference of Heterogeneous Treatment Effects Using Random Forests. *Journal of the American Statistical Association* 113 (523): 1228–1242.

Waldrop, M.M. 2019. News Feature: What Are the Limits of Deep Learning? *Proceedings of the National Academy of Sciences* 116 (4): 1074 LP–1071077.

Watson, D., and L. Floridi. 2018. Crowdsourced Science: Sociotechnical Epistemology in the e-Research Paradigm. *Synthese* 195 (2): 741–764.

Watson, D., J. Krutzinna, I.N. Bruce, C.E.M. Griffiths, I.B. McInnes, M.R. Barnes, and L. Floridi. 2019. Clinical Applications of Machine Learning Algorithms: Beyond the Black Box. *BMJ* 364: 1886.

Wu, Y., M. Schuster, Z. Chen, Q.V. Le, M. Norouzi, W. Macherey, … J. Dean. 2016. Google's neural machine translation system: Bridging the gap between human and machine translation. *arXiv* preprint: 1609.08144.

Zhu, J.-Y., T. Park, P. Isola, and A.A. Efros. 2017. Unpaired image-to-Image Translation Using Cycle-Consistent Adversarial Networks. In *2017 IEEE International Conference on Computer Vision (ICCV)*, Venice.

David Watson is doctoral candidate at the University of Oxford and an enrichment student at The Alan Turing Institute. He received his MSc from the Oxford Internet Institute in 2015, studying under the supervision of Professor Luciano Floridi. He went on to become a Data Scientist at Queen Mary University's Centre for Translational Bioinformatics before returning to Oxford for his DPhil in 2017. He is passionate about promoting more interpretable techniques for analysing complex systems in the social and life sciences.

David is a founding member of the Digital Ethics Lab, where his research focuses on the epistemological foundations of machine learning. He develops new methods for explaining the outputs of black box algorithms, with the goal of better understanding causal relationships in high-dimensional systems. In addition to his academic work, David is a regular contributor to The Economist, where he writes articles and builds models for the Graphic Detail and Game Theory blogs.

Chapter 5
Empowerment or Engagement? Digital Health Technologies for Mental Healthcare

Christopher Burr and Jessica Morley

Abstract We argue that while digital health technologies (e.g. artificial intelligence, smartphones, and virtual reality) present significant opportunities for improving the delivery of healthcare, key concepts that are used to evaluate and understand their impact can obscure significant ethical issues related to patient engagement and experience. Specifically, we focus on the concept of empowerment and ask whether it is adequate for addressing some significant ethical concerns that relate to digital health technologies for mental healthcare. We frame these concerns using five key ethical principles for AI ethics (i.e. autonomy, beneficence, non-maleficence, justice, and explicability), which have their roots in the bioethical literature, in order to critically evaluate the role that digital health technologies will have in the future of digital healthcare.

Keywords Digital health technology empowerment · Patient engagement · Mental health · Artificial intelligence · Bioethics

5.1 Introduction

The way that healthcare services are set to operate is likely to change drastically over the next decade as a result of key digital health technologies (DHTs) (e.g. telemedicine, wearables and smartphones, artificial intelligence, and genomics). Some of these technologies are being deployed within formal healthcare settings and are already impacting the way that patients access healthcare services (e.g. telemedicine and digital therapies), how they are monitored or diagnosed (e.g. sensors/wearables, smartphones, social media), and how healthcare services are governed and administered (e.g. electronic health records, machine learning) (The Topol Review

C. Burr (✉)
Digital Ethics Lab, Oxford Internet Institute, University of Oxford, Oxford, UK
e-mail: christopher.burr@oii.ox.ac.uk

J. Morley
Oxford Internet Institute, University of Oxford, Oxford, UK

C. Burr, S. Milano (eds.), *The 2019 Yearbook of the Digital Ethics Lab*,
Digital Ethics Lab Yearbook, https://doi.org/10.1007/978-3-030-29145-7_5

Board 2019). Other technologies are being used by individuals in more informal ways, embedded within their daily activities as part of a more personal concern for self-tracking of health and well-being (Lupton 2016).

In this paper, we explore the ethical impact of some of these key technologies and the concepts used to critically evaluate them, focusing primarily on their role in mental healthcare in the United Kingdom—though many of the issues we discuss are applicable to wider healthcare services. According to the Adult Psychiatric Morbidity Survey (NatCen Social Research 2016), one in six adults surveyed in England in 2014 met the criteria for a common mental disorder (CMD).[1] The World Health Organisation (WHO) also notes that depression is the single largest contributor to global disability and a major contributor to suicide deaths, which number close to 800,000 per year. As part of NHS England's long-term plan, significant investment for mental health services has been promised, with data and technology set to play a central role in transforming their delivery (NHS England 2019). This investment is vital, as mental healthcare is in urgent need of new approaches, and digital technologies, such as artificial intelligence (AI), will likely have a critical role in easing the burden that mental health conditions have on individuals and society. Furthermore, this specific focus is important from a parity of care perspective, in order to ensure that the opportunities associated with DHTs are equally distributed. However, aiming for parity does not mean that we should assume the implications, both positive and negative, of the increasing use of DHTs are equal. Mental healthcare poses unique ethical challenges due to the need to consider wider psychological and social factors, many of which interact with biological factors in complex ways that are not fully understood.[2] We approach these challenges from the perspective of a broader concern about the nature of *patient empowerment*—a concept that has received a large amount of attention in recent years (Chiauzzi et al. 2016; Spencer 2015; Bravo et al. 2015)—and in relation to the key technologies identified as having a central role to play in the delivery of mental healthcare services.

In Sect. 5.2, we discuss the idea that technology can empower service users to take charge of their own digitally-mediated care, supported by myriad streams of user-generated data and co-curated with various DHTs, including AI. This idea has caught the attention of many developers, stakeholders, and policy makers, but the empowerment narrative rests on some questionable conceptual and ethical foundations. We will argue that genuine empowerment depends on the prior removal of certain barriers to *engagement*, which patients suffering from a variety of mental health conditions face. To support this argument, in Sect. 5.3, we adopt a bioethical perspective in order to critically evaluate the role that DHTs play in removing these

[1] The report defines a CMD as comprising different types of depression and anxiety, which cause marked emotional distress and interfere with daily function, but do not usually affect insight or cognition. CMDs are typically contrasted with major psychiatric disorders, such as schizophrenia (NatCen Social Research 2016).

[2] For instance, the acknowledgement that "neurobiology does not fully account for the emergence of mental distress" formed the basis of one of the criticisms brought against the DSM-V in an open letter signed by 15,000 individuals of 50 professional organisations (Kamens et al. 2017, p. 682).

barriers, as well as the possible unintended consequences that arise from their implementation. In Sect. 5.4, we stress that if harder governance measures are adopted to protect people from the unintended consequences that present the highest level of risk, these measures must be developed in a way that is tolerant of value pluralism. In Sect. 5.5, we conclude with a brief summary of the main points discussed in the article.

5.2 Mental Health and Empowerment

A recent review commissioned by the previous UK Secretary of State for Health and Social Care, Jeremy Hunt, explores how technological developments are likely to impact the future of healthcare in the NHS (The Topol Review Board 2019). Included alongside this review is an individual report that focuses specifically on mental healthcare and the key DHTs[3] that are identified as likely to have a significant impact over the next 20 years (Foley and Woollard 2019). The role and scope of these technologies differs widely but the report notes that they "have the potential to reduce the administrative burden, allow treatment in more convenient settings, and *empower* patients and their carers to take on some of the tasks currently performed in the clinic" (Foley and Woollard 2019, p. 25, emphasis added).

The use of the term 'empower' here is important, and reflects a growing emphasis and usage of the concept, most notably within the literature discussing digital health and well-being (Burr et al. 2019; Morley and Floridi 2019). In the case of mental healthcare, a significant challenge for promoting empowerment is the fact that certain psychiatric disorders impact the individual's decisional capacity, affecting their choice of whether to engage with some service (e.g. an online CBT programme), or, more broadly, restricting their ability to make their own healthcare decisions.[4] Different disorders impact decisional capacity in myriad ways. For instance, in a review of the medical ethical and empirical literature on depression and decisional capacity, Hindmarch et al. (2013) found that being in a depressive episode impacts an individual's ability to *appreciate* the significance of information that may be relevant to healthcare decisions. In other words, information that may be treated similarly from a quantitative perspective (i.e. it is of equal quality and quantity) is not always the same from a qualitative perspective (in terms of meaning) (Floridi 2010). The latter perspective depends on the individual who is consuming the information, as well as the prior beliefs they bring to bear on the information,

[3] The 13 DHTs the report identifies are telemedicine, sensors/wearables, smartphones, digital therapies, social media, genotyping microarrays, neuroimaging, electronic health records and patient health records, healthcare data collections, natural language processing, artificial intelligence, virtual reality (VR), and augmented reality (AR)

[4] Typically, decisional capacity is divided into four sub-categories: the capacity to express a choice, the ability to understand relevant information, the ability to appreciate the significance of the information, and the ability to reason with the information (Charland 2015; Grisso and Appelbaum 1998).

how it is perceived and what affordances arise between the user and their environment (Nagy and Neff 2015). These types of assessment and considerations are important for identifying the specific barriers that exist in the case of specific mental health conditions, which may prevent DHTs from increasing patient empowerment.

However, it is not sufficient to restrict our focus in this paper to the issues of decisional capacity alone—understanding and critically evaluating the concept of empowerment requires a broader focus. A key concern is that so-called 'empowering technologies' focus too narrowly on monitoring and providing information to an individual, on the assumption that a more informed process of deliberation is sufficient for empowerment (Morley and Floridi 2019). However, there are many problems with this assumption.

First, and foremost, it is not clear *exactly how* digitally-mediated access to information will empower people. This is primarily because, despite its common use, empowerment is a term that is used both loosely and inconsistently (Roberts 1999) and is, consequently, embedded in a range of competing discourses that have highly variable aims: from the need to give people choice to the importance of providing people with an opportunity to change their position in society (Starkey 2003). All these variable conceptualizations are in use in the wider health promotion discourse (Sheehan 2014) but, as has been highlighted elsewhere (Morley and Floridi 2019), the narrative that is used in the context of digitising healthcare services (including mental health services) positions empowerment as a self-reflexive and transformative process (Garcia et al. 2014).

At first, this view of empowerment might not appear to be problematic. Indeed, there have been some early findings that this process can result in, at least moderate, positive impacts on the mental health of adolescents (Kenny et al. 2015) if appropriate evidence-based design recommendations are followed (Bakker et al. 2016). This means that mental health-focused DHTs that aim to 'empower' individuals by taking action to actively improve their mental health through a process of self-reflection are likely to play an important part in the future of mental health care, especially in terms of making mental health support more accessible and reducing barriers to seeking help (Bakker et al. 2016). These opportunities should not be ignored. However, this conception of empowerment raises unique ethical issues, such as how it can be leveraged in ways that overlook socioeconomic factors that determine whether an individual can benefit from the use of a mental health DHT in the manner described. Moreover, the self-reflexive process presumes that an individual actively *wants* and *feels able to* engage with the process in the first place (e.g. to download an app, open it and register a user name)—this presumption is far from guaranteed in a wide variety of mental health disorders. Thus, the overarching argument tends to ignore the fact that there are many factors that moderate an individual's ability and motivation to even *engage* with this active process of self-reflection.

Such moderating factors (or variables) are well articulated by the Engagement Capacity Model (ECM) (Sieck et al. 2019), which stresses that an individual may fail to engage with healthcare services if they feel unable to do so due to (a) low resources, (b) low self-efficacy (competence), or (c) low willingness. These variables are themselves the result of a dynamic interplay between an individual, their environment, and the corresponding behaviours creating a complex feedback loop where each of these factors constantly influence each other. For example, a change in an individual's environment, such as a reduction in income and consequential decision that paying for a smartphone contract is no longer affordable, might reduce the amount of resources they feel they have available to them to improve their mental health, in turn reducing their level of willingness to engage with the mental health services that are available (e.g. those accessible via a desktop computer at the library), making them less likely to consider engaging with the self-reflexive process of empowerment, and as a consequence lowering the confidence they have in their capacity (self-efficacy) to take the steps necessary to improve their mental health.

Genuine empowerment, therefore, requires attending to the wider psychosocial factors that could constrain an individual's ability to engage with healthcare services, both online and offline. For instance, far greater attention needs to be paid to the unequal distribution of mHealth resources throughout society and the existence of considerable perverse incentives within the system that will discourage the lowering of barriers to adoption. For example, while it may be better for the system and for the individual themselves to 'self-treat' at home through the use of a mindfulness app there are likely to still be incentives in the system for health practitioners to want to see the person in a clinical setting so that it generates a payment.

Our intention, in highlighting these complex sociotechnical and (later) bioethical issues, is not to present the future of digitally-enhanced mental health service provision as dystopian or impossible to achieve. We believe that it is possible to capitalise on the opportunities presented by DHTs in a responsible manner, but this requires making it clear that DHTs are not neutral technologies.[5] As such, there is a responsibility on all parts of the system to encourage the design of DHTs that, in complete awareness of the complex space within which they operate, actively re-ontologise the way that mental health care services are delivered, with the goal of genuine improvement to the patient experience, as determined within the bounds of long-established bioethical principles that we will now discuss.

[5] In Morley and Floridi (2019), one of the authors defends a view of framing DHTs as 'digital companions', which can have significant (positive and negative) effects on relationships key to maintaining positive mental health, such as those between: (a) clinical advice and behaviour change; (b) perception of self and behaviour change; (c) need for social interaction and desire to socialise.

5.3 Engagement and DHTs: Five Principles to Guide Critical Evaluation

In this section we present several conceptual and ethical concerns that need to be addressed if we are to achieve the goal of increasing patient engagement and, in turn, empowerment. These concerns are structured according to the principles outlined in Floridi et al. (2018), which comprise the four traditional principles of biomedical ethics (i.e. beneficence, non-maleficence, autonomy, and justice (Beauchamp and Childress 2013)) as well as an additional principle (i.e. explicability) that is included to capture specific ethical issues that arise with the use of AI. These five principles were found to be well-represented in several significant policy documents that address the ethical issues with AI (see Floridi et al. 2018), and are well-suited to the present article because of their grounding in biomedical ethics.

5.3.1 Autonomy

In biomedical ethics, the principle of autonomy incorporates respect for both an individual's *right to decide* and *freedom of whether to decide* (Beauchamp and Childress 2013). The motivation behind the latter component, as Sen (2010, p. 18) notes, is that "[t]he freedom to choose our lives can make a significant contribution to our well-being, but going beyond the perspective of well-being, the freedom itself may be seen as important [...] we are under no obligation to seek only our own well-being, and it is for us to decide what we have good reason to pursue." In short, although humans have a right to decide, we also have the freedom to choose how and whether to exercise that right. However, freedom alone is insufficient for autonomy—agency is also required and provides the basis for social recognition of one's right to decide, including the capacity to express informed consent.

Contemporary theories of relational autonomy maintain that an individual's agency, or capacity for intentional action, is in large part determined by their sociocultural environment.[6] These approaches contrast with procedural accounts of autonomy, which view autonomous decision-making in more cognitivist terms and may downplay the significance of the wider environmental dynamics that contribute to overt choice behaviour (see Owens and Cribb 2013 for a discussion).

Relational theories of autonomy help bring into stark relief the need to design and evaluate DHTs at a level of abstraction that articulates the socially embedded (or situated) nature of the user, in order to fully appreciate the interpersonal differences in capacity for engagement (e.g. time demands, literacy levels, finances,

[6]A related idea is captured in the well-known *capability approach*, which focuses on the real opportunities for action that different sociocultural environments afford, the individual differences in people's abilities (or capacity) to transform resources in ways conducive to their well-being, and the unequal distribution of such opportunities throughout society (Sen 2010).

social support). For example, Lucas et al. (2017, p. 2, emphasis added) explored whether virtual human interviewers could "increase *willingness* of service members to report PTSD symptoms", by reducing barriers to engagement that may result from the perceived stigma that comes from reporting symptoms to a human interviewer. They show how such a technology has the potential to increase an individual's relational autonomy, by creating a wider set of opportunities for seeking treatment and respecting the barriers to engagement that certain mental health conditions present—in this case the barrier was low willingness caused by a concern regarding perceived stigma. In this manner, retaining an emphasis on relational autonomy may help ensure that DHTs do not end up embodying overly-individualistic values of what it means to 'live well' but rather help demonstrate the prudential value of social relatedness.

Thus, although DHTs can create new opportunities available to individuals by altering the landscape of affordances that a user perceives (Bruineberg and Rietveld 2014), respect for individual autonomy also requires acknowledgement of the different values that individuals bring to bear when choosing whether to engage. This is often embodied in the idea that the *right* to choose is not a *duty* to choose (Beauchamp and Childress 2013). This aspect of autonomy can cause difficulties for technology designers and developers, as well as the healthcare professionals that use their products. Two concerns are significant.

Firstly, there is a concern that can arise when insufficient consideration is given to the scope of autonomy. For example, a patient may autonomously decide to *dis-empower* themselves, in order to have someone else (e.g. their doctor or caregiver) make decisions on their behalf. Alternatively, an individual experiencing depression may be fully informed about their mental health and the options available to them in terms of recovery, but nevertheless autonomously decide not to engage with the variety of DHTs available to them—their mental health may be an important part of their self-identity and how they make sense of the world.[7] Examples such as these pose challenges for determining the efficacy of a DHT. As White et al. (2016, p. 2) note, delivering mental health services is problematised by the challenge of specifying what constitutes a "'good outcome' for people in the particular contexts in which they are living their lives". An individual may autonomously decide that their own journey of recovery requires learning to live within acceptable limitations that are intrinsically chosen and governed, rather than based on extrinsic and optimal standards represented by the outcome measure chosen by the healthcare provider.

Secondly, there is a concern that can arise when too much consideration is given to the scope of autonomy. For example, if a technology developer focuses too narrowly on the day-to-day decisions of a user (e.g. whether to adhere to a self-directed course of therapy delivered via an mHealth technology), they may fail to appreciate

[7] This perspective is captured by the *recovery approach* (Anthony 1993, p. 527), which maintains that recovery "is a deeply personal, unique process of changing one's attitudes, values, feelings, goals, skills, and/or roles. It is a way of living a satisfying, hopeful, and contributing life even with limitations caused by illness. Recovery involves the development of new meaning and purpose in one's life as one grows beyond the catastrophic effects of mental illness."

how a single decision fits within a patient's broader healthcare regime. As Kukla (2005, p. 37) states: "The bulk of our health care activities take the form, not of crisis management and punctate decision-making, but of ongoing practices, including large amounts of self-management and surveillance, wherein we are inducted into standards set by medical institutions with which we have prescribed forms of direct contact." The point here is that the individual decision of whether to adhere to a course of treatment on any day, typically made multiple times during a course of treatment, may be the wrong level of abstraction to focus on when determining whether a user's autonomy is respected. The meaningful choice that requires consideration is the initial choice of whether to engage in a course of treatment and how to integrate the treatment into ongoing practices, as opposed to the subsequent choices that may result from individual prompts (or nudges)—perhaps delivered via smartphone notifications and serving to remind a user to continue with a self-determine course of therapy (e.g. CBT).

5.3.2 *Beneficence*

The principle of beneficence typically emphasises the promotion of patient welfare but can also be extended to include the welfare of the caregivers. Consideration of how to 'do good' in the context of healthcare and DHTs, therefore, need not, and perhaps should not, be limited to the individual patient—deploying a new DHT in a healthcare pathway can be highly beneficial for patients, but could prove to be overly-demanding for clinical staff.

Novel technologies are creating new opportunities to 'do good', by unlocking possible treatment options that did not exist previously (Fernández-Caballero et al. 2017). However, ensuring that the principle of beneficence is upheld when designing, implementing, and using DHTs requires that we have some way of measuring a wide range of outcomes and that the measures used are suitable for the context in which they are deployed (e.g. clinical, epidemiological, or allocational decisions).[8] This can prove to be challenging for a number of reasons.

In order to determine whether DHTs 'do good' it is important to consider how effective they are in bringing about their stated goals—this includes a *comparative evaluation* against relevant existing services. However, depending on the type of comparative analysis being conducted, certain measures may prove to be limited. For instance, alongside other key performance indicators that commissioners use to assess the overall quality of care, patient-reported outcome measures (PROMs) can provide a valuable source of information about a patient's subjective attitudes towards a procedure or treatment. As Nelson et al. (2015, p. 1) notes, "the systematic use of information from PROMs leads to better communication and decision making between doctors and patients and improves patient satisfaction with care".

[8] See Hausman (2015) for an argument that claims that no single measure can adequately capture the value of health outcomes across all three contexts.

However, PROMs can be either specific or generic, and in the case of the former, can be specific in myriad ways (e.g. disease- or condition-specific, population-specific).[9] This leads to certain constraints on their applicability. For instance, if the PROM has been validated for a specific population (e.g. elderly patients) this can rule out comparisons with the wider population due to differences in the dimensions being assessed (e.g. an instrument for measuring adolescent well-being will focus on different factors from well-being of elderly patients due to different expectations concerning typical levels of functioning.

DHTs, such as sensors/wearables, smartphones, and social media are enabling new forms of data collection and measurement when combined with techniques such as big data analytics and machine learning. However, DHTs are not immune to the aforementioned limitations on measurement, and technology designers must consider what to measure and how best to measure it during the design process. Furthermore, technology designers also face additional ethical challenges that go beyond the choice of measurement tool.

One such challenge, is the need to balance the evidence-standard required of health interventions, exemplified by the reproducible results of randomised-controlled trials, with the opportunity presented by DHTs to deliver far more personalised care. If too much emphasis is put on optimising the outcome for an individual 'user' during the designing, testing and evaluating phases, then it would be ethically wrong to launch that product at scale on the market—where it would be used by individuals with grossly different socioeconomic circumstances—due to the chances of it having a negative impact on those that do not match the 'profile' of the individual for which it was tailored. If, however, the opposite was true and the focus was on reproducibility of the results, we risk missing the opportunity to improve outcomes for individuals who have more specific needs that have, up until now, been unmet by the provision of generic mental health services.

Another key ethical concern is that although subjective reports are a valuable source of information about how a patient may evaluate the positive impact of some intervention, treatment or therapy, the way the information is collected, stored, and used could raise concerns among users. This is especially important in the case of mental health, where concerns over privacy can be particularly significant. For instance, a DHT designer may be aware that some biometric signals carry mutual information about an individual's mood or emotional state or that natural language processing techniques can be used to infer information about common mental health disorders such as depression and anxiety (Burr and Cristianini 2019). Moreover, they may be aware that such techniques can be used to bypass the need for explicit user input (e.g. completion of a questionnaire), allowing them to be used at scale without high costs. Although the reliability and validity of using digital footprints or biometric signals to bypass traditional forms of psychometric assessment is currently inadequate for clinical use, this does not prevent the use of such techniques in the wider ecosystem of mHealth apps and IoT devices (Bellet and Frijters 2019). As such, from the perspective of a designer, the decision not to utilise such techniques

[9] Examples can be found at: http://phi.uhce.ox.ac.uk/inst_types.php

within a health and wellness app could be judged as a missed opportunity and a failure to "do good".

However, the use of such a technique to measure the effectiveness of a possible intervention may not necessarily be seen the same way by the user, who may have decided to present themselves in public in such a way that their mental health condition is not obvious to their friends, family or colleagues. This ability to choose the "face" we wear in public, therefore, could be undermined by a designer's attempt to use novel techniques (e.g. big data and machine learning) to measure our inner lives by bypassing the need for explicit feedback (e.g. a self-reported questionnaire) (Bellet and Frijters 2019; Burr and Cristianini 2019). In turn, the discovery of such techniques by a user, who may have wished to keep their mental health condition private, could lead to self-surveillance of future online interactions that end up overriding the initial desire to "do good".[10] The simple point here, well-known to bioethicists, is that consideration of how best to meet the principle of beneficence goes hand in hand with a requirement of considering the possible risks of harm.

5.3.3 Non-maleficence

Avoiding harm is sometimes treated as an overriding principle in the delivery of healthcare (i.e. 'above all do no harm'), although there are many instances of where this fails to be useful in practice and sometimes morally indefensible in principle (see Beauchamp and Childress 2013). As such, it is typically agreed in bioethics that independent of context, there is no a priori rank ordering of the norms of beneficence and non-maleficence. Nevertheless, the bias towards the principle of non-maleficence can be seen in the NICE Evidence Standards Framework, which is used for evaluating DHTs deployed in the NHS and places a significant emphasis on demonstrating how proposed DHTs should be evaluated according to the proportional risk that their use would pose within the healthcare system (Greaves et al. 2018). The framework is founded on a *proportionate approach to risk*, which categorises DHTs according to their function so that more rigorous standards are applied to DHTs that have the potential for causing greater harm. For example, DHTs that are designed for 'active monitoring' of patients—included in the highest risk tier of the framework—should ideally be supported by a high-quality randomised controlled study that demonstrates how the DHT has comparative utility according to relevant clinical outcomes in the target population, using validated condition-specific measures. Again, here we see the need to consider the scope of measures deployed for assessing DHTs and their potential impacts on service users (see previous section).

Unfortunately, the NICE framework notes that its evaluative scope is limited and less relevant to DHTs that are "downloaded or purchased directly by users (such as

[10] This is likely one of the primary motivations behind the backlash to a study by Facebook that demonstrated how user's emotional states could be manipulated (Kramer et al. 2014).

through app stores)" and is "not [yet] designed for use with DHTs that incorporate artificial intelligence using adaptive algorithms" (National Institute for Health and Care Excellence 2018). This limited scope is understandable when we consider the variation in *standards of due care* that are relied upon in order to avoid negligence. In the first instance, an app developer does not have the same professional duty of care to an individual that a doctor does to a patient. In the second, the adaptive nature of the algorithms in question may place epistemic limits on the duty of care that can be exercised due to the lack of explainability inherent in some forms of AI (Watson et al. 2019). Nevertheless, the fact that app developers are not yet beholden to the same duty of care that governs the obligations of a formal caregiver does not mean that they are exempt from giving *appropriate consideration* to possible risks and benefits that their product may cause. How we delineate and specify the concept of 'appropriate consideration' though, must instead make reference to a broader ethics of social responsibility. It is, perhaps, for these reasons that so many organisations are currently at work trying to specify codes of conduct (Department of Health and Social Care 2019) or empirically-informed design guidelines (Calvo and Peters 2014), which can help provide ethical support for the development and use of DHTs in wider contexts.

A central challenge for the development of such ethical frameworks is how to deal with trade-offs between maximising opportunities and minimising risks. Several specific trade-offs arise in relation to the *over-use* and *under-use* of DHTs for mental health.

Firstly, and in relation to the *over-use* of DHTs, while there is broad consensus that CBT is an effective treatment for common mental health disorders such as anxiety and depression, CBT is not harmless. As such, there are potential risks that could emerge from over-use of DHTs for CBT, such as deterioration of existing symptoms, emergence of new symptoms, and strains on family relations (Schermuly-Haupt et al. 2018). Such risks may also help explain the findings of a study performed by Breedvelt et al. (2019), which analysed GP's attitudes to mHealth interventions for depression, and found that GPs thought that unguided use of such interventions (e.g. automated self-care) is likely to be less effective than guided care. In short, although the proliferation of therapy-based apps may provide greater access, and in turn reduce barriers to engagement for those who need support, there is a trade-off between improved access or scalability on the one hand, and potential decrease in efficacy and possible increase in the risk of harm on the other.

Another instance of the possible over-use of DHTs can be found in the ongoing debate around the automated monitoring of suicidal ideation on social media. Others have already raised concerns about the ethical challenges raised by mental health professionals using social media as a way of monitoring patients, including the tension between the principles of beneficence and non-maleficence (Lehavot et al. 2012). A notable concern in relation to using DHTs to automatically monitor individuals is that the reliability and validity of such techniques is currently insufficient for clinical use (Burr and Cristianini 2019). Therefore, there is a risk that if deployed at scale, such techniques would likely lead to a high-rate of false positives, which in turn could result in the over medicalisation and stigmatisation of otherwise healthy and normal attitudes, behaviours and cognitions.[11]

Secondly, and in relation to the *under-use* of DHTs for mental health, it can be argued that an over-cautious approach to mitigating risk can stifle research and lead to harm by failing to advance treatment options. This is particularly relevant in the case of IoT devices and ubiquitous computing where there is a genuine opportunity to gather valuable environmental data (or 'ecologically valid' data) that could help researchers to understand how the environment affects the presentation of mental health disorders. For instance, one epidemiological study used Google Trends data and NHS prescription data for antidepressants to explore the distribution and prevalence of seasonal affective disorder (Lansdall-Welfare et al. 2019), while another used Twitter data (i.e. NLP) to discover a diurnal variation in emotions (Lansdall-Welfare et al. 2019; Dzogang et al. 2018). Both of these population-level studies were done using publicly-available datasets but required extensive forms of data collection and expensive data storage. Greater collaboration between researchers and technology companies who already have access to this data, as well as additionally valuable meta-data that is not publicly available, would likely extend our scientific and medical knowledge about possible risk factors for mental health disorders. It is also possible that, as more is understood about how environmental factors co-determine mental health, DHTs and the information that we gather from them could contribute to raising the standards of due care—as the evidence base grows the number of unintended consequences from lack of knowledge shrinks. This potential for DHTs, particularly those involving the use of artificial intelligence to spark human curiosity that can lead to better outcomes (Holm 2019), is one reason why governments should take a proportionate risk-based approach to the ways in which such DHTs are regulated.

5.3.4 Justice

Although DHTs could be used to optimise back-end operational processes for efficiency purposes (e.g. to release time for clinicians to ensure the right care is delivered in the right place at the right time and to improve equity of care (Nelson et al. 2019)), it is also likely that their use will have impacts on society in ways that are unequally distributed. For instance, there could be economic inequalities (e.g. those who have to rely on free-apps are far more likely to experience privacy harms due to the exploitative monetisation of their data (Polykalas and Prezerakos, 2019)) or epistemic inequalities (e.g. those with higher levels of health and media literacy

[11] Such a concern is reminiscent of concerns raised in an open letter to the DSM-V, which noted how lowering diagnostic thresholds for certain categories (e.g. ADD) could lead to *epidemiological inflation*, and in some cases could lead to the inappropriate prescription of pharmacological substances to vulnerable populations (e.g. the use of neuroleptics in children diagnosed with disruptive mood dysregulation disorder) (Kamens et al. 2017, p. 682).

who are better placed to make use of developments). However, there are also more specific concerns that can be discussed.

In addition to DHTs that are employed and embedded within formal healthcare systems, there are many more DHTs that can be accessed through third-party services (e.g. app stores). The quality and variety of these DHTs is vast, including apps that teach mindfulness-based stress reduction, online community support forums, and services that connect users with chatbots or human wellness coaches. We here focus on the latter.

Wellness coaching often has similar goals to formal healthcare services and can include NLP-based chatbots that deploy some form of CBT or paid-for online services that connect users to another human. It has been reported that some of these services are reliant on unlicensed "coaches" who deliver simple forms of motivational therapy or emotional-health coaching (Barras 2019), rather than a clinically recognised form of mental health therapy. While improving access on one level, and perhaps even extending the set of opportunities for engagement, these services also raise several ethical concerns.

Primarily these concerns stem from the fact that the logic underpinning many of these ideas is overly technologically deterministic, presenting the 'problem' of emotional wellbeing as something with a well-defined causal chain that can be 'solved' algorithmically (Janssen and Kuk 2016). This approach assumes that a DHT is a neutral collection of code and data rather than a node in a much broader social *system* composed of human and artificial agents (Ananny and Crawford 2018), the impact of which needs to be assessed not in silico but in socio. When such a social systems approach to analysis (Crawford and Calo 2016), instead of a product analysis, is taken it becomes much clearer that when the effects of many small, seemingly neutral, interactions (e.g. one user 'talking' to an NLP-based chatbot) are aggregated at a societal level the impact can be morally significant (Floridi 2013). For instance, if these chatbot or video-based consultation services do little more than provide paid-for access to someone to talk to, it can be argued that they end up commercialising (and perhaps replacing) an important social function that has typically been provided by friends and families. This could result in the commodification and diminishment of social relationships by reducing the opportunity for an actual friend to cultivate virtues such as empathy, or compassionate listening. Moreover, a genuine friend or family member may also be able to offer more insightful support, due to a wider understanding of the contextual factors (e.g. lifestyle, previous experiences). Alternatively, if these services end up drawing users away from formal healthcare services, which are governed by stricter evidence standards (see previous section), they could result in harm to the user due to inadequate care.

Although aspects of these concerns may fall more naturally within the remit of the principle of non-maleficence (i.e. avoid harm), there is also a social justice concern related to the fact that these services may further increase social inequalities in access to forms of treatment by creating a market that is only available to segments of society, and perhaps more importantly, the compounding effects of isolation that result from shifting the burden of care. Here, the aggregate effect is the loss of community. People will rely less on their neighbours, friends and family to provide them with advice, which will give them less opportunities to build up trusting relationships that hold together divergent and contrasting views (Durante 2010), and undermine the likelihood that responsibility (burden of care) for maintaining the wellbeing of each node (individual) is evenly distributed across the network (Floridi 2016a). Instead, this responsibility is shifted solely to the individual, which can potentially be very damaging to that individual's mental wellbeing for two primary, interconnected, reasons: (1) the individual becomes increasingly isolated, unable to benefit from the cathartic social support captured by the 'a problem shared, is a problem halved' idiom; and (2) the individual feels too much backward-facing moral responsibility (blame) for having experienced a deterioration in their mental wellbeing and feels increasingly unable to interact with other 'blameless' individuals, resulting in further isolation (Wardrope 2015).

5.3.5 *Explicability*

Much of the current literature about explicability in the context of artificial intelligence and 'black-box' decision-making focuses on the need to make it possible for an individual to understand *how* an algorithm made a decision through the use of specific statistical or visualisation techniques such as Local Interpretable Model-Agnostic Explanations (LIME) (Ribeiro et al. 2016) or SHapely Additive exPlanations (SHAP) (Lundberg and Lee 2017).[12] In the context of medical care, and particularly mental healthcare, this focus is necessary but not sufficient as it does not reflect the fact that explanations are social and contextual, about more than causal attribution (Miller 2019), and reliant on meaningful dialogue between user, developer and model (Mittelstadt et al. 2019). In short, purely quantitative explanations fail to take into account the need to make a result, or specific piece of advice, *meaningfully interpretable* (or understandable to a specific end-user (Guidotti et al. 2018)).

What counts as interpretable, and therefore actionable, advice is not an agreed standard (Doshi-Velez and Kim 2017; Dosilovic et al. 2018). Instead, what counts for one individual may not count as such to another individual with a different set of epistemic and normative standards, experiences, and baseline knowledge (Binns 2018). This is particularly related to variance in health literacy level, which has been shown to have a significant influence on an individual's ability to evaluate the quality, reliability and actionability of a healthcare information source (Chen et al. 2018). For example, those with lower health literacy levels are more likely to rely on social media sources of health advice, including mental health advice, than traditional online sources, such as websites providing clinically-validated information (Chen et al. 2018). This may be because, in the absence of an ability to determine

[12] Both LIME and SHAP are methods that can be used to 'explain' the output of any machine learning model, typically used for 'explaining' classifiers.

the difference in credibility between the two sources, these individuals rely more heavily on bandwagon heuristics and conflate popularity (e.g. likes and shares) with credibility and reliability (Borah and Xiao 2018). In the context of mental health, a lack of such considerations is particularly concerning as it means that those with low eHealth literacy, presented with conflicting information or recommendations about how to improve their health, are potentially more at risk than others of suffering from health anxiety (so-called 'cyberchondria') (McMullan et al. 2019) and more vulnerable to poor-quality and potentially harmful advice.

This is a concern from an equity of care perspective due to the following cycle: (a) lower levels of eHealth literacy have been found to be associated with other disadvantaging sociodemographic factors (Paige et al. 2017); (b) individuals with a lower income are more likely to rely on unregulated (and free) online sources of mental health care provision; (c) the poorer quality of advice delivered through these unregulated services means that individuals are unlikely to see an improvement in their mental state; (d) this lowers their self-efficacy; (e) this lessens their willingness to engage with mental health services; (f) this increases the risk of these individuals feeling unable to participate in society, both socially and economically; which (g) lessens their chances of improving their circumstances or their eHealth literacy, creating a situation of cumulative disadvantage. As such, we can acknowledge the importance of keeping the patient as a key part of the decision-making process as much as possible, in order to mitigate the worst effects that result from a lack of awareness.

The only way such nuances in design needs for mental health DHTs are going to be elicited is if the 'users' are treated as part of the solution, rather than as a problem that needs to be overcome (Aitken et al. 2019). This requires all parts of the system (e.g. designers, commissioners, policymakers, etc.), committing to the use of techniques such as those encapsulated under the headings of value sensitive design (Friedman et al. 2017) or responsible research and innovation (Jirotka et al. 2017; Stahl and Wright 2018; Stilgoe et al. 2013), which stresses the importance of considered and extensive stakeholder engagement throughout the development, deployment and use of DHTs. Not only will such a commitment improve the design of the technology and ensure it achieves positive outcomes for its users (e.g. as DeepMind Health found by developing their Streams App *with,* rather than *for,* clinicians in the Royal Free Hospital (DeepMind Health 2019)), but also meet the requirements of perceived usefulness and ease of use, to enhance the likelihood of adoption.

Such engagement practices can, therefore, be seen as a way of improving the social responsibility of DHTs by encouraging their designers and commissioners to take into account the expectations of stakeholders with regards to the impacts of the DHT on individuals, society and the wider system (Zhao 2018). As such they are a means of moving from principles to practice (Winfield and Jirotka 2018) and are a key 'tool' in the governance toolbox alongside impact assessments, judicial review, model repositories (Edwards and Veale 2018), and best practice guidelines or codes of conduct. However, in cases where the risks to end-users, in this case patients, are at their highest, it might be that these governance approaches are insufficient. For example, Hall et al. (2017) assessed the information for consumers' of 15 direct-to-consumer genetic testing companies available in the UK against the UK Human Genetics Commission (HGC) best practice principles and failed to find one provider compliant with all of the principles. Given that the results from these tests often include the statistical likelihood of the individual developing a specific disease, the risk posed to the individual's psychological integrity by not presenting this information in an interpretable format, is quite high (Andorno 2004). Instances of such high risk may result in calls for a move up from ethically-aligned standards to ethically-aligned regulation (Winfield and Jirotka 2018). While this may well be necessary to protect patient safety, it is important that the transition from "soft ethics" to governance and legislation (Floridi 2018) is done in a way that is proportionate and capable of producing regulation that is neither too semantically strict, flexible nor overly unpredictable (Arvan 2018).

5.4 Allowing for Contextual Flexibility

All ethical principles, including the bioethical principles that we have used as a means of guiding our critique, constrain behaviours. However, the way that they constrain behaviours may not always be interpreted consistently across different contexts (e.g. between different cultures, peoples and organisations) (Turilli 2007). This creates a tension between the need for universal principles, such as non-maleficence, beneficence, autonomy, justice and explicability, and the need to respect differences in their implementation, application, and relative weighting of importance (Binns 2018). For example, a clinical researcher might have a different interpretation of justice and give it a different weighting than a policy-maker. In addition, patients and clinicians are likely to interpret 'harm' (non-maleficence) differently.

If regulation is designed in a way that makes the interpretation of these principles too 'strict' it will limit society's ability to reflect on them (i.e. flexibly interpret, discuss and evaluate), making it harder to judge whether or not they have been adequately applied in different circumstances (D'Agostino and Durante 2018). However, if regulation is designed in a way that is too open to interpretation it will fail to protect society from the risks that have been highlighted (Floridi 2016b). There is no simple or straightforward way out of this tension. Ethics in this sense is a practice of ongoing discussion and critical engagement, and as such any set of ethical guidelines or principles should be treated as "living documents" that require continuous investment to maintain (Floridi et al. 2018).

5.5 Conclusion

Discussing the clinical applications of machine learning, Watson et al. note how the "opportunity costs of not using our best available tools for disease detection and treatment are substantial—12 million people a year receive misdiagnoses in the United States, with about six million facing potential harm as a result. Nearly one third of all preventable deaths in the United Kingdom are attributable to misdiagnosis" (2019, p. 2). As we have demonstrated, additional opportunity costs exist in the context of failing to use DHTs effectively for delivering mental healthcare. However, to ensure that these opportunities are pursued in an ethically responsible manner, it is vital that those responsible for delivering healthcare understand the importance of framing the challenges in the appropriate way—the concepts we use matter.

In this paper, we critically evaluated the concept of empowerment as it applies to DHTs and mental healthcare, showing how an insufficient consideration of wider psychological and socioeconomic factors runs the risk of missed opportunities for patient engagement and a misunderstanding of the role that key bioethical principles play in shaping healthcare delivery. Different mental health disorders will present different barriers to engagement and must be considered in relation to the situated nature of the individual concerned. To better articulate these concerns, we deployed five principles related to the ethical development and use of artificial intelligence, which are grounded in the literature on bioethics. These principles served as a structure to frame our discussion of some of the specific ethical issues that arise with the use of DHTs for mental healthcare—there will obviously be many more that we have not considered. It is well understood in the bioethical literature that these *prima facie* principles are general guidelines (Beauchamp and Childress 2013), which serve to establish more specific rules that could be used to assist the design and development of relevant DHTs. As such, they can only serve as a starting point in the ethical evaluation of specific technologies with specific uses in specific contexts. However, as we have shown, their higher-order level of abstraction can be of significant value in drawing attention to relevant ethical differences between the use of DHTs in healthcare systems broadly construed and the use of DHTs in the narrower context of mental healthcare.

It is vital that we continue to scrutinise the design, development, and use of DHTs in all areas of healthcare. While traditional ethical principles will still play a valuable role, the novel features of DHTs (e.g. artificial intelligence) alter their nature and specificity when applied to these new contexts. Therefore, and to appropriate a term from computer science, if we wish to avoid creating vulnerabilities that arise from being locked-in to a *legacy system of values* we must be willing to regularly evaluate our use of normative concepts. If we fail to do this, we may be unable to determine whether DHTs are genuinely empowering all users or simply serving as a costly distraction that prevents our healthcare system from serving those who need the most support.

Acknowledgements CB conducted this research as part of the Ethics of Digital Well-Being project, funded by a grant from Microsoft Research and awarded to Professor Luciano Floridi.

Statement of Contribution CB and JM contributed equally to the design, research, and writing of this article.

References

Aitken, M., M.P. Tully, C. Porteous, S. Denegri, S. Cunningham-Burley, N. Banner, et al. 2019. Consensus Statement on Public Involvement and Engagement with Data-Intensive Health Research. *International Journal of Population Data Science* 4 (1). https://doi.org/10.23889/ijpds.v4i1.586.

Ananny, M., and K. Crawford. 2018. Seeing Without Knowing: Limitations of the Transparency Ideal and Its Application to Algorithmic Accountability. *New Media & Society* 20 (3): 973–989. https://doi.org/10.1177/1461444816676645.

Andorno, R. 2004. The Right Not to Know: An Autonomy Based Approach. *Journal of Medical Ethics* 30 (5): 435–439. https://doi.org/10.1136/jme.2002.001578.

Anthony, W.A. 1993. Recovery from Mental Illness: The Guiding Vision of the Mental Health Service System in the 1990s. *Psychosocial Rehabilitation Journal* 16 (4): 11–23. https://doi.org/10.1037/h0095655.

Arvan, M. 2018. Mental Time-Travel, Semantic Flexibility, and A.I. Ethics. *AI & Society*. https://doi.org/10.1007/s00146-018-0848-2.

Bakker, D., N. Kazantzis, D. Rickwood, and N. Rickard. 2016. Mental Health Smartphone Apps: Review and Evidence-Based Recommendations for Future Developments. *JMIR Mental Health* 3 (1): e7. https://doi.org/10.2196/mental.4984.

Barras, C. 2019. Mental Health Apps Lean on Bots and Unlicensed Therapists. *Nature Medicine*. https://doi.org/10.1038/d41591-019-00009-6.

Beauchamp, T.L., and J.F. Childress. 2013. *Principles of Biomedical Ethics*. 7th ed. New York: Oxford University Press.

Bellet, C., and P. Frijters. 2019. Big Data and Well-being. In *World Happiness Report 2019,* ed. J. Helliwell, R. Layard, and J. Sachs. Retrieved from https://worldhappiness.report/ed/2019/big-data-and-well-being/.

Binns, R. 2018. Algorithmic Accountability and Public Reason. *Philosophy & Technology* 31 (4): 543–556. https://doi.org/10.1007/s13347-017-0263-5.

Borah, P., and X. Xiao. 2018. The importance of 'Likes': The Interplay of Message Framing, Source, and Social Endorsement on Credibility Perceptions of Health Information on Facebook. *Journal of Health Communication* 23 (4): 399–411. https://doi.org/10.1080/10810730.2018.1455770.

Bravo, P., P.J. Barr, I. Scholl, G. Elwyn, M. McAllister, G. Elwyn, and M. McAllister. 2015. Conceptualising Patient Empowerment: A Mixed Methods Study. *BMC Health Services Research* 15 (1). https://doi.org/10.1186/s12913-015-0907-z.

Breedvelt, J.J., V. Zamperoni, D. Kessler, H. Riper, A.M. Kleiboer, I. Elliott, et al. 2019. GPs' Attitudes Towards Digital Technologies for Depression: An Online Survey in Primary Care. *British Journal of General Practice* 69 (680): e164–e170. https://doi.org/10.3399/bjgp18X700721.

Bruineberg, J., and E. Rietveld. 2014. Self-Organization, Free Energy Minimization, and Optimal Grip on a Field of Affordances. *Frontiers in Human Neuroscience* 8. https://doi.org/10.3389/fnhum.2014.00599.

Burr, C., and N. Cristianini. 2019. Can Machines Read Our Minds? *Minds and Machines*. https://doi.org/10.1007/s11023-019-09497-4.

Burr, C., M. Taddeo, and L. Floridi. 2019. The Ethics of Digital Well-being: A Thematic Review. *SSRN Electronic Journal*. https://doi.org/10.2139/ssrn.3338441.

Calvo, R.A., and D. Peters. 2014. *Positive Computing: Technology for Wellbeing and Human Potential*. Cambridge: MIT Press.

Charland, L.C. 2015. Decision-Making Capacity. In *The Stanford Encyclopedia of Philosophy* (Fall 2015), ed. E.N. Zalta. Retrieved from https://plato.stanford.edu/archives/fall2015/entries/decision-capacity/

Chen, X., J.L. Hay, E.A. Waters, M.T. Kiviniemi, C. Biddle, E. Schofield, et al. 2018. Health Literacy and Use and Trust in Health Information. *Journal of Health Communication* 23 (8): 724–734. https://doi.org/10.1080/10810730.2018.1511658.

Chiauzzi, E., P. DasMahapatra, E. Cochin, M. Bunce, R. Khoury, and P. Dave. 2016. Factors in Patient Empowerment: A Survey of an Online Patient Research Network. *The Patient – Patient-Centered Outcomes Research* 9 (6): 511–523. https://doi.org/10.1007/s40271-016-0171-2.

Crawford, K., and R. Calo. 2016. There is a Blind Spot in AI Research. *Nature* 538 (7625): 311–313. https://doi.org/10.1038/538311a.

D'Agostino, M., and M. Durante. 2018. Introduction: The Governance of Algorithms. *Philosophy & Technology* 31 (4): 499–505. https://doi.org/10.1007/s13347-018-0337-z.

DeepMind Health. 2019, April 15. Retrieved from https://deepmind.com/applied/deepmind-health/working-partners/how-were-helping-today/.

Department of Health and Social Care. 2019, Feb 19. *Code of Conduct for Data-Driven Health and Care Technology*. Retrieved 15 April 2019, from GOV.UK website: https://www.gov.uk/government/publications/code-of-conduct-for-data-driven-health-and-care-technology/initial-code-of-conduct-for-data-driven-health-and-care-technology.

Doshi-Velez, F., and B. Kim. 2017. Towards a Rigorous Science of Interpretable Machine Learning. ArXiv:1702.08608 *[Cs, Stat]*. Retrieved from http://arxiv.org/abs/1702.08608.

Dosilovic, F.K., M. Brcic, and N. Hlupic. 2018. Explainable Artificial Intelligence: A Survey. In *2018 41st International Convention on Information and Communication Technology, Electronics and Microelectronics (MIPRO)*, 0210–0215. https://doi.org/10.23919/MIPRO.2018.8400040.

Durante, M. 2010. What Is the Model of Trust for Multi-agent Systems? Whether or Not E-trust Applies to Autonomous Agents. *Knowledge, Technology & Policy* 23 (3–4): 347–366. https://doi.org/10.1007/s12130-010-9118-4.

Dzogang, F., S. Lightman, and N. Cristianini. 2018. Diurnal Variations of Psychometric Indicators in Twitter Content. *PLoS One* 13 (6): e0197002. https://doi.org/10.1371/journal.pone.0197002.

Edwards, L., and M. Veale. 2018. Enslaving the Algorithm: From a "Right to an Explanation" to a "Right to Better Decisions"? *IEEE Security & Privacy* 16 (3): 46–54. https://doi.org/10.1109/MSP.2018.2701152.

Fernández-Caballero, A., E. Navarro, P. Fernández-Sotos, P. González, J.J. Ricarte, J.M. Latorre, and R. Rodriguez-Jimenez. 2017. Human-Avatar Symbiosis for the Treatment of Auditory Verbal Hallucinations in Schizophrenia Through Virtual/Augmented Reality and Brain-Computer Interfaces. *Frontiers in Neuroinformatics*: 11. https://doi.org/10.3389/fninf.2017.00064.

Floridi, L. 2010. *Information: A Very Short Introduction*. Oxford/New York: Oxford University Press.

———. 2013. Distributed Morality in an Information Society. *Science and Engineering Ethics* 19 (3): 727–743. https://doi.org/10.1007/s11948-012-9413-4.

———. 2016a. Faultless Responsibility: On the Nature and Allocation of Moral Responsibility for Distributed Moral Actions. *Philosophical Transactions of the Royal Society A: Mathematical, Physical and Engineering Sciences* 374 (2083): 20160112. https://doi.org/10.1098/rsta.2016.0112.

———. 2016b. Tolerant Paternalism: Pro-ethical Design as a Resolution of the Dilemma of Toleration. *Science and Engineering Ethics* 22 (6): 1669–1688. https://doi.org/10.1007/s11948-015-9733-2.

———. 2018. Soft Ethics, the Governance of the Digital and the General Data Protection Regulation. *Philosophical Transactions of the Royal Society A: Mathematical, Physical and Engineering Sciences* 376 (2133): 20180081. https://doi.org/10.1098/rsta.2018.0081.

Floridi, L., J. Cowls, M. Beltrametti, R. Chatila, P. Chazerand, V. Dignum, et al. 2018. AI4People—An Ethical Framework for a Good AI Society: Opportunities, Risks, Principles, and Recommendations. *Minds and Machines* 28 (4): 689–707. https://doi.org/10.1007/s11023-018-9482-5.

Foley, T., & Woollard, J. 2019. *The Digital Future of Mental Healthcare and Its Workforce*. Retrieved from topol.hee.nhs.uk.

Friedman, B., D.G. Hendry, and A. Borning. 2017. A Survey of Value Sensitive Design Methods. *Foundations and Trends® in Human–Computer Interaction* 11 (2): 63–125. https://doi.org/10.1561/1100000015.

Garcia, J., N. Romero, D. Keyson, and P. Havinga. 2014. Reflective Healthcare Systems: Mirco-cylce of Self-Reflection to Empower Users. *Interaction Design and Architecture(s)* 23 (1): 173–190.

Greaves, F., I. Joshi, M. Campbell, S. Roberts, N. Patel, and J. Powell. 2018. What Is an Appropriate Level of Evidence for a Digital Health Intervention? *The Lancet* 392 (10165): 2665–2667. https://doi.org/10.1016/S0140-6736(18)33129-5.

Grisso, T., and P.S. Appelbaum. 1998. *Assessing Competence to Consent to Treatment: A Guide for Physicians and Other Health Professionals*. New York: Oxford University Press.

Guidotti, R., A. Monreale, S. Ruggieri, F. Turini, F. Giannotti, and D. Pedreschi. 2018. A Survey of Methods for Explaining Black Box Models. *ACM Computing Surveys* 51 (5): 1–42. https://doi.org/10.1145/3236009.

Hall, J.A., R. Gertz, J. Amato, and C. Pagliari. 2017. Transparency of Genetic Testing Services for 'Health, Wellness and Lifestyle': Analysis of Online Prepurchase Information for UK Consumers. *European Journal of Human Genetics* 25 (8): 908–917. https://doi.org/10.1038/ejhg.2017.75.

Hausman, D. 2015. *Valuing Health: Well-being, Freedom, and Suffering*. New York: Oxford University Press.

Hindmarch, T., M. Hotopf, and G.S. Owen. 2013. Depression and Decision-Making Capacity for Treatment or Research: A Systematic Review. *BMC Medical Ethics* 14 (1). https://doi.org/10.1186/1472-6939-14-54.

Holm, E.A. 2019. In Defense of the Black Box. *Science* 364 (6435): 26–27. https://doi.org/10.1126/science.aax0162.

Janssen, M., and G. Kuk. 2016. The Challenges and Limits of Big Data Algorithms in Technocratic Governance. *Government Information Quarterly* 33 (3): 371–377. https://doi.org/10.1016/j.giq.2016.08.011.

Jirotka, M., B. Grimpe, B. Stahl, G. Eden, and M. Hartswood. 2017. Responsible Research and Innovation in the Digital Age. *Communications of the ACM* 60 (5): 62–68. https://doi.org/10.1145/3064940.

Kamens, S.R., D.N. Elkins, and B.D. Robbins. 2017. Open Letter to the DSM-5. *Journal of Humanistic Psychology* 57 (6): 675–687. https://doi.org/10.1177/0022167817698261.

Kenny, R., B. Dooley, and A. Fitzgerald. 2015. Feasibility of "CopeSmart": A Telemental Heath App for Adolescents. *JMIR Mental Health* 2 (3): e22. https://doi.org/10.2196/mental.4370.

Kramer, A.D.I., J.E. Guillory, and J.T. Hancock. 2014. Experimental Evidence of Massive-Scale Emotional Contagion Through Social Networks. *Proceedings of the National Academy of Sciences* 111 (24): 8788–8790. https://doi.org/10.1073/pnas.1320040111.

Kukla, R. 2005. Conscientious Autonomy: Displacing Decisions in Health Care. *Hastings Center Report* 35 (2): 34–44. https://doi.org/10.1353/hcr.2005.0025.

Lansdall-Welfare, T., S. Lightman, and N. Cristianini. 2019. Seasonal Variation in Antidepressant Prescriptions, Environmental Light and Web Queries for Seasonal Affective Disorder. *The British Journal of Psychiatry*: 1–4. https://doi.org/10.1192/bjp.2019.40.

Lehavot, K., D. Ben-Zeev, and R.E. Neville. 2012. Ethical Considerations and Social Media: A Case of Suicidal Postings on Facebook. *Journal of Dual Diagnosis* 8 (4): 341–346. https://doi.org/10.1080/15504263.2012.718928.

Lucas, G.M., A. Rizzo, J. Gratch, S. Scherer, G. Stratou, J. Boberg, and L.-P. Morency. 2017. Reporting Mental Health Symptoms: Breaking Down Barriers to Care with Virtual Human Interviewers. *Frontiers in Robotics and AI* 4. https://doi.org/10.3389/frobt.2017.00051.

Lundberg, S., and S.-I. Lee. 2017. A Unified Approach to Interpreting Model Predictions. ArXiv:1705.07874 *[Cs, Stat]*. Retrieved from http://arxiv.org/abs/1705.07874.

Lupton, D. 2016. *The quantified self*. Cambridge: Polity Press.

McMullan, R.D., D. Berle, S. Arnáez, and V. Starcevic. 2019. The Relationships Between Health Anxiety, Online Health Information Seeking, and Cyberchondria: Systematic Review and Meta-analysis. *Journal of Affective Disorders* 245: 270–278. https://doi.org/10.1016/j.jad.2018.11.037.

Miller, T. 2019. Explanation in Artificial Intelligence: Insights from the Social Sciences. *Artificial Intelligence* 267: 1–38. https://doi.org/10.1016/j.artint.2018.07.007.

Mittelstadt, B., C. Russell, and S. Wachter. 2019. Explaining Explanations in AI. In *Proceedings of the Conference on Fairness, Accountability, and Transparency – FAT*'19*, 279–288. https://doi.org/10.1145/3287560.3287574.

Morley, J., and L. Floridi. 2019. *Against Empowerment: How to Reframe the Role of mHealth Tools in the Healthcare Ecosystem (Draft)*.

Nagy, P., and G. Neff. 2015. Imagined Affordance: Reconstructing a Keyword for Communication Theory. *Social Media + Society* 1 (2): 205630511560338. https://doi.org/10.1177/2056305115603385.

NatCen Social Research. 2016. Adult Psychiatric Morbidity Survey. Retrieved 3 April 2019, from NHS Digital website: https://digital.nhs.uk/data-andinformation/publications/statistical/adult-psychiatric-morbidity-survey/adult-psychiatric-morbidity-survey-survey-of-mental-health-and-wellbeing-england-2014

National Institute for Health and Care Excellence. 2018. *Evidence Standards Framework for Digital Health Technologies*. Retrieved from https://www.nice.org.uk/Media/Default/About/what-we-do/our-programmes/evidence-standards-framework/digital-evidence-standards-framework.pdf.

Nelson, A., D. Herron, G. Rees, and P. Nachev. 2019. Predicting Scheduled Hospital Attendance with Artificial Intelligence. *Npj Digital Medicine* 2 (1): 26. https://doi.org/10.1038/s41746-019-0103-3.

Nelson, E.C., E. Eftimovska, C. Lind, A. Hager, J.H. Wasson, and S. Lindblad. 2015. Patient Reported Outcome Measures in Practice. *BMJ* 350 (feb10 14): g7818–g7818. https://doi.org/10.1136/bmj.g7818.

NHS England. 2019. *The NHS Long Term Plan*. Retrieved from NHS website: https://www.longtermplan.nhs.uk/wp-content/uploads/2019/01/nhs-long-term-plan.pdf.

Owens, J., and A. Cribb. 2013. Beyond Choice and Individualism: Understanding Autonomy for Public Health Ethics. *Public Health Ethics* 6 (3): 262–271. https://doi.org/10.1093/phe/pht038.

Paige, S.R., J.L. Krieger, and M.L. Stellefson. 2017. The Influence of eHealth Literacy on Perceived Trust in Online Health Communication Channels and Sources. *Journal of Health Communication* 22 (1): 53–65. https://doi.org/10.1080/10810730.2016.1250846.

Polykalas, S.E., and G.N. Prezerakos. 2019. When the Mobile App is Free, The Product Is Your Personal Data. *Digital Policy, Regulation and Governance* 21 (2): 89–101. https://doi.org/10.1108/DPRG-11-2018-0068.

Ribeiro, M.T., S. Singh, and C. Guestrin. 2016. "Why Should I Trust You?": Explaining the Predictions of any Classifier. ArXiv:1602.04938 *[Cs, Stat]*. Retrieved from http://arxiv.org/abs/1602.04938.

Roberts, K.J. 1999. Patient Empowerment in the United States: a Critical Commentary. *Health Expectations* 2 (2): 82–92. https://doi.org/10.1046/j.1369-6513.1999.00048.x.

Schermuly-Haupt, M.-L., M. Linden, and A.J. Rush. 2018. Unwanted Events and Side Effects in Cognitive Behavior Therapy. *Cognitive Therapy and Research* 42 (3): 219–229. https://doi.org/10.1007/s10608-018-9904-y.

Sen, A. 2010. *The Idea of Justice*. London: Penguin.

Sheehan, M. 2014. Reining in Patient and Individual Choice. *Journal of Medical Ethics* 40 (5): 291–292. https://doi.org/10.1136/medethics-2014-102161.

Sieck, C., D. Walker, S. Retchin, and A. McAlearney. 2019. *The Patient Engagement Capacity Model: What Factors Determine a Patient's Ability to Engage?* Retrieved 30 March 2019, from Catalyst website: https://catalyst.nejm.org/patient-engagement-capacity-model/?utm_campaign=Connect%20Weekly&utm_source=hs_email&utm_medium=email&utm_content=70937477&_hsenc=p2ANqtz-9iyYCA7cZ07BERqjc6bZfyUmsoykOeFDRfMu9O-AAxkEwMcmOIxeQ6s7AjzvfxHDfuTuPrEeL3FZwMVEVDa8DRGkFSPAw&_hsmi=70937477.
Spencer, G. 2015. Troubling' Moments in Health Promotion: Unpacking the etHics of Empowerment: G. Spencer. *Health Promotion Journal of Australia* 26 (3): 205–209. https://doi.org/10.1071/HE15049.
Stahl, B.C., and D. Wright. 2018. Ethics and Privacy in AI and Big Data: Implementing Responsible Research and Innovation. *IEEE Security & Privacy* 16 (3): 26–33. https://doi.org/10.1109/MSP.2018.2701164.
Starkey, F. 2003. The 'Empowerment Debate': Consumerist, Professional and Liberational Perspectives in Health and Social Care. *Social Policy and Society* 2 (4): 273–284. https://doi.org/10.1017/S1474746403001404.
Stilgoe, J., R. Owen, and P. Macnaghten. 2013. Developing a Framework for Responsible Innovation. *Research Policy* 42 (9): 1568–1580. https://doi.org/10.1016/j.respol.2013.05.008.
The Topol Review Board. 2019. *The Topol Review: Preparing the Healthcare Workforce to Deliver the Digital Future*. Retrieved from topol.hee.nhs.uk.
Turilli, M. 2007. Ethical Protocols Design. *Ethics and Information Technology* 9 (1): 49–62. https://doi.org/10.1007/s10676-006-9128-9.
Wardrope, A. 2015. Relational Autonomy and the Ethics of Health Promotion. *Public Health Ethics* 8 (1): 50–62. https://doi.org/10.1093/phe/phu025.
Watson, D.S., J. Krutzinna, I.N. Bruce, C.E. Griffiths, I.B. McInnes, M.R. Barnes, and L. Floridi. 2019. Clinical Applications of Machine Learning Algorithms: Beyond the Black Box. *BMJ*: l886. https://doi.org/10.1136/bmj.l886.
White, R.G., M.G. Imperiale, and E. Perera. 2016. The Capabilities Approach: Fostering Contexts for Enhancing Mental Health and Wellbeing Across the Globe. *Globalization and Health* 12. https://doi.org/10.1186/s12992-016-0150-3.
Winfield, A.F.T., and M. Jirotka. 2018. Ethical Governance is Essential to Building Trust in Robotics and Artificial Intelligence Systems. *Philosophical Transactions of the Royal Society A: Mathematical, Physical and Engineering Sciences* 376 (2133): 20180085. https://doi.org/10.1098/rsta.2018.0085.
Zhao, W.-W. 2018. Improving Social Responsibility of Artificial Intelligence by Using ISO 26000. *IOP Conference Series: Materials Science and Engineering* 428: 012049. https://doi.org/10.1088/1757-899x/428/1/012049.

Christopher Burr is a philosopher of cognitive science and artificial intelligence. His research explores philosophical and ethical issues related to the opportunities and risks that digital technologies pose for mental health and well-being.

He has held previous posts at the University of Bristol, where he explored the ethical and epistemological impact of big data and artificial intelligence and completed his PhD in 2017.

Research Interests: Philosophy of Cognitive Science and Artificial Intelligence, Ethics of Artificial Intelligence, Philosophy of Technology, Decision Theory, and Philosophy of Mind.

Jessica Morley is an MSc student at the Oxford Internet Institute, supervised by Professor Luciano Floridi. She is also a Tech Lead for AI at NHSx. In both capacities Jess focuses on the use of data-driven health and care technologies.

Jess previously studied for a B.A. in Geography at Oxford University, where she explored the impact of social media on the spread of cultural ideas.

Research interests: AI, Personalised Healthcare, mHealth, ethics.

Chapter 6
Towards the Ethical Publication of Country of Origin Information (COI) in the Asylum Process

Nikita Aggarwal and Luciano Floridi

Abstract This article addresses the question of how 'Country of Origin Information' (COI) reports—that is, research developed and used to support decision-making in the asylum process—can be published in an ethical manner. The article focuses on the risk that published COI reports could be misused and thereby harm the subjects of the reports and/or those involved in their development. It supports a situational approach to assessing data ethics when publishing COI reports, whereby COI service providers must weigh up the benefits and harms of publication based, inter alia, on the foreseeability and probability of harm due to potential misuse of the research, the public good nature of the research, and the need to balance the rights and duties of the various actors in the asylum process, including asylum seekers themselves. Although this article focuses on the specific question of 'how to publish COI reports in an ethical manner', it also intends to promote further research on data ethics in the asylum process, particularly in relation to refugees, where more foundational issues should be considered.

Keywords Asylum · Country of origin information (COI) · Data ethics · Dual use research · Refugees · Human rights · Open access

N. Aggarwal (✉)
Faculty of Law, University of Oxford, Oxford, UK

Oxford Internet Institute, University of Oxford, Oxford, UK
e-mail: nikita.aggarwal@law.ox.ac.uk

L. Floridi
Oxford Internet Institute, University of Oxford, Oxford, UK

The Alan Turing Institute, London, UK

C. Burr, S. Milano (eds.), *The 2019 Yearbook of the Digital Ethics Lab*,
Digital Ethics Lab Yearbook, https://doi.org/10.1007/978-3-030-29145-7_6

6.1 Introduction

'Country of Origin Information' (COI) is an umbrella term describing the diverse body of information used to support decision-making in the asylum process. COI is used both by governmental agencies to assess asylum claims, as well as by asylum seekers and their legal advisers, *inter alia* to substantiate the claimant's risk of persecution in their country of origin (or transit), and the credibility of their testimony.

The sources of COI vary. They include generic information (for example, news bulletins and maps) as well as reports specifically produced and compiled for use in asylum proceedings (hereinafter, 'COI reports').[1] COI reports can be thematic, country-specific, or case-specific (produced on request for specific claimants). They are developed by a variety of organizations, but primarily by non-profit organizations (for example, the charity Asylos)[2]; national government agencies (for example, the UK Home Office)[3]; and regional and international governmental agencies (for example, the European Asylum Support Office (EASO)[4] and UN High Commissioner for Refugees (UNHCR)) (hereinafter, 'COI service providers').[5]

As such, COI reports typically provide detailed information on conditions in countries from which asylum seekers originate (or through which they transit)—based on fieldwork and/or desk research (Van der Kist et al. 2019)—in order to substantiate claims for asylum in host countries on the basis of, *inter alia*, refugee and human rights grounds.[6] Notably, for the purposes of seeking asylum as a refugee, it must be demonstrated that the claimant is unable or unwilling to return to their country of origin due to a 'well-founded fear of being persecuted for reasons of race, religion, nationality, membership of a particular social group or political opinion' (United Nations 1951).[7]

As things stand, however, there are evident procedural weaknesses in the development and use of COI for asylum decision-making. In particular, there is a lack of consistently applied standards for developing COI, especially with respect to the

[1] For the sake of simplicity, we refer to COI 'reports', however in practice these can take the form (inter alia) of reports, fact sheets, responses to specific queries and documentation packages, see ACCORD (2013, p. 17).

[2] See https://asylos.eu/about-asylos/

[3] See https://www.gov.uk/government/collections/country-policy-and-information-notes

[4] See https://coi.easo.europa.eu/

[5] See http://www.unhcr.org/uk/country-reports.html

[6] See ACCORD (2013, p. 12) et seq. *Inter alia*, the UNHCR (2011) has underscored in its guidance the importance for decision-makers to have knowledge about conditions in an applicant's country of origin in order to assess asylum claims (para 42). Within the EU, the EU Asylum Procedures Directive 2005 stipulates that border authorities must examine 'precise and up-to-date information…obtained from various sources' (Art 8(2)(b) Council Directive 2005/85/EC).

[7] Article 1(A)(2), UN 1951 Convention Relating to the Status of Refugees http://www.unhcr.org/3b66c2aa10.html. This Convention is grounded in Article 14 of the Universal Declaration of Human Rights 1948, recognizing the right of persons to 'seek and to enjoy in other countries asylum from persecution' http://www.un.org/en/udhrbook/pdf/udhr_booklet_en_web.pdf

accuracy, relevance and reliability of information, and transparency of sources, as well as for the relative evidentiary value to be given to different COI sources by decision-makers in asylum proceedings.[8] Amongst other things, this lack of consistency enables claimants and national border agencies to 'cherry pick' different COI to suit their case, with claimants seeking to substantiate the risk of persecution or human rights violation in their country of origin, and border agencies often seeking to downplay the gravity of the threat.[9]

A further weakness in the current system is that asylum seekers and their legal advisers usually have more limited access to COI than host country authorities. This asymmetry of information aggravates the existing power imbalance between asylum seekers and host country governments, putting them at a disadvantage in presenting and substantiating their claims, and undermining the fairness of the asylum procedure, in particular the principle of 'equality of arms as regards access to information'.[10] Ultimately, lack of access to information to substantiate a claim impedes the fundamental rights of individuals to seek and enjoy asylum from persecution, as enshrined in the Universal Declaration of Human Rights (United Nations 1948).[11]

One way to mitigate this problem is for COI reports to be more widely disseminated, including through wider publication. Whilst some COI reports are already made publicly available (such as those produced by dedicated public COI units), many COI reports—especially case-specific ones produced by non-profits— remain unpublished, and stay within the organizations that develop them. Wider sharing of COI reports could also help to reduce 'survey fatigue' of asylum-seeking groups due to repetitious assessment of the risks they face, and could furthermore reduce data security risks by significantly reducing the amount of data that needs to be collected and stored in relation to those groups (Hayes 2017). However, the publication of these reports also raises various ethical and legal concerns that must be addressed.

The rest of this article examines only the principal *ethical* concerns relating to the publication of COI reports by COI service providers and proposes a way for addressing them. The legal implications pertain primarily to restrictions on the processing of personal (sensitive) data—in the EU, pursuant to the EU General Data Protection Regulation (GDPR).[12] However, note that, in practice, many COI service providers are unwilling to risk publishing COI reports that disclose personally iden-

---

[8] See IAS (2009). For a critical assessment of the use of COI by the UK Home Office, see UK Independent Chief Inspector of Borders and Agencies (2017). Examples of COI standards and methodologies that have been promulgated include: ACCORD (2013), UNHCR (2004), European Comission (2008), and EASO (2012).

[9] See for example the 'Eritrea Controversy' (the 2014 decision of the Danish authorities to suspend refugee status determination for Eritrean asylum seekers, and subsequent volte-face, was based on a politicized COI report produced by the Danish Immigration Service as part of a strategic effort to pursue restrictive asylum policies) (Van der Kist et al. 2019).

[10] See Art 16(1) of the EU Asylum Procedures Directive 2005 (n 6), and ACCORD (2013), Principle 2.2.2 (p 37).

[11] See n 7 and Asylos and Haagsma (2017).

[12] Regulation (EU) 2016/679 on the protection of natural persons with regard to the processing of personal data and on the free movement of such data, and repealing Directive 95/46/EC.

tifiable information (even on the basis of consent of the data subjects, as permitted under the GDPR), on the grounds that this could expose the subjects of the report to further persecution.[13] As such, our assumption in this article is that personal data would generally be anonymised or pseudonymised before publication of the report (by removing any identifiers from which natural persons can be identified, either directly or indirectly), in which case the obligations under the GDPR, which only apply to the processing of personal data, would cease to apply (in case of anonymisation) or apply only to a limited extent (in case of pseudonymisation).[14]

6.2 How to Address Ethical Concerns When Publishing COI Reports

6.2.1 Dual-Use Risk

One of the principal ethical concerns relating to the publication of COI reports is that the information contained in the reports could be misused. This could involve: misuse by (other) asylum claimants to support false claims (for example, by falsely co-opting a narrative of persecution described in a COI report); misuse by governmental or non-governmental actors in the claimant's country of origin to further persecute individuals or groups who are the subjects of the reports; and/or misuse by prospective host countries to deny meritorious claims—for example, by selecting only the negative portions of a report and using them out of context. Although the anonymisation of personal data mitigates these misuse risks to some extent, it is insufficient to eliminate the risks fully, e.g. in the case of co-option of an anonymised narrative, or because of proxy and secondary information that may enable re-identification of data subjects.[15]

From an ethical perspective, the starting point in evaluating and managing the risk of misuse is the principle of harm prevention. There are two key considerations in implementing this principle: the foreseeability and probability of potential harm due to misuse, and whether such harm outweighs the reasonably foreseeable and probable benefits flowing from the widening of access to COI reports. On the one hand, categorically prohibiting the publication of all COI reports due to the possibility of misuse would curtail the potential beneficial uses of these reports—notably, helping to redress the asymmetry of information and power between asylum seekers and host country authorities. It would also contradict the ethos and expectations of openness and collaboration that underpin scientific and social-scientific research (as discussed further below), as well as the rights and duties of COI service providers

[13] See further ACCORD (2013), Principle 2.2.4 (p 38).

[14] See n 12, Recital 26, and Article 4(1) (defining 'personal data' as 'any information relating to an identified or identifiable natural person').

[15] See further UNHCR (2018) at paragraph 2.4.2 (discussing the risk of re-identification when sharing aggregate data).

to publish their research.[16] On the other hand, to commit categorically to the publication of COI reports in all cases may enable the occurrence of preventable harms due, *inter alia*, to misuse of the reports.

This dilemma calls for a more situational approach that balances, on a case-by-case basis, and in accordance with the principle of proportionality, the benefits and harms of publication.[17] This approach is in line with that generally taken by academic institutions when assessing the publication of dual-use research, for example, in the context of peer-review journals and institutional pre-publication review.[18] However, the potential for misuse is not solely an intrinsic property of COI reports, but also an imposed property (Bezuidenhout 2013). That is, the potential misuse of COI reports also depends on how they are used by other actors in the asylum claim and appeal process, in potentially new contexts unrelated to those in which the reports were conceived, and in combination with other information, possibly including other COI reports.

This imposed nature of the dual-use risk in COI research limits a COI service provider's ethical responsibility to mitigate potential misuse, given that the risk of misuse is highly context-dependent, and its foreseeability necessarily more limited. Accordingly, the principle of proportionality demands that COI service providers consider the potential negative uses of their research and take reasonable measures to prevent reasonably foreseeable and probable misuse, to the extent proportionate to the information known to the COI service provider at the time of the risk assessment. As such, it does not require that providers prevent misuse that is not reasonably foreseeable or probable, nor take unreasonable measures to prevent misuse (Kuhlau et al. 2008).[19] Ultimately, if misuse is reasonably foreseeable, and such misuse would likely outweigh the potential benefits of publication, granting full open access to the reports would not be advisable.

In this regard, the 'zones of risk' approach, proposed under the Common EU Guidelines for Processing COI, offers a useful framework for assessing the risks involved in the publication of COI reports.[20] For example, a COI service provider might take the view that, even with anonymisation of personally identifiable information, publishing COI reports detailing instances of persecution in particular countries still runs a high risk of the individual subjects of the report being

[16] See European Commission (2005), European Charter for Researchers, which recognizes 'research freedom' as the first general principle https://euraxess.ec.europa.eu/sites/default/files/am509774cee_en_e4.pdf, p 11.

[17] Kuhlau et al. (2008) describe this as a 'duty to *consider* whether to refrain from publishing or sharing sensitive information when the information is of such a character that it could invite misuse'. See further UNDG (2017) for an articulation of the situational approach to data ethics in the context of the UN Sustainable Development Goals.

[18] However, Bezuidenhout (2013) notes that, at least as of 2011, no papers were refused publication, as part of the open science journal reviews, on the grounds of dual-use potential.

[19] The scope of 'reasonable' measures must be assessed relative to professional and resource capacity. Thus, what is considered reasonable care or precaution by a volunteer COI service provider with limited financial resources will differ from the measures expected to be taken by a large, well-funded COI service provider (Kuhlau et al. 2008).

[20] See n 8, p 22 et seq.

re-identified and further persecuted (e.g. due to proxy information, combination with secondary information, and/or because they are a small ethnic minority whose cause is widely known). Alternatively, even if the individual subjects are not identifiable, it may be possible to easily identify and persecute the wider ethnic group to which they belong. The publication of COI in this context could thus result in group-level ethical harms (Floridi 2014).[21]

On the one hand, if these risks are deemed to be reasonably foreseeable and probable, and the COI service provider could mitigate them by limiting access to its reports, it should either avoid publication or opt for restricted and carefully monitored publication, for example, through a subscription-based access policy. Alternatively, the reports could be shared on an individual basis with selected third parties, subject to a confidentiality agreement. On the other hand, if the COI service provider considers that these risks are highly unlikely, and do not outweigh the benefits to those vulnerable individuals or groups of publishing the reports (or, if the risk would not be mitigated by withholding publication), it would be appropriate to make the reports more widely available. Moreover, increasing access to COI for claimants through wider publication could itself counteract the potential for misuse of information by the host country government (for example, through cherry-picking information or using it out of context to deny meritorious claims), by strengthening the asylum claimants' evidence against such attempted misuse.

Publication of COI reports should furthermore be subject to ex post mechanisms to safeguard against unforeseen risks if the initial risk assessment proves to be wrong, or the risk assessment changes due to new evidence—for example, where following publication a COI service provider becomes aware that its published COI reports are being used to falsify claims. These mechanisms for accountability should also be made available to asylum seekers, who should be able to hold COI service providers and other actors in the asylum claim-handling process accountable for the use and sharing of their information (Kaurin 2019). It should be noted, however, that the duty to report ex post about activities of concern is not universally accepted, at least in the scientific research community, as it may be considered to demand treachery (Kuhlau et al. 2008). However, self-reporting of ethical misconduct appears at least to be encouraged in the academic context.[22]

Finally, given the imposed and therefore inherently less foreseeable nature of dual-use risk in publishing COI reports, it is important to take a collective approach towards conceptualizing and apportioning ethical responsibility for such risk (Bezuidenhout 2013). In this sense, the asylum claims community as a whole, encompassing all actors that take 'custody' of published COI reports, assumes a collective responsibility to address dual-use risks. *Inter alia*, this should include collective discussion and educational efforts to develop a 'culture of awareness and responsibility'[23] within the field of asylum research and decision-making, including

[21] See also Taylor et al. (2017).

[22] See for example SSRN, question 12, https://www.ssrn.com/en/index.cfm/ssrn-faq/#ssrn_copyright

[23] See Institute of Medicine and National Research Council (2006), ch 4.

through the development and application of codes of ethics and practice relating to the dissemination of COI reports by COI service providers.[24] It should also include greater education of asylum seekers about the use of their information, and their rights to control such use through data protection mechanisms and to assess their own risks throughout the asylum process (Kaurin 2019).[25]

6.2.2 *Open Access*

The ethics of publishing COI reports must also be evaluated as part of the wider movement for 'open access' to research. The principle of open access encourages the global and free distribution of knowledge, in the form of publication (Mauthner and Parry 2013), and is based on the notion that information is a public good, which society and individuals have an obligation to make as widely accessible as possible, and which individuals should be able to access as a basic right (Willinsky 2006).[26] It could also be said that the advent of digital publishing and the Internet affords the practical tools and platforms by which to 'do the right thing' by granting open access to research, and a duty to share (if one is recognized) is rooted in this technological affordance (Willinsky and Alperin 2011).

This ethical duty to share research with the public, and the public's right to access research, is arguably stronger in the case of research that has been funded by the public (Arzberger et al. 2006).[27] That is, the public has a right to know what research outputs it has contributed towards financing, as well as to engage with the resulting outcomes (Bishop 2009). At the same time, certain forms of research may be considered, by their very nature, public goods that should be made publicly available, regardless of how they were funded. It could be argued that COI reports fall in this category, given that the protection of refugees is a public and humanitarian concern.[28]

However, the principle of open access, where acknowledged, is not unconditional, with recognized exceptions, *inter alia* where there is a risk of misuse (as discussed above), national security concerns, and/or a need to protect confidentiality, privacy, and intellectual property rights. These exceptions are typically addressed through anonymisation of personal and sensitive information, license agreements specifying the rights and responsibilities of data depositors, archives and end users,

[24] See further Kuhlau et al. (2008) discussing the formulation of ethical codes and guidelines to address dual use concerns in scientific and policy communities.

[25] See further OHCHR (2018), 3–6 ('Participation').

[26] See further the Budapest Open Access Initiative (BOAI) Declaration (2002), https://www.budapestopenaccessinitiative.org/read

[27] See for example OECD (2007) noting that 'publicly funded research data are a public good, produced in the public interest'. Parker (2013) refers to the 'researcher's social licence' and the responsibility of 'those who spend public money to contribute to the dissemination of knowledge'.

[28] By way of analogy, Langat et al. (2011) refer to the 'public notion of health' as intimately tied to notions of social justice and equity.

and in some cases limitations on access to, and use of, the data (Bishop 2009).[29] In addition, the duties and rights of access to research embodied in the open access principle need to be balanced against the rights and duties of (co-)researchers, as well as the requestors and subjects of research (Mauthner and Parry 2013).

The latter set of responsibilities includes not only safeguarding the security and safety of both researchers and research subjects, but also honouring the trust and preferences of the research subjects. For example, researchers may use the promise of restricting further use of a participant's data as a way of building trust and to induce participation in the research (Bishop 2009). Or, participants may simply not wish to have the reports published, even if their personal data is (technically) anonymised, particularly in light of the misuse risks described above. Thus, notwithstanding the absence of any *legal* obligations to obtain consent for the publication of personal data that has been anonymised, researchers arguably still have an *ethical* duty to obtain participants' consent to such publication and reuse. Obtaining 'informed consent' in this context requires data subjects to be given adequate information at the time of collection about the purposes and risks associated with sharing their data, including potential future uses of that data and unintended consequences, as well as powers to access the resulting COI reports and, where feasible, object to publication or further dissemination.[30]

In this regard, the publication of COI reports raises further political and epistemic questions about the integrity of taking information out of its context of production and reusing and repurposing it. *Inter alia*, the inherent imbalance of power between the organizations and communities that produce and use COI reports, and the vulnerable individuals and communities that are typically the subjects of those reports, risks reproducing and/or exacerbating exploitative relations between nations, and between data users and data producers, as problematized by feminist and post-colonial scholars (Mauthner and Parry 2013). Reliance on the 'informed consent' of research subjects appears insufficient to assuage concerns of exploitation, in light of this unequal power dynamic (Kaurin 2019).

A related concern is the need to respect the right of research subjects to self-identify the parameters of their population, rather than having them imposed externally by COI researchers (OHCHR 2018). On the other hand, the use of data for new purposes, and to reach different conclusions, is inherent to the nature of research and scholarly debate. As such, it can be argued that it is not necessary, from an epistemological perspective, for participants to have an ongoing role in the interpretation of their data or research conclusions (Bishop 2009). These questions certainly merit further and deeper consideration, but they are not within the scope of this article.[31]

---

[29] Copyright laws generally permit 'fair use' of protected works for (personal or scholarly) non-commercial purposes. See SSRN's Copyright policy at question 11, https://www.ssrn.com/en/index.cfm/ssrn-faq/#ssrn_copyright

[30] On the importance of informed consent and information provision in supporting the digital agency of refugees, see further Kaurin (2019).

[31] On the politics of knowledge production in the context of COI, see further Van der Kist et al. (2019).

6.3 Conclusions

This article has highlighted some of the key ethical issues that should be considered when publishing COI reports relating to asylum claims. It has advocated for a situational approach that weighs the benefits and harms of publication based, inter alia, on the foreseeability and probability of harm due to potential misuse of the research, the public good nature of such research, and the need to balance the rights and duties of the various actors in the asylum process, including both the public as well as the requestors and subjects of the research. Of course, the feasibility of such an approach will depend on the resources that a COI service provider has at its disposal. For smaller organizations with a low volume of COI reports, a case-by-case approach is more likely to be administratively feasible. In contrast, for organizations with a large volume of publications, a more standardized policy for sharing COI may be required.[32]

COI service providers should furthermore consider additional mechanisms for increasing the availability and visibility of their reports, beyond conventional publication. This includes collaborating with existing COI-sharing platforms to disseminate reports, for example ecoi.net[33] and the Refworld database,[34] and more generally engaging in outreach and educational efforts to increase awareness of, and therefore access to, COI research amongst asylum seekers and their legal advisers.

Acknowledgements The authors would like to thank Asylos for the fruitful interactions on a report about how to ethically publish COI reports, which contributed to inform some of the research presented in this article. Asylos is an international network of volunteers who research vital information to support people fleeing war, violence, persecution and grave threats with claiming their right to asylum. Research for this article has been supported by Privacy and Trust Stream - Social lead of the PETRAS Internet of Things research hub. PETRAS is funded by the Engineering and Physical Sciences Research Council (EPSRC), grant agreement no. EP/N023013/1; and by a Microsoft academic grant.

References

ACCORD (Austrian Red Cross). 2013. *Researching Country of Origin Information: Training Manual.* https://www.coi-training.net/site/assets/files/1021/researching-country-of-origin-information-2013-edition-accord-coi-training-manual.pdf.

Arzberger, P., et al. 2006. Promoting Access to Public Research Data for Scientific, Economic, and Social Development. *Data Science Journal* 3: 135–152.

Asylos, and J. Haagsma. 2017. Research Under Pressure: Challenges to Researching Country of Origin Information for Asylum Claims. https://www.asylos.eu/research-under-pressure.

[32] See also n 19.

[33] See https://www.ecoi.net/en/document-search/?asalt= and http://www.refworld.org/type,COUNTRYREP,,,,,0.html.

[34] See https://www.refworld.org/type,COUNTRYREP,,,,,0.html.

Bezuidenhout, L. 2013. Data Sharing and Dual-Use Issues. *Science and Engineering Ethics* 19 (1): 83–92.

Bishop, L. 2009. Ethical Sharing and Reuse of Qualitative Data. *Australian Journal of Social Issues* 44 (3): 255.

Budapest Open Access Initiative (BOAI). 2002. *Declaration* https://www.budapestopenaccessinitiative.org/read.

EASO. 2012. Country of Origin Information Report Methodology. https://coi.easo.europa.eu/administration/easo/PLib/EASO_COI_Report_Methodology.pdf.

European Commission. 2005. *European Charter for Researchers*. https://euraxess.ec.europa.eu/sites/default/files/am509774cee_en_e4.pdf.

———. 2008. *Common EU Guidelines for Processing Country of Origin Information (COI)*. https://www.sem.admin.ch/dam/data/sem/internationales/herkunftslaender/coi_leitlinien-e.pdf.

Floridi, L. 2014. Open Data, Data Protection, and Group Privacy. *Philosophy and Technology* 27 (1): 1–3.

Hayes, B. 2017. Migration and Data Protection: Doing No Harm in an Age of Mass Displacement, Mass Surveillance and "Big Data". *International Review of the Red Cross* 99 (1): 179–209.

Immigration Advisory Service (IAS). 2009 May. *The Use of Country of Origin Information in Refugee Status Determination: Critical Perspectives*. http://www.refworld.org/pdfid/4a3f2ac32.pdf.

Institute of Medicine and National Research Council. 2006. *Globalization, Biosecurity, and the Future of the Life Sciences*. Washington, DC: The National Academies Press.

Kaurin, D. 2019. Data Protection and Digital Agency for Refugees. World Refugee Council Research Paper no. 12. https://www.cigionline.org/publications/data-protection-and-digital-agency-refugees.

Kuhlau, F., S. Eriksson, K. Evers, and A. Höglund. 2008. Taking Due Care: Moral Obligations in Dual Use Research. *Bioethics* 22 (9): 477.

Langat, P., et al. 2011. Is There a Duty to Share? Ethics of Sharing Research Data in the Context of Public Health Emergencies. *Public Health Ethics* 4 (1): 4–11.

Mauthner, N., and O. Parry. 2013. Open Access Digital Data Sharing: Principles, Policies and Practices. *Social Epistemology* 27 (1): 47–67.

OECD. 2007. *OECD Principles and Guidelines for Access to Research Data from Public Funding*. https://www.oecd.org/sti/sci-tech/38500813.pdf.

Office of the United Nations High Commissioner for Human Rights (OHCHR). 2018. *A Human Rights-Based Approach to Data*. https://www.ohchr.org/Documents/Issues/HRIndicators/GuidanceNoteonApproachtoData.pdf.

Parker, M. 2013. The Ethics of Open Access Publishing. *BMC Medical Ethics* 14: 16.

Taylor, L., L. Floridi, and B. van der Sloot, eds. 2017. *Group Privacy – New Challenges of Data Technologies*. Cham: Springer.

Willinsky, J. 2006. *The Access Principle: The Case for Open Access to Research and Scholarship*. Cambridge: MIT.

Willinsky, J., and J.P. Alperin. 2011. The Academic Ethics of Open Access to Research and Scholarship. *Ethics and Education* 6 (3): 217–223.

UK Independent Chief Inspector of Borders and Agencies. 2017. *An Inspection of the Home Office's Production and Use of Country of Origin Information*. https://asylumresearchcentre.org/wp-content/uploads/2018/05/An_inspection_of_the_production_and_use_of_Country_of_Origin_Information.pdf.

United Nations. 1948. Universal Declaration of Human Rights. http://www.un.org/en/udhrbook/pdf/udhr_booklet_en_web.pdf.

———. 1951. Convention Relating to the Status of Refugees. http://www.unhcr.org/3b66c2aa10.html.

United Nations Development Group (UNDG). 2017. *Data Privacy, Ethics and Protection – Guidance Note on Big Data for Achievement of the 2030 Agenda*. https://undg.org/document/data-privacy-ethics-and-protection-guidance-note-on-big-data-for-achievement-of-the-2030-agenda/.

United Nations High Commissioner For Refugees (UNHCR). 2004. *Country of Origin Information: Towards Enhanced International Cooperation.* http://www.refworld.org/docid/403b2522a.html.
———. 2011. *Handbook and Guidelines on Procedures and Criteria for Determining Refugee Status.* http://www.unhcr.org/uk/publications/legal/3d58e13b4/handbook-procedures-criteria-determining-refugee-status-under-1951-convention.html.
———. 2018. *Guidance on the Protection of Personal Data of Persons of Concern to UNHCR.* https://www.refworld.org/docid/5b360f4d4.html.
Van der Kist, J., et al. 2019. In the Shadow of Asylum Decision-Making: The Knowledge Politics of Country-of-Origin Information. *International Political Sociology* 13: 68–85.

Nikita Aggarwal is a Research Associate at the Digital Ethics Lab, as well as a Research Fellow and doctoral candidate at the Faculty of Law. Her research examines changes to the regulatory landscape occasioned by the proliferation of data-driven technology, particularly due to advances in machine learning ('artificial intelligence'). Her other areas of interest include internet policy and regulation more generally, as well as the ethics of data-driven technology.

As the Research and Course Design Fellow in Law and Technology under the ESRC-funded project 'Unlocking the Potential of AI for English Law', she is researching the educational skills gaps in legal education and training generated by recent technological development, and is helping to design and deliver a more interdisciplinary approach to law and technology education at the University.

Prior to entering academia, Nikita was an attorney in the legal department of the International Monetary Fund, where she advised on financial sector law reform in the Euro area and worked extensively on initiatives to reform the legal and policy frameworks for sovereign debt restructuring. She previously practiced as an associate with Clifford Chance LLP, where she specialized in EU financial regulation and sovereign debt restructuring.

She earned her law degree (LLB) from the London School of Economics and Political Science, and is a solicitor of England and Wales.

Research interests: Artificial Intelligence, Machine Learning, Big Data, Regulation, Ethics, Law.

Luciano Floridi is the OII's Professor of Philosophy and Ethics of Information at the University of Oxford, where he is also the Director of the Digital Ethics Lab of the Oxford Internet Institute. Still in Oxford, he is Distinguished Research Fellow of the Uehiro Centre for Practical Ethics of the Faculty of Philosophy, and Research Associate and Fellow in Information Policy of the Department of Computer Science. Outside Oxford, he is Faculty Fellow of the Alan Turing Institute (the national institute for data science) and Chair of its Data Ethics Group; and Adjunct Professor ("Distinguished Scholar in Residence") of the Department of Economics, American University, Washington D.C.

He is deeply engaged with emerging policy initiatives on the socio-ethical value and implications of digital technologies and their applications. And he has worked closely on digital ethics (including the ethics of algorithms and AI) with the European Commission, the German Ethics Council, and, in the UK, with the House of Lords, the Cabinet Office, and the Information Commissioner's Office, as well as with multinational corporations (e.g. Cisco, Google, IBM, Microsoft, and Tencent). Currently, he is a Member of the EU's Ethics Advisory Group on Ethical Dimensions of Data Protection, of the Royal Society and British Academy Working Group on Data Policy, of Google Advisory Board on "the right to be forgotten", of the Advisory Board of Tencent's Internet and Society Institute, and of NEXA' Board of Trustees. He is the Chairman of the Ethics Advisory Board of the European Medical Information Framework (a €56 million EU project on medical informatics).

Research interests: Information and Computer Ethics (aka Digital Ethics), Philosophy of Information, and the Philosophy of Technology, Epistemology, Philosophy of Logic, and the History and Philosophy of Scepticism.

Chapter 7
Deciding How to Decide: Six Key Questions for Reducing AI's Democratic Deficit

Josh Cowls

Abstract Through its power to "rationalise", artificial intelligence (AI) is rapidly changing the relationship between people and the state. But to echo Max Weber's warnings from one hundred years ago about the increasingly rational bureaucratic state, the "reducing" power of AI systems seems to pose a threat to democracy—unless such systems are developed with public preferences, perspectives and priorities in mind. In other words, we must move beyond minimal legal compliance and faith in free markets to consider public opinion as constitutive of legitimising the use of AI in society. In this chapter I pose six questions regarding how public opinion about AI ought to be sought: what we should ask the public about AI; how we should ask; where and when we should ask; why we should ask; and who is the "we" doing the asking. I conclude by contending that while the messiness of politics may preclude clear answers about the use of AI, this is preferable to the "coolly rational" yet democratically deficient AI systems of today.

Keywords Artificial intelligence · Max Weber · Legitimacy · Bureaucracy · Public opinion · Digital ethics

7.1 Introduction

Artificial intelligence (AI) suffers from, it can be argued, a democratic deficit. This may seem like a curious ascription, as "democratic deficit" is a label usually applied only to public entities including sub-national, national or supranational institutions like the United States or the European Union. In its canonical usage, a democratic deficit is said to apply when "ostensibly democratic organizations or institutions in

J. Cowls (✉)
Oxford Internet Institute, University of Oxford, Oxford, UK

The Alan Turing Institute, London, UK
e-mail: josh.cowls@oii.ox.ac.uk

C. Burr, S. Milano (eds.), *The 2019 Yearbook of the Digital Ethics Lab*,
Digital Ethics Lab Yearbook, https://doi.org/10.1007/978-3-030-29145-7_7

fact fall short of fulfilling what are believed to be the principles of democracy" (Levinson 2006). AI, meanwhile, in both conception and application, has long been bound up with the logic and operations of big business (Penn 2018) and its inception can be dated to a landmark conference held at Dartmouth University in the summer of 1956 (Moor 2006).

Today, however, we find AI put to use in an increasing array of socially significant settings, from sifting through CVs to swerving through traffic. While many of these use cases certainly continue to serve these corporate interests, it is not only businesses, but also governments of all stripes that have shown a willingness to explore the potential power of AI to patrol and cajole the movements and mindsets of citizens (see e.g. Dodd 2017; Hvistendahl 2017; Harwell 2018). Political parties and non-governmental organisations have also been keen to embrace the power of algorithm-driven campaigning and activism. Crucially, because the technical expertise required to develop and deploy AI far outweighs the capacities of the ordinary person as citizen or consumer, there is a growing accountability gap between those who create AI systems and those who are subject to them (Whittaker et al. 2018). In this chapter, therefore, I argue that we should think of AI—conceived of as the technical architecture that permits computers to "behave in ways that would be called intelligent if a human were so behaving", to use the definition offered in the conference proposal above (McCarthy et al. 1955)—as having a democratic deficit. I then offer tentative pathways through which we can consider how this deficit may be reduced, by posing six questions, each of which pinpoints a conceptual obstacle which must be overcome as a way to reduce the deficit. Each question sheds light on a different aspect of the democratic deficit that afflicts AI. Since AI is already being put to use in myriad domains, and its political and ethical significance understood in many different ways, these questions are consciously preliminary and exploratory. Before taking each of these questions in turn, it is first necessary to situate the debate about AI's democratic deficit within a wider historical context.

7.2 What Makes the Use of Technology Legitimate in Society?

One hundred years ago, the sociologist Max Weber gave a lecture, "Politics as a vocation", to a student union in Bavaria. The starting point of Weber's lecture was what would become one of his most famous ideas: that "a state is that human community which (successfully) lays claim to the *monopoly of legitimate physical violence* within a certain territory" (Weber 1994: 310, emphasis in original). The key word—and the one from which the rest of Weber's argument follows—is "legitimate". Since the state is considered the sole source of legitimate physical violence, then for Weber politics can be defined as "striving for a share of power or for influence in the distribution of power"—the power, that is, to legitimately inflict violence (Weber 1994: 311). The violent revolutions and civil wars in the decades after his speech lend empirical weight to the significance Weber places on physical violence as the means by which "legitimate" power is both obtained and maintained. The state's legitimacy itself, however, comes not from winning wars or quashing rebellions, but instead from three distinct sources: "traditional rule", as exercised by "the patriarch and the patrimonial prince"; "charismatic rule" as exercised by the "warlord or the plebiscitarian ruler, the great demagogue and leader of a political party"; and domination "by virtue of legality, by virtue of belief in the validity of legal statute and the appropriate judicial 'competence' founded on rationally devised rules" (311–312).

Since it focuses on politics as a vocation, much of the remainder of the speech is concerned with the second source of legitimacy, charisma. But one hundred years on, it is the third, "rational-legal" source of legitimacy, as it has come to be known in scholarship, that has the greatest bearing on the implications of AI for democratic society. For Weber, the "unique character of modern western society" was epitomised by the trend of "growing rationalisation in all spheres of social life" (Lassman and Speirs 1994: xviii). Among examples of such "rationalisation" in pre-digital society we can consider the standardisation of measurement and the regularisation of tax collection (Scott 1998). This "rationalisation" is characterised by what Gellner calls "coherence or consistency, the like treatment of like cases, regularity, what might be called the very soul or honour of a good bureaucrat", and "efficiency, the cool rational selection of the best available means to given, clearly formulated and isolated ends; in other words, the spirit of the ideal entrepreneur" (Gellner 2008: 20). Gellner's two-part explication of Weber's rationalisation, which fuses the consistency of the bureaucrat with the efficiency of the entrepreneur, is remarkably anticipatory of, and applicable to, the emergence of an algorithmic society. As ideals, "consistency" and "efficiency" epitomise the promised benefits of AI, a supposedly impartial, value-free technology, in terms of both its machinations and its motivations. Consider for example some of the promised benefits of artificial intelligence in healthcare. As the Radiological Society of North America recently proclaimed, AI is showing "tremendous potential in the clinic through a growing number of applications that improve efficiency, quality and overall productivity" (Dargan 2019). AI, we are led to believe, will rationalise the world around itself, detecting insights invisible to human eyes, and using these insights to make even more accurate predictions and powerful calculations.

Weber, however, was no cheerleader for the increasing rationalisation he observed. For all its appealing efficiency and rationality as a mode of domination—surely, in his day and ours, preferable to the vain politician?—Weber saw the increased risk to individual human freedom that the bureaucratic, mechanistic state posed. As Collins paraphrases, Weber saw that "partly due to rationalisation and routinisation, power [becomes] even harder to locate, much less control" (Collins 1998: 56). The wider implications of these advances are stark. And this bureaucratic power can be self-perpetuating, as "rational domination no longer requires the external support of this legitimation since, in the form of bureaucracy, this form of domination disciplines its population (as well as its own apparatus) and thus *creates its own conditions for effectiveness* and with this legitimates itself" (Schroeder 1998: 83). At a time in which opaque algorithmic decision-making is accorded ever greater prominence and reverence, Weber's warning from a century ago seems starkly prescient. Nor can the rationalisation of the bureaucrat be easily detached from that of the entrepreneur. In other words, the interplay between the rise of the legal-rational mode of legitimation as reified by AI on the one hand, and the capitalist framework within which AI technology is devised on the other, is considerable and entrenched. For Weber, "legal-rational domination is indispensable for modern capitalism, because [it] requires calculability and predictability" (Schroeder 1998: 85). Today, more so than ever, promises of calculability and predictability are what undergird the bottom lines of big business, not least the major technology firms of Silicon Valley. Nor is the notionally Communist China's revolutionary use of calculation and prediction in its "social credit" system unreliant on commercially developed solutions (Kobie 2019).

The preceding discussion has served to situate Weber's oft-quoted aphorism about legitimacy within the wider context of his political philosophy. Whether or not we take his claims to be true, Weber's insights complicate common assumptions about the legitimacy of technology in democratic society. It is true that, to the extent that we live in a territory that has free and open elections and a free market, people still enjoy the notional power to vote with their ballot paper, as citizens, and their purse strings, as consumers. However, as Weber's discussion of increasing rationalisation in society makes clear, free elections and free markets are not by themselves enough to ensure that "rationalising" technological systems such as AI are *socially preferable* in their design and deployment. Even in liberal systems, the logics of capitalism and bureaucracy can conspire to reduce populations to mere units of analysis, calculable and predictable. The processes necessary for the "achievement" of modernisation, as Weber saw it, include "the rationalisation of all aspects of social reality" (Whimster 1998: 76). But this in turn would "unlock immense powers that stand beyond the moral ken of human beings."

Put simply, when it comes to AI the moral stakes are high. The potential power of AI threatens to rationalise, and in doing so reduce, the complexity of human experience to its most calculable and predictable elements. Moreover, certain characteristics of AI, including the datasets upon which it is developed and the practices through which it is embedded, only augment the ethical risks of this powerful technology used in the service of bureaucratic and entrepreneurial interests. Here we may consider two sets of constraining characteristics. The first are technical: in short, it is difficult to make many types of AI systems explain themselves. The absence of a basic understanding of how a given implementation of AI works, at the level of either individual decisions or system functionality, obscures the ability to hold AI and its developers and deployers to account (Wachter et al. 2016). The second set of constraints are economic. The power of network effects makes it increasingly difficult to exercise true consumer choice: if all my friends are on one social network, or if all my purchasing history is held by a single shopping site, my desire to leave these services for preferable equivalents is counterbalanced by the inconvenience of doing so. This problem was not created by AI but is certainly exacerbated by its increasing ubiquity as the algorithmic "secret sauce" that powers the ranking of items in news feeds, search results, and shopping suggestions. And this of course presumes that people have any sort of choice, however compromised or problematic; this kind of agency is not enjoyed by those fleeing digitally mediated persecution (see e.g. Miles 2018), or those deprived of a free choice of internet services (Solon 2017).

Upstream of these constraints, however, lie more fundamental questions about the basic legitimacy of using AI in society. Dogged engineering and diligent policy-making may improve algorithmic transparency or soften network effects—but we may still find ourselves facing larger questions about exactly the sort of societies we want, and how we want to use AI to help us get there, within the technical and political constraints already discussed. Opening the black box doesn't remove the risk of Black Mirror-style social control; indeed, in some sense China's "social credit" system depends on a managed degree of system *transparency* to marshal behaviour (Kobie 2019). And while firmer antitrust regulation may be a necessary step to open up, if not break up, the quasi monopolistic tech firms of today, it may not be sufficient; many of the firms under threat ultimately today were themselves the indirect beneficiaries of earlier action against Microsoft (Brandom 2018). Nor will mere compliance or limited electoral democracy alone enable us to harness the genuine power of AI and related technologies to propel social good. A good example here is climate change. AI could prove an enormous boon in helping deal with the extraordinary coordination complexity that effectively mitigating climate change will require. But this in turn will require both enormous investment and political will, both of which rest on securing public consent.

All of which obliges us to consider strategies beyond the ballot box to reduce AI's democratic deficit, and to start reshaping this technology to help us reshape society in desirable ways (Patel 2019). Of course, the appealingly simple idea of "democratising AI" (Webb 2019) masks millennia of debates over what this democratisation should look like—involving Weber and many others—and how it should be pursued and preserved. But (permitted, if I may be, a *reductio ad absurdum*), this risks a kind of infinite regress, since before we know what democracy should look like, we need to know how we should decide what democracy should look like, but before that we need to decide how to decide, and so on. However, the sudden ubiquity of AI in society (not to mention the many other urgent issues that AI may itself help us address) encourages us to break out of this infinite regress and move rather more swiftly and pragmatically. In this spirit, it seems to me that we need to answer six important, practical questions before we can hope to meaningfully reduce AI's democratic deficit. I introduce these key questions in turn.

7.3 Reducing AI's Democratic Deficit: Key Questions

7.3.1 What Should We Ask About AI?

The first and most basic question concerns what exactly are the features and applications of AI about which we need societal input. This is the realm of definitions and domains. First, we need a sensible definition of AI—or perhaps better yet, an alternative term that better encompasses what AI is and can do. While it is beyond the scope of this chapter to invent and defend a different term, it is worth nothing that alternative phrasings, such as "*Autonomous and Intelligent Systems*"—as used by the Institute of Electrical and Electronics Engineers in its Ethically Aligned Design initiative—may preclude some of the more hyperbolic hopes and fears around AI (The IEEE Initiative on Ethics of Autonomous and Intelligent Systems 2017). Second, and more complicated, we may need to know at the outset of any public consultation what it is about the way in which AI is developed and deployed that is of societal significance. Should the focus be on the ethical principles that should govern AI in general, on the application of AI systems in particular settings, or on the very anatomy of an AI system and the resources it draws upon (Crawford and Joler 2018)? Some organisations, such as the Ada Lovelace Institute, have adopted a wide remit to research and deliberate on "the impact of AI and data-driven technologies on different groups in society" (Ada Lovelace Institute n.d.). Yet not all domains are created equal, and it is clear that in the most pressing areas of (potential) application, such as health, specific action is needed, as demonstrated by Nesta's recent report on "creating a people-powered future for AI in health" (Loder and Nicholas 2018), and in the Alan Turing Institute's Data Ethics Group on a code of conduct for digital health (Hitrova 2019). Similarly, self-driving cars clearly introduce new social and ethical questions—above and beyond the classic "trolley problem" (Cowls 2017)—and therefore merit closer consideration.

Nor should we neglect to squarely address the new conceptual challenges that AI poses. Following the canonical definition quoted above, a democratic deficit hinges on the extent to which the performance of a given public institution "fulfils what are believed to be the principles of democracy." Yet this presumes a degree of agreement about what these principles are believed to be. Again, this risks circularity, since the process by which these principles are set down is itself subject to fundamental questions. However, some convergence is possible: a recent synthesis of six high-level documents of ethical principles for AI (Floridi and Cowls 2019) found that an important ethical principle that is "new" to AI, compared with other forms of patient-oriented ethics like bioethics, is explicability—that is, the ability to understand how an AI decision was reached, and how to hold accountable those responsible for it. The UK's Information Commissioner's Office and the Alan Turing Institute are taking this question forward with work to address the technical and ethical complexities of "explainable AI" (Hall and Pesenti 2017).

Of course, these are somewhat false dichotomies: we can, and should, adopt both a broad perspective on AI's capabilities and risks, and a deep focus on the specific challenges that AI poses in particular domains. This in turn will require asking different questions in different ways for different purposes. In other words, another consideration is *how* we should seek societal perspectives on the impact of AI.

7.3.2 How Should We Ask About AI?

The sociologist Pierre Bourdieu once argued that "public opinion does not exist" (Bourdieu 1979: 124). He cited three basic assumptions about public opinion that, he argued, do not hold: first, that everyone has an opinion; second, that everyone agrees on the question; and third, that everyone's opinion is of the same value. We will tackle the final allegedly flawed assumption in the following section but address the first two points here. It is certainly true that presuming at the outset that a given issue is *salient* to a particular person or sample of people is foolhardy. The salience of a given issue can vary over time, and has been shown to affect the strength of feeling that people hold on issues as diverse as gay rights and European integration (Franklin and Wlezien 1997; Lax and Phillips 2009). At present, the salience of digital technology seems to be lacking, at least when its perceived importance is formally measured against other political questions. This can be hard to demonstrate, since many "issue importance" polls pose a forced choice to respondents, in which technology is not one of the issues asked about (Pew Research Center 2016). All the same, it does seem that public awareness of technology is relatively lacking compared to more traditional concerns such as employment and social issues. Of course, this general problem about a lack of public awareness or interest can be avoided by designing public opinion research in a way that prioritises the issues one wishes to address. At a time when various pressing policy questions jostle for attention, it is not surprising that the time and inclination that an ordinary person has to focus on AI is limited. But by carving out some time and space for focused consultation about the serious issues that AI raises, it would not be surprising to find that, *contra* Bourdieu, most people do indeed "have an opinion".

Yet this does not resolve Bourdieu's second contention that "everyone agrees on the question". Indeed, taking this line of reasoning further, neither should we presume that everyone agrees on how the question ought to be asked. Above, I have referred rather generically to "public opinion research", but the methods of eliciting this public opinion are disparate, and the choice of method is likely to yield quite different responses. Representative opinion polls are often seen as the default method of eliciting public opinion in a way that can be standardised, summarised and compared with earlier poll results. But particularly in the case of complex and often opaque digital technologies, opinion polls are but one instrument, and a rather blunt one at that. Many organisations are instead turning to focus groups, roundtables, citizens' juries, and other immersive methods for eliciting public opinion (see e.g. Balaram 2017; O'Connor 2018). These exercises deliver not (only) headline numbers, but also more nuanced, sensitive articulation of the key ethical values and social concerns shaping people's perceptions of how AI technology should or should not function in different contexts. For example, in a recent "citizen's jury" conducted by the Information Commissioner's Office, jurors believed that explanations of AI decisions were more important in recruitment and criminal justice than in healthcare (Hubbard 2019).

Finally, a third category of opinion research into perspectives on AI employs experimental approaches. This includes MIT's "Moral Machine" project, which recreates the "trolley problem" for self-driving cars, by asking online participants to choose which direction an out-of-control car should swerve, in order to save some fictional hypothetical individuals by mowing down others (Awad et al. 2018). Such exercises may prove problematic, both by focusing attention on rather hypothetical questions about self-driving cars at the expense of deeper and more urgent concerns (Cowls 2017), and because research suggests that responses to hypothetical dilemmas are not necessarily predictive of real-life dilemma behaviour (Wilson 2018). Nonetheless, experimental approaches are an interesting complement to other qualitative and quantitative methods for creating a rich understanding of public values, such as justice and fairness, as it relates to AI (Binns et al. 2018). But whether it is opinion polls, focus groups or simulations, gaining perspectives on AI inevitably involves deciding who, exactly, to speak to—another key question.

7.3.3 Who Should We Ask About AI?

Any attempt to engage with and understand public perspectives on AI needs to grapple with a rather hard truth up front: that the design and development of AI systems is carried out by a small, clustered coterie of engineers and other experts, most of whom work for corporations. In other words, a tiny fraction of humans are building the systems that are, or soon will be, used by many if not most of the rest of humanity; in contrast to earlier forms of patient-oriented ethics, we are almost all "patients" now (Floridi 1999). Nor, crucially, may we assume that this small group is representative of humanity as a whole, whether measured along the dimensions of race, gender, class, religion, sexuality, ability, nationality, and so on. The effects of this inequality are likely to be pernicious (Leslie 2019). Reducing this aspect of AI's democratic deficit is likely to involve several complementary responses: diversifying its workforce; debiasing (as far as possible) the datasets that are used to train AI systems; and consulting with "diversely diverse" groups of citizens about their preferences for and responses to AI design and use.

Where we want to speak of what "the public" thinks about AI (or any other issue), the first port of call has tended to be public opinion polls, which strive for overall representativeness. But, notwithstanding the critiques of opinion polling noted above (as well as other methodological challenges like falling response rates), in many contexts it is also unhelpful to think of "the public" as a single entity. Moreover, while nobody sincerely thinks that "the public" has, or can have, a single opinion, the value of the mere *exercise* of working towards consensus has been debated. While political theorists like John Rawls (2009), Jurgen Habermas (1989) and Kwasi Wiredu (2001) have, in their own ways, championed the idea that societal consensus, or something like it, is possible and desirable, others such as Amartya Sen (2009), Chantal Mouffe (2005), Nancy Fraser (1990) and Catherine Squires (2002) have (again, in their own ways) critiqued both the plausibility and the preferability of such an approach. While it is impossible to resolve these decades of debate here, for present purposes it seems most sensible to adopt an "all of the above" approach. Having an overall sense of representative public opinion will be of use in some cases, and as Reuben Binns has persuasively argued, algorithmic accountability can be usefully framed in terms of the ideal of "public reason" (Binns 2018). But in practice, it will also be important to engage directly with particular groups who are most likely to be affected by a given application of AI. These groups need not be small—consider consulting the millions of people engaged in gig economy work, for their perspectives on the algorithmic ranking or routing deployed on their platforms (e.g. Wood et al. 2019)—but they are likely to be salient. And in particular, greater attention should be paid to those individuals and groups who have typically been left behind or left worse off by technological change. Happily, this intention is reflected in the remit of new bodies set up to address the question of AI's democratic deficit. The UK's Centre for Data Ethics and Innovation has recently committed in its ways of working not merely to conduct "public engagement" per se, but more specifically to "ensure the inclusion of marginalised groups and those most affected by technological developments in the debate" (Department for Digital, Culture, Media and Sport 2019). This follows the Ada Lovelace Institute's stated aim to "convene diverse voices to create a shared understanding of the ethical issues arising from data and AI" (Ada Lovelace Institute 2018). Whilst not everything can be boiled down to a single "debate", nor is a truly "shared understanding" perhaps strictly possible, the commitment of these organisations to promoting previously underrepresented views and values should be welcomed. Yet these two organisations are both based in the UK. The question of "who" we should ask about AI invites questions in turn about "where" and "when" we should ask.

7.3.4 Where and When Should We Ask About AI?

A recent opinion piece claimed, seemingly without irony, that "ethics" would be "Europe's silver bullet in [the] global AI battle" (Delcker 2019). While some of the greatest treatises on ethics have emerged in the context of warfare, nonetheless it is a little jarring to read that ethics itself can serve as a "bullet" in a "battle" with implicitly amoral global competitors. More jarring still, though, was the presumption of a European monopoly on technology ethics. While the European Commission has indeed sought to make sustainability and trustworthiness central to its AI strategy (European Commission 2019), the notion that Europe is implicitly ethical (or worse yet that ethics is implicitly European) is a dangerous one. For one thing, many of the highest-profile statements of principles for ethical AI are global, including the IEEE's Ethically Aligned Design as well as the Asilomar Principles (2017) and the Montreal Declaration (2017). But more importantly, to see Europe as the sole or even chief steward of ethical technology is a mistake (Floridi 2019). We need instead to work towards, at least aspirationally, not merely an international but also an intercultural ethics of technology, consisting of contributions from the full range of global traditions.[1]

Of course, for the purposes of law and policymaking, the traditional Westphalian notion of bounded sovereignty is still influential. It is therefore perfectly legitimate for national governments to address their own AI democratic deficit in terms most relevant to their populations. But to focus on the nation state as the sole or pre-eminent information agent in a given society is increasingly naive, as multi-agent systems that transcend physical borders become ever more prominent and cross-border problems become more prevalent (Floridi 2014).

Moreover, seeing the American and Chinese *states* as geopolitical foes is to miss most of the people that reside there and the rich tapestry of their experiences and traditions—whether this is, say, the shocking racism encountered by an African-American woman navigating the web (Noble 2018), or the contributions of Confucianism to the ethics of technology (Wong 2012). Neither, better yet, should the debate over the ethics of AI be framed as tripartite between the US, China and Europe, a classic global-northern assumption; whether out of genuine inclusivity, or just the narrower interests of geopolitical risk, market share or talent acquisition, policymakers would be wise not to ignore the rapid innovation and increasing skills of other regions (see e.g. Snow 2019), nor to miss the earlier effects of datafication and "legibility" in the service of international development (Taylor and Broeders 2015). Nor need the question of "where" we should ask about AI restrict us to geography—as noted above, focusing on underrepresented or overlooked groups within the context of a particular place enables a richer set of perspectives to be gathered (Binns et al. 2018) and more inclusive, effective responses.

The idea of generating policy or industry "responses" to the impact of AI, or any other technology, obliges us to grapple with the final question of *when* any exercise in public engagement or consultation should occur. At any rate, it is self-evident that we must avoid an "oil spill" approach to AI, focused entirely on environmental clean-up, community regeneration and legal restitution after the seemingly inevitable damage is done. This suggests instead an "ethics by design" approach, a principle recently adopted by the International Conference of Data Protection and Privacy Commissioners (ICDPPC 2018).[2] But in addition to the questions raised above about how and with whose input an ethical AI system should be built, even if "ethics by design" is necessary, it may not be sufficient. The training of algorithmic

[1] Note, however, that this is likely to result in a plural and quite possibly irreconcilable set of perspectives that do not constitute a single technology "ethics".

[2] Definitions of "ethics by design" vary, but the ICDPPC Declaration encompasses technical measures to ensure that privacy rights are protected; ex ante and ex post impact assessment; and the identification of requirements for fair use and the protection of human rights in AI systems. For a more detailed and applied example of "ethics by design" (though it does not use the term), see Leslie (2019).

systems, however ethically, typically involves a "one-stop shop" approach, which can preclude these systems from mimicking the "habit reversal" seen in humans (Delacroix 2017). This raises the risk that an AI system trained in this way will, in Delacroix's words, "leap morally away" (Delacroix 2017: 3). The explanation of how an AI system works can be offered (with some limitations), either before (ex ante) or after (ex post) a system has delivered a decision (Wachter et al. 2016). We may usefully apply this framing when we consider societal input into the operations of AI systems as well. *When* we seek people's perspectives on AI, then, may be before, during and after a given system is in place.

7.4 Conclusion: Why Should We Ask at All—And Who Are "We" to Ask, Anyway?

I have sketched some key considerations around who is asked about the design and implementation of AI; when, where, and how they are asked; and what they are asked about. These are all vital questions, but the question of "why" they should be asked is of even more fundamental importance, which it may be valuable to restate in closing. I have argued that there is a democratic deficit associated with AI systems, resulting from several sets of constraints—technical and economic, but also political and ethical—that emerge from the characteristics of many sorts of AI and the varied social circumstances in which it is deployed. As one of the foremost theorists of political legitimacy argued a century ago, the project of modernisation depends on ever greater rationalisation, in the interests of both bureaucracy and capitalism, and making human behaviour and relations more calculable and predictable. Such a trend, which is already being amplified by the use of AI by both governments and businesses, leaves little space for individual human freedom or group identity. This insight helps to explain why traditional ballot-box politics and free market economics is struggling to respond to the severe risks and dangers of AI systems—not least to vulnerable populations—on one hand, nor to unlock their potential to enhance social good on the other.

The answer, instead, is to ask people what they want from AI in ways that move beyond electoral politics and free market economics. This may offer another, less obvious benefit. While the hypes and fears around AI are often greatly overstated, nonetheless the fact that some amount of "smart" decision-making agency is being increasingly ascribed to non-human entities for socially significant decisions presents an opportunity. It obliges us to make more concrete the views and values that should shape our societies. With the rise of the internet, much has been made of the idea that we now reveal our innermost thoughts, feelings and worries online by making them digital (Burr and Cristianini 2019), through seemingly anonymous Google searches (Stephens-Davidowitz 2013) or half-written-but-unpublished Facebook posts (Golbeck 2013). But training AI systems to operate equitably may come to work the other way around. By making manifest people's views and values, in the diverse ways discussed above, it may no longer be that digital technology reveals who we supposedly really are, but instead, that we make technology act more like us. In this sense, then, we should not just aspire for AI to reason *publicly*, through system transparency and explainability, but also for it to reason *public-like*, reflecting not society as it is, but society as we think it should be. Asking people for their perspectives, preferences and priorities for what AI should do is the first, essential step in that process.

This is of course aspirational. AI systems today seem more likely to amplify rather than limit existing inequities (Angwin et al. 2016) and to radicalise rather than reconcile opposing views (Tufekci 2018). As I have shown, the reasons for this are bound up in structural factors which stretch beyond technology itself but which have shaped its creation and adoption, not least among these factors is the logic of capitalism—including "surveillance capitalism" (Zuboff 2019). But this notion of asking people what they want from AI also carries danger, because it ascribes enormous power to whoever is doing the asking. We are unlikely to satisfactorily resolve the Rawlsian infinite regress I described above, whereby before we can decide how AI should decide, we need to decide to decide how AI should decide, and so on. Instead, we should be more pragmatic, by vesting the responsibility (and adequate resources) for managing this process in equitable public institutions, civil society organisations, and other non-profits who together may be seen to represent society as a whole and/or assemblages within it, especially those who stand to lose the most from AI that is designed and deployed in a negligent or malevolent way. In and of itself, this would mark a stark contrast with the status quo, whereby those who have the most to gain, in profit and power, have the most sway.

We should also be content with incomplete, incoherent or even contradictory answers to the questions people are asked—not only between people, but also within their own contributions. And we should explore in turn ways that even disparities such as this can be accommodated, rather than subdued, by the functioning of algorithmic systems. Even the apparently straightforward assumption that decision-making systems such as search engines should be designed to yield only the "best" result should not be taken at face value (Crawford 2016). Politics is messy. But this messiness is far preferable to the faux-omnipotence and apparently "cool rationality" of AI today, a logic that more often serves the purposes of its purveyors rather than of citizens more generally. Put another way, it is far preferable that AI systems not merely be "trained" on our data—hoovered up with minimal consent—and deployed only with power and profit in mind, but instead be designed and deployed in ways that respect—better yet, revere—the preferences, perspectives and priorities of people (Cowls et al. 2019). To do so successfully would be to close the democratic deficit that presently afflicts AI.

Acknowledgements Josh Cowls is the recipient of a doctoral scholarship from The Alan Turing Institute.

References

Ada Lovelace Institute. 2018. *About Us*. Retrieved 8 April 2019. https://www.adalovelaceinstitute.org/about-us/.

———. n.d. *Ada Lovelace Institute*. Retrieved 8 April 2019. https://www.adalovelaceinstitute.org/.

Angwin, Julia, Jeff Larson, Surya Mattu, and Lauren Kirchner. 2016. Machine Bias. *ProPublica*. Retrieved 8 April 2019. https://www.propublica.org/article/machine-bias-risk-assessments-in-criminal-sentencing.

Asilomar AI Principles. 2017. *Principles Developed in Conjunction with the 2017 Asilomar Conference [Benevolent AI 2017]*.

Awad, Edmond, Sohan Dsouza, Richard Kim, Jonathan Schulz, Joseph Henrich, Azim Shariff, Jean-François Bonnefon, and Iyad Rahwan. 2018. The Moral Machine Experiment. *Nature* 563 (7729): 59.

Balaram, Brhmie. 2017. *The Role of Citizens in Developing Ethical AI – RSA*. Retrieved 8 April 2019. https://www.thersa.org/discover/publications-and-articles/rsa-blogs/2017/10/the-role-of-citizens-in-developing-ethical-ai.

Binns, Reuben. 2018. Algorithmic Accountability and Public Reason. *Philosophy & Technology* 31 (4): 543–556.

Binns, Reuben, Max Van Kleek, Michael Veale, Ulrik Lyngs, Jun Zhao, and Nigel Shadbolt. 2018. *"It's Reducing a Human Being to a Percentage"; Perceptions of Justice in Algorithmic Decisions*.

Bourdieu, Pierre. 1979. Public Opinion Does Not Exist. *Communication and Class Struggle* 1: 124–130.

Brandom, Russell. 2018. Is Google's $5 Billion Antitrust Fine a Microsoft Moment? *The Verge*. Retrieved 8 April 2019. https://www.theverge.com/2018/7/18/17587620/google-european-commission-billion-fine-microsoft-antitrust.

Burr, Christopher, and Nello Cristianini. 2019. Can Machines Read Our Minds? *Minds and Machines*.

Collins, Randall. 1998. Democratization in World-Historical Perspective. In *Max Weber, Democracy and Modernization*, 14–31. Secaucus: Springer.

Cowls, Josh. 2017. AI's "Trolley Problem" Problem. *The Alan Turing Institute*. Retrieved 8 April 2019. https://www.turing.ac.uk/blog/ais-trolley-problem-problem.

Cowls, Josh, Thomas King, Mariarosaria Taddeo, and Luciano Floridi. 2019. *Designing AI for Social Good: Seven Essential Factors*. SSRN Scholarly Paper. ID 3388669. Rochester: Social Science Research Network.

Crawford, Kate. 2016. Can an Algorithm Be Agonistic? Ten Scenes from Life in Calculated Publics. *Science, Technology, & Human Values* 41 (1): 77–92.

Crawford, Kate, and Vladan Joler. 2018. Anatomy of an AI System.

Dargan, Richard. 2019. Artificial Intelligence Boosts Efficiency and Quality in Radiology Practice. *Radiological Society of North America*. Retrieved 10 June 2019. https://www.rsna.org/en/news/2019/March/Artificial-Intelligence-Boosts-Efficiency.

Delacroix, Sylvie. 2017. *Taking Turing by Surprise? Designing Autonomous Systems for Morally-Loaded Contexts*. . SSRN Scholarly Paper. ID 3025626. Rochester: Social Science Research Network.

Delcker, Janosch. 2019. Europe's Silver Bullet in Global AI Battle: Ethics. *POLITICO*. Retrieved 8 April 2019. https://www.politico.eu/article/europe-silver-bullet-global-ai-battle-ethics/.

Department for Digital, Culture, Media and Sport. 2019. Centre for Data Ethics (CDEI) 2 Year Strategy. *GOV.UK*. Retrieved 8 April 2019. https://www.gov.uk/government/publications/the-centre-for-data-ethics-and-innovation-cdei-2-year-strategy/centre-for-data-ethics-cdei-2-year-strategy.

Dodd, Vikram. 2017. Met Police to Use Facial Recognition Software at Notting Hill Carnival. *The Guardian*, August 5.

European Commission. 2019. Ethics Guidelines for Trustworthy AI. *Digital Single Market – European Commission.* Retrieved 8 April 2019. https://ec.europa.eu/digital-single-market/en/news/ethics-guidelines-trustworthy-ai.

Floridi, Luciano. 1999. Information Ethics: On the Philosophical Foundation of Computer Ethics. *Ethics and Information Technology* 1 (1): 33–52.

———. 2014. The Rise of the MASs. In *Protection of Information and the Right to Privacy – A New Equilibrium?, Law, Governance and Technology Series*, ed. L. Floridi, 95–122. Cham: Springer International Publishing.

———. 2019. Translating Principles into Practices of Digital Ethics: Five Risks of Being Unethical. *Philosophy & Technology* 32 (2): 185–193.

Floridi, Luciano, and Cowls, Josh. 2019. A Unified Framework of Five Principles for AI in Society. *Harvard Data Science Review*.

Franklin, Mark N., and Christopher Wlezien. 1997. The Responsive Public: Issue Salience, Policy Change, and Preferences for European Unification. *Journal of Theoretical Politics* 9 (3): 347–363.

Fraser, Nancy. 1990. Rethinking the Public Sphere: A Contribution to the Critique of Actually Existing Democracy. *Social Text* (25/26): 56–80.

Gellner, Ernest. 2008. *Nations and Nationalism*. Santa Barbara: Cornell University Press.

Golbeck, Jennifer. 2013. Facebook Wants to Know Why You're Self-Censoring Your Posts. *Slate Magazine*. Retrieved 8 April 2019. https://slate.com/technology/2013/12/facebook-self-censorship-what-happens-to-the-posts-you-dont-publish.html.

Habermas, J. 1989. *The Structural Transformation of the Public Shere*. Boston: MIT Press.

Hall, Wendy, and Jérôme Pesenti. 2017. *Growing the Artificial Intelligence Industry in the UK*. Department for Digital, Culture, Media & Sport and Department for Business, Energy & Industrial Strategy. Part of the Industrial Strategy UK and the Commonwealth.

Harwell, Drew. 2018. Amazon Met with ICE Officials over Facial-Recognition System That Could Identify Immigrants. *Washington Post*. Retrieved 8 April 2019. https://www.washingtonpost.com/technology/2018/10/23/amazon-met-with-ice-officials-over-facial-recognition-system-that-could-identify-immigrants/.

Hitrova, Christina. 2019. Turing's Data Ethics Group Supports the Development of the NHS Code of Conduct for Data-Driven Health and Care Technology. *The Alan Turing Institute*. Retrieved 8 April 2019. https://www.turing.ac.uk/blog/turings-data-ethics-group-supports-development-nhs-code-conduct-data-driven-health-and-care.

Hubbard, Alex. 2019. When It Comes to Explaining AI Decisions, Context Matters. *Information Commissioner's Office*. Retrieved 10 June 2019. https://ai-auditingframework.blogspot.com/2019/06/when-it-comes-to-explaining-ai.html.

Hvistendahl, Mara. 2017. In China, a Three-Digit Score Could Dictate Your Place in Society. *Wired*, December 14.

International Conference of Data Protection and Privacy Commissioners. 2018. *Ethics and Data Protection in Artificial Intelligence*. Retrieved 8 April 2019. https://icdppc.org/public-consultation-ethics-and-data-protection-in-artificial-intelligence-continuing-the-debate/.

Kobie, Nicole. 2019. The Complicated Truth about China's Social Credit System. *Wired UK*, January 21.

Lassman, Peter, and Ronald Speirs. 1994. *Weber: Political Writings*. Cambridge: Cambridge University Press.

Lax, Jeffrey R., and Justin H. Phillips. 2009. Gay Rights in the States: Public Opinion and Policy Responsiveness. *American Political Science Review* 103 (3): 367–386.

Leslie, David. 2019. *Understanding Artificial Intelligence Ethics and Safety*.

Levinson, Sanford. 2006. How the United States Constitution Contributes to the Democratic Deficit in America. *Drake L Review* 55: 859.

Loder, John, and Lydia Nicholas. 2018. Confronting Dr Robot. *Nesta*. Retrieved 8 April 2019. https://www.nesta.org.uk/report/confronting-dr-robot/.

McCarthy, J., M. L. Minsky, N. Rochester, and C. E. Shannon. 1955. A Proposal for the Dartmouth Summer Research Project on Artificial Intelligence.

Miles, Tom. 2018. U.N. Investigators Cite Facebook Role in Myanmar Crisis. *Reuters*, March 12.

Montreal Declaration for a Responsible Development of Artificial Intelligence. 2017. Montreal Declaration for a Responsible Development of Artificial Intelligence. Announced at the Conclusion of the Forum on the Socially Responsible Development of AI.

Moor, James. 2006. The Dartmouth College Artificial Intelligence Conference: The next Fifty Years. *AI Magazine* 27 (4): 87–87.

Mouffe, Chantal. 2005. *The Return of the Political*. Vol. 8. London: Verso.

Noble, Safiya Umoja. 2018. *Algorithms of Oppression: How Search Engines Reinforce Racism*. New York: NYU Press.

O'Connor, Dan. 2018. *Can AI Improve Health for Everyone? We Want to Fund Research to Find out | Wellcome*. Retrieved 8 April 2019. https://wellcome.ac.uk/news/can-ai-improve-health-everyone-we-want-fund-research-find-out.

Patel, Reema. 2019. *Public Deliberation Could Help Address AI's Legitimacy Problem in 2019*. Retrieved 8 April 2019. https://www.adalovelaceinstitute.org/public-deliberation-could-help-address-ais-legitimacy-problem-in-2019/.

Penn, Jonnie. 2018. AI Thinks like a Corporation—and That's Worrying – Open Voices. *The Economist*. Retrieved 8 April 2019. https://www.economist.com/open-future/2018/11/26/ai-thinks-like-a-corporation-and-thats-worrying.

Pew Research Center. 2016. *Top Voting Issues in 2016 Election*. Retrieved 8 April 2019. https://www.people-press.org/2016/07/07/4-top-voting-issues-in-2016-election/.

Rawls, John. 2009. *A Theory of Justice*. Cambridge: Harvard University Press.

Schroeder, Ralph. 1998. From Weber's Political Sociology to Contemporary Liberal Democracy. In *Max Weber, Democracy and Modernization*, 79–92. Secaucus: Springer.

Scott, James C. 1998. *Seeing like a State: How Certain Schemes to Improve the Human Condition Have Failed*. New Haven: Yale University Press.

Sen, Amartya Kumar. 2009. *The Idea of Justice*. Cambridge: Harvard University Press.

Snow, Jackie. 2019. How Africa Is Seizing an AI Opportunity. *Fast Company*. Retrieved 8 April 2019. https://www.fastcompany.com/90308114/how-africa-is-seizing-an-ai-opportunity.

Solon, Olivia. 2017. "It's Digital Colonialism": How Facebook's Free Internet Service Has Failed Its Users. *The Guardian*, July 27.

Squires, Catherine R. 2002. Rethinking the Black Public Sphere: An Alternative Vocabulary for Multiple Public Spheres. *Communication Theory* 12 (4): 446–468.

Stephens-Davidowitz, Seth. 2013. Dr. Google Will See You Now. *The New York Times*. Retrieved 8 April 2019. https://www.nytimes.com/2013/08/11/opinion/sunday/dr-google-will-see-you-now.html?rref=collection%2Fbyline%2Fseth-stephens-davidowitz&action=click&contentCollection=undefined&region=stream&module=stream_unit&version=latest&contentPlacement=16&pgtype=collection.

Taylor, Linnet, and Dennis Broeders. 2015. In the Name of Development: Power, Profit and the Datafication of the Global South. *Geoforum* 64: 229–237.

The IEEE Initiative on Ethics of Autonomous and Intelligent Systems. 2017. Ethically Aligned Design, V2.

Tufekci, Zeynep. 2018. YouTube, the Great Radicalizer. *The New York Times*, June 8.

Wachter, Sandra, Brent Mittelstadt, and Luciano Floridi. 2016. *Why a Right to Explanation of Automated Decision-Making Does Not Exist in the General Data Protection Regulation* . SSRN Scholarly Paper. ID 2903469. Rochester: Social Science Research Network.

Webb, Amy. 2019. Build Democracy into AI. *POLITICO*. Retrieved 8 April 2019. https://www.politico.eu/article/build-democracy-into-ai-combat-china/.

Weber, Max. 1994. *Weber: Political Writings*. Cambridge: Cambridge University Press.

Whimster, Sam. 1998. The Nation-State, the Protestant Ethic and Modernization. In *Max Weber, Democracy and Modernization*, 61–78. New York: Springer.

Whittaker, Meredith, Kate Crawford, Roel Dobbe, Genevieve Fried, Elizabeth Kaziunas, Varoon Mathur, Sarah Mysers West, Rashida Richardson, Jason Schultz, and Oscar Schwartz. 2018. AI Now Report 2018. AI Now Institute at New York University.

Wilson, Clare. 2018. Trolley Problem Tested in Real Life for First Time with Mice. *New Scientist*. Retrieved 8 April 2019. https://www.newscientist.com/article/2168648-trolley-problem-tested-in-real-life-for-first-time-with-mice/.

Wiredu, Kwasi. 2001. Democracy by Consensus: Some Conceptual Considerations. *Philosophical Papers* 30 (3): 227–244.

Wong, Pak-Hang. 2012. Dao, Harmony and Personhood: Towards a Confucian Ethics of Technology. *Philosophy & Technology* 25 (1): 67–86.

Wood, Alex J., Mark Graham, Vili Lehdonvirta, and Isis Hjorth. 2019. Good Gig, Bad Gig: Autonomy and Algorithmic Control in the Global Gig Economy. *Work, Employment and Society* 33 (1): 56–75.

Zuboff, Shoshana. 2019. *The Age of Surveillance Capitalism: The Fight for the Future at the New Frontier of Power*. New York: Profile Books.

Josh Cowls is a DELab researcher and DPhil student at the Oxford Internet Institute. He is the recipient of a doctoral studentship from the Alan Turing Institute, where he is also the Research Associate in Data Ethics as part of the public policy programme. Josh's doctoral research focuses on the ethics and politics of algorithmic decision-making systems. His wider research agenda centres on democratic decision-making in the digital era, and he is the author or co-author of work on data ethics, state surveillance, online agenda-setting, and the use of web archives in publications such as New Media & Society, Minds and Machines, and in numerous edited volumes. Josh is the Convenor of the Turing's Ethics Advisory Group, a member of its Data Ethics Group, and sits on the Digital Catapult Machine Intelligence Garage's Ethics Committee.

Chapter 8
Prayer-Bots and Religious Worship on Twitter: A Call for a Wider Research Agenda

Carl Öhman, Robert Gorwa, and Luciano Floridi

Abstract The automation of online social life is an urgent issue for researchers and the public alike. However, one of the most significant uses of such technologies seems to have gone largely unnoticed by the research community: religion. Focusing on Islamic Prayer Apps, which automatically post prayers from its users' accounts, we show that even one such service is already responsible for millions of tweets daily, constituting a significant portion of Arabic-language Twitter traffic. We argue that the fact that a phenomenon of these proportions has gone unnoticed by researchers reveals an opportunity to broaden the scope of the current research agenda on online automation.

Keywords Automatic prayers · Twitter bots · Digital afterlife industry · Islam · Online death

8.1 Introduction

Online social life is increasingly automated. From virtual assistants that help with day-to-day tasks, to chatbots providing companionship or preserving the memory of deceased family members (Öhman and Floridi 2018), industry has been quick in realizing the potential of the development. At the same time, online social

---

Originally published in Minds and Machines April 1 2019. Cite as: Öhman, C., Gorwa, R. & Floridi, L. Minds & Machines (2019). https://doi.org/10.1007/s11023-019-09498-3

C. Öhman (✉)
Oxford Internet Institute, University of Oxford, Oxford, UK
e-mail: carl.ohman@oii.ox.ac.uk

R. Gorwa
Department of Politics and International Relations, University of Oxford, Oxford, UK

L. Floridi
Oxford Internet Institute, University of Oxford, Oxford, UK

The Alan Turing Institute, London, UK

C. Burr, S. Milano (eds.), *The 2019 Yearbook of the Digital Ethics Lab*,
Digital Ethics Lab Yearbook, https://doi.org/10.1007/978-3-030-29145-7_8

automation is also used for political goals, including automated "bot" accounts on social networks that attempt to influence elections and other key political events (Gorwa and Guilbeault 2018). These trends have rightly attracted much attention, both publicly and in the research community. However, one major area of online automation has largely been overlooked so far: religious worship. In this article, we provide the first large-scale analysis of the religious use of online automation technologies. More specifically, the article focuses on a particularly wide-spread phenomenon, what we call Islamic Prayer Apps, which, despite their popularity, have so far gone unnoticed by the research community. We argue that the spread and social significance of these applications calls for a broadening of the scope of current research on online automation in general, and on social media bots in particular.

8.2 Islamic Prayer Apps

It is increasingly popular amongst Muslim social media users to employ services that automatically post prayers on one's behalf. In this article, we shall refer to such services as Islamic Prayer Apps. These apps vary in their business model and popularity, but share the same goal: to facilitate and automate worship. This does not mean that the apps replace the mandatory "5-times-aday" prayer rituals. While documented services simply send or post reminders for local prayer times (Wyche et al. 2008), the Islamic Prayer Apps seem to facilitate additional public supplication (دُعَاء "dua"), which may be understood as a humble asking for an event to occur or a wish to be fulfilled.

Believers in Islam may phrase their own personal supplications, but there is also an array of examples in the Quran to choose from. Based on these examples, the apps enable the user to post automatically their supplications on social networking sites, like Twitter and Facebook. Du3a.org is a typical example: the site's landing page (see Fig. 8.1) features some Quranic quotes and popular prayers, and a sidebar encourages visitors to share the site on different social networks, like Facebook and Pinterest, claiming that 26 million visitors have done so already. But the most salient feature is perhaps the button prompting visitors to subscribe to the service. Upon doing so, visitors are redirected to Twitter, where they are asked to authorize the application to use their account and post on their behalf. After a few hours, Du3a begins to post a > 140 character supplication from the user's account every second hour, alongside a site URL (and until recently a "recycling" emoji).

Because Du3a.org includes the service's URL in every tweet that is sent out from the user's account, its traffic can be measured using Twitter's Streaming application programming interface (API), which provides live access to up to 1% of Tweets on the global platform. By querying for the dur3a.org URL, we collected tweets posted over a 48-h period, in June 2018. During this time, 3.8 million tweets containing the URL were posted (See Fig. 8.2). It should be noted however, that Du3a at the time appeared to release one tweet per hour from the users' accounts, a frequency which

Fig. 8.1 Screenshot of Du3a's landing page

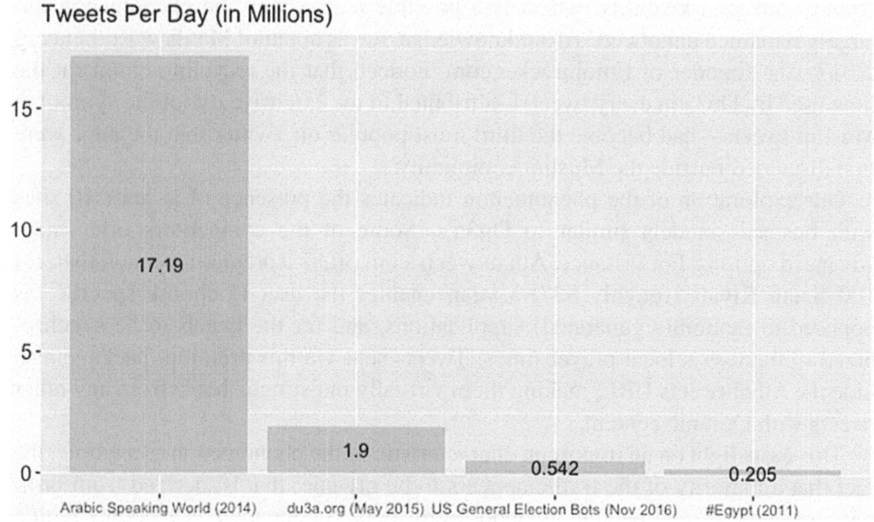

Fig. 8.2 Illustration of average tweets per day

recently seems to have slowed down to one every second hour. About 50% of the users self-identify as located in Saudi Arabia and Egypt, suggesting that, at least in the case of Du3a, the phenomenon is predominantly Arabic (other countries represent approximately 1% each).

The number of 1.9 million tweets per day—coming just from Du3a, one of many Islamic Prayer Apps—demonstrates how much traffic can be generated through automation. To put the numbers in context (see Fig. 8.2), Bruns et al. (2013) collected 205,000 tweets on the Arab-Spring related hashtag #egypt on its busiest day, when President Hosni Mubarak resigned amidst intense public pressure. During the 2016 US election, when significant popular attention focused on the role of automated accounts, Bessi and Ferrara (2016) estimated an upper bound of 3.8 million tweets from automated accounts on political topics in the week leading up to voting day (an average of about 540 thousand tweets per day). In other words, according to our exploratory analysis, a single automated prayer app generated almost as many tweets in 2 days as accounts believed to be automated did in the whole week leading up to the US election. Yet, contrary to the US general election, Du3a continues its activity every day of the year. And insofar as we were able to ascertain, this activity has been going on for about 5 years. While exact numbers are difficult to determine, an analysis of Arabic Social Media (2014) estimated that, in 2014, 17.19 million tweets were sent daily from users in the entire Arab world, suggesting that automated prayer may be responsible for a substantial proportion of Twitter in Arabic speaking countries. Thus, at least in terms of sheer numbers, the expression of worship may rank among the most significant phenomena on Twitter overall.

Du3a.org, like most Islamic Prayer Apps, does not use hashtags which can "trend" and gain visibility, which is a possible reason why the phenomenon has largely remained unnoticed. To our knowledge, it was not until Matthew Rothenberg (2017), the founder of Emojitracker.com, noticed that the recycling emoji (at the time used by Du3a in every tweet)—attributed to the extensive use of the symbol in Muslim tweets—had become the third most popular on Twitter that the apps were first discussed outside the Muslim community.

Our exploration of the phenomenon indicates the presence of at least 10 sites with business models similar to Du3a's. Some of the competitors offer more advanced options. For instance, Athantweets.com offers a premium version that, for 100 Saudi Riyals (roughly $27) a year, enables the user to choose specific (as opposed to randomly generated) supplications, and for the tweets to be synchronized to the user's local prayer times. Tweets sent via this premium package also hide the Athantweets URL, making them virtually indistinguishable from any other tweets with Quranic content.

This casts light on an important characteristic of the phenomenon as a whole, the fact that a majority of the traffic appears to be organic; that is, derived from ordinary accounts of real people, as opposed to 'bots', understood as accounts with a fake identity set up purely for the purpose of disseminating content. A qualitative close-reading of a few dozen twitter accounts using Du3a shows that, whereas some of the accounts appeared to be created specifically to use these prayer services, most appeared to be ordinary users, who tweeted everyday messages, photos, and commentary interspersed with the automated messages. In other words, much of the traffic appears to be created by authentic accounts, operated by legitimate users, who creatively automate a facet of their online activity while also using the service as they would do ordinarily.

8.3 Religious Context

It is too soon to try to explain the specific role that the Islamic Prayer Apps play in the everyday life of their users. Much more work on both the qualitative properties of the phenomenon (such as that of Bell 2006) as well as further analysis of the quantitative ones is needed. "Even though there is almost 1.2 billion Muslims …" as Akma and Abdul Razak (2013, p. 6) point out, "… there is too little research done on the techno-spiritual application from the Islamic perspective." Looking more closely at some of the accounts captured in our data collection, we see that there seem to be many possible motivations behind the use of such services. One account, for instance, notes that the reason it is set up is to pray for "my brother [name]," suggesting that users might be setting up such accounts to cast prayers on behalf of friends and family.

Arguably, one of the core functions of the automated prayer apps is tied to their explicit promise to continue posting even after the user's death. For instance, the slogan of Zad-Muslim.com reads "Register now so your account would tweet now and after you die." Similarly, Dur3a.org promises that "your account will tweet in your life and in your death." This is more than a mere detail. While the posthumous prayer apps resonate with traditions in many different religions, it is notable that such features have emerged within Islam. According to the Quran, one does not receive one's judgement immediately upon death. Instead, those who pass away must wait in their graves for Allah to end Earth and make His final judgment of each respective individual. In order to be eventually sent to paradise, a Muslim's sins must be outweighed by his or her good deeds. But in between the time of death and the final judgement day, a number of factors may posthumously increase their standing in the eyes of Allah. The Prophet Muhammed specifically mentioned three things that can improve one's afterlife reward this way: the continuous effects of charity; the provision of knowledge used by future generations; and virtuous descendants who pray for you (Sahih Muslim 1330, 42: 7064).

Islamic scholars debate about how this should be interpreted (see for instance Al-Halbali 2016). However, most interpreters agree that the reward of the afterlife, at least to some degree, is subject to posthumous improvement. Because contributing to the dissemination of Islam is considered an inherent good, it is less important whether this activity is performed by someone personally, or through knowledge that one helps disseminating. So, the hypothesis is that putting in motion an app to post supplications on one's behalf after one's death could help increase one's chances of a good afterlife.

With few exceptions, the Islamic community has thus far accepted the incorporation of new technologies into religious practice, especially when it comes to realizing their missionary potential. In her book When Religion Meets New Media,

Campbell (2010, p. 96) describes this new emphasis on technology, noting that "Engagement with media is a religious imperative, one which Muslims will be held accountable for in the afterlife." Thus, it seems that the dissemination of Islam through media may have profound implications in both life and death. Yet, little is known about the attitudes of the larger Islamic community when it comes to Islamic Prayer Apps, which undoubtedly ties religious practice closer to online technologies. And research is needed to study the specific role that these apps may play within the lives and religious practices of their users. Likewise, little, if anything, is known about the stance of social media platforms themselves on this widespread phenomenon.

Unlike a platform such as Facebook, which now has a "memorialization" feature, Twitter handles deceased users by permanently taking down their accounts after some months of inactivity (Twitter n.d.). However, an account that has subscribed to a Islamic Prayer App will not go inactive after the user's death. It will keep tweeting, and will therefore not be identified as inactive or abandoned. This means that the huge presence of the Islamic Twitter supplications will likely continue to grow long after the account holders have died. An array of similar applications, albeit with a secular framing of "immortalizing one's social media presence", have been launched mainly targeting secular Western audiences (Öhman and Floridi 2017). However, such a project of social media immortalization still remains fringe in comparison to the Islamic Prayer Apps. Considering their popularity, it may, even within only a few decades, become increasingly difficult to differentiate between traffic generated by living and deceased users—and not because of the futurist community in Silicon Valley, but because of Islamic worshipers.

8.4 Broader Implications

Religion has always been one of the most significant aspects of human life, individually, socially, as well as technologically. It should not be surprising if it is now emerging as a possible key driver for the mainstream adoption of social technology. Islam is not the only religion incorporating creative automation technologies into worship. The iTunes App Store contains more than 6000 applications related to spirituality and religion (Buie and Blythe 2013, p. 2315). In early 2019, Pope Francis launched a new app called "Click to Pray,"[1] with which Catholics may participate in the Pope's prayers and share them on social media. Similarly, the Church of England's new voice activation feature for Amazon's Alexa allows owners of the device to ask it to read daily prayers (BBC 2018). This could be understood as part of a larger movement; after all, the offering of a wax candle in a church can now often be replaced by the turning on of an electric one. In a narrow capacity, technological services can even substitute for priests, answering religious questions like "Who is God?" or what it means to believe in Jesus. Similarly, Jewish communities

[1] https://clicktopray.org/

have started employing new technologies to automate home facilities during the Sabbath (Woodruf et al. 2007), and members of diverse religious communities can now chat and make prayer requests to religious chatbots, such as those created by the Californian start-up Prayerbot. These examples, alongside the scale of the Islamic Prayer Apps, show that religion is far from a small or marginal force in contemporary social automation.

The case of the Islamic Prayer App also provides valuable insights into the complex, fast-evolving discourse on Twitter bots and online automation policy. Much recent literature on social bots focuses on false accounts set up during elections, and other political events, to inflate engagement metrics and help spread problematic political content (Ferrara et al. 2016). In contrast, Islamic Prayer Apps share no hashtags, and do not appear to try and influence the social network, instead remaining unobtrusively out of view. As well, because many of the observed accounts appear to be ordinary users who have partially "botified" or automated their accounts, they complicate the existing discourse, which is often methodologically and conceptually predicated on the assumption that "bots" and "not bots" exist as two distinct categories that can be easily separated (Gorwa and Guilbeault 2018; Stieglitz et al. 2017). Many Twitter users rely on a variety of publicly available services, from Twitter's own platform 'Tweetdeck' to 'If This Then That' to automate parts of their online activity. But how exactly should such behavior be understood? And what are the ethical ramifications?

There have been many positive uses of automated social media accounts, which have been deployed creatively by journalists (Lokot and Diakopoulos 2016), activists fighting corruption (Savage et al. 2016), and those promoting institutional transparency (Ford et al. 2016), but religious uses have been largely unexplored. The Islamic Prayer Apps we analysed here arguably represent one of the largest examples to date of Twitter automation being deployed organically in a creative and culturally significant way. The fact that a phenomenon of these unprecedented proportions has gone unnoticed by researchers shows the limitations of our current scope. To quote Bell (2006, p. 155): "We appear to be stubbornly secular in our imaginings of home and leisure contexts of computing." Indeed, now is the time to broaden the conversation.

Acknowledgements Our sincere thanks to Bence Kollanyi, for assistance with data collection.

References

Akma, N., and F.H. Abdul Razak. 2013. On the Emergence of Techno-Spiritual: The Concepts and Current Issues. In *Computer and Mathematical Sciences Graduates National Colloquium 2013 (SISKOM2013)*.

Al-Halbali, I.J. 2016. *The Three That Follow to the Grave*. Birmingham: Dar As-Sunnah Publishers.

Arab Social Media Report. 2014. Twitter in the Arab Region. Available at: http://arabsocialmediareport.com/Twitter/LineChart.aspx. Accessed 12 June 2018.

BBC. 2018. Church of England offers prayers read by Amazon's Alexa. BBC.com. https://www.bbc.co.uk/news/uk-44233053. Accessed 27 Mar 2019.
Bell, G. 2006. No More SMS from Jesus: Ubicomp, Religion and Techno-Spiritual Practices. In *UbiComp 2006: Ubiquitous Computing. UbiComp 2006*, Lecture Notes in Computer Science, ed. P. Dourish and A. Friday, vol. 4206. Berlin/Heidelberg: Springer. https://doi.org/10.1007/11853565_9.
Bessi, A., and E. Ferrara. 2016. Social Bots Distort the 2016 US Presidential Election Online Discussion. First Monday. https://doi.org/10.5210/fm.v21i11.7090.
Bruns, A., T. Highfield, and J. Burgess. 2013. The Arab Spring and Social Media Audiences. *American Behavioral Scientist* 57 (7): 871–898.
Buie, E., and M. Blythe. 2013. Spirituality: There's an App for That! (But Not a Lot of Research). CHI 2013 Extended Abstracts, April 27–May 2 2013, Paris.
Campbell, H.A. 2010. *When Religion Meets New Media*. London: Routledge.
Ferrara, E., O. Varol, C.B. Davis, F. Menczer, and A. Flammini. 2016. The Rise of Social Bots. *Communications of the ACM* 59 (7): 96–104.
Ford, H., E. Dubois, and C. Puschmann. 2016. Keeping Ottawa Honest—One Tweet at a Time? Politicians, Journalists, Wikipedians and Their Twitter Bots. *International Journal of Communication* 10: 4891–4914. ISSN 1932–8036.
Gorwa, R., and D. Guilbeault. 2018. Unpacking the Social Media Bot: A Typology to Guide Research and Policy. *Policy and Internet*. https://doi.org/10.1002/poi3.184.
Lokot, T., and N. Diakopoulos. 2016. News Bots: Automating News and Information Dissemination on Twitter. *Digital Journalism* 4 (6): 682–699. https://doi.org/10.1080/21670811.2015.1081822.
Öhman, C., and L. Floridi. 2017. The Political Economy of Death in the Age of Information: A Critical Approach to the Digital Afterlife Industry. *Minds and Machines*. https://doi.org/10.1007/s11023-017-9445-2.
———. 2018. An Ethical Framework for the Digital Afterlife Industry. *Nature Human Behavior*. https://doi.org/10.1038/s41562-018-0335-2.
Rothenberg, M. 2017. Why the Emoji Recycling Symbol is Taking Over Twitter. Medium. Available at: https://medium.com/@mroth/why-the-emoji-recycling-symbol-is-taking-over-twitter-65ad4b18b04b. Accessed 25 Apr 2018.
Sahih Muslim. 1330. Sahih Muslim Vol. 7, Book of Zuhd and Softening of Hearts, Hadith 7064. Retrieved from: http://www.iupui.edu/~msaiupui/042.smt.html. Accessed 27 Mar 2019.
Savage, S., A. Monroy-Hernandez, and T. Höllerer. 2016. Botivist: Calling Volunteers to Action Using Online Bots. In *Proceedings of the 19th ACM conference on computer-supported cooperative work & social computing*, pp. 813–822. ACM.
Stieglitz, S., F. Brachten, B. Ross, and A.-K. Jung. 2017. Do Social Bots Dream of Electric Sheep? A Categorisation of Social Media Bot Accounts. arXiv:1710.04044 [Cs]. Retrieved from http://arxiv.org/abs/1710.04044.
Twitter. (n.d.) Inactive Account Policy. Available at: https://help.twitter.com/en/rules-and-policies/inactive-twitter-accounts. Accessed 27 Mar 2019.
Woodruf, A., S. Augustin, and B. Foucault. 2007. Sabbath Day Home Automation: "It's Like Mixing Technology and Religion". CHI 2007, April 28–May 3, 2007, San Jose/California.
Wyche, S. P., Caine, K. E., Davison, B., Arteaga, M., & Grinter, R. E. (2008). Sun Dial: Exploring Techno-Spiritual Design Through a Mobile Islamic Call to Prayer Application. In *CHI 2008*, April 5–April 10, 2008. Florence: ACM.

Carl Öhman is a doctoral candidate at the Oxford Internet Institute, supervised by Professor Luciano Floridi.

Carl's doctoral dissertation looks at the ethical and political challenges that arise from the growing volume of 'digital human remains' – data left by deceased users – on the internet. This includes questions of post-mortem privacy, the right to access and control over the personal data of the deceased, and the relationship between information and time. In addition to this project, Carl is also researching the ethics of Deepfake pornography.

Carl graduated from Oxford 2016 with the award-winning thesis The Political Economy of Death in the Age of Information: A Critical Approach to the Digital Afterlife Industry. Prior to the OII, Carl studied for a B.A. in Sociology and Comparative literature at Uppsala University Sweden.

Research interests: Digital Afterlife, Time, Immortality, Information Ethics, Economic Sociology, Critical Theory, Personal Identity.

Robert Gorwa (@rgorwa) is a PhD candidate in the Department of Politics and International Relations, University of Oxford. Robert primiarily works on platform regulation, content moderation, and other transnational digital policy challenges, with recent work published in Information, Communication & Society, Internet Policy Review, and other journals.

He is currently a fellow at the Weizenbaum Institute for the Networked Society in Berlin, and is affiliated with the Reuters Institute for the Study of Journalism and the Centre for Technology and Global Affairs and Oxford, the Project on Democracy and the Internet at Stanford University, and the Max Bell School of Public Policy at McGill University. He holds a MSc from the Oxford Internet Institute, and a BA in International Relations from the University of British Columbia, Canada.

He contributes to the Los Angeles Review of Books and has written for Wired Magazine UK, the Washington Post, Foreign Affairs, and a host of other popular outlets.

Luciano Floridi is the OII's Professor of Philosophy and Ethics of Information at the University of Oxford, where he is also the Director of the Digital Ethics Lab of the Oxford Internet Institute. Still in Oxford, he is Distinguished Research Fellow of the Uehiro Centre for Practical Ethics of the Faculty of Philosophy, and Research Associate and Fellow in Information Policy of the Department of Computer Science. Outside Oxford, he is Faculty Fellow of the Alan Turing Institute (the national institute for data science) and Chair of its Data Ethics Group; and Adjunct Professor ("Distinguished Scholar in Residence") of the Department of Economics, American University, Washington D.C.

He is deeply engaged with emerging policy initiatives on the socio-ethical value and implications of digital technologies and their applications. And he has worked closely on digital ethics (including the ethics of algorithms and AI) with the European Commission, the German Ethics Council, and, in the UK, with the House of Lords, the Cabinet Office, and the Information Commissioner's Office, as well as with multinational corporations (e.g. Cisco, Google, IBM, Microsoft, and Tencent). Currently, he is a Member of the EU's Ethics Advisory Group on Ethical Dimensions of Data Protection, of the Royal Society and British Academy Working Group on Data Policy, of Google Advisory Board on "the right to be forgotten", of the Advisory Board of Tencent's Internet and Society Institute, and of NEXA' Board of Trustees. He is the Chairman of the Ethics Advisory Board of the European Medical Information Framework (a €56 million EU project on medical informatics).

Research interests: Information and Computer Ethics (aka Digital Ethics), Philosophy of Information, and the Philosophy of Technology, Epistemology, Philosophy of Logic, and the History and Philosophy of Scepticism.

Chapter 9
What the Near Future of Artificial Intelligence Could Be

Luciano Floridi

Abstract The chapter looks into the possible developments of Artificial Intelligence (AI) in the near future and identifies two likely trends: (a) a shift from historical to synthetic data; and (b) a translation of difficult tasks (in terms of abilities) into complex ones (in terms of computation). It is argued that (a) and (b) will be pursued as development strategies of AI solutions whenever and as far as they are feasible.

Keywords Artificial intelligence · Big data · Complexity · Foresight analysis · Historical data · Synthetic data

9.1 Introduction

Artificial Intelligence (AI) has dominated recent headlines, with its promises, challenges, risks, successes, and failures. What is its foreseeable future? Of course, the most accurate predictions are retrodictions, made with hindsight. But if some cheating is not acceptable, then smart people bet on the uncontroversial or the untestable. On the uncontroversial side, one may mention the increased pressure that will come from law-makers to ensure that AI applications align with socially acceptable expectations. For example, everybody expects some regulatory move from the EU, sooner or later. On the untestable side, some people will keep selling catastrophic forecasts, with dystopian scenarios taking place in some future that is sufficiently distant to ensure that the Jeremiahs will not be around to be proven wrong. Fear always sells well, like vampire or zombie movies. Expect more. What is difficult, and may be quite embarrassing later on, is to try to "look into the seeds of time, and say which grain will grow and which will not" (*Macbeth*, Act I, Scene III), that is,

L. Floridi (✉)
Oxford Internet Institute, University of Oxford, Oxford, UK

The Alan Turing Institute, London, UK
e-mail: luciano.floridi@oii.ox.ac.uk

C. Burr, S. Milano (eds.), *The 2019 Yearbook of the Digital Ethics Lab*, Digital Ethics Lab Yearbook, https://doi.org/10.1007/978-3-030-29145-7_9

to try to understand where AI is more likely to go and hence where it may not be going. This is what I will attempt to do in the following pages, where I shall be cautious in identifying the paths of least resistance, but not so cautious as to avoid any risk of being proven wrong.

Part of the difficulty is to get the level of abstraction right (Floridi 2008a, b), i.e. to identify the set of relevant observables ("the seeds of time") on which to focus because those are the ones that will make the real, significant difference. In our case, I shall argue that the best observables are provided by an analysis of the *nature of the data* used by AI to achieve its performance, and of the *nature of the problems* that AI may be expected to solve.[1] So, my forecast will be divided into two, complementary parts. In section two, I will discuss the nature of the data needed by AI; and in section three, I will discuss the scope of the problems AI is more likely to tackle successfully. I will conclude with some more general remarks about tackling the related ethical challenges. But first, let me be clear about what I mean by AI.

9.2 AI: A Working Definition

AI has been defined in many ways. Today, it comprises several techno-scientific branches, well summarised in Corea (2019), p. 26 (see Fig. 9.1).

Altogether, AI paradigms still satisfy the classic definition provided by John McCarthy, Marvin Minsky, Nathaniel Rochester, and Claude Shannon in their seminal "Proposal for the Dartmouth Summer Research Project on Artificial Intelligence", the founding document and later event that established the new field of AI in 1955:

> For the present purpose the artificial intelligence problem is taken to be that of making a machine behave in ways that would be called intelligent if a human were so behaving. (Quotation from the 2006 re-issue in McCarthy et al. 2006)

As I have argued before (Floridi 2017), the classic and foundational definition is obviously a counterfactual: *were* a human to behave in that way, that behaviour *would* be called intelligent. Because it offers a counterfactual criterion of identification rather than a definition in terms of necessary and sufficient conditions, it avoids the charge of circularity typical of other attempts that reintroduce in the *definiens* the same key term occurring in the *definiendum*, as in "The designing and building of *intelligent* [my italics] agents that receive percepts from the environment and take actions that affect that environment." (Russell and Norvig 2010).

The counterfactual does not suggest that the machine *is* intelligent or even *thinking*. The latter scenario is a fallacy, and smacks of superstition. Just because a dishwasher cleans the dishes as well as, or even better than, I do does not mean that it

[1] For a reassuringly converging review based not on the nature of data or the nature of problems, but rather on the nature of technological solutions, based on a large scale review of the fortcoming literture on AI, see "We analyzed 16,625 papers to figure out where AI is headed next" https://www.technologyreview.com/s/612768/we-analyzed-16625-papers-to-figure-out-where-ai-is-headed-next/ (accessed 16 June 2019).

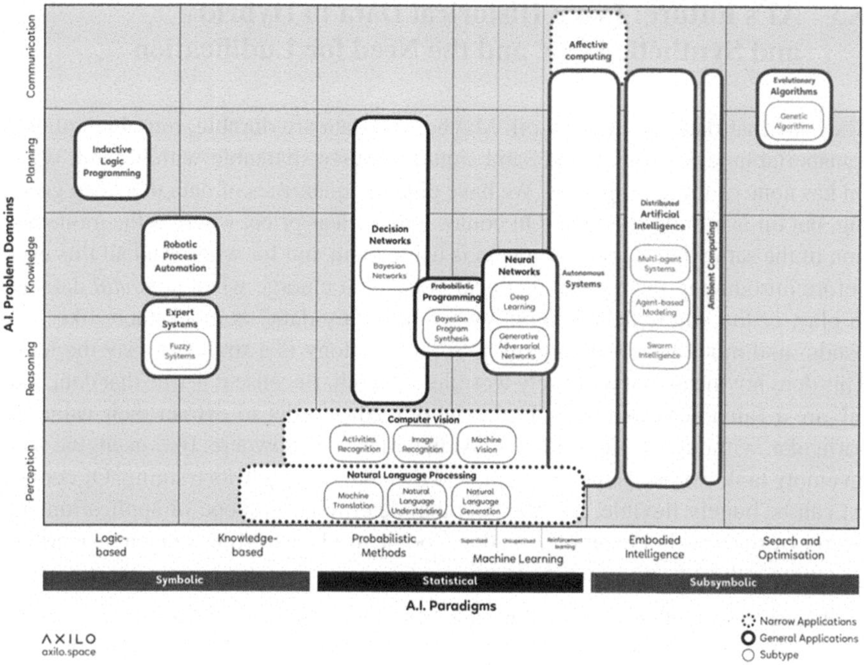

Fig. 9.1 There are many kinds of technologies that are called AI, here is an AI Knowledge Map (AIKM). (Source: Corea 2019, p. 21)

cleans them *like* I do, or needs any intelligence in achieving its task. The same counterfactual understanding of AI underpins the Turing test (Floridi et al. 2009), which, in this case, checks the ability of a machine to perform a task in such a way that the *outcome* would be indistinguishable from the outcome of a human agent working to achieve the same task (Turing 1950).

The classic definition enables one to conceptualise AI as a growing resource of interactive, autonomous, and often self-learning (in the machine learning sense, see Fig. 9.1) *agency*, that can deal with tasks that would otherwise require human intelligence and intervention to be performed successfully. This is part of the ethical challenge posed by AI, because artificial agents are:

> sufficiently informed, 'smart', autonomous and able to perform morally relevant actions independently of the humans who created them [...]. (Floridi and Sanders 2004)

Although this aspect is important, it is not a topic for this article, and I shall return to it briefly only in the conclusion.

In short, AI is defined on the basis of outcomes and actions and so, in what follows, I shall treat AI as a *reservoir of smart agency on tap*. The question I wish to address is: what are the foreseeable ways in which such a technology will evolve and be used successfully? Let us start from the data it needs.

9.3 AI's Future: From Historical Data to Hybrid and Synthetic Data, and the Need for Ludification

They say that data are the new oil. Maybe. But data are durable, reusable, quickly transportable, easily duplicable, and simultaneously shareable without end, while oil has none of these properties. We have gigantic quantities of data that keep growing, but oil is a finite resource. Oil comes with a clear price, whereas the monetisation of the same data depends on who is using them and for what. And all this even before introducing the legal and ethical issues that emerge when *personal* data are in play, or the whole debate about ownership ("my data" is much more like "my hands" and much less like "my oil"). So, the analogy is a stretch, to say the least. This does not mean that is entirely worthless though. Because it is true that data, like oil, are a valuable resource, and must be refined in order to extract their value. In particular, without data, algorithms—AI included—go nowhere, like an engine with an empty tank. AI needs data to *train*, and then data to *apply* its training. Of course, AI can be hugely flexible, it is the data that determine its scope of application and degree of success. For example, in 2016 Google used DeepMind's machine learning system to reduce its energy consumption:

> Because the algorithm is a general-purpose framework to understand complex dynamics, we plan to apply this to other challenges in the data centre environment and beyond in the coming months. Possible applications of this technology include improving power plant conversion efficiency (getting more energy from the same unit of input), reducing semiconductor manufacturing energy and water usage, or helping manufacturing facilities increase throughput.[2]

It is well known that AI learns from the data it is fed, and progressively improves its results. If you show an immense number of photos of dogs to a neural network, in the end it will learn to recognize dogs increasingly well, including dogs it never saw before. To do this, usually one needs huge quantities of data, and it is often the case that the more the better. For example, in recent tests a team of researchers from the University of California in San Diego trained an AI system on 101.6 million electronic health record (EHR) data points (including text written by doctors and laboratory test results) from 1,362,559 paediatric patient visits at a major medical centre in Guangzhou, China. Once trained, the AI system was able to demonstrate:

> [...] high diagnostic accuracy across multiple organ systems and is comparable to experienced pediatricians in diagnosing common childhood diseases. Our study provides a proof of concept for implementing an AI-based system as a means to aid physicians in tackling large amounts of data, augmenting diagnostic evaluations, and to provide clinical decision support in cases of diagnostic uncertainty or complexity. Although this impact may be most evident in areas where healthcare providers are in relative shortage, the benefits of such an AI system are likely to be universal. (Liang et al. 2019)

---

[2] https://deepmind.com/blog/deepmind-ai-reduces-google-data-centre-cooling-bill-40/ (accessed 16 June 2019).

However, in recent times AI has improved so much that, in some cases, we are moving from an emphasis on the quantity of large masses of data, sometimes improperly called Big Data (Floridi 2012), to an emphasis on the quality of data sets that are well curated. For example, in 2018, DeepMind, in partnership with Moorfields Eye Hospital in London, UK, trained an AI system to identify evidence of sight-threatening eye diseases using optical coherence tomography (OCT) data, an imaging technique that generates 3D images of the back of the eye. In the end, the team managed to:

> demonstrate performance in making a referral recommendation that reaches or exceeds that of experts on a range of sight-threatening retinal diseases after training on *only 14,884 scans* [my italics]. (De Fauw et al. 2018, p. 1342)

I emphasise "only 14,884 scans" because "small data" of high quality is one of the futures of AI. AI will have a higher chance of success whenever well-curated, updated, and fully reliable data sets become available and accessible to train a system in a specific area of application. This is quite obvious and hardly a new forecast. But it is a solid step forward, which helps us look further ahead, beyond the "Big Data" narrative. If quality matters, then provenance is crucial. Where do the data come from? In the previous example, they were provided by the hospital. Such data are sometimes known as historical, authentic, or real-life (henceforth I shall call them simply historical). But we know that AI can generate its own data. I am not talking about metadata, or secondary data about its uses (Floridi 2010). I am talking about its primary input. I shall call such entirely AI-generated data synthetic. Unfortunately, the term has an ambiguous etymology. It began to be used in the 1990s to refer to historical data that had been anonymised before being used, often to protect privacy and confidentiality. These data are synthetic only in the sense that they have been synthesised from historical data, e.g. through "masking".[3] They have a lower resolution, but their genesis is not an artificial source. The distinction between the historical data and those synthesised from them is useful, but this is not what I mean here, where I wish to stress the completely and exclusively artificial provenance of the data in question. It is an ontological distinction, which may have significant implications in terms of epistemology, especially when it comes to our ability to explain the synthetic data produced, and the training achieved by the AI using them (Watson et al. 2019). A famous example can help explain the difference.

In the past, playing chess against a computer meant playing against the best human players who had ever played the game. One of the features of Deep Blue, the IBM's chess program that defeated the world champion Garry Kasparov, was

> an effective use of a Grandmaster game database. (Campbell et al. 2002, p. 57)

But AlphaZero, the last version of the AI system developed by DeepMind, learned to play better than anyone else, and indeed any other software, by relying only on

---

[3] Masking is any information process used to conceal (hide or "mask") sensititive or private information, e.g. by replacing or making unavailable part of the relevant data https://www.tcs.com/blogs/the-masking-vs-synthetic-data-debate (accessed 16 June 2019).

the rules of the game, with no data input at all from any external source. It had no external, historical memory whatsoever (only its own):

> The game of chess represented the pinnacle of artificial intelligence research over several decades. State-of-the-art programs are based on powerful engines that search many millions of positions, *leveraging handcrafted domain expertise and sophisticated domain adaptations*. [my italics, these are the non-synthetic data]. AlphaZero is a generic reinforcement learning and search algorithm—originally devised for the game of Go—that achieved superior results within a few hours […] *given no domain knowledge except the rules of chess* [my italics]. (Silver et al. 2018, p. 1144)

AlphaZero learnt by playing against itself, thus generating its own chess-related, synthetic data. Unsurprisingly, Chess Grandmaster Matthew Sadler and Women's International Master Natasha Regan,

> who have analysed thousands of AlphaZero's chess games for their forthcoming book Game Changer (New in Chess, January 2019), say its style is unlike any traditional chess engine. "It's like discovering the secret notebooks of some great player from the past," says Matthew.[4]

Truly synthetic data, as I am defining them here,[5] have some wonderful properties. Not only do they share those listed at the beginning of this section (durable, reusable, quickly transportable, easily duplicable, simultaneously shareable without end, etc.). They are also clean and reliable (in terms of curation), they infringe no privacy or confidentiality at the development stage (though problems persist at the deployment stage, because of the predictive privacy harms Crawford and Schultz 2014), they are not immediately sensitive (sensitivity during the deployment stage still matters), if they are lost it is not a disaster because they can be recreated, and they are perfectly formatted to be used by the system that generates them. With synthetic data, AI never has to leave its digital space, where it can exercise complete control on any input and output of its processes.[6] This explains why they are so popular in security contexts, for example, where AI is deployed to stress-test digital systems in a way that reduces the possibility of causing real-world harm. And sometimes synthetic data can also be produced more quickly and cheaply that historical data. AlphaZero became the best chess player on earth in nine hours (it took 12 h for shogi, and 13 days for Go).

Between historical data that are more or less masked (impoverished through lower resolution, e.g. through anonymisation) and purely synthetic data, there is a

[4] https://deepmind.com/blog/alphazero-shedding-new-light-grand-games-chess-shogi-and-go/ (accessed 16 June 2019).

[5] One may argue that the data generated by AlphaZero are as synthetic as the data that would be generated by a human player playing against herself. This is correct—this is the idea behing the very process of synthesising anything from anything else—but also irrelevant here. Syntehtic data is used to stress the fact that the data avaialbel to the AI system are generated (mind, not collected, because the collecioth could be of data generated by humans, for example) entirely by the AI system.

[6] Put more epistemologically, with synthetic data AI enjoys the privileged position of a maker's knowledge, who knows the intrinsic nature and working of something because it made that something (Floridi 2018).

variety of more or less *hybrid* data, which you can imagine as the offspring of historical and synthetic data. The basic idea is to use historical data to obtain some new synthetic data that are not merely impoverished historical data. A good example is provided by Generative Adversarial Networks (GANs), introduced by Goodfellow et al. (2014):

> Two neural networks—a Generator and a Discriminator [my capitals in the whole text]—compete against each other to succeed in a game. The object of the game is for the Generator to fool the Discriminator with examples that look similar to the training set. […] When the Discriminator rejects an example produced by the Generator, the Generator learns a little more about what the good example looks like. […] In other words, the Discriminator leaks information about just how close the Generator was and how it should proceed to get closer. […] As time goes by, the Discriminator learns from the training set and sends more and more meaningful signals back to the Generator. As this occurs, the Generator gets closer and closer to learning what the examples from the training set look like. *Once again, the only inputs the Generator has are an initial probability distribution (often the normal distribution) and the indicator it gets back from the Discriminator. It never sees any real examples* [my italics].[7]

The Generator learns to create synthetic data that are like some known input data. So, there is a bit of a hybrid nature here, because the Discriminator needs to have access to the historical data to "train" the Generator. But the data generated by the Generator are new, not merely an abstraction from the training data. So, not a case of parthenogenesis, like AlphaZero giving birth to its own data, but close enough to deliver some of the very appealing features of synthetic data nevertheless. For example, synthetic human faces created by a Generator pose no problems in terms of privacy, consent or confidentiality at the development stage (thus, for example, the debate on GANs and Deepfakes concerns the problems at the deployment stage).[8]

Many methods to generate hybrid or synthetic data are already available or being developed, often sector specific. There are also altruistic trends to make such data sets publicly available (Howe et al. 2017). Clearly, the future of AI lies not just in "small data" but also, or perhaps mainly, in its increasing ability to generate its own data. That would be a remarkable development, and one may expect significant efforts to be made in that direction. The next question is: what factor can make the dial in Fig. 9.2 move from left to right?

The difference is made by the genetic process, i.e. by the rules used to create the data. *Historical data* are obtained by *recording rules*, as they are the outcome of some observation of a system behaviour. *Synthesised data* are obtained by *abstracting rules* that eliminate, mask or obfuscate some degrees of resolution from the historical data, e.g. through anonymisation. *Hybrid* and truly *synthetic data* can be generated by *constraining rules* or *constitutive rules*. There is no one-to-one mapping, but it is useful to consider hybrid data as the data on which we have to rely,

[7] https://securityintelligence.com/generative-adversarial-networks-and-cybersecurity-part-1/ (accessed 16 June 2019).

[8] https://motherboard.vice.com/en_us/article/7xn4wy/this-website-uses-ai-to-generate-the-faces-of-people-who-dont-exist (accessed 16 June 2019).

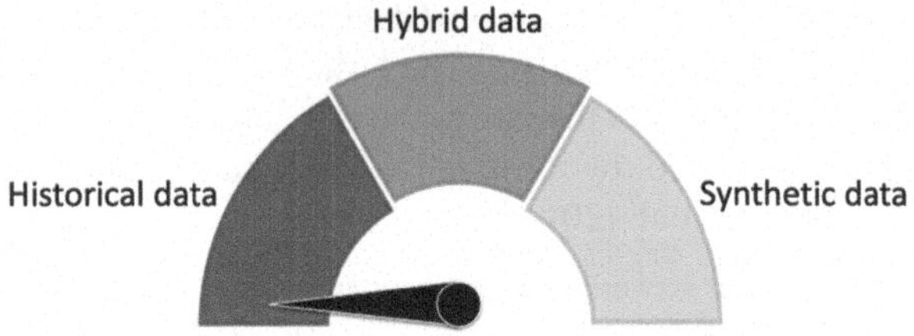

Fig. 9.2 Shifting from entirely historical to truly synthetic data

using constraining rules, when we do not have constitutive rules that can generate synthetic data from scratch. Let me explain.

The dial moves easily towards synthetic data whenever AI deals with "games"—understood as any formal interactions in which players compete according to rules and in view of achieving a goal—the rules of which are *constitutive* and not merely *constraining*. The difference is obvious if one compares chess and football. Both are games, but in chess the rules establish the legal and illegal moves before any chess-like activity is possible, so they are generative of all and only the acceptable moves. Whereas in football, a previous activity—let's call it 'kicking a ball'—is "regimented" or structured by rules that arrive *after* the activity. The rules do not and cannot determine the moves of the players, they simply put boundaries to what moves are "legal". In chess, as in all board games whose rules are constitutive (draughts, Go, Monopoly, shogi…), AI can use the rules to play any possible legal move that it wants to explore. In nine hours, AlphaZero played 44 million training games. To have a sense of the magnitude of the achievement consider that the *Opening Encyclopedia 2018* contains approximately 6.3 million games, selected from the whole history of chess. But in football, this would be meaningless because the rules do not make the game, they only shape it. This does not mean that AI cannot play virtual football; or cannot help identifying the best strategy to win against a team whose data about previous games and strategies are recorded; or cannot help with identifying potential players, or training them better. Of course, all these applications are now trivially feasible and already occur. What I mean is that when (1) a process or interaction can be transformed into a game, and (2) the game can be transformed into a *constitutive-rule* game, then (3) AI will be able to generate its own, fully synthetic data and be the best "player" on this planet, doing what AlphaZero did for chess (in the next section I shall describe this process as *enveloping* Floridi 2014a). To quote Wiener:

> The best material model of a cat is another, or preferably the same, cat. (Rosenblueth and Wiener 1945, p. 316)

Ideally, the best data on which to train an AI are either the fully historical data or the fully synthetic data generated by the same rules that generated the historical data. In any board game, this happens by default. But insofar as any of these two steps (1)–(2) is difficult to achieve, the absence of rules or the presence of merely constraining rules is likely to be a limit. We do not have the actual cat, but only a more or less reliable model of it. Things can get more complicated once we realise that, in actual games, the constraining rules are simply conventionally imposed on a previously occurring activity, whereas in real life, when we observe some phenomena, e.g. the behaviour of a kind of tumour in a specific cohort of patients in some given circumstances, the genetic rules must be extracted from the actual "game" through scientific (and these days possibly AI-based) research. For example, we do not know and perhaps we may never know what the exact "rules" for the development of brain tumours are. We have some general principles and theories according to which we understand their development. So, at this stage (and it is unclear whether this may well be a permanent stage), there is no way to "ludify" (transformation into a game in the sense specified above, I avoid "gamifying", which has a different and well-established meaning) brain tumours into a "constitutive-rule game" (think of chess) such that an AI system, by playing according to the identified rules, can generate its own synthetic data about brain tumours that would be equivalent to the historical data we could collect, doing for brain tumours what AlphaZero has done for chess games. This is not necessarily a problem. On the contrary, AI, by relying on historical or hybrid data (e.g. brain scans) and learning from them, can still (and indeed increasingly) outperform experts,[9] and expand its capabilities beyond the finite historical data sets provided (e.g., by discovering new patterns of correlations), or deliver accessible services where there is no expertise. It is already a great success if one can extract enough constraining rules to produce reliable data in silico. But without a reliable system of constitutive rules, some of the aforementioned advantages of synthetic data would not be available in full (the vagueness of this statement is due to the fact that we can still use hybrid data).

Ludification and the presence or absence of constraining/constitutive rules are not either-or hard limits. Recall that hybrid data can help to develop synthetic data. What is likely to happen is that, in the future, it will become increasingly clear when high-quality databases of historical data may be absolutely necessary and unavoidable—when you need the actual cat, to paraphrase Wiener—and hence when we will have to deal with issues about availability, accessibility, legal compliance with legislation, and, in the case of personal data, privacy, consent, sensitivity and other ethical questions. However, the trend towards the generation of as-synthetic-as-possible (synthesised, more or less hybrid, all the way to fully synthetic) data is likely to be one of AI's holy grails, so I expect the AI community to push very hard in that direction. Generating increasingly non-historical data, making the dial move as far as possible to the right, will require a "ludification" of processes, and for this reason I also expect the AI community to be increasingly interested in the gaming industry, because it is there that the best expertise in "ludification" is probably to be found. And in terms of negative results, mathematical proofs about the impossibility of ludifying whole kinds or areas of processes or interactions should be most welcome in order to clarify where or how far an AlphaZero-like approach may never be achievable by AI.

[9] See for example Microsoft's "Project InnerEye—Medical Imaging AI to Empower Clinicians", https://www.microsoft.com/en-us/research/project/medical-image-analysis/ (accessed 16 June 2019).

9.4 AI's Future: From Difficult Problems to Complex Problems, and the Need for Enveloping

I have already mentioned that AI is best understood as a reservoir of agency that can be used to solve problems. AI achieves its problem-solving goals by detaching the ability to perform a task successfully from any need to be intelligent in doing so. The App in my mobile phone does not need to be intelligent to play chess better than I do. Whenever this detachment is feasible, some AI solution becomes possible in principle. This is why understanding the future of AI also means understanding the nature of problems where such a detachment may be technically feasible in theory and economically viable in practice. Now, many of the problems we try to solve through AI occur in the physical world, from driving to scanning labels in a supermarket, from cleaning flows or windows to cutting the grass in the garden. The reader may keep in mind AI as robotics in the rest of this section, but I am not discussing only robotics: smart applications and interfaces in the Internet of Things are also part of the analysis, for example. What I would like to suggest is that, for the purpose of understanding AI's development when dealing with physical environments, it is useful to map problems on the basis of what resources are needed to solve them, and hence how far AI can have such resources. I am referring to *computational resources*, and hence to degrees of *complexity*; and to *skill-related resources*, and hence to degrees of *difficulty*.

The degrees of complexity of a problem are well known and extensively studied in computational theory (Arora and Barak 2009; Sipser 2012). I shall not say much about this dimension but only remark that it is highly quantitative and that the mathematical tractability it provides is due to the availability of standard criteria of comparison, perhaps idealised but clearly defined, such as the computational resources of a Turing Machine. If you have a "metre", then you can measure lengths. Similarly, if you adopt a Turing Machine as your starting point, then you can calculate how much time, in terms of steps, and how much space, in terms of memory or tape, a computational problem consumes to be solved. For the sake of simplicity—and keeping in mind that finely-grained and sophisticated degrees of precision can be achieved, if needed, by using tools from complexity theory—let's agree to map the complexity of a problem (dealt with by AI in terms of space–time = memory steps required) from 0 (simple) to 1 (complex).

The degrees of difficulty of a problem, understood in terms of the skills required to solve it, from turning on and off a light to ironing shirts, need a bit more of a stipulation to be mapped here because usually the relevant literature, e.g., in human motor development, does not focus on a taxonomy of problems based on resources needed, but on a taxonomy of the performance of the human agents assessed and their abilities or skills demonstrated in solving a problem or performing a task. It is also a more qualitative literature. In particular, there are many ways of assessing a performance and hence many ways of cataloguing skill-related problems, but one standard distinction is between gross and fine motor skills. Gross motor skills require the use of large muscle groups to perform tasks like walking or jumping,

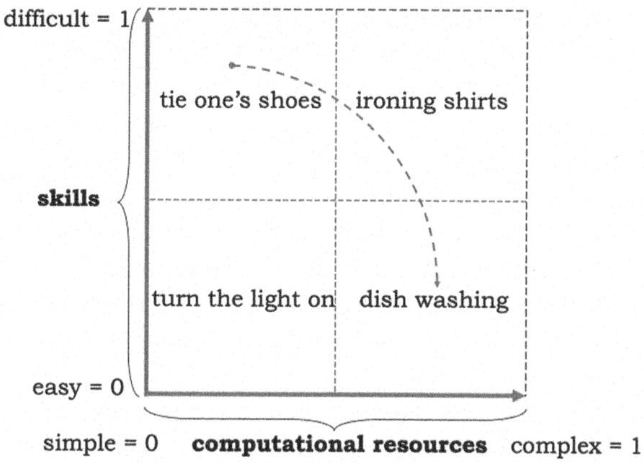

Fig. 9.3 Translating difficult tasks into complex tasks

catching or kicking a ball. Fine motor skills require the use of smaller muscle groups, in the wrists, hands, fingers, and the feet and toes, to perform tasks like washing the dishes, writing, typing, using a tool, or playing an instrument. Despite the previous difficulties, you can see immediately that we are dealing with different degrees of difficulty. Again, for the sake of simplicity—and recalling that finely-grained and sophisticated degrees of precision can be achieved, if needed, by using tools from developmental psychology—let's agree to map the difficulty of a problem (dealt with by AI in terms of skills required) from 0 (easy) to 1 (difficult).

We are now ready to map the two dimensions in Fig. 9.3, where I have added four examples.

Turning the light on is a problem whose solution has a very low degree of complexity (very few steps and states) and of difficulty (even a child can do it). However, tying one's own shoes requires advanced motor skills, and so does lacing them, thus it is low in complexity (easy), but it is very high in difficulty. As Adidas CEO Kasper Rorsted remarked in 2017:

> The biggest challenge the shoe industry has is how do you create a robot that puts the lace into the shoe. I'm not kidding. That's a complete manual process today. There is no technology for that.[10]

Dishwashing is the opposite: it may require a lot of steps and space, indeed increasingly more the more dishes need to be cleaned, but it is not difficult, even a philosopher like me can do it. And of course, top-right we find ironing shirts, which is both resource-consuming, like dishwashing, and demanding in terms of skills, so it is both complex and difficult, which is my excuse to try to avoid it. Using the previous examples of playing football and playing chess, football is simple but difficult, chess is easy (you can learn the rules in a few minutes) but very complex, this is why AI can win against anyone at chess, but a team of androids that wins the world cup is science fiction.

---

[10] https://qz.com/966882/robots-cant-lace-shoes-so-sneaker-production-cant-be-fully-automated-just-yet/ (accessed 16 June 2019).

The reader will notice that I placed a dotted arrow moving from low-complexity high-difficulty to high-complexity low-difficulty.[11] This seems to me the arrow that successful developments of AI will follow. Our artefacts, no matter how smart, are not really good at performing tasks and hence solving problems that require high degrees of skilfulness. However, they are fantastic at dealing with problems that require very challenging degrees of complexity. So, the future of successful AI probably lies not only in increasingly hybrid or synthetic data, as we saw, but also in translating difficult tasks into complex tasks.

How is this translation achieved? By transforming the environment within which AI operates into an AI-friendly environment. Such translation may increase the complexity of what the AI system needs to do enormously but, as long as it decreases the difficulty, it is something that can be progressively achieved more and more successfully. Some examples should suffice to illustrate the point, but first, let me introduce the concept of *enveloping*.

In industrial robotics, the three-dimensional space that defines the boundaries within which a robot can work successfully is defined as the robot's *envelope*. We do not build droids like Star Wars' C3PO to wash dishes in the sink exactly in the same way as we would. We envelop environments around simple robots to fit and exploit their limited capacities and still deliver the desired output. A dishwasher accomplishes its task because its environment—an openable, waterproof box—is structured ("enveloped") around its simple capacities. The more sophisticated these capacities are, the less enveloping is needed, but we are looking at a trade-off, some kind of equilibrium. The same applies to Amazon's robotic shelves, for example. It is the whole warehouse that is designed to be robot-friendly and not necessarily human-friendly. Ditto for robots that can cook[12] or flip hamburgers,[13] which already exist. Driverless cars will become a commodity the day we can successfully envelop the environment around them. This is why it is plausible that in an airport, which is a highly controlled and hence more easily "envelopable" environment, a shuttle could be an autonomous vehicle, but not the school bus that serves my village, given that the bus driver needs to be able to operate in extreme and difficult circumstances (countryside, snow, no signals, no satellite coverage etc.) that are most unlikely (mind, not impossible) to be enveloped. In 2016, Nike launched HyperAdapt 1.0, its automatic electronic self-lacing shoes, not by developing an AI that would tie them for you, but by re-inventing the concept of what it means to adapt shoes to feet: each shoe has a sensor, a battery, a motor, and a cable system that, together, can adjust fit following an algorithmic pressure equation.[14] Enveloping used to be either a standalone phenomenon (you buy the robot with the required envelop, like a dishwasher or a washing machine) or implemented within the walls of industrial buildings,

[11] I am not the first to make this point, see for example: https://www.campaignlive.co.uk/article/hard-things-easy-easy-things-hard/1498154 (accessed 16 June 2019).

[12] http://www.moley.com/ (accessed 16 June 2019).

[13] https://misorobotics.com/ (accessed 16 June 2019).

[14] Strange things happen when the software does not work properly: https://www.bbc.co.uk/news/business-47336684 (accessed 16 June 2019).

carefully tailored around their artificial inhabitants. Nowadays, enveloping the environment into an AI-friendly infosphere has started to pervade all aspects of reality and is happening daily everywhere, in the house, in the office, and in the street. We have been enveloping the world around digital technologies for decades, invisibly and without fully realising it. The future of AI also lies in more enveloping, for example, in terms of 5G and the Internet of Things, but also insofar as we are all more and more connected and spend more and more time "onlife", and all our information is increasingly born digital. In this case too, some observations may be obvious. There may be problems, and hence relative tasks that solve them, that are not easily subject to enveloping. Yet here it is not a matter of mathematical proofs, but more of ingenuity, economic costs, and user or customer preferences. For example, a robot that irons shirts can be engineered. In 2012, a team at Carlos III University of Madrid, Spain, built TEO, a robot that weighs about 80 kg and is 1.8 m tall. TEO can climb stairs, open doors and, more recently, has been shown to be able to iron shirts (Estevez et al. 2017), although you have to put the item on the ironing board. The view, quite widespread, is that:

> 'TEO is built to do what humans do as humans do it,' says team member Juan Victores at Carlos III University of Madrid. He and his colleagues want TEO to be able to tackle other domestic tasks, like helping out in the kitchen. Their ultimate goal is for TEO to be able to learn how to do a task just by watching people with no technical expertise carry it out. 'We will have robots like TEO in our homes. It's just a matter of who does it first,' says Victores.

And yet, I strongly doubt this is the future. It is a view that fails to appreciate the distinction between difficult and complex tasks and the enormous advantage of enveloping tasks to make them easy (very low difficulty), no matter how complex. Recall that we are not building autonomous vehicles by putting robots in the driving seat, but by rethinking the whole ecosystem of vehicles plus environments, that is, removing the driving seat altogether. So, if my analysis is correct, the future of AI is not full of TEO-like androids that mimic human behaviour, but is more likely represented by Effie,[15] Foldimate[16] and other similar domestic automated machines that dry and iron clothes. They are not androids, like TEO, but box-like systems that may be quite sophisticated computationally. They look more like dishwasher and washing machines, with the difference that, in their enveloped environments, their input is wrinkled clothes and their output is ironed ones. Perhaps similar machines will be expensive, perhaps they may not always work as well as one may wish, perhaps they may be embodied in ways we cannot imagine now, but you can see how the logic is the correct one: do not try to mimic humans through AI; exploit what machines, AI included, do best. Difficulty is the enemy of machines, complexity is their friend, so envelop the world around them, design new forms of embodiment to embed them successfully in their envelop, and at that point progressive refinements, market scale, and improvements will become perfectly possible.

---

[15] https://helloeffie.com/ (accessed 16 June 2019).

[16] https://foldimate.com/ (accessed 16 June 2019).

9.5 Conclusion: A Future of Design

The two futures I have outlined here are complementary and based on our current and foreseeable understanding of AI. There are unknown unknowns, of course, but all one can say about them is precisely this: they exist, and we have no idea about them. It is a bit like saying that we know there are questions we are not asking but cannot say what these questions are. The future of AI is full of unknown unknowns. What I have tried to do in this article is to look at the "seeds of time" that we have already sowed. I have concentrated on the nature of data and of problems because the former are what enable AI to work, and the latter provide the boundaries within which AI can work successfully. At this level of abstraction, two conclusions seem to be very plausible. We will seek to develop AI by using data that are as much as possible hybrid and preferably synthetic, through a process of ludification of interactions and tasks. In other words, the tendency will be to try to move away from purely historical data. And we will do so by translating, as much as possible, difficult problems into complex problems, through the enveloping of realities around the skills of our artefacts. In short, we will seek to create hybrid or synthetic data to deal with complex problems, by ludifying tasks and interactions in enveloped environments. The more this is possible the more successful AI will be. Which leads me to two final comments.

Ludifying and enveloping are a matter of *designing*, or sometimes re-designing, the realities with which we deal (Floridi 2019). So, the foreseeable future of AI will depend on our design abilities and ingenuity. It will also depend on our ability to negotiate the resulting (and serious) ethical, legal and social issues (ELSI), from new forms of privacy (predictive or group-based) to nudging and self-determination. The very idea that we are increasingly shaping our environments (analog or digital) to make them AI-friendly should make anyone reflect (Floridi 2013). Anticipating such issues, to facilitate positive ELSI and avoid or mitigate any negative ones, is the real value of any foresight analysis. It is interesting to try to understand what the paths of least resistance may be in the evolution of AI. But it would be quite sterile to try to predict "which grain will grow and which will not" and then to do nothing to ensure that the good grains grow, and the bad ones do not (Floridi 2014b). The future is not entirely open (because the past shapes it), but neither is it entirely determined, because the past can be steered in a different direction. This is why the challenge ahead will not be so much digital innovation per se, but the governance of the digital, AI included.[17]

[17] I would like to thank all members of the Digital Ethics Lab, OII, Univeristy of Oxford, for many discussions about some of the topics covered in this article, Nikita Aggarwal, Josh Cowls, Jessica Morley, David Sutcliffe, and Mariarosaria Taddeo for their hugely helpful coments on several drafts, and the editors of the volume, Christoper Burr and Silvia Milano, for their constructive feedback on the last version.

Funding This research was partly supported, at different stages, by Privacy and Trust Stream—Social lead of the PETRAS Internet of Things research hub (PETRAS is funded by the Engineering and Physical Sciences Research Council (EPSRC), grant agreement no. EP/N023013/1), Facebook, Google, and Microsoft.

References

Arora, Sanjeev, and Boaz Barak. 2009. *Computational Complexity: A Modern Approach*. Cambridge: Cambridge University Press.

Campbell, Murray, A. Joseph Hoane Jr., and Feng-hsiung J. Hsu. 2002. Deep Blue. *Artificial Intelligence* 134 (1–2): 57–83.

Corea, Francesco. 2019. *An Introduction to Data*. New York: Springer.

Crawford, Kate, and Jason Schultz. 2014. Big Data and Due Process: Toward a Framework to Redress Predictive Privacy Harms. *BCL Review* 55: 93.

De Fauw, Jeffrey, Joseph R. Ledsam, Bernardino Romera-Paredes, Stanislav Nikolov, Nenad Tomasev, Sam Blackwell, Harry Askham, Xavier Glorot, Brendan O'Donoghue, Daniel Visentin, George van den Driessche, Balaji Lakshminarayanan, Clemens Meyer, Faith Mackinder, Simon Bouton, Kareem Ayoub, Reena Chopra, Dominic King, Alan Karthikesalingam, Cían O. Hughes, Rosalind Raine, Julian Hughes, Dawn A. Sim, Catherine Egan, Adnan Tufail, Hugh Montgomery, Demis Hassabis, Geraint Rees, Trevor Back, Peng T. Khaw, Mustafa Suleyman, Julien Cornebise, Pearse A. Keane, and Olaf Ronneberger. 2018. Clinically Applicable Deep Learning for Diagnosis and Referral in Retinal Disease. *Nature Medicine* 24 (9): 1342–1350.

Estevez, David, Juan G Victores, Raul Fernandez-Fernandez, and Carlos Balaguer. 2017. Robotic Ironing with 3D Perception and Force/Torque Feedback in Household Environments. In *2017 IEEE/RSJ International Conference on Intelligent Robots and Systems (IROS)*.

Floridi, Luciano. 2008a. The Method of Levels of Abstraction. *Minds and Machines* 18 (3): 303–329.

———. 2008b. Understanding Epistemic Relevance. *Erkenntnis* 69 (1): 69–92.

———. 2010. *Information: A Very Short Introduction*. Oxford: Oxford University Press.

———. 2012. Big Data and Their Epistemological Challenge. *Philosophy & Technology* 25 (4): 435–437.

———. 2013. *The Ethics of Information*. Oxford: Oxford University Press.

———. 2014a. *The Fourth Revolution – How the Infosphere is Reshaping Human Reality*. Oxford: Oxford University Press.

———. 2014b. Technoscience and Ethics Foresight. *Philosophy & Technology* 27 (4): 499–501.

———. 2017. Digital's Cleaving Power and Its Consequences. *Philosophy & Technology* 30 (2): 123–129.

———. 2018. What the Maker's Knowledge Could Be. *Synthese* 195 (1): 465–481.

———. 2019. *The Logic of Information*. Oxford: Oxford University Press.

Floridi, Luciano, and Jeff W. Sanders. 2004. On the Morality of Artificial Agents. *Minds and Machines* 14 (3): 349–379.

Floridi, Luciano, Mariarosaria Taddeo, and Matteo Turilli. 2009. Turing's Imitation Game: STILL an Impossible Challenge for All Machines and Some Judges—An Evaluation of the 2008 Loebner Contest. *Minds and Machines* 19 (1): 145–150.

Goodfellow, Ian, Jean Pouget-Abadie, Mehdi Mirza, Bing Xu, David Warde-Farley, Sherjil Ozair, Aaron Courville, and Yoshua Bengio. 2014. Generative Adversarial Nets. In *Advances in Neural Information Processing Systems*.

Howe, Bill, Julia Stoyanovich, Haoyue Ping, Bernease Herman, and Matt Gee. 2017. Synthetic Data for Social Good. arXiv:1710.08874.

Liang, Huiying, Brian Y. Tsui, Hao Ni, Carolina C.S. Valentim, Sally L. Baxter, Guangjian Liu, Wenjia Cai, Daniel S. Kermany, Xin Sun, Jiancong Chen, Liya He, Jie Zhu, Pin Tian, Hua Shao, Lianghong Zheng, Rui Hou, Sierra Hewett, Gen Li, Ping Liang, Xuan Zang, Zhiqi Zhang, Liyan Pan, Huimin Cai, Rujuan Ling, Shuhua Li, Yongwang Cui, Shusheng Tang, Hong Ye, Xiaoyan Huang, Waner He, Wenqing Liang, Qing Zhang, Jianmin Jiang, Wei Yu, Jianqun Gao, Wanxing Ou, Yingmin Deng, Qiaozhen Hou, Bei Wang, Cuichan Yao, Yan Liang, Shu Zhang, Yaou Duan, Runze Zhang, Sarah Gibson, Charlotte L. Zhang, Oulan Li, Edward D. Zhang, Gabriel Karin, Nathan Nguyen, Xiaokang Wu, Cindy Wen, Jie Xu, Wenqin Xu, Bochu Wang, Winston Wang, Jing Li, Bianca Pizzato, Caroline Bao, Daoman Xiang, Wanting He, Suiqin He, Yugui Zhou, Weldon Haw, Michael Goldbaum, Adriana Tremoulet, Chun-Nan Hsu, Hannah Carter, Long Zhu, Kang Zhang, and Huimin Xia. 2019. Evaluation and Accurate Diagnoses of Pediatric Diseases Using Artificial Intelligence. *Nature Medicine* 25: 433–438.

McCarthy, John, Marvin L. Minsky, Nathaniel Rochester, and Claude E. Shannon. 2006. A proposal for the Dartmouth Summer Research Project on Artificial Intelligence, August 31, 1955. *AI Magazine* 27 (4): 12.

Rosenblueth, Arturo, and Norbert Wiener. 1945. The Role of Models in Science. *Philosophy of Science* 12 (4): 316–321.

Russell, Stuart J., and Peter Norvig. 2010. *Artificial intelligence: A modern approach.* 3rd, International ed. Boston/London: Pearson.

Silver, David, Thomas Hubert, Julian Schrittwieser, Ioannis Antonoglou, Matthew Lai, Arthur Guez, Marc Lanctot, Laurent Sifre, Dharshan Kumaran, Thore Graepel, Timothy Lillicrap, Karen Simonyan, and Demis Hassabis. 2018. A General Reinforcement Learning Algorithm that Masters Chess, Shogi, and Go Through Self-Play. *Science* 362 (6419): 1140–1144.

Sipser, Michael. 2012. *Introduction to the Theory of Computation.* 3rd ed. Boston: Cengage Learning.

Turing, Alan Mathison. 1950. *Computing machinery and intelligence.* Minds and Machines 59: 433–460.

Watson, David S., Jenny Krutzinna, Ian N. Bruce, Christopher E.M. Griffiths, Iain B. McInnes, Michael R. Barnes, and Luciano Floridi. 2019. Clinical Applications of Machine Learning Algorithms: Beyond the Black Box. *British Medical Journal* 364: 1886.

Luciano Floridi is the OII's Professor of Philosophy and Ethics of Information at the University of Oxford, where he is also the Director of the Digital Ethics Lab of the Oxford Internet Institute. Still in Oxford, he is Distinguished Research Fellow of the Uehiro Centre for Practical Ethics of the Faculty of Philosophy, and Research Associate and Fellow in Information Policy of the Department of Computer Science. Outside Oxford, he is Faculty Fellow of the Alan Turing Institute (the national institute for data science) and Chair of its Data Ethics Group; and Adjunct Professor ("Distinguished Scholar in Residence") of the Department of Economics, American University, Washington D.C.

He is deeply engaged with emerging policy initiatives on the socio-ethical value and implications of digital technologies and their applications. And he has worked closely on digital ethics (including the ethics of algorithms and AI) with the European Commission, the German Ethics Council, and, in the UK, with the House of Lords, the Cabinet Office, and the Information Commissioner's Office, as well as with multinational corporations (e.g. Cisco, Google, IBM, Microsoft, and Tencent). Currently, he is a Member of the EU's Ethics Advisory Group on Ethical Dimensions of Data Protection, of the Royal Society and British Academy Working Group on Data Policy, of Google Advisory Board on "the right to be forgotten", of the Advisory Board of Tencent's Internet and Society Institute, and of NEXA' Board of Trustees. He is the Chairman of the Ethics Advisory Board of the European Medical Information Framework (a €56 million EU project on medical informatics).

Research interests: Information and Computer Ethics (aka Digital Ethics), Philosophy of Information, and the Philosophy of Technology, Epistemology, Philosophy of Logic, and the History and Philosophy of Scepticism.

Index

C. Burr, S. Milano (eds.), *The 2019 Yearbook of the Digital Ethics Lab*, Digital Ethics Lab Yearbook, https://doi.org/10.1007/978-3-030-29145-7

The manufacturer's authorised representative in the EU is Springer Nature Customer Service Centre GmbH, Europaplatz 3, 69115 Heidelberg, Germany. If you have any concerns regarding our products, please contact ProductSafety@springernature.com

Printed and bound by CPI Group (UK) Ltd, Croydon, CR0 4YY
30/09/2026
02225608-0012

To Ángeles

Preface

I was about fifteen when my father, after watching my attempts at milking, decided to sell the family farm. The truth is I lacked not just milking skills, but also those needed for mending the bailer, fixing burst pipes, or understanding basic crop rotations. Historians, when they actually noticed farmers, used to complain about them being 'backward' or 'uncooperative'. This is no longer fashionable, and today they note their lack of human capital. While business historians happily write at length on the actors that innovated and built successful companies, most agricultural historians remain strangely quiet about farmers.

My interest in farms, and farming, therefore started at an early age, but I too was initially drawn to questions of production and productivity, without seeing the farm as a business. I first discussed writing a book on European agriculture with Eric Jones in UC Davis in 1992. I found the challenge too great then but, thirty or so years later, the field is still empty and there lacks a general monograph on the Continent's agriculture in the interwar years. A lot older, but probably not much wiser, I finally decided to write the book. The task has been made much easier by the appearance of a considerable secondary literature on different countries, but I have been delighted in discovering a number of classics such as those by Henry Roberts on Romania, or Jozo Tomasevich on Yugoslavia.

Many colleagues in the Universidad Carlos III de Madrid have had an enormous influence on my work over the years, including Carlos Álvarez, Stefano Battilossi, Alan Dye, Eva Fernández, Francesco Galassi, Markus

Lampe, Rich Sicotte, Leandro Prados de la Escosura, Pedro Fraile, Stefan Houpt, Joan Rosés, Antonio Tena, and Zacarias Moutoukias. More recently, I have benefited from suggestions from Miguel Artola, Jordi Domenech, Robert Fishman, Dacil Juif, Laura Maraval, Pablo Martinelli, Sergio Riesco, Ignacio Sánchez-Cuenca, and Emiliano Travieso.

Spanish agricultural history has been unusually dynamic in the past three decades, and I have had the good fortune to talk at length with many specialists, including Antonio Miguel Bernal, Elisa Botella, Miguel Cabo, Francisco Cobo, Josep Colomé, Rosa Congost, Luis Germán, Domingo Gallego, Luis Garrido, Manuel González de Molina, Iñaki Iriarte, Gabriel Jover, Mikeas Lana, Enrique Montañés, Vicente Pinilla, Jordi Planas, Ramón Ramón-Muñoz, Ricardo Robledo, Jesus Sanz, and David Soto Fernández.

I have presented numerous works at the conferences of the European History Rural Organization (EURHO) and *Historia Agraria*, and thank especially Jakub Benes, Paul Brassley, Richard Hoyle, Dulce Freire, and Socrates Petmezas for comments.

My visits to UC Davis were for many years a source of inspiration, and I have benefitted over time from many conversations with Greg Clark, Jim Lapsley, Peter Lindert, Alan Olmstead, Paul Rhode, and Alan Taylor.

Special thanks is due to Lourenzo Fernández Prieto and Juan Pan-Montojo who have gone to enormous lengths to comment on my earlier works. Samuel Garrido also made frequent and constructive criticisms. Juan Carmona deserves a special thanks, as we have written and published many articles and books together.

In England, Pepe, Madeleine, Kate, and Joyce were encouraging as always, but Lindy and Miles are sorely missed.

At Palgrave Macmillan it has been a pleasure to work with Ellie Duncan, who edited the book. I also thank Aishwarya Balachandar and Chitra Gopalraj for transforming my text into the finished product.

A large part of this book has been written in Moralina de Sayago, and I am deeply appreciative to many people for building the house, and providing a congenial place to work. Carlos and Pilar also provided emergency computer aid and good entertainment, while Charo allowed me to work in her vineyard.

Yet without the support of Ángeles, I would have had neither the time nor the inspiration to have written this book. It is dedicated to her.

Moralina de Sayago, Spain
March 2024

James Simpson

Contents

List of Tables

CHAPTER 1

Introduction

European hostilities opened with the First Balkan War in 1912, but the 'long First World War' only finished with the Greco-Turkish War of 1919–22 and the Irish Civil War of 1922–23. With peace came hopes of building of more democratic and fairer societies. Rapid technological change promised to revolutionize the lives of ordinary citizens in both the workplace and home, and governments, which had traditionally been reluctant to intervene in markets, had experienced some success at managing economic activity during the hostilities. In Eastern Europe especially, the creation of new nation states transformed political identities, while democratic constitutions and universal male suffrage everywhere augured for more representative governments. If the landed elites had wielded considerable political influence before 1914, it was now the family farmer who had become the dominant force in agriculture, and by far the largest group of voters in most countries. Never before, and probably never since, did Europe's family farmers enjoy such a position of strength to influence economic and political outcomes.

Yet most Europeans, instead of enjoying rising living standards and the consolidation of tolerant, liberal democracies, experienced economic depression which provided fertile ground for new political ideas that sought to radically redefine, if not replace, liberal capitalism and parliamentary democracy. Farmers were rarely the instigators of these changes,

J. Simpson, *Family Farmers, Land Reforms and Political Action*, Palgrave Studies in Economic History,
https://doi.org/10.1007/978-3-031-67281-1_1

although their numerical importance and wider concerns over food security, ensured that they played a major role in regime change. At the extremes, Hitler made the family farm central to his vision of the future of the German race, while for Stalin it was an obstacle to industrialization, and he confiscated them to form giant collectives to feed the rapidly growing cities. Farmers across much of Eastern Europe were attracted to Agrarianism, a political movement which prioritized their needs and was seen as an alternative development model to those of capitalism and communism. Farmers in Scandinavia also played a central role in social democracy which broke with liberal capitalism by establishing corporatist agreements to set prices and wages across the economy. Farmers, even in countries with historical traditions as different as England, France, or Italy, convinced their governments to intervene in markets on an unprecedented scale in the 1930s.

Economic historians frequently show how farmers respond to shifts in farm prices and production costs without explaining the political economy that determined them in the first place. By contrast, political theorists tend to study how landowners and farmers lobbied governments to influence policy, but ignore their impact on farming, food security, or economic growth. This book integrates both literatures, shedding light on topics such as the effectiveness of land reform, why farmers are sometimes reluctant to adopt new farming methods, or why some governments responded to the demands of farmers for market intervention, while others choose to ignore them.

There are a great many national studies of agriculture for the 1920s and 1930s, although surprisingly few that consider all Europe, especially countries in Eastern Europe. Yet many of the problems of the period, such as low farm prices, insufficient land, or need to design new institutions to allow governments to help farmers, were common to all countries. This book advances several new theories which helps to place the family farmer at the centre of change during this particularly turbulent period. How European farmers adapted to market instability by changing farming methods or building new organizations to influence government policy are crucial to understanding long-run economic growth and political change during the period.

Farmers found plenty of reasons for optimism when hostilities finally ended. The early twentieth century witnessed a massive fall in land inequality, leading to the family farm becoming the dominant unit of production everywhere and, outside industrial Europe, farmers were now the largest political constituency. The creation of new national frontiers, liberal constitutions, and a greatly extended suffrage produced a 'democratic spring', offering farmers the possibilities to create an alternative future, especially in Southern and Eastern Europe. Yet for this to happen, family farmers had to organize and fill the political void left by landed elites to exploit their electoral strength. In general, they were unsuccessful.

Family farmers generally failed to develop coherent, alternative ideologies or establish effective mass political organizations. Farmers outside a few small homogenous societies such Denmark were divided along commodity and cultural cleavages (religion, ethnicity, and nationalism), making it difficult to construct strong representative organizations. Governments in Western and Southern Europe had struggled since the 1870s to reconcile the contradictory demands of urban consumers for cheap (imported) food and their farmers for high prices. The traditional cultural divisions that existed between urban and rural societies deepened with the post-war inflation (and high food prices), reducing the possibilities for politicians to bridge the interests of the two worlds. In Eastern Europe, the growing export markets for cereals in the half century before 1914 could only be exploited by keeping farm wages low.

In general, governments were reluctant to prioritize agriculture. The Great War ended with many Europeans angry with their new national frontiers (Bulgaria, Hungary, and Germany), and others fearful that their territorial gains might disappear (France, Romania). The fact that rich countries had visibly smaller and more productive agricultural sectors encouraged governments to pursue policies that transferred resources from agriculture to industry. Denmark was the great exception, but it depended on a thriving export market for its food products, something that was difficult for other countries to emulate, especially given the economic conditions of the 1930s. Furthermore, economic orthodoxy required governments to implement austerity measures to tackle the post-war inflation, balance-of-payments shortages, and negotiate new foreign loans. Only with the collapse of international trade in the 1930s were the 'shackles' of economic orthodoxy finally broken, and democratic and non-democratic societies alike experimented with the alternative policies.

The new Eastern European governments conducted major land reforms involving the transfer of 20 million hectares of farmland, equivalent to a fifth of the total. With the exceptions of parts of Hungary and Poland, most landed estates were broken-up and given to small farmers and landless workers. These reforms created a successful barrier against the spread of communism from Russia, and potentially helped integrate more farmers into national politics. Farm ownership also encouraged the new farmers to work the land better and produce more. They might have become more productive if sufficient land had been available to allow them to adopt the new mechanical technologies found in cereal production (as was happening in North America), or if markets had existed to encourage them to specialize in high-value, labour-intensive farming (such as milk, oranges), or even if they had been able to find part-time employment when there was insufficient work on their farms. Unfortunately, not only was there too little land to create competitive farms, but the land reforms took place in a context of low prices. The result was that farmers prioritized the preservation of their new properties (and only source of employment) by reducing market activities to become more self-sufficient. In Poland, large farms of over 50 hectares accounted for only 17% of the arable land, but produced 21.5% of output and a massive 44.5% of sales of food. Most Eastern European families therefore continued to be poor, although landownership allowed them to consume more of their own food.

The Great Depression shook Europe's economies and sometimes threatened governments and democracy itself. The collapse in farm prices led those farmers who could not easily become more self-sufficient to form lobbies, but support was usually only forthcoming when two conditions were met. Governments were generally more accommodating when farmers' demands helped reduce balance-of-payments constraints, a problem which had been greatly aggravated by countries returning to the Gold Standard and having to repay debt. Western European farmers especially benefitted from policies that encouraged the import substitution of basic foods for the domestic market. A second factor was the extent that farm lobbies could persuade governments that there were greater political returns from helping them rather than other producer groups or consumers. This favoured those farmers in specialist lobbies, especially the 'electoral' commodities of wheat, wine, milk, or sugar beet, rather than the whole sector. Some farmers were given the right to form a monopoly to regulate their markets, with all producers obliged to participate. The Great Depression thus led to radical changes in farm organization in parts of North-Western Europe, and this helped guarantee government support even when economies eventually recovered. By contrast, when collective action failed and governments were unable, or unwilling, to intervene, farmers became more self-sufficient.

Government intervention in agriculture therefore produced three very distinct results which contributed to the major political changes of the 1930s. In the first, family farmers, in countries such as England and Wales, Switzerland, or France, were already well-organized and integrated into competitive mass political parties before 1914, and they successfully influenced farm policies during the 1930s, regardless of whether the government was conservative or socialist. In Scandinavia, farmers build strong agrarian parties which joined with other parties to establish social democracy, with governments intervening to protect the interests of both farmers and organized labour. The result was that farm prices in North-Western Europe were double those of Eastern Europe by the 1930s because of their protected markets and legalized farm monopolies. Democracy was also often strengthened, with farm groups and governments creating new institutions that would ensure long-term prosperity.

In a second group of countries, the Great Depression led to a weakening of electoral democracy, as the failure of governments to intervene left farmers with no option other than to reduce market operations, consume more of their own production, and participate less in active politics. This was especially common in Eastern Europe, where the influence of the Agrarian Parties was limited by their ideological weakness, and divisions along national, ethnic, and religious cleavages. The result was frequently 'pseudo' democracy, with governments ignoring liberal constitutions and using electoral corruption which made universal male suffrage irrelevant.

Finally, fascism found space to take root when governments failed to intervene or pursued policies that favoured *some* farm groups at the expense of others, especially if these could not then become more independent of markets. Support for electoral democracy might diminish when governments favoured grain growers, with the extra costs of animal feed being passed onto livestock farmers. Or when they approved significant wage demands for farm workers at a time of falling farm prices. Or simply deciding to help Serbs but not Croats. Mussolini in Italy, Hitler in Germany, or Franco in Spain would enjoy the support, at least initially, of large groups of farmers.

The book is organized around 11 chapters. Chapter 2 shows that agriculture was still the leading sector in much of interwar Europe, with farm productivity greatest in countries with the highest per capita incomes and fewest workers employed in farming. High productivity was achieved by farmers having either more land, allowing them to use their farm implements and work animals with greater efficiency, or enjoying favourable natural resource endowments and access to rich markets to specialize in labour-intensive, high-value commodities, such as horticultural or dairying.

Government interest in agriculture was driven by concerns over food security, and the belief in some circles that agriculture could be taxed to develop industry, and farm exports provide the necessary foreign currency to import machinery and raw materials. The debate was most intense in the Soviet Union, where the efforts to encourage farmers to produce large amounts of cheap food for urban consumers were seriously compromised by the ideological need to avoid the reappearance of a class of capitalist farmers ('kulaks'). Stalin's collectives would successfully increase food supplies for the cities at massive social costs, with ten million famine deaths.

Many countries adopted new constitutions and universal male suffrage following the Great War, encouraging the belief that future economic growth might benefit all social groups. Yet the democratic spring was usually short-lived. One problem was that the possibilities for political agreements between urban and rural groups became seriously diminished. In particular, the traditional rural and urban cleavages deepened during the hostilities and post-war austerity, as urban groups responded to inflation with historically unprecedented industrial strikes and factory occupations, while farmers benefited from the high prices, and inflation eroded farm debts and eased cash-flows. Furthermore, if the industrial proletariat was growing in most cities, the numbers of farm workers were declining as the family farm increased in importance.

The interwar years marked the hegemony of the family farm in Europe. Family farms had the major advantage in that they encouraged good work, as families benefitted directly from producing more and improving product quality, although the seasonal nature of farming implied many farms were too small to keep the family fully employed during the whole year. This problem could have been alleviated by choosing either more labour-intensive, high-value products, or increasing farm size and mechanizing peak-time operations. Chapter 3 explains why most European farmers could do neither.

Cereals were widely cultivated in Europe, both on large, mechanized farms and small, marginal holding. Many farmers in North-Western Europe practised mixed husbandry and produced feed for their livestock, to reduce risk and spread farm work more evenly over the calendar year. However, cereals were also grown across large areas of Eastern and Southern Europe because they could be consumed by the family or fed to their work animals when they could not be sold. In the 1930s, the significant amount of land under cereals often signalled farming difficulties, as in Western Europe farmers were usually dependent on tariffs and in Eastern Europe, they reflected the partial retreat by farmers from markets.

Natural resource endowments and weak markets frequently limited alternatives to labour-intensive cereals. Dairy farming was ideal for the family farmer, as it provided a good income and constant work over the year when farms were sufficiently close to consumers. Some farms located further from their markets benefited from the rapid technological change that produced significant economies of scale in the modern dairies, and Danish dairy farmers created highly competitive cooperatives to sell in international markets.

Small farmers, especially in southern climates, specialized in viticulture, although a significant number of the 1.5 million French producers were part-time growers, producing wine for family consumption. Technological change favoured large-scale producers of cheap table wines, but profitability remained low for much of the period because of persistent overproduction in producer countries and import restrictions in foreign markets. Small farmers faced significant entry barriers to producing and marketing high-value commodities, such as fine wines, or citrus fruit. Markets became more segmented in the period, leaving most family farmers having to compete on price, rather than quality.

Chapter 4 looks at the significant changes in the thinking about the role of the state and market intervention. To be effective, governments had to allocate scarce resources to increase state capacity, a process that was often slow and with frequent changes in direction. State capacity was the outcome of political bargaining over how to raise the necessary resources and establish spending priorities, involving complex decisions such as over whether to modernize the armed forces or develop drought-resistant seeds.

Rising cereal imports from the 1870s saw Western Europe's landed elites lobby, often successfully, for higher tariffs to protect their rents.

Governments found tariffs simple to collect, with the additional advantages of providing them with revenue and easing balance-of-payments constraints. The First World War required a massive increase in state capacity for economic planning and market intervention, and governments needed to encourage farmers to maintain output despite having less labour and fertilizers, and then sell to consumers at affordable prices. Rationing was required everywhere.

Much of this state capacity became redundant with the ending of hostilities, although different demands on governments quickly appeared with the new boundaries, constitutions, and democracies. A gap emerged between the interest of voters for social expenditure (pensions, unemployment benefits) and the belief in financial and political circles that a return to economic prosperity required economic orthodoxy, and an end to budget deficits and the return to the gold standard. It was only with the Great Depression that governments began to rethink priorities and develop new capacity to stimulate their economies. Governments generally remained reluctant to invest in R&D in agriculture because the political returns were too slow to appear. The major exceptions were when investment promised to reduce food imports (and ease the balance-of-payments) and, increasingly in the 1930s, when farmers built strong organizations to lobby for specific needs, allowing governments to appreciate better the potential political returns.

Land ownership was an important source of income inequality in pre-industrial Europe, and the landed elite usually opposed moves towards greater democracy. Yet by the interwar period, they had lost most of their economic and political power, both through market-induced changes which diminished their incomes, or government-sponsored land and tenancy reforms. The family farm was left as the most important production unit in much of Europe. Chapter 5 shows how this occurred.

From the eighteenth century, the long-run decline in feudal relations in the countryside accelerated in the face of political revolutions and changing commercial opportunities which often left a new, more market oriented, landed elite in power. Nevertheless, from the 1870s, the growing integration of the Atlantic economy made large farms in Western Europe increasingly unprofitable as farm wages rose, and cereal prices and rents fell. By the Great War many large estates had been broken-up and sold. In Eastern Europe, by contrast, large estates benefited from improved transportation and the stagnant labour costs caused by rapid population growth, until they too disappeared with the land reforms of the 1920s.

Economic change was accompanied by political transformation, with the landed elites losing their political power in two distinct ways. In most of North-Western Europe, they responded to parliamentary attacks from urban-based groups by forming their own parties, often with the help of the Church. Mass political parties in countries such as Britain, Belgium, Denmark, Netherlands, Norway, and Sweden were coordinated by a central office and paid officials, that recruited members from across most of the country, and determined policy. The electoral success of these conservative parties led in time to changes in their core constituencies, and the decline in influence of the landed elites and the Church. By the interwar years, not only had family farmers been assimilated politically and the influence of the landed elites significantly diminished, but these conservative parties were usually strong enough to withstand the pressure to move further to the right, and fascism.

By contrast, across much of Eastern and Southern Europe, the political elites could maintain their political influence using a mixture of electoral manipulation and fraud. Those political parties that existed were organized around individuals, with little or no central co-ordination, and were frequently at risk from external manipulation from well-organized lobbies. The events of the First World War and land reforms effectively ended many, requiring new parties to be build, potentially giving significant political power to the newly enfranchised family farmer.

Chapter 6 looks at how land reforms changed economic incentives in farming, and their impact on farm output and the living standards of the poorest groups in society. Results differed according to whether land reform took place in transforming economies such as Czechoslovakia or Spain, where the relative importance of the farm sector had already begun to decline because of industrialization, or in agricultural-based societies, where agriculture still employed two-thirds or more of the active population. Governments everywhere found that there was too little land to distribute, not just because the expropriated estates had been cultivated reasonably efficiently, but also because weak economic growth kept significant amounts of labour employed in agriculture. Consequently, farmers were reluctant to invest, and their farm implements and work animals were frequently underutilized because farms were too small. Land reform, however, successfully provided a minimum subsistence for many families during the Great Depression, restricted communist influence in the region, and avoided major rural conflicts, such as took place in Italy and Spain where large numbers of landless workers were still found.

Farmers had traditionally enjoyed significant benefits from the social networks found in the relatively closed village societies, and they used these in the interwar period to develop new forms of organization. Voluntary associations, and especially cooperatives, provided the link between the family farm and the lengthening food chains and mass competitive political parties. Yet as Chapter 7 argues, despite enjoying significant social capital, most European farmers either did not belong to a cooperative, or they enjoyed only limited benefits from membership.

Cooperatives in theory allowed farmers to both continue benefitting from the strong work incentives associated with the family farm and capture the growing economies of scale found in the bulk purchase of farm inputs such as working capital or artificial fertilizers, and in the processing and marketing of farm produce. Yet successful cooperatives not only required farmers to be able to work together, they also had to be financially viable. Danish cooperatives were the pioneers, although the unique conditions of the country's dairy industry made their institutional transfer to other countries difficult, especially given the high start-up costs of cooperatives and the export problems that farmers faced in the depressed economic conditions of the period.

One major obstacle was that despite strong social capital helping to create village-level cooperatives, the real benefits often came from the much greater scale that cooperative federations offered. This required individual cooperatives to work together, with their members now being unknown to each other. In North-Western Europe, the Church, and sometimes political parties, helped to provide the necessary trust to build federations, but this was rarely possible across much of Eastern and Southern Europe. Governments sometimes intervened, seeing the cooperative as a means to extend their influence into village society, which inevitable discouraged many farmers from joining.

Chapter 8 argues that most farm workers preferred either loyalty to their employers or exit for higher paid urban employment, rather than use voice, and form rural trade unions to demand better work conditions. In Eastern Europe, land reform significantly reduced the number of landless workers, and trade unions in this region were also frequently repressed by governments. In Western Europe, organizing farm labour, even with trade unions, proved difficult because of the highly varied nature of farm work, while permanent and casual workers often had conflicting interests.

Nevertheless, governments increasingly included farm workers with other workers when they legislated minimum wages and fixed the length of the workday or included them as part of broader packages to support farming.

Italy and Spain were the major exceptions, as the persistence of electoral fraud and political influence of the landed elites allowed governments to repress rural trade unions for longer. Given the limited possibilities for exit, some farm workers turned to anarcho-syndicalism to protect their living standards. In Italy, following the Great War, the government failed to intervene in rural conflicts, encouraging landowners and farmers to arm fascist groups to restore their traditional control of labour markets. By contrast, governments continued to police rural Spain in the early 1930s, although armed fascist groups quickly appeared following the 1936 military coup.

The Great Depression saw food prices halve on world markets and forced governments to defend their currencies in the face of rapidly falling exports. Chapter 9 extends the earlier discussions on farm associations, state capacity, and the lengthening food chains, to explain the paradox of why Western European governments, with relatively few farmers, were generally more willing to intervene to help than in those countries where farmers were more numerous. All governments tried to steady farm prices by reducing imports but faced significant challenges to avoid the accumulation of costly surpluses. This created incentives for specialist producers who organized along commodity lines to negotiate price support in exchange for limiting individual farmer's output. By the 1930s, farmers in countries, such as Germany, France, Italy, or Switzerland, came to enjoy a monopoly in their domestic internal markets, with food prices double those of world levels. Delegating regulatory powers to farmers participating in voluntary organizations, rather than imposing decisions on them from above, was both more effective and usually strengthened democracy. Outside North-Western Europe the efforts to form dynamic village-level organizations failed because farmers sold too little, while weaker state capacity made intervention less effective and impartial. Farmers in these areas preferred to withdraw further from markets, reducing their political influence.

The numerical importance of the family farm and the extension of the suffrage encouraged some farmers to lobby governments, but others supported political parties that sought to overthrow parliamentary government (Chapter 10). Agrarians in particular believed that family farmers, male suffrage, and farm cooperatives could allow them to prioritize their needs over those of industry, creating a ‘third way’ that avoided capitalism, and the eventual ‘voluntary’ sale of the family farm, and communism, which expropriated them to form giant collectives. Agrarianism failed as a political movement because it was ideologically confusing and contradictory, and because small farmers faced high costs to build effective mass political parties. Instead, most agrarian parties remained populist, with farmers dividing politically along cultural cleavages, especially nationalism.

The events of 1917 showed the revolutionary potential of landless farmers and encouraged governments in the successor nations to implement land reforms. The growing economies of scale in cereal farming led to the mass collectivization of Soviet agriculture, but few farmers would freely vote to surrender their land. The result was that most farmers were conservative, and socialist parties in countries such as England and Spain had difficulties to attract the farm vote. Nevertheless, the depth of the economic depression, and the fact that no single political party could retain power indefinitely in a democracy, encouraged farm groups in North-Western Europe to negotiate across party lines. In France and the UK, farm associations gained important concessions which continued regardless of the political party in power. Farm parties in Scandinavia formed governments with Social Democrats, supporting social transfers for urban workers in exchange for high farm prices. Therefore, although the short-term impact of the economic depression created major difficulties for farmers, the long-term impact in these countries was favourable, with farm organizations working permanently with governments to support the sector.

While some farmers defended democracy, others proved enthusiastic supporters of authoritarian governments, and their massive support was crucial for both Mussolini and Hitler gaining power. Yet if the family farm and *volk* provided stability and useful ideological support for these regimes, armies depended on healthy farmers and modern armaments of mass destruction. Hitler, given the demands of rapid re-armament, choose commercial farming and the rapid rural exodus to the higher farm prices that were necessary for the stability of the family farm. Instead more land was to be found with war, and *Lebensraum* or the colonial settlement of Eastern Europe.

The economic and political influence that the family farm enjoyed in the interwar years was considerably greater than anything that had gone before or would come after 1945. Ironically, its very success in responding to market incentives hastened its demise as consumers purchased proportionally less food as they became richer, and small farmers and farm labour were attracted by higher urban living standards.

CHAPTER 2

Agriculture and the Pursuit of Economic Growth

Contemporaries observed how agriculture in rich countries was usually more productive and employed fewer people than poorer ones. In the words of two English economists:

> A decline in the proportion of the population engaged in agriculture is ... an inevitable concomitant of economic progress and an improving standard of life; and it is impossible to lay down, on *a priori* grounds, any limits to the extent to which this proportion may eventually decline. (Astor and Rowntree 1939: 50)

Economic growth offered agricultural workers better paid urban employment, something which was especially attractive given the seasonal and physical nature of much of farming. Industrialization also increased the supply of new agricultural technologies, helping farmers to offset their loss of workers and utilize their land more intensely. Farm specialization, modern food processing industries, and falling transport costs produced lengthening commodity chains, suggesting that a vibrant and rapidly changing agriculture was both a cause, and the result, of economic growth.

Yet most Europeans were not rich on the eve of the Great Depression, and only in four of the 23 countries considered in this book did agriculture employ less than a quarter of the nation's labour force, and

J. Simpson, *Family Farmers, Land Reforms and Political Action*, Palgrave Studies in Economic History,
https://doi.org/10.1007/978-3-031-67281-1_2

in two-thirds of them it remained the largest sector. The extremes were significant, with England and Wales having just 6% of their labour force in agriculture, against close to 80% in countries such as Bulgaria, Romania, or Yugoslavia. A major concern for contemporaries was therefore to understand why farming had developed so much faster in some countries than others, and what governments could do to make farmers more productive.

The First World War highlighted the need for a country to possess a modern industry capable of providing the necessary armaments to defend itself and an efficient agriculture to feed its urban population and army. Agriculture in the large 'peasant' populations of Russia, Italy, Austria-Hungary, the Ottoman Empire, and Germany had manifestly failed, causing widespread urban hunger (Broadberry and Harrison 2005). Modernising agriculture therefore was moving up the list of government priorities in most countries even before hostilities had ended.

The Peace Treaties brought hopes that renewed economic growth would alleviate the poverty in which many Europeans lived. Many countries adopted new constitutions and extended the suffrage, with more representative governments promising a democratic spring. Yet these hopes were dashed, not least by the austerity measures that governments imposed to control inflation, and generate the necessary foreign exchange to pay interest on the massive loans that had been borrowed during the hostilities. Europeans faced wage cuts and unemployment instead of higher living standards and social transfers to those in need. The democratic spring, especially in Southern and Eastern Europe, failed to take root.

This chapter looks at agriculture and questions of economic development and political change in interwar Europe. The first section considers the difficulties in measuring long-run economic growth and agrarian change, and the diversity of European agriculture. This is followed by explaining why some countries had relatively small and dynamic agricultural sectors, but others suffered from low productivity, limited work opportunities, and poor living standards. Section three examines the debates over 'late industrialization', especially in the light of the Russian Revolution, and the implications that this had for government policies. The final section shows some of the difficulties that family farmers faced in influencing government policy following the Great War, despite universal male suffrage making them the largest group of voters in most countries.

2.1 Long-Run Economic Growth and Agricultural Change

Living standards, as measured by GDP per capita, grew at an annual average of around 1.0% across Europe in the half century before the First World War, with growth being strongest in Scandinavia, and weakest in Eastern Europe (Table 2.1). The UK was the country with the highest GDP per capita in 1913, being 88% more than the European average, followed by countries such as Germany (+56%), France (+21%), and Italy (+2%). At the other extreme were countries such as Serbia, at just 40% of the European average, Bulgaria (54%), Russia (58%), and Austria-Hungary (96%).

Growth rates between 1913 and 1937, and their regional distribution, were little different to what they had been in the previous quarter of a century (Table 2.2). By 1937, GDP per capita averaged \$4984 in North-West Europe, a third higher than the European average. In Southern Europe, the figure was \$2728, or 74% of the average, while Central Europe was divided between the more industrial north (Czechoslovakia and Hungary), with a GDP per capita of \$2695, and Bulgaria, Poland, Romania, and Yugoslavia, where the figure fell to 1568\$, just two-fifths of Europe's average.[1] The UK again had the highest per capita income, five times greater than that of Romania or Yugoslavia. Individual countries during the interwar years experienced significant short-term fluctuations in growth, influenced by factors including whether they were on the winning or losing side during the First World War, or the length of time they remained on the Gold Standard in the 1930s (Feinstein et al. 1997: Table 1.6).

Table 2.1 Comparative European growth rates, 1870–1913

Growth rates (% per year)	*GDP*	*Population*	*GDP per capital*
Early industrializers	1.80	0.57	1.23
Later industrializers	2.51	1.01	1.50
Nordic countries	2.53	0.91	1.62
Mediterranean countries	1.70	0.73	0.97
Russia, Romania, Bulgaria	2.38	1.62	0.76
Total Europe	2.13	1.05	1.08

(\$ in 1990 international prices)
Source Broadberry and Klein (2012: Table 4).

Table 2.2 Economic growth and structural change in Europe, 1913–1937

	% Workers in agriculture 1930	*GDP per capita 1937 $*	*Annual GDP per capita growth 1913–1937*	*Population change (1920–39)*	*Infant mortality 1930–31*	*Per capita productivity in agriculture*
UK	6	6249	1.1	9.0	63*	319
Belgium	17	4967	1.1	12.5	88	220
Switzerland	21	6171	1.5	8.4	50	194
Netherlands	21	4786	1.3	28.7	51	259
Germany	29	4836	1.1	13.9	84	195
Austria	32	3256	–0.5	3.8	104	134
Denmark	35	5601	1.6	17.1	77	354
Noway	35	4180	2.3	10.8	46	116
France	36	4207	1.1	7.0	77	176
Sweden	36	4565	2.1	7.4	56	146
Czechoslovakia	37	2747	1.1	14.0	136	105
Italy	47	3469	1.1	15.6	110	73
Ireland	48	2952	1.1	−5.0	69	93
Portugal	48	1753	1.4	27.0	143	53
Hungary	53	2607	1.0	14.2	157	78
Greece	54	2509	2.2	43.5	117	50
Spain	56	1799	−0.5	20.2	117	105
Finland	65	3638	2.0	15.5	75	65
Poland	65	1916	1.0	29.9	142	49
Yugoslavia	79	1273	1.1	31.0	159	38
Romania	79	1206	−1.0	28.2	178	48
Bulgaria	80	1496	1.0	30.0	147	47
Total Europe	38	3217	1.1	19.3	n.a.	100
USSR	86	2267	1.5	27.0	181	39

Infant mortality per 1000 live births. *Refers to England and Wales.
Sources Column (a) Feinstein et al. (1997: table 4.1); columns (b) and (c), Broadberry and Klein (2012: table 7); columns (d) and (e) Kirk (1946: table 3) and appendix 2; column (f) Moore (1945: table 3).

Countries in Table 2.2 are listed by the relative size of their agricultural workforce, which suggests a correlation between the prosperity of a country measured by per capita income, and the share of its active population working outside agriculture. Indeed, four of the five countries that had less than 30% of their workforce in agriculture in 1930 were found among the top five European countries listed by GDP per capita, with Germany being the only outsider. At the other extreme, Yugoslavia, Romania, and Bulgaria made up the tail in both categories.

Countries with low per capita incomes consequently had relatively large numbers working in agriculture, the sector where labour productivity was usually below, and often considerably below, levels found in industry or the service sectors.One cause of economic growth was therefore the movement of relatively unproductive farm labour into urban employment, especially industry. In Austria, for example, changes in the allocation of labour between sectors are estimated to have contributed 40% of GDP growth between 1870 and 1910, while in Germany and Hungary, the figure was perhaps a quarter (Schulze 2007: 200). Although contemporaries might not see growth in this way, they did spot that farming methods in urban-based societies were visibly more productive than those found in agricultural-based ones, where farmers were often considered as being 'backward', and hostile to new technologies and change. In reality, as this book argues, the causes of low agricultural productivity, and why farmers continued with traditional farming methods, usually reflected a lack of market opportunities.

The World Bank suggests that the opportunities and the nature of economic development at any particular moment are determined by the relative size of the agricultural sector (World Bank 2007: 1–2). Sources of economic growth in agricultural-based countries, where farming employs around two-thirds of the labour force, are inevitably closely linked to changes within the farm sector itself or in food processing industries and farm services. At the other extreme, in urban-based countries, agriculture's contribution to economic growth declines, despite the fact that large urban markets and high incomes create strong incentives for agricultural specialization. Rich countries can also attract food imports, which encouraged farm specialization in poorer countries, at least before international trade collapsed during the Great Depression.

Most European countries in the interwar period can be categorized as being located somewhere between these two extremes as 'transforming countries', where the industrial sector was still too small to be the sole motor of growth. Rural political tensions in interwar Europe were perhaps greatest in this group, as governments had difficulties helping the comparatively large number of farmers adjust to market volatility, while the lack of effective safety nets saw unemployed urban workers return to the family farm during economic depressions.

There are well-known limits to using national accounts to measure long-run historical economic development, such as shown in Table 2.2 (Macekura 2020; Angrist et al. 2021). One difficulty is that the statistical capacity of most countries was weak in areas of data collection and production of statistics, while historians lack household surveys or per capita household consumption data to contrast results. Farm production is often underestimated, a problem made more difficult by the need to measure both market and non-market production, given that an unknown, but sometimes important part of production in rural areas was for self-consumption. Vegetable plots, the family cow, or vineyard could make an important non-monetary contribution to household consumption which frequently escaped the statistician. Estimates for commercialization in agriculture range from 83% of output in Switzerland (1931–46), 80% in Italy (1930s), 75% in France (1938) to just 35–40% in Bulgaria, Romania, and Greece (1920) (Federico 2006: table 8.10). Yet these figures were never fixed, and farmers shifted in and out of markets according to opportunities. Few farmers followed strict profit and loss calculations in their decision-making as most were primarily concerned with preserving the family farm, resulting in market transactions and consumption being reduced to a minimum in the 1930s.

The statistical need to allocate individuals to a single economic sector also creates important distortions, as the resilience of the small family farm was precisely its ability to move between market and non-market activities, and for family labour to slip periodically in and out of farming. Therefore, in Czechoslovakia in 1930, an estimated 44% of the farms had less than two hectares, but 60% of these farmers had other occupations.[2] In the agricultural-based societies especially, there is evidence that many alternative sources of part-time employment, such as cottage industries and traditional transportation activities, were declining in the interwar period, something that the new Agrarian political parties hoped to reverse (Mitrany 1930: 224–5; 1951: 23). In agricultural-based societies today, an estimated 30 or 40% of income in rural areas comes from non-agricultural sources, a figure which is identical to one estimate for the Soviet Union in 1925–6.[3] Workers in urban-based economies were themselves sometimes part-time farmers, keeping a few animals in their backyards, or working on the family farm during their summer holidays.[4]

The fact that women are normally excluded from the census figures also seriously distorts our understanding of farming, which was very much a family-based activity, with few farms being operated by a single male alone. Therefore, the total civilian labour force in Austria-Hungary fell by 24% during the First World War because most of the female population were already working as 'family helpers' in agriculture, and unable to replace those male workers mobilized by the military (Schulze 2005: 81).[5]

Choosing a sector to allocate different economic activities along the food chain creates other difficulties in growth accounting. Farmers in traditional agriculture, unlike those in urban-based economies, often grow, process, and then sell their farm produce themselves in neighbouring markets. A recent World Bank report notes that as rising economic prosperity leads to agriculture's contribution falling from 40 to less than 10% of GDP, that of 'agribusiness (including agricultural trade and distribution services) typically rises from under 20% of GDP to more than 30% before declining as economies become industrial' (World Bank 2007: 135). The measurement of agricultural success in Denmark in the 1920s is highly dependent on whether the value added in farmer-owned dairy cooperatives and bacon factories are considered as farming activities, or industrial ones (Henriksen 2009: 118–9). In Britain, the 1.1 million workers found in agriculture in 1921, required a further 1.4 million in the processing and distribution of food and drinks (Astor and Murray 1933: Tables 3 and 19).

Finally, while GDP provides an indicator of changes in output, it says nothing of other dimensions of well-being, such as health, education and literacy, political rights, or pollution. The interwar years looks much less bleak when achievements in life expectancy and education are considered alongside the weak growth in GDP per capita (Prados de la Escosura 2022: ch.2).

Measuring agricultural productivity can be distorted when it is limited to dividing total farm output by the total numbers given as employed in agriculture in the population censuses. Agricultural labour productivity can appear very different when measured by the number of days actually worked, rather than the calendar year. As later chapters will argue, living standards were frequently higher when some family workers could find off-farm work during the slack season of the farm year.

Despite these measurement difficulties, many farmers in the period showed considerable ability to adapt and increase output in the face of rising population growth and growing land scarcity. European agriculture successfully supported a population that virtually doubled in the century after 1850, and fed it better. Diets in all agricultural-based societies, and significant regions of transforming ones, remained poorer than those in urban societies, limiting children's learning capacities, affecting health, and sometimes causing early death.[6] Life in the countryside was hard and novels, such as Émile Zola's *La Terre*, Blasco Ibáñez's *La barraca*, or Ignazio Silone's *Fontamara*, did much to undermine any romantic attachment for farm life among their urban readers. Nevertheless, most family farmers did *not* want to give up their properties for a city life and, as their political voice grew, demanded government policies to maintain the viability of their farms and preserve their way of life.

2.2 Why Were so Many European Farmers Poor?

Historians have found it difficult to create satisfactory historical series for agricultural output and productivity for countries outside Western Europe. Direct estimates falter for a variety of reasons, including a lack of accurate information for most farm products other than cereals; the difficulties in selecting representative price series to allow adequate cross-country comparisons; the problems associated with measuring both the size of the agricultural workforce and the area of farmland, especially as some countries had extensive areas of rough pasture (or land cropped only occasionally). The significant changes in national frontiers that took place in the period under discussion also make measuring long-run change difficult.

Nevertheless, several broad conclusions can be advanced from a small sample of countries on the eve of the First World War (Table 2.3). First, output per worker (O/W) was two or three times higher in Europe's urban-based economies than its agricultural-based ones. Second, the difference in output per hectare (O/H) varied significantly, even among the urban-based economies. Finally, high labour output was the result of either farmers producing significant amounts on a small area of land, or being able to farm a much larger area of less productive land. Low farm incomes in Europe were usually the result of farmers having too little land, and growing low value cereals rather than labour-intensive, high-value products. The contrast between North-Western and Eastern Europe was especially striking, as in Yugoslavia it was noted that 'on a given unit of land four times as many people produce three times less wheat than in Denmark' (Seton-Watson 1945–1967: 98). Explaining why farmers in some countries are so much more productive than others is at the heart of development economics. Theories that link a country's poor agriculture to farmers' ignorance or a stubborn resistance to change, have long been rejected as too simplistic. Instead, other arguments associated with farm structure, market incentives, natural resources, and government policy are usually advanced

The ownership of landed estates and large farms provided political privileges, collateral for loans, or means to increase human capital through private education, helping to perpetuate inequality. Yet, as this book shows, most farms were small and family operated, allowing farmers to use their labour during periods of low seasonal demand in the agricultural year to improve their properties by constructing fences, digging drainage ditches, or planting trees and vines. Small farmers at times of low farm prices only turned to the village money lender when forced to buy food for day-to-day consumption or to keep their livestock alive.[7] Landless labourers were less fortunate, although in most regions their numbers were declining significantly, not just because of possibilities of better paid urban employment, but also because changes in factor prices and the extensive land reforms following the Great War allowed many to become family farmers.

Family farmers were often highly resourceful and, with well-functioning markets and strong consumer demand, quickly shifted resources to specialize for niche markets. Adam Smith's comments in

Table 2.3 Land and labour productivities in selected countries, c.1910

	Output/worker	*Output/hectare*	*Hectares/worker*
Denmark	147	202	8.3
UK	100	100	11.4
Netherlands	92	237	4.4
France	82	136	6.9
Germany	118	205	6.6
Italy	45	161	3.2
Spain	32	55	6.7
Poland	47	129	na
Russia	43	70	na
Hungary	50	106	na
Austria	50	129	na
USA	136	35	44.1

UK = 100

Sources Based on O'Brien and Prados de la Escosura (1992) and Van Zanden (1991)

1776 that 'commerce and manufactures' in English cities were the 'cause and occasion of the improvement and cultivation of the country' remained just as true in interwar Europe (Smith 1776–1970: 515). In Italy therefore, 'it was the growth of Northern industry that led to the growth of Northern agriculture, and not vice versa', explaining why the North-South income gap widened in the interwar years, and why Southern farmers preferred more extensive farming (Martinelli 2014).[8]

Diets in Europe's urban-based and agricultural-based economies were marked less by differences in calorie consumption as by the relative importance of animal protein, fruit, and vegetables in diets (Table 2.4). Consumers in agricultural-based societies spent around two-thirds of their budgets on food, with cereals and potatoes accounting for a significant share, discouraging specialized farm production.[9] In a transforming economy such as Spain, per capita incomes increased by 45% and calorie consumption by 16% between 1900 and 1931, but meat consumption rose by 40% and dairy products more than doubled, although the average Spaniard still ate only 13 kilos of meat, 1.5 kilos of cheese, and drank 54 litres of milk in 1930.[10] They rarely consumed oranges, but Spanish exports to rich industrial markets boomed. It was weak domestic demand and limited access to export markets that left many farmers in Southern and Eastern Europe dedicating significant amounts of their land and labour to low-yield cereals and potatoes. These crops were 'safe' as they could be consumed by the family or fed to their animals when they could not be sold (Chapter 6).

Farmers in North-Western Europe benefitted not only from a strong demand for high-value foods but also generally enjoyed more favourable natural resource endowments to switch out of cereals to labour-intensive crops and livestock. By contrast, a major restriction in much of Southern and Eastern European agriculture was the need to follow dry-farming practices. European agriculture even today can be divided into two large blocks determined primarily by rainfall, and especially whether a country experiences a long summer drought or not. Although annual rainfall in Oxford is little different to that in Cordoba, and is 50% more in Naples than in Paris, the long summer droughts and high evaporation rates in southern Spain and Italy require quite different farming practices to those found in southern England or northern France (Martínez-Alier 1971: 25; Yates and Warriner 1943: 8).

China's recent history suggests that when conditions are highly favourable, poor agricultural-based economies can see rapid economic

Table 2.4 European per capita food consumption on the eve of the Second World War

	UK	*Denmark*	*Germany*	*France*	*Italy*	*Ireland*	*Greece*	*Spain*
GDP per capita, 1937	6249	5601	4836	4207	3469	2952	2509	1799
% Workers in agriculture	6	35	29	36	47	48	54	56
Annual per capita cons. (kg.)								
Cereals (as flour)	95.3	93.9	113.0	123.7	160.4	131.4	163.0	146.4
Potatoes	82.5	120.0	187.0	143.2	36.6	195.4	13.6	109.4
Vegetables	54.5	58.0	51.9	143.2	55.8	53.2	27.0	114.6
Fresh fruit	41.7	30.1	42.0	29.4	33.7	19.5	49.0	57.0
Sugar	44.5	50.5	26.3	24.3	7.9	38.1	10.9	11.6
Fats (excl. butter)[1]	12.1	19.6	14.3	11.2	10.6	2.9	13.8	14.4
Butter[1]	9.2	7.0	6.7	4.4	1.1	10.6	0.9	0.3
Total fats	21.3	26.6	21.0	15.6	11.7	13.5	14.7	14.7
Cheese	4.0	5.4	4.4	6.4	5.3	0.3	8.5	1.5
Milk	107.3	166.7	138.6	85.5	37.3	146.6	42.0	60.6
Meat[2]	62.6	74.6	52.8	55.2	20.1	54.9	19.5	28.1
Fish	20.6	32.4	14.1	14.7	11.8	6.5	12.4	25.0
Eggs	12.8	7.5	7.4	9.0	7.3	15.8	4.2	4.9
Daily per capita cons.								
Calories	3.110	3.450	3.040	2.880	2.520	3.400	2.600	2.760
Protein (grams)	80	93	85	96	77	99	84	88
Total calories (% from cereals and potatoes)	35	33	47	51	65	50	61	59
Total protein (% from animal products)	55	61	51	43	29	48	27	28

Sources Table 2.2; Yates (1960: table 2.4). Notes: [1]Fat content; [2]Carcase weight.

growth and major agricultural change. Chinese agriculture in the late 1970s employed almost 70% of the labour force and the country's citizens lived on less than 2,300 calories per day. However, between 1978 and 2007, GDP per capita grew at a phenomenal 8% annually, while farm employment shrank from 69 to 26% of the total labour force, and total factor productivity in agriculture grew by over 4% a year. China's farming was revolutionized, not just because of the significant government investment in R&D and extensions programs, but also because family farmers enjoyed major market incentives to change their farming systems (Zhu 2012: 109–112).

European governments influenced domestic farm prices through their decisions over whether to allow cheap imports, and sometimes by funded scientific research to develop drought-resistant seeds, find a solution to phylloxera in viticulture, or organize the mass testing and culling of cattle following outbreaks of foot-and-mouth (Chapter 4). They also created land registries, established national weights and measures, and set food hygiene standards. Yet European states, especially in the agricultural-based societies, generally played only a modest role in helping farmers adapt to changing markets. Unlike China between 1978 and 2007, the interwar years witnessed low prices, and the longest and deepest economic recession of the twentieth century. Government intervention in Europe in this period was sometimes radical, but in areas of supporting farm prices rather than increasing output.

2.3 The Late Industrialization Debate: Agriculture Versus Industry

Many economists believed that the key to explaining growth from the late nineteenth century was free trade, the discipline imposed by the Gold Standard, and the absence of government intervention in economies. The demands of the First World War required fresh ideas, leading to new forms of economic organization, with governments mediating between private business and trade unions to resolve production and supply problems.[11] War highlighted the advantages of having a modern industrial sector and efficient food chains, while the ease that national boundaries were redrawn following the hostilities showed that states needed to build an effective military deterrent to defend their territories. Although these were strong arguments for governments to pursue rapid industrialization, the newly enfranchised farmers, especially in the agricultural-based economies, had their own, very different demands.

Contemporaries debated whether it was industrial development that sparked agricultural change, or rather the needs of farmers that created the incentives for new industries. A balanced growth might in theory result from farmers responding to the growing demand for food in domestic and export markets by using more industrial inputs (fertilizers, machinery, etc.,), and greater rural prosperity creating new markets for manufactured goods (Johnson and Mellor 1961: 571–81). Farm exports could provide the foreign exchange needed to purchase strategic imports of raw materials and capital goods, and a more prosperous agriculture deliver the taxes for government to modernize infrastructure. The development of modern food processing industries and distribution networks created a steppingstone for the transition from an agricultural to an industrial society.

Just as in China in the late twentieth century, there is evidence that agriculture and industry developed in parallel in interwar Europe, with each sector reinforcing the other. The Danish experience has already been mentioned, with the needs for its dairy industry leading to the development of specialist manufacturing industries. In the Po Valley in Northern Italy, the rapid growth in the use of artificial fertilizers and the mechanization of agriculture provided markets for new industries, and changes in farm output stimulated specialized food businesses (Cobo Romero 2012: 237–9). In Valencia (Spain), the rapidly growing export markets for oranges and domestic demand for fresh vegetables also produced forward and backward linkages with the rest of the economy (Palafox 1985), while by the late nineteenth century a pioneering flour industry had developed in Hungary (Schulze 1997). East Anglia (England) was home to a dynamic farm implements industry, and Germany's chemical industry was highly dependent for agriculture's demand for fertilizers (Perkins 1982: 87; Dixon 2018). Nevertheless, as the First World War had shown, many of Europe's agricultural regions still enjoyed only weak linkages with modern industry (Broadberry and Harrison 2005).

Exogenous shocks to the agricultural sector can sometimes set-off rapid changes in farming. Europe's railways were built with the aim of promoting mining and manufacturing industries, state building, or for military purposes, rather than developing agriculture. Yet agricultural products quickly became an important item of freight, leading to regional specialization, such as dairying in England's East Midlands, or wine production in France's Midi. Likewise, the construction of large reservoirs to store water were primarily built for hydroelectricity, but would revolutionize farming in dry areas, mostly after the Second World War.

While balanced economic growth was indeed possible, the agricultural sector appeared to grow more slowly than industry, with farming offering fewer economies of scale compared to those associated with the Second Industrial Revolution, and found in iron and steel making, automobiles, or chemical production. Creative destruction also saw new industrial enterprises drive inefficient ones out of business, but was rare in European agriculture, as suggested by the small number of farmers that went bankrupt (Chapter 9). Farmers often appeared risk averse, in part because their human capital was closely associated with their knowledge of the production possibilities of their own land, making them unwilling to gamble the future of their farms. Few farmers, once they had started a family, left their villages permanently.

If some farmers saw cities as an opportunity to specialize and improve their living standards, many believed they were a source of economic and social instability. Even moderate industrialization threatened to increase income inequality, with long-run food prices declining in relative terms, while urban growth created significant opportunities to acquire wealth (Kuznets 1955).[12] How the benefits of economic growth were distributed were influenced by the political context of industrialization. From the seventeenth century, the British government dismantled institutional obstacles to mechanization, rapidly making redundant the skills of hundreds of thousands of rural workers, rather than protecting craft guilds. The law was forcefully employed in the early nineteenth century against the Luddites, who destroyed textile mills and machinery, and Captain Swing and his followers, who burnt ricks and threshing machines (Frey 2019). French visitors at this time were shocked by the misery and squalor of its industrial cities, just as many British travellers wrote at length on France's 'traditional' and 'immobile' agriculture, and rural poverty. [13] However, as O'Brien and Keyder (1978: 194) argue, the more we learn 'about the social history of French towns and the pace and pattern of internal migration in France, it becomes harder to condemn people's decisions to remain where they were born as irrational'. Seton-Watson (1945–1967: 128), writing of Eastern Europe in 1945, also noted the long-run benefits of industrialization for farmers, 'but this long term utility is obscured, for the first years at least, by the burden which it puts upon the poorest classes of the population'. Even commercial farmers selling in foreign markets must have thought that economic growth was 'zero-sum', with one person's gain being another's loss, as middlemen and shippers appeared to capture a rising share of the retail price of their products. Many European farmers were therefore sceptical, if not hostile, to government policies for rapid industrialization, in this period.

By far the most ambitious attempt at government-directed industrialization took place in the Soviet Union. The 1917 Revolution witnessed massive land invasions which the Bolshevik government legitimized to guarantee the political support of farmers. In the countryside, private property and food markets were allowed to operate relatively freely during the New Economic Policy (NEP) period between 1921 and 1928. Although agricultural and industrial production had regained their prewar levels by 1926, 'more rapidly than anyone had anticipated', the greater land equality resulted in smaller sales of grain. Large farms were crucial for creating marketable surpluses as just 10 or 11% of growers supplied 56% of the grain sold in 1927/8 in European USSR.[14] The NEP therefore faced two irreconcilable objectives: to encourage farmers to market sufficient food for urban consumers, while at the same time avoiding the appearance of a new capitalist class of farmers, as demanded by Marxist orthodoxy.

Harvest failures were inevitable in agriculture, but sufferings could be limited if sufficient storage existed to keep surpluses after good years, or foreign exchange available to supplement domestic supplies with imports in poor ones. Urban consumers were not only especially vulnerable, they were also highly visible, living close to the centres of government, and it was the severe food shortages that led to the political unrest that helped the Bolsheviks to power in 1917. The Bolsheviks were essentially an urban party, and the wellbeing of the industrial proletariat was considered crucial for industrial development.[15] As Chayanov and other agricultural economists noted at the time, family farmers would increase their production when suitable consumer goods were available in the shops but not if their crops were going to be confiscated by the government. When the Soviet government cut the prices of grain but not those of industrial goods in 1927 and 1928, rationing was needed in urban areas, and grain procurement campaigns launched in the countryside (Davies 1980; Wheatcroft 1990; Allen 2003: 78–86). Laws were passed against 'hoarding and speculating', and attacks became more frequent on the kulaks, a term which had become used to describe 'capitalist' farmers (Davies 1980: 23). The government found that although grain could be obtained by turning rural society against the kulaks, these inevitably then planted less, and some disposed of their work animals, farm equipment, and land (Applebaum 2018: 87–8).

The debate over agriculture's role in industrialization was more advanced in the Soviet Union than elsewhere, and its agricultural economists highlighted the diversity of the country's farming systems.[16] Soviet agriculture consisted of perhaps 25 million households and farming, as in much of Eastern Europe, was labour-intensive with most farms too small to fully employ a plough team. Stalin by the late 1920s believed that large collective farms and mechanization, especially tractors, offered a solution to both increasing market surpluses of food *and* eliminating the chance of a new class of capitalist farmers emerging in the countryside. A second revolution in the countryside was now engineered by the government, creating some 250,000 collectives from millions of small farms, and 'state coercion, including the use of violence, replaced the market relations' (Davies 2010: 51).[17]

Marxist economists believed that the economics of scale associated with collectives would provide the necessary capital and labour for industry, and cheap food for urban consumers. Collectives allowed the government to plan agriculture and control farm surpluses, ending the old village-level decision-making institutions. Farm production declined, not least because of the weak work incentives associated with collectives, but the quantities of food made available for non-farm consumption almost doubled in a decade, and urban consumption of basic foods such as bread, potatoes, and cabbages rose at the expense of rural areas. Mechanization allowed the slaughter of around 15 million horses between 1929 and 1938, freeing sufficient land to feed the equivalent of about 30 million people (Ellman 2014: 195; Allen 2003: 79, 135–6). Alongside the inefficiencies of the collectives, the social costs were enormous, with perhaps 10 million people dying from starvation, and millions more sent to detention camps in Siberia. In particular, Stalin used the terror-famine of 1932–3 in an attempt to crush the family farmer, and destroy Ukrainian nationalism (Conquest 1986; Applebaum 2018; Naumenko 2021).

The dilemma across much of Eastern and Southern Europe was that most farmers did not want to lose their land, but the small size of most farms made cereal farming highly inefficient, especially when tractors became more readily available from the 1930s. Engels in 1895 had argued that the growth of the franchise in industrializing countries would benefit the proletariat and lead to socialism, but it was the small family farmers across Eastern and Southern Europe that suddenly became the largest political constituency after the First World War (cited in Paxton 2005: 3). Agrarian parties saw the possibilities of democracy, land reform, and cooperatives creating a new development model that prioritized their interests, as Alexander Stamboliiski, the Bulgarian leader of the Agrarian Party and head of government noted in 1923, 'today there are only two interesting experiments: the experiment of Lenin and my own' (Toshkov 2019). Yet despite their numerical superiority, farmers everywhere found it difficult to advance their interests over those of smaller, but better organized groups in society.

2.4 Farmers and the Political and Economic Instability Following the First World War

The Armistice of November 1918 failed to end hostilities over large areas of central-eastern Europe and violence continued in some places until as late as 1923. In a matter of months, the old Austria-Hungarian, Russian, and Ottoman Empires were broken-up, and the Peace Treaties redrew political boundaries, rewarding the victorious powers at the expense of Germany and Soviet Russia (Connelly 2020: ch.12; Findlay and O'Rourke 2007: 441; Wolf et al. 2011: 918–23). Germany lost 13% of its territory and a tenth of its population, benefitting especially France (Alsace-Lorraine), and the restored Polish state (Poznam, large areas of west Prussia, and parts of industrial Silesia). Soviet Russia lost most of its western non-Russian territories, leading to the creation of the three Baltic states (Estonia, Latvia, and Lithuania), and surrendering land to Poland and Romania. The break-up of Austria-Hungary saw the creation of three independent states: Austria (restricted to Austria province); Hungary (reduced to less than a third of its old territory); and Czechoslovakia (made up from the former Austrian regions of Bohemia, Moravia, Silesia, and the Hungarian ones of Slovakia, and Carpathian Ruthenia). Serbia-Croatia-Slovenia (later Yugoslavia) was formed from the former Austrian provinces of Dalmatia, Slovenia, and the annexed Bosnia-Hercegovina. Rumania received Bukovina (from Austria), Transylvania and the border districts of Partium (from Hungary), Dobrudja (from Bulgaria), and Bessarabia (from Russia). The new Polish state was created out of territories from Germany, Russia, and Austro-Hungary (Galicia). Bulgaria, which fought alongside the Central Powers, lost relatively little territory, but this included the fertile agricultural regions of Dobrudja and Thrace and its access to the Aegean. It also suffered from a massive inflow of refugees. Ukraine, with a population of 43 million, became 'the nation that nobody knows', being divided between Soviet

Russia, Poland, Romania, and Czechoslovakia (Tiltman 1934: 192–3). By contrast, with the notable exception of the Irish Free State, boundary changes were limited in Western Europe.

The attempts to create new states on the principle of national self-determination led some becoming 'mini-empires ... every bit as multi-ethnic as the vanquished land empires they had replaced' (Mazower 1999: 40–1).[18] Yet whereas legitimacy in the old empires had been based on dynastic loyalty, in the successor states it was now ethnicity. Furthermore, as Mazower notes (1999: 55), 'neither minority nor majority believed in assimilation', resulting in the new democracies being 'exclusionary and antagonistic in their ethnic relations'.[19] Large numbers of people suddenly found themselves living in what had effectively become a foreign country, complicating the problems of achieving stable governments. Some 30 and 40% of Germans lived outside the diminished German state, while Czechs accounted for little more than half the population of Czechoslovakia, and Serbs only 43% of those in Yugoslavia (Connelly 2020: 360, 375). A third of the population in the new Polish nation were not Polish (Gerwarth 2017: 215). Political stability was maintained in Czechoslovakia only because the Sudeten Germans choose not to participate in government, but the Serbian elite faced fierce opposition from Radíc's Croatian Peasant Party (Connelly 2020: 377–80). Rural populations could mobilize on local issues in the interwar years, but these ethnic divisions often made it harder at the national level (Brett 2018). The successor countries of Eastern Europe also ended the 'prewar economics' as new customs units and tariffs were created, and restrictions to the migration of seasonal workers (Berend and Ránki 1974: 172–3; Gerwarth 2017: ch. 13).

Nevertheless, the ending of hostilities and new national boundaries produced optimism that liberal democracy would allow greater political participation, and that the benefits from economic growth would be more fairly shared. By late 1920, only the Soviet Union of Europe's 27 nation states lacked a constitution 'enshrining parliamentary elections, competing political parties, and guarantees for minorities' (Mann 2004: 37; Capoccia 2005: 7). Europe's post-war 'democratic spring' however was extremely fragile and short-lived, failing in part because farmers and workers were deeply divided.

The prevailing economic orthodoxy clashed with demands for a fairer societyand policies that implied higher government expenditure on social transfers such as war pensions, health care, or unemployment benefits

(Eichengreen 1996: chs. 3–4). Economic discipline had been abandoned during the hostilities, and large budget deficits led to high levels of debt and soaring inflation. With peace, economists believed that strict budgetary and monetary discipline was needed to restore competitiveness and attract the necessary foreign loans to buy crucial imports. The new governments therefore faced the choice of either implementing highly unpopular budgetary cuts that would increase unemployment and reduce wages, or resort to inflationary financing and being cut-off from international capital markets. Reparations made the situation even worse, and the Austrian and German governments initially rejected the deflationary policies required to pay them, especially as they hurt their voters while benefitting French and British taxpayers.[20] The French government also hoped that German reparations would make it unnecessary for it to deflate its own economy. The result was that while war and post-war prices in Europe roughly tripled, those in Germany increased by a trillionfold, in Russia by four billionfold, in Poland by two and half millionfold, in Austria by two thousandfold, and in France, by sevenfold (DeLong 2022: 183–6). Controlling inflation was only the beginning, as economic orthodoxy linked future economic prosperity with a return to free trade, fixed exchange rates, and the Gold Standard, as well as an end to wartime economic management by governments.

Protests against austerity were generally organized by urban groups, but even if the entire working class had voted socialist, it would have been insufficient to form a government on its own. The question of electoral agreements, and especially participating in 'bourgeois' governments, split the labour movement in the 1920s (Bartolini 2000: 97; Berman 2006). By contrast, trade union activity was much more visible, and revolutionary. In Western Europe, trade unions had seen a rapid growth in members, especially among unskilled workers, as governments ceased to negotiate with them after the War, and inflation rapidly eroded living standards.[21] The events of 1917 in Russia showed the possibilities of direct action, inspiring revolutionary movements on the streets of Germany, and factory occupations in Northern Italy. Unlike Russia however, urban workers attracted little, or no support, from farm workers and farmers. Within a short time, the Left had been defeated, both in the street and the ballot box, and the 'middle-classes' swept back to power. While conservatives in North-Western Europe formed democratically elected governments, in Eastern Europe the young democracies quickly gave way to what Seton-Watson called ‘pseudo-democracies’, and in Southern Europe to authoritarian regimes, as discussed in later chapters.

The strikes and factory occupations in the immediate post-war years against austerity only deepened the traditional cleavages found between urban and rural societies. Cultural differences traditionally ran deep, with rural society being usually more religious and preferring the Church to the State in the education of their children and setting moral values. Farmers often disliked losing their children to urban employment, while those farm labourers who aspired to own some land in the future, resented the Left’s attacks on private property. Across Europe, rural society saw cities as being morally corrupt, and producing unhealthy individuals who were unsuited to be soldiers. Urban intellectuals, by contrast, were shocked by the apparently primitive nature of village society, and supposedly backward nature of much of farming. During the Great War, farmers generally believed that they had made greater sacrifices than urban workers not least in providing men in uniforms, while urban groups complained that farmers had benefitted unduly from the widespread food shortages and high prices.

The post-war austerity also probably hurt agriculture less. Governments in Eastern Europe responded to the Soviet threat by rapidly implementing major land reforms (Chapter 6). Farmers also enjoyed the short-term benefits from inflation, as the real value of their debts fell, although in the longer-term it discouraged banks and individuals from advancing new loans. Balance-of-payments constraints encouraged governments to raise tariffs, protecting many farmers from foreign competition. Some farmers benefitted even when governments preferred to allow cheap imports. In Denmark and the Netherlands, governments prioritized dairy and meat exports, sectors dependent on imports of cheap animal feed. In Britain, economists argued that foreign markets for its manufactured goods required maintaining food imports, once again helping livestock farmers. Less fortunate were many Eastern and Southern European exporters, which found many of their traditional markets closed by the 1930s.

By the early 1920s, land reforms had ended the Bolshevik threat in Eastern Europe and the revolutionary labour movements in cities such as Turin, Milan, Berlin, Munich, and Budapest were crushed. The consolidation of the family farm took place even as the young electoral democracies struggled and often failed in the face of government austerity and political reaction. Yet economic recovery was brief, as economies collapsed in the early 1930s.

2.5 Conclusions

Europe's population, excluding the Soviet Union, increased by 16% in the two decades after 1920, and became generally better fed and enjoyed higher living standards (Table 2.2; Svennilson 1954: 236–7). Europe's agriculture was highly varied, with farmers being more productive in the rich industrial regions than on the tiny 'peasant' holdings found in agrarian-based societies. Poor farmers, as will be shown, were remarkably quick in allocating resources to areas which promised to improve their living standards. The persistence of rural poverty and poor farming methods was the result of farmers being unable to switch into high-value labour-intensive farming because they lacked access to rich consumers. The criticisms of farming methods by government experts and foreign travellers need to be placed in the context of interwar Europe, namely the economic depressions of the early 1920s and 1930s, and austerity, which severely restricted farming opportunities.

The growing market integration in the Atlantic economy had radically transformed many aspects of European agriculture even before the Great War. One important change was the increase in the global supply of new farm technologies which widened the gap in farming methods and productivity in European cereal farming (Chapter 3). The attempts by governments to pursue rapid industrialization in the 1920s and 1930s required cheap food for urban workers, although most countries lacked the necessary foreign exchange to import it. Soviet collectivization was only an extreme response to the common problem facing nearly all European governments, namely how to encourage farmers to produce food in sufficient quantities to ensure adequate and cheap supplies for urban consumers. What made the Soviet experiment so very different, and virtually guaranteed its failure, was the ideological need to increase production without 'capitalist' farmers. The political solution of collectivization led to millions of deaths, but it gave the state control over agriculture production, and rapid mechanization helped guarantee a supply of cheap grains for urban consumers.

The optimism produced with the ending of hostilities, the creation of new nation states, liberal constitutions, and democracy was often short-lived. Farmers, despite representing the largest numbers of voters in most countries, found it difficult to influence government policy. Eastern Europe's land reforms successfully stopped the spread of communism and gave farmers greater resources to survive as austerity reduced market opportunities, but growing self-sufficiency also limited their interest in national politics. By contrast, many farmers in North-Western Europe were already fully integrated into mass political parties by 1914, and enjoyed suitable political channels to voice their discontent. Only in parts of Hungary, Italy, Poland, and Spain did a politically influential landed elite continue to be found. Nevertheless, the post-war settlements and land reform changed politics in two major ways. The extension of the suffrage was accompanied by a deepening of the urban-rural cleavage because farmers generally managed better during the post-war austerity. At the same time, as family farmers came to dominate agriculture, the class cleavage was weakened, but the boundary changes in the successor states created minorities, deepening instead nationalist cleavages.

Notes

1. Averages are weighted by the size of countries. North-Western Europe includes Austria, Belgium, Denmark, Finland, France, Germany, Ireland, Netherlands, Norway, Sweden, Switzerland, and the UK; Southern Europe, Greece, Italy, Portugal, and Spain; Eastern Europe, Bulgaria, Czechoslovakia, Hungary, Poland, Romania, and Yugoslavia. Russia is excluded.
2. Most of those who lived in the poor agrarian provinces of Slovakia and Ruthenia worked only in agriculture, while farms of this size in much of Poland and the Balkans were also the family's sole income (Warriner 1939: 143–5).
3. Haggblade et al. (2007) in Lipton (2009: 141). The Soviet Union estimate of 39% in Davies (1980: 12).
4. In North Wales, even as late as the 1960s, a few industrial workers returned to the family farm for the harvest.
5. The official female participation rate in agriculture was 58% in 1913.
6. For food availability and needs in contemporary low-income societies, see Banerjee and Duflo (2011: ch. 2).
7. Yugoslavian farmers, for example, found it too risky to purchase feed to fatten their livestock for the market, and only bought it when animals were in danger of starvation (Tomasevich 1955:

506). Binswanger and Deininger (1997), for land ownership and capital market imperfections in contemporary low-income countries.

8. Kopsidis and Wolf (2012), for a similar explanation for the East-West gradient in nineteenth-century Prussian agriculture.
9. Allen (2017) calculates 64% of total expenditure is spent on food in developing countries today to meet a 'Basic Needs Poverty Line' of 2,100 calories per day, and 50% in middle-income OECD countries such as Turkey or Mexico. Banerjee and Duflo (2007: 146) suggest that among the world's extremely poor today, even before basic necessities are met, 'for every 1% increase in the food expenditure, about half goes into purchasing more calories, and half goes into purchasing more expensive (and presumably better tasting) calories'.
10. Per capita income in Prados de la Escosura (2007: S27); and diets in Simpson (1989: cuadro 5). Figures for meat exclude poultry and entrails.
11. The state, in countries such as Germany and France, gave 'new regulatory authority to delegates of business, labor, or agriculture, not merely though informal consultation but also through official supervisory boards & committees' (Maier 1975: 11).
12. The great majority of farmers earned less than those employed in industry and professional occupations (Royal Institute of International Affairs 1932: 58).
13. The standard of living debate has spawned a huge literature, see especially Feinstein (1998), Clark (2005), Allen (2009).
14. Sales between farmers are excluded. Some 26 of the 77 million tons of grain produced in 1926 was sold 'either on the market or direct to other peasants' (Davies 1980: 13, 27).
15. Only 494 peasants belonged to the Bolshevik party on the eve of the Revolution, and in October 1928 there were 198,000 members, equivalent to 14.5% of the total (Davies 1980: 51).
16. See Chayanov (1986), for an illustration of the wealth of Russian rural studies before 1917.
17. Collectives in the Ukraine were formed from an average of 90 small farms, with extremes ranging from just 14 to over 500 (Davies 2010: 47, 51; Naumenko 2021: 169).
18. By contrast, the 'core states of the vanquished land empires: the Weimar Republic, Austria, Hungary, Bulgaria and the Turkish

Republic, founded in October 1923' became ethnically more homogenous (Gerwarth 2017: 214–5).

19. Five per cent of the population were considered belonging to minorities in Western Europe, but a quarter in Eastern Europe (Mazower 1999: 55).
20. Germany was caught in a vicious circle, as attempts to limit imports threatened to cut it off from vital raw materials, thereby reducing manufacturing exports, and hence requiring further reductions to imports (Eichengreen 1996: 132).
21. Even trade union membership in Britain doubled between 1914 and 1920 to 8.4 million, while in Italy almost four million workers participated in labour disputes following the end of the hostilities (Mattei 2022: 76–77).

References

Allen, R.C. 2017. "Absolute Poverty: When Necessity Displaces Desire." *American Economic Review* 107 (2): 3690–3721.

Allen, Robert C. 2009. "Engels' Pause: Technical Change, Capital Accumulation, and Inequality in the British Industrial Revolution." *Explorations in Economic History* 46 (4): 418–435.

Allen, Robert C. 2003. *Farm to Factory. A Reinterpretation of the Soviet Industrial Revolution.* Princeton: Princeton University Press.

Angrist, Noam, Pinelopi Koujianou Goldberg, and Dean Jolliffe. 2021. "Why Is Growth in Developing Countries So Hard to Measure?" *Journal of Economic Perspectives* 35 (3): 215–242.

Applebaum, Anne. 2018. *Red Famine. Stalin's War on Ukraine.* Milton Keynes: Penguin.

Astor, Viscount, and Keith Murray. 1933. *The Planning of Agriculture.* Oxford: Oxford University Press.

Astor, Viscount, and B. Seebohm Rowntree. 1939. *British Agriculture the Principles of Future Policy.* London: Penguin.

Banerjee, Abhijit V., and Esther Duflo. 2007. "The Economic Lives of the Poor." *Journal of Economic Perspectives* 21 (1): 141–167.

Banerjee, Abhijit V., and Esther Duflo. 2011. *Poor Economics. A Radical Rethinking of the Way to Fight Global Poverty.* New York: Public Affairs.

Bartolini, Stefano. 2000. *The Political Mobilization of the European Left, 1860–1980.* Cambridge: Cambridge University Press.

Berend, Ivan T, and Gyorgy Ránki. 1974. *Economic Development in East-Central Europe in the 19th and 20th Centuries*. New York: Columbia.

Berman, Sheri. 2006. *The Primacy of Politics. Social Democracy and the Making of Europe's Twentieth Century*. Cambridge: Cambridge University Press.

Binswanger, Hans P., and Klaus Deininger. 1997. "Explaining Agricultural and Agrarian Policies in Developing Countries." *Journal of Economic Literature* XXXV (December): 1958–2005.

Brett, Daniel. 2018. "Indifferent but Mobilized: Rural Politics during the Interwar Period in Eastern and Western Europe." *Central Europe* 16 (2): 65–80. https://doi.org/10.1080/14790963.2019.1624461.

Broadberry, S., and Alexander Klein. 2012. "Aggregate and Per Capita GDP in Europe, 1870–2000: Continental, Regional and National Data with Changing Boundaries." *Scandinavian Economic History Review* 60: 79–107.

Broadberry, Stephen, and Mark Harrison. 2005. "The Economies of World War I: an Overview." In *The Economics of World War I*, edited by Stephen Broadberry and Mark Harrison, 3–40. Cambridge: Cambridge University Press.

Capoccia, Giovanni. 2005. *Defending Democracy: Reactions to Extremism in Interwar Europe*. Baltimore: Johns Hopkins University Press.

Chayanov, A.V. 1986. *The Theory of Peasant Economy*. Manchester: Manchester University Press.

Clark, Gregory. 2005. "The Condition of the Working Class in England, 1209–2004." *Journal of Political Economy* 113 (6): 1307–1340.

Cobo Romero, Francisco. 2012. *¿Fascismo o democracia? Campesinado y política en la crisis del liberalismo europeo, 1870–1939*. Granada: Universidad de Granada.

Connelly, John. 2020. *From People into Nations. A History of Eastern Europe*. Princeton: Princeton University Press.

Conquest, Robert. 1986. *The Harvest of Sorrow. Soviet Collectivisation and the Terror-Famine*. London: Hutchinson.

Davies, R.W. 1980. *The Soviet Offensive. The Collectivisation of Soviet Agriculture*. Cambridge, Mass.: Harvard.

Davies, R.W. 2010. *Soviet Economic Development from Lenin to Khrushchev*. Cambridge: Cambridge University Press.

DeLong, J.Bradford. 2022. *Slouching Towards Utopia*. London: Basic.

Dixon, Marion W. 2018. "Chemical Fertilizers in Transformations in World Agriculture and the State System, 1870 to Interwar Period." *Journal of Agrarian Change* 18: 768–786.

Eichengreen, Barry. 1996. *Globalizing Capital. A History of the International Monetary System*. Princeton: Princeton University Press.

Ellman, Michael. 2014. *Socialist Planning*. 3 ed. Cambridge: Cambridge University Press.

Federico, Giovanni. 2006. *Feeding the World. An Economic History of Agriculture, 1800–1900*. Princeton: Princeton University Press.

Feinstein, Charles. 1998. "Pessimism Perpetuated: Real Wages and the Standard of Living in Britain During and After the Industrial Revolution." *The Journal of Economic History* 58 (3): 625–658.

Feinstein, Charles, Peter Temin, and Toniolo. 1997. *The European Economy Between the Wars*. Oxford: Oxford University Press.

Findlay, Ronald, and Kevin H. O'Rourke. 2007. *Power and Plenty. Trade, Wars, and the World Economy in the Second Millennium*. Princeton: Princeton University Press.

Frey, Carl B. 2019. *The Technology Trap. Capital, Labor, and Power in the Age of Automation*. Princeton University Press: Princeton.

Gerwarth, Robert. 2017. *The Vanquished. Why the First World War Failed to End, 1917–1923*: London: Penguin.

Haggblade, S., P. Hazell, and T. Reardon. 2007. *Transforming the Rural Nonfarm Economy: Opportunities and Threats in the Developing World*. Baltimore: Johns Hopkins.

Henriksen, Ingrid. 2009. "The Contribution of Agriculture to Economic Growth in Denmark, 1870–1939." In *Agriculture and Economic Development in Europe since 1870*, edited by Pedro Lains and Vicente Pinilla, 117–47. Abingdon: Routledge.

Johnson, Bruce F., and John W. Mellor. 1961. "The Role of Agriculture in Economic Development." *American Economic Review* 51 (4): 566–593.

Kirk, Dudley. 1946. *Europe's Population in the Interwar Years*. Edited by League of Nations. Princeton: Princeton University Press.

Kopsidis, MIchael, and Nikolaus Wolf. 2012. "Agricultural Productivity across Prussia during the Industrial Revolution: A Thünen Perspective." *The Journal of Economic History* 72: 634–670.

Kuznets, Simon. 1955. "Economic Growth and Income Inequality." *American Economic Review* 45: 1–28.

Lipton, Michael. 2009. *Land Reform in Developing Countries. Property Rights and Property Wrongs*. Abingdon: Routledge.

Macekura, Stephen. 2020. *The Mismeasure of Progress: Economic Growth and its Critics*. Chicago: Chicago University Press.

Maier, Charles S. 1975. *Recasting Bourgeois Europe. Stabilization in France, Germany, and Italy in the Decade After World War I*. Princeton: Princeton University Press.

Mann, Michael. 2004. *Fascists*. Cambridge: Cambridge University Press.

Martinelli, Pablo. 2014. "Van Thünen South of the Alps: Access to Markets and Interwar Italian Agriculture." *European Review of Economic History* 18: 107–143.

Martínez-Alier, Juan. 1971. *Labourers and Landowners in Southern Spain*. Oxford: Oxford University Press.

Mattei, Clara E. 2022. *The Capital Order. How Economists Invented Austerity and Paved the Way to Fascism*. Chicago: Chicago University Press.

Mazower, Mark. 1999. *Dark Continent. Europe's Twentieth Century*. London: Penguin.

Mitrany, David. 1930. *The Land and the Peasant in Rumania. The War and Agrarian Reform (1917–21)*. London: Milford.

Moore, Wilbert. 1945. *Economic Demography of Eastern and Southern Europe*. Geneva: League of Nations.

Naumenko, Natalya. 2021. "The Political Economy of Famine: The Ukrainian Famine of 1933." *The Journal of Economic History* 81 (1): 156–197.

O'Brien, Patrick, and Leandro Prados de la Escosura. 1992. "Agricultural Productivity and European Industralization, 1890–1980." *The Economic History Review* 45: 514–536.

O'Brien, Patrick, and Cagler Keyder. 1978. *Economic Growth in Britain and France, 1780–1914: Two Paths to the Twentieth Century*. London: Allen & Unwin.

Palafox, Jordi. 1985. "Exportaciones, demanda interior y crecimiento económico en el País Valenciano." In *La modernización económica de España*, edited by N. Sánchez Albornoz, 319–43. Madrid: Alianza.

Paxton, Robert O. 2005. *The Anatomy of Fascism*. London: Penguin.

Perkins, J. A. 1982. "The Agricultural Revolution in Germany 1850–1914." *Journal of European Economic History* 10: 71–118.

Prados de la Escosura, Leandro. 2007. "Growth and Structural Change in Spain, 1850–2000: A European Perspective." *Revista de Historia Económica/Journal of Iberian and Latin American Economic History* 25 (1): 147–181.

Prados de la Escosura, Leandro. 2022. *Human Development and the Path to Freedom. 1870 to the Present*. Cambridge: Cambridge University Press.

Royal Institute of International Affairs. 1932. *World Agriculture, an International Survey: A Report by a Study Group of the Royal Institute of International Affairs*. London: Oxford University Press.

Schulze, Max-Stephan. 2005. "Austria-Hungary's Economy in World War I." In *The Economics of World War I*, edited by Stephen Broadberry and Mark Harrison, 77–111. Cambridge: Cambridge University Press.

Schulze, Max-Stephan 1997. "The Machine-Building Industry and Austria's Great Depression after 1873." *The Economic History Review* 50 (2): 282–304.

Schulze, Max Stephan. 2007. "Origins of Catch-up Failure: Comparative Productivity Growth in the Habsburg Empire, 1870–1910." *European Review of Economic History* 11: 189–218.

Seton-Watson, Hugh. 1945: 1967. *Eastern Europe Between the Wars 1918–1941*, 3rd ed. New York: Harper.

Simpson, James. 1989. "La producción agraria y el consumo español en el siglo xix." *Revista de Historia Económica* 7 (2): 355–388.
Smith, Adam. 1776: 1970. *The Wealth of Nations*. London: Penguin.
Svennilson, Ingvar. 1954. *Growth and Stagnation in the European Economy*. Edited by United Nations Economic Commission for Europe. Geneva: United Nations.
Tiltman, Hubert H. 1934. *Peasant Europe*. London: Jarrolds.
Tomasevich, Jozo. 1955. *Peasant, Politics, and Economic Change in Yugoslavia*. Stanford: Stanford University Press.
Toshkov, Alex. 2019. *Agrarianism as Modernity in 20th century Europe. The Golden Age of the Peasantry*. London: Bloomsbury.
Van Zanden, J.L. 1991. "The First Green Revolution: the Growth of Production and Productivity in European Agriculture, 1870–1914." *The Economic History Review* 44: 215–239.
Wheatcroft, Stephen G. 1990. "Agriculture." In *From Tsarism to the New Economic Policy*, edited by R.W. Davies, 79–103. Basingstoke: Macmillan.
Wolf, Nikolaus, Max-Stephan Schulze, and Hans-Christian Heinemeyer. 2011. "On the Economic Consequences of the Peace: Trade and Borders After Versailles." *Journal of Economic History* 71 (4): 915–949.
World Bank. 2007. *Agriculture for Development. World Development Report 2008*. Washington D.C.
Yates, P.Lamartine. 1960. *Food Production and Manpower in Western Europe*. London: Macmillan.
Yates, P.Lamartine, and Dorren Warriner. 1943. *Food and Farming in Post-War Europe*. Oxford: Oxford University Press.
Zhu, Xiaodong. 2012. "Understanding China's Growth: Past, Present, and Future." *Journal of Economic Perspectives* 26 (4): 103–124.

CHAPTER 3

Farmers and the Dynamics of Agricultural Change in Interwar Europe

European agriculture successfully fed a population that doubled in the century after 1850 although, as contemporaries were aware, significant regional differences in farming practices and performance existed.[1] Denmark was at one extreme, with its farming being 'almost exclusively a family venture' and employing a third of the working population as late as 1930 (Yates 1940: 59). Farm products accounted for a massive 80% of total exports and, given that net farm exports were 75% of agricultural production, a single family produced enough to feed twelve others (Henriksen 2009: 119–121).[2] Exceptionally, labour productivity in Danish agriculture was as high as other sectors of its economy (Crafts 1985: 56; Henriksen 2009: 117–23).[3] Bulgaria was at the other extreme, having suffered greatly during the two Balkan wars (1912 and 1913), and then seeing major boundary changes and population movements after finding itself on the losing side during the First World War. Bulgaria's agriculture employed four-fifths of the total active population and contributed almost 70% of GNP in both 1892 and 1929, with net agricultural exports being minimal. However, even in Bulgaria, farm output increased sufficiently to feed a population that grew by 70% between these years (Ivanov and Tooze 2007: table 2).[4]

Farmers in North-Western Europe generally faced fewer obstacles than those in Southern and Eastern Europe to increasing output and

J. Simpson, *Family Farmers, Land Reforms and Political Action*, Palgrave Studies in Economic History,
https://doi.org/10.1007/978-3-031-67281-1_3

improving living standards. Land was scarce almost everywhere, but in richer countries, urban markets attracted underemployed farm labour and allowed farmers to specialize in high-value farm products. The ample summer rainfall that fell across North-Western Europe permitted intensive farming practices, unlike many areas of Eastern and Southern Europe where dry-farming techniques had to be used. North-Western Europe's relatively small farm sectors, and the greater political mobilization of its farmers, also led to tariffs and food prices being higher than elsewhere by the 1930s (Chapter 9). Europe was therefore divided between those areas where farmers enjoyed higher prices, practised intensive 'mixed' farming, could mechanize to compensate for growing labour shortages and used artificial fertilizers to save land, and those regions that experienced low farm prices, had underemployed farm labour, and weak productivity growth. These conditions created another division, between commercial farmers who were more likely to specialize for the urban markets, and 'peasant' farmers who had higher levels of self-sufficiency, above all at times of market instability. A third, smaller area, consisted of specialist export orientated farming in the Mediterranean, involving products such as fresh fruit, vegetables, dried fruit, nuts, and tobacco.

This chapter looks at some of the restrictions that European farmers faced to becoming more productive. It begins with farm organization, and the implications that the family farm had for agricultural change. It then considers cereal farming, which was most appropriate for large farms, followed by dairy farming and viticulture, activities traditionally more suited to the family farm. Finally, it examines two specialist Mediterranean commodities, currants from Greece and oranges from Spain. Farmers were usually highly resourceful and responded to market opportunities, but outside North-Western Europe, natural resource endowments, farm technologies, and weak markets often resulted in family farmers failing to fully utilize their labour, limiting incomes.

3.1 The Economics of Farm Organization

A major factor for successful farming was to ensure sufficient labour was available to meet the seasonal peaks in agricultural demand, while at the same time proving enough work to keep labourers occupied during the slack periods of the year. Large farmers traditionally preferred to employ only a few full-time workers, and then hire large numbers of casual ones to meet the peak demand for operations such as mowing and harvesting.

Far more common were small farms which could not fully employ all the family during the whole year, requiring some members to work part-time in other activities. There was no shortage of entrepreneurs in rural society in interwar Europe, as not only did many operate their own farms, but large numbers were also involved in part-time businesses.[5]

Determining the optimal farm structure has generated a large theoretical and empirical literature. Arthur Young, writing in the late eighteenth century, favoured the large English tenanted estates as he believed they encouraged scientific, capital-intensive, and market-oriented farming based on mixed husbandry, rather than French 'peasant' agriculture, which he thought grossly misallocated resources (Mingay 1975). Large farmers however generally preferred farming activities that required little labour as its supervision was costly, especially when many activities were carried out simultaneously across the farm. The exact timing and care required in many tasks was crucial to maximize harvest size and keep animals healthy, and shoddy work could have significant consequences, with poor pruning permanently damaging vines, or careless sowing only being discovered at the harvest. Even then, employers would find it difficult to attribute whether the poor yield was caused by careless work, or to other factors such as the weather (Allen and Lueck 2002: 34–5). Large farms, by using only small amounts of labour, could create major social problems in the countryside at times of rapid population growth.

These difficulties in monitoring wage labour led many contemporaries to disagree with Arthur Young, and economists today stress the advantages of the family farm, as its members have strong incentives to work carefully and quickly, encouraging labour-intensive farming that maximizes output. Economic and political changes produced a major decline in the number of large farms and estates over much of Europe, so that by the 1920s the family farm was the dominant production unit (Chapters 5 and 6). The amount of land needed was determined not just by the size and age composition of the family, but also by soil quality and climate, nature of farming technologies, distance to markets, and level of consumer demand. In southern Spain, for example, a family farmer could earn a reasonable living on less than a hectare of irrigated land when it was close to a town, but three hectares were thought necessary for vines, almost 30 hectares for cereals, and perhaps 125 hectares for rough grazing (Carmona and Simpson 2003: cuadro 1.1).[6] Boserup (1965: 28–34) suggests that with traditional labour-intensive farming, growing population pressure encouraged farmers to increase output by intensifying production, such as by sowing cereals instead of natural pasture, or converting marginal cereal land to vines and olives. Low farm prices and the collapse of world trade after 1930 would significantly limited incentives for these types of change.

Another debate was over whether it was better for farmers to own their land or rent it. Farm ownership offered obvious attractions, but resulted in many farms being either too small, or overburdened farmers with mortgage payments. Buying land also risked leaving farmers with insufficient working capital, and farmers in the 1930s often found it easier to renegotiate rental contracts with landowners than mortgages with banks.[7] Tenant rights improved from the late nineteenth century, helping to safeguard farmers against eviction, linking rents with farm prices, and compensating tenants for their improvements.[8] Very different trajectories in landownership therefore developed over time, and if in England only one-third of farmland was worked by landowners in the late 1920s, the figures were three-fifths in France and Italy, and four-fifths or more in Germany, Switzerland, Denmark, Norway, and Sweden (League of Nations 1939: 14, 18, 25, 28, 33).[9]

Most farmers were not specialists and needed considerable knowledge on growing crops, animal care, the processing and marketing of farm produce, as well as being able to mend machinery or fix leaking roofs. Literacy had traditionally been less important in a world that used oral contracts, but by the 1920s it had become another requisite almost everywhere. A farm ladder sometimes existed that allowed landless youths to learn their trade on a neighbouring farm, save money, and obtain a reputation for hard work. The next rung on the ladder was to rent some land and then perhaps buy a plot or two. In Western Europe, the increase in farm wages and fall in land prices in the half century before the Great War helped this upward mobility. With luck, enough land could be accumulated for farmers to become rentiers by the time old age restricted their ability to work. Inheritance also offered a path to landownership, and one that was much less depended on an individual's farming skills (Griffiths 2007: 275). The increase in life expectancy and growing mechanization of heavy farm work delayed the age when land was handed down.

No country produced statistics that were sufficiently detailed to allow the number of family farms to be measured accurately or show how these changed over time. Nevertheless, the combination of land reform and sale of large estates probably made the period between 1914 and 1939 the heyday of the European family farm as, except in the Soviet Union, the amount of land found in farms of between two and 100 hectares increased everywhere.[10] Many of these farms were heavily fragmented with plots being dispersed over the village, often the result of inheritance laws. Fragmented holdings helped reduce the risks of a total harvest failure caused, for example, by localized hailstorms. It also gave flexibility to the farm ladder, allowing a farmer to acquire one field at a time, resulting in even relatively small farms consisting of several dozen plots. By the 1920s, this fragmentation was being seen as wasting labour time and an obstacle to mechanization, especially when impersonal credit and insurance markets were appearing (Dovring 1965: ch. 2; McCloskey 1991; Carmona and Simpson 2003: ch. 7). Consequently, while the land question in interwar Italy and Spain remained associated with landless workers and the need for land reform, in France or Belgium it had been replaced by the need to consolidate small plots into a single farm.

Many of these farms were too small to provide an adequate living for the family. Small plots sold for proportionately more than larger ones, because families produced more per hectare by planting labour-intensive crops and were less concerned by the marginal return of their labour than meeting their consumption needs. As a result, they worked longer hours, and with greater intensity, than what would have been profitable for large farmers using hired labour. Jean Jaurès, the French Socialist leader, suggested that the difference between large and small property was not just one of degree but also of kind, as 'one was a form of capital, the other a form of labour' (cited in Mitrany 1951: 35), and it was frequently commented that day wages were greater than what a family earned on their own land. For Kautsky, 'peasants' survived not because they were efficient, but because they 'eat too little and work too much' (Hussain and Tribe 1981: 27).

This 'self-exploitation' suggests that family farms were perhaps less efficient than sometimes claimed, but families could sometimes supplement their incomes by working part-time for others. One study argues that across the world today, this non-farm work sets a shadow wage, encouraging families to work their land only when it was *more profitable* than labouring for others. In other words, the essential farming activities were undertaken, but not those that made only a marginal difference to farm output. At the other extreme, modern, labour-saving farm equipment such as tractors allows time-bound operations to be carried out better than using traditional technologies, and at the optimal moment. Foster and Rosenzweig argue that this produces a 'U-shaped' relationship between farm productivity and scale, being highest on both the large farms using wage labour and modern technologies *and* on small part-time, family operated farms. It was lowest among farmers prone to 'self-exploitation', whose only source of employment was their farm (Foster and Rosenzweig 2022). This has two important lessons for interwar Europe. First, *hourly* labour productivity on large farms using modern motor-powered machinery would be higher than that achieved on family farms. Indeed, as Chapter 6 suggests, it was also usually true with traditional technologies, as casual labour was only employed when there was enough work. The significant poverty found in areas of large estates was caused not so much by low wages, but rather by workers facing long periods of seasonal unemployment (Simpson and Carmona 2020: 161). A second factor was that opportunities of off-farm work might reduce farm output but increase the living standards of the family. The appearance of cheap manufactured imports in the interwar years was therefore a mixed blessing, as they made traditional domestic producers uncompetitive, eliminating opportunities for part-time work.

Contemporary worries of 'surplus' farm labour, especially in Eastern Europe, were not just the result of a lack of part-time non-farm work, but also because agriculture was the employer of last resort, with farms having to support unemployed urban 'family' workers at times of economic downturns. Yet the major concern was the limited opportunities for farm specialization and employment in the interwar years, as the remainder of the chapter will show.

3.2 Cereal Farming: Between Economies of Scale and Self-Sufficiency

Wheat was Europe's major bread grain, providing half of all calories in many countries, with most farmers dedicating at least part of their land and labour to its production. Imports in Norway, Switzerland, Belgium, the UK, Ireland, and the Netherlands accounted for over half their needs in 1934–8, but countries such as France (98%), Germany (89%), Italy (94%), and Spain (100%) had become virtually self-sufficient (United Nations and Food and Agriculture Organization 1954: Table 19), Cereals required little labour during much of the year, but the heavy peak demands for the sowing and harvesting operations restricted the area that a family farmer could cultivate using traditional technologies.

Cereals were cultivated using several distinctive farming systems. World prices were set by family farmers in the New World from the 1870s, as they mechanized peak-time operations and extended their farms to incorporate large amounts of virgin land. Some Eastern European exporters remained internationally competitive before 1914 because farmers employed cheap labour for the essential peak time tasks, or rented the land to families who were willing to work for less than the going wage. On the eve of the Great War, the combination of extensive cereal rotations with unsown fallow and manured by large sheep flocks was still a common sight across large areas of Eastern and Southern Europe.[11] Land reforms made most of Eastern Europe's cereal farms too small to be competitive, especially as summer droughts caused low cereal yields and the shortage of natural grass made animal feed expensive, creating an insoluble bottleneck to increasing livestock densities. Mineral fertilizers and better seed selection helped farmers to extend the area of cultivation but offered only limited possibilities for improving yields under dry-farming conditions before the 1960s (Simpson 1995a: 251–2; Pujol-Andreu 2011).[12]

By contrast, cereals in North-Western Europe were often part of complex farming systems, with grain being fed on-farm to animals. Cereal yields in some favoured areas had been improved by planting nitrogen-fixing crops such as beans and peas in the fallow from the seventeenth century or earlier.[13] These pulses, as well as new root crops such as turnips and, later, potatoes and sugar beet, improved the supply of winter feed, thereby avoiding the massive autumn slaughter of cattle, and alleviating the bottle-neck to increasing herd size. Artificial fertilizers from the late nineteenth century further enhanced yields on some soils, although cereal prices had to be sufficiently high to offset their extra costs (Thompson 1968; Bairoch 1989; Van Zanden 1991). In northern France, wheat yields rose by 280% between 1750 and 1929, while labour productivity when measured by wheat produced per day worked, improved by 475%, with half this figure being achieved after 1892 (Grantham 1991).[14] Rotations became more fodder-intensive, permitting higher stocking levels which produced more manure, although by 1900 commercial fertilizers and new plant strains were 'beginning to lift crop yields above the ... limits set by manure-intensive husbandry'. Labour productivity increased both because of higher yields and the major savings found in soil preparation, harvesting, and post-harvesting activities. Horses were preferred to oxen because of their greater speed in field work and haulage, while metallurgic advances allowed the mass production of bolts and screws, making iron farm implements lighter and stronger. The 50% reduction in the weight and mechanical resistance of metal ploughs allowed farmers for the first time to use heavy harrows and row cultivators (Grantham 1991).[15]

German farmers used artificial fertilizers at unprecedented levels from the late nineteenth century, as some changed from rotational farming and a crop sequence to support the necessary livestock to manure the fields, to a 'free economy' (*freie Wirtschaft*), which allowed them to decide annually which crops they wanted to cultivate and, in some cases, disperse entirely with their animals (Perkins 1982: 88–9). German farmers by 1914 used three times more artificial fertilizers per hectare than those in France (Perkins 1982: 86, 114). This level of specialization was rare because its profitability depended on favourable market prices for both artificial fertilizers and farm products. Most European farmers preferred instead to produce their own animal feed or buy cheap imports. Indeed, Germany's growing dependence on artificial fertilizers contrasted with Britain's massive imports of cheap cereals, which led to farmers converting their arable to pasture, inadvertently creating a fertile 'land bank' that was used during the First World War to increase domestic cereal production (Chapter 4).

Traditional cereal production required little labour, but it was heavily concentrated in the sowing, harvesting, and threshing operations (Table 3.1). Peak-time labour shortages encouraged a switch from 'lower to higher working capacity tools', such as the heavy hook and scythe, which replaced the sickle in much of Europe outside the Mediterranean in the nineteenth century (Collins 1969: 85).[16] The development of new wheat varieties with non-shattering qualities and stiffness of straw helped the diffusion of new harvesting machinery (Malenbaum 1953: 95). One important constraint was that the profitability of labour-saving, animal-powered harvesting machinery was highly dependent on finding suitable employment for the animals during the rest of the year. Even so, by the 1920s, reapers and reaper-binders were being found in southern Russia, not because they reduced costs, but because they lifted the capacity constraints imposed by the harvest operations on the area that a family could dedicate to cereals with its own labour (Chayanov 1986: 188–9).[17]

While family farms in North America increased in size because of inexpensive land, cheap work animals, and new, labour-saving farm machinery, most European farmers were seriously constrained by the amounts of land that could be brought under the plough and the fragmented nature of

Table 3.1 Changing labour requirements in grain production

	Traditional methods	*Modern machinery*
Ist ploughing	2.0	0.5
Ist harrowing	0.6	0.1
2nd ploughing	2.0	–
2nd harrowing	0.6	–
Seeding	0.5	0.1
3rd harrowing	0.6	–
Harvesting	4.0	0.1
Carting	1.0	1.0
Threshing	8.0	0.4
Total	19.4	2.4

Source Allen (2003: table 4.5)

farms.[18] Large producers in regions such as East Anglia (England) or Ile-de-France did remain competitive as tractors cut the labour costs for preparing the land for sowing and the harvest operations were fully mechanized (Brown 1989: 100–3; Perren 1995: 48). The same was also true on some of the latifundios in southern Europe, although mechanization here left many landless labourers without alternative employment (Reis 1982; Cabral Chamorro 2000). In Eastern Europe, however, the small family farms significantly reduced the potential for labour-saving machinery, and the Danubian Countries (Bulgaria, Hungary, Rumania, and Yugoslavia) saw their share of world's wheat exports fall from 15 to 6% between 1909/13 and 1927/31 (Hevesy 1940: app. 10).[19]

Land constraints, cheap labour, and fragmented farms therefore limited the number of tractors in Europe to 270 thousand in 1939, or 17% of those found in North America, despite similar areas of arable (Svennilson 1954: 250).[20] In Germany, tractor numbers jumped from 24,183 to 66,000 between 1933 and 1939, but in England there were still only 40,000 in 1938, mostly found on farms of over 120 hectares (Wunderlich 1961: 184; Howkins 2003: 65). Figures elsewhere were less, with 26,792 tractors in France in 1929, 23,662 in Italy in 1931, and 4,000 in Spain in 1932 (Yates 1940: 258; Schmidt 1938: 59; Simpson 1995a: 245).

Yet family farmers showed interest in new technologies when they promised to increase output or redistribute workloads better over the year. Farmers in Galicia (northern Spain), a region of minuscule and heavily fragmented farms, accounted for just 5% of the nation's cereals but 20% of its threshing machines, as these reduced the labour demands in harvesting, a task which coincided with hay-making and milking (Fernández Prieto 1997: 139–42).[21] Much of Europe's rural poverty was not the result of family farmers being uninterested in improving production techniques, but rather the lack of incentives and resources needed for them to change.

New World cereal farmers expanded cultivation during the high prices of the First World War and, following the hostilities, continued to increase output as European production recovered, leading to global overproduction and the collapse in prices in the late 1920s (Table 3.2). Some European producers diversified away from cereals, but many more benefited from tariffs and other forms of protection that raised domestic prices well above world levels (Chapter 9). In agricultural-based economies especially, small family farmers continued to grow cereals because they offered alternatives *after* the harvest of either selling the crop if prices were attractive, or using them for their family and animals when they were not.[22] Family farmers survived because greater self-sufficiency in grains was a logical response to unfavourable market conditions, rather than irrational behaviour as many state agronomists and foreign travellers believed (Kopsidis 2012). It explains, for example, why desperately poor sharecroppers in Extremadura (Spain) grew cereals on tiny plots alongside large latifundios producing the same crop, using labour-saving technologies.

The fact that in Northern Europe many farmers sold relatively small amounts of their produce and grew crops to feed their animals also offered some protection against low cereal prices. As the American economist Karl Brandt noted at the height of the Great Depression, large, specialized

Table 3.2 Long-run changes in wheat cultivation and output

	New World Exporters			*European exporters*			*European importers**		
	Acreage	*Output*	*Yield*	*Acreage*	*Output*	*Yield*	*Acreage*	*Output*	*Yield*
1899–04	124	124	100	110	108	99	99	109	109
1909–14	140	151	108	120	129	108	101	115	114
1924–29	188	220	117	142	132	92	90	109	120
1934–39	209	184	88	163	165	101	101	141	140

1889–94 = 100; * Spain is excluded

Source calculated from Malenbaum (1953: appendices, tables 1 and 2). European exporters include Bulgaria. Hungary, Romania, Yugoslavia, and Poland

farms prospered in good times but suffered at times of depression. He continued (in (Royal Institute of International Affairs 1932: 278):

> ... I do not believe that there is any proof to-day that the American wheat farmer in Kansas is really able to produce wheat at a cheaper rate than the European peasant farmer. The latter produces all kinds of grain as by-products in the range of many other products, and has a very different criterion of costs, because work is well distributed all the year round and because manuring utilizes another by-product.

This diversity, made possible by Northern Europe's ample summer rainfall, was common on all farms, regardless of size. In England, it was noted in the late 1930s that 'farming is such a complex interlocking enterprise that it is not always easy to abandon the cultivation of a single crop – however unprofitable it may be', while in Denmark changes in 'one part of the farm ... necessitated changes in other areas' (Astor and Rowntree 1939: 128; Jensen 1937: 282). This flexibility contrasts with areas where low summer rainfall required extensive cereal farming, and mechanization threatened to eliminate even the little work available. For Warriner (1939: 97), low yields in Eastern Europe were the result of land being 'cultivated which, with the present resources of the world, ought not to be cultivated at all as arable land and need not be, if the farm population of these countries were free to move'.

3.3 Dairy Production and Market Specialization

Dairying was considered as an ideal occupation for family farmers because it produced a high-valued product that required plenty of skilled labour with few seasonal peaks, and a constant income over the year.[23] Liquid milk was especially valuable if farmers could sell directly to the consumer, but manufacturing butter and cheese for more distant markets could also be highly profitable.[24] From the late nineteenth century major advances were achieved in those areas of North-Western Europe which benefited from good natural pastures, rapid communications, and high consumer incomes. Europe's dairy industry however remained heavily segmented, and some 22% of the milk in France was fed to calves, leaving a third for drinking, 31% for making butter, and 14% for cheese (International Institute de Agriculture 1924: 25). Poor communications, low incomes, and expensive feed restricted dairy specialization, although the multi-purpose house cow was common when pastures were abundant.

Milk's high nutritional value made it an important food during the early stages of the European nutritional transition (Hernández Adell and Pujol-Andreu 2016: 187). However, it was highly perishable, especially in the absence of pasteurization and refrigeration, requiring production to be located near to consumers, or connected to them by good communications. Milk could also transmit disease, most notably bovine tuberculosis and, while it had become England's most valuable farm commodity by the 1930s, the medical profession remained 'torn between a general belief in the valuable nutritional qualities of milk and legitimate misgivings as to the quality of much of the milk supplied' (Astor and Rowntree 1939: 60). Converting milk into butter or cheese, when done under hygienic conditions, helped extend product life, although the small scale of farm production restricted market opportunities.[25] The skimmed milk left after butter- and cheese-making could be fed to pigs, as suggested by the Danish saying that 'the pig hangs on the cow's tail'.[26] Calves were slaughtered for veal, or fattened for beef, and milch cows used for meat once their productive life had ended. On the eve of the Great War, the relative importance of animal produce in final agricultural output was positively linked to living standards when measured by GDP per capita (Table 3.3).

The Danish dairy farm was heavily export orientated, specializing in high quality butter and bacon. Milk was easily transported across the comparatively flat country, while the fact that no farm was more than

Table 3.3 Final agricultural output and GDP per capita in different European countries, c.1910

	Denmark	*UK*	*Germany*	*Neth*	*France*	*Italy*	*Spain*	*Bulgaria*	*Portugal*
Non-animal	18	25.3	33.7	38.0	54.9	68.1	68.3	66.3	76.9
Animal	82	74.7	66.3	62.0	45.1	31.9	31.7	34.7	23.1
GDP per capita, 1913	3768	5176	4181	3539	3245	2721	2057	1450	1257

Sources Just (2010: table 9.1), O'Brien and Prados de la Escosura (1992: table 3), Ivanov and Tooze (2007: table 2), Broadberry and Klein (2012: table 7), Lains (2009: 343)

50 kilometres from the coast facilitated rapid and cheap communications to industrial Britain and the Rhineland (Yates 1940: 27–8, 40). The short grazing season required cows to be stall-fed for seven months, but improved breeding, the introduction of all-year milking, and the greater use of bought-in animal feed helped increase milk yields from an annual 1,000 litres per cow in 1860 to 2,700 litres in 1914, and over 3,000 litres by the 1930s.[27] Family labour was kept fully employed, and the fact that 70% of cows were found in herds of less than fifteen animals made it easy to monitor their health and adapt feeding routines for individual animals to maximize milk production.[28] The growing use of written records, accounting practices, and systematic recording of milk yields by cattle associations also improved farming practices and animal breeding (Lampe and Sharp 2015: 1133; Yates 1940: 39).

Danish family farmers benefitted from the changes in factor prices in the second half of the nineteenth century and profited from the advances in animal breeding and feeding practices achieved by 'elite' farmers. While the family farm was efficient for milking, it lacked the necessary scale to process the milk and market the butter and bacon competitively. From the mid-1880s, Danish farmers created cooperatives which used new technologies (steam-powered separators, refrigeration, pasteurization) to capture the growing economies of scale found in manufacturing and help enforce the necessary quality controls to protect the 'Danish' brand in international markets. An affluent and educated class of family farmers successfully organized producer-driven commodity chains that accounted for 80% of the country's exports and build influential lobbies to defend their interests (Chapter 9). Danish cooperatives became an international model for how a highly adaptive 'peasant' farming could respond positively to rapid technological change by creating new institutional structures (Lampe and Sharp 2018: ch.11). Yet few European farmers, especially outside the North Sea area, were as well placed geographically *and* had the luck to develop expertise in an agricultural commodity (butter) which 'combined both a relatively high-income elastic of demand and an industrial production technology' that farmers could control (Lampe and Sharp 2018: 18).[29]

Specialized dairy farming grew much more slowly in Southern and Eastern Europe because of poor pastures and expensive feed, high transport costs, and weak consumer demand. High urban milk prices allowed stall-fed animals in Madrid to produce yields of almost 3,000 litres a year by 1930, but production accounted for less than 3% of the country's total.[30] Instead, Northern Spain produced almost three-quarters of Spain's milk, benefitting from cheap feed because of abundant summer rainfall, but located so far from urban markets that farmers had no incentive to increase annual yields above 1,000 litres (Simpson 1995a: table 8.6). Nevertheless, the region of Galicia once again provides a classic example of inventive farmers struggling under the constraints of insufficient land and geographical isolation.[31] Farmers, often on miniscule holdings, increased farm output by 73% per hectare and 82% per worker between 1910 and 1930, by when livestock products accounted for 44% of total output (Simpson 1995b: app. 2c). Farmers, despite the lack of fast, cheap communications with Madrid or the industrial Basque Country, showed great ingenuity and hard work in improving soil quality by using natural compost as fertilizer, and growing a wide variety of labour-intensive crops (maize, potatoes, vines).[32] There was a growing local interest in scientific plant breeding and veterinary science, and Galician farmers specialized in a breed of cattle most suited to local conditions, namely a multi-purpose animal that provided calves to be sold; milk for home consumption; sufficient strength to plough or transport farm produce; manure that would replenish soils; and still be suitable for meat when their working life was over (Fernández Prieto 2001: 131–2).

Although Galician farmers enjoyed ample summer rainfall, those in much of Southern and Eastern Europe suffered from poor natural pastures. For Warriner (1939: 98), 'the line which divides the regions of intensive and extensive live-stock production can be drawn across Central Europe; on one side of it is Germany, the Western half of Czechoslovakia and Hungary west of the Danube; and east of it the Hungarian Plain, Slovakia, Jugoslavia, Rumania, and Central Poland'. Nevertheless, the primacy of cereals encouraged even small farmers to own a work animal to prepare the land for sowing, resulting in most cows being underfed as farmers could rarely afford to purchase feed. Milk supplies in the few large cities were often primitive and only 20% in Belgrade in the early 1930s was purchased from stores, with the rest bought directly from traders and farmers arriving from neighbouring villages, a large percentage of which was considered unfit for consumption (Tomasevich 1955: 514, 605).[33]

3.4 Vines, Grapes, and Wines

While natural resource restrictions in the Mediterranean regions made intensive cereal and livestock husbandry difficult, their warm summers and mild winters were ideal for viticulture, olive and fruit trees, crops that could provide significant and remunerative employment for family workers *and* high output per hectare. Wine production in France, Italy, and Spain accounted for almost three-quarters of world production on the eve of the Second World War, and with Portugal and Romania, four-fifths. Yet the area of vines in Europe increased by only 0.5% between 1900/09 and 1930/39, and production by 15%.[34] Viticulture, despite its importance in Southern Europe, had become a mature industry by the interwar years.

Most grapes and wines were produced on family-owned farms. Vineyards were rarely rented because tenants would be tempted to maximize short-term output, thereby damaging the productive life of the vineyard, although sharecropping was common in places such as Beaujolais, Tuscany, and Catalonia (Carmona and Simpson 2023). In France there were perhaps 1.5 million winegrowers, with the vast majority combining wine-making with other activities, and much of their production being for home consumption (Lachiver 1988).[35] The labour-intensive nature of viticulture, especially in the clearing and planting of vines, and the fact that they thrived on marginal soils for other crops, made it ideal for poor labourers to create an asset.[36] In Italy, approximately three-quarters of all vines, accounting for half production, were grown alongside other crops as a means to reduce risk (Federico and Martinelli 2023: 2). Traditional wine-making was skilled, but unscientific, and quality varied significantly from year-to-year, being heavily influenced by the weather and levels of hygiene under which it was made. Most wines were consumed locally before the railways appeared, and drunk, or distilled, within the year.[37]

The organization and production of 'fine' wines, such as port, sherry, claret, or champagne were very different, but accounted for less than five percent of volume.[38] Production was highly specialized, land prices high, and owners used a wide variety of formal and informal labour contracts to guarantee the supply of quality grapes (Carmona and Simpson 2012). Fine wines were often exported, increasingly under private or collective brands (regional denominations) (Simpson 2011). Most attempts by producers of cheap wines to switch to fine wines were unsuccessful, even when the vineyard was well-located, planted with healthy vines, and owned by a skilled producer. Significant capital requirements were needed to build and equip a modern winery, and then mature the wine for several years. As quality was also highly dependent on the vintage, little or no wine could be sold in poor years if the winery's reputation was to be maintained. Even if producers met these conditions, they still had to convince consumers it was worth paying a premium for their wine, develop a brand that was easy to identify, and be willing to protect it from imitations in the courts. These were formidable problems and the large modern wineries that began appearing in Rioja (Spain) from the late nineteenth century enjoyed only limited success in the interwar period, while even the established Bordeaux growers made heavy losses at times (Mees 2023: chs.9–10; Roudié 1994: ch. 7).

The appearance of phylloxera, a plant louse introduced in France in 1863 from the United States, eventually destroyed virtually all of Europe's vines. Phylloxera was especially destructive in the Midi (southern France) in the 1870s and 1880s but replanting with phylloxera-resistant American vines led to a wine revolution. Commercial viticulture moved from the hills to the plains, and the heavy use of artificial fertilizers, pesticides, and fungicides with the new grape varieties and hybrids produced large quantities of cheap watery wines. These were made more drinkable by blending them with strong Algerian wines. New technologies greatly increased the scale of wine-making (*la viticulture industrielle*) and, by controlling the temperature during fermentation, large volumes of consistently drinkable table wines were now produced in hot climates (Augé-Laribé 1907). By the interwar years the Midi and colonial Algeria accounted for half of all France's production (Table 3.4).

Table 3.4 Wine output in France, the Midi, and Algeria, 1870s–1930s

	France	*Midi*	*Algeria*	*Midi & Algeria share of total (%)*
1870–9	5158	1506	23	29.5
1880–9	2989	895	128	32.8
1890–9	3621	1486	396	46.8
1900–9	5583	2223	678	46.3
1910–9	4319	2081	758	55.8
1920–9	5998	2646	948	51.5
1930–9	5876	2512	1717	55.7

Source Lachiver (1988: 582–611). The Midi includes the *départements* of the Aude, Gard, Hérault and Pyrénées-Orientales

The profitability of these large vertically integrated, capital-intensive wineries were threatened by the mass production of cheap 'artificial' wines made from industrial alcohol. The Griffe Law of 1889 made selling wines made from anything other than fresh grapes illegal, but enforcement remained slack. Against a background of low prices, the large Midi producers organized regional demonstrations against artificial wines, culminating in half a million people taking to the streets in Montpellier in June 1907. The government responded by giving legal powers to the *Confédération générale des vignerons du Midi* (CGV), the winegrowers' association, to police and initiate legal proceeding against those making or selling artificial wines. The granting of powers to a private body created a precedent not just for the French wine industry, but also for future relations between governments and the farm sector everywhere (Chapter 9).

All European governments taxed alcohol consumption heavily and restricted imports to protect their domestic industries, causing wine exports to decline by half in the interwar period.[39] Consumption in producer countries grew only slowly because of the low price and income elasticities of demand for wine.[40] The long-run tendency for overproduction was caused a combination of weak demand and by growers being reluctant to uproot plants during periods of low prices because of the high costs of creating vineyards. Instead, growers responded to swings in demand by varying their use of fertilizers and pesticides, causing the industry to lurch 'from crisis to crisis' (Lachiver 1988: ch.8).

The high transport costs and family nature of production implied that despite the growing importance of large-scale wine-making, an important part of the industry remained small scale. In Italy the largest 7,932 wineries had an average capacity of over 1,400 hectolitres (equivalent to 200,000 bottles, or 56 hectares of vines), but they accounted for only a third of production in 1938 (Federico and Martinelli 2018: tables 5.2, 5.4). In France, family wineries with a capacity of less than 400 hectolitres (or ten hectares) accounted for half the Midi's wine and 86.5% in the rest of the country in 1934 (Galet 2004, my calculation). Influential French writers, such as Charles Gide (1926), Michel Augé-Laribé (1907), or Adrian Berget (1902), saw cooperatives as the solution to the need of small growers to improve wine quality, by allowing them to benefit from the new scientific wine-making methods overseen by qualified chemists, as well as strengthening their bargaining position in the lengthening commodity chains (Simpson 2000). Nevertheless, despite some notable exceptions in the Midi and Catalonia, cooperative wine-making would be largely a post-World War II phenomenon (Fernández and Simpson 2017; Garrido 2022).

Viticulture, in spite of its slow growth in interwar Europe, remained an important part of agriculture, and wine was an integral part of diets in producer countries. Yet both the direction of technological change and the failure to create a strong cooperative movement had major economic and political consequences. The interests of winegrowers were more diverse than those of cereal farmers, with fine wine producers looking to limit output and create restrictive regional appellations, while large producers in the Midi, La Mancha, or Puglia, wished to maximize volume to lower unit costs. In France, in particular, the shift of viticulture from the hills to the plains produced a distinction between intensive, high-yielding 'capitalist' viticulture, and low-yield, labour-intensive, 'peasant' farming (Carmona and Simpson 1999: 307; 2012: 902). Where the steep terrain made ploughing difficult, such as the Priorat in Catalonia, vines were not replanted after phylloxera (Perpinyá i Grau 1932). Viticulture remained important, but many Europeans worked their vines only part-time, and wine was a supplementary income for farmers and families working in other professions, such as shopkeepers, teachers, and craftsmen.

3.5 Mediterranean Family Farmers and Export Specialization

Just as many farmers in the rich industrial regions of North-Western Europe could specialize in intensive livestock farming, so those in the Mediterranean regions enjoyed growing export demand for labour-intensive fruit and horticulture crops. In the half century before the Second World War, crops such as citrus fruit (Spain, Italy), dried fruits (Greece, Spain), tobacco (Greece, Bulgaria) made a significant contribution to regional economic development. This growth might have been even stronger if California (and to a lesser extent, Florida) had not developed their own specialist production, shutting European producers out of the rapidly growing US market. After looking at specialist production of currants in Greece and oranges in Spain, the nature of Californian competition is discussed briefly.

Greek currants had long been exported from the Peloponnese to the United Kingdom for use in confectionery, but it was French demand to meet the phylloxera-induced wine shortages that sent exports and prices soaring in the early 1880s. Currants accounted for 55% of all Greek exports by 1886–90 but prices halved after French growers replanted their vines and new taxes were imposed that made raisin wines uncompetitive (Morilla Critz et al. 2000: 221, Sempé 1898: 102; Simpson 2011: 60–63). Growers, as elsewhere, were reluctant to uproot their vines because of the marginal nature of the land and the possibilities, however remote, that prosperity might return one day (Mazower 1991: 82–3). Instead, the Peloponnese witnessed large-scale emigration in the two decades before 1914.[41]

Unlike vines, the area suitable for producing citrus fruit was severely limited by the risks from late frosts and the need for irrigation during the hot summers. In Spain, orange orchards covered over 73,000 hectares by 1936, mostly around Valencia, with four-fifths of growers having less than a hectare, and over 85% of the crop exported (Garrido 2010; Pinilla and Ayuda 2009: 200; Font de Mora 1954: 309). Exports grew from 510 thousand tons in 1910/14 to 937 thousand in 1929/33, equivalent to half the world's total in both dates, and accounted for 12% of all Spanish exports by the 1930s (Simpson 1995a: table 9.5; Prados de la Escosura 1988: table 6.6). Indeed, for most of the period it was cheaper to send the fruit from Valencia to northern Europe by boat than by rail to Madrid.[42] The growing export demand encouraged the development of tube-well technologies to create new areas of irrigated land, although orchards also displaced other crops on the older irrigated areas. The heavy planting costs and intensive use of artificial fertilizers and pesticides created significant backward linkages, while preparing and packing the fruit for export added a further 50% to the farm-gate price (Abad García 1984; Palafox 1985; Simpson 1992: 133–6). Cooperatives were formed to select, pack, and ship the oranges, but struggled to guarantee quality, as ripe and unripe fruit were often mixed and sold in the final markets (Garrido 2014). Even so, profitability was sufficiently high for the area of orchards to double from 20,000 to 40,500 hectares in Valencia between 1922 and 1932 (Simpson 1995a: table 6.7).

Mediterranean Europe enjoyed considerable export success in specialist fruit and horticulture products, but commodity chains were often weak, and quality poorer than that of Californian producers. Protective tariffs from the 1870s helped transform California's agriculture from one of extensive cereals to intensive crops, with 'massive investments in transportation networks, water supply systems, and biological learning' leading to the output of citrus, raisins, prunes, figs, almonds, and walnuts all increasing by 'nearly a 100-fold' between the early 1880s and early 1930s (Morilla Critz et al. 1999: 318). Yet, despite producing and delivering better quality products to consumers than most European farmers, they experienced only limited success in world markets, highlighting both the achievements of some Mediterranean farmers, but also the obstacles for them to develop new markets (Morilla Critz et al. 1999: 318).

The success of California is perhaps surprising given the labour-intensive nature of horticulture and fact that farm wages were 'four to eight times' higher than those in the Mediterranean (Morilla Critz et al. 1999, 2000: 208). According to one US study, while labour requirements in wheat in 1939 were only 22 man-hours per hectare, lemon production required 706 hours, grapes 457 hours, oranges 385 hours, and prunes 284 hours (Cooper et al. 1943, cited in Morilla Critz et al. 1999: 321). California's farms were heavily mechanized, and horses, tractors, and small trucks moved freely between widely spaced trees. Californian farmers could also draw on a highly mobile casual labour force which was contracted for specific tasks. By contrast most farms in Valencia were family owned and worked by hand, requiring little wage labour, and allowing significantly greater density of trees than in California (415 against 220 per hectare), and achieving slightly better yields (2.6 boxes per tree against 2.4).

Farm operations represented only *one* phase in the lengthening commodity chains, and in the United States, machinery was also widely used in the cleaning, grading, processing, packaging, and shipping of produce. Producers, by improving grading and quality controls, removed substandard fruit, allowing the use of brand names, and developing reputations for quality. US oranges, for example, sold for over three times those of Spanish ones on international markets, and almost twice the price of those from Italy and South Africa, between 1922 and 1926 (Morilla Critz et al. 1999: 324). However, production costs in Spain were much lower, resulting in Californian producers selling quality fruit at the top end of the market, but Spanish growers capturing the much larger, cheaper segments (Table 3.5). This type of market segmentation was also found with other commodities, most notably wine and olive oil (Ramón Muñoz 2000).

Table 3.5 Production and shipping costs of oranges delivered to the UK, c.1934

	South Africa	*California*	*Brazil*	*Spain*	*Palestine*
Growing fruit	2.50	2.75	1.33	1.00	2.00
Handling	2.75	2.17	2.67	3.00	3.50
Inland transport	1.25	0.67	0.83	0.00	0.00
Freight	2.92	3.67	3.50	1.08	1.17
Other costs	1.50	1.50	1.50	1.50	1.75
TOTAL	10.92	10.76	9.83	6.50	8.42
Duty	0.00	2.50	2.50	1–2.5	1–2.5
TOTAL	10.9	13.3	12.3	7.6–9.1	9.4–10.9
% Share of UK market 1931*	9.3	8.1	10.8	57.4	12.6
TOTAL	10.92	13.26	12.33	7.58–9.08	9.42–10.92

Figures in shillings per box

Sources Neumark (1938: 113), cited in Pinilla and Ayuda (2009, table 7.4), Abad García (1984: 254)

[a]Figures for California include other US states, and those for Palestine include Egypt. Other countries accounted for 1.7% of total.

3.6 Conclusions

The increase in the global supply of new farm technologies from the late 1870s significantly widened the gap found in farming methods and productivity between industrial and agricultural-based economies. Growing market integration implied that farm prices were no longer fixed locally, but by national if not international shifts in supply and demand. Economic development changed the nature of cyclical fluctuations within the sector, as farm profitability became increasingly linked to the business cycle, rather than the weather.

Small family farmers transformed European agriculture in the half century prior to the Second World War. The family farm was highly flexible, shifting labour between commodities to take advantage of swings in market demand. Family labour moved out of agriculture for short periods when more remunerative employment was available, but usually returned at moments of peak demand in the agricultural year. The fact that family farms preferred traditional technologies and were slow to modify farming systems usually reflected market opportunities, rather than a reluctance to change. Yet if world trade in agricultural products increased three times faster than farm output between 1870 and 1914, both indicators stagnated and moved together in the interwar years (Federico 2006: 28).[43] Many of the difficulties of interwar farming are to be explained by the fewer export opportunities, rather than any supposed inferiority of the family farm to large farms using wage labour.

The commodities discussed in this chapter illustrate the varied nature of Europe's farming. Natural resource endowments in the North-West were particularly favourable for livestock and labour-intensive farming, but the lack of summer rainfall made these activities difficult elsewhere. Rich consumers and cheap animal feed encouraged commercial dairy farming, with cows producing milk yields in excess of 3,000 litres a year, while in less favourable areas they rarely exceeded 1,000 litres, and the animals were kept for a variety of uses, including ploughing and transport. Artificial fertilizers promised to transform arable farming, but their profitability required cereal prices to be above, and often considerably above, world levels. Mechanization of the cereal harvest could bring large savings in labour *and* increase the area that a family could cultivate, but the extra work animals had to be profitably employed during the rest of the year.

Viticulture was traditionally a crop suited for small farmers, especially in areas of dry-farming. Yet small growers now found it increasingly difficult to compete against large producers because of the economies of scale they enjoyed in wine-making with cheap table wines, while they lacked the necessary capital to produce fine wines. Specialization in high-value Mediterranean export crops such as oranges or tobacco were also highly profitable at times, but the absence of suitable land limited the areas of production, while prosperity often depended as much on trade policies of North-Western European countries as farm efficiency.

Family farmers were highly competitive but found themselves at an increasing disadvantage in the lengthening food chains, both as buyers of farm inputs and the processing, storing, and marketing of farm output. California's horticultural farmers benefitted greatly from government-funded scientific research, access to large amounts of cheap capital, efficient storage and rapid transport, and modern marketing methods that attracted consumers, and limited fraud and mislabelling. Yet without the Federal government protecting their domestic markets, even California's farmers would have struggled. Government intervention was important, everywhere.

Notes

1. From 208 million in 1850 to 393 million in 1950, excluding Russia.
2. Assumes that creameries and bacon factories were agricultural, rather than industrial concerns.
3. Productivity growth in agriculture in developed economies is often faster than other sectors of the economy (Federico 2006: 2).
4. Agriculture contributed 29% of Bulgaria's exports in 1929 (Feinstein et al. 1997: 59). Dietary improvements in Bulgaria are discussed in Chapter 6.
5. For contemporary rural societies, Banerjee and Duflo (2011: 208–12, 233).
6. The areas assume a gross income of 5,000 pesetas. Caziot (1914) suggested a figure of between 8 and 20 hectares in France, depending on region, soil fertility, and type of crop, while the Peasant Party in Romania gave a figure of 3 hectares in the highlands, 5 hectares in lowlands, and 10 hectares in the newly settled regions (Mitrany 1930:194).
7. Yates (1940: 138, 208) for the advantages of renting over ownership in Belgium and the Netherlands, although rented farms were in 'a much more dilapidated condition'.
8. The three Fs—Fair rent, Fixed tenure, and Free sale. Conditions were such by 1945 that many tenants in Belgium, France, or the Netherlands preferred to invest in livestock and farm machinery rather than buy more land (Swinnen 2002: 391).
9. Figures for Denmark, Norway, and Sweden refer to the number of holdings, not area.
10. Tatu Vanhanen (1984) provides figures for the relative importance of the family farm in 119 countries between 1850 and 1979, which he defines as being 'mainly cultivated by the holder family or, if leased, tenancy does not make the tenant cultivator socially and economically dependent on the landowner' (35). Although it is not clear how Vanhanen came by his estimates, he shows the family farm increasing in importance during the period in all European countries, except for Portugal where it remained stable, and his figures generally coincide with those that will be shown in Table 6.2.

11. The sheep were folded at night and trampled their manure into the soil. For Germany, Perkins (1982: 78), and the decline in Spanish numbers, González Garrido (1941: 399–402).
12. In the United States, significant scientific research was required just to keep cereal yields stable (Olmstead and Rhode 2002).
13. For different interpretations of these changes, see the contributions in Campbell and Overton (eds) (1991). Changes had begun in the Middle Ages in the Po Valley (Italy) and parts of the Netherlands (Federico 2006: 88–89). Transport improvements also encouraged regional specialization and higher wheat yields in seventeenth-century England (Kussmaul 1990: ch. 5).
14. Northern France and south-eastern United States were notable exceptions to the general shift to mechanize and extend cultivation in dry lands (Malenbaum 1953: 96).
15. Mangon (1875), for a contemporary calculation of potential energy savings with draught animals and farm implements.
16. The sickle remained popular in Mediterranean countries because less grain was lost (Simpson 1995a: 155).
17. Olmstead and Rhode (2001: 676) make a similar argument for the diffusion of the tractor in the interwar period in the United States.
18. The US family cereal farm increased tenfold in size between 1914 and the 1970s (Drache 1976, cited in Offer 1989: 112).
19. These refer to post-First World War boundaries. New World producers also benefitted from cheaper transportation and lower storage and marketing costs.
20. There was one tractor per 615 hectares in Europe, compared to one per 138 hectares in North America. Figures exclude the Soviet Union.
21. The small size and uneven nature of many fields made the use of mechanical reapers very difficult.
22. Feed grains in this period sold for about 20% less than wheat, a difference which exceeded 'any advantage which wheat might have in nutritive content' (Malenbaum 1953: 75).
23. Seasonal peaks were not entirely eliminated, as cereals and haymaking were usually associated with dairy farming.
24. In theory, surplus milk could be used for manufacturing powdered or condensed milk, but few farmers were sufficiently close to a factory.

25. Small quantities were used to produce powdered and condensed milk.
26. In Denmark 94% of all skimmed milk after butter production was fed to pigs (Yates 1940: 46).
27. Year-round milking also allowed cooperative dairy equipment to be more fully utilized (Henriksen and O'Rourke 2005; Henriksen 2009: 125). Milk yields in Lampe and Sharp (2015: 1136), Yates (1940: 39).
28. In the late nineteenth century, one milkmaid could look after up to 20 cows. Only 6.6 farmers had more than 20 cows (Yates 1940: 43). Even if milk was not processed on-farm, additional labour was needed for cleaning the shippen, producing and preparing the animal feed, and pig farming.
29. For farmers controlling commodity chains, Gereffi et al. (1994), Simpson (2011: 77–9).
30. It is assumed that there were 14,000 cows in urban dairies in Madrid, each producing 3,000 litres of milk a year. Calculated from Hernández Adell and Pujol-Andreu (2016: 192, app. 1.3).
31. In 1930 male workers had on average just 2.7 hectares, and the first Cadastre (1959) shows that the number of holdings outnumbered the total active population by a 26 to 1 (Malefakis 1970: 17–18).
32. Per capita meat consumption in Madrid was still around 30 kilos per annum in 1930 (Gómez Mendoza and Simpson 1988: app. 2).
33. Blasco Ibañez, in his novel *La Barraca*, describes women from the neighbouring villages taking their cows to be milked in the streets of Valencia.
34. Production figures refer to 1930–9 and include the French colony Algeria, being 63% and 72%, respectively, when it is excluded. Area figures exclude Russia (Anderson et al. 2017: tables 121; 132).
35. In Italy, small growers numbered 'hundreds of thousands' (Federico and Martinelli 2018: 130).
36. In Zaragoza growers planted vineyards, which they then sold to purchase plots of irrigated land (Rivera y Casanova 1897: 93–4).
37. Fine wines were always produced within easy reach of a navigable river or seaport.
38. Lachiver (1988: 496), gives 10%, but this figure refers to regional appellations, not all of which were fine wines. Other estimates are 4.5% Italy in 1938 and 6.7% in Spain in 1932 (Federico and

Martinelli 2018: Table 5.4 and Spain, Ministerio de Agricultura 1933: cuadro 68).

39. Falling from an average of 9.4 million hectolitres in 1909–13 to 8.1 million in 1928–32, and 4.7 million in 1934–8 (Pinilla 2014: table T.1). Fine wine producers also struggled.
40. Federico et al. (2019), estimate an income elasticity of 0.5 and a price elasticity of –0.3 for Italy in the half century prior to the Great War.
41. Greek currants production actually increased by 6% between 1886–90 and 1909–13, and was only 10% lower in 1921–5 than the late 1880s (Morilla Critz 1995: 303–4, my calculations). For emigration, see especially Petmezas (2009: 359).
42. It cost five times more to send a box of oranges to Madrid in 1914 than to ship to New York (Morilla Critz et al. 1999: fn. 10). Only when it became harder to export in the 1930s did some producers take more serious the domestic market.
43. This author notes that the calculations require 'some daring assumptions'.

References

Abad García, Vicente. 1984. *Historia de la Naranja (1781–1939)*. Valencia: Comité de Gestión de la Exportación de Frutos Cítricos.

Allen, Douglas W., and Dean Lueck. 2002. *The Nature of the Farm. Contracts, Risk, and Organization in Agriculture*. Cambridge, Massachusetts and London: MIT Press.

Allen, Robert C. 2003. *Farm to Factory. A Reinterpretation of the Soviet Industrial Revolution*. Princeton: Princeton University Press.

Anderson, K., S. Nelgen, and V. Pinilla. 2017. *Global Wine Markets, 1860 to 2016: A Statistical Compendium*. Adelaide: University of Adelaide.

Astor, Viscount, and B. Seebohm Rowntree. 1939. *British Agriculture the Principles of Future Policy*. London: Penguin.

Augé-Laribé, Michel 1907. *Le problème agraire du socialisme: la viticulture industrielle du Midi de la France*. Paris: Giard & Brère.

Bairoch, Paul. 1989. "Les trois révolutions agricoles du monde développé: rendements et productivité de 1800 a 1985." *Annales ESC* (2): 317–353.

Banerjee, Abhijit V., and Esther Duflo. 2011. *Poor Economics. A Radical Rethinking of the Way to Fight Global Poverty*. New York: PublicAffairs.

Berget, Adrien. 1902. *La coopération dans la viticulture européenne: étude d'économie rurale et d'histoire agronomique*. Lille: A. Decos.

Boserup, Ester. 1965. *The Conditions of Agricultural Growth*. New York: Aldine.

Broadberry, S., and Alexander Klein. 2012. "Aggregate and Per Capita GDP in Europe, 1870–2000: Continental, Regional and National Data with Changing Boundaries." *Scandinavian Economic History Review* 60: 79–107.

Brown, Jonathan. 1989. *Agriculture in England: A Survey of Farming, 1870–1947*. Manchester: Manchester University.

Cabral Chamorro, Antonio. 2000. *Renovación tecnológica y mecanización de la agricultura en Cádiz (1850–1932)*. Cadiz: Universidad de Cádiz.

Campbell and Overton, eds. 1991. *Land, Labour and Livestock: Historical Studies in Agricultural Productivity*. Manchester: Manchester University Press.

Carmona, Juan, and James Simpson. 1999. "The "Rabassa Morta" in Catalan Viticulture: The Rise and Decline of a Long-Term Sharecropping Contract, 1670s–1920s." *The Journal of Economic History* 59: 290–315.

Carmona, Juan, and James Simpson. 2003. *El laberinto de la agricultura española. Instituciones, contratos y organización entre 1850 y 1936*. Zaragoza: PUZ.

Carmona, Juan, and James Simpson. 2012. "Explaining Contract Choice: Vertical Co-ordination, Sharecropping, and Wine, Europe 1850–1950." *The Economic History Review* 65 (3): 887–909.

Carmona, Juan, and James Simpson. 2023. "Landlords and Sharecroppers in Wine Producing Regions: Beaujolais, Catalonia and Tuscany, 1800–1940." In *Global Agricultural Workers from the 17th to the 21st Century*, edited by Rolf Bauer and Elise van Nederveen Meerkerk, 91–113. Leiden & Boston: Brill.

Caziot, Pierre. 1914. *La Valeur de la terre en France*. Paris: Baillière.

Chayanov, A.V. 1986. *The Theory of Peasant Economy*. Manchester: Manchester University Press.

Collins, E.J.T. 1969. "Labour Supply and Demand in European Agriculture, 1800–1880." In *Agrarian Change and Economic Development. The Historical Problems*, edited by E. L. Jones and S.J Woolf. London: Methuen.

Cooper, M.R., W.C.Holley, and H.W.Hawthorne. 1943. *Labor Requirements for Crops and Livestock, Farm Management Reports no. 40*. Washington: DC: USDA.

Crafts, N.F.R. 1985. *British Economic Growth during the Industrial Revolution*. Oxford: Claredon.

Dovring, Folke. 1965. *Land and Labor in Europe in the Twentieth Century: A Comparative Survey of Recent Agrarian History*. The Hague M. Nijhoff.

Drache, H.M. 1976. "Midwest Agriculture: Changing with Technology." *Agricultural History*: 290–302.

Federico, Giovanni. 2006. *Feeding the World. An Economic History of Agriculture, 1800–1900*. Princeton: Princeton University Press.

Federico, Giovanni, and Pablo Martinelli Lasheras. 2023. "Risk Management in Traditional Agriculture: Intercropping in Italian WIne Production." *European Review of Economic History*. https://doi.org/10.1093/ereh/head017.

Federico, Giovanni, and Pablo Martinelli. 2018. "Italy to 1939." In *Wine Globalization. A New Comparative History*, edited by Kym Anderson and Vicente Pinilla, 130–52. Cambridge: Cambridge University Press.

Federico, Giovanni, A Nuvolari, and Michelangelo Vasta. 2019. "The Origins of Regional Divide: Evidence from Real Wages, 1861–1913." *The Journal of Economic History* 79 (1): 63–98.

Feinstein, Charles, Peter Temin, and Toniolo. 1997. *The European Economy Between the Wars*. Oxford: Oxford University Press.

Fernández, Eva, and James Simpson. 2017. "Producer Cooperatives, Institutional Change, and Politics in the Wine Industry, 1880–1980." *The Economic History Review* 70 (1): 122–142.

Fernández Prieto, Lourenzo. 1997. "Selección de innovaciones en una agricultura atlántica de pequeñas explotaciones. Galicia, 1900–1936. La adopción de las trilladoras mecánicas." *Noticiario de Historia Agraria* (14): 133–163.

Fernández Prieto, Lourenzo. 2001. "Caminos del cambio technológico en las agriculturas españolas contemporáneas." In *El pozo de todos los males. Sobre el atraso en la agricultura española contemporanea*, edited by J. Pujol, M. González de Molina, L. Fernández Prieto, D. Gallego Martínez and R. Garrabou, 95–146. Barcelona: Crítica.

Font de Mora, R. 1954. *El Naranja, su cultivo, explotación y comercio*, 3rd. ed. Madrid: Espasa-Calpe.

Foster, Andrew D., and Mark R. Rosenzweig. 2022. "Are There Too Many Farms in the World? Labor Market Transaction Costs, Machine Capacities, and Optimal Farm SIze." *Journal of Political Economy* 130: 636–680.

Galet, Pierre. 2004. *Cépages et vignobles de France. Tome III Les vignobles de France*. 2 vols. Paris: Tec & Doc.

Garrido, Samuel. 2010. "Oranges or "Lemons"? Family Farming and Product Quality in the Spanish Orange Industry, 1870–1960." *Agricultural History* (Spring): 224–243.

Garrido, Samuel. 2014. "Plenty of Trust, Not Much Cooperation: Social Capital and Collective Action in Early Twentieth Century Eastern Spain." *European Review of Economic History* 18 (4): 416–432.

Garrido, Samuel. 2022. "Por qué buena parte del vino europeo procede de compañías con mala reputación: las bodegas cooperativas en España y más allá." *Historia Agraria* (88): 7–40. https://doi.org/10.26882/histagrar.088e06g.

Gereffi, Gary, Miguel Korzeniewicz, and Roberto Korzeniewicz. 1994. "Introduction: Global Commodity Chains." In *Commodity Chains and Global*

Capitalism, edited by Gary Gereffi and Miguel Korzeniewicz. Westport and London.

Gide, Charles. 1926. *Les associations coopératives agricoles*. Paris: Association pour l'enseignement de la coopération.

Gómez Mendoza, A., and James Simpson. 1988. "El consumo de carne en Madrid durante el primer tercio del siglo XX." *Moneda y Crédito* 186: 57–91.

González Garrido, Justo. 1941. *La Tierra de Campos*. Valladolid: Santarén.

Grantham, George. 1991. "The Growth of Labour Productivity in the Production of Wheat in the Cinq Grosses Fermes of France, 1750–1929." In *Land, Labour and Livestock: Historical Studies in Agricultural Productivity*, edited by B. Campbell and M. Overton, 340–63. Manchester: Manchester University Press.

Griffiths, Clare V.J. 2007. *Labour and the Countryside. The Politics of Rural Britian*. Oxford: Oxford University Press.

Henriksen, Ingrid. 2009. "The Contribution of Agriculture to Economic Growth in Denmark, 1870–1939." In *Agriculture and Economic Development in Europe since 1870*, edited by Pedro Lains and Vicente Pinilla, 117–47. Abingdon: Routledge.

Henriksen, Ingrid, and Kevin O'Rourke. 2005. "Incentives, Technology and the Shift to Year-Round Dairying in Late Nineteenth-Century Denmark." *The Economic History Review* 58 (3): 520–554.

Hernández Adell, Ismael, and Josep Pujol-Andreu. 2016. "Economic Growth and Biological Innovation: The Development of the European Dairy Industry." *Rural History* 27 (2): 187–212.

Hevesy, Paul de. 1940. *World Wheat Planning and Economic Planning in General*. London, New York, Toronto: Oxford.

Howkins, Alun. 2003. *The Death of Rural England. A Social History of the Countryside since 1900*. London: Routledge.

Hussain, Athar, and Keith Tribe. 1981. *Marxism and the Agrarian Question. German Social Democracy and the Peasantry 1890–1907*. London: Macmillan.

International Institute de Agriculture. 1924. *Milk and Milk Products. Statistical Survey*. Rome: IIA.

Ivanov, M, and Adam Tooze. 2007. "Convergence or Decline on Europe's Southeastern Periphery? Agriculture, Population, and GNP in Bulgaria, 1892–1945." *The Journal of Economic History* 67: 672–703.

Jensen, E. 1937. *Danish Agriculture: its Economic Development*. Copenhagen: Schultz.

Just, F. 2010. "The Scandinavian Food System between Organization and State." In *Managing Crises and De-globalization. Nordic Foreign Trade and Exchange, 1919–39*, edited by S.O Olsson, 121–36. London: Routledge.

Kopsidis, MIchael. 2012. "Peasant Agriculture and Economic Growth: The Case of Southeast Europe c.1870–1940 reinterpreted." EHES Working Paper, 28.

Kussmaul, Ann. 1990. *A General View of the Rural Economy of England, 1538–1840*. Cambridge: Cambridge University Press.
Lachiver, Marcel. 1988. *Vins, vignes et vignerons. Histoire du vignoble français*. Paris: Fayard.
Lains, P. 2009. "Agriculture and Economic Devlopment in Portugal, 1870–1973." In *Agriculture and Economic Development in Europe since 1870*, edited by Pedro Lains and Vicente Pinilla, 333–52. London & New York: Routledge.
Lampe, Markus, and Paul Sharp. 2015. "Just Add Milk: A Productivity Analysis of the Revolutionary Changes in Nineteenth-Century Danish Dairying." *The Economic History Review* 68 (4): 1132–1153.
Lampe, Markus, and Paul Sharp. 2018. *A Land of Milk and Butter: How Elites Created the Modern Danish Dairy Industry*. Chicago: Chicago University Press.
League of Nations. 1939. *The Land Tenure Systems in Europe: Contributions by the International Institute of Agriculture, European Conference of Rural Life*, Geneva.
Malefakis, Edward. 1970. *Agrarian Reform and the Peasant Revolution in Spain: Origins of the Civil War*. New Haven: Yale University Press
Malenbaum, Wilfrid. 1953. *The World Wheat Economy, 1885–1939*. Cambridge, Mass.: Harvard.
Mangon, Hervé. 1875. *Travaux, instruments et machines agricoles*. Paris: Dunod.
Mazower, Mark. 1991. *Greece and the Inter-War Economic Crisis*. Oxford: Clarendon.
McCloskey, Donald. 1991. "The Prudent Peasant: New Findings on Open Fields." *The Journal of Economic History* 51–2: 343–55.
Mees, Ludger. 2023. *The History of Rioja Wine. Tradition and Invention. Routledge Studies of Gastronomy, Food and Drink*. London & New York: Routledge.
Mingay, G.E., ed. 1975. *Arthur Young and his Times*. London and Basingstoke: Macmillan.
Mitrany, David. 1930. *The Land and the Peasant in Rumania. The War and Agrarian Reform (1917–21)*. London: Milford.
Mitrany, David. 1951. *Marx Against the Peasant. A Study in Social Dogmatism*. London: Weidenfeld.
Morilla Critz, José. 1995. "La irrupción de California en el mercado de productos vitícolas y sus efectos en los países mediterráneos (1865–1925)." In *California y el Mediterráneo*, edited by José Morilla Critz. Madrid: Ministerio de Agricultura, Pesca y Alimentación.
Morilla Critz, Jose, Alan L. Olmstead, and Paul W. Rhode. 1999. ""Horn of Plenty": The Globalization of Mediterranean Horticulture and the Economic Development of Southern Europe, 1880–1930." *The Journal of Economic History*. 59 (2): 316–352.

Morilla Critz, José, Alan Olmstead, and Paul Rhode. 2000. "International Competition and the Development of the Dried-Fruit Industry, 1880–1930." In *The Mediterranean Response to Globalization before 1850*, edited by Sevket Pamuk and Jeffrey G. Williamson, 199–232. London & New York: Routledge.

Neumark, S.D. 1938. *The Citrus Industry of South Africa*. Johannesburg.

O'Brien, Patrick, and Leandro Prados de la Escosura. 1992. "Agricultural Productivity and European Industralization, 1890–1980." *The Economic History Review* 45: 514–36.

Offer, Avner. 1989. *The First World War: an Agrarian Interpretation*. Oxford: Clarendon.

Olmstead, Alan L., and Paul W. Rhode. 2001. "Reshaping the Landscape: The Impact and Diffusion of the Tractor in American Agriculture, 1910–1960." *Journal of Economic History* 61 (3): 663–698.

Olmstead, Alan L., and Paul W. Rhode. 2002. "The Red Queen and the Hard Reds: Productivity Growth in American Wheat, 1800–1940." *Journal of Economic History* 62 (4): 929–966.

Palafox, Jordi. 1985. "Exportaciones, demanda interior y crecimiento económico en el País Valenciano." In *La modernización económica de España*, edited by N. Sánchez Albornoz, 319–43. Madrid: Alianza.

Perkins, J. A. 1982. "The Agricultural Revolution in Germany 1850–1914." *Journal of European Economic History* 10: 71–118.

Perpinyá i Grau, Ramón. 1932. *La crisi del Priorat*. Barcelona: Agricultura i Ramaderia.

Perren, R. 1995. *Agriculture in Depression, 1870–1940*. Cambridge: Cambridge University Press.

Petmezas, Socrates D. 2009. "Agriculture and Economic Growth in Greece, 1870–1973." In *Agriculture and Economic Development in Europe since 1870*, edited by Pedro Lains and Vicente Pinilla, 353–74. London & New York: Routledge.

Pinilla, V. 2014. "Wine Historical Statistics: a Quantitative Approach to its Consumption, Production and Trade, 1840–1938." Working Paper, DT-SEHA 1409.

Pinilla, V., and María Isabel Ayuda. 2009. "Foreign Markets, Globalization and Agricultural Change in Spain, 1850–1935." In *Markets and Agricultural Change in Europe from the 13th to the 20th Century*, edited by V. Pinilla, 173–208. Turnhout: Brepols.

Prados de la Escosura, Leandro. 1988. *De imperio a nación. Crecimiento y atraso económico en España (1780–1930)*. Madrid: Alianza.

Pujol-Andreu, Joseph. 2011. "Wheat Varieties and Technological Change in Europe, 19th and 20th centuries: New Issues in Economic History." *Historia Agraria* (54): 71–103.

Ramón Muñoz, Ramón, ed. 2000. *Specialization in the International Market for Olive Oil before World War II*. Edited by Sevket Pamuk and Jeffrey G. Williamson, *The Mediterranean Response to Globalization before 1950*. London and New York: Routledge.

Reis, J. 1982. "Latifúndio e progresso técnico: a difusao da debulha mecanica no Alentejo, 1860–1930." *Análise Social* 18: 371–433.

Rivera y Casanova, Julian. 1897. *La tierra labrantía y el trabajo agrícola en la provincia de Zaragoza*. Madrid: Péant.

Roudié, Philippe. 1994. *Vignobles et vignerons du Bordelais (1850–1980)*, 2nd ed. Bordeaux: Presses Universitaires de Bordeaux.

Royal Institute of International Affairs. 1932. *World Agriculture, an International Survey: A Report by a Study Group of the Royal Institute of International Affairs*. London: Oxford University Press.

Schmidt, Carl T. 1938. *The Plough and the Sword. Labor, Land, and Property in Fascist Italy*. New York: Columbia.

Sempé, Henri. 1898. *Régime économique du vin. Production, consommation, échange*. Bordeaux and Paris.

Simpson, James. 1992. "Los limites del crecimiento agrario: España, 1860–1936." In *El desarrollo económico en la Europa del Sur: España e Italia en perspectiva histórica*, edited by Leandro Prados de la Escosura and Vera Zanagni, 103–38. Madrid: Alianza.

Simpson, James. 1995a. *Spanish Agriculture: the Long Siesta, 1765–1965*. Cambridge: Cambridge University Press.

Simpson, James. 1995b. "Spanish Agricultural Production and Productivity 1890–1936." In *The Economic Development of Spain since 1870*, edited by Pablo Martín-Aceña and James Simpson, 181–220. Aldershot: Edward Elgar.

Simpson, James. 2000. "Cooperation and Cooperatives in Southern European Wine Production." In *Advances in Agricultural Economic History*, edited by K. Kauffman, 95–126. Stamford, Connecticut: JAI Press.

Simpson, James. 2011. *Creating Wine: the Emergence of a World Industry, 1840–1914*. Princeton: Princeton University Press.

Simpson, James, and Juan Carmona. 2020. *Why Democracy Failed: The Agrarian Origins of the Spanish Civil War*. Cambridge: Cambridge University Press.

Spain, Ministerio de Agricultura. 1933. *Anuario estadístico de las producciones agrícolas. Año 1932*. Madrid: Palomeque.

Svennilson, Ingvar. 1954. *Growth and Stagnation in the European Economy*. Edited by United Nations Economic Commission for Europe. Geneva: United Nations.

Swinnen, J.F.M. 2002. "Political Reforms, Rural Crises, and Land Tenure in Western Europe." *Food Policy* 27: 371–94.

Thompson, F.M.L. 1968. "The Second Agricultural Revolution, 1815–1880." *The Economic History Review* 21: 62–77.

Tomasevich, Jozo. 1955. *Peasant, Politics, and Economic Change in Yugoslavia*. Stanford: Stanford University Press.
United Nations and Food and Agriculture Organization. 1954. *European Agriculture. A statement of Problems*. Geneva: United Nations.
Van Zanden, J.L. 1991. "The First Green Revolution: the Growth of Production and Productivity in European Agriculture, 1870–1914." *The Economic History Review* 44: 215–239.
Vanhanen, Tatu. 1984. *The Emergence of Democracy. A Comparative Study of 119 States, 1850–1979*. Helsinki.
Warriner, Doreen. 1939. *Economics of Peasant Farming*. Oxford: Oxford University Press.
Wunderlich, Freida. 1961. *Farm Labour in Germany 1810–1945*. Princeton: Princeton University Press.
Yates, P. Lamartine. 1940. *Food Production and Manpower in Western Europe*. London: Longmans Green.

CHAPTER 4

Agriculture and the State

Governments faced significant logistical difficulties to keep their hundreds of thousands of soldiers sufficiently well-armed and fed during the First World War. The Great Depression then created the very different problems of mass unemployment, falling prices, and the collapse in international trade. The two events contributed to radical changes in economic thinking about the role of the state, and led to orthodox monetary and fiscal policies being finally abandoned for reflationary and redistributive ones. As governments began to intervene more in the economy, it raised questions of whether the 'backward' farming methods, rural poverty, and high illiteracy rates still found in many countries were the inevitable results of late economic development, or rather those of a disinterested state. This chapter tries to provide some answers.

The development of effective state capacity was essential if the young democracies of the post-war years were to survive. Governments needed to be able to secure their frontiers, impose law and order, collect taxes, enforce contracts, and regulate markets to protect both consumers and producers. Successful law enforcement and the provision of efficient and impartial public services required a strong state, and were crucial in well-functioning democracies. The level and nature of state capacity at any one moment were the result of *previous* political decisions on investment priorities (Besley and Persson 2011: 12), such as whether to build

J. Simpson, *Family Farmers, Land Reforms and Political Action*, Palgrave Studies in Economic History,
https://doi.org/10.1007/978-3-031-67281-1_4

a battleship to defend the country's frontiers or invest instead in research laboratories to improve wheat yields. This could create significant problems for new governments that wanted to pursue radically different agendas to those of previous ones, especially as legislation was implemented by civil servants who were sometimes less than enthusiastic to serve the new regime, such as the Weimar Republic in November 1918, or the Spanish Republic in April 1931. For Sam Huntington, a significant gap can quickly emerge 'between the expectations of newly mobilized populations and their government's ability or willingness to accommodate their participation in politics' (in Fukuyama 2014: 48).

The World Bank identifies two interrelated challenges for agricultural development programs: one of political economy associated with how rents are to be redistributed, and the need to strengthen governance to implement policies effectively (World Bank 2007: 22).[1] This chapter is primarily concerned with the first, with governance being discussed in Chapter 9. It begins by briefly discussing state capacity and looks at the different incentive structures facing farm groups and others to organize lobbies. The rest of the chapter examines the development of capacity in several key areas. Tariffs were frequently used to keep domestic farm prices higher than international ones and had the advantage of being easy to implement, produced taxes for governments, and were politically visible to farmers. However, they alienated some important groups (consumers, organized labour, and industry) and distorted producer incentives. Section three considers the demands that the Great War placed on governments, and how questions of food security led to experiments at managing the food chain. The last section argues that government investment in agricultural research and extension services was often concerned with reducing the country's dependence on food imports, rather than gaining the political support of farmers. Progress was also limited because the biological technologies developed in North America and North-Western Europe were generally inappropriate for the labour-intensive farming found across large areas of Eastern and Southern Europe.

4.1 State Capacity and Interest Groups

Knowledge and farming practices in traditional societies were essentially local, being largely incomprehensive to outsiders, especially the state. Farm contracts were frequently oral rather than written, and the size of fields were measured by the eye and their ownership common knowledge among the villagers. Local differences were sometimes seen in the weights and measures used, while the language spoken in a village could be distinct from that of the government (Scott 1998: 25–7; Gellner 1983: ch.2). Traditionally, villagers considered the state as an intruder, interested only in taxation, conscripting the young, and enforcing statute laws that trampled over the rights enshrined by local custom. For Carlo Levi (1947, 1982: 78), the state for Southern Italian peasants in the 1930s was 'more distant than heaven and far more of a scourge because it was always against them' (in Banfield 1958: 36, 87). In Eastern Europe, the new political frontiers sometimes radically transformed relations, so if some had previously seen the state as 'a distant protector', they now suddenly found it both closer, and a 'source of oppression' (Judt and Snyder 2013).[2]

The state tried to impose uniformity across its territories and extend its reach through laws and administrative routines, to reduce the localism of traditional village society. As Scott (1998: 35) writes, 'the very concept of the modern state presupposes a vastly simplified and uniform property regime that is legible and hence manipulable from the center'. Governments created land registries, cadastral maps, and eliminated common property, which was 'fiscally illegible and hence fiscally less productive' (Scott 1998: 39). Opposition came not just from village society, but also from the local landed elites and Church, two groups that resented the expansion of the state in their spheres of influence. Most governments, even on the eve of the Great War, continued to possess remarkably little knowledge of rural communities and different types of agriculture found in their country.

State capacity developed along various dimensions, including the creation of a army to protect national frontiers; a fiscal system and institutions necessary to promote economic growth; information systems to facilitate decision-making and to implement policies impartially; and the legitimacy needed to encourage citizens to cooperate and provide the necessary information that the state required to arbitrate in their daily lives (Centeno and Ferraro 2013: 10–13). Advances in one sphere certainly did not imply an automatic expansion in other areas, as the creation of new state capacity was the outcome of political bargaining over how to raise the necessary resources and establish spending priorities. Some groups found it easier to organize than others, perhaps because they were culturally homogenous (nationality, ethnicity, religion), or agents lived in close geographical proximity (sharing the same clubs, etc.) (Olson 1965).[3] The incentives to lobby were greatest when a relatively small group had low organizational costs to capture potentially large rents (Wilson 1980: 367–70; Bates 1981: 88–89). By contrast, when both the costs and benefits were widely distributed among participants there were few incentives to organize lobbies. Agency capture and policy sclerosis resulted when a small group enjoyed significant benefits (and therefore had strong incentives to defend them), and the costs were widely distributed across the population.

In traditional rural societies, it was generally the landed elites and Church who had the resources to organize to influence government policy. The growth of commerce and widening of political representation created opportunities for new entrants, and by the late nineteenth-century specialist industrial groups and railway companies had developed important lobbies. Farmers, being numerically larger than other groups, faced significant difficulties to organize, even after the suffrage was extended.

According to Sheingate (2001: 24), the incentives for lobbies to organize 'tells us very little about the relationship between interest-group power and government capability'. Governments needed the active cooperation of the population (*legitimacy*) to intervene effectively. Villagers were much more likely to pay taxes if they thought that they were being fairly assessed, requiring governments to possess sufficient information on the individual's income and wealth, and the ability to act impartially. The move from an agricultural-based society dominated by an aristocratic elite to an urban-based one with universal (male) suffrage changed the nature of the information and incentive problems for the state, but did not diminish them. In fact, it was specialist farm groups in *industrial* societies that created the voluntary associations that were able, and willing, to help implement government legislation in exchange for market support (Chapter 9).

A simple cost–benefit analysis might suggest that governments would be more likely to respond to those interest groups which offered the greatest electoral support, when costs were similar. Yet governments in interwar Europe faced significant economic constraints which limited their options. Tariffs in Eastern and Southern Europe represented a fifth or more of tax revenues in the late 1920s, so a move to either free trade, or stopping imports entirely, risked a major loss of income.[4] However, balance of payment constraints and the need to service foreign debts required most governments to restrict imports, especially following the collapse of world trade after 1929. Therefore, although the strength of farm organizations and lobbies is crucial for understanding the extent and nature of intervention, the economic constraints on government decision-making also need to be considered.

4.2 Government and Markets

European landowners from the sixteenth century had benefitted from both rising rentals as the population grew faster than the area cultivated, and cheap labour-intensive consumer goods and services (Hoffman et al. 2002). Thomas Malthus in 1798 presented a deeply pessimistic vision of these different trajectories of population growth and food supplies. In areas with poor communications, farmers sometimes had difficulties in selling their crops after good harvests, while cities faced starvation after poor ones because of high transport costs.[5] Paris on the eve of the French Revolution was filled by people looking for food following a series of poor harvests, just as the 1848 Revolutions took place against another backdrop of hunger in Europe.

It was the combination of falling transport costs and growing foreign imports that first eliminated famines and the Malthusian threat hanging over Europe and, from the late nineteenth century, significantly improved urban living standards.[6] Population continued to rise at an accelerating rate, but 'the relative price of food stopped rising, and eventually started to fall, and the ratio of wages to land rents started to rise' (Finlay and O'Rourke 2007: 385). By the 1870s, international freight rates had fallen sufficiently for wheat grown in the southern hemisphere to compete in European markets. Tropical commodities, such as sugar, coffee, tea, and cocoa, which had been luxuries in much of Western Europe before the Napoleonic wars, now became items of mass consumption. Freight costs collapsed in three distinct segments of the commodity chain: the railways connecting farmers to ports; the steam engines on the shipping routes between exporting and importing countries; and the railways between the port and urban consumers. The impact of cheap imported grains for European farmers was quick and devastating. As one Spanish commentator lamented in 1880, it had become cheaper to bring wheat from California to the ports of Barcelona or Bilbao, than from the inland regions of Palencia or Arévalo (Costa 1880–1911: 124). By 1913, North-Western Europe was importing an increasing amount of food and beverages from the rest of the world which was paid for by exporting manufactured goods

Table 4.1 World trade in primary products between 1876/80 and 1913

	Imports		*Exports*	
	1876/80	*1913*	*1876/80*	*1913*
UK & Ireland	1297	2596	111	760
North-West Europe	1714	5894	800	3064
Other Europe	490	1689	714	1793
Total	3501	10,179	1625	5617
% of world total	80.2	74.3	45.9	46.1

$ million, in 1913 prices. North-West Europe includes Finland, Sweden, Norway, Denmark, Germany, Belgium, Netherlands, France, Switzerland, and Austria. Other Europe includes Russia. *Source* Yates (1959: 227, 229)

(Table 4.1). Cereal exports from Eastern and Southern Europe grew, but their trade surpluses in food were shrinking in the face of New World competition.

The growth in international trade transformed world agriculture. North American family farmers benefited from technological changes that allowed them to extend the area that they could cultivate and significantly reduce unit costs and cereal prices (Chapter 3). By contrast, productivity growth in farming in tropical areas was restricted by the unlimited supplies of cheap land and labour which allowed production to spread to new countries to meet the rising demand from industrial societies.[7] Commodity chains were however transformed by organizational changes in the roasting, packing, and branding of coffee, rather than in the production of the beans on the farm (Bates (1997) for coffee and Simpson (2011) for wine). It was often the entrepreneurial skills of importing merchants that was key in relocating production from one country to another in response to changes in demand and their need to control costs.

The Heckscher-Ohlin trade model suggests that a country will export goods that are intensive in the factor of production that they possess in abundance and import those goods in which it is scarce. In the Atlantic economy, the New World imported manufacturing goods (labour was scarce) and exported agricultural products (land was abundant). Growing international trade threatened the profits of domestic owners of scarce factors of production, which was land in Western Europe (Rogowski 1990; O'Rourke and Williamson 1994). Therefore, the flood of cheap imports from the 1870s and large-scale emigration promised higher real wages, falling farm rents, and a collapse in farm profits which threatened to transform agriculture. The landed elites now organized and lobbied governments to intervene to protect their interests. Numerous government enquiries were established to determine the state of agriculture, followed in many cases with tariffs being implemented 'to protect agriculture' by raising domestic prices.[8]

The success of farm lobbies before 1914 can be explained by the political influence of the landed elites in *all* European countries, and their ability to associate their private interests (land rents) with those of a much wider constituency, family farmers (and farm profits). Rural elites, by lobbying for tariffs, helped to strengthen hierarchical loyalties in the countryside. Although Ricardian trade theory suggests that farming would have remained profitable under conditions of free trade, as landowners would have been forced eventually to reduce rents, this ignores the population pressure on the land, and the willingness of family farmers to work for less than the going wage (Koning 1994: 27). Urban workers also feared that a flood of unemployed farm labourers looking for work in the cities would reduce their wages. Individual groups within the food chain sometimes had very different interests, threatening inter-class conflicts, and increasing the difficulties for governments to respond (Table 4.2). In addition, merchants were often divided between local millers supporting farmers (and protection), and those who wanted free trade because of their investments in new flour mills in the ports.

The extent that free trade could change farming is illustrated in England and Wales, where urban lobbies proved to be too strong for landowners, and tariff-free imports saw farm rents dropping by 27%, farm wages increasing by 31%, and the area of wheat falling by about half

Table 4.2 Objectives and policy demands in European cereal production in the 1920s

Pressure group	*Demands*
Landowners	High rents
Farmers- owneroccupiers	High wheat prices + low wages*
Farmer-tenants	Low rents + low wages*
Farm workers	High wages

* Farmers as employers wanted low wage costs, but not those that worked part-time as casual labourers

between 1870 and 1913. On the eve of the Great War, the country imported about two-thirds of all its calorific needs, compared to a fifth in tariff-protected Germany (Afton and Turner 2000: tables 36.2a, 39.6, 42.10; Offer 1989: 25; Olson 1963: 74; Turner 2000: 224). The cost of Britain's imports was more than covered by its manufacturing exports. In Denmark and the Netherlands, significant numbers of farmers also welcomed imports because cheap grains helped make their livestock products internationally competitive. Yates and Warriner (1943: 45), two English experts writing in 1943, firmly believed that Danish and Dutch farming as a result had performed much better over the previous half century than in tariff-protected France, Germany, or Italy, 'in respect to improvement in crop yields per acre, increase in livestock numbers, up-grading in quality of livestock (e.g. milk yield per cow) and so on'. By contrast, Ireland was obliged to accept free trade, and adjusted not through trade but by emigration, with its population falling by 33% and its agricultural population by 47% between 1851 and 1911 (Turner 1966: table 6.6). Those Irish farmers that remained had more land and became considerably more productive.

The situation in Eastern Europe was however very different as countries were net-food exporters, especially cereals. Just as in the New World, falling transport costs after 1870 encouraged farmers to increase the cultivated area, but it was large estates, not family farms, that benefitted most from exports, and their owners generally used cheap labour or sharecroppers rather than modern farm machinery. Circumstances changed radically after the First World War when the land reforms in the successor states broke-up the large estates, and created family farms (Chapter 6).

Once vested interests were created in agriculture, they often became 'deep rooted and politically difficult to eradicate', and the introduction of temporary measures 'allowed to drift into a permanent policy' (Astor and Murray 1933: 104). Even before 1929, tariffs in most European countries were higher on agricultural imports than they had been in 1914 (Liepmann 1938). What changed was that it was no longer the landed elites who represented the sector, but rather organizations of family farmers.

4.3 Government and War

The Great War was Europe's first major conflict in a century and showed the devastating capability of the new weaponry produced by industrial societies. In addition to the millions that died on the battlefields, hunger reappeared in some regions on a scale that many had believed had been consigned to history, and the influenza epidemic of 1918 killed a further 20 million worldwide. Hostilities in Western Europe officially ended in November 1918, although they continued to rage in Central and Eastern Europe for several more years. In Germany, the controlled economy (*Zwangswirtschaft*) began in autumn 1914, and only ended in the autumn of 1923 (Moeller 1986: 7).

War required enormous increases in state capacity, as governments had to learn to plan and co-ordinate the massive transfer of civilian resources for military use. German government expenditure increased from less than 10% of GDP before 1914, to 59%, while figures peaked at 50% in France and 37% in the UK (Broadberry and Harrison 2005: table 1.5). Governments learnt to mediate between private companies and trade unions to ensure that resources were not wasted, and sufficient food was produced and distributed to both military and urban consumers.

The hostilities, by persisting for so long, placed a severe strain on agriculture, depriving farmers not only of their sons, but also of work animals and fertilizers, as the nitrates were now used for munitions. Although it was initially believed that countries with large farm populations and food exports would have a decisive advantage over those with small farm sectors and dependent on imports, the opposite proved to be the case. Russia's seemingly 'vast reserves of domestic manpower and food' were not effectively mobilized, and its cities suffered massive shortages because of government price controls and compulsory food purchases, which made farmers reluctant to produce, especially as the war economy turned out few consumer goods for them to purchase (Gatrell 2005: 236, 258–9).

Most governments had problems encouraging farmers to increase production of high calorific foods at official prices. Austria-Hungary had been self-sufficient in grains before 1914, but the combination of war destruction, the loss of farm labour, work animals, and artificial fertilizers contributed to a drop in per capita consumption of bread grains by between 30 and 45%. Government policy also led to shortages, as farmers found it more profitable to produce animal feed rather than bread grains, even though cattle and pig numbers fell dramatically during the war. Food riots broke out in Vienna as early as the spring of 1915. With growing shortages, food-producing regions such as Bohemia, Moravia, Silesia, and Galicia restricted their sales to other areas, and the Austrian government seized barges on the Danube in April 1918 that were transporting Romanian grain to Germany, because there was none in Vienna to feed its population (Schulze 2005: 91–7). Yet some farmers prospered, and it was widely believed that French farmers became 'notoriously rich' from their dealings on the black market as consumers suffered from food shortages (Hautcoeur 2005: 199).[9]

The war-effort in Britain was an extreme case, with less than 10% of its workforce employed in agriculture, and importing two-thirds of its calorific needs in 1913. The small number of private, vertically integrated commodity chains that already supplied large quantities of food to customers were easily adapted to the war economy.[10] Imports allowed the government to set domestic cereal prices sufficiently high to encourage farmers to plough-up pastureland for grain. Basic foods were only rationed from late in 1917, although the Ministry of Food was responsible for 85% of the food supply by the end of the war (Olson 1963: 95). Food was a decisive factor in the outcome of the war, and while British males continued to consume around 3,400 calories a day, the figure for German males fell to half this figure by 1918, with women consuming even less (Mann 2012: 160; Offer 1989: chs. 3–4).

Wartime economic planning and market intervention required a massive increase in state capacity, which inevitably became less relevant with the ending of hostilities, while the spread of democracy created new demands on governments. A wide gap quickly emerged between voters' interests in social expenditure (pensions, unemployment benefits), and the belief in financial and political circles that balanced budgets and the return to the gold standard were essential for the renewal of economic prosperity. The War had been funded by countries rapidly increasing their money supply, with inflation and high food prices causing labour disputes to reach unprecedented levels, including factory occupations in Germany and Italy (Feinstein et al. 1997: 24).[11]

In the absence of a Marshall Plan and international banking agreements, economic orthodoxy required countries to raise interest rates, balance budgets, and reduce imports to protect currency reserves. Some countries responded quickly by implementing austerity, with price stability being achieved with rising unemployment and economic depression (the Scandinavian countries, Britain, and the Netherlands). Others, such as Belgium, France and Italy, were slower to act, and inflation persisted for longer, with hyperinflation in Austria, Germany, Hungary, Poland, and Russia destroying the life-savings of millions.

Food exports in the successor states in Eastern Europe were a major source of foreign exchange, though the new governments usually lacked mechanisms to collect taxes other than those on trade.[12] Romania had been the world's fifth largest wheat exporter before 1914, and these virtually disappeared in the early 1920s, not just because of weak international demand, but also because of monetary instability, and the fact that a third of government revenue came from tariffs, of which half were from exports in 1928 (Mitrany 1930: 343, 438–9). With the Great Depression and collapse in world trade, it proved relatively easy for Western European farm lobbies to obtain protection from foreign competition because governments once again needed to limit imports to save foreign exchange, hitting farmers in Eastern Europe especially hard.

4.4 Government, Agricultural Science, and Farm Technologies

Economic historians have often emphasized the importance for government intervention to accelerate agricultural change. Stiglitz (2001: xiii), for example, has argued that the 'burst of productivity in agriculture that provided the basis of industrialization' in the United States in the late nineteenth century was the result of government research, teaching, and extension services. The rapidly expanding agricultural frontier incorporated new climatic regions, and faster communications facilitated the spread of plant and animal diseases and pests, such as cotton weevil, phylloxera, or stem rust. Without biological innovations, Olmstead and Rhode (2002, 2008) believe that US wheat yields would have been little more than half those actually achieved in 1914. The remarkable growth in Chinese agricultural productivity after 1978 was also made possible by previous government investment in green revolution technologies such as improved seeds, fertilizers, and irrigation (Naughton 2007: ch.2). Yet in both cases, the economic climate for private investment was also highly favourable, with US farmers benefitting from the growing international markets after the 1870s, and Chinese ones from the rapidly expanding domestic market after 1978. This was not the case in interwar Europe. While governments had encouraged farmers to increase output almost regardless of cost during the First World War, the situation in the 1920s, and especially the 1930s, was very different. In the industrial-based economies particularly, crop yields remained flat, as the benefits from new technologies were offset by farmers reducing labour inputs because of low farm prices.

The major differences in farming practices across Europe suggested that existing technologies in use offered considerable possibilities for improvements on many farms. Wheat yields in 1930, for example, averaged three tons per hectare in Denmark and the Netherlands, but just one ton in Greece, Romania, and Spain. Cows produced two or three times more milk in North-Western Europe, than elsewhere. Winegrowers in the France's Midi obtained yields that were four times greater than those in Spain, although rice and orange producers in that country were among the world's most productive (Simpson and Carmona 2020; table 2.1; Simpson 1995; table 6.5; International Institute de Agriculture 1934). Differences in mechanical technologies were highly visible following the introduction of tractors, combine harvesters, or modern wine-making equipment. However, farming practices varied as much *within* countries, as between them. A survey of 600 dairy herds 'in the chief dairying districts' of the England and Wales showed that production costs of a litre of milk varied by a factor of over four.[13] Similar differences were no doubt found in other countries, though governments rarely collected this type of information.

Even existing technologies therefore promised to significantly change farming practices, although one expert, writing at the end of the period, believed that agricultural science was 'putting within our reach the power of producing all the food we need with but a fraction of the present farming population of the world' (Yates 1940: 17). Some contemporaries explained low productivity and rural poverty by distinguishing between 'modern, commercial farming' and the seemingly largely self-sufficient 'peasant' agriculture, where farmers were considered as being too 'ignorant' or lacking motivation ('stubborn') to implement change. Others, and more in keeping with development economists today, believed that farmers persisted with traditional methods because of weak factor and product markets. Poor farmers only borrowed from the village money lender for essential consumption needs rather than for investment because of the 'usurious' interest rates charged (Chapter 6). There was no shortage of suggestions for how governments should intervene to modernize traditional agriculture. Seton-Watson (1945–1967: 105–6), for example, identified seven areas needed for Eastern Europe, including technical education, cheaper credit, the consolidation of scattered holdings to create compact farms, new crops, better local and international transport, public works (such as land reclamation, irrigation, etc.), and cooperatives.

As with other areas of state capacity, the amount of agricultural research and the fields that a country prioritized reflected internal political negotiations. There were high fixed costs associated with R&D, and the slow economic returns made it politically less visible than other forms of farm support. It was usually limited to those biological technologies which private entrepreneurs were reluctant to finance, because the benefits were public goods, and consequently costless to transfer to other users. Improved seed varieties, for example, could be shared with other farmers or countries (nonexcludable), and information exchanged freely (nonrival). These weakened incentives for agricultural-based and transforming countries to dedicate their scarce resources for original research, as opposed to free-riding on the efforts of other countries (World Bank 2007: 166). Governments attempted to identify the most promising results achieved in the more advanced economies, and then adapt them to their own agriculture. A major problem was that the supply of these new technologies reflected the needs and factor endowments of North America and North-Western Europe, rather than those of Eastern and Southern Europe. In fact, there were few biological advances to be borrowed that were appropriate to improve crop yields in their dry-farming regions before the 1960s. Farm machinery, by contrast, was more easily adapted for use across a wide range of geographical regions but these were patented by manufacturers, and generally less viable in economies where labour was cheap and capital scarce. Indeed, while labour shortages were a growing problem in agriculture in parts of North-Western Europe, elsewhere the challenge was to create more employment in the face of a growing population and limited supply of new land.

Given the location specific nature of agriculture, farmers themselves created formal and informal spaces to exchange information and ideas. The contribution of pure science to technological change was modest before the mid-nineteenth century, but inquisitive and practical individuals helped advance farming knowledge. Robert Bakewell, for example, a well-known eighteenth-century English farmer, had made significant progress in the selective breeding of cattle and sheep, 'without knowing Mendelian genetics' (Mokyr 2002: 48–9). Agricultural societies sprung up in many countries at both the national and local levels to 'advance progress', with the role of the state normally limited to awarding prizes or pensions to individuals who had used their own resources to make discoveries (Mokyr 2018). Agricultural shows also became increasingly common during the nineteenth century, featuring ploughing competitions or local experts judging animals by what they believed were the necessary physical characteristics to be more productive. Farmers could watch displays of farm machinery in operation, and exchange information with their manufacturers. These were normally annual events, although weekly market provided a more informal setting to exchange information, as well as listening to new political ideas.

Governments at times were forced to intervene in the face of an imminent disaster which threatened massive economic losses. In France, for example, the fear that phylloxera would destroy the country's vines, led to a major increase in scientific research in the 1870s. However, even here, the government initially resorted, without success, to the traditional practice of offering prizes to encourage private research.[14] Furthermore, once government scientists had developed practical solutions (grafting European varieties on American rootstock or the use of hybrids), it was usually left to private enterprise to provide the millions of new vines needed. The limited interest in state-sponsored research resulted in a lack of trained scientists, although when governments did establish agricultural colleges, the students, often farmer's sons, frequently preferred to work in the urban sector, rather than remain in agriculture.[15]

Western European governments in the interwar years often faced contradictory demands from consumers who wanted cheap food,and cereal farmers who needed prices that were above those on world markets to remain competitive. A major incentive for government investment in R&D was therefore to make cereals cheaper for consumers *and* more profitable for farms to produce, so as to reduce the need to import, and save scarce foreign exchange. Italy on the eve of the First World War was dependent on wheat imports for 22% of its needs, a figure that had grown to a third by 1919–22, at a time of high world prices and shortages, encouraging Mussolini to launch the *Batalle de Trigo* in 1925 to make the country self-sufficient. The government-sponsored research to develop new seed varieties and better cultivation methods, and significant investment was made in land reclamation, resulting in the area under wheat increasing by 7% between 1922–7 and 1932–7, yields growing three time faster, and imports falling from 30 to 7% of national consumption. By 1936, the country was approaching self-sufficiency, creating new difficulties for the government to maintain stable farm prices after good harvests. Furthermore, the 'one-sidedness of the wheat policy' negatively affected tree crops and livestock production, so that the wheat policy cost according to one estimate between '5 and 10 per cent of the total earning of many workers' (Salvemini 1931 in Schmidt 1938: 58, 68). Real wages and food availability declined between the early 1920s and late 1930s (Cohen 1979: 83–5). Unsurprisingly, those regions best suited to cereals suffered less during the 1930s, together with those areas where underemployed farm labour could find work in urban areas, or where farmers were able to switch into labour-intensive, high-value products (Chiapparino and Morettini 2023: fig, 5.7).

In Greece, a similar concern to reduce imports led to governments encouraging cereal production, with the wheat harvest more than doubling between 1928–32 and 1933–37, as the area increased by 43% and the yields by 47%. During the Great Depression, Greece 'massively' expanded wheat production at the height of the crisis', having 'few parallels in Europe' (Mazower 1991: table 9.4, 244). Once again, government concerns over the balance-of-trade determined farm policy, distorting incentives for those farmers who specialized in other commodities.

Danish agriculture's achievements rested on the common interests and flexible communications between farmers, cooperatives, *and* the state. Indeed, government agencies were crucial in helping to maintain export competitiveness, which accounted for 80% of agricultural output. The high degree of homogeneity of Danish farming made government support considerably easier than in most countries. Farms were usually of between 15 and 30 hectares and family operated, and land utilization was 'extraordinary' uniform, with 90% of farms having the same proportion of arable and pasture, and following similar crop rotations (Yates 1940: 29, 36). Practically all farmers belonged to a dairy and bacon-curing cooperative, and sometimes several others. Most were members of the Farmer Society and Smallholder Society, whose national federations combined to create a single peak association, the Agricultural Council of Denmark to advise the Government on policy. Strong farm organizations and electoral strength helped farmers to articulate specific demands, making it easier for governments to respond. As a result, the Farmer and Smallholder Societies employed over 300 fully-trained farm advisors, which were partly government subsidized (Yates 1940: 81–2). Close collaboration was found in areas such as animal breeding, disease control, and export quality standards. The high literacy of Danish farmers not only made them more open to novel technologies, but the new demands of measuring and recording farm activities encouraged parents to educate their children for longer. Danish agriculture was distinguished not so much by the achievements of a few highly innovative family farmers, but rather the near absence of bad ones.[16] The lesson, as discussed in greater detail in later chapters, was that strong local voluntary organizations such as cooperatives could help formulate the demands of farmers, creating the necessary incentives for politicians to respond to them, rather than other groups.

Unlike Danish agriculture, which was characterized by homogeneous farm structures, farming practices, and output, French farmers organized along regional, ideological, and commodity lines. From the 1870s, rural France had witnessed a struggle between the conservatives, who had traditionally controlled the countryside, and republicans, who saw the state as an efficient instrument to help them gain political influence among rural voters. Indeed, the creation of the Ministry of Agriculture in 1881 by the Gambetta government was considered by some as an endeavour to increase the political influence of republicans among farmers as much as to improve farming. France's weak political party system before 1914 encouraged the development of a centralized agricultural bureaucracy, which in turn led to the 'creation of state-sponsored farm organizations engaged in national politics and policy debate'.[17] The institutional structure determined the amount and nature of government research and extension, although implementation and its effectiveness depended on the response of local farmers to state agencies. In Finistère (Brittany), for example, conservatives considered the attempts by the state to change local farming practices as a major threat to social stability and rural autonomy (Berger 1972: 69–71). Local associations existed, but village society was organized here in a way that tried to limit whenever possible the influence of central government, leaving many cooperatives as little more than fertilizer stores (Berger 1972: 82, 85–6).

The attempts by government agencies to speed agrarian change were therefore frustrated in areas where traditional hierarchical relationships still existed, as elites resented the presence of government appointed specialists. By the interwar years however, the growing influence of family farm organizations and falling farm prices led to greater intervention. At the extreme, in Nazi Germany, the giant *Reichsnährstand* (RNS), a highly centralized corporation which planned to increase food production and its distribution, simply absorbed the decentralized systems of farm associations that already existed (Chapter 10). Even here, however, the 'RNS officials were simply out of touch with the grassroots' in the important area of plant breeding, and suffered from a lack of individuals at the village level who were both 'brown and expert' (Harwood 2010: 600).

4.5 Conclusions

By the interwar period, governments everywhere were intervening in farm markets. They were also active, to differing degrees, in their attempts to control plant and animal diseases, or protect farmers from fraud when purchasing inputs such as chemical fertilizers, or consumers when buying food. Most governments intervened to some extent to create mechanisms to regulate rents, protect tenants against unfair eviction, or compensate them for improvements that they had made to their farms (the 'Three Fs') (Douglas 1976). All countries carried out some agricultural research, and extension and education programs were becoming increasingly more common. Yet the economic context of the interwar period was generally unfavourable for government research that aimed to make farming more scientific, as the collapse in farm prices from the late 1920s discouraged farmers from experimenting and increasing investment. Unlike the United States, where the rapid growth in the use of tractors was closely linked to state support, European governments usually resorted to tariffs on imported farm machinery to save scarce foreign exchange.[18]

The low agricultural productivity found in large areas of Eastern and Southern Europe, and pockets of North-West Europe, was due in part to a disinterested state. Many governments, especially in Europe's agricultural-based and transforming economies, had very limited knowledge of their agriculture on the eve of the Great Depression. They lacked basic information of why farmers preferred a particular crop mix or form of cultivation, making it impossible to know what improvements might be successfully transferred from other regions or countries. This was not just a question of economic development, as the Russian government in the 1920s had better information about their farmers, and their farming decisions, than most industrial-based societies. In Southern Poland and large parts of Yugoslavia, it was unknown whether the rural population was growing faster than agricultural output in the three decades before the Second World War (Yates and Warriner 1943: 48–9). Spain lacked basic information in the early 1930s on the amount of cultivable land that was available for land reform, or the numbers who needed to be settled. Nevertheless, this provides a good example of the endogenous nature of state capacity, as the political demands for land reform finally created the necessary incentives to collect systematically farm-level studies (Simpson and Carmona 2017, 2020).

As the Danish case suggests, voluntary associations were needed to design and channel the needs of farmers effectively to their government to devise R&D programs that were relevant, and would have the active support of farmers. Farm record keeping was rare and while nearly one in twenty Danish farmers kept accounts by the end of the period, only a few hundred French farmers out of millions did (Yates and Warriner 1943: 96). Why farmers in most countries failed to build dynamic farm groups to demand government intervention will be discussed in Chapter 7. The importance of priorities being set by farmers, rather than by government, is illustrated by the distortions that were created in their attempts at achieving wheat self-sufficiency in Italy and Greece.

Notes

1. Pasour and Rucker (2005: 8) note that 'the challenge in improving public policy is to develop an institutional framework that will induce actors in the political process to serve the general welfare, just as Adam Smith's "invisible hand" induces market participants to do so'.
2. Snyder, commenting on Kafka, who migrated 'uncomfortably back-and forward across his various identities—Jewish, Czech, German' in the interwar years.
3. See Fraile Balbín (1991: ch. 6.4) for Spain.
4. Tariffs accounted for 32% of government revenue in Bulgaria in 1928/9; 45% in Romania (1925); 25% in Yugoslavia (1929/30); 25% in Poland (1925/6); 20% in Hungary (1925/6); and 17% in Czechoslovakia (Drabek 1985: 413).
5. Lindert (1991: 29–83) notes that British farmers were encourage to produce more because of export bounties which created a minimum price for grain, but most other European countries looked to protect domestic consumers with maximum prices, discouraging farmers from growing more.
6. Irish food exports to Britain were important before the 1840s (Jones 1981: 67).
7. European emigrants were attracted to high wage in temperate regions but the wage ceiling in tropical areas was low, being set by Indian and Chinese workers (Lewis 1978: 191).

8. Vivier (2014), with chapters on Britain, Denmark, France, Hungary, Ireland, Italy, the Netherlands, and Spain.
9. Augé-Laribé and Pinot (1927: 2) argue that were rumours were spread because of the poor information available on prices and output.
10. Meat, for example, was imported by just 6 companies who retailed it in their 3,545 shops, accounting for 41% of national sales (Jeffreys 1954: 183–7).
11. The United Kingdom was unusual in that a third of its war expenditure was met by higher taxes.
12. At the end of the 1920s, 80% of Bulgaria's exports were food (and tobacco); 60% of Hungary's; and almost 50% of Romania's and Yugoslavia's (Drabek 1985: 407).
13. From 5 to 21d per gallon (Astor and Rowntree 1939: 188).
14. The prize of 300,000 francs offered in June 1873 was never awarded, despite attracting 696 entries by October 1876 (Ordish 1972: 68, 70). Considerable state and local investment went into identifying which grafts were best suited to local conditions (Paul 1996).
15. Only one in 20 who attended higher agricultural education in Belgium, went back into agriculture (Yates 1940: 224). See also Tomasevich (1955: 463) and Federico (2006: 109).
16. Yates (1940: 40), for example, writes that there are few 'really bad cows' in Denmark.
17. Sheingate (2001: 30) concludes that, 'created in order to attract the political loyalties of farmers, agricultural ministries and farm organizations operated in lieu of formal political parties in France'.
18. For the United States, see Clarke (1994).

References

Afton, Bethanie, and Michael Turner. 2000. "The Statistical Base of Agricultural Performance in England and Wales, 1850–1914." In *The Agrarian History of England and Wales, 1850–1914*, edited by E.J.T. Collins, 1757–2140. Cambridge: Cambridge University Press.

Astor, Viscount, and Keith Murray. 1933. *The Planning of Agriculture*. Oxford: Oxford University Press.

Astor, Viscount, and B. Seebohm Rowntree. 1939. *British Agriculture the Principles of Future Policy*. London: Penguin.

Augé-Laribé, Michel, and Pierre Pinot. 1927. *Agriculture and Food Supply in France during the War, Carnegie Endowment for International Peace*. New Haven: Yale.

Banfield, Edward. 1958. *The Moral Basis of Backward Society*. Illinois: The Free Press.

Bates, Robert H. 1981. *Markets and States in Tropical Africa. The Political Basis of Agricultural Policies*. Berkeley: University of California.

Bates, Robert H. 1997. *Open Economy Politics: The Politics and Economics of the International Coffee Market*. Princeton: Princeton University Press.

Berger, Suzanne. 1972. *Peasants Against Polticis. Rural Organizaion in Brittany 1911–1967*. Cambridge, Mass.: Harvard.

Besley, Timothy, and Torsen Persson. 2011. *Pillars of Prosperity. The Political Economics of Development Clusters*. Princeton: Princeton University Press.

Broadberry, Stephen, and Mark Harrison. 2005. "The Economies of World War I: an Overview." In *The Economics of World War I*, edited by Stephen Broadberry and Mark Harrison, 3–40. Cambridge: Cambridge University Press.

Centeno, Miguel A, and Agustin E Ferraro. 2013. "Republics of the Possible. State building in Latin America and Spain." In *State and Nation Building in Latin America and Spain. Republics of the Possible*, edited by Miguel A Centeno and Agustin E. Ferraro, 3–24. Cambridge: Cambridge University Press.

Chiapparino, Francesco, and Gabriele Morettini. 2023. "International Markets, Policy, and Mobility. 'Rural Italies' in the 1930s Recession." In *Agriculture and the Great Depression. The Rural Crisis of the 1930s in Europe and the Americas*, edited by Gérard Béaur and Francesco Chiapparino, 77–96. Abingdon: Routledge.

Clarke, Sally H. 1994. *Regulation and the Revolution in United States Farm Productivity*. Cambridge: Cambridge University Press.

Cohen, Joh S. 1979. "Fascism and Agriculture in Italy: Policies and Consequences." *The Economic History Review* 32 (1): 642–54.

Costa, Joaquin. 1880:1911. "El cultivo de cereal es antieconómico en España." In *Agricultura Armónica*. Madrid.

Douglas, Roy. 1976. *Land, People and Politics. A History of the Land Question in the United Kingdom, 1878–1952*. London: Allison & Busby.

Drabek, Z. 1985. "Foreign Trade Performance and Policy." In *The Economic History of Eastern Europe 1919–1975. Economic Structure and Performance between the Two Wars*, edited by M.C. Kaser and E.A. Radice, 379–531. Oxford: Clarendon.

Federico, Giovanni. 2006. *Feeding the World. An Economic History of Agriculture, 1800–1900*. Princeton: Princeton University Press.

Feinstein, Charles, Peter Temin, and Toniolo. 1997. *The European Economy Between the Wars*. Oxford: Oxford University Press.

Findlay, Ronald, and Kevin H. O'Rourke. 2007. *Power and Plenty. Trade, Wars, and the World Economy in the Second Millennium*. Princeton: Princeton University Press.

Fraile Balbín, Pedro. 1991. *Industrialización y grupos de presión. La economía política de la protección en España, 1900–1950*. Madrid: Alianza.

Fukuyama, Francis. 2014. *Political Order and Political Decay. From the Industrial Revolution to the Globalisation of Democracy*. London: Profile.

Gatrell, Peter. 2005. "Poor Russia, Poor Show: Mobilising a Backward Economy for War, 1914–1917." In *The Economics of World War I*, edited by Stephen Broadberry and Mark Harrison, 235–75. Cambridge: Cambridge University Press.

Gellner, Ernest. 1983. *Nations and Nationalism*. Oxford: Blackwell.

Harwood, Jonathan. 2010. "The Fate of Peasant-Friendly Plant Breeding in Nazi Germany." *Historical Studies in the Natural Sciences* 40 (4): 569–603.

Hautcoeur, Pierre-Cyrille. 2005. "Was the Great War a Watershed? The Economics of World War I in France." In *The Economics of World War I*, edited by Stephen Broadberry and Mark Harrison, 169–205. Cambridge: Cambridge University Press.

Hoffman, Philip, David Jacks, Patricia Levin, and Peter Lindert. 2002. "Real Inequality in Europe since 1500." *The Journal of Economic History*: 322–355.

International Institute de Agriculture. 1934. *International Yearbook of Agricultural Statistics, 1933–4*. Rome: IIA.

Jeffreys, James B. 1954. *Retail Trading in Britain, 1850–1950*. Cambridge: Cambridge University Press.

Jones, E.L. 1981. "Agriculture, 1700–80." In *The Economic History of Britain since 1700. vol 1. 1700–1860*, edited by Roderick Floud and Donald McCloskey. Cambridge University Press: Cambridge.

Judt, Tony, and with Timothy Snyder. 2013. *Thinking the Twentieth Century*. London: Vintage.

Koning, Niek 1994. *The Failure of Agrarian Capitalism: Agrarian Politics in the U.K., Germany, the Netherlands and the USA, 1846–1919*. London and New York: Routledge.

Levi, Carlo. 1947: 1982. *Christ Stopped at Eboli*. Harmondsworth: Penguin.

Lewis, W. Arthur. 1978. *Growth and Fluctuations, 1870–1913*. London: Allen & Unwin.

Liepmann, H. 1938. *Tariff Levels and the Economic Unity of Europe*. London.

Lindert, Peter, ed. 1991. *Historical Patterns of Agricultural Policy*. Edited by C.P. Timmer, *Agriculture and the State: Growth, Employment, and Poverty in Developing Countries*. Ithaca & London.

Mann, Michael. 2012. *The Sources of Social Power. 3. Global Empires and Revolution, 1890–1945*. Cambridge: Cambridge University Press.

Mazower, Mark. 1991. *Greece and the Inter-War Economic Crisis*. Oxford: Clarendon.

Mitrany, David. 1930. *The Land and the Peasant in Rumania. The War and Agrarian Reform (1917–21)*. London: Milford.

Moeller, Robert G. 1986. *German Peasants and Agrarian Politics, 1914–1924. The Rhineland and Westphalia*. Chapel Hill: North Carolina.

Mokyr, Joel. 2002. *The Gifts of Athena: Historical Origins of The Knowledge Economy*. Princeton: Princeton University Press.

Mokyr, Joel. 2018. "Bottom-Up or Top-Down? The Origins of the Industrial Revolution." *Journal of Institutional Economics* 14 (6): 1003–1024.

Naughton, Barry. 2007. *The Chinese Economy. Transitions and Growth*. Cambridge, Mass.: MIT.

O'Rourke, Kevin, and Jeffrey G. Williamson. 1994. "Late Nineteenth-Century Anglo-American Factor-Price Convergence: Were Heckscher and Ohlin Right?" *The Journal of Economic History* 54 (4): 892–916.

Offer, Avner. 1989. *The First World War: an Agrarian Interpretation*. Oxford: Clarendon.

Olmstead, Alan L., and Paul W. Rhode. 2002. "The Red Queen and the Hard Reds: Productivity Growth in American Wheat, 1800–1940." *Journal of Economic History* 62 (4): 929–966.

Olmstead, Alan L., and Paul W. Rhode. 2008. *Creating abundance. Biological innovation and American agricultural development*. Cambridge: Cambridge University Press.

Olson, M. 1965. *The Logic of Collective Action*. Cambridge: Harvard University Press.

Olson, Mancur. 1963. *The Economics of the Wartime Shortage: A History of British Food Supplies in the Napoleonic War and in World Wars I and II*. Durham: Duke.

Ordish, George 1972. *The Great Wine Blight*. London: Dent.

Pasour, E.C., and Randal R. Rucker. 2005. *Plowshares and Pork Barrels. The Political Economy of Agriculture*. Oakland: The Independent Institute.

Paul, Harry W. 1996. *Science, Vine, and Wine in Modern France*. Cambridge: Cambridge University Press.

Rogowski, Ronald. 1990. *Commerce and Coalitions: How Trade Affects Domestic Political Alignments*. Princeton: Princeton University Press.

Salvemini, Gaetano. 1931. "Mussolini's Battle of Wheat." *Political Science Quartely* 46 (March): 25–40.

Schmidt, Carl T. 1938. *The Plough and the Sword. Labor, Land, and Property in Fascist Italy*. New York: Columbia.

Schulze, Max-Stephan. 2005. "Austria-Hungary's Economy in World War I." In *The Economics of World War I*, edited by Stephen Broadberry and Mark Harrison, 77–111. Cambridge: Cambridge University Press.

Scott, James C. 1998. *Seeing like a State*. New Haven: Yale.

Seton-Watson, Hugh. 1945: 1967. *Eastern Europe between the Wars 1918–1941*, 3 ed. New York: Harper.

Sheingate, Adam D. 2001. *The Rise of the Agricultural Welfare State. Institutions and Interest Group Power in the United States, France, and Japan*. Princeton: Princeton University Press.

Simpson, James. 1995. *Spanish Agriculture: the Long Siesta, 1765–1965*. Cambridge: Cambridge University Press.

Simpson, James. 2011. *Creating Wine: the Emergence of a World Industry, 1840–1914*. Princeton: Princeton University Press.

Simpson, James, and Juan Carmona. 2017. "Too Many Workers or Not Enough Land? Why Land Reform Fails in Spain During the 1930s." *Historia Agraria* (72): 37–68.

Simpson, James, and Juan Carmona. 2020. *Why Democracy Failed: The Agrarian Origins of the Spanish Civil War*. Cambridge: Cambridge University Press.

Stiglitz, Joseph E. 2001. "Foreword." In *The Great Transformation*, edited by Karl Polanyi, vii–xvii. Massachusetts: Beacon.

Tomasevich, Jozo. 1955. *Peasant, Politics, and Economic Change in Yugoslavia*. Stanford: Stanford University Press.

Turner, M.E. 1966. *After the Famine. Irish Agriculture 1850–1914*. Cambridge: Cambridge University Press.

Turner, Michael E. 2000. "Agricultural Output, Income and Productivity." In *The agrarian history of England and Wales*, edited by E.J.T. Collins, 224–320. Cambridge: Cambridge University Press.

Vivier, Nadine. 2014. *The Golden Age of State Enquiries. Rural Enquiries in the Nineteenth Century*. Turnhout: Brepols.

Wilson, James Q. 1980. "The Politics of Regulation." In *The Politics of Regulation*, edited by James Q. WIlson, 357–95. New York: Basic Books.

World Bank. 2007. *Agriculture for Development. World Development Report 2008*. Washington D.C.

Yates, P. Lamartine. 1940. *Food Production and Manpower in Western Europe*. London: Longmans Green.

Yates, P. Lamartine. 1959. *Forty Years of Foreign Trade: A Statistical Handbook with Special Reference to Primary Products and Under-developed Countries*. London: Allen and Unwin.

Yates, P.Lamartine, and Dorren Warriner. 1943. *Food and Farming in Post-War Europe*. Oxford: Oxford University Press.

CHAPTER 5

When Do Landed Elites Voluntarily Give Up Power? The Europe Experience

Barrington Moore (1967) argued in his highly influential *Social Origins of Democracy and Dictatorship* that the interwar dictatorships were the result of the landed elites having maintained their political power during the early stages of industrialization and forming coalitions with a politically dependent bourgeoisie and state. By contrast, democracies appeared, and were sustained, in those countries where a strong, independent bourgeoisie had developed. Moore's study was built around just six historical cases (England, France, the United States, China, Japan, and India), with comments on a couple more (Germany and Russia), but Rueschemeyer et al. (1992: 8) extended the geographical area and concluded that when the 'landed upper-classes' were dependent on 'a large supply of cheap labor', they were 'consistently anti-democratic'.

In fact, and contrary to these assertions, by the early 1920s most of Europe's landed elites had either sold their estates, usually to their tenants, or seen them confiscated by the new governments in Eastern Europe, benefiting small farmers. The political authority of these landed elites was therefore significantly curtailed, requiring other explanations for the emergence of fascism in interwar Europe (Mahoney 2003).[1] As a new literature suggests, it was how the elites lost their power which mattered most, and whether the extension of the suffrage created a durable democracy, or ended in an authoritarian government. In particular, democracy's

J. Simpson, *Family Farmers, Land Reforms and Political Action*, Palgrave Studies in Economic History,
https://doi.org/10.1007/978-3-031-67281-1_5

survival in the interwar years depended on the sequence of events, and whether the landed elite were responsible for creating a hierarchical mass political party *before* male suffrage was widened (Luebbert 1991; Kalyvas 1996; Ertman 2009; Fukuyama 2014; Ziblatt 2017). This happened in much of North-West Europe, as the combination of long-run changes in factor prices, and the need for landed elites and Church to respond to parliamentary attacks from well-organized urban interests threatened both their economic and political powers. The conservative parties they formed enjoyed considerable electoral success, attracting new political entrepreneurs, and in the process diminishing the political influence of the landed elites. By contrast, in Eastern Europe, changes in factor prices *strengthened* the economic position of the landed elites, which only ended with the government-sponsored land reforms after the First World War.

This chapter begins by examining the historiography concerning land inequality, and its impact on economic growth, rural poverty, and participatory politics. It then shows how the interests of the landed elites changed over time, as the growing economic opportunities brought about by trade and industrialization provided incentives to dismantle Old Regime privileges, producing a new and more diverse elite. This is followed by looking at why their economic and political influence began to diminish in Western Europe from the late nineteenth century. In Eastern Europe, by contrast, rising population densities allowed the landed elites to continue to benefit from low wages and high rents, and their political influence remained strong until the Great War because of a restricted suffrage and electoral fraud. Southern Europe fell somewhere between these two extremes, with the landed elites successfully protecting their farm incomes through tariffs and adapting to political challenges by developing new forms of electoral fraud and patronage.

5.1 Landed Elites in Comparative Historical Perspective

Long-run changes in land inequality and political authority present formidable measurement problems for the historian. Traditionally, not only is there a lack of good information on the physical area that an individual or family owned, but there is also virtually none on land quality, and its actual or potential value. This is hardly surprisingly given that an influential landed elite was inevitably reluctant to use the limited state resources to measure its own wealth! In Britain and France, it was only following the bitter debates on the extent of land inequality in the late nineteenth century that governments began to collect the necessary statistical information.[2] In Spain, political conditions discouraged the necessary investment until the early 1930s, amid a major land reform (Simpson and Carmona 2020: 70–4).

Land inequality in traditional agrarian-based societies helped elites create rent-seeking opportunities and establish institutions that perpetuated their political authority, providing private benefits but slowing economic development (Acemoglu and Robinson 2012; Bates 1981; Engerman and Sokokoff 2012). Long-run economic growth was also harmed by elite governments having few incentives to provide public goods, such as an equitable tax system or effective banking systems, and there is considerable evidence that levels of schooling, literacy, and numeracy were lower in regions of large estates (Galor et al. 2009; Baten and Juif 2014). Even when public expenditure on education was not especially low, it was often skewed towards secondary and university education, benefiting the more affluent and perpetuating inequality (Nuñez 1991). By contrast, 'inclusive' institutions were more likely to be found in regions where landownership was egalitarian, helping to foster earlier industrialization and democracy.

A large historical literature therefore suggests that the landed elite was likely to oppose an extension of the suffrage, seeing it as a threat to their political authority and ability to enforce laws, or collect and spend taxes in their territories. Controlling the levers of political power was important, especially as land was a highly visible and immobile source of wealth, which could be easily taxed or confiscated. Acemoglu and Robinson argue that landed elites would only willingly surrender political power when they believed that the costs of preserving it outweighed the benefits. This might occur when the threat of revolution made (further) expenditure on repression too high and risky, or when income inequality was sufficiently low in a society that a major extension of the franchise could not produce significant transfers of wealth (Acemoglu and Robinson 2006: ch.2). In fact, the elites often had highly diverse interests, which made collective action difficult for them, especially following the disappearance of feudalism.

The numbers of landless labourers were significant in some regions, and rural poverty widespread in all of Europe's agricultural-based societies. Although 'labour-repressive' contracts had become rare in Europe by 1900, many farmers still required significant supplies of cheap labour, especially for the harvest, and complaints about restrictions to workers' mobility, or discrimination against trade unionists, were common in areas of large estates. Yet workers usually lacked the necessary organization to make income redistribution a danger for the landed elites, and in the interwar period rarely produced a political threat to governments (Chapter 8).

Nevertheless, the landed elites in some historical contexts have been seen in a more favourable light. English landowners in the seventeenth and perhaps eighteenth-centuries supposedly made important contributions to economic growth by developing commercial agriculture and stimulating farming innovations. Although these elites were reluctant to pay taxes to fund the schooling of the children of their tenants and workers, many invested in other sectors of the economy, while at the same time rich industrialists bought significant numbers of estates (Thomson 2001: ch.1). Large farms were much more likely to create marketable surpluses than smaller ones (Chapter 6). Robert Bates (1981: 95) has argued that hierarchical arrangements can allow landed elites to help overcome problems of free-riding among small farmers, and large landowners in countries such as Denmark and France helped small farmers to innovate (Lampe and Sharp 2018; Cleary 1989: 2–3) and, alongside the Church, played a major role in supporting voluntary associations such as farm cooperatives which integrated farmers into national politics and increased farm prosperity (Chapter 7).

The influence of the landed elite could therefore vary greatly, especially as the legal privileges and economic opportunities associated with land and the aristocracy were rarely stable but changed from the mid-eighteenth century across Europe. All the evidence suggests that the landed estate had significantly declined by the early 1920s, and the political authority of the landed elites was in retreat in most countries. Although land inequality persisted in regions of Germany, Italy, and Spain, offering some support for Moore's thesis, fascism was usually strongest in areas of small family farms, rather than areas of landed estates 'dependent' on cheap labour (Luebbert 1991: 309).

5.2 From Aristocratic Elites to Capitalist Farmers

European societies on the eve of the French Revolution were hierarchical, privileged social orders, with limited social mobility. The nature of land ownership was highly complex, with land being 'subject to many superimposed layers of tenancy, lordship, management and sovereignty which often overlapped' (van Bavel and Hoyle 2010: 12). Landed elites obtained their wealth and power from a variety of source, including land they farmed with workers (demesne), rental incomes, and feudal dues from a wide range of rights and privileges over the land and labour of others. Significant amounts of land belonged to the Church, municipalities, or was held by the nobility under strict-settlement laws and could never be sold. Labour obligations were common, and mobility restricted, especially in Eastern Europe. Yet from the late eighteenth century, and at differing speeds, feudal rights were eliminated with many of the landed estates being broken up and sold, and lease law totally reformed.

The French Revolution in 1789 was not caused by rural unrest, but farmers were quick to seize the land they rented and terminate the seigneurial regime, while the government moved rapidly to nationalize the Church's lands and abolished tithes. By 1815, the French nobility had lost much 'of its social and economic privileges ... its monopoly of high offices in the state, church, and military; feudal dues and services; much of its land; and its special fiscal and legal rights' (Berman 2019: 75). Despite this, land inequality remained significant, and large estates were common in France during the nineteenth century (Chevet 2009).

As Napoleon's armies swept across Europe, they abolished many aspects of feudal society. The restored monarchies after 1815 tried to reverse these changes, but the 'old' regime privileges were opposed not just by the growing urban middle classes who wanted a greater participation in government, but also by commercial farmers who looked to benefit from the expanding markets. The 1848 revolutions saw governments threatened by groups of urban intellectuals, artisans, and young nationalists across Europe. The events of 1848, just as with the French Revolution, took place against the background of widespread harvest failures, with those in Ireland in particular leaving a million dead. Yet even in North-Western Europe, the size of the urban middle classes was still small and family farmers showed little interest in further reforms once the remaining seigneurial dues had been eliminated, seeing them as a threat to their religion and traditional village life (Bayly 2004).[3] These farmers frequently opposed the privatization and loss of common land rights; were worried about the developing market economy, especially the usurious rates they had to pay to the village moneylender, or the low prices that merchants offered for their goods; and, of course, they resented the growing tax demands by the state. Opposition could lead to open conflict, such as the three Carlist Wars in nineteenth-century Spain, brigandage (Italy), or Jacqueries (Romania in 1907).[4] The swift conservative reaction in rural areas following the 1848 reforms would be repeated after the brief revolutionary period following the Great War.

The landed elites in Eastern Europe were able to maintain many of their privileges for longer, but institutional restrictions to land and labour markets were also seen by some large farmers as barriers to the growing commercial opportunities offered by trade. The 1848 revolutions led to the emancipation of the serfs and elimination of feudalism in Hungary and the western (Austria and Bohemia) provinces of the Habsburg Empire. In Poland, following the emancipation of the serfs in Russia in 1864, all villein services were abolished and the land was taken over by the farmers. In Southeastern Europe, the Ottoman Empire had centralized land in the hands of the state, with the landlords being state officials without ownership rights, and cultivation carried out by serfs. The 1859 Paris Convention abolished serfdom in Rumania, but landownership continued to be concentrated. By contrast, the abolition of Turkish feudalism during the early nineteenth century in Serbia, and in 1878 in Bulgaria, created an agriculture of small family farmers (Berend and Ránki 1974: ch.2).

Mitrany argued that the large estates persisted in Eastern Europe not because of any economic superiority over small farms, but rather because the abolition of feudal servitudes brought 'the great landlords' greater wealth and influence under the prevailing social and political conditions (Mitrany 1951: 43, 110). The large estates in Hungary and Poland, and the Ukraine exported grain to Western Europe, and during the three decades before the First World War, wheat output nearly doubled in Hungary; increased two and half times in Bulgaria; three-fold in Romania; and almost fourfold in Serbia, with yields and the area sown increasing (Berend and Ránki 1974: 55). In Spain, commercial cereal production was also highly profitable, although in this case demand came from an increasingly protected domestic market. As massive amounts of common lands were privatized, forests cut down to make railway sleepers, and pastures ploughed up for grain, leading to a *decline*, rather than *increase*, in the number of farm animals (GEHR 1978–1979; González de Molina et al. 2014). Complaints of falling yields and growing inequality, especially concerning the loss of common lands, were becoming common even before the flood of cheap New World cereals.

The ending of feudal privileges in much of Europe was therefore linked to a growing commercial agriculture, changing how the landed elite obtained their wealth, and allowing a new generation of more market-orientated landowners and farmers to replace the old nobility. The new elites benefitted from the greatly increased land market, which allowed them to buy farms from groups of the old nobility that could not adapt, as well as large amounts of the Church, municipal, and common lands. The difficulties of the traditional nobility to sustain their living standards filled contemporary novels by authors such as Turgenev or Hardy. Land ownership and authority over labour were no longer determined by 'rights' and 'privileges' but reflected market strength. When labour shortages began to appear because of industrialization and emigration, farmers strengthened paternalism and used interlinked contracts to help guarantee an adequate supply of willing and loyal workers, or tenants to rent their land (Chapter 8). Therefore, although the 'feudal' elites might have largely disappeared, land ownership remained highly concentrated, and holdings of over 100 hectares still accounted for at least a third, if not a half, of land at the end of the nineteenth century in most countries (Table 5.1). Wealth inequalities would be considerably greater if landless labourers are included to the figures.

Many contemporaries in the late nineteenth century expected farm size to continue to grow, as they believed that mechanization would produce economies of scale in farming as it had done in modern industry. Yet surprisingly, the direction of change in virtually all countries from the late nineteenth century was exactly the opposite, and by the interwar period the economic influence of the landed elites had declined significantly, and the family farm had become the dominant organizational structure. How this happened is treated in the rest of this chapter.

Table 5.1 Land concentration in different countries, circa 1900

	Size of holdings has	*% of all holdings*	*% of all land area*
Austria 1900	100+	0.6	48.3
Bavaria 1895	100+	0.1	2.6
Bohemia 1900	100+	0.5	32.8
Bulgaria 1897	100+	0.1	6.5
Denmark 1901	120+	2.9	23.0
England & Wales 1895*	121+	3.4	38.1
France 1892	40+	2.4	37.0
Hungary 1895	570+	0.2	32.3
Prussia 1907	100+	0.5	26.0
Sweden 1895	100+	0.9	12.0
Rumania 1897	100+	0.6	48.3

* Excludes holdings of less than 0.4 hectares

Sources Berend and Ránki (1974: 32, 37, 39), Afton and Turner (2000: 1844–5), Chevet (2009: 43), Jensen (1937), Osmond (2003: tables 3.5, 3.6), Myrdal and Morell (2011: tables 2.2, 2.3)

5.3 The Landed Elites and the Creation of Mass Political Parties in North-Western Europe

In contrast to the violent overthrow of the traditional aristocracy in revolutionary France, the new landed elites would only gradually lose their political and economic powers in North-Western Europe. During the half century following the Battle of Waterloo, they created lobbies and, on occasions, even directed rural protests, but they were generally able to keep the suffrage limited, and influence government by a combination of electoral fraud and control of state executives. Politics in most countries remained highly 'personal' and organized around influential individuals, with parties lacking a centralized bureaucracy. As the suffrage was gradually extended under pressure from urban groups, the landed elites in some countries found that there were limits to how far they could continue to determine electoral outcomes through patronage, corruption, and electoral fraud. The alternative was for themselves to build modern political parties, which were often surprisingly successful.

From around the 1870s, rural labour markets tightened and wages rose as growing numbers of farm workers left the land for the cities or emigrated to the New World. At the same time, the growing integration of international commodity markets exerted a significant downward pressure on land prices and rents, further diminishing the profitability of the large estate (Table 5.2) (O'Rourke and Williamson 1999). Free-trade in farm products therefore threatened not just a massive redistribution of incomes away from agriculture to urban consumers, but also within agriculture itself, so that the number of days that a farm labourer needed to work to buy a hectare of land halved between 1875 and 1912 in countries such as Denmark, Great Britain, and Sweden.

In Scandinavia, the landed elites had actually given up much of their land even before the 1870s. In Sweden, farmers with freeholds owned around 60% of the total area, and the nobility just 15%; in Denmark, landowners were restricted from raising rents, expanding their demesne, or evicting tenants; while in Norway large estates were of little importance (Olsson and Morell 2010). Most Scandinavian farmers benefitted from low cereal prices after 1870, as it made their livestock enterprises more profitable. Therefore, the major shifts in relative wage-rent ratios in this region helped both consolidate the family farm and align the interests of farmers and their demands for cheap cereals with those of urban workers and their employers.

Change was slower elsewhere in Western Europe because governments usually responded to the petitions of the landed elites to raise tariffs on imported foods. Yet everywhere the ratio of wages to land rents increased,

Table 5.2 Factor prices in Europe and the United States, 1875–1913

	US	*France*	*Germany*	*Great Britain*	*Denmark*	*Sweden*
Real wages 1875–1913						
1877	100	100	100	100	100	100
1902	136	132	131	122	204	152
1912	142	122	135	126	252	181
Real land prices, 1875–1913						
1877	100	100	100	100	100	100
1902	154	82	98	70	85	76
1912	275	85	108	58	112	81
Wage-rental ratios, 1875–1913						
1877	100	100	100	100	100	100
1902	88	162	134	174	239	199
1912	52	144	125	216	224	224

Source O'Rourke (1997: table 5)

helping farm workers to accumulate savings to buy land and encouraging large landowners to sell at least part of their estates.[5] In the words of Findlay and O'Rourke (2007: 402), 'on balance, it appears that the new transport technologies were so cost-reducing that their effects swamped those of rising European and American protectionism'. The introduction of the Code Napoleon in the early nineteenth century also had long-run implications in countries such as France, Belgium, and the Netherlands, as it now gave all children—not just the eldest male—the right to inherit on the death of their parents. In France, there were few landless farm workers over thirty by 1906, as by this age they had either become farmers in their own right, or left the land permanently to work for higher wages in other sectors of the economy (Sicsic 1992: 680, based on Garden 1988). Unsurprisingly, the years between 1919 and 1945 have been described as 'the triumph of the family farm' (Jessenne and Vivier 2010: 143). Farmers in North-Western Europe were forced to look elsewhere for labour, and on the First World War large numbers of Spanish and Italian workers were found in France, and Russian and Polish workers in Eastern Germany (Smith 1975: 373; Frader 1991: table 1; Koning 1994: 104).

Just as farm profits were being squeezed by falling prices and rising wages, large landowners experienced organized parliamentary attacks over their political privileges from the new, urban-based liberal parties. These groups also challenged the Church's traditional control over education and the family. Whenever possible, the landed elites responded by creating new forms of 'electoral fraud, manipulation, clientelism and corruption that *substituted* for the "old corruption" of deference and coercion'. When this failed, the landed elites set about building their own hierarchical, mass competitive political parties to win elections fairly (Ziblatt 2017: 34–5).

In Britain, agriculture employed only a quarter of the workforce by the 1840s, less than half the figure found elsewhere. The landed elites failed to stop the Corn Laws Act being passed in 1846, and between 1870 and 1914 saw their rents fall by 27% and labour costs rose by 31% (Afton and Turner 2000: tables 39.6, 42.9, 42.10, 44.1). At the same time, the rapidly growing cities demanded an extension of the franchise and the end of election rigging, which was prominent in 'safe' rural seats. New election rules and the secret ballot forced Britain's Conservative Party to change from being an 'elite' to a 'mass' political party, and it was so successful that it governed continuously between 1886 and 1906, save for 34 months (Ziblatt 2017: 110). As with most Western

European conservative parties, the British Conservative Party used religion for cross-class mobilizing, along with Empire and Nationalism (the Union with Ireland). The enduring success of the Conservative Party can be attributed to its hierarchical party organization and centralized administration which helped coordinate policies to attract support from outside groups, and control those within, with its paid officials allowing it to mobilize nationally. The switch from a party dominated by an elite to a popular mass one was greatly facilitated by the Primrose League, a vast network of family-based social associations it organized across the country, with reputably 1.5 million members by 1901 (Ziblatt 2017: 83–7). Therefore, although the Conservative Central Office determined the political issues to prioritize, and could exclude ideas that it deemed unsuitable, the Party's extensive grass-roots organizations and electoral successes allowed for new ideologies to develop, and for its core constituencies to change over time. As Ziblatt (2017) argues, the British landed elites only surrendered political power when they believed that the Conservative Party had created an organizational structure to win elections and form governments.

Yet in a democracy, no political party, however competitive, could guarantee power indefinitely. Following the Liberal Party's electoral landslide in 1906, Lloyd George passed the 'People's Budget' (1909) which introduced not just a progressive tax on income and land, but also death duties, both measures that produced a huge economic burden for owners of large estates, and country houses. The landed elites also saw their political influence curtailed with the loss of a permanent veto on parliamentary business in the reformed House of Lords (1911 Parliament Act). A 'revolution in landownership' followed, with perhaps a quarter of all England's land being sold between 1918 and 1921, as estates were broken up and sold to their tenants (Thompson 2007; Beckett and Turner 2007).

In Ireland, the shifts in factor prices coupled with the successful independence movement produced even greater changes, as the number of owner-occupiers increased from just 3% of all farms in 1870s to a massive 97% by 1929 (Hooker 1938: 120). Land transfers in Ireland were heavily politicized, with landowners separated from their tenants and workers along religious and national cleavages. As farm prices fell, the Anglo-Protestant landowners initially refused to reduce rents, which led to rent strikes and rural violence during the Land Wars (1879–1881). Gladstone's Land Act (1881) established a Land Commission to adjudicate on a 'fair rent', leading to reductions of about a fifth across the country

(Dooley 2022: 12). Nevertheless, many landowners avoided the controls by limiting their leases to eleven months rather than a year and remained unwilling to sell their land. Significant sales only followed the 1903 Land Act, a land reform which paid landowners the generous price of 25 years of rental income and a 12% bonus (Chapter 6). Even so, some landowners continued to keep a few tenanted holdings, as well as their demesnes, to pay for the upkeep of their houses. Political conflicts resulted in arson, with almost 300 large houses being destroyed during the War of Independence (1919–1921) and especially the Civil War (June 1922–May 1923). As Dooley (2022: 161) notes, this, and the general intimidation of landowners, 'was an effective stratagem to drive the owner away, leaving lands available for redistribution'. Yet Dooley also concludes that, 'even without revolution, hundreds of great houses would have been (and were) abandoned across Ireland from the 1920s, a trend that was equally evident across Britain as their owners could no longer afford their upkeep' (Dooley 2022: 223).

A very different story unfolded in Germany. The German Conservative Party (DKP) represented the landed elite, and it remained a party of notables until 1918, relying not on grass-roots organizations to create a competitive mass political party to win elections legitimately, but rather on 'state-assisted electoral fraud and anti-socialist election-time coalitions with other parties of the right' (Ziblatt 2017: 173). The DKP was a large, but weak party, lacking a central organization to nominate candidates, mobilize voters, and impose parliamentary discipline. Instead, it was captured by the Agrarian League, the *Bund der Landwirte* (BdL), a well-organized interest group that represented agricultural concerns. Unlike the DKP, the BdL did have a highly centralized bureaucracy, employing 700 people by the turn of the century, and was as active in helping farmers as it was in lobbying to protect the interests of landowners. According to Ziblatt (2017: 199), 'between 1898 and 1912, not only was every single Reichstag Conservative Party MP endorsed by and programmatically committed to the BdL, but also one-third of Conservative Party MPs were simultaneously high level BdL functionaries'.

Therefore, unlike other North-Western European countries, the German landed elites did not need to build a competitive mass political conservative party before 1914 because they already controlled government sufficiently. Unlike Britain and elsewhere, conservative parliamentary representatives remained dependent on the narrow group interests of cereal farmers, effectively limiting changes to its core constituencies as the economy developed over time.

Stathis Kalyvas (1996) has shown that the Catholic Church worked with the landed elites to develop mass competitive conservative parties.[6] Across much of North-Western Europe from the 1860s, centralizing and state-building governments threatened the economic and political privileges of both the landed elites and Catholic Church. Furthermore, well-organized, urban-based liberal parties launched parliamentary attacks on the Church over its control of education and the family, and the landed elites for their privileges and political influence in village society.[7] Given the diminishing possibilities of controlling parliaments through electoral fraud, these attacks created incentives for the two groups to organize together and build new political parties to compete with the urban-based ones. The Catholic Church in countries such as Belgium, the Netherlands, Austria, Germany, or Italy helped recruit voters, with the political leadership provided by the landed elites. Family farmers became drawn into national politics as the landed elites and Church helped them form their own associations and cooperatives, thereby strengthening the family farm within the marketplace, and formalizing better their political demands (Chapter 7). The new parties enjoyed considerable success, assisted by the 'blind belief' of many liberals in secular progress, and their 'elitist underestimation of the power of the masses coupled with a complete unfamiliarity with rural reality' (Kalyvas 1996: 106). Kalyvas argues that the electoral success of the new parties attracted other ambitious politicians, who realized that power lay with the electorate and a secular party, which in time marginalized both the landed elites and the Church politically. By extending their social base, confessional party also found it easier to work with other, non-confessional parties in government.

5.4 The Consolidation of Large Estates in Eastern Europe Before 1914

Feudalism persisted for longer in Eastern Europe, and the growing market integration reinforced, rather than weakened, the position of large landowners and farmers, especially as industrialization was often weak. Neither was the political influence of landed elites seriously challenged by urban liberals, making it unnecessary for them to establish competitive political mass parties, especially as traditional mechanisms of paternalism for allocating land, hiring workers, or lending capital remained unchallenged. Land ownership in Eastern Europe was only significantly changed with the land reforms following the Great War.

Just as in the New World, railway construction cut freight rates and helped link farmers to markets, leading to a major increase in the area cultivated and a rise in land prices. By contrast, rapid population growth and weak urban demand restricted wage growth. The Russian export boom saw annual agricultural output increase by 2.8% between the mid-1880s and 1913, with the area cultivated growing by 1.3% and labour inputs by 1.4%, compared to a GDP growth of 3.3% (Allen 2003: 24–8, figures from Gregory, 1982). Land rentals increased sevenfold between 1861 and 1901 but farm workers saw no increase in real wages. Land ownership was 'the way to participate in the Russian wheat boom' (Shanin, 1986: 147 cited in Allen, 2003: 43) and explains why the peasants were so quick to seize farms in 1917. Hungarian farmers enjoyed protected markets within the Habsburg Empire, which led to the 'consolidation of large, centrally operated estates', perhaps unique in Europe before 1914 (Kopsidis 2009: 288–90). Again, land rents increased in the long-run, but wages tended to stagnate, with short-term fluctuations according to levels of emigration and harvest mechanization (Eddie 1967: 307–9). Real wages in the western regions of the Habsburg Empire grew slowly between the 1850s and 1914 but stagnated in eastern and south-eastern areas (Cvrcek 2013: 20, figures 4a and 4b).

Land ownership was highly concentrated in Romania, but it was farmed in small plots by tenants and sharecroppers. The area of wheat increased from 700–900,000 hectares in the 1860s to two million hectares by the early twentieth century (Chirot and Ragin 1975: 430). The rapid rise in rents after 1870, and acute shortage of land, led to violent assaults on large farms in March 1907, with an estimated 11,000 being killed during the revolt and repression (Roberts 1951: 3, 15; Roszkowski 1995: 26, 49).[8] In some countries, smallholdings were already common and in Serbia, a country of almost no landless labour, real wages for unskilled urban workers remained stagnant at low levels during the half century prior to the First World War (Mijatović and Milanović 2021).

Land inequality, as in Ireland, was often accompanied by deep national and religious cleavages. In the Baltic, large estates averaging around 2,000 hectares, and covering about three-fifths of the land area, often belonged to German and, less frequently, Russian and Polish landowners.[9] Large estates also covered two-fifths of the area of the Old Polish territories. In Greater Poland, Pomerania, and Upper Silesia, estates were usually owned by German landlords, but further east, they were more likely to be Polish. In Bohemia and Moravia large estates were also in hands of foreigners, with the Kingdom of Bohemia being referred to as the Kingdom of Schwarzenberg, because of the family's massive holdings (Roszkowski 1995: 42–4). In Hungary, the area of farms of over 575 hectares accounted for about 40% of the land area between 1867 and 1914, while middle-sized properties (29–575 hectares) represented only two-ninths of the total acreage and tended to decline (Eddie 1967: table 1).[10] Some 13,949 estates covered more than ten million hectares, averaging 777 hectares each, and 45% of the total area. There were regional differences, but in general most were in the hands of Hungarian landowners. Land in Bulgaria and Serbia, by contrast, belonged predominantly to small and medium-sized farmers.

Eastern Europe in 1900 was therefore dominated by large estates, often owned by individuals whose nationality was distinct from those who worked the land. The introduction of universal male suffrage in Bohemia and Moravia in 1907 saw the growth of an Agrarian Party but in most other countries small farmers remained weakly organized, despite their constant demands for land. It was political circumstances, rather than concerns about inequality, which explains the nature and timing of land reforms after 1918, and why many estates were transferred with little compensation to landless and tenant farmers on 'a wave of revolutionary and nationalist enthusiasm' (Warriner 1939: 145–6).

5.5 The Persistence of Landed Elites in Southern Europe

The presence of large estates and a politically influential landed elite often persisted in Southern Europe for longer than elsewhere. The rural exodus was delayed by late industrialization, with agriculture still employing around half the labour force in 1930. Cereal farmers were sheltered by high tariffs but, although labour costs rose less than those in North-Western Europe, the numbers of landless workers still declined. Italy, just as in England and Wales, witnessed massive sales in the immediate post-war years (948 thousand hectares), equivalent to 4.5% of farmland, benefitting especially tenant and sharecropping families, and would probably have been even greater but for the success of fascism in destroying rural labour organizations (Martinelli 2015).[11]

In Spain, the share of the farm population that owned or rented some land increased from 51% to 70% between 1890 and 1930, and the number of landless workers halved, to slightly under a million (Carmona et al. 2019: tables 2, 3). The large latifundios were also slowly being broken up, and in Cordoba (southern Spain) they declined from an average of 2,000 hectares in the mid-eighteenth century to 1,300 hectares a century later, before falling to 700 hectares by the 1930s. By this date, most landowners possessed only a single farm, which they worked themselves rather than being an absentee landowner (López Ontiveros and Mata Olmo 1993: 45–6). Yet if the relative importance of family farms was growing, many were too small to support a family, and there were significant numbers of landless workers concentrated in southern Spain.

Crucially, neither the landed elites nor the Catholic Church in Southern Europe felt sufficiently threatened by the liberals in their national parliaments to attempt to build mass competitive political parties before 1914. Furthermore, when the suffrage was extended, the rural elites were able to develop new informal techniques of electoral fraud, manipulation, clientelism, and corruption to maintain their political control. In Spain, despite universal male suffrage from 1890, the so-called *turno pacifico* was an agreement between the two main political parties, the Conservatives and Liberals, to alternate in government. The winning party, and allocation of parliamentary seats, took place prior to the elections, and it was left to the village cacique, or local party boss, to use his patronage to obtain the necessary votes. Similar systems allowed parties to alternate power through the rigging of elections in Italy (*trasformismo*) and Portugal (*rotativismo*) (Ziblatt 2017: 34–5). As a result, the combination of weak state capacity and manipulated elections strengthened the political authority of the local elites, as patron-client networks were extensively used to 'accomplish political work which, in constitutional principle, should have been carried on by independent citizens, representative assemblies, bureaucrats, and public-minded public officials' (Tilly et al. 1975: 90–1).

The persistence of a landed elite and the appearance of fascism in Italy, Portugal, and Spain during the 1920s and 1930s suggest possible linkages to support Barrington Moore's thesis. Both Mussolini's seizure of power in 1922, and Spain's military coup d'état in 1936, took place against a background of rural conflicts (Chapter 8). However, fascist activists usually showed more interest in breaking-up labour organizations than preserving the large estates, while large landowners objected to greater state intervention that fascists demanded, and the industrial biases of their economic policies.

5.6 Conclusion

The political and economic influence of the landed elites by the mid-1920s had diminished significantly across much of Europe. Two distinct models have been identified to explain this demise: a 'bottom-up' process, where the landed elites played an important role in helping to organize small farmers in mass competitive political parties, whose success in time would undermined their own political control; and 'top-down' one, where government implemented land reforms to break up the large estates. Although the small farm became the dominant production unit in both cases, and the numerical importance of family farmers promised to transform domestic politics, the outcomes were actually very different. In North-Western Europe, the landed elites had to adapt in the decades before 1914 to the extension of the suffrage and falling profits, as the centre of the economy shifted away from agriculture to the urban sectors. Landowners were perhaps too successful, as the new mass political parties that they helped create were taken over by more ambitious political entrepreneurs. In Eastern and Southern Europe, by contrast, the landed elites could continue to use corruption and bribery to retain their political hold, reflecting the continuation of traditional hierarchical structures in the countryside. With the sudden appearance of the 'democratic spring', no real political parties existed to represent the demands of the new voters.[12] The Eastern European land reforms successfully removed the economic and political powers of significant sections of the landed elites but proved to be an imperfect substitute to the slower changes that took place in North-Western Europe (Chapter 6).

Notes

1. Mahoney (2003: 137, 145) who describes the *Social Origins* as 'the single most important book in the comparative historical research tradition', believes that Moore's 'specific hypotheses

about democracy and authoritarianism' have 'only limited and highly conditional support'.
2. See especially Bateman (1883), Thompson (1963), and Lindert (1987). Richard Cobden and John Stuart Mill in the mid-1860s linked the extension of the franchise with the need for some form of land reform. For France, Augé-Laribé and Pinot (1927: 2–3).
3. The Swing Riots and the destruction of steam threshing machines in southern England in the 1830s illustrate that villagers might turn to violence to protect their interests in a rapidly transforming economy.
4. Tilly et al. (1975: 122–3) for brigandage in Italy; for Romania, Marin (2018).
5. The wage-rent ratio increased by a factor of 2.7 between 1870 and 1914 in Britain, in Sweden by 2.6, in Denmark by 3.1, and in Ireland by 5.6. By contrast the figures were 2.0 in France and 1.4 in Germany (O'Rourke and Williamson 1999: 62).
6. Religious affiliations divided German conservatives, and the DKP represented Protestant (and Prussian), rather than Catholic interests.
7. Kalyvas (1996: 51) notes that 'Liberals, strong among the rising industrial and urban bourgeoisie, stood for state rationalization and centralization and fought against local particularisms and privileged bodies such as monarchies, established churches, and hereditary aristocracies'.
8. The Fischer family alone controlled some 200,000 hectares.
9. In Estonia, 1,149 estates occupied an average of 2,000 hectares, while in Latvia, 1,410 estates averaged 2,100 hectares. The figures for Lithuania were probably similar (Roszkowski 1995: 41–2).
10. A significant part of this land was held in mortmain and could not be sold. Despite regional diversity, Eddie (1967: 300) argues that perhaps even more striking was 'the general countrywide similarity in the pattern of landholdings'.
11. Figures refer to between 1920 and 1923. Sales were less important in area where conflicts between socialists and fascists was greatest.
12. Ortega y Gasset noted at the time of Spain's Second Republic in 1931 that, 'with the exception of the Socialist Party, all the other parties that engage in politics are not really parties nor anything worthy of it' (in Linz 1967: 228).

References

Acemoglu, Daron, and James A. Robinson. 2006. *Economic Origins of Dictatorship and Democracy*. Cambridge: Cambridge University Press.

Acemoglu, Daron, and James A. Robinson. 2012. *Why Nations Fail. The Origins of Power, Prosperity and Poverty*. Princeton: Princeton University Press.

Afton, Bethanie, and Michael Turner. 2000. "The Statistical Base of Agricultural Performance in England and Wales, 1850–1914." In *The Agrarian History of England and Wales, 1850–1914*, edited by E.J.T. Collins, 1757–2140. Cambridge: Cambridge University Press.

Allen, Robert C. 2003. *Farm to Factory. A Reinterpretation of the Soviet Industrial Revolution*. Princeton: Princeton University Press.

Augé-Laribé, Michel, and Pierre Pinot. 1927. *Agriculture and Food Supply in France during the War, Carnegie Endowment for International Peace*. New Haven: Yale.

Bateman, John. 1883. *The Great Landowners of Great Britain and Ireland*. London.

Baten, Joerg, and Dácil Juif. 2014. "A Story of Large Landowners and Math Skills: Inequality and Human Capital Formation in Long-Run Development, 1820–2000." *Journal of Comparative Economics* 42: 375–401.

Bates, Robert H. 1981. *Markets and States in Tropical Africa. The Political Basis of Agricultural Policies*. Berkeley: University of California.

Bayly, C.A. 2004. *The Birth of the Modern World 1780–1914*. Malden,MA: Blackwell.

Beckett, John, and Michael E. Turner. 2007. "End of the Old Order? F.M.L. Thompson, the Land Question, and the burden of ownership in England, c1880–c1925." *Agricultural History Review* 55 (2): 269–88.

Berend, Ivan T., and Gyorgy Ránki. 1974. *Economic Development in East-Central Europe in the 19th and 20th Centuries*. New York: Columbia.

Berman, Sheri. 2019. *Democracy and Dictatorship in Europe; From the Ancien Régime to the Present Day*. Oxford University Press.

Carmona, Juan, Joan Rosés, and James Simpson. 2019. "Spanish Land Reform in the 1930s: Economic Necessity or Political Opportunism?" *The Economic History Review* 72 (2): 669–90.

Chevet, Jean-Michel. 2009. "Reconsidering A Rural Myth: Peasant France and Capitalist Britain." *Agricultural History Review* Supplement: 37–54.

Chirot, Daniel, and Charles Ragin. 1975. "The Market, Tradition and Peasant Rebellion: The Case of Romania in 1907." *American Sociological Association* 40 (4): 428–44.

Cleary, Mark. 1989. *Peasants, Politicians and Producers: The Organisation of Agriculture in France Since 1918*. Cambridge: Cambridge University Press.

Cvrcek, Tomas. 2013. "Wages, Prices, and Living Standards in the Habsburg Empire, 1827–1910." *Journal of Economic History* 73 (1): 1–37.

Dooley, Terence. 2022. *Burning the Big House. The Story of the Irish Country House in a Time of War and Revolution*. New Haven & London: Yale.

Eddie, Scott M. 1967. "The Changing Pattern of Landownership in Hungary, 1867–1914." *The Economic History Review* 20 (2): 293–310.

Engerman, Stanley, and Kenneth L. Sokokoff. 2012. *Economic Development in the America since 1500. Endowments and Institutions*. Cambridge: Cambridge University Press.

Ertman, Thomas. 2009. "Western European Party Systems and the Religious Cleavage." In *Religion, Class Cleavages, and Welfare States*, edited by Kees van Kersbergen and Philip Manow, 39–55. Cambridge: Cambridge University Press.

Findlay, Ronald, and Kevin H. O'Rourke. 2007. *Power and Plenty. Trade, Wars, and the World Economy in the Second Millennium*. Princeton: Princeton University Press.

Frader, Laura Levine 1991. *Peasants and Protest: Agricultural Workers, Politics, and Unions in the Aude, 1850–1914*. Berkeley, Los Angeles and London: University of California Press.

Fukuyama, Francis. 2014. *Political Order and Political Decay. From the Industrial Revolution to the Globalisation of Democracy*. London: Profile.

Galor, Oded, Omer Moav, and Dietrich Vollrath. 2009. "Inequality in Landownership, the Emergence of Human-Capital Promoting Institutions, and the Great Divergence." *The Review of Economic Studies* 76 (1): 149–79.

Garden, M. 1988. "L'évolution de la population active." In *Historie de la population française, vol..3*, edited by Dupâquier, 243–68. Paris: Presses Universitaires de France.

GEHR. 1978–9. "Contribución al análisis histórico de la ganadería española, 1865–1929." *Agricultura y Sociedad* (viii and x):129–182 and 105–169.

González de Molina Navarro, Manuel, Juan Infante Amate, and Antonio Herrera González de Molina. 2014. "Cuestionando los relatos tradicionales: desigualdad, cambio liberal y crecimiento agrario en el Sur peninsular (1752–1901)." *Historia Agraria* (63): 55–88.

Gregory, Paul R. 1982. *Russian National Income, 1885–1913*. Cambridge: Cambridge University Press.

Hooker, E.R. 1938. *Re-adjustments of Agricultural Tenure in Ireland*. Chapel Hill: North Carolina.

Jensen, E. 1937. *Danish Agriculture: its Economic Development*. Copenhagen: Schultz.

Jessenne, Jean-Pierre, and Nadine Vivier. 2010. "Northern France, 1750–2000." In *Rural Economy and Society in Northern-western Europe, 500–2000. Social Relations: Property and Power*, edited by Bas van Bavel and Richard Hoyle. Turnhout: Brepols.

Kalyvas, Stathis N. 1996. *The Rise of Christian Democracy in Europe*. Ithaca and London: Cornell.
Koning, Niek 1994. *The Failure of Agrarian Capitalism: Agrarian Politics in the U.K., Germany, the Netherlands and the USA, 1846–1919*. London and New York: Routledge.
Kopsidis, Michael. 2009. "Agricultural Development and Impeded Growth: The Case of Hungary, 1870–1914." In *Agriculture and Economic Development in Europe Since 1870*, edited by Pedro Lains and Vicente Pinilla, 286–310. London: Routledge.
Lampe, Markus, and Paul Sharp. 2018. *A Land of Milk and Butter: How Elites Created the Modern Danish Dairy Industry*. Chicago: Chicago University Press.
Lindert, Peter H. 1987. "Who Owned Victorian England? The Debate over Landed wealth and Inequality." *Agricultural History* 61 (4): 25–51.
Linz, Juan J. 1967. "The Party System of Spain: Past and Future." In *Party Systems and Voter Alignments: Cross-National Perspectives*, edited by Seymour M. Lipset and Stein Rokkan. New York: The Free Press.
López Ontiveros, Antonio, and Rafael Mata Olmo. 1993. *Propiedad de la Tierra y Reforma Agraria en Córdoba (1932–1936)*. Córdoba: Universidad de Córdoba.
Luebbert, George M. 1991. *Liberalism, Fascism, or Social Democracy. Social Classes and the Political Origins of Regimes in Interwar Europe*. Oxford: Oxford University Press.
Mahoney, James. 2003. "Knowledge Accumulation in Comparative Historical Research: The Case of Democracy and Authoritarianism." In *Comparative Historical Analysis in the Social Sciences*, edited by James Mahoney and Dietrich Rueschemeyer, 131–74. Cambridge: Cambridge University Press.
Marin, Irina. 2018. *Peasant Violence and Antisemitism in Early Twentieth-Century Eastern Europe*. London/New York/Shanghai: Palgrave Macmillan.
Martinelli, Pablo. 2015. "A Spontaneous Land Reform in Post-World War I Italy? "Red Fear" and the Formation of New Peasant Ownership." International Conference European Rural History Organization (EURHO), Girona.
Mijatović, Boško, and Branko Milanović. 2021. "The Real Urban Wage in an Agricultural Economy Without Landless Farmers: Serbia, 1862–1910." *The Economic History Review* 74 (2): 424–48.
Moore, Barrington. 1967. *Social Origins of Dictatorship and Democracy: Lord and Peasant in the Making of the Modern World*. London: Allen Lane.
Myrdal, J., and Matts Morell. 2011. "Statistical Appendix." In *The Agrarian History of Sweden 4000BC to AD2000*, edited by Mats Morell, C.-J. Gadd and J. Myrdal, 285–301. Lund: Nordic Academic Press.
Nuñez, Clara Eugenia. 1991. "El gasto público en educación en la España contemporánea." *Hacienda Pública Española*: 121–46.

O'Rourke, Kevin. 1997. "The European Grain Invasion, 1870–1913." *The Journal of Economic History* 57 (4): 775–801.
O'Rourke, Kevin, and Jeffrey G. Williamson. 1999. *Globalization and History. The Evolution of a Nineteenth-Century Atlantic Economy*. Cambridge, Massachusetts and London.
Olsson, Mats, and Mats Morell. 2010. "Scandinavia, 1750–2000." In *Rural Economy and Society in North-western Europe, 500–2000. Social Relations: Property and Power*, edited by Bas J.P van Bavel and Richard Hoyle, 315–47. Turnhout: Brepols.
Osmond, Jonathan. 2003. "Land, Peasant and Lord in German Agriculture since 1800." In *Germany. A New Social and Economic History. 3, Since 1800*, edited by Sheilagh Ogilvie and Bob Scribner, 71–105. London: Hodder.
Roberts, Henry L. 1951. *Rumania. Political Problems of an Agrarian State*. New Haven: Yale University Press.
Roszkowski, Wojciech. 1995. *Land Reforms in East Central Europe after World War One*. Warsaw: Institute of Political Studies Polish Academy of Science.
Rueschemeyer, Dietrich, Evelyne Huber Stephens, and John Stephens. 1992. *Capitalist Development and Democracy*. Cambridge: Polity.
Shanin, Teodor. 1986. *Russia as a 'Developing Society'*. London: Macmillan.
Sicsic, Pierre. 1992. "City-Farm Wage Gaps in Late Nineteenth Century France." *The Journal of Economic History* 52: 675–695.
Simpson, James, and Juan Carmona. 2020. *Why Democracy Failed: The Agrarian Origins of the Spanish Civil War*. Cambridge: Cambridge University Press.
Smith, Harvey. 1975. "Work Routine and Social Structure in a French Village: Cruzy, Hérault in the Nineteenth Century." *Journal of Interdisciplinary History* 5: 357–382.
Thompson, F.M.L. 1963. *English Landed Society in the Nineteenth Century*. London: Routledge & Kegan Paul.
Thompson, Michael. 2007. "The Land Market, 1880–1925: A Reappraisal Reappraised." *Agricultural History Review* 55 (2): 289–300.
Thomson, F.M.L. 2001. *Gentrification and the Enterprise Culture. Britain 1780–1980*. Oxford: Oxford University Press.
Tilly, Charles, Louise Tilly, and Richard Tilly. 1975. *The Rebellious Century*. Cambridge, Mass.: Harvard University Press.
van Bavel, Bas J.P, and Richard Hoyle. 2010. "Introduction." In *Social Relation: Property and Power*, 1–23. Turnhout: Brepols.
Warriner, Doreen. 1939. *Economics of Peasant Farming*. Oxford: Oxford University Press.
Ziblatt, Daniel. 2017. *Conservative Parties and the Birth of Democracy*. Cambridge: Cambridge University Press.

CHAPTER 6

Land Reform and Farming in Interwar Europe

Why are some land reforms more successful than others? Interwar Europe provides an opportunity to answer this question as many countries, at different levels of economic development carried out major reforms at one moment or another. This chapter argues that although redistributive land reforms provided some economic and political stability during this particularly turbulent period of history, policymakers were divided between meeting the economic and political needs of those farmers living in acute poverty, and increasing efficiency and the production of cheap food for urban consumers.

Interwar Europe has been described as the 'Golden Age of the Peasantry', as the family farm because the dominant unit of production, occupying the space left following the demise of the large, landed estate. Land reforms took place across all of Eastern Europe, parts of Scandinavia and Southern Europe, as well as in several North-Western European countries (Ireland, Germany). In Eastern Europe, land reforms were specifically pro-poor, involving the break-up and settlement of marginal farmers and landless workers on private estates and state land in the aftermath of the First World War, by governments eager to widen their political support in the successor states.

The land reform literature suggests that creating small, family-operated farms changes work incentives, encouraging the new owners to work the

J. Simpson, *Family Farmers, Land Reforms and Political Action*, Palgrave Studies in Economic History,
https://doi.org/10.1007/978-3-031-67281-1_6

land better and increase output, thereby improving living standards for the poorest groups in society, as well as empowering them politically. The political background to Europe's land reforms often differed greatly, but the economic constraints of insufficient land and weak consumer demand in the interwar years were common to all. The challenges also differed between those land reforms taking place in transforming economies, where the relative importance of agriculture was declining because of growing industrialization, and those in agricultural-based societies, where the sector still employed half or more of the active population.

Land reform was generally a poor substitute to the market-led changes in land ownership that had taken place in much of North-Western Europe in the half century after the 1870s, where the numbers of family farms grew as a result of the long-run shifts in factor prices which made the large private estates unprofitable, and family farmers were integrated into competitive, mass political parties (Chapter 5). By contrast, although land reforms successfully created employment for the poor and helped maintain their food consumption during the depths of the economic depression, they limited market specialization, slowing the supply of cheap food for the cities. The fact that farmers received insufficient land and withdrew from markets also restricted their incentives to organize cooperatives and political parties.

The chapter is divided into five sections. The first examines the political and economic arguments for land reform, and its impact on inequality and farm productivity. This is followed by a survey of European reforms in the interwar years. Sections three and four consider the experience of land reform in agrarian societies, where three-quarters or more of the active population worked in agriculture (Bulgaria, Romania, and Yugoslavia), and in transforming economies, where the rural exodus was already strong (Czechoslovakia, Ireland, and Spain). Section five concludes.

6.1 Farm Size, Market Specialization, and the Arguments for Land Reform

Some contemporaries in the late nineteenth century expected that the growing economies of scale and the division of labour found in industry would spread to agriculture, as seemed to be the case on the massive wine-producing estates appearing in southern France (Augé-Laribé 1907; Simpson 2011: 53–7). Lenin, and other Marxists, believed that capitalism would make small farms uncompetitive, forcing their owners to join the proletariat. Yet others, and not only those on the Left, thought that large estates owed their existence to political privilege, if not 'theft', rather than any economic efficiency (Warriner 1939: 11–2).[1] Recent literature has also noted that landed elites tend to create political institutions that stifle economic growth, restrict the suffrage, hamper human capital formation, and distort the expansion of state capacity (Galor et al., 2009; Acemoglu and Robinson 2012; Engerman and Sokokoff 2012; Baten and Juif 2014). Low incomes and high-income inequality, rudimentary farming techniques, few schools and illiteracy, and limited political voice were indeed common when land ownership was concentrated across large areas of Eastern and Southern Europe on the eve of the Great War.

The economic arguments for land reform in low-income countries involve not just questions of social justice, but are closely linked to increasing farm efficiency. Large farmers prefer crops and farming methods that minimize labour inputs because of the high supervision costs associated with using wage workers. Land concentration can give landowners monopsony powers in labour markets when alternative work opportunities are scarce and result in significant unemployment (Martinelli 2014 and Robledo Hernández 2022). Small farmers, by contrast, use family labour and can choose production systems that allow them to work much longer hours to maximize output on their land (Chapter 3). An inverse relationship is therefore found in low-income countries between farm size and output per hectare (Lipton 2009: ch.2). Nonetheless, this is much less true in more developed economies, where large farmers have access to capital markets, and mechanization can reduce labour requirements, including those of skilled work.[2] The greater power and efficiency of machinery improves work quality and allows time-bound operation to be carried out at the optimal moment. Consequently, Foster and Rosenzweig (2022) argue that, from a global perspective, there is a U-shaped relationship between farm productivity and scale, being high on both very small plots in less developed economies *and* the mechanized large farms in more developed economies.[3]

Land reform inevitably creates winners and losers, but the distinct goals of equality and efficiency, and the fact that Europe's land reforms took place in countries at very different levels of development, make any generalizations concerning their success difficult. It raises questions not only of how to measure the economic and political sustainability of a land reform, but also whether results should be viewed in the short term, or rather in the context of long-run development. Land reform often produces conflicting results, changing some aspects of rural society which might be expected to improve economic performance, but creating obstacles to them elsewhere. One risk was that the reduction in income inequality and better diets among the rural poor produced by land reform came at the expense of less food for urban consumers, or a reduced demand for manufactured goods. In land-scarce societies, long-run rural prosperity was closely linked to small family farmers being able to shift out of low yield crops such as cereals, and into more labour-intensive, and higher-value products. Yet it was considerably easier to increase the *marketable* supply of food if land reform prioritized only farms that could fully employ a family's labour and work animals. As planners in the Soviet Union found in the 1920s, there was a dilemma over whether to satisfy farmers' demand for land, even though properties were far too small to be efficient, or meet instead industry's needs for a regular supply of cheap *domestically* produced foodstuffs. Market-orientated family farmers were also likely to have greater incentives to build voluntary associations which strengthened democracy. Some governments preferred however to maximize the number of recipients from land reform to increase their potential support in rural areas (Unwin 1980: 134).

The period between the recovery from war and the fall in farm prices in the late 1920s is too short to fully assess the results of the land reforms but some of the advantages, and difficulties, associated with them were already apparent. These shortcomings were magnified by the fact that they took place in a very different macroeconomic context to those in East Asia after the Second World War, where the rapid growth of the world economy helped farmers in Japan, South Korea, or Taiwan to specialize in high-value farm products (Griffin et al. 2002).

6.2 The Nature of Land Reforms in Interwar Europe

The new governments in Eastern Europe faced enormous popular expectations after the sufferings caused by war, food shortages, and disease. The growing communist threat, not just in Russia, but also in countries such as Germany, Hungary, and Italy, encouraged democratic forces to move swiftly to consolidate their governments. Land reform was attractive to parties across the political spectrum, whether to help overthrow the old 'bourgeois' governments or to ensure the conservatism of a landowning peasantry (Lipton 2009; Albertus 2015). The motives for land reform were therefore political, rather than economic, and access to land, took priority over farming efficiency. Large farms, with the exceptions of Hungary and western Poland, were broken up, and landlords as a political class ceased to be important. In the Balkans, inequalities in landownership were smaller, and land reform led to a change in ownership rather than farming methods. In Romania, only a sixth of the country's large estates had previously been worked by their owners, so the 'real change was not from large-scale to small-scale, from organised capitalistic to simple peasant farming, but rather from farming for the market to farming for subsistence' (Mitrany 1951: 118). By contrast, redistributive land reforms in Western Europe were less important, with the exceptions of the nationalist struggle in Ireland, and democratic Spain in the early 1930s. Land reform across Eastern Europe affected perhaps 20 million hectares of farmland, or almost a fifth of the total area (Table 6.1).[4]

Major land reforms were common in regions where landowners were foreign, or the native aristocracy had lost its political importance, resulting in their impact being smaller in Hungary and Poland, where the native landed elites had played an important role in public life and the nationalist movements (Seton-Watson 1945–1967: 77). The nationalist character of

Table 6.1 Experience of land reform in interwar Europe

	GDP per capita 1929	*% population in agriculture*	*Area parcelled 000s has.*	*Area parcelled % total area*	*No of beneficiaries thousands*	*No of farms 1935 millions*	*Size of holdings allocated*
Estonia	—	—	1204	27.9	84	—	14.4
Lativia	—	—	1700	27.7	145	—	11.8
Lithuania	—	—	740	16.9	72	—	10.4
Baltic states	—	—				0.85	
Bulgaria	1128	75	133	6.0	173	0.7	0.8
Romania	1102	72	3630	12.3	1369	3.2	2.7
Yugoslavia	1364	76	2480	10.0	669	—	3.3
Czechoslovakia	2918	33	1292	12.5	643	1.6	2.0
Hungary	2537	51	727	8.5	685	1.3	1.1
Poland	2118	60	2654	7.0	734	3.3	3.6
Ireland	2952	48	6057	71.0	433	—	—
Spain	2724	50	672	1.2	100	—	—
Germany	4051	29	930	2.0	78	—	12.0

Sources Broadberry and Klein (2012: table 7); Moore (1945: tables 2, 3, 19); Roszkowski (1995: table 9, 12); Warriner)1939: 3); Foley-Fisher and McLaughlin (2016: table 1); Farquharson (1976: 155)

the reform was reflected in who received the land, as landless Hungarians in Transylvania, Slovakia, Bačka, and Banat received less than Romanians or Serbians. Governments also looked to colonize frontier areas where the minority populations were seen as being hostile to the new state. Thus 'Poles, Serbs and Romanians were settled respectively among Ukrainians, White Russians, Albanians and Bulgarians' in Eastern Poland, Macedonia, and Dobrudja (Seton-Watson1945–1967: 79).

Land reform was both extensive and rapid, creating a more egalitarian structure of land ownership in the successor states than generally found in North-Western Europe (Table 6.2). Some 18% of all agricultural land in Eastern Europe was transferred, benefiting two million landless workers and 1.5 million tenants (Royal Institute of International Affairs 1932: 149). Landless labourers in Bulgaria, Romania, and Yugoslavia came to make up less than ten percent of the farm population compared to a third or more in most North-Western European countries. Perhaps half of farmers in Hungary were beneficiaries of land reform by 1935, two-fifths in Czechoslovakia and Romania, and a quarter in Bulgaria and Poland (Table 6.1)[5]

The timing of land reforms can be crucial to their chances of success, because during economic upturns the growing demands of the urban economy provide opportunities for 'surplus' labour to leave farming, allowing more land to be given to proven farmers. By contrast, at times of economic depression, the numbers of workers who wanted 'free' land increased, risking that profit, market-orientated farming be reversed to a more subsistence-based one. The economic cycles influenced the amount of land that could be profitably farmed and, despite a relatively egalitarian structure of land ownership, most of the new farms were too small to fully employ the family and a plough team. Indeed, even if *all* land had been redistributed, farms would have averaged only 13 hectares in Germany and Poland, 12 hectares in Spain (or 14 hectares in areas of large estates), 8.4 hectares in Czechoslovakia, 6 hectares in Hungary and Romania, and 5.3 hectares in Yugoslavia (Roszkowski 1995: ch. 5; Tooze 2006: 179; Simpson 1995). Yet an estimated 7 to 15 hectares were required to support a family in Yugoslavia, 15 or 16 hectares in Romania, 20 hectares in Germany, and 24 hectares in the area of large estates in Spain (Tomasevich 1955: 371; Mitrany 1930: 193; Simpson and Carmona 2017; Tooze 2006: 179). What distinguished Germany in this period was not that there was insufficient land for family farms, but rather the choice of Hitler of *Lebensraum*, and the use of military conquest and ethnic cleansing

Table 6.2 Land inequality and landless workers in select European countries, circa 1930

	Percentage of Farm Area				*Percentage of undertakings*				*Farm workers*
	1 to 5 ha	*5 to 10 ha*	*10 to 50 ha*	*50+ ha*	*1 to 5 ha*	*5 to 10 ha*	*10 to 50 ha*	*50+ ha*	*% of farm population*
Bulgaria	29.1	37.3	32.0	1.6	57.4	30.3	12.2	0.1	10.7
Czechoslovakia	20.0	19.5	39.4	21.1	59.7	21.9	17.4	1.0	38.1
Estonia	2.5	6.1	73.3	18.1	17.6	16.2	61.0	5.2	19.5
Hungary	14.6	12.0	22.1	51.3	67.7	17.3	13.3	1.7	46.6
Latvia	2.3	7.8	64.6	25.3	15.7	19.5	57.7	7.1	-
Lithuania	3.7	13.9	67.3	15.1	18.6	27.2	51.4	2.8	21.2
Poland	14.8	17.0	20.9	47.3	64.2	24.8	10.5	0.5	-
Romania	28.1	20.0	19.7	32.2	75.0	17.1	11.3	0.3	-
Yugoslavia	28.0	27.0	35.3	9.7					
Greece	16.9	11.7	21.6	49.8	79.3	14.3	5.9	0.5	-
Italy	17.5	13.6	26.3	42.6	66.7	18.2	13.4	1.7	43.3
Portugal	28.0	27.5	17.0	17.5					
Spain	18.8	7.1	15.0	59.1	78.5	8.6	10.6	2.3	30.4
Germany	12.9	16.7	44.2	26.2	50.2	24.1	23.8	1.9	22.9
Netherlands	13.0	18.2	59.0	8.8	47.3	23.7	27.9	1.1	65.3
Sweden	14.4	19.2	46.0	20.4	48.9	25.5	23.6	2.1	-
Switzerland	18.1	26.6	40.5	14.8	51.2	29.0	19.0	0.8	21.3
		0 to 10 ha	10 to 50 ha	50+ ha		0 to 10 ha	10 to 50 ha	50+ ha	
Belgium		45.0	46.0	9.0		81.0	18.0	1.0	36.9
Denmark		16.5	68.0	15.5		52.0	46.0	2.0	36.3
England & Wales		6.7	28.1	65.2		35.0	41.7	23.3	63.1
France		20.0	50.0	30.0		62.0	34.0	4.0	35.1

Sources Moore (1945: table 8), League of Nations (1939), Yates (1940: 129, 203, 274, 361, 438), Grigg (1992: 92), Howard (1935: tables 1, 2), Tomasevich (1955: 385), Carmona et al. (2019: table 3)

in Eastern Europe to settle German families (Tooze 2006: 179; Snyder 2015: 19).[6]

This shortage of farmland at a time of growing population growth was an important constraint, forcing governments to choose between creating viable family farms and maximizing the number of settlers, even though they received too little land to live on. They also had to decide who was to benefit from land reform, which offered opportunities for political parties to allocate resources to their supporters. All governments, except for Bulgaria, inserted clauses that rewarded veterans and families of those who were killed in war (Jackson 1966: 10; Dooley, 2022, for Ireland). Governments everywhere found it difficult to identify both those most in need, and the production potential of the land to be distributed. Half a hectare of fertile land close to the farmhouse could produce as much as ten hectares divided into several plots at a distance of ten kilometres from the village. In fact, the under-cultivation of many of the traditional estates was precisely because they were located at significant distances from where the workers lived. Problems of distance might be resolved following land reform by mechanization (which encouraged the maintenance of large farms and collectives), or by constructing new settlements (which greatly increased the scope, but also the cost, of land reform). The great majority of beneficiaries from land reform wanted their own land, and not work it in collectives, and governments lacked the resources to build more than a limited number of new farms. The political rewards derived from land reform could be extended over time if the political party in government continued to use state resources to support the new settlers, by providing working capital, seeds, and support for cooperatives.[7]

6.3 Land Reform in the Balkans

Land reform in the agricultural-based societies faced distinct problems to those carried out in more developed countries. Although land reform reduced inequality, the major challenge was whether the short-term benefits would simply support a rapidly growing population, or rather help instead to diversify the economy by creating alternative, non-farm employment, essential for long-term growth, and freeing society from Malthusian restrictions. As Foster and Rosenzweig (2022: 42) argue, when the shadow price for family labour is set by the outside market, marginal farm work will be sacrificed when wage employment offers a better return. This help explains the frequent mention of farm workers earning more than small farmers in Europe (Roszkowski 1995: 42, for Hungary). However, little alternative work existed, and most farmers in the Balkans struggled because their farms were too small and relatively few opportunities for market specialization existed in the interwar period.

Bulgaria lost a net 7% of its cultivated land between 1913 and 1919, including its most fertile region (Dobruja), and had to find space to settle almost half a million refugees (Ivanov and Tooze 2007: 692). The country was already one of small family farmers and land reform left just 1.6% of land in holdings of over 50 hectares, and allowed 80% of farmers to own their land (Table 6.2).[8] Land reform reinforced family farm ownership, but holdings were miniscule, equivalent to 1.6 hectares per male worker by 1935 (Warriner 1939: 3). Even before land reform, a slow shift was apparent away from extensive cereals into labour-intensive farming, and the 1920s and 1930s saw greater specialization in crops such as grapes, tobacco, fruit, or vegetables, as well as pig farming (Ivanov and Tooze 2007: fig. 2).[9] Agricultural produce accounted for 90% of Bulgaria's exports before 1914, of which 70% were cereals and 8% tobacco, but by the late 1920s, tobacco exports had grown to 39%, and cereals fallen to 25%. Labour-intensive agriculture resulted in output per hectare growing by 50% between 1911 and 1939 but living standards grew by much less, as the farm population increased by 40% (Ivanov and Tooze 2007: 694).

Romania, by contrast, was greatly enlarged by the Peace Treaties and it experienced four regional land reforms, affecting a fifth of the total land area by the early 1920s. Farms of over 100 hectares fell from 40 to 10% of the total area, leaving half the land in holdings of between 1 and 10 hectares. Two-thirds of those eligible received some land, but in insufficient amounts, averaging only 2.7 hectares of arable and 1.1 hectares of communal grazing and forestry. The few large estates that remained were farmed by their owners, 'a radical break with the past' (Mitrany 1930: 250–1).

Romania had been the world's fifth largest wheat exporter before 1914, but these markets now virtually disappeared,[10] and farmers dedicated more resources to maize, barley, industrial crops, and cattle breeding, activities better suited to small farms. Romania by 1930 became Europe's largest maize producer, although cultivation techniques remained largely unchanged and yields were just a third of those found in the United States.[11] Government policies pursued unfavourable farm policies, with food exports suffering not only because of international market instability, but also from export taxes until 1927, and then a rising exchange rate.[12] Cooperatives were generally under state control and ineffective,[13] and farmers were taxed at rates that were effectively double what they could borrow from credit institutions (Mitrany 1930: 425, 427). Land reform was however highly profitable for the government, as while landowners received minimal compensation paid in long-term bonds, the new farmers were eager to pay cash immediately to the government to register the land in their names.[14]

In the new state of Yugoslavia, some 2.5 million hectares were distributed to 669 thousand families. The experience of land reform varied significantly across this highly diverse geographical region, but small family farms again came to dominate in most places, leaving only a tenth of the land in holdings of over 50 hectares by 1930 (Tomasevich 1955).

Land reforms in the Balkans therefore reduced inequality by creating societies of small family farmers with few landless workers, but they failed to significantly increase farm incomes. A major constraint was the lack of new land that could be profitably brought under the plough, even though the lower supervision costs found in using family labour, rather than wage labour, might be expected to allow the cultivated area to increase. In fact, because large farmers had greatly extended the area of cereals in response to high export prices before 1914, the weaker prices of the 1920s and 1930s threatened to make unprofitable the commercial cultivation of even the existing area (Warriner 1939, 97). In addition, the advantage of low supervision costs that family farmers enjoyed to produce labour-intensive, high-value, agricultural products were severely limited by weak consumer demand, poor credit markets, high transport and distribution costs, and unfavourable natural resources. Livestock farming, for example, was severely constrained by the poor quality and highly seasonal character of natural pastures, the high cost of feed, low incomes, and weak market structure (Chapter 3).[15] The presence of irrigated market gardening in areas around towns showed that small farmers could thrive when favourable natural resources and strong consumer demand coincided, but the need to use dry-farming techniques across large areas of the Balkans restricted the potential for increasing farm incomes, while the export possibilities for specialist crops suited to dry-farming, such as the vine and olive, remained weak in interwar Europe (Ayuda et al., 2020; Ramón Muñoz 2010).

Given the limited alternatives, many family farmers dedicated relatively large amounts of their (unpaid) labour to cereals, achieving lower yields than found on the capital-intensive larger farmers. Grains could be easily stored, used to pay taxes, or fed to animals if prices were low. As a result, rural diets improved because of an increase in on-farm consumption rather than market specialization (Mitrany 1930: 488).[16] In Romania, meat consumption increased from 10 kilos per capita before 1914 to 17 kilos in 1923, leading one contemporary to write that although land reform had failed to 'mitigate his poverty of cash resources or to raise the taxable capacity of the nation as a whole', it had 'enabled the ... peasant ... to feed his family and escape from actual hunger' (Michael 1929: 488; Tiltman 1934: 116, both cited in Roszkowski 1995: 165). However, the same author notes that by the early 1930s this required cutting all cash expenditure to the minimum. In Romania, high taxes turned matches into luxuries, and farmers (illegally) used instead dried moss and flints (Tiltman 1934: 158, 247). In Yugoslavia, in the four years between 1929/30 and 1933/34, indirect taxes accounted for 76% of government revenue, resulting in kerosene consumption falling by 24%, matches by 33%, tobacco by 28%, cigarette paper by 59%, at a time when population increased by 7% (Tomasevich 1955: 643, 687). Cereals and self-sufficiency might be a logical response given these market conditions but, as Warriner (1939: 26) noted, 'where land is short, agricultural self-sufficiency means, not a choice of stability in preference to wealth, but instability and poverty together'.

Many of the new farmers therefore used their land and labour for growing extensive cereals, at a time when family farmers in North America were benefitting from tractors and new harvesting and threshing machinery, which allowed them to cultivate a significantly greater area with their own labour (Olmstead and Rhode 2001). The modern farm equipment generally produced higher yields than using traditional labour-intensive technologies. The miniscule size of many properties in Eastern Europe resulted in the paradoxical situation of both under investment and over investment on them. Family farmers, given the time constraints in agriculture, wanted to guarantee having a plough team available to prepare their land, and cart crops from the fields, resulting in most work animals and farm implements being underused (Tomasevich 1955: 439). In Romania, only half of farmers had a plough, but these were used to work an average of just seven hectares (Roberts 1951: 58). The number of work animals per hectare across much of Eastern Europe was in fact as 'high, and sometimes higher, than in the regions of intensive livestock peasant farming of Western Europe' (Warriner 1939: 158). However, the highly seasonal nature of demand in farming, and small amount of off-farm work during the rest of the year, implied that many work animals were in poor condition.

This underinvestment in farm equipment and low cereal yields in countries such as Romania, Bulgaria, and Yugoslavia is reflected in Table 6.3. In agrarian societies, farmers restricted their borrowing to buying food and paying for other essential day-to-day expenditures rather than investing in farm inputs (Table 6.4). In Yugoslavia, only a third of farmers were in debt, no doubt the result of the high interest rates that

Table 6.3 Agricultural inventory and wheat yields, 1930

	Farm inventory lei / hectare	*Wheat kilos/ hectare*
Romania	1.000	860
Bulgaria	2.000	1.320
Poland	3.000	1.440
Germany	15.000	2.070
Switzerland	42.000	2.250

Source Roberts (1951: 58).

most had to pay to private money lenders. Land reform therefore tended to drain capital from productive agriculture in two ways: it encouraged the new farmers to use their limited savings to purchase the land and, by splitting up large farms, resulted in capital being used for subsistence needs rather than productive investment. This, combined with weak farm prices during the period, created a significant poverty trap for many of the new owners.[17]

Large capital investments in machinery suffered because of land reform and the economic crisis, leading to half of Eastern Europe's 40,000 tractors in 1929 disappearing 'owing to defaults in payment' and 'most of the rest are rotting in the fields' because of the lack maintenance and spare parts (Tiltman 1934: 253). In Yugoslavia, imports of agricultural equipment (by weight) fell by 94% between 1928 and 1932–5, and the

Table 6.4 Composition of farm debt by farm size in Yugoslavia, 1932

	Farm size in hectares						
	Landless	*0–2*	*2–5*	*5–10*	*10–20.*	*20–50*	*50+*
Buying of land	8.8	16.1	21.2	32.4	28.2	49.4	71.9
Buying of livestock	1.9	3.7	6.6	5.8	3.6	2.1	0.3
Buildings	7.8	15.0	16.5	13.3	14.5	9.0	12.4
Production purposes	10.5	5.9	6.9	3.4	9.2	7.4	11.5
Family expenditure	26.8	15.3	16.2	9.5	5.9	4.6	0.3
Paying of debts	2.9	12.4	12.0	26.8	25.9	25.7	3.6
Buying food	41.4	31.6	20.6	8.7	12.8	1.8	0.0
	100	100	100	100	1000	100	100

Source Komadinić (1934:.51), based on an unpublished survey for the Chartered Agricultural Bank, cited in Tomasevich (1955: table 45).

consumption of artificial fertilizers was 'profoundly affected by the respective phases of prosperity and depression being just a fifth in 1932–5 of what they had been in 1928–9' (Tomasevich 1955: 441, 447).

The political consequences of land reform and agrarianism are discussed in Chapter 10, but the real poverty that many Balkan families suffered should not hide some of the improvements that were taking place. Life expectancy at birth in Bulgaria increased from 46.3 years in 1926 to 51.8 in 1936, and in Romania, from 40.0 years in 1920 to 42.3 in 1930 (Prados de la Escosura 2015; Morys and Ivanov 2021: table 10.5). The Malthusian trap was avoided, helped by fertility in Bulgaria halving between late 1920s and mid-1930s, 'one of the most rapid demographic transitions on record' (Ivanov and Tooze 2007: 693). Literacy in this country increased from 18% of population in 1900 to 55% in 1938, and 92% in 1946, while in Romania it rose from 35% in 1910 to 57% in 1930 (Ivanov and Tooze 2007: 693; Morys and Ivanov 2021: table 10.5). Although legislation in Romania in 1864 had guaranteed free and universal education, the government provided virtually no schools, and half the children received no education. Land reform now allocated land for villagers to build or renovate buildings, and 7500 schools were established in just four years (Mitrany 1930: 510–4). Land reform in the agrarian-based economies of South-east Europe helped to alleviate poverty, especially in the face of the collapse of the region's exports during the Great Depression, and the inability of government, and their often-corrupt bureaucracies, to provide alternative social transfers.

6.4 Land Reform in Transforming Economies

The impact of land reform in Europe's transforming economies, where labour was already leaving agriculture in considerable numbers, was very different to that in agrarian economies, where it had hardly begun. Economic development could produce significant regional differences in agriculture, with farmers being a much smaller part of the active population in industrial areas than agricultural ones (Rosés and Wolf 2019). Farm policies that were attractive to farmers in one region were often opposed, not just by urban groups, but by farmers elsewhere. While farmers in agrarian-based societies adapted to the weak markets of the early 1930s by increasing self-sufficiency, and in industrial societies by lobbying for government support, in transforming economies, farm organizations and state capacity were usually much weaker.

Czechoslovakia was Eastern Europe's most developed economy in 1930, with a higher per capita income than in Italy, and with only 37% of its workforce employed in agriculture (Table 6.5). It possessed modern food-processing industries, including sugar factories, breweries, fruit processing plants, and ham-curing. A major land reform resulted in 12.5% of all land (including woodland) or 1.3 million hectares, changing hands between 1918 and 1938. A number of large estates escaped, especially in western half of the country, while some of the poorest failed to receive any land, leaving two-fifths of the agricultural workforce landless, and a recent study talking of a 'stolen revolution' (Doležalová 2021), although estates of over 100 hectares accounted for only 10.7% of the land.

Even before land reform, no inverse relation between farm size and output existed in Czechoslovakia, as large farms enjoyed both *higher* crop yields and dedicated *more* of their land to labour-intensive crops such as barley and sugar beet, than small farms (Table 6.6). Large farms had fewer animals per hectare, but these were bigger as they were kept for beef, while family farms preferred smaller animals for dairying (Brdlík 1933: 114). Large farmers also marketed a higher share of their output. The fact that large farmers in Czechoslovakia were often the first movers to intensive farming is perhaps not unexpected, given the recent studies on the role of large dairy estates in Denmark and Sweden in promoting change on small farms in the mid-nineteenth century (Lampe and Sharp 2018; Morell and Söderhäll 2019).

Table 6.5 Land reform in transforming economies

	Per capita income in 1929 ($ 1990)	*% of labour in agriculture*	*Farm workers % of ag. population*	*The extent of land reform*	*Political change after land reform*
Italy	2721	47	43.4	minor	Mussolini
Czechoslovakia	2918	37	38.1	significant	Agrarians pact
Spain	2057	56	27.3	minor	Military coup
Germany	4051	29	29.9	minor	NSDAP
Ireland	2952	48	10.8	significant	Independence

Sources Tables 6.1, 6.2 and 8.1.

Table 6.6 Yields per hectare (QM) in Czechoslovakia by farm size, 1909-13

	Wheat	*Rye*	*Barley*	*Oats*	*Potatoes*	*Sugar beet*
0-2 has.	15.3	14.7	16.6	15.5	100	203
2-5 has.	16.3	15.4	16.4	17.4	111	291
5-20 has.	17.5	15.5	17.7	17.0	110	295
20-100 has.	18.6	16.3	18.7	17.7	114	307
100+ has.	20.0	18.9	21.9	19.8	116	296

Source Brdlík (1933: table 14).

Major regional differences existed in Czechoslovakia, with agriculture employing only 28.4% of the labour force in Bohemia in 1921, half the figure found in Slovakia (58.7%) (Luebbert 1991: 293). Farming was more productive in the proximity of the industrial centres in the west, which combined high consumer demand with large and medium-sized holdings, high rainfall, good clay, and loam soils. Cattle were usually stall-fed on hay, roots, sugar-beet pulp. By contrast, farmers dedicated more resources to low value produce in poorer Slovakia (Table 6.7). In the industrial west (Bohemia and Moravia), the inverse relation between farm size and output per hectare did exist, as farms of less than 50 hectares were cultivated more intensely and produced more per hectare than those of over 50 hectares (Meissner 1955: tables 2 and 3).

Land reform in Czechoslovakia, especially in Slovenia, gave labourers and small farmers access to land, but farming remained market orientated in the industrializing regions. Farm cooperatives and government polices played their part. By 1930, there were 11,029 agricultural cooperatives, with about two-thirds of farmers being members. Individual cooperatives were grouped into associations reflecting not just the characteristics

Table 6.7 Regional differences in farming in Czechoslovakia, 1930-4

	Crop yields - Qm per has.		*Animals per 100 has*	
	Wheat	*Rye*	*Cattle*	*Pigs*
Bohemia	18.9	20.0	71	51
Slovakia	14.4	13.5	32	33
Total	15.9	17.5	52	40

Source Warriner (1939: 99–100)

of different farm commodities and regions in which they were located, but also the nationality and political allegiances of their members (Brdlík 1933: 126). In Bohemia, there was a farm movement in late nineteenth century, and the Agrarian Party won 12% of the vote in Czechoslovakia in 1920, making it the largest party in a heavily fragmented parliament (Brdlík 1933: 100). During the interwar years, the Agrarian Party played a major role in providing a stable government and its leader, Jan Malypetr, helped inspire Czechoslovakia's 'New Deal', which invested large sums in new infrastructure projects, legislated to protect workers, and supported farm incomes.[18]

Output per hectare was greater on large farms in other Eastern European countries, such as Hungary or Poland in this period (Roszkowski 1995: tables 21, 25). In Poland in 1933–4, farms with more than 50 hectares possessed 17% of arable land, harvested 21.5% of all crops, and supplied 44.5% of grain for local and export markets. Large Polish farms sold almost five times more per hectare than small farms (Roszkowski 1995: 158). Higher yields were the result of the more efficient farm equipment used for soil preparation and sowing (tractors, ploughs, harrows, seed drills), and the use of chemical fertilizers, whenever cereal prices made their use profitable.[19]

Rapid economic growth in Spain during the three decades before the Great Depression also saw the agricultural workforce fall by almost a million and the number of landless workers by 40%, as family farmers increased from 61 to 73% of the agricultural workforce (Carmona et al. 2019). The first democratic government of the Second Republic passed a land reform law in 1932, at a time when economic depression closed urban markets for surplus farm labour, and made agriculture the employer of last resort (Malefakis 1970; Robledo Hernández 2014). Unlike Eastern Europe, there were no foreign landowners, and differences quickly appeared over whether the objective of land reform was to provide viable family farms (the preference of the Ministry of Agriculture) or settle the maximum numbers of landless workers (Simpson and Carmona 2017: 53–4).[20] Weak state capacity contributed to the slowness of reform, with only slightly more than 10,000 families being settled on 100,000 hectares by the end of 1934. As labour was legally free to form trade unions (Domenech 2013), these organized land invasions in Western Spain, resulting in 33,000 families being given temporary settlement rights on 100,000 hectares in 1932, and 110,921 families on 572,035 hectares in 1936.

Spain had enjoyed stable frontiers for centuries, but significant regional inequalities had appeared with economic growth, with Andalucia dropping from being the second richest region in 1860 (out of seventeen), to twelve by 1930 (Rosés et al., 2010). In southern Spain, almost two-thirds of the active population continued to work in agriculture, with two-fifths being landless. Large landowners enjoyed significant local political power, controlling the economic opportunities for many families (Cobo Romero and Rodríguez 2021). Yet outside this region, small family farmers dominated, with most being opposed to land reform. This was especially true of the small Agrarian Party, as well as the major centre-right party, the CEDA, which enjoyed strong support among the family cereal farmers of Castile-Leon and wanted higher wheat prices and cheap labour. Consequently, the well-organized landless workers of the Socialist FNTT and Anarchist CNT syndicates became hostile not just to large farmers, but also to their small tenant farmers and workers who preferred paternalistic loyalties to those of voice.

Just as in Romania or Yugoslavia a decade or so earlier, families in Spain received far too little following the land reform and the invasions—perhaps a fifth of the 25 hectares needed with dry-farming. The difficulties of cultivating extensive cereals efficiently on small plots led to some anarchist groups to demand collectives and mechanization, although most farmers preferred private property (Caro Cancela 2001). Short-term solutions following land invasions led to the shortening of crop rotations, complaints of soil mining, and the ploughing-up of vital winter pastures. The question of whether a land reform should encourage farmers to specialize for urban markets or rather meet the subsistence needs of the rural poor was summarized by the Socialist deputy Cabrera, who noted that in parts of La Mancha the use of land 'as pasture was much more remunerative but condemned whole villages … to starve because of the limited work it provided at a time of unemployment' (in Ladrón de Guevara 1993: 246).

The significant regional inequalities in transforming economies such as Czechoslovakia, Italy, and Spain created contrasting demands over whether to encourage commercial farming or resolve traditional land inequalities. In Czechoslovakia, the political success of the nationalistic Agrarian Party in Bohemia was helped by land reform widening its social base, and the party's decision to participate in government (Doležalová 2021: 10). By contrast, the large numbers of landless labourers in Italy (post-First World War) and Spain (early 1920s and 1930s) were organized by Marxist and anarchist syndicates which at times of economic depression challenged the legitimacy of the Liberal state. Rural unrest over land reform in Italy led to fascism, while the Spanish countryside became deeply divided, as reflected in the extremely close election results in most southern provinces in 1936 (Snowden 1986; Díaz del Moral 1928–1973; Riesco Roche 2006). This failure of land reforms in Italy and Spain can perhaps be seen as a counterfactual for elsewhere, with Eastern Europe generally enjoying significantly greater social stability after land ownership was widened, although government repression was frequently used against communism (or anarchism).

Nationalism in Ireland, perhaps even more than in the successor states of Eastern Europe, was the driving force behind land reform, although the creation of Irish Free State in 1922 took place *after* the land question had been largely resolved and the vast majority of tenant farmers had become owners of the land. The Irish land reforms were Europe's most extensive, with a series of laws between 1891 and 1934 transferring roughly three-quarters of all the country's land to tenants. It was also Europe's land reform that provided most benefits to *both* parties, with landlords being generously compensated by an immediate lump sum equivalent to 22.5 years of rental income, and their old tenants becoming landowners with mortgages of up to 100% of the value of the land, to be repaid over 66 years (Foley-Fisher and McLaughlin 2016: 77–8). These generous terms were made possible by the British government funding the operation and guaranteeing the necessary bonds that were issued on the stock market. As Foley-Fischer and McLaughlin (2016: 100) note, 'without the issue of land bonds and the simultaneous purchase of these securities by the UK savings bank funds, land reform would have ground to a halt'.

The Irish land reforms were a success, especially as farmers could freely export to industrial Britain, and underemployed labour emigrate. Between 1912 and 1925–6, labour productivity in Irish agriculture increased by about 50%, but then stagnated over the next twelve years, as livestock exports from the Irish Free State to Britain fell sharply (Ó Gráda 1994: table 15.3). Significant numbers of Irish farmers had mortgages, and these largely maintained their interest payments during the worst moments of the political conflicts, helped greatly by inflation reducing their real burden. Difficulties arose however during the Great Depression, when deflation increased interest payments in real terms, leading to non-payment and the 'economic war' between the Irish Free State and the British government in 1932 (Chapter 7).

Finally, land reform in Germany saw some 77,865 families settled on 930 thousand hectares between 1919 and 1938. As Hitler converted the NSDAP into a mass political party, he gained the support of the small family farmer (*Bauer*) by protecting them from market instability through the giant food cartel (*Reichsnährstand*) and new inheritance laws (*Erbhofgesetz*) (Farquharson 1976; Cobo Romero 2012: ch.3). However, the challenge, as in many countries, was how to meet the needs of the large numbers of family farmers with insufficient land and increase output to feed industrial workers at a time of low prices without recourse to imports (Chapter 10). Stalin recognizes this and, because 'capitalist' kulaks were ideologically unacceptable, forced small farmers into giant collectives. Hitler's equally brutal solution was a dream to repopulate lands in Poland and the Ukraine with German farmers.

6.5 Conclusions

Several conclusions from the experience of land reform in interwar Europe can be advanced. First, a contradiction existed over whether the objective of land reform was to reduce the traditional inequality found *within* the agricultural sector or, alternatively, to tackle the fall in farm incomes relative to urban dwellers that appears with rapid economic growth, and the Kuznets Curve.[21] In the former, land reform in the agricultural-based economies helped farm workers gain access to land and, by *reducing* agriculture's links with the urban economy, increased farm consumption at a time of economic difficulty. Yet if greater self-sufficient helped improve diets and led to a fall in rural poverty, it threatened to weaken agriculture's demand for capital and consumer goods, delaying economic development. The problem became important because as countries struggled with balance-of-payments' constrains, governments after land reform were faced with the decision over whether to encourage commercial farming, and allow successful farmers to purchase the property of those that were struggling ('natural selection'), or protect instead the beneficiaries of land reform indefinitely (Roberts 1951: 150–8).

Land reform therefore differed to agrarian reforms, and those policies that tried to strengthen the family farm in transforming economies by further *integrating* it in the market economy, improve productivity and profitability, and encourage unneeded labour to move to the cities. The political dilemma of deciding the most suitable type of land reform was vividly highlighted by the Spanish experience in the depth of the 1930s recession.

Land reform proved to be a poor substitute for the market-led changes of North-Western Europe before 1914 where the landed elites, to further their own interests, had helped integrate small farmers into competitive mass political parties and provided important services, such as assisting farmers to establish cooperatives. Although paternalistic relations were often biased in the favour of landowners and large farmers, they provided a system to allocate the limited amounts of credit, land and work, and then monitor a client's performance. These selection mechanisms automatically ended with land reform, and new ones had to be created. Attempts in Eastern Europe to resolve this problem with farm cooperatives were generally unsuccessful (Chapter 7).

Eastern Europe's land reforms in the interwar period were carried out in a period of democratic transition and, as a significant number of voters worked in agriculture, their political demands were inevitably very different to those found in industrial societies. Yet even if an agrarian party had overcome the deep nationalist cleavages found in most countries, the combination of rapid population growth, weak market demand (both national and international), and small amounts of agricultural land implied that living standards would inevitably struggle to grow, regardless of its policies. In fact, the effectiveness of land reforms proved to be severely restricted by the austerity policies imposed by most governments, which strangled most of the young democracies at the outset. Just as with land reform, agrarian ideology suffered from the contraction that higher farm incomes required a commercial agricultural and a growing urban economy, which would threaten to undermine traditional village societies, something that many agrarians wished to protect in the first place.

Notes

1. A British Independent Labour Party pamphlet noted in 1901 that 'robbery by force or cunning has played a much greater part than merit in the building up of estates', in Griffiths (2007: 28).
2. As early as the mid-nineteenth century, the planting of vines in straight rows and use of secateurs rather than knives for pruning reduced the skills that wage labourers needed, and allowed a

foreman to control with 'ease the quantity and quality of work of each of his workers' (Guyot 1861: 19).

3. These authors also argue that the high fixed costs associated with hiring labour benefit those farmers who can employ significant numbers of workers.
4. Differences exist between the area expropriated and what farmers received because forestry was sometimes kept by the state, and governments needed time and investment to create small farms.
5. Figures have been cultivated by dividing the number of beneficiaries from land reform by the number of farmers in 1935.
6. Mussolini invaded Ethiopia partly to obtain more land.
7. The classic example is Mexico, where land reform created a significant political clientele for the PRI, but at the expense of lower long-run economic growth (Albertus et al. 2016).
8. In 1926, 80.6% of farmers only worked their own land; 13.3% rented more than 50% of their land; 3.5% rented less than 50% of the land; and 2.6% rented all their farm (Molloff 1933: 50).
9. According to Molloff (1933: 58), 'in the technique of tilling the land, sowing, and taking care of the plants and harvesting, definite progress has been made during the last few years, even if it is not yet reflected in yields'.
10. The 27 tons of butter and 400 tons of cheese that Transylvania exported in 1921 had also virtually disappeared three years later (Mitrany 1930: 440).
11. Maize yields in Romania average a ton per hectare (Mitrany 1930: 320–1). All cereals were sold with significant impurities.
12. Tariffs produced about a third of government revenue, and half of this came export taxed in 1928 (Mitrany 1930: 438).
13. In Romania, half the rural population belonged to a cooperative bank, but 'the immense majority of the members only participates with infinitesimal shares'. Loans were often used to create political allegiances (Mitrany 1930: 385, 407).
14. Landowners paid about 3.2% of pre-war price in depreciated bonds 'The former landowners ... were receiving the sums due to them from the State but tardily and in depreciated bonds; while the peasants were pressed to part with the money just when they most needed it' (Mitrany 1930: 417, 421).
15. Warriner (1939: 151) notes that 'wherever intensification by increasing live-stock production was possible ... the extension of peasant farming meant an improvement in the welfare of the peasant community, since it implied more employment'.

16. In the Old Kingdom, wheat became increasing used for bread, and a baker was now found in 'almost every village', and pellagra had disappeared (Mitrany 1930: 488).
17. For the literature on poverty gaps, see especially Kraay and McKenzie (2014) and Banerjee and Duflo (2011). Governments everywhere found it especially hard to help marginal farmers following land reform.
18. Along with the 4 other Czech and Slovak parties—the National Democrats, National Socialists, Social Democrats, and the Catholic People's Party. The party leaders 'became quasi-dictators in their own organizations, expecting unquestioned support' (Connelly 2020: 380, 413).
19. Warriner (1939: 125) notes that in Germany, in East Prussia and Pomerania, high yields were obtained because tariffs made heavy fertilizing profitable but 'in the parts of Poland formerly included in Germany the farming system is now much less intensive than it was before the War, and yields per head have declined'.
20. On the 596-hectare *Merinillas Alto* estate (Badajoz), 119 families were eventually settled instead of the proposed 23.
21. Kuznets suggested income inequalities increased with economic development given the greater opportunities for professionals and high paid workers in the commercial and industrial sectors.

References

Acemoglu, Daron, and James A. Robinson. 2012. *Why Nations Fail. The Origins of Power, Prosperity and Poverty*. Princeton: Princeton University Press.

Albertus, Michael. 2015. *Autocracy and Redistribution. The Politics of Land Reform*. Cambridge.

Albertus, Michael, Alberto Diaz-Cayeros, Beatriz Magaloni, and Barry R. Weingast. 2016. "Authoritarian Survival and Poverty Traps: Land Reform in Mexico." *World Development* 77: 154–170.

Augé-Laribé, Michel 1907. *Le problème agraire du socialisme: la viticulture industrielle du Midi de la France*. Paris: Giard & Brère.

Ayuda, M.I., H Ferrer-Pérez, and V. Pinilla. 2020. "Explaining World Wine Exports in the First Wave of Globalization, 1848–1938." *Journal of Wine Economics* 15 (3): 263–283.

Banerjee, Abhijit V., and Esther Duflo. 2011. *Poor Economics. A Radical Rethinking of the Way to Fight Global Poverty*. New York: Public Affairs.

Baten, Joerg, and Dácil Juif. 2014. "A Story of Large Landowners and Math Skills: Inequality and Human Capital Formation in Long-Run Development, 1820–2000." *Journal of Comparative Economics* 42: 375–401.

Brdlík, Vladislav. 1933. "Czechoslovak Agriculture." In *Agricultural Systems of Middle Europe: A Symposium*, edited by O.S. Morgan, 87–136. New York: Macmillan.

Broadberry, S, and Alexander Klein. 2012. "Aggregate and Per Capita GDP in Europe, 1870–2000: Continental, Regional and National Data with Changing Boundaries." *Scandinavian Economic History Review* 60: 79–107.

Carmona, Juan, Joan Rosés, and James Simpson. 2019. "Spanish Land Reform in the 1930s: Economic Necessity or Political Opportunism?" *The Economic History Review* 72 (2): 669–690.

Caro Cancela, Diego. 2001. *Violencia política y luchas sociales: La Segunda República en Jerez de la Frontera*. Jerez: Ayuntamiento de Jerez.

Cobo Romero, Francisco. 2012. *¿Fascismo o democracia? Campesinado y política en la crisis del liberalismo europeo, 1870–1939*. Granada: Universidad de Granada.

Cobo Romero, Francisco, and Francisco de Paula Garrido Rodríguez. 2021. *La Republica en los pueblos. Conflicto, radicalización y exclusion en la vida política local durante la Segunda República Española (1931–1936)*. Granada: Comares Historia.

Connelly, John. 2020. *From People into Nations. A History of Eastern Europe*. Princeton: Princeton University Press.

Díaz del Moral, Juan. 1928: 1973. *Historia de las agitaciones campesinas andaluzas*. Madrid: Alianza.

Doležalová, Antonie. 2021. "A Stolen Revolution. The Political Economy of the Land Reform in Interwar Czechoslovakia." *Scandinavian Economic History Review* 61 (3): 278–300.

Domenech, Jordi. 2013. "Rural Labour Markets and Rural Conflict in Spain Before the Civil War (1931–36)." *Economic History Review* 66 (1): 86–108.

Dooley, Terence. 2022. *Burning the Big House. The Story of the Irish Country House in a Time of War and Revolution*. New Haven & London: Yale.

Engerman, Stanley, and Kenneth L. Sokokoff. 2012. *Economic Development in the America since 1500. Endowments and Institutions*. Cambridge: Cambridge University Press.

Farquharson, John E. 1976. *The Plough and the Swastika: The NSDAP and Agriculture in Germany 1928–45*. London: Sage.

Foley-Fisher, Nathan, and Eoin McLaughlin. 2016. "Capitalising on the Irish Land Question: Land Reform and State Banking in Ireland, 1891–1938." *Financial History Review* 23 (1): 71–109. https://doi.org/10.1017/S0968565016000019.

Foster, Andrew D., and Mark R. Rosenzweig. 2022. "Are There Too Many Farms in the World? Labor Market Transaction Costs, Machine Capacities, and Optimal Farm SIze." *Journal of Political Economy* 130: 636–680.

Galor, Oded, Omer Moav, and Dietrich Vollrath. 2009. "Inequality in Landownership, the Emergence of Human-Capital Promoting Institutions, and the Great Divergence." *The Review of Economic Studies* 76 (1): 149–179.

Griffin, Keith, Azizur Rahman Khan, and Amy Ickowitz. 2002. "Poverty and the Distribution of Land." *Journal of Agrarian Change* 2 (3): 279–330.

Griffiths, Clare V.J. 2007. *Labour and the Countryside. The Politics of Rural Britain*. Oxford: Oxford University Press.

Grigg, David B. 1992. *The Transformation of Agriculture in the West*. Oxford & Cambridge, Mass.: Blackwell.

Guyot, Jules 1861. *Culture de la vigne et vinification*. 2nd ed. Paris: Librairie Agricole de la Maison rustique.

Howard, Louise E. 1935. *Labour in Agriculture. An International Survey*. Oxford: Oxford University Press.

Ivanov, M, and Adam Tooze. 2007. "Convergence or Decline on Europe's Southeastern Periphery? Agriculture, Population, and GNP in Bulgaria, 1892–1945." *The Journal of Economic History* 67: 672–703.

Jackson, George D. 1966. *Comintern and Peasant in East Europe 1919–1930*. New York: Columbia.

Komadinié, Milan J. 1934. *Problem seljčkih dugova*: Belgrade.

Kraay, Aart, and David McKenzie. 2014. "Do Poverty Traps Exist? Assessing the Evidence." *The Journal of Economic Perspectives* 28 (3): 127–148.

Ladrón de Guevara, Maria Paz. 1993. *La Esperanza Republicana. Reforma agraria y conflicto campesino en la provincia de Ciudad Real (1931–1939)*. Ciudad Real: Diputación.

Lampe, Markus, and Paul Sharp. 2018. *A Land of Milk and Butter: How Elites Created the Modern Danish Dairy Industry*. Chicago: Chicago University Press.

League of Nations. 1939. *The Land Tenure Systems in Europe: Contributions by the International Institute of Agriculture, European Conference of Rural Life*. Geneva.

Lipton, Michael. 2009. *Land Reform in Developing Countries. Property rights and property wrongs*. Abingdon: Routledge.

Luebbert, George M. 1991. *Liberalism, Fascism, or Social Democracy. Social Classes and the Political Origins of Regimes in Interwar Europe*. Oxford: Oxford University Press.

Malefakis, Edward. 1970. *Agrarian Reform and the Peasant Revolution in Spain: Origins of the Civil War*. New Haven: Yale University Press

Martinelli, Pablo. 2014. "Latifundia Revisited: Market Power, Land Inequality and Agricultural Efficiency. Evidence from Interwar Italian Agriculture." *Explorations in Economic History* 54: 79–106.

Meissner, Frank. 1955. "Economies of Scale in Relation to Agrarian Reforms in Czechoslovakia." *The American Slavic and East European Review* XIV (Feb.): 67–83.

Michael, Louis G. 1929. *Agricultural Survey of Europe. The Danube Basin, Technical Bulletin 126*. Washington D.C.: US Government Printing Office.

Mitrany, David. 1930. *The Land and the Peasant in Rumania. The War and Agrarian Reform (1917–21)*. London: Milford.

Mitrany, David. 1951. *Marx Against the Peasant. A Study in Social Dogmatism*. London: Weidenfeld.

Molloff, J.S. 1933. "Bulgarian Agriculture." In *Agricultural Systems of Middle Europe: A Symposium*, edited by O.S Morgan, 41–85. New York: Macmillan.

Moore, Wilbert. 1945. *Economic Demography of Eastern and Southern Europe*. Geneva: League of Nations.

Morell, Mats, and Martin Söderhäll. 2019. "Smallholders' and Large Estates' Reaction to Changed Market Conditions 1860–1910." *Scandinavian Economic History Review* 67 (3): 312–331.

Morys, Matthias, and Martin Ivanov. 2021. "Population and Living Standards: Central, East and South-East Europe, 1918–1939." In *The Economic History of Central, East and South-East Europe. 1800 to the Present*, edited by Matthias Morys, 243–74. London: Routledge.

Ó Gráda, Cormac. 1994. *Ireland. A New Economic History 1780–1939*. Oxford: Clarendon.

Olmstead, Alan L, and Paul W. Rhode. 2001. "Reshaping the Landscape: The Impact and Diffusion of the Tractor in American Agriculture, 1910–1960." *Journal of Economic History* 61 (3): 663–698.

Prados de la Escosura, Leandro. 2015. "World Human Development 1870–2007." *The Review of Income and Wealth* 61: 220–247.

Ramón Muñoz, Ramón. 2010. "Globalisation and the International Markets for Mediterranean Export Commodities: the Case of Olive Oil, 1850–1938." Ph.D., European University Institute, Ph.D.

Riesco Roche, Sergio. 2006. *La Reforma agraria y los orígenes de la Guerra Civil (1931–1940)*. Madrid: Biblioteca Nueva.

Roberts, Henry L. 1951. *Rumania. Political Problems of an Agrarian State*. New Haven: Yale University Press.

Robledo Hernández, Ricardo. 2014. "Sobre el fracaso de la reforma agraria andaluza en la Segunda Republica." In *La cuestión agraria en la Historia de Andalucía. Nuevas perspectivas*, edited by Manuel González de Molina, 63–96. Sevilla.

Robledo Hernández, Ricardo. 2022. *La tierra es vuestra: la reforma agraria, un problema no resuelto. España 1900–1950*. Barcelona: Pasado y Presente.

Rosés, Joan Ramón, Julio Martínez-Galarraga, and Daniel A. Tirado. 2010. "The upswing of regional income inequality in Spain (1860–1930)." *Explorations in Economic History* 47 (2): 244–257.

Rosés, Joan, and Nikolaus Wolf. 2019. "Regional Economic Development in Europe, 1900–2010: A Description of Patterns." In *The Economic Development of Europe's Regions. A Quantitative History Since 1900*, edited by Joan Rosés and Nikolaus Wolf, 3–41. Abingdon: Routledge.

Roszkowski, Wojciech. 1995. *Land Reforms in East Central Europe after World War One*. Warsaw: Institute of Political Studies Polish Academy of Science.

Royal Institute of International Affairs. 1932. *World Agriculture, an International Survey: A Report by a Study Group of the Royal Institute of International Affairs*. London: Oxford University Press.

Seton-Watson, Hugh. 1945: 1967. *Eastern Europe between the Wars 1918–1941*. 3 ed. New York: Harper.

Simpson, James. 1995. "Spanish Agricultural Production and Productivity 1890–1936." In *The Economic Development of Spain since 1870*, edited by Pablo Martín-Aceña and James Simpson, 181–220. Aldershot: Edward Elgar.

Simpson, James. 2011. *Creating Wine: the Emergence of a World Industry, 1840–1914*. Princeton: Princeton University Press.

Simpson, James, and Juan Carmona. 2017. "Too Many Workers or not Enough Land? Why Land Reform Fails in Spain during the 1930s." *Historia Agraria* (72): 37–68.

Snowden, Frank. 1986. *Violence and Great Estates in the South of Italy: Apulia, 1900–1922*. Cambridge: Cambridge University Press.

Snyder, Timothy. 2015. *Blood Lands. Europe Between Hitler and Stalin*. London: Vintage.

Tiltman, Hubert H. 1934. *Peasant Europe*. London: Jarrolds.

Tomasevich, Jozo. 1955. *Peasant, Politics, and Economic Change in Yugoslavia*. Stanford: Stanford University Press.

Tooze, Adam. 2006. *The Wages of Destruction. The Making and Breaking of the Nazi Economy*. London: Penguin.

Urwin, Derek W. 1980. *From Ploughshare to Ballot Box: the Politics of Agrarian Defence in Europe*. Oslo: Universitetsforlaget.

Warriner, Doreen. 1939. *Economics of Peasant Farming*. Oxford: Oxford University Press.

Yates, P. Lamartine. 1940. *Food Production and Manpower in Western Europe*. London: Longmans Green.

CHAPTER 7

Family Farmers: From Cooperatives and Voluntary Associations to Political Parties

Europe's landed elites had lost most of their lands by the early 1920s, leaving the family farm as the dominant unit of production, and giving farmers strong incentives to work long hours and specialize in labour-intensive, high-value farm commodities. Although family farmers saw their bargaining position weakened by the rapidly lengthening food chains, the extension of (male) suffrage and new constitutions promised to give them greater political voice. Nevertheless, despite their numerical strength, farmers usually found it difficult to organize effective parliamentary representation and fill the political void left by the landed elites. The post-war 'democratic spring' failed in many countries as the political elites followed economic orthodoxy by imposing austerity and returning to the Gold Standard rather than prioritizing the creation of employment. Even the more established democracies struggled in the face of economic depression, and their increasingly authoritarian neighbours during the period. This chapter shows why civic society was often too weak to resist the 'Despotic Leviathan', and why farmers, by far the largest group of voters in most societies, failed to 'cooperate, organize collectively, and take up political participation' so as to limit the power of the state, and advance their interests (Acemoglu and Robinson 2019: 45).[1]

Family farmers were villagers, giving them important economic and social benefits, as well as obligations, that influenced their individual

J. Simpson, *Family Farmers, Land Reforms and Political Action*, Palgrave Studies in Economic History,
https://doi.org/10.1007/978-3-031-67281-1_7

decision-making. As a result, farmers needed not just physical capital for purchasing land or farm inputs and human capital, to resolve day-to-day work problems, but also social capital to cooperate with their neighbours. Village networks contributed to the formation of this social capital, and farmers by the turn of the twentieth century were working together to build producer and credit cooperatives to become more competitive. For some contemporaries, the success of Danish cooperatives was the result of deep social capital in village society, just as the supposed 'individualism' of farmers explained why so many cooperatives failed elsewhere. However, a circular argument that assumes that deep social capital produced dynamic cooperatives, and the presence of cooperatives is explained by social capital, fails to identify how much social capital was needed, and of what type.[2] This chapter argues that significant social capital existed in most European villages, but that many farmers failed to dedicate the necessary resources to establish cooperatives because they were simply not profitable.

This chapter looks at how farmers organized. The first section considers the benefits from belonging to a village society and the constraints it imposed on individual behaviour and decision-making. Village society was rarely static, but transformed over time by economic development, changes in political boundaries, and the growth in state capacity. This is followed by explaining why farm cooperatives frequently failed to meet the expectations of contemporaries, and suggests that their relative small size and commodity-specific characteristics often limited their effectiveness, especially in the depressed markets of the interwar years. Section three looks at the relation between cooperatives and the state, with voluntary associations in Denmark contributing to the creation of competitive cooperatives, but the Romanian state seeing them as a means to control rural society. The last section argues that a combination of weak voluntary associations and deep cleavages in rural society undermined the electoral advantage that the large numbers of farm voters offered the Agrarian parties.

7.1 Farmers as Villagers

Europe's farmers lived and worked in village societies. Even though neighbouring villages might differ greatly, they all shaped how farmers thought and responded to market incentives. Social mobility before the eighteenth- and nineteenth-century liberal reforms was often limited by legal privileges and illiteracy. Gellner argues that the nobility, military, and Church hierarchies combined to form a horizontally segmented elite with their own distinctive *literate culture*, isolating them from village society. The timing and nature of the dismantling of feudalism, and the opening of land and labour contracts to market forces, influenced how villages subsequently developed. Social segmentation often continued after feudal rights had been abolished, because neither the landed elites nor the state, at least initially, had incentives to try to homogenize village society and culture across regions. While market integration offered opportunities for some farmers, others saw the secular culture of the urban commercial classes as a threat to traditional village society. The rural world was conservative but not necessarily passive, and it was quite capable of responding to supposedly excessive demands by outsiders. The French and Russian Revolutions began in the cities, but their eventual success depended on the support of the countryside.

The village helped shape both social relations and economic opportunities for farmers. The strong work incentives associated with the family farm could not disguise the fact that it was too small to carry out some activities efficiently, while governments were frequently slow to help at time of crises. By contrast, village communities created public goods, such as a well-kept road or monitor common lands that guaranteed households a minimum amount of employment and access to free resources such as firewood. These traditional village organizations were usually successful because of self-interest, as most families saw that their economic and social benefits outweighed their costs. However, village-level public goods also worked because families lived in close proximity, and frequent face-to-face communications generated high levels of trust. Individuals who did not meet their obligations or 'abused' the system in some way were highly visible and their free-riding could be reproached by their neighbours. No farmer could pasture an extra animal on the village common or miss a social activity without it going noticed. Village society therefore influenced decision-making, sometimes discouraging individuals to participate in activities that might increase their incomes if they were likely to be censured by their neighbours. Farmers consequently made production decisions to protect both their farms and the entitlement rights associated with belonging to the community.

Many farmers also organized themselves into small groups. In the poor villages of Extremadura (western Spain), it was common for a dozen or two landless labourers to form an association to rent part of a large estate each year to sow a crop of cereals, with the association itself allocating the work and dividing the income among its members. Landowners would have been reluctant to rent to individuals as these lacked the necessary farm implements and work animals, but members of the association could pool their resources, as well as acquire a reputation for good cultivation and paying the rent (Carmona and Simpson 2014).

Social capital can sometimes have negative consequences. A network that encouraged good behaviour and exchange among its members might exclude some individuals, thereby reinforcing inequality if employment opportunities were allocated only to those within a closed group. In interwar Europe especially, group boundaries were often formed along ethnic or religious cleavages, as well as rivalries between villages. Villagers need not have been openly antagonistic, but they simply joined different clubs, or worshiped in another church (Brett 2018). Strong social capital was as easily used to lobby governments to slow the speed of innovation or create other obstacles to change, as it was to build a competitive cooperative.

The pre-industrial village was hardly idyllic, regardless of the amount of social capital present. The moments of diversion captured in Bruegel the Younger's paintings hid the huge amounts of hard physical work required in traditional farming (Steckel and White 2012). Farm wages in Germany peaked at between just 35 and 45 years, and then declined (Wunderlich 1961: 235). Many villagers suffered from poor nutrition and early ageing, living in societies that were often under the Malthusian threat. Ó Gráda (1999: 30–3) suggests that poverty in nineteenth-century Ireland was a major cause of the lack of schooling and illiteracy. Neither did strong social capital imply the existence of a 'moral economy', where village institutions acted primarily as a defence against capitalism and change.[3] Villages were not egalitarian, and most farmers wanted to acquire more land, enjoy better housing, or buy new consumer goods. The extent of safety-nets to support the poor in hard times would always be limited because of the difficulties in determining who was most in need, and whether a family's poverty was the result of bad luck, idleness, or excessive drinking after a good harvest (Popkin 1979: 17–8).

Village conflicts over the distribution of resources were therefore frequent, while the economic opportunities created by the liberal reforms encouraged some families to consider whether to bend or break the accepted norms, and establish new ones. Social capital could not avoid conflicts between families that might fester for generations and were found in *all* villages. Their importance varied greatly, with tensions existing beneath the surface of village life, and being largely invisible to outsiders. Occasionally they erupted, something that was tragically common in interwar Europe. In one Spanish village, 'Los Olivos', political power and patronage networks switched several times between two political groups in the early 1930s, ending only when 38 Socialists men, or 12% of village males, were murdered within the year of the outbreak of the Civil War, leaving their family members 'terrorized and humiliated' (Collier 1987: 146; see also Rey 2008; Caro Romero and Rodríguez 2021; and for Greece, Kalyvas 1996).

In North-Western Europe, economic development and growth of the state was transforming village societies long before 1918, while change in Eastern Europe was greatly accelerated by the events of the Great War.[4] Eugene Weber (1977: 69) has shown that French as late as 1870 was still a foreign tongue for half the country's citizens who conversed instead in Alsatian, Basque, Breton, Catalan, Corsican, Flemish, or Gascon. Over the next half century, village loyalties broke down and 'peasants' were turned into 'French citizens' by the combination of free and universal elementary education taught in French, faster and cheaper travel (roads and railways), and military service.[5] Even so, France remained a patchwork of local agricultures with their own cultures and political demands, leading Charles De Gaulle to supposedly complain of the difficulties of governing a nation with 'two hundred and forty-six different kinds of cheese'.

The French state could build on pre-existing foundations of local identity, as 'peasants and their ancestors had lived in France from time immemorial and had no other memory to draw on' (Connelly 2020: 60). This was usually much less true elsewhere. Economic life in Austria-Hungary Empire, despite its customs and monetary union and relatively developed infrastructure, had major ethno-linguistic cleavages. Even before 1914, the impact of declining transport costs that helped integrate markets was offset by 'non-distance-related barriers to interregional exchange, such as ethnic or linguistic differences' pulling in the opposite direction (Schulze and Wolf 2012: 671). The *Risorgimento* created a unified Italy only on paper, as localism continued to determine much of political life, and the Italian state was 'incapable of exerting its control effectively and uniformly throughout the territory nominally under its jurisdiction' (Tilly et al. 1975: 87–9). Across Southern Europe, land inequality and weak factor markets encouraged paternalism, and the powers of the village elites or 'bosses' increased as the state extended its presence in the late nineteenth century, and economic growth created more rents to distribute.[6]

The political break-up of the 'great autocratic empires' of Russia, Austria-Hungary, Hohenzollern Germany, and Ottoman Turkey made state building especially contentious. Mazower (1999: 58) notes that the discrimination in Eastern Europe against minority rights 'was above all the work of modernizing liberals who were trying to create a national community through the actions of the state'. Minorities saw their schools closed and resettlement schemes to change the ethnic mix were undertaken, especially in the border areas of Eastern Galicia and Macedonia. When Hitler interpreted global politics in terms of race, and the state as the expression of the racial *Volk*, it was perhaps inevitable that he also saw German minorities in other countries as 'racial comrades', giving the mother country the right to protect them from their host government (Mazower 1999: 70–4).

7.2 Institutional Innovation and Cooperatives

The frequent face-to-face meetings between neighbours in small communities produced the social capital needed to organize modern farm cooperatives that began to appear in the decade or two before 1914, which contemporaries hoped would change farming. Cooperatives offered members economies of scale in the buying of inputs (seed, fertilizers, pesticides, etc.); the provision of cheap working capital; the possibilities of sharing new production and storage technologies or hiring specialist technicians; and strengthening their negotiating position for selling farm products in the lengthening food chains.[7] They could also impose discipline on farmers to meet the necessary quality standards to sell in distant markets.[8] Voluntary associations such as cooperatives helped to mobilize rural society politically, providing new channels for farmers to negotiate with governments over policy. Yet despite considerable contemporary interest, most European farmers did not belong to a cooperative in 1939. Even in Denmark, where their success was greatest, the relative importance of cooperatives varied significantly by farm activity (Table 7.1).[9]

Contemporaries frequently explained the limited numbers of cooperatives by the excessive 'individualism' and the lack of trust among farmers. Yet, as noted, farmers had almost daily face-to-face contact with their

Table 7.1 Danish farm processing and trading cooperative in 1936

	Per cent of total processing and trading in cooperative hands
Dairies	91
Butter exports	51
Bacon production	86
Meat exports	30
Purchasing cattle feed	67
Eggs export	28
Purchasing new seed	40
Purchasing fertilizers	38

Source Yates (1940: 79).

neighbours, and cooperative by-laws were adopted that strengthened group solidarity. Potential members usually had to possess some capital (thereby eliminating the poorest groups in society), and behavioural norms, such as religious practice (assistance at mass), avoidance of taverns, or political allegiance were used to filter out 'undesirable' members (Galassi 2000: 89–91). Cooperatives were therefore not open to everyone, and those who did become members were expected to make significant commitments. The decision to create a cooperative winery, for example, required farmers to abandon their old winemaking facilities, and sign long-term financial contracts with their neighbours to borrow the necessary capital and then build the new facilities.

A major obstacle to creating a cooperative was the opposition from the traditional village middlemen, whose business was now being threatened. As the planning and building of cooperative facilities took place over several years, members risked retaliatory action from them, including the refusal to process their produce. The success of dairy and wine cooperatives owed much to the fact that the processing of the milk and grapes had traditionally been done by farmers themselves rather than by local businesses. By contrast, the storing and milling of cereals, the transformation of olives into olive oil, or the commercial slaughter of cattle were all carried out by local firms who usually successfully opposed the creation of cooperative before 1939.

Unlike private enterprises, cooperatives had to resolve several free-riding problems if the greater scale of production was going to improve product quality and reduce unit costs. Poor quality milk supplied by one member, for example, would contaminate the production of all members.

Danish dairy cooperatives successfully enforced quality, because the daily production implied that farmers would have had significant problems finding an alternative outlet if they were expelled from the cooperative for supplying poor quality milk (Henriksen 1999). By contrast, cooperative wine remained poor because the annual harvest made it too expensive to monitor the grape quality of members other than by their weight and sugar content. This created incentives to plant high yielding vines, and uproot those of better quality, but lower yields (Simpson 2011: 73–4; Fernández and Simpson 2017: 126–7).[10] Some cooperative managers refused to sell wine because of the subjective nature of measuring quality, especially in a highly volatile market, which could leave them open to accusations of dishonesty if the price negotiated was less than expected (Clique 1931; Simpson 2011: 71–4). Wine cooperatives were especially strong in the Midi in France, and Catalonia in Spain, but as late as 1938, only a fifth of French wine was produced in cooperatives, and less than a tenth in Italy and Spain (Planas 2017; Simpson 2000: table 5; 2011: 71–6). The dense social capital produced by centuries-old collectively owned water-rights in Eastern Spain was also insufficient to resolve the new-collective action problems associated with guaranteeing the quality of orange exports along the lengthening commodity chain in foreign markets (Garrido 2014).

The absence of a village cooperative could also be explained by the high capital costs of building the necessary installations, or simply their low economic returns. Crop-specific characteristics affected the demand for working capital. In cereal cultivation, needs were traditionally relatively small, and for several centuries in Spain had been met by village savings banks (Carmona and Simpson 2019). From the late nineteenth century the growing use of chemical fertilizers and new farm machinery increased credit needs, but cooperatives were slow to appear. In North-Western Europe, the need for working capital also increased as farmers shifted out of cereals and into livestock (Suesse and Wolf 2020).

Cooperatives found that supplying credit and insurance was risky given the homogenous nature of village agriculture, creating similar cash needs and risks of crop failure among farmers. This lack of diversity was rudely tested after the inflationary years following the Great War, when many credit cooperatives went bankrupt as prices fell in countries such as Denmark, Germany, and Spain (Yates 1940: 79; Moeller 1986: 142; Simpson and Carmona 2020: 135–6). The rapidly changing nature of commercial agriculture and the lengthening of commodity chains therefore required other types of institutional arrangements that could operate on a much greater scale than just the village. Credit and insurance were provided more efficiently, and with lower risks, if the bank covered diverse farming regions over a large geographical area. The solution to many of these problems was for village cooperatives to join cooperative federations, allowing them to draw on wider capital markets, coordinate sales so as not to depress prices, and increase their political influence.

Village-level social capital was insufficient to create regional federations as members from different villages were unknown to each other, requiring a trusted outside group to help organize them. In France, the deep ideological divide and political competition between those that wanted to restore the monarchy and those who defended the Third Republic provided the necessary political incentives. Rural elites established the influential *Société des agricultures de France* in 1867 to propagate agricultural modernization and ensure the loyalty of family farmers but, from the 1870s, republican parties also competed for the farm vote (Cleary 1989). This rivalry between republican and monarchical groups strengthened village-level associations, with the numbers of syndicates growing from 2,069 in 1900 to 15,000 in 1929, and membership increasing from 512,000 to 1.5 million (Sheingate 2001: 92; Barral 1968: 107–9; Cleary 1989: 36–8). Nevertheless, despite these apparently impressive figures, most farmers were not members, and many cooperatives did little more than buy fertilizers in bulk (Unwin 1980: 103; Berger 1972: 82).

Elsewhere in North-Western Europe, the parliamentary competition between urban liberals and rural elites (and the Church) led to competitive mass political parties being build, encouraging the creation of networks of voluntary associations and cooperative (Chapter 5). In Eastern and Southern Europe, by contrast, political competition remained much weaker, and it was left to the state to organize farmers.

7.3 Cooperatives and the State

By the interwar years, some governments saw farm cooperatives as a useful channel of communications with farmers, as well as the key to transforming agriculture at a time of growing concerns over food security. Some of the potential benefits of cooperatives and the state from working together included resolving information problems and reducing transaction costs. Governments, for example, could help solve collective action problems by giving cooperatives legal powers to collect payments from all producers, regardless of whether they were members, to be spent on creating commercial brands, marketing, and advertising, or buying surplus production to support prices. Governments could also allocate R & D investment to meet the specific needs of cooperative members. Most governments had limited bureaucracies and faced significant problems collecting basic information, such as how much land had been sown with spring wheat or the size of stocks that small farmers were holding on the eve of a harvest. Therefore, in return for government help, a cooperative network might help increase state capacity by providing the organizational structure to gather village-level information to assist governments regulate markets, monitor agreements over farm-level production controls in exchange for price support, or enforce controls to limit the spread of plant or animal diseases. Furthermore, a successful export-driven cooperative commodity chain helped governments by acquiring foreign currency. Yet the 'dark' side of state power was that cooperatives could be used to increase government vigilance over farmers, rather than making them more competitive in the market place. A brief look at cooperatives in Denmark, Ireland, and Romania helps illustrate both the role of social capital, and when voluntary associations benefitted from working with governments, and when they simply became an instrument of its control.

Danish cooperatives were highly successful in implementing quality controls along the international food chains for commodities such as butter, pork, or eggs. The average dairy cooperative in 1928 had just 145 members owning 1,025 milch cows, living within a two or three-mile radius of the cooperatives (Jensen 1937: 324). From the mid-nineteenth century, winter Folk High Schools operated when there was relatively little farm work, helping to increase not just literacy, but build a strong civic society with their democratic ideas and community spirit. Their contribution to Danish agriculture and cooperatives was widely recognized. Sir Michael Sadler in 1936, after noting that Danish 'peasants' in the nineteenth century were 'still unprogressive, sullen and suspicious, averse to experiment, incapable of associated enterprise', claimed that farmers now were 'forward looking, cheerful, scientifically minded, resourceful, co-operative' (in Yates 1940: 75).

While the Danish state played only a limited role in establishing and running cooperatives, it was crucial for creating the favourable conditions for agriculture (Ashley and Adams 1924: 63). This included reducing rural discontent by providing small plots to the landless and helping smallholders; supporting research and development to improve farm performance; and proving the legislative framework for farmers to become commercially more efficient. It was the Danish cooperatives that organized the full-time agricultural advisors to help farmers, but half the costs were paid by state (Yates 1940: 81–2). The Federation of Danish Creamery Associations acted as a lobby as well as in an advisory capacity to individual cooperative creameries, collecting and circulating statistical information.[11] The success of Danish cooperatives depended on their ability to compete in foreign markets, which absorbed 80% of food production, and the extent that the interests of the state and cooperatives were aligned was highlighted in their joint responses to the export problems after 1929 (Yates 1940: 99). In Denmark, family farmers and the state worked together through the cooperative movement.

Ireland also had an important dairy industry, but farmers were slower to create cooperatives and mechanize butter production, with exports to England being of poorer quality, and selling for less, than Danish butter. Ó Gráda (1977, 2006: 140–5) has explained the slower diffusion of Irish cooperatives by the smaller numbers and lower density of cows than in Denmark (creating higher transport costs for cooperatives), and the much greater presence of the private dairies. Some Irish farmers found it more profitable to supply the liquid milk market or specialist livestock breeding rather than butter production. Differences in natural resource endowments also influenced decision-making in the two countries. Irish farmers enjoyed milder winters and an extended grazing-season compared to Danish farmers, allowing animals to be fed more cheaply. The failure of Irish farmers, just as those in New Zealand, to switch to winter dairying was because the higher costs associated with stall-feeding made it unprofitable, rather than any ignorance. Therefore, while the relative price of beef and butter encouraged winter dairying in Denmark, it discouraged it in Ireland (Crotty 1966: 72–7, in Ó Gráda 2006: 147). It was the different commercial opportunities facing livestock farmers that explain the greater interest of Danish farmers in cooperatives. As a result, although butter accounted for 18% of Irish output in 1910–14, total livestock products represented over four-fifths of the final agricultural output (Turner 1966: table 4.5).

Distrust frequently existed between the Protestant government and Catholic farmers, leading Kevin O'Rourke (2007: 1375) to argue that the 'suspicion between Catholics and Protestants, and tenants and landlords, spilled over into Nationalist suspicion of the cooperative movement'.[12]

These barriers to developing a stronger cooperative movement disappeared with the creation of the Irish Free State, but the economic situation also changed. The new Irish government continued to pursue orthodox fiscal and monetary policies to encourage exports, but agriculture suffered from the Great Depression and faced barriers to the British market during the 'Economic War' (1932–8). The farming community split, with the National Farmers' and Ratepayers' League (NFRL) being founded in 1932 to defend an open economy, which was opposed by many smallholders who wanted a protected one.[13]

Cooperative societies existed in Romania for renting land before the First World War, with the area increasing from 133,000 hectares in 1908 to 410,000 hectares in 1916 (Roberts 1951: 21; Mitrany 1930: 399–400). A strong civic society also drove collective action to demand land reform in Bessarabia and other areas (Roberts 1951: 34). Yet cooperatives generally remained weak in the interwar years, not so much because of a lack of social capital, but rather because of government imposed austerity and the lack of high-value export commodities that could have made them profitable. The costs of creating voluntary cooperatives usually did not compensate for the marginal improvements that they offered Rumanian farmers. Many farmers were also reluctant to participate in them because the government saw cooperatives as a useful instrument for controlling rural society. Rumanian cooperatives had little in common with Danish ones especially as the management, according to one writer, 'frequently exploited the peasants' ignorance and inexperience to its own benefit. The cooperatives were not really cooperative ventures but rather official institutions, financed, directed, and controlled by the state and therefore completely subject to political vicissitudes' (Roberts 1951: 64; see also Warriner 1939: 41; Riley 2010: 119).

7.4 Farmers and Agrarian Parties

It is often argued that democracies failed in interwar Europe because the electorate became disillusioned with the austerity programmes imposed on them at times of economic depression. This raises the question of why voters were not able to organize more effectively, and present alternative policies that reflected better their interests. The agricultural sector is a good place to look for an answer, as the family farmer dominated electorates across much of Europe. The organizational difficulties facing farmers in creating cooperatives, which might have not only improved material conditions of their members, but also given them a much greater political voice, suggest why Agrarian parties frequently disappointed.

Agrarianism in the aftermath of the First World War, especially in the Danubian countries of Bulgaria, Romania, and Yugoslavia, appeared to offer farmers a more optimistic future than capitalism, and the threat of having to sell the family farm and move to the city, or seeing it absorbed in a giant communist collective. The Agrarians wanted to locate industries in the countryside rather than the cities, using local resources and employing underemployed seasonal farm labour. The combination of land reform, democracy, and cooperatives was considered part of an alternative path to economic development (Toshkov 2019: 17). Agrarianism failed in part because of its ideological shortcomings, especially the contradictions of its economic policy, but also because of the substantial difficulties that existed to build effective mass political parties from a large, but often divided rural society.

The break-up of Europe's old land empires and creation of new nation states resulted in some countries having not one, but several agrarian parties. The agrarian parties therefore operated in diverse political settings, reflecting not just their different historical inheritances, but the country's wartime experience, and the nature of post-war settlement. The most radical expression of Agrarianism was the Bulgarian Agrarian National Union (BANU), under the leadership of Aleksandar Stamboliiski. The BANU finished second in the 1913 elections, benefiting from Stamboliiski's anti-war views, for which he was imprisoned in 1915. Following his release, BANU won the March 1920 elections and implemented a land reform which eliminated the few remaining estates, leaving less than two percent of land in farms of over 50 hectares, and only a tenth of the agricultural population landless (Table 6.2). Nevertheless, nearly four-fifths of Bulgarians were still farmers, and the small farm size left their owners extremely poor.

Bulgaria's politics in the post-war period were typical of many countries which attempted to transplant Western political institutions when the state was still weak, there was no tradition of competitive mass political parties, and rural and urban society were deeply divided culturally. Stamboliiski prioritized education, and made secondary education compulsory, built new schools, and revised the curriculum (Toshkov 2019: 64). Nevertheless, his attempts to displace urban influence from institutions, especially filling the state bureaucracy with party activists, alienated the powerful while failing to attract effective allies. His political isolation was increased when he alarmed the king with talk of forming a republic, and the armed forces resented the budgetary restrictions that he imposed on them (Connelly 2020: 373). Following the military coup d'état in June 1923, Stamboliiski was brutally murdered by Macedonians, who had been infuriated by his attempts to improve relations between Bulgaria and Serbia. BANU was now banned in Romania, and the party in exile in Prague split between moderates and communists. In reality, however, BANU had never been 'a political party in the strict sense of the word', being built around the personal leadership of Stamboliiski, with no true party programme and an unknown membership. The fact that BANU won just 52% of the votes in its largest victory in 1923 suggests that Stamboliiski lacked the support of many farmers (Bideleux 2020: 291). It also emphasized the need for agrarian parties to be willing to cooperate with urban-based parties if they wanted to form a stable government (Table 7.2).

There was considerable regional income inequality in the new state of Yugoslavia, with a steep gradient running from Kosovo, Bosnia, and Macedonia to the richer Zagreb, 'and still richer Ljubljana' (Connelly 2020: 349). Political parties were deeply divided along nationalist lines. The Serbian Radical Party dominated Yugoslavia's National Assembly, not

Table 7.2 Major European agrarian parties in the interwar years

	Party & estimated date of origin	*Electoral strength*	*Political tendency*
Bulgaria	Agrarian Union 1889 (BANU)	Large	Agrarian
Czechoslovakia	Czech Republican 1896	Medium	Moderate
Denmark	Venstre 1888	Large	Moderate/Conservative
Ireland	Farmers 1923	Weak	Conservative
Poland	Piast 1913	Medium	Moderate
	Wyzwolenie 1915	Medium	Agrarian
	Stronnictwo Ludowe 1931	Weak (?)	Radical (?)
Romania	National Peasant 1926	Large	Agrarian/moderate
Spain	Agrarian 1931	Very weak	Conservative
Sweden	Agrarian (Centre) 1921	Medium	Moderate
Yugoslavia	Croat Peasant 1904	Medium	Agrarian / nationalist
	Serbian Agrarian League	Weak	Agrarian

Source Based on Urwin (1980: 167–8).

least because it was well situated to reward its supporters, thereby closing the space for the Serbian Agrarian League. By contrast, the Croatian Peasant Party under Stjepan Radić attracted widespread support as voters were alienated by Serbia's move towards a centralized state, and filled administrative posts, including the police, in Croatia with Serbians. The Peasant Party widened its membership after Radić was killed in Parliament, creating a united front against Belgrade, and King Alexander's dictatorship. In the last free elections of 1927 it won 63 of the 67 of Croatia's seats in the Yugoslavian parliament, but fought on a nationalist ticket, not an agrarian one (Tiltman 1934: 57). Although the Croatian Peasant Party was originally a 'social revolutionary movement' it had become transformed into 'a nationalist organization directed by the urban middle class' (Seton-Watson 1945–1967: 227).

In Romania, the National Party of Transylvania and the Peasant Party of the Old Kingdom merged in 1926 to make the National Peasant Party (*Partidul National-Taranesc* or PNT), and formed a government after winning the December 1928 elections with 78% of the votes, and capturing 348 of the 387 seats (Bideleux 2020: 293). The PNT attempted to reverse its predecessors' policies of industrial self-sufficiency and advance others more favourable for small, family farmers. It failed, in part because it chose to impose austerity measures to meet the demands of foreign investors after 1929, ignoring agricultural interest. King Carol ended its power in 1931, and the party fragmented into new agrarian groups, with some joining the Iron Guard, 'a supernationalist and anti-semitic organization which captured the imagination of frustrated Romanians in the 1930s' (Roszkowski 1995: 208–9).[14]

In Poland, agrarian parties were also initially divided along ethnic cleavages reflecting the old political boundaries and class cleavages, and between those who wanted a more radical land reform, and those who looked for consolidation, and the implementation of an agrarian programme.[15] The two main agrarian parties were the conservative Piast (from former Austrian Galicia) and the radical Wyzwolenie (former Russia central Poland). The Piast, opposed by Wyzwolenie, was influential in passing the moderate land reform in 1925. However, party splits led to two communist regional farm parties appearing (Independent Peasant Party, based in Eastern Poland, and Belorussian Hramada), with their own more radical land reforms. Political repression and economic depression saw the Piast and Wyzwolenie merge to create the Peasant Party (*Stronnictwo Ludowe* or SL) in March 1931, which looked to protect democracy and extend the land reforms (Connelly 2020: 383; Jackson 1966: ch. 8; Roszkowski 1995: 201–3).[16] The government expelled the SL leadership, restricting the party's activities, but the massive protests against urban monopolies and authoritarian rule in August 1937 threatened to overthrow the government.

Politics in Hungary were dominated by the demands to reverse the Trianon Peace Treaty, which saw the country lose two-thirds of its territory. The failure of Bela's Communist Revolution and the limited land reforms left the landed elite in control of government. Rural democracy was greatly diminished by the fact that, 'without parallel in contemporary Europe', the secret ballot was not used in the countryside (Varga 2014: 114–5). A number of farm parties existed, but these were split between those who already owned some land, and those who were landless and demanded a more radical land reform.[17] Agriculture, and the needs of the family farm, became a priority for the ultra-conservative Gömbös government (1932–6), with its policies being heavily influenced by those of Nazi Germany.

Agrarian parties were often much more successful in transforming economies than in agrarian societies, especially when they worked with other political parties. This was especially true in Czechoslovakia and Scandinavia, where farming was dominated by relatively wealthy owner-occupiers, and poor farmers and landless workers were either few in number or had limited political influence. In Czechoslovakia, nationalist cleavages again dominated politics, with the Bohemian Agrarian Party, arguably Eastern Europe's most effective agrarian party, owing its success to the support from non-farm groups in industrial Bohemia (Roszkowski 1995: 204–5).[18] In 1920 it was the largest party, and during the interwar years played a major role in the 'committee of five' (*Pětka*) which provided relatively stable governments.[19] The Agrarian leader, Jan Malypetr in the 1930s helped to organize a Czech 'New Deal' by supporting large fiscal deficits for new infrastructure projects and legislation to protect workers in exchange for stabilizing agricultural incomes (Connelly 2020: 413). In the words of Luebbert (1991: 291), 'Social Democrats and Agrarians in Czechoslovakia actually did what their Scandinavian counterparts have merely been credited with having done: they used large fiscal deficits to stimulate a recovery'. In Scandinavia, the homogenous nature of rural society and strong networks of voluntary organizations gave family farmers a significant political voice (Chapter 10).

Finally, the Green International also failed to speak with a single voice. Founded in Prague in May 1928, it looked to strengthen the 'peasant' movements by exchanging information, providing moral support to family farmers, and strengthening local movements through their connections with an international organization (Jackson 1982: 147; Cabo Villaverde 2018). Seventeen agrarian parties were represented at its first General Assembly in May 1929, but it lacked funds to create a centralized bureaucracy, and policy divided once more over nationalist interests.[20] The optimism of the family farmer movements in Eastern Europe in the early 1920s ended in political failure usually well before the economic crisis in the 1930s. In the words of Seton-Watson (1945–1967: 257):

Everywhere in Eastern Europe much had been expected of the Peasant Parties, and everywhere these expectations were disappointed. Some of these parties were rendered helpless by terror exercised from above (Bulgaria and Poland). Others collapsed from internal decay (Serbia and Romania). Others came under the control of the urban bourgeoisie (Czechoslovakia) or of nationalist intellectuals (Croatia). In one country, Hungary, no Peasant Party existed.

7.5 Conclusions

Democracies need a vibrant civil society to survive, with local voluntary associations integrated into regional or national organizations, to help assimilate individuals into political parties. Across Europe, farmers had traditionally participated in village-level organizations, creating deep social capital that could be used to build farm cooperatives from the turn of the twentieth century. These gave family farmers the possibilities of greater scale in the purchase of inputs (fertilizers, pesticides, machinery), in the processing of agricultural products (butter, wine), and in their marketing in the lengthening food chain. Yet, with the exception of Denmark, relatively few farmers belonged to one, and many of those that did, saw few benefits. Some authors have emphasized the importance of culture and education for cooperative success (Fernández 2014; Henrich 2020) but, as this chapter has argued, strong market incentives were essential if farmers were going to dedicate the necessary resources in time and money.

Farmers faced considerable difficulties to create their own political parties because of their traditional limited contracts with the world outside their villages. The landed elites and Church had helped coordinate farmers in North-Western Europe in the half century before 1914, but this option was not possible in Eastern Europe following the land reforms. The attempts by Agrarians to transform politics were short-lived. Their ideological contradictions in pursuing economic development while at the same time protecting the family farm from market competition were visible not just in rural Eastern Europe, but also in Nazi Germany. Attempts to create agrarian parties were hampered by the heterogeneity of rural societies, problems of leadership, the difficulties to cooperate with non-farm groups, and the strength of nationalist cleavages found in most countries. Indeed, the success of the Croatian Peasant Party was due to the fact that it represented all Croatians, not just farmers, in the heavily fragmented Yugoslavian parliament. In Romania's Old Kingdom, the National Peasant Party owed its ideological origins to a literary movement, and its leaders were mainly professionals and intellectuals, rather than farmers (Roberts 1951: 89).

As farmers responded to economic depression after 1930 by limiting market transactions, their interest in forming new village-level cooperatives declined. Yet with the fall in farm prices, growing numbers of governments, especially in Western Europe, saw cooperatives as a potential intermediary between itself and small farmers to channel state resources and help intervene directly in farm markets. At the same time, especially in Eastern Europe, authoritarian governments were attracted by the political opportunities that the cooperative movement offered them to control rural society, and capture the farm vote, in those countries where elections still provided some sort of legitimacy for the government.

Nevertheless, the presence of strong voluntary associations, social capital, and mass competitive political parties could not guarantee the survival of democracy. The Nazis successfully infiltrated voluntary organizations, especially those of farm groups, and were able to rapidly mobilize politically to seize power. The *Volksgemeinschaft*, a truly national ideology, was shared by millions of Germans of all classes, and used to bolster fascism, as discussed in Chapter 10.

Notes

1. These authors provide a wide-ranging study of democracy, and the need for both a strong state *and* civic society.

2. Portes (1998: 19) notes that social capital, 'as a property of communities and nations rather than individuals, ... is simultaneously a cause and an effect'.
3. For a discussion and criticism of the 'moral economy', see Scott (1976), Popkin (1979), and Bates (1990: 36–41).
4. Major changes also took place in Eastern Europe before 1914, such as the decline of systems of extended families and common property ownership in the Balkans (Tiltman 1934: 86–8; Tomasevich 1955: 178–186).
5. Youngsters were taught national and patriotic sentiments, and the benefits of taxation and military service. Bilinguals by 1920 were more awkward in patois than in French and 'the majority and, most important, the young were on the side of the national language' (Weber 1977: 79, 332).
6. The Mafia also benefitted, as noted in Dimico et al. (2017), Acemoglu et al. (2020).
7. Cleary (1989: 167) notes that 'if technical changes—the mechanisation of arable and pastoral farming or the drive for ever greater production and productivity', were the 'most visible aspect of the transformation of rural France, the spread of new forms of cooperation and association' were 'no less important'.
8. Chayanov (1986: 268), writing in 1925 before collectivization in the Soviet Union, noted that a collective 'obliges the small producer to change his farm's organization plan according to cooperative selling and processing policy, to improve his techniques, and to transfer to improved methods of tillage and livestock farming, insuring a fully standard product, subjecting it to careful sorting, processing, packing, and canning according to world market demand'.
9. Yates (1940: 78) wrote that 'almost every farmer belongs both to a butter-making and to a bacon-curing cooperative and every second farmer purchases some of his feeding-stuffs through cooperative societies'. The average family belonged to 3 or 4 cooperatives, with some as many as 8 or 9.
10. The Burgundy cooperatives in the late 1920s were the exception that proves the rule, as the region's high wine prices allowed growers to dedicate enough time to monitor the vineyards and grape quality of other cooperative members (Clique 1931: 21–60).

11. Marketing associations usually competed with each other (Jensen 1937: 330–1).
12. For a criticism of its methodology and conclusions, see Ó Gráda (2006: 141–3).
13. The 'Economic War' began in 1932 when the Fianna Fail government refused to pay land annuities as stipulated in the Treaty Settlement of 1921 to compensate the former landowners who had lost their land. Many smallholders had been unable or unwilling to pay (Ó Gráda 1994: 411–6).
14. The agrarian splinter groups included the Peasant Party of Nicolae Lupu, Democratic Peasant Party of Stere, and the Ploughman's Front of Petru Groza.
15. The moderate *Piast* party found its support in the area that had previously been Austria, and the more radical *Wyzwolenie* (Liberation) from the old Russian territories.
16. The Independent Peasant Party claimed 75,000 members when it was dissolved in 1927, and the Belorussian Hramada, some 150,000 members.
17. The Smallholders Party in the early 1920s enjoyed little success. In 1937 a new National Peasant Party issued a Twelve Point Program that included demands for universal suffrage and a radical land reform. The anti-Semitic, fascist Arrow Cross Party also demanded land reform, but neither did well in the 1939 elections (Roszkowski 1995: 205–7).
18. German speakers in Czechoslovakia supported the League of Farmers in the 1930s.
19. Along with the 4 other Czech and Slovak parties—the National Democrats, National Socialists, Social Democrats, and the Catholic People's Party. The party leaders 'became quasi-dictators in their own organizations, expecting unquestioned support' (Connelly 2020: 380).
20. These parties were from Austria, Bulgaria, Czechoslovakia (2), Estonia, Finland, France, Latvia, Lithuania, Netherlands, Poland, Romania, Switzerland (2), and Yugoslavia (3) (Jackson 1982: 148).

References

Acemoglu, Daron, Giuseppe De Feo, and Giacomo De Luca. 2020. "Weak States: Causes and Consequences of the Sicilian Mafia." *Review of Economic Studies* 87 (2): 537–581.

Acemoglu, Daron, and James Robinson. 2019. *The Narrow Corridor. How Nations Struggle for Liberty*. London: Penguin.

Ashley, William, and W.G.S. Adams. 1924. "Report." In *Agricultural Tribunal Final Report*. London.

Barral, Pierre. 1968. *Les agrariens français de Méline à Pisani*. Paris: Armand Colin.

Bates, Robert H. 1990. "Macropolitical Economy in the Field of Development." In *Perspectives on Positive Political Economy*, edited by James E. Alt and Kenneth A. Shepsle, 31–54. Cambridge: Cambridge University Press.

Berger, Suzanne. 1972. *Peasants against Politics. Rural Organization in Brittany 1911–1967*. Cambridge, Mass.: Harvard.

Bideleux, Robert. 2020. "The Peasantries and Peasant Parties of Interwar East Central Europe." In *Interwar East Central Europe, 1918–1941. The Failure of Democracy-building, the Fate of Minorities*, edited by Sabrina P Ramet, 272–316. London: Routledge.

Brett, Daniel. 2018. "Indifferent but Mobilized: Rural Politics during the Interwar Period in Eastern and Western Europe." *Central Europe* 16 (2): 65–80. https://doi.org/10.1080/14790963.2019.1624461.

Cabo Villaverde, Miguel Angel. 2018. "Los partidos agrarios en Europa hasta 1945." In *Del pasado al futuro como problema. La historia agraria contemporánea española en el siglo XXI*, edited by David Soto Fernández and José-Miguel Lana Berasáin, 235–56. Zaragoza: PUZ.

Carmona, Juan, and James Simpson. 2014. "Los contratos de cesión de la tierra en Extremadura en el primer tercio del siglo XX." *Historia Agraria* 63: 183–213.

Carmona, Juan, and James Simpson. 2019a. "El microcrédito antes de las cooperativas. Pósitos y crédito público agrario en España en vísperas de la Gran Guerra." *Historia Agraria* 19 (77).

Caro Romero, Francisco, and Paula Garrido Rodríguez. 2021. *La Republica en los pueblos. Conflicto, radicalización y exclusión en la vida política local durante la Segunda República Española (1931–1936)*. Granada: Comares.

Chayanov, A.V. 1986. *The Theory of Peasant Economy*. Manchester: Manchester University Press.

Cleary, Mark 1989. *Peasants, Politicians and Producers: The Organisation of Agriculture in France Since 1918*. Cambridge: Cambridge University Press.

Clique, Hubert 1931. *Les caves coopératives de vinification en Bourgogne*. Paris: Recueil Sirey.

Collier, George. 1987. *Socialists of Rural Andalusia. Unacknowledged Revolutionaries of the Second Republic*. Stanford: Stanford University Press.

Connelly, John. 2020. *From People into Nations. A History of Eastern Europe*. Princeton: Princeton University Press.

Crotty, R.D. 1966. *Irish Agricultural Production*. Cork: Cork University.

Dimico, Arcangelo, Alessia Isopi, and Ola Olsson. 2017. "Origins of the Sicilian Mafia: The Market for Lemons." *Journal of Economic History* 77 (4): 1083–1115.

Fernández, Eva. 2014. "Trust, Religion, and Cooperation in Western Agriculture, 1880–1930." *The Economic History Review* 67 (3): 678–698.

Fernández, Eva, and James Simpson. 2017. "Producer Cooperatives, Institutional Change, and Politics in the Wine Industry, 1880–1980." *The Economic History Review* 70 (1): 122–142.

Galassi, Francesco. 2000. "A Measure of Culture: Trust and Defection in Southern Italy." In *Cultural Factors in Economic Growth*, edited by Mark Casson and Andrew Godley, 69–110. Berlin: Springer.

Garrido, Samuel. 2014. "Plenty of Trust, Not Much Cooperation: Social Capital and Collective Action in Early Twentieth Century Eastern Spain." *European Review of Economic History* 18 (4): 416–432.

Henrich, Joseph. 2020. *The Weirdest People in the World*. London: Allen Lane.

Henriksen, Ingrid. 1999. "Avoiding Lock-in: Co-operative Creameries in Denmark, 1882–1903." *European Review of Economic History* 9 (3): 365–397.

Jackson, George D. 1966. *Comintern and Peasant in East Europe 1919–1930*. New York: Columbia.

Jackson, Marvin R. 1982. "Agricultural Output in Southeastern Europe, 1910–1938." *ACES Bulletin* 24 (4).

Jensen, E. 1937. *Danish Agriculture: its Economic Development*. Copenhagen: Schultz.

Kalyvas, Stathis N. 1996. *The Rise of Christian Democracy in Europe*. Ithaca and London: Cornell.

Luebbert, George M. 1991. *Liberalism, Fascism, or Social Democracy. Social Classes and the Political Origins of Regimes in Interwar Europe*. Oxford: Oxford University Press.

Mazower, Mark. 1999. *Dark Continent. Europe's Twentieth Century*. London: Penguin.

Mitrany, David. 1930. *The Land and the Peasant in Rumania. The War and Agrarian Reform (1917–21)*. London: Milford.

Moeller, Robert G. 1986. *German Peasants and Agrarian Politics, 1914–1924. The Rhineland and Westphalia*. Chapel Hill: North Carolina.

O'Rourke, Kevin. 2007. "Culture, Conflict and Cooperation: Irish Dairying before the Great War." *The Economic Journal* 117 (October): 1357–1379.

Ó Gráda, Cormac. 1977. "The Beginnings if the Irish Creamery System." *The Economic History Review* 25: 284–305.

Ó Gráda, Cormac. 1994. *Ireland. A New Economic History 1780–1939*. Oxford: Clarendon.

Ó Gráda, Cormac. 1999. *Ireland Before and After the Great Famine*. 2nd ed. Manchester: Manchester University Press.

Ó Gráda, Cormac. 2006. "Irish Agriculture after the Land War." In *Land Rights, Ethno-Nationality, and Sovereignty in History*, edited by Stanley Engerman and Jacob Metzer, 131–52. London & New York: Routledge.

Planas, Jordi. 2017. "State Intervention in Wine Markets in the Early Twentieth Century. Why Was it so Different in France and Spain?" *Revista de Historia Económica* 35 (2): 175–206.

Popkin, Samuel. 1979. *The Rational Peasant. The Political Economy of Rural Society in Vietnam*. Berkeley: University of California.

Portes, A. 1998. "Social Capital. Its Origins and Applications in Modern Sociology—Dark Side of Social Capital." *Annual Review of Sociology* (24): 1–24.

Rey, Fernando del 2008. *Paisanos en lucha: exclusión política y violencia en la Segunda República española*. Madrid: Biblioteca Nueva.

Riley, Dylan. 2010. *The Civic Foundations of Fascism in Europe: Italy, Spain, and Romania, 1870–1945*. Baltimore: John Hopkins.

Roberts, Henry L. 1951. *Rumania. Political Problems of an Agrarian State*. New Haven: Yale University Press.

Roszkowski, Wojciech. 1995. *Land Reforms in East Central Europe after World War One*. Warsaw: Institute of Political Studies Polish Academy of Science.

Sadler, Michael. 1936. "Introduction." In *The Folk High Schools of Denmark*, edited by Holger Begtrup, Hans Lund and Peter Manniche. Oxford.

Schulze, Max-Stephan, and Nikolaus Wolf. 2012. "Economic Nationalism and Economic Integration: the Austro-Hungarian Empire in the late Nineteenth Century." *The Economic History Review* 65 (2): 652–673.

Scott, James C. 1976. *The Moral Economy of the Peasant. Rebellion and Subsistence in Southeast Asia*. New Haven: Yale University Press.

Seton-Watson, Hugh. 1945: 1967. *Eastern Europe between the Wars 1918–1941*. 3nd ed. New York: Harper.

Sheingate, Adam D. 2001. *The Rise of the Agricultural Welfare State. Institutions and Interest Group Power in the United States, France, and Japan*. Princeton: Princeton University Press.

Simpson, James. 2000. "Cooperation and Cooperatives in Southern European Wine Production." In *Advances in Agricultural Economic History*, edited by K. Kauffman, 95–126. Stamford, Connecticut: JAI Press.

Simpson, James. 2011. *Creating Wine: the Emergence of a World Industry, 1840–1914*. Princeton: Princeton University Press.

Simpson, James, and Juan Carmona. 2020. *Why Democracy Failed: The Agrarian Origins of the Spanish Civil War*. Cambridge: Cambridge University Press.

Steckel, Richard H., and William J. White. 2012. Engines of Growth: Farm Tractors and Twentieth-Century U.S. Economic Welfare. In *NBER Working Paper 17879.*

Suesse, Marvin, and Nikolaus Wolf. 2020. "Rural Transformation, Inequality and the Origins of Micro-Finance." *Journal of Development Economics* 143. https://doi.org/10.1016/j.jdeveco.2019.102429.

Tilly, Charles, Louise Tilly, and Richard Tilly. 1975. *The Rebellious Century*. Cambridge, Mass.: Harvard University Press.

Tiltman, Hubert H. 1934. *Peasant Europe*. London: Jarrolds.

Tomasevich, Jozo. 1955. *Peasant, Politics, and Economic Change in Yugoslavia*. Stanford: Stanford University Press.

Toshkov, Alex. 2019. *Agrarianism as Modernity in 20th century Europe. The Golden Age of the Peasantry*. London: Bloomsbury.

Turner, M. E. 1966. *After the Famine. Irish Agriculture 1850–1914*. Cambridge: Cambridge University Press.

Urwin, Derek W. 1980. *From Ploughshare to Ballot Box: the Politics of Agrarian Defence in Europe*. Oslo: Universitetsforlaget.

Varga, Zsuzsanna. 2014. "Challenges and Responses: Dilemmas of Agrarian Modernization in Interwar Hungary." In *Agriculture in the Age of Fascism. Authoritarian Technocracy and Rural Modernization, 1922–1945*, edited by Lourenzo Fernández Prieto, Juan Pan Montojo and Miguel Cabo, 113–37. Turnhout: Brepols.

Warriner, Doreen. 1939. *Economics of Peasant Farming*. Oxford: Oxford University Press.

Weber, Eugen. 1977. *Peasant into Frenchmen. The Modernization of Rural France, 1870–1914* London: Chatto & Windus.

Wunderlich, Freida. 1961. *Farm Labour in Germany 1810–1945*. Princeton: Princeton University Press.

Yates, P. Lamartine. 1940. *Food Production and Manpower in Western Europe*. London: Longmans Green.

CHAPTER 8

Farm Labourers: Exit, Loyalty, or Voice?

European countries in the interwar years witnessed the consolidation of three very different political-economic regimes: liberal democracy, social democracy, and fascism. For Luebbert (1991: 1), these were 'above all' political responses to accommodate or crush the 'demands of the working classes'. In most accounts the sources of this political instability are to be found in the urban labour markets, rather than agricultural ones. Although farm labourers were the largest group of workers in many countries, and the lowest paid in all of them, they only seriously threated liberal democracy in Italy and Spain, usually preferring elsewhere 'exit' or 'loyalty', rather than 'voice'.[1]

Labour accounted for between a third and two-thirds of farm costs in this period, but a significant part was supplied by unpaid family workers, and relatively few workers were entirely dependent on farm wages for their livelihood (Howard 1935: 229–30; Toth 1982: table 2). Wage labourers can be divided between those employed on annual contracts, and those contracted by the task. The supply of full-time farm workers was limited by the growing importance of the family farm and the pull of better paid urban work, while the high organizational costs peculiar to farm work restricted their disruptive powers. Farmers could not compete with urban wages because full-time workers had to be paid during the slack winter months, and labour productivity in agriculture was constrained by the

J. Simpson, *Family Farmers, Land Reforms and Political Action*, Palgrave Studies in Economic History,
https://doi.org/10.1007/978-3-031-67281-1_8

low levels of mechanization found on most farms. The number of permanent workers would have been even less if employers had not provided additional non-monetary benefits to keep their best people, or if the urban-based trade unions had not feared a flood of cheap labour driving down their members' wages, especially as labour shortages in the countryside risked higher food prices. Only in those regions where a significant number of landless workers continued to depend on highly seasonal farm employment did organized farm labour threaten political stability.

Labour conflicts tended to be concentrated in areas of large cereal farms because of the traditional need for significant numbers of harvest workers, while the temporal distribution of conflicts reflected changes in associational power, and in particular the legal possibilities for workers to form a trade union and oblige farmers to participate in collective bargaining. Europe's harvest workers, operating in very different cultural and political settings, followed 'strikingly similar' cycles of labour unrest, stretching in time from the Swing riots in southern England in the 1830s, to those on Andalucía's *Campiña* in southern Spain a century later.[2] These conflicts generally evolved in three stages. In the first, rural trade unions were still illegal and workers carried out wildcat harvest strikes in response to farmers failing to raise wages at a time of high food prices. A second phase, which became common across much of Western Europe after 1914, was associated with government attempts to allow collective bargaining in the countryside. The legalization of trade unions lowered the organizational costs for collective action among the large numbers of casual harvest workers, but farmers were still reluctant to negotiate with them, or respect agreements that had been previously reached. The final stage, increasingly common by the end of the period, saw governments incorporate labour legislation as part of wider packages to help farmers.

This chapter begins by examining the nature of farm work, and the difficulties associated with calculating the number of agricultural workers. The highly seasonal nature of much of the work implied that a sizeable number of families worked on both their own land and for harvest wages, which are not reflected in the censuses. Section two looks at the nature of farm work and labour contacts. Despite the major growth in associational power after 1918, the strong seasonal fluctuations in labour demand, together with the adverse economic conditions of the interwar period, created difficulties for labour movements. Section three looks more closely at the cycles of labour unrest and the cereal harvest, which were often triggered when governments relaxed the repression of trade unions. The final section explains why exceptionally large concentrations of farm workers in Italy and Spain choose voice rather than loyalty and exit, contributing to regime change.

8.1 Who Were the Wage Labourers in European Agriculture?

The fact that crops grow slowly but ripen quickly shaped not just the farming calendar, but the entire agricultural economy, especially labour contracts (Howard 1935: 3). Farmers could choose between hiring sufficient workers on annual contracts to guarantee enough labour for the harvest, but at the expense of having to support them during the slack winter months, or instead hire the necessary workers for winter work on annual contracts, and then compete in the tight summer markets for harvest labourers. Farm workers can therefore be divided between a relatively small group of professional full-time workers and a much larger one of casual labourers, drawn from a wide variety of backgrounds, including small farmers and urban wage labourers.

Full-time farm workers were normally hired annually and were essential to the organization of large farming enterprises.[3] Traditionally, farm servants had been contracted at the autumn hiring fairs and were common in the rain-fed agricultures of North-Western Europe, where more regular farm work was found over most of the year. They were rarer in dry-farming regions, which had a higher share of the land under cereals, and livestock farming was extensive, rather than intensive (Reher 1998; Simpson and Carmona 2020: 90). Farm servants were traditionally young and unmarried, and sought to gain experience and save money before returning to the family farm or renting land themselves, perhaps a first step on the farm ladder (Simpson and Carmona 2023: ch. 3 for France and Spain). They frequently ate at their employer's table and identified with small family farmers, a class they aspired to join, rather than the labour unions that appeared from the turn of the twentieth century (Yates 1940: 307).

Farm servants still accounted for almost two-fifths of Denmark's agricultural population as late as 1934, but numbers had been declining in many countries since the late nineteenth century (Yates 1940: 58). Nevertheless, the need for some permanent workers remained, and these benefitted from better legal rights in the decades immediately before the

Great War. Permanent workers formed 'the élite of the agricultural proletariat' possessing 'the vast traditional' manual skills required in farming, as well as the authority to oversee casual workers, especially at harvest time (Howard 1935: 60). They included older workers with specialized skills, such as herdsmen or shepherds, who looked after what they considered to be 'their' animals, and normally showed strong loyalty to their employer (Howkins 1985: 161). While many farming tasks required 'considerable dexterity, co-ordination and judgement', others relied on physical exertion, with a third of agricultural labour in Germany in the 1930s being employed in transportation (Mitch 1994: 10; Wunderlich 1961: 184). Even so, farmers rarely hired more than a few permanent workers, and in France only 8,262 out of a total of 2,514,637 farms in 1926 had more than ten full-time workers, found especially on the vineyards of the Midi and cereal and beet districts around Paris (Augé-Laribé 1932: 47–8).

The number of full-time workers declined in much of Europe because of the attractions of high-wage urban employment and the growing possibilities for labourers to own a small farm. Before 1914, the opportunities for temporary emigration to the Americas allowed young workers to save money, and an estimated 30–40% of emigrants from northern Portugal, Croatia, Serbia, Hungary, and Poland, and 40–50% from Italy, returned home in the early twentieth century, often to buy a farm (Baines 1991: 39). In Western Europe in particular, the import of cheap grains from the 1870s made large farms uncompetitive, while rising wages and stagnant or falling rents helped workers onto the lower rungs of the ladder (Chapter 5). In France, the rural proletariat was constantly disintegrating, 'as members break away, either to become landowners or join the industrial proletariat in the manufactories' (Augé-Laribé and Pinot 1927: 116). Vacant labouring positions in France were increasingly filled by Czech, Italian, Polish, and Spanish workers, and foreigners accounted for one-seventh of all Germany farm workers by 1914. Changes in factor prices were weaker in Southern Europe but even here rising real wages and falling land prices implied that labourers needed to work fewer days to buy their farm (Carmona et al. 2019). In Eastern Europe, by contrast, the opportunities for high paid urban work were scarcer, but rising wages from the late nineteenth century in Hungary encouraged some farmers to mechanize the harvest operations, while landowners in Romania chose to split their estates into small plots for tenants and sharecroppers, rather than working it themselves (Berend and Ránki 1974: 49; Mitrany

1930–1968: 282–3). Most would become owner-occupiers with the land reforms of the early 1920s.

This long-run tendency for the numbers of farm labourers to decline was sometimes interrupted and reversed. Agriculture was the employer of last resort in most countries, and urban workers drifted back to eat and work on the family farm when they became unemployed or join the pool of landless village workers, and migrant workers had to return home (Yates 1940: 285–6). Germany, for example, experienced several distinct employment cycles in the interwar period. A major labour shortage on farms followed the First World War when 700,000 prisoners and most of the 350,000 foreign workers left. This was soon more than compensated by the 'hundreds of thousands' of Germans arriving from the lost territories of the Reich, demobilized soldiers, and those escaping urban hunger. After 1923, industrial recovery led to a new rural exodus, creating labour shortages in agriculture by the late 1920s. With the Great Depression the country-to-city exodus was again briefly reversed and population growth saw the numbers of farm labourers increasing, although low farm prices encouraged employers to cut labour costs by mechanizing or shifting out of labour-intensive farming (Wunderlich 1961: 54–5). Labour shortages appeared once more in Nazi Germany, as workers flocked to the cities and growing restrictions imposed on using foreign workers, despite the government's attempts to increase food self-sufficiency.

The diverse and highly seasonal nature of farming makes it impossible to know with any certainty the relative share of permanent and casual workers in agriculture. Indeed, most small farmers worked a few days of the year for wages, while 'full-time' workers often had a plot of land or kitchen garden. The seasonal fluctuations in labour demand were rarely reflected in population censuses, as they recorded employment on a single day of the year. The treatment of women especially was 'subject to most extraordinary vagaries' (Howard 1935: 52). Few women were employed full-time in agriculture, but most played a vital role, not just in the house, but on the farm itself, supplying the additional labour needed at the peak-times of the year, as well as daily tasks such as milking, keeping poultry, or working the kitchen garden. Women in Galicia (Northern Spain) ran the farm on their own for several months a year when their husbands were away on temporary employment. In Ireland, the combination of low nuptiality and high levels of permanent emigration among young adults resulted in the brothers and sisters sometimes working a farm together

(Guinnane 1997: 230–2). The family farm, as its name implies, was very much a joint venture.

The figures in Table 8.1 must therefore be considered as only very approximate, and the different methodologies used to compile them make comparisons between countries dangerous. However, several general comments can be made. First, in industrial economies such as the United Kingdom or the Netherlands, full-time agricultural labourers accounted for over 60% of the total farm population, compared to between 20 and 30% in most other countries. Second, in countries such as Bulgaria or Yugoslavia, most farmers were self-employed, and there were few large farms that required part-time workers. In fact, the lack of off-farm seasonal employment, and the possibility of earning high harvest wages, explains why so many smallholders remained so poor. By contrast, large cereal farms in countries such as Hungary or Spain employed few permanent workers, but continued to depend on large numbers of temporary harvest workers, something that is missing from the official statistics.

8.2 Contracts and Rising Farm Wages

The highly seasonal nature of labour demand and the fact that agriculture remained the employer of last resort in many countries created difficulties for both farmers to manage their labour supply and workers to organize collective action. When farmers hired labour on annual contracts, they were effectively subsidizing workers during the dead season of the agricultural year and needed guarantees that they would not quit just prior to the periods of peak labour demand. In the past this had given rise to 'coercive' contracts, where force, or the threat of force, played 'a central role in convincing workers to accept employment or its terms' (Acemoglu and Wolitzky 2011: 555). The master-servant contracts had made it illegal for anyone to hire a worker who had broken a contract, and the legislation was usually actively enforced by the local authorities. This legal protection for employers was eroded as labour markets tightened from the late nineteenth century, but permanent workers on the large Polish farms even in the early 1930s often required a discharge certificate from their former employer to find new work (Gnoinski 1933: 67).[4] In Western Europe especially, economic conditions had encouraged farmers to turn to paternalism rather than coercion to motivate and encourage good work. In Italy, for example, the latifundio system depended in the nineteenth century 'primarily on the masters' and workers' 'recognition

Table 8.1 Wage workers in European agriculture, 1920s

	Numbers employed in agriculture (000 s)	*% of workers employed in agriculture*	*Numbers of agricultural workers*	*Agricultural paid workers as % of total agricultural*	*Farm workers as % of active population*
Austria (1930)	1718	31.9	450	26.6	8.5
Belgium (1920)	611	19.1	224	36.9	7.0
Bulgaria (1920)	2149	82.4	229	10.7	8.8
Czechoslovakia (1921)	2346	40.3	896	38.1	15.3
Denmark (1920)	461	33.8	167	36.3	12.3
Estonia (1922)	402	65.6	78	19.5	12.8
Finland (1920)	1018	68.9	367	36.0	24.8
France (1926)	8130	37.7	2852	35.1	13.2
Germany (1925)	14,388	30.5	3273	22.9	7.0
Eng. & Wales (1921)	975	6.8	615	63.1	4.3
Scotland (1921)	162	10.1	103	63.1	6.4
Hungary (1920)	2127	58.2	987	46.6	27.2
Ireland (1926)	672	52.1	139	20.7	10.8
Italy (1921)	9783	55.3	4238	43.3	23.9
Lithuania (1923)	1088	79.4	231	21.2	16.8
Netherlands (1920)	622	23.6	406	65.3	15.4
Norway (1920)	336	36.8	107	32.0	11.8
Portugal (1930)	1897	48.0	na	na	na
Romania (1930)	8231	77.2	na	na	na
Spain (1930)	3712	46.0	1014	27.3	12.6
Sweden (1920)	963	40.7	226	23.5	9.6
Switzerland (1920)	460	25.9	98	21.3	5.5

Source Howard (1935: tables 1 and 2) and for Spain, Simpson and Carmona (2020: table 4.3), refers to male workers only

of reciprocity in their relations': the master being entitled to loyalty, gratitude, and good service, and the worker to help, gifts, job security and consideration of their family needs (Petrusewicz 1996: 185).

Farmers, rather than attempting to compete directly with urban wages, therefore preferred to supplement low wages which rewarded all workers equally, by giving trusted workers perks, such as a vegetable plot, free firewood and grazing for their animals, or subsidized housing (Howard 1935: 234). Permanent workers were also sometimes allowed to hire family members for seasonal work (Móricz 1933 for Hungary and Gnoinski 1933: 67 for Poland). Families, contingent on good work on the Soviet collective farms, had the right to a house, half a hectare of land, work implements, and livestock which, according to one director, 'saved the majority of households from starvation' (Belov 1956: 179, in Naumenko 2021: 165). However, the fact that paternalism linked workers to the fortunes of agriculture inevitably resulted in living standards remaining low during the interwar period. There were also limits to their effectiveness. Some French farmers had to recruit from outside their districts, making it difficult for them to assess potential candidates, and a common complaint was that many of 'the youngest, cleverest, and most progressive elements' that were hired promptly left for industrial work (Augé-Laribé 1932: 51; Howard 1935: 41). Farmers also frequently used interlinked contracts to guarantee help in the harvest from their tenants or other farmers who had borrowed money from them. This could be mutually beneficial, as casual work provided an important supplement to the family economy of small proprietors, although it might clash with the labour demands on their own holdings. Finally, investment to provide running water, electricity, and tractors made farm employment potentially much more attractive to workers.

These problems, together with the huge variety of local conditions, make it virtually impossible to measure long-run changes in real wage costs for farmers with any accuracy. Instead, Table 8.2 shows the *direction* of wage movements and prices of major farm commodities in two very different economies, a 'certain' county in free-trade England and in protectionist Spain. In both cases, wages during the period rose much faster than farm prices.

Some farmers, in the face of these weak farm prices and rising wage costs, converted fixed costs associated with annual labour contracts into variable ones, by employing temporary workers instead. There was a long tradition of using migrant gang labour to collect the cereal harvest on

Table 8.2 Relative movements of farm wages and prices in England and Spain

	England 'a certain county'				*Spain*		
	wheat	*barley*	*beef*	*mutton*	*wheat*	*wine*	*olive oil*
1914	100	100	100	100	100	100	100
1928–30	158	138	125	124	167	250	159
1932	233	169	139	190	173	292	176

Sources Astor and Murray (1933: table IX) and Simpson (1985: appendix 3)

the large estates in countries such as Spain and Hungary, but by the turn of the twentieth century they were being used as well in specialist, labour-intensive tasks (Florencio Puntas and López Martínez 2000). The large vineyard owners in southern France hired gangs of 10 to 15 skilled workers to prune their vines (Smith 1975; Frader 1991: 75), and they were also used in sugar-beet production in northern Europe. Farmers avoided having to pay workers during the slack seasons, and they benefitted from the fact that the work was organized by the gangs themselves. More novel was the growing use of reapers and threshing machines, which reduced the need for casual harvest workers on large farms and allowed some family farmers to dispense entirely with their farm servants.[5]

The long-run shifts in wages and farm prices encouraged changes in farming practices. Cereal yields in England after the First World War stagnated because of the lower intensity of cultivation, despite farmers using better strains of seeds and the availability of artificial fertilizers. The high labour requirements for root crops caused the area to decline, as farmers switched to cheap imported animal feed instead, while the area of grass, 'a crop pre-eminently suited to the climate and labour conditions of the country', increased (Astor and Rowntree 1939: 83, 107). One large farm in Wiltshire (England) employed in 1931 just '25% or 30% of the number of men' that it had done just twenty-five years earlier (Street 1932–1948: 11).

There are few farm-level studies available, but those for nearly 200 farms in Sweden suggest that mechanization and changes in farming methods and cropping led to labour demand falling by 21% between 1913 and 1928, with the drop being similar on both small and large farms (Table 8.3). Change was generally easier in the rain-fed agricultures of North-Western Europe, as the low summer rainfall limited alternatives for farmers over large areas of Southern and Eastern Europe.

Table 8.3 Decline in the demand for farm labour in Sweden

Size of farms	*Number of man-days' work per 100 hectares*		
	1913	*1920*	*1928*
Over 50 hectares	3.352	3.049	2.678
Under 50 hectares	4.101	3.718	3.209
All farms	3.586	3.258	2.844
Index 1913 = 100	100	91	79

Source International Labour Office (1933: 792)

The fact that farming activities often took place over large areas on isolated farms created organizational problems that were significantly greater than those faced by industrial workers on the new assembly lines in large factories. Another obstacle was the diversity of farm work, which was reflected in the different labour contracts used, and segregated workers into distinct groups. On the large estates in Andalucía (southern Spain), for example, three distinctive sets of farm workers can be identified: those on permanent contracts; temporary village labourers; and migrant workers. Each group had quite different objectives, creating cleavages within the regional labour movement, and limiting effective collective action. Permanent workers were few in numbers and lived on isolated farms, which gave them few opportunities for contact with others on similar contracts. As they were guaranteed stable employment, even those who resented the demands of their employers had much to lose by joining temporary workers during a strike. Migrant workers also happily accepted piece-work contracts to maximize their daily wage to minimize their time away from home. By contrast, the several thousand landless workers and their families living in the local village wished to extend the available work. The future Spanish Socialist Minister, Fernando de los Ríos (1925: 844), hardly an enemy of organized labour, reported a conversation with a village dayworker who explained to him that they tried to work slowly because, 'if we work hard, there will be too many of us by half'.

8.3 Exercising Voice: Waves of Unrest and the Limits to Collective Bargaining

Many of the rural conflicts in Europe in the century following the Napoleonic Wars arose from the tensions produced by the changing economic and political relations between lord and peasant, or the growing influence of the central state on village society.[6] Farm workers by the late nineteenth century began to organize into 'syndicates' or labour unions, and demand better work conditions, especially during the cereal harvest. The cereal harvest was a time-bound operation, and the labour needed for a couple of weeks in the year was traditionally far greater than the local supply, giving workers potentially significant disruptive power, especially as farmers had to collect it quickly to avoid risking the loss of their entire annual income. Conflicts tended to follow a three-stage process over several decades, beginning with village-level protests at a time of low cereal prices, a tightening labour markets, but weak and illegal trade unions. The next stage saw massive harvest disruptions as governments relaxed their repression of trade unions. The state now responded by either forcing employers to negotiate, or banning unions once more. The cycle, which began in the village, was completed when farm workers had their wages and employment conditions set by national or regional authorities.

Rural life was centred on the village, and even in rural Norfolk (England) in the early 1920s the 'culture and consciousness of the rural poor' was generally local rather than national (Howkins 1985: xii). The first phase of the cycle was 'reactive' protests by villagers in response to what they considered as an abuse of power by large farmers. Although labour organizations were still illegal, village workers found it relatively easy to organize because they knew each other, but it was necessary to remain anonymous to avoid being blacklisted and forced to leave their homes and villages to find work (Howkins 1985: 35; Montañés and Simpson 2015: 120). Employers could count on a compliant state that was quick to repress local conflicts to stop them spreading, and ensure the speedy collection of the harvest. Some of the most spectacular successes were found in southern England in the 1830s, when villagers destroyed hay ricks and threshing machinery that threatened to significantly reduce casual winter work, delaying their use by several decades (Hobsbawm and Rudé 1973). By contrast, workers generally avoided damaging crops and property if it reduced employment opportunities.

From the late nineteenth century, a series of changes began to favour farm workers. Labour markets began to tighten as workers moved to the towns or emigrated, while governments started to pass legislation that allowed syndicates or trade unions to negotiate with their employers. Conflicts usually arose whenever farmers responded to falling cereal prices by cutting wages and governments no longer arrested workers for picketing, such as in France or Hungary in the 1890s, Italy or Spain in the years immediately following the First World War. Yet a surge in labour unrest was generally short-lived, as agreements had to be renegotiated annually because the amount of work that was available depended on the size of the local harvest; the ability of employers to pay better wages on the level of cereal prices; or the possibilities of farmers using non-union labour on which political party controlled local government.

Workers had to create labour organizations that operated over a much wider area than the village if they were to be able to restrict the use of outside labour. Large centralized union, especially if they had government recognition, found it easier to negotiate agreements, and could sometimes enforce a closed shop to avoid employers blacklisting union members.[7] Agricultural workers formed trade unions in countries such as England (Joseph Arch in the 1870s), Italy (1884), followed by Scotland, Denmark, Sweden, the Netherlands (1900), Hungary (1905), Austria (1902 and 1906), and Germany (1909) (Howard 1935: 184). However, as Clair Griffiths (2007: 185) notes for England, agricultural trade unionism in the early twentieth century was notable for having no continuous history.

The early unions frequently struggled to keep members. Farm disputes were highly localized, making national organizations reluctant to intervene. Indeed, central organizations saw strikes as being costly and difficult to control, while a national strike was impossible because the harvest began, and finished, on different dates even within relatively small regions. Farm workers often saw little point in paying union dues to an organization that they believed took local democracy away from them and determined if, and when, they could go on strike. Yet workers sometimes questioned whether it was necessary to pay their dues when unions appeared to do nothing, despite having successfully avoided a costly conflict by negotiating a settlement with employers.

If farm workers had difficulties to form trade unions in regions where labour was becoming scarce, the problems were even greater in those areas where numbers were still growing and surplus to requirements.

Workers in Jerez de la Frontera (southern Spain) created anarchist syndicates which, whenever repression was relaxed, paralysed the whole city in pursuit of their demands, such as during the 'peasant assault' of 1892; the waves of labour conflicts between 1910 and 1923; and again in the 1930s (Montañés and Simpson 2015). Successful harvest strikes depended on the local authorities allowing picketing and restricting the use of migrant workers and machinery. The fact that day wages in Jerez were maintained in real terms between 1911 and 1936 reflects both the success of sustained union activity and the town council's concern of having 5,000 often desperate and well-organized landless workers within the city walls.

The years immediately following the First World War witnessed another great burst of union activity and strikes in Western Europe, before farm prices collapsed once more. Repressing trade unions was now seen as being incompatible with democracy, and the International Labour Office (ILO) as early as 1921 demanded that governments introduce legislation for social reforms, giving farm workers the same entitlements as industrial workers (Howard 1935: 172).[8] Farmers everywhere opposed the new labour organizations and compulsory collective bargaining, while the attempts to introduce a uniform 8-hour day were considered impractical because of the seasonal fluctuations in labour demand, and the fact that the workday was much shorter in the winter than summer, especially in northern Europe. As the French government noted, an 8-hour day in agriculture could only be 'a sort of legal make-believe consisting entirely of exceptions' (Howard, 1935: 132). Legislation reflected these difficulties, with Poland fixing a workday of 6¼ hours in winter, but 11½ hours in summer. Germany, by contrast, divided the year into three blocks of 8-, 10-, and 11-hour days, but allowed farmers to allocate the time as they wished, thereby effectively creating an 11-hour day for both sowing and harvesting.[9]

By 1933, collective bargaining was in use agriculture in at least eleven European countries, including Austria*, Czechoslovakia, Denmark, Germany*, England, Wales, Scotland, Italy, Netherlands, Poland, Spain*, Sweden*, although these rights were being curtailed by the 'recent political changes' in those countries marked with an asterisk (Howard 1935: 171–4).[10] Farm labour in this third stage was either successfully organized and integrated into the wider government policy for agriculture, or instead governments failed to intervene sufficiently, and large numbers of poor workers who could not leave the land threatened liberal democracy itself.

8.4 The Political Legacy of Farm Workers' Activism

Whether farm labour in the interwar period became successfully integrated within liberal democracy, or instead was crushed politically, was closely associated with the groups that helped organize it (Luebbert 1991: 1). Traditional top-down hierarchical organizations, often Catholic, helped reinforce paternalistic ties based on 'loyalty', offering workers a sense of belonging in rural society, and were especially effective when discontented workers could exit, and find well-paid urban employment. By contrast, when socialist or anarchist groups found a ready audience among farm workers who had few possibilities of obtaining land *and* where there were few opportunities for exit, they threatened not only to increase employers' costs, but challenge the legitimacy of the government. The level of support for these syndicates fluctuated significantly but could be massive when an economic depression coincided with the government relaxing repression, such as when a million Italian rural workers went on strike in 1920 (Berman 2006: 128). However, as Luebbert (1991: 285–6) notes, when a socialist movement mobilized 'a significant fraction' of the rural proletariat, it 'contained the seeds of its own failure, for it would become enmeshed in rural class conflict and alienate the family peasantry'. Family farmers were usually significantly more numerous and saw labour organizations as part of an alien urban culture which threatened not just their businesses, but traditional village lifestyles.

Liberal England was perhaps an unlikely place for government intervention in labour markets. During the First World War, the combination of shortages and strong urban demand tightened labour markets, and the government established a fixed working week and a minimum wage for farm workers in 1917, something that '50 years of trade union agitation' had failed to achieve (Howkins 1985: 121).[11] This was part of a wider package that guaranteed prices of wheat and oats for farmers, fixed rents for tenants, and gave the government powers to oblige farmers to bring land into cultivation. By the end of the war, nearly half of farm labourers were union members (Howkins 2003: 34–5). Although the Agricultural Act was repealed in June 1921 (the so-called great betrayal), minimum farm wages were quickly re-established in the Agricultural Wages Act of 1924 (Howkins and Verdon 2009).

In Germany, the two major farm workers' unions—the Socialist 'German Agricultural Workers' Union' (DLV) and the Christian 'Central

Union of Agricultural Workers' (ZV)—resorted to strikes when employers refused to participate in collective bargaining. The number of strikes declined rapidly after 1924 as trade unions leant to use their political powers to influence arbitration policy in collective agreements, 'a much easier way to improve conditions of work than by risky and unpopular strikes' (Wunderlich 1961: 105–8). A combination of social provisions and tight labour markets helped improve conditions for farm labourers during the Weimar Republic. The National Socialists ended all independent unions, and conditions for workers became determined by corporatist settlements for the sector, rather than by individual employers. Tight labour markets kept living standards relatively high, with 1.45 million workers leaving agriculture between 1933 and 1939, creating a deficit of about 750,000, as foreign workers were limited and the government was obsessed with increasing food self-sufficiency (Wunderlich 1961: 154, 297, 301–2).[12] In France, the electoral victory of the Popular Front in 1936 set off a 'social explosion' across the economy, involving two and half million strikers in 17,000 separate conflicts (Shorter and Tilly, 1974: 127). Agriculture was relatively unaffected, and the elected government survived the challenges from organized labour, unlike those in Italy in the early 1920s, and, perhaps, Spain in the 1930s.

Workers in both Italy and Spain had traditionally been excluded from the political process because of rigged elections and trade unions being banned. Even when the Italian and Spanish Socialist parties eventually began to compete electorally, they were slow to show interest in the plight of farm labourers. Therefore, and unlike France or Germany, many workers failed to equate electoral democracy with the possibility of better living conditions, and turned instead to revolutionary syndicalism, and the belief that changes could be only achieved by overthrowing the political system. Anarchism was particularly strong in villages with large numbers of landless workers and weak farm ladders, organizing harvest time strikes, especially at moments when governments relaxed their repression (Simpson and Carmona 2020: 207–159).

In Italy, the strike waves of 1885, 1890–3, 1896–7, 1900–2, and 1908 were concentrated in Lombardy, Veneto, Emilia, and Sicily and associated with a 'decreasing willingness or ability of government to repress' organized labour.[13] Agricultural employers responded by forming their own regional associations and the National Confederation of Agriculture in 1911, just at the moment when the Socialist Party and labour movement split into reformist and revolutionary sections (Tilly et al. 1975: 165). The government was forced to make major concessions during the War, but when the veterans from the Bari, Lecce, and Murge brigades returned home, they were greeted not by land reform and full employment, but rather by 'convicts and Austrian prisoners of war being used in place of local workers to till the fields' (Snowden 1986: 158).[14] Labour conflicts became particularly bitter across the very different agricultural regions of the Po Valley, Tuscany, and Apulia.

Agriculture in the Po Valley area was dominated by large farms specializing in mixed husbandry, rice, sugar, and fruit. Although small farms were also common, significant numbers of landless workers (*braccianti*) were needed, and these organized strikes across the region in the immediate post-war years. In 1920, squads of Fascists left their urban bases in Milan and Ferrara, and descended on the small towns and villages, destroying union property, and attacking Socialists and Communists (Chiapparino and Morettini 2023: 80–1; Cobo Romero 2012: 276–7; Tilly et al. 1975: 176–7).

The conflicts in central Italy were associated with the centuries-old *mezzadria* sharecropping contract, which had traditionally been seen as having resolved the social question. Sharecropping created common interests between landowners and tenants for good cultivation, as output was divided between them, often in equal parts, and families frequently worked the same farm over several generations, despite contracts being renewed annually. In the early 1920s, the long-run fall in land prices (the landowner's contribution) and the rise in labour costs (the sharecropper's part) saw sharecroppers' living standards declining relative to urban workers. Sharecroppers, who usually considered themselves as independent tenant farmers, found themselves earning little more than wage labourers (Snowden 1989: 11–2). The Tuscan countryside had remained untouched by rural protests before the Great War, but then the breakdown in the traditional hierarchical social order that had tied the *mezzadro* 'to master, land, and family' led to 'a new network of horizontal class bonds' being forged that 'provided the collective consciousness that was a major premise of revolt' (Snowden 1989: 32, 54). Sharecroppers demanded that contracts be renegotiated, a problem further complicated by the need to apportion the growing amounts of capital needed for commercial farming between the two parties.[15] The landowners responded with massive, politically motivated evictions of sharecroppers in 1921 and 1922, replacing them with workers provided by the local *fasci*. Support for the *fasci* came not only from landowners, but also from many small farmers, landless workers, and small businessmen, who found the 'collective and communitarian doctrines of socialism ... menacing or at least incomprehensible' (Snowden 1989: 90, 167, 183, 190).

The large estates in the southern province of Apulia provide the third major region for Italian rural fascism. Farmers responded to legalized trade unions and strikes by leaving land uncultivated or eliminating unnecessary work. Given the disinterest of the Italian Socialist Party in the problems of southern agriculture, it was the local anarcho-syndicate that organized strikes and land invasions, while the landowners, in contrast to those of the Po valley and Tuscany, lacked cohesion (Snowden 1986: 96). Highly localized strikes 'coalesced into a single regionally organized challenge to the power of property' across Apulia greatly helped by workers winning the local elections in October and November 1920 and the control over whether to allow picketing and restrict the use of migrant labour and harvest machinery. The failure of the central government to respond to the strikes and land occupations encouraged landowners and employers to resolve their own divisions and fund armed fascist squads who, using motor transport, descended in large numbers on villages to attack trade unionists and their properties. By August 1922, 'the era of strikes, cooperatives, and socialist local government was over', and in October, Mussolini 'marched' on Rome (Snowden 1986: 167–82, 200).

In fascist Italy, just as later in Nazi Germany, corporatist settlements were introduced, with 1,607 collective agreements being signed between the Confederation of Agricultural Employers and its 543,486 members, and the Confederation of Agricultural Workers, with 1,654,340 between 1927 and 1932 (Biagi 1934: 313). Most farm workers saw their living standards fall significantly because the weak pull of urban markets created significant amounts of rural under-employment, and the anti-labour policies pursued by the regime (Schmidt 1938: 117; Ramón Muñoz 2010: 260).

The situation in southern Spain during the Bolshevik Triennium (1918–20) and then the *Primer Bienio* of the Second Republic (1931–3) was remarkably similar to that of Apulia in Italy in the immediate aftermath of the First World War. A large population of landless and near-landless workers, who had no possibilities of climbing the farm ladder and whose numbers had been swollen because of return migration, demanded work on the large estates, and an end to a political system based on electoral fraud and paternalism. The success of the Socialist Party in the municipal elections in southern Spain saw the patronage system being reversed, and used to reward their own followers, rather than those of the traditional village bosses, the *caciques*. Small farmers and tenants found they had to pay higher wages to collect their harvest and were legally required sometimes to employ workers they did not need. Although the latifundios contributed little more than three per cent of Spain's GDP, and employed just five per cent of the nation's workforce, the well-organized Socialist FNTT and Anarchist CNT threatened not just the economic viability of the large estates, but the government itself. Indeed Spain by 1931 was a country of family farmers, accounting for around a third of the country's electorate, and outnumbering landless workers even in the regions of large estates.[16] Rural Spain became heavily divided and, in the comparatively free elections of February 1936, almost as many people in the latifundios provinces voted for parties of the Right, as they did for those of the Popular Front.

8.5 Conclusions

Rural workers, despite being a significant group within agriculture, generally had limited political influence in interwar Europe. As this chapter has argued, workers faced major organizational difficulties to improve their living standards, being a highly diverse group with very different economic interests, and with a significant number believing that long-run loyalty to their employers offered greater rewards than those that could be achieved through voice. Harvest strikes were common in some regions, but workers usually resented ceding local control to a centralized, but distant union organization.

Farm workers in Western European generally benefitted from the tightening of labour markets after the 1870s, as cities attracted low paid farm labour. When food security became an important policy objective after the First World War, governments increasingly included farm labour in wider agreements to restore farm profitability, and slow the rural exodus. In Eastern Europe, by contrast, the agrarian problem remained linked almost exclusively to access to land for workers, which was largely resolved by the land reforms.

The events in Italy and southern Spain were unusual because the landed elites had maintained a significant level of political control allowing governments to repress organized labour for longer. Farm workers had become accustomed to acting outside political parties and, by organizing massive strikes when restrictions to trade unions were relaxed, could sometimes threatened the governments itself. They were, however, unsuccessful. In Italy, by refusing to intervene, the government left space for armed fascist groups, which were much better organized than the workers, to restore the traditional influence of landowners and farmers in the countryside. Fascist groups were slower to appear in Spain because the government generally maintained law and order in the countryside, but when the military rose in July 1936, and quickly swept over large areas of southern Spain, 'fascist' hit squads went methodically village by village arresting those who they believed had challenged the traditional order (trade unionists, local government officials, teachers...), and murdered many of them. Few villages were spared, with one estimate giving 150,000 killed, and today their remains are still being recovered from mass graves (Preston 2012: xviii).[17]

Italy and Spain were unusual in having large concentrations of landless workers. As Huntington (1968: 375) famously noted, 'no group is more conservative than a landowning peasantry, and none is more revolutionary than a peasantry that owns too little land or pays too high a rental'. Historically, it was extraordinary that the majority of those who worked the land in interwar Europe were either landowners, or aspired to be one, and had little time for parliamentary socialism, let alone anarchism or communism.

Notes

1. Hirschman (1970) for the distinction between exit, loyal, and voice.
2. Silver (2003: 32) identifies a similar cycle for the automobile industry.
3. Howard (1935: 254–5) notes that they were known as '*deputatists* and farm-servants of the north, east, and centre of Europe; the *statare* of Sweden, the *komorniky* of Poland; the *valets de ferme* of Belgium and France; the *garzone* ...of Italy; the ploughmen, stockmen, and ordinary farm-labourers or orramen of England, Wales, and Scotland'.
4. Howard (1935: 103) claims that it had been common, if not universal, for the police to force deserting workers to return to their masters but, by the 1930s, except for Hungary, 'all these penal systems are now either formally or in practice abolished'.

5. Buylla (1904), for the conflicts over the elimination of full-time workers in Castile-Leon (Spain) in the early 1900s.
6. Rural protests and 'peasant' wars were frequent across large areas of the world during the twentieth century. Wolf (1971) and Mason (2004).
7. Half of the original agricultural trade union membership of Scotland emigrated Howard (1935: 184).
8. Silver (2003:14) notes that associational power was embedded in the state legal framework, and included factors such as the right to form trade unions or the obligation of employers to bargain collectively with them.
9. The attempts in Czechoslovakia (1918) and Italy (1923) to introduce an 8-hour day were quickly reversed. Howard (1935: 120–3, and 131).
10. In the Netherlands, nearly a quarter of farm workers were covered by collective bargaining agreements in 1936, and the Ministry of Agriculture enforced a settlement if negotiations failed. In Belgium, minimum wages were also fixed by *Commissions Paritaires*, representing both employers and workers (Yates 1940: 142–3, 215).
11. Wages were to be set at the local (country) level. The board had representatives of workers and farmers, as well as government-appointed members.
12. The National Socialist trade union was the German Labour Front (DAF).
13. Over 6,000 strikes took place between 1878 and 1903 (Tilly et al. 1975: 155–7).
14. A government promise of land reform followed the military disaster of Caporetto, when 40,000 soldiers were killed, 280,000 taken as prisoners of war, and 350,000 deserted. The Italian economy contracted by 14% in 1919 and another 8% in 1920.
15. Carmona and Simpson (1999) discuss long-run change in farm prices and industrial wages in sharecropping contracts. For changes in farming, Galassi (1986), and specialized viticulture, Biagioli (2002: 42–2) and Carmona and Simpson (2023).
16. There were perhaps 900,000 landowners and tenants and 570,000 landless workers in the latifundios provinces (Carmona et al. 2019: tables 1, 2, and 3). Cobo Romero (2003) for a discussion in the province of Jaen.

17. A further 50,000 were murdered by supporters of the Republican Government.

References

Acemoglu, Daron, and Alexander Wolitzky. 2011. "The Economics of Labor Coercion." *Econometrica* 79 (2): 555–600.

Astor, Viscount, and Keith Murray. 1933. *The Planning of Agriculture*. Oxford: Oxford University Press.

Astor, Viscount, and B. Seebohm Rowntree. 1939. *British Agriculture the Principles of Future Policy*. London: Penguin.

Augé-Laribé, Michel. 1932. "Labour Conditions in French Agriculture." *International Labour Review* 25 (1): 23–57.

Augé-Laribé, Michel, and Pierre Pinot. 1927. *Agriculture and Food Supply in France during the War, Carnegie Endowment for International Peace*. New Haven: Yale.

Baines, D.E. 1991. *Emigration from Europe 1815–1930, Studies in Economic History and Social History*. Basingstoke: Macmillan.

Belov, Fedor. 1956. *The History of a Soviet Collective Farm*. London: Routledge & Kegan Paul.

Berend, Ivan T., and Gyorgy Ránki. 1974. *Economic Development in East-Central Europe in the 19th and 20th Centuries*. New York: Columbia.

Berman, Sheri. 2006. *The Primacy of Politics. Social Democracy and the Making of Europe's Twentieth Century*. Cambridge: Cambridge University Press.

Biagi, H. 1934. "The Regulation of Collective Employment Relations in Agriculture in Italy." *International Labour Review* 29 (3): 309–19.

Biagioli, Giuliana. 2002. "La mezzadria poderale nell'Italia Centro-settentrionale in età moderna e contemporánea." *Rivista Di Storia Dell'agricoltura* 42: 53–101.

Buylla, Adolfo. 1904. *Memoria acerca de la información agraria en ambas Castillas*. Edited by Instituto de Reformas Sociales. Madrid: Minuesa de los Ríos.

Carmona, Juan, Joan Rosés, and James Simpson. 2019. "Spanish Land Reform in the 1930s: Economic Necessity or Political Opportunism?" *The Economic History Review* 72 (2): 669–90.

Carmona, Juan, and James Simpson. 1999. "The "Rabassa Morta" in Catalan Viticulture: The Rise and Decline of a Long-Term Sharecropping Contract, 1670s–1920s." *The Journal of Economic History* 59: 290–315.

Carmona, Juan, and James Simpson. 2003. *El laberinto de la agricultura española. Instituciones, contractos y organización entre 1850 y 1936*. Zaragoza: Prensas Universitarias de Zaragoza.

Carmona, Juan, and James Simpson. 2023. "Landlords and Sharecroppers in Wine Producing Regions: Beaujolais, Catalonia and Tuscany, 1800–1940." In *Global Agricultural Workers from the 17th to the 21st Century*, edited by Rolf Bauer and Elise van Nederveen Meerkerk, 91–113. Leiden & Boston: Brill.

Chiapparino, Francesco, and Gabriele Morettini. 2023. "International Markets, Policy, and Mobility. 'Rural Italies' in the 1930s Recession." In *Agriculture and the Great Depression. The Rural Crisis of the 1930s in Europe and the Americas*, edited by Gérard Béaur and Francesco Chiapparino, 77–96. Abingdon: Routledge.

Cobo Romero, Francisco. 2003. *De Campesinos a Electores. Modernización agraria en Andalucía, politización campesina y derechización de los pequeños propietarios y arrendatarios. El caso de la provincia de Jaén, 1931–1936*. Madrid: Biblioteca Nueva.

Romero, Cobo, and Francisco. 2012. *¿Fascismo o democracia? Campesinado y política en la crisis del liberalismo europeo, 1870–1939*. Granada: Universidad de Granada.

de los Rios, Fernando. 1925. "The Agrarian Problem in Spain." *International Labour Review*: 830–851.

Puntas, Florencio, and Antonio, and Antonio López Martínez. 2000. "El trabajo asalariado en la agricultura de la Baja Andalucía, Siglos XVIII-XIX." *Historia Agraria* 21: 99–126.

Frader, Laura Levine. 1991. *Peasants and Protest: Agricultural Workers, Politics, and Unions in the Aude, 1850–1914 Berkeley*. Los Angeles and London: University of California Press.

Galassi, Francesco. 1986. "Reassessing Mediterranean Agriculture: Retardation and Growth in Tuscany, 1870–1914." *Rivista Di Storia Economica* 3: 91–121.

Gnoinski, J. 1933. "The Conditions of Agricultural Workers in Poland in 1930 and 1931." *International Labour Review* 27 (1): 66–78.

Griffiths, Clare V.J. 2007. *Labour and the Countryside. The Politics of Rural Britain*. Oxford: Oxford University Press.

Guinnane, Timothy W. 1997. *The Vanishing Irish: Households, Migration, and the Rural Economy in Ireland, 1850–1914* Princeton: Princeton University Press.

Hirschman, Albert O. 1970. *Exit, Voice, and Loyalty: Responses to Decline in Firms, Organizations, and States*. Cambridge, MA: Harvard University Press.

Hobsbawm, Eric, and George Rudé. 1973. *Captain Swing*. Harmondsworth: Penguin.

Howard, Louise E. 1935. *Labour in Agriculture. An International Survey*. Oxford: Oxford University Press.

Howkins, Alun. 1985. *Poor Labouring Men. Rural Radicalism in Norfolk 1870–1923*. London: Routledge & Kegan Paul.
Howkins, Alun. 2003. *The Death of Rural England. A Social History of the Countryside since 1900*. London: Routledge.
Howkins, Alun, and Nicola Verdon. 2009. "The State and the Farm Worker: The Evolution of the Minimum Wage in Agriculture in England and Wales, 1909–24." *Agricultural History Review* 57: 257–74.
Huntington, Samuel. 1968. *Political Order in Changing Societies*. New Haven: Yale.
ILO. 1933. "The Labour Question in Swedish Agriculture." *International Labour Review* 27 (June): 789–801.
Luebbert, George M. 1991. *Liberalism, Fascism, or Social Democracy. Social Classes and the Political Origins of Regimes in Interwar Europe*. Oxford: Oxford University Press.
Mason, T.David. 2004. *Caught in the Crossfire. Revolutions, Repression, and the Rational Peasant*. Lanham: Rowan & Littlefield.
Mitch, David. 1994. "Learning by Doing Among Victorian Farmworkers: A Case Study in the Biological and Cognitive Foundations of Skill Acquisition." *LSE Working Papers in Economic History*, 16/94.
Mitrany, David. 1930:1968. *The Land and the Peasant in Rumania*. New York: Greenwood.
Montañés, Enrique, and James Simpson. 2015. "Casual Workers, Collective Action and Anarcho-Syndicalism in Southern Spain: Jerez de la Frontera, 1882 to 1933." *Agricultural History Review* 63 (1): 113–31.
Móricz, Miklos. 1933. "Landless Agricultural Workers in Hungary." *International Labour Review* 28 (4): 513–50.
Naumenko, Natalya. 2021. "The Political Economy of Famine: The Ukrainian Famine of 1933." *Journal of Economic History* 81 (1): 156–197.
Petrusewicz, Marta. 1996. *Latifundium : Moral Economy and Material Life in a European Periphery*. Ann Arbor: Michigan University Press.
Preston, Paul. 2012. *The Spanish Holocaust, Inquisition and Extermination in Twentieth-century Spain*. London: Harper.
Muñoz, Ramón, and Ramón. 2010. *Globalisation and the International Markets for Mediterranean Export Commodities: The Case of Olive Oil, 1850–1938*. Ph: D., European University Institute, Ph.D.
Reher, David Sven. 1998. "Family Ties in Western Europe: Persistent Contrasts." *Population and Development* 24 (2): 203–34.
Schmidt, Carl T. 1938. *The Plough and the Sword. Labor, Land, and Property in Fascist Italy*. New York: Columbia.
Shorter, Edward, and Charles Tilly. 1974. *Strikes in France, 1870–1968*. Cambridge: Cambridge University Press.

Silver, Beverly. 2003. *Forces of Labor: Workers' Movements and Globalization since 1870*. Cambridge: Cambridge University Press.
Simpson, James. 1985. *Agricultural Growth and Technological Change: The Olive and Wine in Spain, 1860–1936*. Ph: D., University of London, Ph.D., University of London.
Simpson, James, and Juan Carmona. 2020. *Why Democracy Failed: The Agrarian Origins of the Spanish Civil War*. Cambridge: Cambridge University Press.
Smith, Harvey. 1975. "Work Routine and Social Structure in a French Village: Cruzy, Hérault in the Nineteenth Century." *Journal of Interdisciplinary History* 5: 357–382.
Snowden, Frank. 1986. *Violence and Great Estates in the South of Italy: Apulia, 1900–1922*. Cambridge: Cambridge University Press.
Snowden, Frank. 1989. *The Fascist Revolution in Tuscany, 1919–1922*. Cambridge: Cambridge University Press.
Street, A.G. 1932: 1948. *Farmer's Glory*. London: Faber.
Tilly, Charles, Louise Tilly, and Richard Tilly. 1975. *The Rebellious Century*. Cambridge, Mass.: Harvard University Press.
Toth, Tibor. 1982. "Profitability and Cost-Efficiency in Hungarian Agriculture in the 1930s." *Journal of European Economic History* 11 (1): 157–64.
Wolf, Eric R. 1971. *Peasant Wars of the Twentieth Century*. London: Faber.
Wunderlich, Freida. 1961. *Farm Labour in Germany 1810–1945*. Princeton: Princeton University Press.
Yates, P. Lamartine. 1940. *Food Production and Manpower in Western Europe*. London: Longmans Green.

CHAPTER 9

The Great Depression: Commodity Chains, Farm Organizations, and State Capacity

By the early 1930s, the price of commodities such as wheat in France, milk in Denmark, or wine in Italy, had all fallen to half the levels they had been just a few years earlier (Sheingate 2001: 16; Yates 1940: 45; Simpson 2000: Fig. 1).[1] Most businesses that experience a decline of this magnitude would go bankrupt, especially if outgoings such as taxes, rent, or interest payments were slower to adjust to the deflationary conditions. Farming in interwar Europe proved more durable, with farmers withdrawing from markets, consuming less, and working harder. While the short-term adaptation of farming to lower prices was important, the major legacy of the Great Depression in industrial-based societies was the success of some farm groups to create new organizations to obtain government intervention to redistribute rents in their favour. These would not only prove difficult to reverse when economic conditions eventually improved but were significantly expanded after the Second World War.

This chapter extends the earlier discussions on farm associations, state capacity, and lengthening food chains to explain why some farm groups were more successful at obtaining government support than others. Governments found market intervention much easier for those goods that they imported, rather than exported, and many farmers in the industrial-based nations of North-West Europe benefitted from higher tariffs that limited foreign competition. However, as countries approached

J. Simpson, *Family Farmers, Land Reforms and Political Action*, Palgrave Studies in Economic History,
https://doi.org/10.1007/978-3-031-67281-1_9

self-sufficiency, other mechanisms, requiring the active collaboration of farmers were needed to avoid costly surpluses from accumulating and depressing markets once more. By contrast, governments in Eastern and Southern Europe struggled to find new markets for their exports of cereals and Mediterranean produce.

Specialist farm producers generally enjoyed greater incentives to organize than those that were less market-orientated, explaining the stronger farm organizations found across much of North-Western Europe (Chapter 7). Governments were also more predisposed to intervene when farm lobbies expressed precise demands, especially if these helped to protect the country's gold and currency reserves. Effective agricultural policymaking became the result of a political bargain between politicians and farm lobbies (World Bank 2007: 43).

This chapter begins by examining the impact of the Great Depression on European agriculture and the demands, and opportunities, it created for farm groups and governments to extend their influence through market intervention. This is followed by looking at wheat, dairy farming, and viticulture, illustrating not just the importance of commodity-specific characteristics in determining the nature of market intervention, but also why government policies often varied significantly for the same commodity across countries. It shows when farm groups and political parties had incentives to work together, allowing the active participation of farm groups in formulating government policy. While governments and farm organization in North-Western Europe from the early 1930 were increasingly working together, they frequently remained highly suspicious of each other elsewhere.

9.1 The Great Depression and European Agriculture

Many Western European governments raised tariffs in response to New World imports and falling cereal prices from the 1870s, slowing the shift out of cereals and the rural exodus (Chapter 4). In Eastern Europe, cereal exporters were forced to cut labour costs to remain competitive. The food shortages caused by the First World War required a very different response, with governments encouraging farmers to increase output to feed urban consumers. Farmers, long before 1929, had come to expect governments to influence farm prices by as much, if not more, than world markets or the weather.

The Great Depression was therefore the third major exogenous shock to hit European agriculture in half a century, once again creating severe problems of overproduction. Prices actually started to fall earlier, with the world's wheat production growing twice as fast as consumption between 1914 and 1939, leading to stocks accumulating (Sheingate 2001: 16; Federico 2005). The global impact of the Depression was fuelled by the rapid contraction of international credit and the implementation of orthodox monetary policies by governments to protect their currencies, leading to cuts in imports and a reduction in the money supply. The result was deflation, rising real interest rates, and a rapid growth in industrial unemployment, reducing the demand for farm products.[2] In those countries where agriculture was still the employer of last resort, unemployed urban workers returned to the family farm, or competed with farm labourers for the diminishing amount of agricultural work (Janicki 2023: 165: Simpson and Carmona 2020: 76–77; Wright 1964: 41). Many governments, even after they left the Gold Standard, remained reluctant to abandon orthodox economics, thereby delaying recovery (Eichengreen 1996).

World agricultural output actually remained relatively stable between 1929 and 1932, but farm prices fell faster than industrial and consumer goods, creating the price scissors effect (Table 9.1). The plummeting world price for farm goods correctly identifies the magnitude of the depression, but their impact on living standards for European farmers are harder to decipher. Not only did farm prices vary significantly by commodity, but government intervention usually kept domestic prices above global levels. Therefore, while the international price of wheat halved between 1929 and 1932, the 'official' price in Spain changed little, although the number of farmers that could actually sell at this price was probably small. The significant volatility of world markets implies that the extent of the price falls is also heavily dependent on the choice of the base years. The choice of 1914 in particular exaggerated price and production falls as this was an unusually good year for most commodities (Federico 2005: 953; Pasour and Rucker 2005: 87). For Astor and Murray (1933: 22), price fluctuations in the last two decades in Great Britain in 1933 were 'so violent that the working of the price system has had the appearance of being anarchic. Agricultural prices in 1920 were 192% higher than in the three pre-War years; in 1932 they were only 12% above'.

The importance of the family farm and government policies explains why the volume of food production remained stable despite rapidly falling

Table 9.1 World production and prices between 1929 and 1932

	Production		*Prices*	
	1929	*1932*	*1929*	*1932*
Industry	100	64	100	64
Food	100	100	100	52
Raw Materials	100	75	100	44

Source Feinstein et al. (1997: table 6.2)

prices. Families on small farms still had to eat, and responded to market uncertainty not by reducing output, but by working harder, buying less, and generally becoming more self-sufficient. By contrast, commercially orientated farmers responded by eliminating non-essential tasks and reducing their purchases of artificial fertilizers, pesticides, and farm implements. As the Royal Institute of International Affairs (1932: 74) noted, many farmers 'are returning to more primitive methods of production, to human and animal labour in place of machines, and are spending less on fertilizers, the production of which showed a remarkable decline in 1930 and 1931'. These reversals would have been greater if governments in industrial-based societies had not supported farm prices. As a result, few European farmers actually lost their farms. In Sweden, for example, only 1,018 farms out of a national stock of about 300,000 were sold at auction in 1932, and 5,000 out of 200,000 farms in Denmark between 1931 and 1933 (Morell 2010: 140–1; Just 2010: 121). In the United States, by contrast, about a sixth of farms were foreclosed between 1921 and 1929 (Alston 1983: table 1, in Federico 2006: 192). As cereal farmers in the New World responded to falling prices by increasing production by extending the area cultivated to benefit from the growing economies of scale associated with the new labour-saving technologies to cut unit costs, world production of wheat actually increased between 1924–9 and 1929–34 by 6.5%, and the area sown by 11.6% (Malenbaum 1953: tables 1, 2).

The Great Depression reinforced the divisions in European agriculture. For Eastern Europe especially, the protectionist policies implemented in the industrial countries limited their export possibilities at a time when their own farm populations were growing rapidly, reducing the land: labour ratios. Most farms in this region were too small to mechanize, while labour-intensive cultivation and specialized livestock farming were not viable given the weak domestic demand and natural resource constraints (Chapter 3). By contrast, Western European farmers benefitted from the 'Lindert paradox', whereby 'the more advanced the nation, the more its government favors agriculture' (Lindert 1991: 29). Farmers in countries such as Germany, France, Italy, or Switzerland enjoyed a monopoly in their domestic markets by the 1930s that left food prices double those of world levels. For Doreen Warriner (1939: 26, 31), it was 'paradoxical' that when economic growth recovered in the late 1930s, the protected Western European countries saw labour leave agriculture once more, while it continued to rise in the unprotected Eastern Europe ones.

The success of farmers in Europe's industrial-based countries in obtaining government support is sometimes explained by the fact that only a relatively small group of farmers benefitted, but the costs were paid by the taxes of a large non-farm population (Lindert 1991: 31). Yet farm groups still had to organize and articulate specific and feasible policy demands, and then convince politicians to prioritize their interests over those of other groups. Governments were reluctant to raise consumer prices at a time of high unemployment, but they usually needed to reduce imports to protect their gold and currency reserves, and tariffs were relatively easy to implement (Table 9.2).

Some countries had traditionally encouraged imports, resulting in cheap bread and animal feed. Britain, in particular continued to prioritize free trade (although after January 1933 it favoured countries of

Table 9.2 Balance of trade constraints on agricultural protection in select countries

	Prioritize cheap food imports	*Dependence on manufacture imports*	*Importance of food exports*	*Importance of manufacturing exports*
UK	Yes	Low	Low	High
Denmark	Yes	High	High	Low
France	No	Low	High	Low
Germany	No	Low	Low	High
Romania	No	High	High	Low
Spain	No	High	High	Low

the Empire), believing it was necessary to guarantee its own manufacturing exports, where it had a comparative advantage, and the freight essential for the country's ship building industries (Astor and Rowntree 1939: 53). In Denmark, cheap imported feed benefitted farmers who specialized in high-quality butter and bacon for export, although after 1931 it faced considerable problems as industrial countries closed their markets. Germany faced the difficult choice of whether to use its limited foreign exchange to prioritize cheap food imports or industrial raw materials. By choosing to protect its grain producers, it raised the cost of animal feed, resulting in a shortage of animal fats for domestic consumers. Southern and Eastern European countries, especially those with large export sectors, faced the greatest difficulties, as they now struggled to find new markets for their agricultural goods, severely restricting their capacity to import manufactures.

Farmers, especially in industrial societies, complained of their weakening position in the lengthening commodity chains, as growing economies of scale appeared in processing and marketing, while motorized transport helped merchants widen their supply networks. New legal standards for food quality could have 'far-reaching repercussions on the organization of agriculture' (Astor and Rowntree 1938: 64). Food prices in London or Paris fell by much less than farm prices. Although all farmers probably wanted to control 'exploitative' middlemen, their other policy demands were often contradictory. A strategy, for example, which raised cereal prices was opposed by livestock farmers, as it implied higher feed costs. Government investment to encourage more scientific farming might increase output (and depress farm prices) or farm machinery cut labour inputs at a time of high unemployment. Yet policies to encourage farmers to create more employment threatened to raise farm costs, reduce labour productivity, and depress farm prices by increasing output.

Most governments in any case struggled to obtain the necessary farm-level information to intervene effectively in markets. The significant variations in prices and crop yields caused production costs to fluctuate massively, with those for wheat in Hungary ranging between 120 and 215 *pengös* a ton in the 1930s (Hevesy 1940: 799). As many farmers followed complex production systems, it was virtually impossible to allocate fixed costs such as rent, depreciation, or interest payments to a single crop. Likewise, variable costs could not be calculated when unpaid family labour was used. These problems were as true in industrial-based as agricultural-based economies. In England and Wales, it was noted that 'farming is such a complex of interlocking enterprises that it is not always easy to abandon the cultivation of a single crop—however unprofitable it may be' (Astor and Rowntree 1939: 128), while Danish farming was 'a specialised system where several products are produced, because thereby each product can be produced more cheaply and the returns of the whole farm business can be increased' (Jensen 1937: 299). Farms that specialized in just a single product were the exception (Royal Institute of International Affairs 1932: ch.4).

Government policies that successfully raised farm prices inevitably risked farmers producing more, thereby depressing prices again (Pasour and Rucker 2005: xx). Price support therefore also had to include commitments from farmers not to extend the area cultivated or use more fertilizers. Governments lacked the necessary farm-level information to monitor and sanction those who broke agreements, so the active support of local farm groups was essential to provide this, and monitor their members to ensure compliance. As Sheingate (2001: 5) notes, effective policy implementation depended on the level of state capacity and this in turn on the 'relationship between interest groups and the State as mediated by institutions'. Farm associations in the industrial-based societies that were built around specific commodities generally proved more effective than single peak organizations covering all farmers.

Farmers everywhere found it difficult to associate their own difficulties with the global imbalances in the supply and demand for foodstuffs, and they had an exaggerated idea of what government intervention could achieve. What is remarkable is that market intervention had less to do with the nature of the political regime, as to the character, depth, and geographical reach of farm-level organizations. Governments, by delegating regulatory powers to farmers in voluntary organizations, rather than imposing decisions on them from above, were both more effective and helped to strengthen democracy (Chapter 10). Many farm groups however, especially those outside of North-Western Europe, remained weakly organized, resulting in governments doing little to support prices, leaving farmers no other option but to withdraw from markets. The rest of this chapter looks more closely at the nature of government intervention and the development of farm organizations with three major commodities: wheat, milk, and wine.

9.2 Wheat Farming During the Great Depression

Wheat was by far the most important food crop traded internationally, with Britain accounting for 27% of world imports between 1927/8 and 1931/2 (Hevesy 1940: app. 9).[3] Most importing countries raised tariffs and other trade barriers, increasing self-sufficiency everywhere, except Denmark (Table 9.3). By the mid-1930s, if not earlier, Czechoslovakia, France, German, Portugal, Spain, and Sweden were effectively 100% autonomous. Whereas in Britain the slogan for cheap food ('Big Loaf, Little Loaf') was perhaps decisive for the Liberal Party's victory in the 1906 elections, in France it was still possible in the 1930s to claim that 'every reduction of the wheat area is regarded as a national disaster' (Royal Institute of International Affairs 1932: 139). Therefore, while wheat prices fell by 52% in Liverpool between 1924 and 1931, they rose by 39% in France, 60% in Germany, and two per cent in Italy, so that wheat prices in February 1931 were two or three times greater in France, Germany, and Italy than Britain (Royal Institute of International Affairs 1932: 180).Although keeping foreign wheat out of a country was relatively easy, governments faced significant problems planning consumption, especially as they risked upsetting two important groups: urban consumers, by creating artificial bread shortages by restricting imports, and farmers, by lowering farm prices by importing too much.

Figures for Belgium include Luxembourg

Source Calculated from Hevesy (1940)

By contrast, Bulgaria, Hungary, and Yugoslavia saw their exports decline as a share of national production between 1922–7 and 1932–7 (Table 9.3). Poland's figures are distorted by its need to import wheat in the mid-1920s, and Romania's exports rose only slightly, from 7 to 10% of total output. All European countries, except for Romania and Yugoslavia, saw domestic wheat production grow in these years, and in ten cases the figure was by over 50%. In the UK, which was still dependent on imports for about four-fifths of its needs in the mid-1930s, the rise was just 5%, and in Spain, which had become virtually self-sufficient by the mid-1920s, output grew by 11%. Significant increases were found among the exporting nations, Bulgaria (53%), Poland (40%), and Hungary (24%) between 1922–7 and 1932–7, but figures in Romania and Yugoslavia dropped marginally.

Domestic wheat consumption varied from just 47 kilos per capita / year in Poland to 179 kilos in France, with part of the difference being

Table 9.3 Europe's growing self-sufficiency in wheat, 1909–1937

						Wheat consumption		*Wheat production*
	Imports as percentage of national consumption				*% change*	*per capita*	*% change*	*% growth in domestic*
					1922–7 to	*kilos*	*1922–7 to*	*output*
	1909–14	*1922–27*	*1927–32*	*1932–37*	*1932–7*	*1932–7*	*1932–7*	*1922–7 to 1932–7*
Austria	48	62	58	42	−33	90	−6	52
Belgium	76	74	75	70	−6	162	−5	28
Czechoslovakia	28	34	28	2	−94	93	−4	63
Denmark	52	45	56	48	6	67	−6	45
Finland	98	86	86	56	−35	53	24	317
France	12	17	16	3	−82	179	−7	16
Germany	37	35	28	5	−87	66	−3	72
Greece	40	66	66	41	−39	141	18	141
Italy	22	30	22	7	−78	162	−9	29
Ireland	93	95	96	79	−17	168	−2	307
Netherlands	82	83	83	59	−28	104	3	180
Norway	93	92	92	88	−4	82	29	138
Portugal	26	34	36	0	−100	58	−5	72
Spain	5	0	5	1	0	149	4	11
Sweden	47	46	29	0	−100	67	2	134
Switzerland	85	82	83	77	−6	136	9	41
UK	77	79	83	77	−2	130	−7	5
	Exports as a share of national production							
	1909–14	1922–27	1927–32	1932–37				
Bulgaria	27	7	7	7	−8	170	51	53
Hungary	34	24	28	23	−4	150	25	24
Poland	28	−10	1	6	155	47	6	40
Romania	16	7	11	10	38	91	−10	−1
Yugoslavia	13	12	12	8	−31	111	26	−1

explained by cheap substitutes, such as rye bread (Denmark, Germany), potatoes (Ireland, Poland), and maize bread (Romania). Consumption, even among relatively wealthy Europeans diverged considerably, from 179 kilos per capita in France, to 130 kilos in the UK, and just 66 kilos in Germany. Rising incomes in the 1920 in a transforming economy such as

Spain encouraged both a switch away from rye to wheat, as well as the start of the move away from bread towards higher-value foods (Flores de Lemus 1926: 1951). The fact that domestic consumption in traditional exporting countries grew by 51% in Bulgaria, 26% in Yugoslavia, and 25% in Hungary, suggests that farmers were eating themselves what they had previously sold. Indeed, the level of bread consumption in Bulgaria was second only to France. Land reform therefore helped reinforce self-sufficiency and alleviate extreme poverty as the landless, or those that had less than a hectare of land, now numbered only 16% of the agricultural population in Romania, 15% in Yugoslavia, and 9% in Bulgaria (Zagoroff et al., 1955: 50).

In Britain, the area of wheat declined by a third in the decade after 1922, but recovered when the Wheat Act (1932) provided some assistance to growers, although it was still only slightly above 700 thousand hectares in 1936 (Brassley 2023: 67–9). Farmers responded to falling prices by reducing the area of labour-intensive cereals and sowing grass instead, leaving the country in the 1930s as 'a carpet of grass with a pattern of arable', when in the 1870s it had been 'a carpet of arable with a pattern of grass' (Astor and Rowntree 1939 : 76). Even in East Anglian, wheat by the early 1930s contributed only 5.3% to farm incomes in a financial study of 1000 farms (Royal Institute of International Affairs 1932: 135).

In France, wheat imports declined from an annual average of 1.4 million tons between 1927 and 1932 to 0.27 million in 1932–7, a drop from 15.5 to 3.1% of national consumption, while the area planted increased by 150,000 hectares (Hevesy 1940: 471, my calculations). France's mediocre harvests in 1930 and 1931 kept prices stable, but the large harvests between 1932 and 1934 caused prices to halve by 1935. The government, in addition to tariffs and import licences, required flour mills to use up to 100% of domestically produced wheat and legislated minimum farm prices. However, many farmers were forced to sell at lower prices to small mills, as the more closely supervised larger ones simply refused to buy at the official price (Tracy 1989: 167–8).

Market intervention on a massive scale was required to plan production, control imports, and release supplies on the domestic market in an orderly fashion over the year to guarantee that all producers received the government stipulated price. In France this implied a huge expenditure on storage facilities and to buy the harvest, which averaged 7.6 million tons between 1925 and 1928. Cooperatives were given privileges that allowed them to become more competitive than private businesses, and the government subsidized the construction of new ones for storage. As a result, the number of wheat cooperatives grew from 750 to 1,205 in just a year, and the Bank of France provided the necessary liquidity for them to hold stocks to support prices (Sheingate 2001: 97–8). However, the threat of overproduction risked having to dump surpluses on the world market, or use them as expensive animal feed, a huge burden on the French exchequer (Hevesy 1940: 470). Therefore farmers in December 1934, in exchange for minimum prices, were prohibited from increasing the area sown or intensifying rotations. All these policies were integrated into a single body, the *Office National Interprofessionnel du Blé* (National Wheat Board) in 1936, whose day-to-day activities were managed by a council consisting of producers, consumers, traders, millers, and bakers (Chatriot 2016). George Monnet, the Minister of Agriculture, believed that a guaranteed market at fixed prices and control over the area cultivated would 'in two- or three-years' time' make planning simpler, as the *Office du Blé* would know 'exactly the wheat production of each farmer' (Hevesy 1940: 451–2). For the agronomist Pierre Fromont, the French Wheat Board constituted an 'attempt at a planned agricultural economy, which, though carried out by a Socialist party, is in fact demanded by the immense majority of the farmers of our country' (Hevesy 1940: 462).

For effective market intervention, the *Office du Blé* required both grain silos and capital to loan to farmers, as well as new institutional arrangements to facilitate the active collaboration of village-level farm associations with the state to monitor and ensure that farmers compiled with the new regulations. In France, the government by the 1930s was able to utilize the extensive network of village-level producer associations to implement policies, which had the additional advantage that the state, by delegating public power to their associations, gained legitimacy among farmers (Sheingate 2001: 90). The *Office du Blé* was not really tested before the Second World War as the poor harvests of 1936 and 1937 significantly reduced enforcement problems, and left stocks minimal for when a large harvest was finally collected in 1938.

Spain had become virtually self-sufficient in wheat by the early 1920s, resulting in expensive bread for consumers, and farmers cultivating large areas of marginal land that left them vulnerable to any drop in prices. In the absence of mass political parties, the rural elites and Catholic Church had failed to provide the necessary resources to help build strong cooperative federations that would have given family farmers an independent, political voice, so the government had no effective producer group to work with as it had in France. As wheat prices fell, the government, in addition to tariffs, set import quotas, minimum farm prices, and required millers to use a fixed amount of domestic wheat. However, poorly enforced price regulations made it difficult for small cereal farmers to find buyers at the official prices. Larger growers, by contrast, found it easier to sell their harvest because of their local political connections, and the fact that they could provide merchants with a greater volume of clean grain, that had been threshed mechanically. The government, without the active support of farm groups, lacked accurate information on the area being planted and available stocks, leading to the politically disastrous decision to import wheat to depress rising prices in 1932 on the eve of what became the country's largest harvest ever. The failure of governments to help family cereal farmers deepened their opposition to the democratic Second Republic (Simpson and Carmona 2020: ch. 6).

In Eastern Europe, farm cooperatives might have made cereal exporters more competitive by reducing the handling, grading, and transportation costs, as suggested by changes among New World exporters. In Canada, the homestead system had produced strong rural communities, and these had built a cooperative network that successfully reduced the storing and marketing costs of cereals. However, many owner-occupiers had mortgages contracted when farm prices were high, making them vulnerable to falling farm prices in the 1930s. Argentinian farmers, by contrast, were tenants and rents followed prices downwards, but they lacked the social capital to form cooperative storage facilities, and consequently exported wheat with impurities in 'expensive and clumsy jute bags' (Solberg 1987: 51, 66, 103, 142).[4] Eastern European cereal farmers also suffered from high storage and transportation costs because of their lack of effective cooperatives and, as landowners, from rising mortgage and interest payments as cereal prices fell. Endeavours by governments to ease the debt burden of farmers and subsidize grain exports had only marginal success (Roberts 1951: 182–4).

The attempts by Eastern European countries, as cereal exporters, to build international organizations to negotiate collective deals between themselves and importing countries failed. Some attempted instead to negotiate bi-lateral deals, threatening to block manufacturing imports from a country if there was no agreement (Royal Institute of International Affairs 1932: 205; Hevesy 1940: chs. 3, 4). Germany was especially interested in the Balkans for agricultural products and raw materials. An asymmetric relation was thereby created between heavily agrarian economies trading primary goods which were easily substituted on world markets, for specialized industrial imports (Petmezas 2023: 130). Success for the Balkan governments was generally limited, and if farm exports increased as the German economy grew by an annual 11% between 1934 and 1938, it was often at the expense of growing political interference from the Nazi government (Neal 1979: 393; Petmezas 2023: 130–2).

9.3 Commercial Dairying and Market Intervention

Livestock producers generally suffered less than wheat farmers in the 1930s (Federico 2006; table 3.7; Cohen 1936). While many farmers in rural Europe benefitted from keeping a house cow or two, commercial dairy farming in some regions had become the largest agricultural sector, supplying liquid milk to rapidly growing urban markets or for the manufacture of butter and cheese (Chapter 3).[5] These segmented markets greatly influenced the extent of the difficulties facing dairy farmers, as Whetham (1978: 250–1) notes for England and Wales:

> One farmer in a parish might have his own retail round and gain more from the fall in the costs of feeds than he lost on a slight fall in prices; his neighbour with a contract to a London wholesaler might find a rising proportion of his output paid for at the falling manufacturing price; a third farmer might have been unable to obtain any buyer and thus be forced back onto the manufacture of butter or cheese; his cousin on a Welsh hill farm might be feeding whole milk to his calves and pigs since butter was almost unsaleable in his local market. They almost all voted in 1933 for a milk marketing scheme.

Milk is highly perishable, and its seasonal supply risked prices collapsing in the summer, when it was abundant, and rising in winter when scarce. Even commercial farmers produced tiny amounts compared to those handled by the small number of distributors in the major urban markets, who were benefitting from the growing economies of scale found in pasteurization and bottling, and the concentration of urban deliveries. In France, milk production involved 'almost every cultivator ... (as) nearly every smallholder had one, two or three cows, yet comparatively few depend on dairying for their sole livelihood', but the *Société Laitière Maggi* had 60 plants across the country, and sold 1.2 million litres daily, or a quarter of Paris's milk consumption through its 1400 retail outlets (Bacon and Cassels 1937: 628–9; Yates 1940: 264). Pasteurization improved keeping quality, and helped reassure reluctant consumers against disease, especially bovine tuberculosis, which still killed two or three thousand people annually in England and Wales, and infected perhaps 40% of the national herd (Astor and Rowntree 1939: 191). However, these new sanitary controls that national and municipal governments imposed further increased the negotiating strength of intermediaries.

Most farmers either milked their cows for home consumption or retailed the milk locally themselves, helping to shield them from low prices and overproduction. Short-term milk surpluses were traditionally converted to butter or cheese, but the high storage costs made it impractical to keep them for any length of time. Commercial farmers were more vulnerable to market downturns, as cows still had to be milked, and while an individual farmer might reduce output by slaughtering a few animals, this did not raise milk prices. Falling prices therefore called for government intervention. As low prices discouraged the voluntary culling of animals, a radical solution was developed that granted monopoly powers to a private organization to tax all milk sales and use the proceeds to compensate those farmers who slaughtered animals and subsidize butter and cheese exports. Producers can be divided into three major groups: those that exported a large share of their production (Denmark, Netherlands, Ireland); commercial farmers that were dependent on their domestic markets (France, UK); and those farmers for whom dairying was essentially a part-time activity (rural areas of North-Western and much of Southern and Eastern Europe). The second and third groups sometimes overlapped, especially in the proximity of large cities such as Paris or Rome.

The Danish dairy industry was unique in that only 18% of milk produced was sold in the domestic market, with the rest being exported as butter or in the form of pork and bacon, with skimmed milk being fed to pigs (Yates 1940: 44, for 1928). Danish cooperatives processed and traded 91% of the country's dairy products, achieving considerable marketing strength through producer-driven commodity chain, and

Table 9.4 Markets for milk in North-Western Europe, c.1930

	Denmark	*Belgium*	*Netherlands*	*France*	*Germany*	*Sweden*	*UK*
Liquid milk	0	24	24	30	30	33	60
Butter	85	64	48	35	54	} 50	13
Cheese	0	2	20	15	4	}	11
Livestock	0	8	4	20	11	0	17
Others	15	2	4	0	2	17	9
	100	100	100	100	101	100	110

Sources Jensen (1937: 249); Yates (1940: 44, 122, 191, 266 and 432); Sorenson and Cassels (1936: 276); Morell (2023: 179)

exporting butter under the collective Lur brand (Jensen 1937: 326; Yates 1940: 79, for 1936). Danish exports suffered when Britain, its largest market, gave preference to its Empire producers, and looked to close its considerable trade deficit with Denmark (Tracy 1989: 206–7).[6] The Danish government responded by attempting to stabilize domestic milk prices, and seek international agreements for new markets (Table 9.4).

The fact that dairy cooperatives were already monitoring production and product quality, and were integrated in the Federation of Danish Creamery Association, made self-regulation relatively easy. Although a levy was imposed on domestic butter sales and the proceeds used to support milk prices, the domestic market absorbed far too little. Attempts were also made to slow the increase in the number of dairy cows, which had risen from 1.8 million in 1903 to 3 million by 1929, before reaching 3.2 million in 1938. A tax was introduced on all slaughtered cattle, creating funds to buy more animals, resulting in some 600,000 animals being sacrificed between 1933 and 1938, many in poor condition and suffering from tuberculosis (Mitchell 1992; Tracy 1989: 210). More drastic was the complicated licensing agreement, 'probably the first marketing quota system to be introduced for an agricultural product in any country', which cut pig numbers from 5.4 million in 1932 to 3 million two years later, allowing bacon prices to double (Tracy 1989: 210).

The Netherlands was also a major butter exporter, but two-thirds of its milk was sold domestically, compared to just a fifth in Denmark. The government created two distinct markets for butter: a high-priced domestic one which helped to subsidize export sales, which recovered rapidly after 1932. Attempts at limiting output by reducing the size of the dairy herd were less successful as farmers again tended to cull their worst animals, and fed the remaining ones better, leading to a growth in milk yields.

In the UK, livestock production accounted for about three-quarters of gross agricultural output in the interwar period, with milk sales at £68 million in 1937–8 being considerably greater than those for potatoes (£14.5 million), the most valuable farm crop, or wheat (£9 million) (Perren 1995: 45–6). This unusual farm structure was the result of international trade, 'with less than 3% of the world's population', the UK in 1930 'took about 99% of the world's exports of bacon and hams, 96% of the mutton and lamb, 63% of the butter, 62 per of the eggs, 59% of the beef, 46% of the cheese, 32% of the wool, and 28% of the wheat and wheat flour' (Murray and Cohen 1934: 5, in Brassley 2023: 60). In 1936, approximately 60% of all the country's milk sales were in the lucrative liquid market, while imported butter accounted for 85% of domestic consumption, and cheese 70% (Sorenson and Cassels 1936: 281–2, 294).

Although farmers even before the Great War complained of a 'Milk Combine' that controlled two-thirds of London's wholesale and a third of its retail trade, prices generally remained strong until the 1930s (Whetham 1978: 145). In England and Wales, the Agricultural Marketing Acts of 1931 and 1933 gave farmers the possibility to create compulsory marketing boards for commodities when supported by two-thirds of all producers (measured by numbers and output), leading to the Milk Marketing Board (MMB) being established in September 1933.[7] The MMB divided the country into eleven different pooling regions, and enjoyed monopoly powers to fix minimum prices for consumers and wholesale prices for distributors, in both the liquid and manufacturing markets for milk, with the proceeds distributed to farmers.[8] The MMB was made up of seventeen member, fourteen elected directly by farmers, with only the Minister of Agriculture having the power to overrule decisions on milk prices when in the public interest. The MMB organized annual sale of almost 4,000 million litres of milk, supplied by 120,000 farmers to 40 million consumers (Sorenson and Cassels 1936: 275–6, 280).[9]

The MMB met the long-standing demands of farmers that the state should support farm prices, without interfering in how they farmed, or what they produced (Perren 1995: 37). It was the country's most successful marketing scheme, but it did not directly handle any milk (and so had no need for storage capacity), and in the 1930s a private company, United Dairies, controlled three-quarters of the London wholesale market, and a third of the retail (Sorenson and Cassels 1936: 293). Neither did the MMB have any regulatory powers over how much individual farmers could produce. The problem of successful market intervention leading to overproduction was resolved by surplus milk being diverted to the manufacture of butter and cheese, with farmers receiving just 25% of the liquid market price (Sorenson and Cassels 1936: 282). The government therefore did not have to establish working relations with farmer organizations to collect farm-level information or monitor production. Milk recording was becoming important at this time, but used to help farmers increase output, rather than restrict it (Whetham 1978: 265–6). In 1935, some 81% of farmers, owning 86% of dairy cows voted to continue the MMB, as only a few large dairy farmers close to urban areas were perhaps less well-off (Sorenson and Cassels 1936: 294).

In France, the widely dispersed and fragmented nature of dairying protected farmers from the economic downturn, especially as almost three-quarters of the retail liquid milk trade was carried out by farmers themselves, and more than half the nation's butter and cheese production was farm-made, often from just two or three cows (Yates 1940: 318–9). Government attempts to improve prices risked diminishing consumption, while efforts to make farming more efficient and reduce unit costs, threatened to flood markets. From the Great War, milk prices were regulated in the important Parisian market, but at levels which favoured consumers, leading to a mass demonstration in September 1928 and risk of a general strike by dairy producers. Official prices were abolished, and instead the *Fédération des Coöpératives et Syndicats Laitière de la Region de Paris* negotiated prices with a federation of small retailers, resulting in milk supplies for Paris increasing by 74% between 1926 and 1934, despite consumption growing by only 18% (Bacon and Cassels 1937: 632). The surplus had to be used for manufacturing, and producer groups were successful in persuading government to restrict butter and cheese imports, and assist farmers to help them improve milk quality to raise domestic consumption. Legislation in 1935 required liquid milk to be sold either pasteurized by large dairies, or from government-inspected farms (Bacon and Cassels 1937: 629). The scheme was voluntary so those farmers that did not want to be controlled could still sell their milk for manufacture.

In Belgium, farmers kept cows as dual-purpose animals, with their meat being considered as valuable as the milk. As a result, at least five different breeds of cattle were found, and the 'majority of dairy farmers have only two, or, at the most, three cows in their stalls' (Yates 1940: 193–4). Almost two-thirds of the milk was used for butter which was of poor quality compared to that of Denmark or the Netherlands, but farmers suffered less in the 1930s because production was overwhelmingly for the domestic market (and imports were easy to keep out); grain imports helped limit feed costs, and farm production was much more diversified. The *Office du Lait* was created in 1938 with the object of improving milk and butter quality to increase domestic sales (Yates 1940: 234).

Swedish agriculture in general was protected from world markets but its domestic market was highly competitive. In 1928, the president of *Sveriges Allmänna Lantbrukssällskap* (SAL), an association of large producers, complained that farmers were reluctant to pay their annual fees, as they believed that the economic benefits from membership could be just as easily obtained by remaining outside (Just 2010: 127). This changed with the Great Depression, and the Crisis Agreement of 1933 which gave farmer and worker organizations the necessary 'resources to monopolize the supply of … agricultural products and labour' (Just 2010: 131). The agreement between the Agrarian Party and the Social Democrats led to the newly founded national association of Swedish dairies (SMR) being given statutory powers to collect a price equalization fee on all milk sold for the liquid and manufactured markets, with the proceeds used to reduce the export price of butter (Morell 2023: 180–1).

Dairy farmers in North-Western Europe therefore enjoyed considerable success in obtaining government support to strengthen their negotiating power in the lucrative liquid milk sales in urban markets, and developed mechanisms to avoid surplus production from depressing milk prices in industrial markets producing butter and cheese. By contrast, across most of Eastern and Southern Europe, farmers were rarely over-reliant on the market, and excess production could be easily transformed into cheese or fed to animals.

9.4 Market Intervention in French and Spanish Wine Production

Even before 1914 the French wine market swung from 'crisis to crisis', in part because the high fixed costs of planting vines made growers reluctant to uproot them during market downturns. The interwar years witnessed technological advances in both the vineyards and wineries, as well as the marketing and bulk transportation, leading to higher yields and better keeping-quality of the wines. The delayed appearance of phylloxera checked the growth in production in Italy and Spain, but prices remained weak given the widespread use of industrial alcohol to strengthen wines (Vaquero Piñeiro et al. 2022; Pan-Montojo 1994: ch. 6). Per capita consumption peaked in France and Spain in 1920–4 (at an annual 168 and 96 litres, respectively), and in Italy in 1906–13 (128 litres) (France. Direction Générale 1934: 463). Alcohol was an important source of government revenue everywhere, and tariffs limited the international wine trade to only 7% of global production (9.8 million hectolitres) in 1909–12, a figure that had halved to 3.5% by 1934–8 (6.3 million hectolitres), if Algerian exports are assumed as French production, and not traded internationally (Pinilla and Ayuda 2007, my calculations).

French wine production increased by only 10% between 1900–07 and 1928–35, slightly faster than population growth (6%), but Algerian imports, as part of metropolitan France, led to domestic supply growing by 24% (Table 9.5). By contrast, the amount of wine actually sold (and taxed) in domestic markets grew by just 12% between the two dates, with the difference classified as untaxed 'family consumption', which leapt by 79%, and accounted for 21.3% of all wine consumption by the early 1930s. This, and the spread of hybrid vines in areas of polyculture, which required little care and expenditure on fertilizers and insecticides, suggests a retreat to self-sufficiency not dissimilar to Eastern Europe cereal producers. In commercial viticulture, labour costs doubled on the large vineyards relative to wine prices, so Midi growers were selling their wines for less than the costs of production in years such as 1928 and 1929.[10]

Table 9.5 French wine production and consumption, 1900–1934

	Annual production millions hls	*Domestic wine available millions hls*	*Taxed consumption millions hls*	*Tax-free consumption millions hls*	*Tax-free as % of total consumption*
1900–1907	55.2	56.2	43.3	11.9	21.5
1920–1927	59.1	63.7	47.2	16.5	27.9
1928–1934	60.7	69.6	48.6	21.3	36.3

Notes Wine availability and consumption refers to France (production + imports - exports).
Sources Warner (1960: 75–6)

The Federation of French Regional Winegrowers' Associations worked with the *Groupe viticole*, an all-party parliamentary group which had 210 deputies in the 1920, and negotiated, among other measures, the division of the alcohol markets between wine and sugar beet producers (Planas forthcoming; Warner 1960: 125). The lobby split when wine prices collapsed in 1932 and small producers, under the socialist politician, Édouard Barthe, formed the *Ligue des petits et moyens viticulteurs* and the *Confédération Nationale des Coopératives Vinicoles*.[11] During the First World War, the burden of wine requisitions had fallen heavily on the large producers, and the legislation and decrees from the early 1930s, usually referred to as the *Statut du Vin* (or *Statut de la Viticulture*), continued to favour the family vineyard over the large estate (Phillips 2016: 196; Loubère 1990: 129–30; Warner 1960: 107–9). Consequently the obligation for reducing the area of French vines, restricting yields, or distilling surplus wine fell more heavily on larger growers, helping to keep producers with less than ten hectares in production.

Cooperatives, which allowed family growers to benefit from the growing economies of scale in wine production, now also assumed the role of stabilizing prices by blocking wine in their cellars, and staggering sales over the year. Government support led to the number of French cooperatives growing from 630 in 1929 to 827 a decade later, and these would be key to market intervention following the Second World War (Fernández and Simpson 2017).

Most French producers competed on price and the alcoholic strength of their wines, but a few select growers, with significantly greater costs in the vineyard, went for quality (Carmona and Simpson 2012). Interest in regional appellation among these winegrowers grew with the collapse of prices in the early 1900s and the belief that merchants were devaluing their product by blending them with cheaper wines produced elsewhere. However, the 1919 Appellation Law simply resulted in legal disputes and led to another 'wave of wine fraud' in the 1930s (Phillips 2016: 238). A new law was passed in July 1935, and the following year the *Comité National des Appellations d'Origine* (CNAO) was created to establish appellations and improve wine quality by greatly extending controls in the vineyard and winery. The Committee was composed of local wine experts and government officials from the agriculture, finance, and justice ministries, and their combined 'knowledge and powers' were expected to improve wine quality. Appellations were granted exemptions from the general legislation affecting ordinary wines and included detailed regulations on what grape varieties could be grown, and the maximum yields permitted, with their members monitoring each other. The tighter quality controls applied by the CNAO led to around half of the wines enjoying appellation status under the 1919 Law being declassified (Loubère 1990: 122).

The French wine lobby therefore split along class lines as government intervention favoured small family growers, and the institutional innovations of the 1930s developed in three distinct areas: limiting wine production in the vineyard and wineries; regulating sales through cooperatives; and monitoring and controlling quality in the fine wine market. The active participation of winegrowers and merchants was required in all cases as they were obliged to keep production and sales records and implement controls to avoid cheating. Nothing similar was found in other wine-producing countries.

In Spain, the *Confederación Nacional de Viticultores* (CNV) was only established in 1924, and its leaders claimed that 'if winegrowers had not been so disorganised for so long, many of the problems and taxes on wine... would not have reached the proportions that they have today' (Planas 2017: 190–1). Yet the CNV in 1926 was unable to stop the influential alcohol lobby from continuing to strengthen wines with industrial alcohol (Pan-Montojo 1994: 282–3; Pan-Montojo and Puig 1995; Fernández 2008). A cross party parliamentary group was only established in 1931 and, although it boasted 150 members by 1935, these often disagreed with each other, and merchants successfully restricted the effectiveness of the few regional appellations established (Planas 2017: 200; Fernández 2008).

Spanish winegrowers were best organized in Catalonia, which in 1936 accounted for around 70% of the nation's wine cooperatives, despite having only 20% of its vines, and 30% of wine production (Planas 2017: 198; forthcoming). Catalan politics became highly competitive when regional autonomy was granted between 1917 and 1924 (and again in the 1930s). Significant amounts of wine were produced by sharecroppers and their lobby (*Unió de Rabassaires*) played an important part in the formation of *Esquerra Republicana de Catalunya*, Spain's fourth-largest political party in the 1931 elections. The sharecroppers' demands were political, rather than economic, namely the full ownership of the vines that they worked. By contrast, the landowners' association (IACSI) believed that the recovery of prices depended on increased wine consumption. The legal disputes over landownership contributed to the growing political division of the period, with Cataluña's legal and political institutions generally supporting the demands of the sharecroppers, and those in Madrid the position of landowners (Colomé et al. 2018; Simpson and Carmona 2020: 221–4; Planas and Soler-Becerro 2022; Carmona and Simpson 2023).

9.5 Conclusions

Government intervention in Western Europe helped many farmers survive the Great Depression but it was never sufficient on its own to return prosperity to the sector. Depression would end, not by changes in the agricultural sector, but rather by the renewed demand created by industrial growth and exports. The speed of a country's recovery was closely associated with how long it persisted with the gold standard and deflationary policies. Germany, for example, which resorted to exchange controls rather than devalue after leaving the gold standard, only saw its 1929 levels of industrial output reached in 1935, although military expenditure a couple of years later pushed it 27% higher (Feinstein et al. 1997 : 171–5). As German urban wages recovered, rural labour began to leave the land in large numbers once more, causing shortages in some areas, as farm prices remained controlled by the government.

Yet if the Great Depression reduced living standards of millions of farmers, and low profitability delayed the speed of technological change, in North-Western Europe it also radically changed the relationship between farm organizations and government. As this chapter suggests, effective state intervention required farmers to organize and express concise demands, while governments needed political and economic incentives to prioritize the sector over others and have the capacity to implement policies efficiently and fairly. Agricultural policy implementation could be highly complex, especially when farmers had to be discouraged from increasing output once prices stabilized. It was only in North-Western Europe that farmers enjoyed sufficiently strong commercial and political incentives to organize, explaining the Lindert paradox, whereby farmers in rich countries receive more government support than in those where they are much more numerous and, in theory, enjoy greater political influence.

National organizations, such England and Wales's NFU, France's *Confédération Nationale des Associations Agricoles*, or Germany's *Reichslandbund*, were generally too large and divided to present unified demands to their government. By contrast, specialist farmers, who created vibrant local organizations integrated into commodity-specific national lobbies, such as those in France for wine (1913), sugar beet (1921), and wheat (1924) were much more successful. This benefitted farmers in North-Western Europe, as the 'the causal relationship between cooperative organisations and peasant prosperity' was reciprocal, not unidirectional (Moore 1945: 112). The Great Depression, by encouraging cooperatives, allowed the farm sector in this region to extend its influence in society, and their grassroots support helped reinforce interest in democratic government among farmers. Elsewhere, such as in Romania, the active participation of farmers in cooperatives remained limited, not just because 'the management ... frequently exploited the peasants' ignorance and inexperience to its own benefit', but also because they were 'official institutions, financed, directed, and controlled by the state, and therefore completely subject to political vicissitudes' (Roberts 1951: 64). This contrast between Eastern Europe, and the limited market participation of small farmers, with those of North-Western Europe, would have important political implications as Chapter 10 shows.

Notes

1. Fishback (2023) provides a useful recent survey.
2. Schultz (1945: 113) notes that in the United States, 'the failure of industrial output to expand during the thirties was the basic factor in the worsening of the agricultural situation. The main cause of the unproductive employment and low earnings in agriculture was the unemployment in industry'.
3. Cotton was the most important agricultural product traded.
4. Eastern European emigrants accounted for 17% of farmers on the Canadian Prairies in 1921 and 1931, but remained outside of the cooperative movement (Solberg 1987: 92, 200).
5. Royal Institute of International Affairs (1932: 5) noted that 'there is little doubt that, contrary to popular belief, milk and milk products and eggs are the two most important products to farmers of the world'. Powder and condensed milk had considerably less value.

6. Danish farms were 80% self-sufficient in feed, limiting the impact of cheap imports. The British National Government implemented the Import Duties Act, which was shortly modified by the Ottawa Agreements Act, that gave market preference to Empire producers. The volume of Britain's butter imports remained stable between 1927–9 and 1938, but those from the Empire increased 43%, and fell by 17% from elsewhere (Tracy 1989: 161).
7. Five marketing schemes were created, but those for milk, hops, and potatoes were less successful than that of milk (Brown 1989: 116).
8. More than 90% of registered producer supported the initiative, although the National Farmers' Union opposed it because it would regulate all farmers. Scotland and Northern Ireland had separate schemes (Whetham 1978: 251).
9. Astor and Rowntree (1939: 196) suggest it was 15 elected by dairy producers, and two co-opted.
10. Wages rose 96% in terms of wine in France between 1910 and 1930s, 147% in Italy, and 130% in Spain (Simpson 2000: table 2; Warner 1960: 72).
11. Voting rights in the Midi's *Confédération Générale des Vignerons* was weighted by area of vines (growers), hectolitres of wine (wine producers), and taxes paid (merchants). In 1929, 5,331 French growers out of a total of 1,573,273 had yields of over 80 hectolitres per hectare (726 of 10,348 in Algeria), and 16.6 million hectolitres of harvest of 62.9 million came from properties that produced more than 500 hectolitres (10.8 million out of 12.3 million harvest in Algeria). (Warner 1960: 10; Planas forthcoming).

References

Alston, Lee J. 1983. "Farm Foreclosures in the United States during the Interwar Period." *The Journal of Economic History* 43: 885–903.

Astor, Viscount, and Keith Murray. 1933. *The Planning of Agriculture*. Oxford: Oxford University Press.

Astor, Viscount, and B. Seebohm Rowntree. 1938. *British Agriculture the Principles of Future Policy*. London: Longmans.

Astor, Viscount, and B. Seebohm Rowntree. 1939. *British Agriculture the Principles of Future Policy*. London: Penguin.

Bacon, L.B, and J.M.Cassels. 1937. "The Milk Supply of Paris, Rome and Berlin." *Quarterly Journal of Economics* 51 (4): 626–48.

Brassley, Paul. 2023. "The 1929 Crisis from the Perspective of a Food-Importing Country—The United Kingdom, 1928–35." In *Agriculture and the Great Depression. The Rural Crisis of the 1930s in Europe and the Americas*, edited by Gérard Béaur and Francesco Chiapparino, 59–76. Abingdon: Routledge.

Brown, Jonathan. 1989. *Agriculture in England: a Survey of Farming, 1870–1947*. Manchester: Manchester University.

Carmona, Juan, and James Simpson. 2012. "Explaining Contract Choice: Vertical Co-ordination, Sharecropping, and Wine, Europe 1850–1950." *The Economic History Review* 65 (3): 887–909.

Carmona, Juan, and James Simpson. 2023. "Cuando el rentista no es derrotado. El caso de la rabassa catalana, 1890–1936." *Historia Agraria* (89): 193–221. https://doi.org/10.26882/histagrar.089e06c.

Chatriot, Alain. 2016. *La politique du blé*. Paris: IGPDE.

Cohen, Ruth Louisa. 1936. *The History of Milk Prices: an Analysis of the Factors Affecting the Prices of Milk and Milk Products*. Oxford.

Colomé, Josep, Jordi Planas, Raimon Soler-Becerro, and Francesc Valls-Junyent. 2018. "The *Rabassaire* Struggle: Long-Term Analysis of a Social and Political Movement." *Internationaal Instituut voor Sociale Geschiedenis*: 1–27.

Eichengreen, Barry. 1996. *Globalizing Capital. A History of the International Monetary System*. Princeton: Princeton University Press.

Federico, Giovanni. 2005. "Not Guilty? Agriculture in the 1920s and the Great Depression." *Journal of Economic History* 65 (4): 949–76.

Federico, Giovanni. 2006. *Feeding the World. An Economic History of Agriculture, 1800–1900*. Princeton: Princeton University Press.

Feinstein, Charles, Peter Temin, and Toniolo. 1997. *The European Economy Between the Wars*. Oxford: Oxford University Press.

Fernández, Eva. 2008. "El fracaso del lobby viticultor en España frente al objetivo industrializador del Estado, 1920–1936." *Historia Agraria* (45): 113–41.

Fernández, Eva, and James Simpson. 2017. "Producer Cooperatives, Institutional Change, and Politics in the Wine Industry, 1880–1980." *The Economic History Review* 70 (1): 122–42.

Fishback, Price V. 2023. "Conclusions - Agricultural Crises and Government Responses During the Interwar Period in the Atlantic Trading Network." In *Agriculture and the Great Depression. The Rural Crisis of the 1930s in Europe and the Americas*, edited by G. Béaur and Francesco Chiapparino, 255–74. Abingdon & New York: Routledge.

Flores de Lemus, A. 1926: 1951. "Sobre una dirección fundamental de la producción rural Española." *Reprinted in Moneda y Crédito* 36: 141–68.

France. Direction Générale. 1934. "Annuaire statistique de la France 1933." 50.

Hevesy, Paul de. 1940. *World Wheat Planning and Economic Planning in General*. London, New York, Toronto: Oxford.

Janicki, Tadeusz. 2023. "The Impact of the Crisis on the Polish Agriculture (1929–35)." In *Agriculture and the Great Depression. The Rural Crisis of the 1930s in Europe and the Americas, 2023*, edited by Gérard Béaur and Francesco Chiapparino, 155–67. Abington & New York: Routledge.

Jensen, E. 1937. *Danish Agriculture: its Economic Development*. Copenhagen: Schultz.

Just, F. 2010. "The Scandinavian Food System between Organization and State." In *Managing Crises and De-globalization. Nordic Foreign Trade and Exchange, 1919–39*, edited by S.O Olsson, 121–36. London: Routledge.

Lindert, Peter, ed. 1991. *Historical Patterns of Agricultural Policy*. Edited by C.P. Timmer, *Agriculture and the State: Growth, Employment, and Poverty in Developing Countries*. Ithaca & London.

Loubère, Leo A. 1990. *The Wine Revolution in France. The Twentieth Century*. Princeton: Princeton University Press.

Malenbaum, Wilfrid. 1953. *The World Wheat Economy, 1885–1939*. Cambridge, Mass.: Harvard.

Mitchell, Brian R. 1992. *International historical statistics, Europe, 1750–1988*. 3rd ed. Basingstoke & New York: Macmillan & Stockton Press.

Moore, Wilbert. 1945. *Economic Demography of Eastern and Southern Europe*. Geneva: League of Nations.

Morell, Mats. 2010. "Trade Crisis and Regulation in the Farm Sector. Sweden in the Interwar Years." In *Managing Crises and De-globalization. Nordic Foreign Trade and Exchange, 1919–39*, edited by Mats Olsson, 137–57. London: Routledge.

Morell, Mats. 2023. "Swedish Agriculture and the Crisis of the 1930s." In *Agriculture and the Great Depression. The Rural Crisis of the 1930s in Europe and the Americas*, edited by G. Béaur and F. Chiapparino, 171–89. Abington & New York: Routledge.

Murray, K.A.H, and R.L.Cohen. 1934. *The Planning of Britain's Food Imports: a quantitative study of the effects of recent legislation*. Oxford: Agricultural Economic Research Institute.

Neal, Larry. 1979. "The Economics and Finance of Bilateral Clearing Agreements: Germany 1934–1938." *The Economic History Review* 32 (3): 391–04.

Pan-Montojo, J., and Nuria Puig. 1995. "Los grupos de interés y la regulación pública del mercado de alcoholes en España (1887–1936)." *Revista de Historia Económica* XIII (2): 251–80.

Pan-Montojo, Juan L. 1994. *La Bodega del Mundo. La vid y el vino en España, 1800–1936*. Madrid: Alianza.

Pasour, E.C., and Randal R. Rucker. 2005. *Plowshares and Pork Barrels. The Political Economy of Agriculture*. Oakland: The Independent Institute.

Perren, R. 1995. *Agriculture in Depression, 1870–1940*. Cambridge: Cambridge University Press.

Petmezas, Socrates D. 2023. *The Effects of the Great Depression on the Agricultural Economy of the Tobacco Exporting Countries of South-Eastern Europe*. Edited by G. Béaur and Francesco Chiapparino, *Agriculture and the Great Depression. The Rural Crisis of the 1930s in Europe and the Americas*. London & New York: Routledge.

Phillips, Rod. 2016. *French Wine. A History*. Oakland: University of Calfornia.

Pinilla, V., and María-Isabel Ayuda. 2007. "The International Wine Market, 1850–1938." In *Wine, Society, and Globalization*, edited by Gwyn Campbell and Nathalie Guibert, 179–99. Basingstoke: Palgrave Macmillan.

Planas, Jordi. 2017. "State Intervention in Wine Markets in the early Twentieth Century. Why was it so Different in France and Spain?" *Revista de Historia Económica* 35 (2): 175–206.

Planas, Jordi. forthcoming. "The Interplay Between Winegrowers Organizations and the State in France and Spain in the early Twentieth Century." In *The Formation of Agricultural Governance. The Interplay between State and Civil Society in European Agriculture, 1870–1940*, edited by Jordi Planas, Anton Schuurman and Yves Segers. Turnhout: Brepols.

Planas, Jordi, and Ramón Soler-Becerro. 2022. "Agricultural Associations and Political Parties in the Transition to Mass Politics in Catalonia, 1890–1936." In *Making Politics in the European Countryside, from the 1780s to the 1930s*, edited by L. Brassart, C. Marache, J. Pan-Montojo and L. Van Molle, 271–92. Turnhout: Brepols.

Roberts, Henry L. 1951. *Rumania. Political Problems of an Agrarian State*. New Haven: Yale University Press.

Royal Institute of International Affairs. 1932. *World Agriculture, an International Survey: a Report by a Study Group of the Royal Institute of International Affairs*. London: Oxford University Press.

Schultz, Theodore W. 1945. *Agriculture in an Unstable Economy*. New York and London: McGraw-Hill.

Sheingate, Adam D. 2001. *The Rise of the Agricultural Welfare State. Institutions and Interest Group Power in the United States, France, and Japan*. Princeton: Princeton University Press.

Simpson, James. 2000. "Cooperation and Cooperatives in Southern European Wine Production." In *Advances in Agricultural Economic History*, edited by K. Kauffman, 95–126. Stamford, Connecticut: JAI Press.

Simpson, James, and Juan Carmona. 2020. *Why Democracy Failed: The Agrarian Origins of the Spanish Civil War*. Cambridge: Cambridge University Press.

Solberg, C.E. 1987. *The Prairies and the Pampas. Agricultural Policy in Canada and Argentina*: Stanford.

Sorenson, Helen, and John M. Cassels. 1936. "The English Milk Market." *Quarterly Journal of Economics* 50 (2): 275–96.
Tracy, Michael. 1989. *Government and Agriculture in Western Europe, 1880–1988*. 3rd ed. New York & London: Harvester Wheatsheaf
Vaquero Piñeiro, Manuel, Paolo Tedesch, and Luciano Maffi. 2022. *A History of Italian Wine. Culture, Economics, and Environment in the Nineteenth through Twenty-First Centuries*. Cham, Switzerland: Palgrave Macmillan.
Warner, Charles K. 1960. *The Winegrowers of France and the Government Since 1875*. New York: Columbia University Press.
Warriner, Doreen. 1939. *Economics of Peasant Farming*. Oxford: Oxford University Press.
Whetham, Edith H. 1978. *The Agrarian History of England and Wales, 1914–1939*. Edited by Joan Thirsk. Vol. 8. Cambridge.
World Bank. 2007. *Agriculture for Development. World Development Report 2008*. Washington D.C.
Wright, Gordon. 1964. *Rural Revolution in France. The Peasantry in the Twentieth Century*. Stanford: Stanford University Press.
Yates, P. Lamartine. 1940. *Food Production and Manpower in Western Europe*. London: Longmans Green.
Zagoroff, S.D, Jeno Végh, and Alexander Bilimovich. 1955. *The Agricultural Economy of the Danubian Countries, 1935–45*. Edited by Food Research Institute. Stanford: Stanford University Press.

CHAPTER 10

Farmers and the Politics of Interwar Europe

The First World War ended the seemingly uninterrupted flow of prosperity in Europe's leading economies, and if liberals struggled to find adequate explanations for its cause, Marxist theorists could point the finger at imperialism, monopolies, and cartels (Milanovic 2019: 702). War was followed by rampant inflation that destroyed the life-savings of millions of people in countries such as Germany, Austria, Hungary, or France, while austerity caused widespread unemployment. The Great Depression, which brought deflation, bank runs, and massive unemployment in its wake, ended any remaining faith in unfettered markets. New ideologies appeared that challenged liberal democracy, offering the possibilities of reshaping markets and protecting workers better from the adverse effects of the business cycle, and even capitalism itself. These new groups, which included agrarians, social democrats, communists, and fascists, competed to remake politics and the market economy.

New ideologies must explain events better than the established ones, but ideas need to be adopted by a political party to become influential (Mann 2004: 79; Berman 2006: 11). Given the heavily rural nature of much of European society, new parties had to define how their policies would affect the family farm, and traditional rural life and village society. Crucially, electoral success also depended on local organizations and mass political parties. This chapter argues that farmers only became

J. Simpson, *Family Farmers, Land Reforms and Political Action*, Palgrave Studies in Economic History,
https://doi.org/10.1007/978-3-031-67281-1_10

politically influential when their parties formed alliances with other non-farm groups, or they established specialist lobbies that could work with governments of all persuasions.

The chapter begins by looking at when farmers became interested in national politics, and how material interests and cultural identities influenced voting behaviour. Section 10.2 considers the limits of Agrarianism, and the contradictory demands of having to protect traditional rural society at the same time as improving the living standards of family farmers in labour-abundant economies. The lack of opportunities for farm specialization in Eastern Europe reduced the incentives of establishing lobbies, thereby increasing the importance of traditional cleavages among voters, especially nationalism. The events of 1917 showed the revolutionary potential of the landless, but land reforms in the successor nations effectively reduced the westwards spread of communism. The economic logic of large, mechanized cereal farms encouraged Stalin to pursue the massive collectivization of Soviet agriculture, but few farmers in a democracy would have voted to give up their land, a handicap that socialist parties suffered when trying to attract the farm vote in countries such as England or Spain. Section 10.4 shows how family farmers created lobbies in France and the UK which successfully influenced governments, regardless of the party in power. In Scandinavia, farm parties worked with other political groupings, and their governments broke with liberal democracy, and intervened in the economy to the benefit of farmers as well as organized labour. The final section considers Nazi Germany and shows how the National Socialists attracted wide support in the 1933 elections among family farmers by appealing to both their material interests and cultural identities. Yet, just as in the Soviet Union, the needs of heavy industry and rearmament would turn government policy against farmers. Unlike Stalin, Hitler's solution to increasing domestic food supplies lay in *Lebensraum*, and the military conquest, ethnic cleansing, and resettlement in Eastern Europe.

10.1 Family Farmers and Political Representation

The implementation of (near) universal male suffrage, the secret ballot, and competitive parliamentary elections threatened to radically change politics overnight by making small farmers the largest political constituency in many countries. Farmers now had to decide which party to support and, if none seemed to adequately represent their interests, whether to create their own political organizations. The success that European family farmers had in filling the political void left by the landed elite, and exploit these new political opportunities, would vary significantly.

Political scientists stress the importance of literacy to encourage voters to actively participate in politics and influence party programmes. In agrarian-based societies especially, poverty limited schooling because of its cost, and the fact that children could be gainfully employed on the family farm. The returns to literacy increased with lengthening food chains, new farm technologies, and obligatory, free primary education, changing in turn how individuals viewed the wider world and the family. Suzanne Berger (1972: 34), writing of rural Brittany in the early twentieth century, argued that villagers became interested in politics only when they began to associate local events and problems of their private life with national policies, such as attributing an outbreak of cholera to government failure rather than divine intervention. The growth in literacy was both a cause, and a result, of the wider integration of farming and village society into national life.

Two theories concerning how voters choose between political parties are advanced in the literature. The rational economic model suggests that decisions are linked to specific issues (ideology), and especially whether voters believe a party will improve their living standards. Before 1914, the major concern had been access to land, but material demands in the interwar period were more likely to be associated with farm prices, something that most governments found difficult to control (Chapter 9).[1] By contrast, Weber's broader 'value rationality' and the group theory of politics considers identity rather than ideology as the factor determining party allegiance (Mann 2004: 357; Brustein 1996: ch.1). For Achen and Bartels (2016: 267), 'the primary sources of partisan loyalties and voting behaviour ... are social identities, group attachments, and myopic retrospections, not policy preferences or ideological principles'. In rural Europe these might include nationality, religion, and ethnicity, although farming systems could also shape wider, cultural identities, with French winegrowing villages being supposedly more egalitarian and democratic than specialist cereal ones (Labrousse 1944: 596; Lachiver 1988: 246), or sharecroppers in central Italy being more left-wing than the owner-occupiers (Linz 1976). The fact that a country sometimes had more than one 'Peasant Party', representing different national or religious groups, inevitably weakened their influence.

It was political parties that determined which policies mattered, and how cleavages became politicalized and shaped politics (Kalyvas 1996: 115). Mass competitive political parties required significant resources to establish village-level groups, build regional networks, and link them to a central office which had the necessary bureaucracy to plan, and money to fight, an election campaign. The labour-intensive nature of family farming limited the pool of individuals who could dedicate the time to become a parliamentary representative or political leader. By contrast, the Church already possessed a hierarchical network, and the fact that it was represented in every parish gave it potentially a major organizational advantage, especially as religion was a major cleavage, separating rural society from the anticlerical liberal and socialist urban parties. Nevertheless, although family farmers might represent a sizeable share of the electorate, they were rarely sufficiently numerous to obtain a parliamentary majority on their own. Just as with urban workers in industrial nations, farmers needed to either work with non-farm groups within a broad, and usually conservative party or, as an agrarian party that pursued electoral agreements with other parties, if their voice was going to be heard in government.

10.2 The Limits to Agrarianism in Eastern Europe

Following the Great War, many farmers in the successor states hoped that universal male suffrage, land ownership (attained by land reform), and cooperatives, would lead to a very different type of society to that of either Western capitalism, or Soviet communism. Interest in agrarianism frequently arose because of the tensions produced by a rapidly developing economy in predominantly traditional rural societies, which saw an increase in inequality and to a relative decline in farm incomes as the size of the agricultural sector shrank. It was not unique to Eastern Europe, as suggested by the US populists in the late nineteenth century. In Spain a movement for 'regeneration' appeared among small farmers around the figure of Joaquin Costa, who wanted to both reverse the nineteenth-century liberal reforms and create modern irrigation systems to make intensive small-scale farming feasible (Gómez Benito ed. 2011). Agrarianism was used to justify ideologically very different farm policies, including those of Nazi Germany. Yet although agrarianism was sometimes effective as a protest movement, especially in traditional rural societies, its ideological and organizational weaknesses made it less useful as a political party.

Once land reform had been achieved, farmers lacked a specific goal that united them to make agrarianism work. Agrarianism appeared ideologically confusing compared to liberalism and its emphasis on free markets and trade, or Marxism and the dictatorship of the proletariat. Instead, as Roberts (1951: 90) noted, 'the immediate and obvious wishes of the peasant—such as more land, more lenient credit, and lower taxes—cannot be the satisfactory basis of a political program unless they can be related to some means of realizing them'. Furthermore, the possibilities that a country could remain agrarian, *and* enjoy growing living standards, was difficult even for contemporaries to envisage in the early 1920s. Some rich agrarian societies existed, most notably the New World grain producers, or Denmark's dairy farmers, but these specialized for export markets, and existed alongside a rapidly growing industrial sector that supported farming. In both cases, the living standards of family farmers grew because of market specialization, which was difficult in Eastern Europe given the small farm size for commercial grain production, and poor natural resource endowments for labour-intensive high-value products. Even the attempts to compete in international markets by farmers exploiting their ample supplies of 'cheap' family labour were often frustrated by the import restrictions imposed by other countries.

Land reform had its limits, as although it helped the asset poor endure the worst years of the Great Depression, it was less successful in preparing farmers to participate in a growing economy, while the lack of farm specialization discouraged political participation. Yet Mellor's law—which argues that the faster agriculture grows, the more rapidly the sector declines in size—suggests that if land reform and cooperatives *had* produced a dynamic agriculture, it would have threatened to undermine traditional village culture and strengthened urban society, the very changes that most agrarians were trying to avoid. This dilemma became apparent after land reform in the debates over 'natural selection', and whether the most successful farmers should be allowed to buy the land of impoverished marginal producers (Roberts 1951: 153–4). Larger commercial farmers not only used capital primarily for production purposes (as opposed for subsistence needs), but marketed much larger quantities, assuring urban food supplies and easing the balance-of-payments problems (Chapter 6). Even the growth in schooling and literacy threatened to increase the influence of urban culture, rather than protecting the village's 'low' culture (Gellner 1983: 72–8).

In Eastern Europe, farm cooperatives failed to strengthen the bargaining position of small farmers in markets or give them greater political voice. Many cooperatives ceased being 'bottom-up' voluntary associations and became instead little more than government instruments to control village society. In Romania, by the 1920s they were 'so entangled with the ... state' that they collected grain as taxes from farmers (Riley 2010: 118, 143). Without strong markets, farmers did not specialize, and without specialization there was limited use for cooperatives in the processing and marketing of food products.

In general, Eastern European farmers therefore did not dedicate the necessary resources to build cooperatives, implying that an essential element for creating competitive mass political parties was absent. Rural politics revolved less around farm issues and economic policies than those of identity. Agrarianism on occasions resembled populism, especially as it was both anti-elite (best seen in the deep urban–rural cleavage), and anti-pluralism, showing little interest in protecting minorities or respecting the ideas of others.[2] Inevitably, and like most other Eastern and Southern European parties of the period, they were built around 'persons and ambitions, not ... conceptions and doctrines' (Roberts 1951: 112). The combination of government-imposed austerity and the lack of export opportunities for their crops left many farmers with scant interest in parliamentary politics and, when they did have the chance to vote, it was for a 'pseudo democracy' rather than liberal democracy (Seton-Watson 1945–1967).

10.3 Communism and Socialism in the Countryside

Orthodox Marxists before 1917 believed that the internal contradictions found in capitalism would lead to its self-destruction, and birth of a socialist society. The implications from this were that political power could *not* be achieved through the ballot box, but rather from the class struggle between capitalists and workers, and that socialism would appear in industrial societies, not rural ones. Marxists believed that most family farmers would be forced to sell their land because of competition from large farmers and join the urban proletariat, leaving a few successful ones to become capitalist farmers. For Engels, 'capitalist large scale production is ... sure to run over their impotent and antiquated system of small scale production as a train runs over a pushcart' (in Hussain and Tribe

1981: 9). As late as 1902, Lenin still argued that small farmers should be helped in their struggle against serfdom, but not against capitalist competition (Jackson 1966: 31). Orthodox Marxists therefore rejected creating socialist organizations such as cooperatives under capitalism because this would delay the proletarianization of small farmers.[3]

Yet by the late nineteenth century it was clear that not only was the demise of the family farm not happening, but they were actually becoming stronger in many regions. When farmers did leave the land, it was more likely to be because of the attractions of high industrial wages, rather than the consequences of competition from larger farms. This resilience of the family farm led to Lenin to rethink the clear separation of 'peasant' farmers and the proletariat in Marxist theory. In Germany, he noted, that there were 3.4 million holdings of less than two hectares, but just 14 per cent of their farmers were economically independent. Lenin now argued that these diminutive holdings were not so much farms, as proletarian households that owned a bit of land.[4] Agriculture and industry were perhaps not so clearly divided as Marxist theory had suggested.

Small farmers showed their revolutionary potential in 1917 when they seized the land that they worked but did not own. Indeed, a major difference between the successful Russian Revolution, where the Bolsheviks encouraged farmers to take over the land, and the failed Hungarian Revolution of March 1919, where Bela Kun insisted on the state owning it, was not lost on contemporaries. Hungary was just one of several European countries to see communist advances, as the Red Army threatened to produce a revolution in Poland in July 1920, and communists enjoyed considerable electoral support in Yugoslavia and Bulgaria in 1919.

The Red Peasant International (Krestintern) was created in 1924 in Russia to help export the Revolution to Eastern Europe. The presence of a poor, land hungry peasantry threatened 'on more than one occasion in 1923 and 1924' to undermine the Marxist thesis of the 'hegemony of the proletariat', and Moscow 'seemed on the verge of declaring that the peasantry was a revolutionary class equal in importance to the proletariat' (Jackson 1966: 54). It never happened. Land reform successfully established societies of small private landowners, which significantly reduced support for communism in rural areas. Agrarian parties and local communists were united only by their opposition to the incumbent government.[5] The banning of most communist parties, and the deep national and ethnic cleavages found in rural Europe, frustrated the few attempts at joint action. Visions of communist peasant societies appearing across Eastern

Europe had disappeared well before Stalin announced the collectivization of Soviet agriculture in 1928.

There was economic logic in creating large, mechanized farms for cereal production, as the relatively small labour requirements were heavily concentrated in the planting and harvesting operations. Indeed, some US experts initially saw the Soviet Union's mechanized collectives as a potential model for their own future, with the combination of tractors, combine-harvesters, and lorries eliminating much of the hard physical work (Fitzgerald 1996). Large-scale cereal production also promised to resolve the seemingly intractable problem facing European agriculture of both making farming profitable and providing cheap bread for urban consumers and feed for livestock farmers. Yet with very few exceptions, the idea of farm collectives was anathema for Europe's farmers. Family farmers saw land not as an input in an economist's model, but a guarantee of a livelihood, as well as a way of life. Regardless of their many ideological differences, farmers were generally united in wanting to protect the family farm, and opposed any party that threatened it.

Even before 1917 orthodox Marxism was increasingly challenged in Europe by revisionists such as Eduard Bernstein in Germany, who attacked its two main pillars of historical materialism and class struggle, and 'argued for an alternative based on the primacy of politics and cross-class cooperation' (Berman 2006: 14). The post-war democratic wave saw revisionism 'blossom' into a movement of its own, as growing numbers of socialists in countries such as Germany, Austria, and Sweden were elected to parliament. The fact that urban industrial workers rarely accounted for more than a third of voters, implied that they needed political support from other parties if they were to form a government in an electoral democracy (Bartolini 2000: 148). Social Democrats increasingly looked to compete for the farm vote, especially as rural electoral districts were over-represented in national assemblies. By the interwar years, the solution to how to help farmers without increasing the living costs for their urban constituents was seen as intervention in the food chains to reduce distribution costs. Danish cooperatives were identified by democratic socialists as a model of how a highly competitive agriculture could produce high incomes for farmers, as well as cheap food for consumers. In Czechoslovakia, the Bavarian Social Democrats also promised to nationalize mortgages (rather than land); create a state monopoly for agrarian credit and farm insurance; limit interest rates; and maintain common property and communal rights (Hussain and Tribe 1981: 95). Yet socialist parties generally struggled to find a convincing programme for dissatisfied farmers and enjoyed little more success than orthodox Marxists in achieving support in rural areas. A brief look at the British and Spanish labour parties illustrates a few of the organizational difficulties they faced.

Land inequality was greater in England and Wales than probably any European country, but not only did small farmers traditionally vote Conservative, but some of the Party's staunchest supporters were found among farm workers in regions of large farms (Urwin 1980: 146). The Conservative Party therefore had already occupied much of the political space in rural areas, where a third of parliamentary constituencies were found, enjoying the support of the Primrose League, a mass social organization with a reportedly 1.5 million members by 1901, widely distributed across the country's shires (Ziblatt 2017: 95–101). The Labour Party's difficulties in attracting the farm vote arose partly from the fact that urban workers were its prime constituency, and these wanted cheap food (and hence low farm prices) and high wages (opposed by those farmers dependent on hired labour for the harvest). Furthermore, urban culture, especially anti-clericalism, was disliked by many rural voters. Suitable parliamentary candidates were difficult to find, as many lived in urban constituencies and had little interest in rural society or knowledge of farming, failing to understand 'the difference between mangolds and swedes' (Griffiths 2007: 134). Yet the Labour Party's attempts to compete in rural areas was also hampered by many voters being ignorant of its policies, severely limiting party membership and the necessary funds to prepare for elections. As Clare Griffiths (2007: 64) notes, 'the major problem which Labour faced across rural Britain was not that villagers were too frightened to vote for the party, but that it would never have occurred to them to do so'.

The British Labour Party at least attempted to engage with rural society, and with small farmers rather than just farmworkers. In Spain, the *Partido Socialista Obrero Español* (PSOE) not only started to recruit late in rural areas but, when it did, it generally ignored farmers (Acosta Ramírez et al. 2009; Bizcarrondo 2008). Indeed, rather than attempt to bridge the class cleavage, the PSOE exploited it for electoral purposes, by looking to organize the landless workers. Unsurprisingly, if this had some success in the regions of latifundios, where about a third of the parliamentary seats were found, it met with hostility elsewhere in the country.[6] The result was that the PSOE was politically isolated, and both unable and unwilling to enter into agreements with other parties to allow it to govern, except briefly in 1931 and 1932.

10.4 Farmers and Reforming Liberal Democracy

Most farmers in North-Western Europe had already been integrated into a range of competitive mass political parties by 1914 and did not feel the need to build their own. In many cases this had been the result of the traditional land elites and Church organizing confessional parties to compete with liberals in the national parliament. Their political success by the early twentieth century resulted in broad-based conservative parties representing a wide variety of interests. Yet the political strength of small farmers owed as much, if not more, to the specialist lobbies that they created. These enjoyed significant support from these conservative parties, but they also learnt to work with other parties in the national parliaments.

In France, the traditional weakness of political parties had encouraged the building of farm lobbies from an early date, while the depth of the economic crisis debilitated the legitimacy of the Third Republic in the countryside. French farmers were heavily divided by regional and class interests, but specialized associations grew around the 'electoral' crops of wheat, supposedly produced by 1.9 million farmers, and wine, with 1.6 million growers (Wright 1964: 43).[7] These enjoyed privileged access to all governments, so while a conservative one was responsible for the *Statut du Vin*, 1931, a socialist Minister of Agriculture in the Popular Front government established the *Office du blé* (1936). Parliamentary debates over market intervention in the 1930s were especially bitter, but these turned on whether it should be the state that determined policies (especially farm prices), or an independent corporate body instead.

The fact that the most successful farm lobbies were commodity-specific, inevitably left some farmers to be poorly represented, creating political space for specialized farm parties. The *Parti Agraire et Paysan Français* (1928) had twelve deputies in the 1936 election, but then split along class lines. By contrast, both Le Roy Ladurie's *Union Nationale des Syndicats Agricoles* (UNSA), and Henri Dorgères's *Comités de Defense Paysanne* (changed to *Syndicate Agricole de Défense Paysannne* in 1936) looked for answers outside parliament, joining in July 1934 to form the short-lived Peasant Front.[8]Henri Dorgères and his Greenshirts were openly fascist and attempted to build a network of agrarian organizations run by farmers (rather than the rural notables) and replace parliamentary politics and class conflicts with professional associations. Party membership jumped from 35,000 in 1935 to perhaps 550,000 in 1939, mostly family farmers enraged at the price cuts for their crops imposed by middlemen (Paxton 1997: 38, 125). Dorgères, against the background of falling farm prices and bankrupt cooperatives, organized tax strikes and demonstrations against distressed farm sales. Physical violence was also directed against striking farm workers who were being organized by the *Confédération Générale du Travail*, which had seen its agricultural membership increase from 7,000 in early 1936 to almost 200,000 a year later (Wright 1964: 68). However, unlike post-war Italy, farmers in general did not need Dorgères's strike breakers because the government continued to police the countryside (Paxton 1997: 67).

If Dorgères organized the 'most serious peasant revolt against the parliamentary Republic since the *chouannerie* of the 1790s', its influence was restricted to the poorer regions of northern and western France. Furthermore, and unlike Hitler or Mussolini, his movement ignored the rural conservative elites, and made no attempt to build support among groups other than small farmers. French rural fascism made only limited progress because most farmers were already adequately represented, especially in commodity-specific lobbies (Paxton 1997: 5, 71–3).

In England and Wales politically active farmers joined the National Union of Farmers (NFU) which was founded in 1908, and enjoyed a membership by the 1920s of more than 100,000, giving it the 'organizational capacity and the monopoly of representation' to negotiate directly with governments (Cox et al. 30, 46). Conservative governments in particular were happy to respond to petitions from the NFU, yet it was a Labour Government (1929–1931), against the background of rural distress, that passed the Agricultural Marketing Act (1931), one of the most important legislative measures to defend farmers against 'middlemen'. This Act allowed producer associations (monopolies) to be established to control prices, leading to the creation of the highly successful Milk Marketing Board in 1933 (Chapter 9).[9]

The task of building farm parties in Scandinavia was made easier by the high levels of ethnic-linguistic homogeneity and the fact that 95 per cent of the population were protestant (Urwin 1980: 192–4). From an early date, rural areas enjoyed high levels of literacy and social capital, reinforced by independent networks of folk high schools. Agriculture was also relatively uniform, given the predominance of medium-sized scattered homesteads and farming practices. However, tensions existed between the wealthier farmers and marginal ones and agricultural workers. In the early 1930s, many farmers not only had problems recruiting reliable labour, but they had become heavily indebted at a time when their markets were rapidly disappearing. The Great Depression saw challenges to economic orthodoxy and liberal democracy everywhere, but it was in Scandinavia that democratic reforms went deepest, with farmers at the front of change.

In Sweden, the economic difficulties of the 1930s created political incentives to bridge the deep ideological cleavages that existed between the Agrarian Party and Social Democrats. When the Swedish Democratic Party (SAP, *Sveriges Socialdemokratiska Arbetareparti*) was in power between October 1921 and April 1923, it still followed classical deflationary economic policies or, in the words of Mark Blyth (2002: 104), 'liberal orthodoxy run by the representatives of the working classes'. The first challenges to this orthodoxy came from the Stockholm School in the mid-1920s, inspired by several brilliant young economists (Gunnar Myrdal, Eric Lindahl, Bertil Ohlin) that developed 'a demand-side model of an economy within a dynamic open-economy framework' (Blyth 2002: 106). The SAP embraced these new ideas to stabilize unemployment, and saw agrarian monopolies and trade unions as the solution to the economic crisis, rather than its cause. Following the 1932 election, party members of the conservative Agrarian Party forced its leadership to form a government with the larger SAP, with the condition that it controlled the Ministry of Agriculture and economic policies were to be expansionary (Urwin 1980: 237–40; Bengtsson 2022). Swedish dairy farmers, given the depth of the crisis, believed that marketing schemes were ineffective without legislation to make them compulsory to all producers, while the SAP needed farm support for their own labour market programme. The fact that the SAP was willing to negotiate with representatives of agriculture, business, and labour created 'a positive-sum trade-off for all parties' (Blyth 2002: 115).[10] As Mats Morell (2023: 184) writes, 'the crisis motivated rapid short-term action but the choice of action, and the political constellations that developed, transformed these measures into a long-time move towards interventionism and corporatism'.

The agrarian problem in Denmark was made more difficult by the fact that exports accounted for four-fifths of milk production, rather than a third as in Sweden (Morell 2023: 185; Just 2010). Danish farming, despite arable systems changing 'more profoundly' between 1860 and 1940 'than any European country', showed 'extraordinary uniformity of land utilization', and 90 per cent of farmers on the eve of the Second

World War had 'almost exactly the same proportion of arable to pasture, and crop their fields in a similar rotation' (Yates 1940: 29). The Danish Venstre was founded in 1888, not as a specifically agrarian party, but rather as part of an urban–rural alliance against absolutism and state bureaucracy. This split in 1905, when smallholders and farmworkers founded the Radical Venstre, and it was these who signed the Kanslergade Agreement with Social Democrats in 1933. This promised increases in public employment and social welfare reforms in exchange for a wage freeze and prohibition on strikes and lockouts, with farmers benefitting from tax reductions, help on mortgage payments, state subsidies to reduce their livestock inventories, and a devaluation of the krone (Luebbert 1991: 267–8).

In Norway, conservative farmers dominated politics until smaller, commercial farmers founded the Norwegian Agrarian Party in 1920, which joined the larger Labour Party in government in 1935 to provide market intervention to help agriculture. In Norway, as elsewhere in Scandinavia, opportunistic behaviour by minority agrarian parties to participate in governments with other political groups transformed politics, and severely restricted the space for fascism. These political alliances between farm groups and the urban working classes preserved the 'democratic competitiveness of liberalism but broke fundamentally with its economics' (Luebbert 1991: 2). Social democracy led to political bargains substituting for market-determined wage and price settlements, while trade unions guaranteed labour market peace. In theory, these corporatist agreements helped all groups, although Luebbert (1991: 312) claims that it was medium-sized family farmers and urban workers who were the main beneficiaries, at the expense of urban middle classes and farm workers. Outside Scandinavia, these attempts by farm groups and urban-based Social Democrats to create a common programme to tackle the economic and social problems of the 1930s were repeated only in Czechoslovakia (Chapter 7).

10.5 German Farmers and the Attractions of Fascism

Germany suffered more than most European countries during the Great Depression, with its economy dropping to its lowest point shortly before the NSDAP seized power in 1933 (Overy 1996: table v; Feinstein et al. ch. 6). Although heavily industrialized, agriculture still employed 30 per cent of workers in 1930, four times the figure of the UK, but German farm workers were only half as productive (Broadberry 2009: tables 3.1, 3.2). Low agricultural productivity resulted in 'modest and monotonous' diets for many, although rising urban incomes was creating demand for dairy produce and meat which farmers struggled to supply in sufficient quantities.[11] German livestock farmers, unlike those of Eastern Europe, faced supply rather than demand constraints, and in particular a lack of cheap feed. Other countries resolved this problem with imports, paid for by exporting agricultural produce (Denmark, the Netherlands) or manufactured goods (Belgium, the UK).[12] France also imported cheap grain (and wines) from its North African colonies, but these were considered part of domestic production. By contrast, German agriculture, even before the Great Depression, was unusually autarchic. The country had been forced to give up its colonies following the First World War, and governments prioritized imports of industrial raw materials over agricultural produce because of the severe shortages of foreign exchange.

German agricultural interests were diverse, with livestock farmers, for example, wanting cheap animal feed, but the large grain producers in East Elbia, protection, and high prices. The National Rural League (Reichs-Landbund or RLB) was formed in 1921 and attempted to create a more decentralized organization than previous groups, provide better representation to family farmers (rather than simply the Junkers), and follow a policy of neutrality with respect to the existing political parties, being opposed to direct state intervention in agriculture (Jones 2020: 59–60).[13] The Weimar governments responded with piecemeal and uncoordinated policies, rather than a coherent, overall plan, so that 'one man's protective measure' became 'another man's higher production costs' (Farquharson 1976: 27). All farmers suffered in the 1930s from low farm prices, while mortgage payments and taxes increased in real terms, leaving many of them disillusioned with the Weimar governments and liberal democracy. Farmers were highly organized, but along regional and commodity lines, with no single political group speaking effectively for the sector.[14] This weakness led farmers in Schleswig–Holstein, against a background of tariffs causing them high feed costs, to protest violently against evictions and taxes, as their own farm prices collapsed in the late 1920s.

The Nazis successfully exploited the discount produced by the military defeat of 1918 and the 'humiliating' peace treaties, hyperinflation and reparations of the post-war years, and massive unemployment of the early 1930s. As late as 1928, the National Socialists (NSDAP) had won only 3 per cent of the vote, with their support coming from a mixture of army veterans and urban middle-classes, especially students, teachers, and civil servants. Their fortunes were changed with the Great Depression, allowing them to argue that the conservative elites and political classes were the cause, rather than the solution, to Germany's growing problems. The NSDAP, unlike other authoritarian parties, initially encouraged popular political participation, and was successful in infiltrating farm organizations from below, gaining wide supported among small family farmers, helping them to win a third of the vote in the July 1933 elections.

Although most farmers were conservative, the experience of war-time controls had rendered them highly suspicious of government intervention, and therefore made them unlikely supporters for the NSDAP. Agriculture also seemed a strange priority for fascism, as Hitler's objective to reverse the post-war settlements required rapid industrialization to rebuild the county's military power. However, farmers were usually strongly anti-communist and, given the economic difficulties of the Depression, were attracted to the Nazi's concern for the primacy of the community (the *volk*) over individual rights, that 'exalted an agrarian utopia free from the rootlessness, conflict, and immorality of urban life' (Paxton 2005: 13, 38). Walther Darré, as the NSDAP's Minister of Agriculture distinguished between the peasant farmer (*Bauer*), who he believed placed community and family before material gain, and the commercial farmer (*Landwirt*) (Farquharson 1976: 59). Ultra-nationalists such as Darré and Hitler wanted to protect the *Bauer*, not just from low farm prices but from market forces in exchange for feeding the nation, providing soldiers for its defence, and shielding the long-term future of the race (Farquharson 1976: 68–70; Tooze 2006: 171). As Darré noted in February 1935, while the agrarian policies of the Soviet Union and fascist Italy looked to maximize output through rationalization, Germany policy was dominated by the ideological issues of blood and race. In the words of Tooze (2006: 180), 'as hard as it may be for us to credit, agrarian ideology is crucial if we are to understand, not the archaism of Hitler's regime, but its extraordinary militancy'.

The NSDAP quickly extended its control over German agriculture, radically changing it in the process. In September 1933 the *Reichsnährstand* (RNS) or State Food Corporation was established, which allowed the government to manage the whole food chain from the farm to the table, effectively ending the free market for agricultural produce.[15] Cartels usually suffer from the free-rider problem, namely groups that remain outside the organization and do not contribute, but who cannot be excluded from the benefits. Cartel members are also temped to cheat on agreements, especially if enforcement is weak. The RNS solved these problems by making membership compulsory for all farmers, and had wide powers to fine, imprison, or close business indefinitely, for those who failed to adhere by the rules. Given Hitler's promise to prioritize agriculture and the family farmer, and the significant material benefits that the RNS offered at a time of low farm prices, opposition was initially limited. The NSDAP quickly absorbed, or closed all farm organizations, and in January 1934 created a new peak association, the *Community of German Farming Profession*. According to Farquharson (1976: 44–5), in 'the space of a few months the whole picture of agrarian organization had been transformed; the historic (and mutually antagonistic) unions had given place at national level to one comprehensive corporation under Darré's control'.[16] The RNS set prices at each stage of the different food chains and exercised 'more or less' direct control over 25% of Germany's GDP, and 40% of the workforce (Tracy 1989: 188).

Many German farms were heavily fragmented because of inheritance laws, and the low prices of the 1930s produced difficulties for farmers to meet their mortgage demands. In response, the NSDAP passed the Hereditary Entitlement Law (*Erbhofgesetz*) in September 1933 that looked to protect the family farm by prohibiting *Bauer* farmers from using land as collateral for loans, or selling it, except for the whole farm to another family member. The scheme benefitted only Germans and covered as much as 55 per cent of farmland. Taken together, the RNS and *Erbhof* gave farmers complete security and guaranteed farm prices, effectively removing the family farm from the market. It was as radical as the liberal reforms of the early nineteenth century, but with the opposite intent, fixing the number of farms indefinitely (Farquharson 1976: 63–7; Tooze 2006: 182). Those siblings who did not inherit had to be compensated, which left many farmers short of capital, and indebted to the state. The fact that the farms of inefficient *Erbhof* farmers could now be confiscated led to some contemporaries to suggest that the discipline of the market had been replaced by that of the state (Farquharson 1976: 122).

Although the *Erbhof* farms were supposed to sustain a family, there was insufficient land available, especially as the direction of technological change was requiring larger, not smaller farms by the early 1930s. This lack of land implied that farmers could not adopt cost-cutting farm machinery, and would struggle to increase productivity sufficiently to provide acceptable living standards unless they were paid higher prices for meat and dairy products.[17]

Land resettlement helped, but it was slow. Even before 1933, some 57,457 families had been settled on 602,110 hectares in the under-populated eastern provinces. Between 1933 and 1938, another 20,408 farms were created on 328,500 hectares (average 16 hectares) by the NSDAP, helping to reduce the need for foreign workers on the large estates and settling land on the German frontier (Farquharson 1976: table 2). Applicants under the NSDAP plan had to show that there had been 'no coloured or Jewish blood' in the family since 1800, as well as evidence that they could produce a sizeable family and were politically sound. Landless workers and small farmers were also effectively excluded because relatively large amounts of capital were needed (Farquharson 1976: 149–59).

A country that was both highly dependent on domestic food production and had a large, but relatively unproductive agriculture, was not unusual in interwar Europe. What was different was Hitler's solution—*Lebensraum*—or the search for 'living space', outside Germany's eastern frontiers. The British Empire had given landless workers and poor farmers from the mother country opportunities to emigrate and create farms, and these supplied massive amounts of food that was paid for by exporting manufacturing products. France's colonies also provided investment and work opportunities for its citizens and supplied considerable amounts of cheap grain and wine in exchange for industrial goods. Even Mussolini's colonial war in Ethiopia was partly to obtain land for its farmers and to provide cheap wheat imports. Some Germans, as early as the First World War, had seen the solution to the country's limited natural resources in Eastern Europe (Ritschl 2005: 42). The NSDAP's farm policy, as Tracy (1989: 200) has noted, was not 'merely based on a desire to pander to the agricultural interest and gain its support' but rather contained a strong internal logic to increase, by force, 'the strength of the German nation'.

The NSDAP's favourable policies for farmers began to change with the Four-Year Plan of 1936, just as the RNS increased its control over individual farms. Despite the National Socialists' promises to revitalize *Bauer* culture, low farm prices and rapidly growing urban demand for labour began to empty the countryside once more.[18] Even the belief that farm workers were heathier than their urban counterparts was questioned, while rural marital fertility continued to decline (Farquharson 1976: 219).

The benefits enjoyed by small farmers from fascism were therefore short-lived. For Paxton (1997: 158), 'triumphant fascism subordinated peasant society to industrial growth, just as liberalism had done and as Soviet communism was doing, in a far more bloody manner, at the same time'. Nevertheless, by the late 1930s, detailed records were available on all of the two million or more holdings of over 5 hectares, equivalent to 90% of the land, giving Hitler 'all the necessary machinery' for controlling food supplies and prices (Farquharson 1976: 173; Tracy 1989: 199).

10.6 Conclusion

The rapid changes in global communications in the half century before 1914 transformed European farming, and it was the landed elites that sought government help to protect farming interests. Yet by the interwar period, the economic and political influence of this social group had been greatly reduced, and it was left instead to small, family farmers to organize and lobby governments, especially during the Great Depression. As this chapter has argued, they were most successful in North-Western Europe, where market-orientated farmers enjoyed greater incentives to build lobbies and to work with other political groups. Farmers in countries such as France and the UK learnt to work not just with conservative political parties but also those of the centre-left, as these parties looked to establish their own support networks in the countryside. In Scandinavia, agrarian parties went even further, as the exceptional difficulties in the 1930s encouraged them to enter government with Social Democrats, supporting social transfers that benefitted urban groups, in return for significant help for the farm sector. Farmers in these countries saw farm profitably restored relatively quickly, and they made the first steps in building the institutional networks necessary to obtain permanent government support for the sector after the Second World War.

Farmers in Eastern and Southern Europe, despite their considerable numbers and universal male suffrage, generally remained politically marginalized, and showed less interest in defending liberal democracy. The industrial and political elites in many of these countries successfully sidestepped restrictions that new constitutions and liberal democracy was supposed to have imposed. In this they were helped by the political weakness of the Agrarian parties, which were divided in their objectives as to whether to continue with the ideas of land reform and provide land for as many families as possible, or those of natural selection, and allowing the most successful family farmers—and the most likely to produce marketable surpluses—to buy the properties of those that struggled. The lack of market specialization discouraged many farmers from building lobbies to influence government policy or participate in politics. When Socialist Parties were not banned outright, their political message rarely found support among poor family farmers. By the 1930s, as Mazower (1999: 25) writes, 'many asked why it should ever have been expected that democracy would flower in Europe'.

Strong associational networks were important for creating effective farm lobbies, but these required not just social capital, but also the promise of financial rewards to encourage farmers to make the necessary investment. However, they were insufficient to guarantee democracy, and in Germany the NSDAP was remarkably successful in infiltrating associations and strengthening its party from below (Ertman 1988; Portes 1998; Satyanath et al. 2017). Both Hitler and Mussolini enjoyed their first mass following among discontented farmers but, once their political power had been assured, industrialization took precedence. The attempts in Nazi Germany to give farmers sufficient land to fully employ their families might have been politically astute, but it risked making farms inflexible to meet changing market demands as well as placing labour productivity on the farm at the base of the 'U-shaped' productivity curve (Foster and Rosenzweig: 2022) (Chapter 6).

Notes

1. US voters over the twentieth century '*consistently* and *systematically* punish(ed) incumbents' for droughts and floods. Emphasis in the original (Achen and Bartels 2016: 128–38).
2. (Guriev and Papaioannou 2022), for a recent survey of populism.
3. Kautsky also criticized helping cooperatives because they perpetuated existing inequalities in agriculture (Hussain and Tribe 1981: 9).
4. These holding represented three-fifths of the total but occupied only 6 per cent of the land area. Kautsky, advanced the same 'highly original' argument which 'departed from the traditional Marxist characterisation of what constitutes a wage labourer' (Hussain and Tribe 1981: 68–70).

5. Two pro-Communist peasant parties were found in Poland, and one in Czechoslovakia (Sub-Carpathian Ruthenia) (Jackson 1966: 99).
6. Even in the latifundio regions, only a third of the population were farm workers (Simpson and Carmona 2020: table 9.2).
7. Beet growers were much fewer, but their organization was equally influential.
8. This split because of personal jealousies and doctrinal conflicts (Wright 1964: 49–54).
9. The Labour minority government of 1924 had also re-established wage regulations in agriculture, and subsidies for growing sugar beet, a labour-intensive crop (Griffiths 2007: 237).
10. The Saltsjöbaden agreement of 1938 united business and labour.
11. Traditional diets comprised of 'bred and jam, potatoes, cabbage and pork, washed down with water and small amounts of milk and beer' (Tooze 2006: 29 and 142).
12. Net imports of wheat and flour in 1929–30, for example, were 73% in Belgium, 35% in Denmark, 2% in France, 24% in Germany, 83% in the Netherlands, and 79% in the UK (Hevesy 1940).
13. The RLB was formed out of a merger between the German Rural League and Agrarian League.
14. The Green Front, an alliance of different agrarian associations was formed in 1929 but quickly collapsed over the question of imports of cheap animal feed (Farquharson 1976: 27).
15. The state controlled imports through the *Reichsstellen* and, although not actually part of the RNS, 'formed an indispensable component to its action' (Tracy 1989:193).
16. The French Ambassador noted that 'the astounding things in this revolution are the speed … but also the facility with which it is everywhere completed, the scant resistance which it encounters' (Farquharson 1976: 49).
17. The amount of farm machinery was growing, but still limited in 1933 (Grant 2009: table 7.6).
18. Even Darré admitted, the 'harmonious balance' in the economy was now lost because of 'the undervaluation (financially) of agricultural work and its last consequence is the land flight' (Farquharson 1976: 195).

References

Achen, Christopher H., and Larry M. Bartels. 2016. *Democracy for Realists. Why Elections do not Produce Responsive Government*. Princeton: Princeton University Press.

Acosta Ramírez, Francisco, Salvador Cruz Artacho, and Manuel González de Molina Navarro. 2009. *Socialismo y democracia en el campo (1880–1930). Los origenes de la FNTT*. Madrid: MAPA.

Bartolini, Stefano. 2000. *The Political Mobilization of the European Left, 1860–1980*. Cambridge: Cambridge University Press.

Bengtsson, Erik. 2022. "The Social Origins of Democracy in Sweden: the Role of Agrarian Politics." *Social History* 47 (4): 419–45. org/https://doi.org/10.1080/03071022.2022.2112865.

Berger, Suzanne. 1972. *Peasants against Politics. Rural Organization in Brittany 1911–1967*. Cambridge, Mass.: Harvard.

Berman, Sheri. 2006. *The Primacy of Politics. Social Democracy and the Making of Europe's Twentieth Century*. Cambridge: Cambridge University Press.

Bizcarrondo, Marta. 2008. *Historia de la UGT (vol. 3): entre la democracia y la revolución, 1931–1936*. Madrid: Siglo XXI.

Blyth, Mark. 2002. *Great Transformations. Economic Ideas and Institutional Change in the Twentieth Century*. Cambridge: Cambridge University Press.

Broadberry, S. 2009. "Agriculture and Structural Change. Lessons from the UK Experience in an International Context." In *Agriculture and Economic Development in Europe since 1870*, edited by Pedro Lains and Vicente Pinilla, 76–94. London: Routledge.

Brustein, W. 1996. *The Logic of Evil: The Social Origins of the Nazi Party, 1915–1933*. New Haven: Yale.

Cox, Graham, Philip Lowe, and Michael Winter. 1991. "The Origins and Early Development of the National Farmers' Union." *Agricultural History Review* 39 (1): 30–47.

Ertman, Thomas. 1988. "Democracy and Dictatorship in Interwar Western Europe Revisited." *World Politics* 50: 475–505.

Farquharson, John E. 1976. *The Plough and the Swastika: The NSDAP and Agriculture in Germany 1928–45*. London: Sage.

Feinstein, Charles, Peter Temin, and Toniolo. 1997. *The European Economy Between the Wars*. Oxford: Oxford University Press.

Fitzgerald, Deborah. 1996. "Blinded by Technology: American Agriculture in the Soviet Union, 1928-1932." *Agricultural History* 70: 459–86.

Foster, Andrew D., and Mark R. Rosenzweig. 2022. "Are There Too Many Farms in the World? Labor Market Transaction Costs, Machine Capacities, and Optimal Farm SIze." *Journal of Political Economy* 130: 636–80.

Gellner, Ernest. 1983. *Nations and Nationalism*. Oxford: Blackwell.

Gómez Benito, Cristóbal, ed. 2011. *Joaquín Costa y la modernizaición de España*. Madrid: Congreso de los Diputados.

Grant, Oliver. 2009. "Agriculture and Economic Development in Germany." In *Agriculture and Economic Development in Europe since 1870*, edited by Pedro Lains and Vicente Pinilla, 178–209. Abingdon: Routledge.

Griffiths, Clare V.J. 2007. *Labour and the Countryside. The Politics of Rural Britain*. Oxford: Oxford University Press.

Guriev, Sergei, and Elias Papaioannou. 2022. "The Political Economy of Populism." *Journal of Economic Literature* LX (3): 753–832. https://doi.org/10.1257/pandp.20181122.

Hevesy, Paul de. 1940. *World Wheat Planning and Economic Planning in General*. London, New York, Toronto: Oxford.

Hussain, Athar, and Keith Tribe. 1981. *Marxism and the Agrarian Question. German Social Democracy and the Peasantry 1890–1907*. London: Macmillan.

Jackson, George D. 1966. *Comintern and Peasant in East Europe 1919–1930*. New York: Columbia.

Jones, Larry Eugene. 2020. *The German Right, 1918–1930*. Cambridge: Cambridge University Press.

Just, F. 2010. "The Scandinavian Food System between Organization and State." In *Managing Crises and De-globalization. Nordic Foreign Trade and Exchange, 1919–39*, edited by S.O Olsson, 121–36. London: Routledge.

Kalyvas, Stathis N. 1996. *The Rise of Christian Democracy in Europe*. Ithaca and London: Cornell.

Labrousse, Ernest. 1944. *La crise de l'economie francaise a la fin de l'ancien regime et au debut de la revolution*. Paris: Presses universitaries de France.

Lachiver, Marcel. 1988. *Vins, vignes et vignerons. Histoire du vignoble français*. Paris: Fayard.

Linz, Juan J. 1976. "Patterns of Land Tenure, Division of Labor, and Voting Behavior in Europe." *Comparative Politics* 8 (3): 365–430.

Luebbert, George M. 1991. *Liberalism, Fascism, or Social Democracy. Social Classes and the Political Origins of Regimes in Interwar Europe*. Oxford: Oxford University Press.

Mann, Michael. 2004. *Fascists*. Cambridge: Cambridge University Press.

Mazower, Mark. 1999. *Dark Continent. Europe's Twentieth Century*. London: Penguin.

Milanovic, Branko. 2019. *Capitalism Alone*. Cambridge, Mass.: Harvard.

Morell, Mats. 2023. "Swedish Agriculture and the Crisis of the 1930s." In *Agriculture and the Great Depression. The Rural Crisis of the 1930s in Europe and the Americas*, edited by G. Béaur and F. Chiapparino, 171–89. Abington & New York: Routledge.

Overy, R.J. 1996. *The Nazi Economic Recovery 1932–1938*. 2nd ed. Cambridge: Cambridge University Press.

Paxton, Robert O. 1997. *French Peasant Fascism*. Oxford: Oxford University Press.

Paxton, Robert O. 2005. *The Anatomy of Fascism*. London: Penguin.

Portes, A. 1998. "Social Capital. Its Origins and Applications in Modern Sociology—Dark Side of Social Capital." *Annual Review of Sociology* (24): 1–24.

Riley, Dylan. 2010. *The Civic Foundations of Fascism in Europe: Italy, Spain, and Romania, 1870–1945*. Baltimore: John Hopkins.

Ritschl, Albrecht. 2005. "The Pity of Peace: Germany's Economy at War, 1914-1918." In *The Economics of World War I*, edited by Stephen Broadberry and Mark Harrison, 41–76. Cambridge: Cambridge University Press.

Roberts, Henry L. 1951. *Rumania. Political Problems of an Agrarian State*. New Haven: Yale University Press.

Satyanath, Shanker, Nico Voigländer, and Hans-Joachim Voth. 2017. "Bowling for Fascism: Social Capital and the Rise of the Nazi Party." *Journal of Political Economy* 125 (4): 478–525.

Seton-Watson, Hugh. 1945: 1967. *Eastern Europe between the Wars 1918–1941*. 3 ed. New York: Harper.

Simpson, James, and Juan Carmona. 2020. *Why Democracy Failed: The Agrarian Origins of the Spanish Civil War*. Cambridge: Cambridge University Press.

Tooze, Adam. 2006. *The Wages of Destruction. The Making and Breaking of the Nazi Economy*. London: Penguin.

Tracy, Michael. 1989. *Government and Agriculture in Western Europe, 1880–1988*. 3rd ed. New York & London: Harvester Wheatsheaf

Urwin, Derek W. 1980. *From Ploughshare to Ballot Box: the Politics of Agrarian Defence in Europe*. Oslo: Universitetsforlaget.

Wright, Gordon. 1964. *Rural Revolution in France. The Peasantry in the Twentieth Century*. Stanford: Stanford University Press.

Yates, P. Lamartine. 1940. *Food Production and Manpower in Western Europe*. London: Longmans Green.

Ziblatt, Daniel. 2017. *Conservative Parties and the Birth of Democracy*. Cambridge: Cambridge University Press.

CHAPTER 11

Conclusions

The growing integration of the Atlantic economy from the 1870s set off changes which by the interwar period had radically altered European agriculture and the role of the state in guaranteeing food security. In Western Europe, international trade led to falling land prices and rising real wages, encouraging landowners to sell their estates, often to their tenants. By contrast, the new trade opportunities benefitted large cereal farmers in Eastern Europe until many of these also lost their farms following the post-war land reforms. Consequently, land inequality by the 1920s had dramatically declined, as Europe went in less than half a century from a society dominated by large landowners to one of small, family farmers. The number of European farmers probably reached a historical peak in the early 1930s, before declining once more as industry recovered, and then collapsing in the post-1945 economic boom. As this book has argued, how these family farmers choose to work their land and organize professionally would have a significant impact on the nature of economic development and political change in the period.

Governments following the Great War sought to prioritize economic development and protect key industries, but they also needed to guarantee adequate supplies of inexpensive food for urban workers. In Western Europe especially, world prices for bread and feed grains were significantly below the levels at which most domestic farmers could compete.

J. Simpson, *Family Farmers, Land Reforms and Political Action*, Palgrave Studies in Economic History,
https://doi.org/10.1007/978-3-031-67281-1_11

Nevertheless, relying on cheap imports required countries to have the necessary foreign exchange at a time when most were struggling, first to re-join the gold standard, and then to remain on it. Some governments were able to import large amounts of grain as it increased their export competitiveness in manufacturing (Britain or Belgium) or in food industries (Denmark or the Netherlands). Most countries however preferred to use their limited foreign exchange to purchase vital industrial imports, relying on domestic farmers to cover their food needs (Chapter 8). This created opportunities for commercial farmers to specialize and establish new institutions to negotiate with governments. As a result, farm prices in North-West Europe were double those of Eastern Europe by the 1930s. In Eastern Europe, farmers suffered because most of their farms were far too small to make commercial grain farming profitable, a problem that could only be resolved by reversing the land reforms to encourage the re-appearance of larger, market-orientated farms, and allowing marginal farmers to disappear.

Rising living standards left European consumers with cash to purchase more attractive foods than just bread or potatoes, benefitting particularly livestock producers in North-Western Europe and those Mediterranean farmers who were able to export high-value fruit and horticultural products. Family farmers were highly competitive because their labour was cheap, but they faced difficulties moving up the quality ladder, and were vulnerable to protectionism closing their markets. Yet for significant numbers of farmers across large areas of Eastern and Southern Europe, high-transport costs, and weak and volatile markets from the late 1920s, discouraged farm investment and specialization.

This book has attempted to understand the challenges and successes of European agriculture in the interwar years. In particular, it has centred on the family farm, which had established itself as the dominant unit of production and made small farmers the largest single group of voters in most countries. It has highlighted several major areas to explain the contribution of European farmers to the economic and political changes of the period.

11.1 Farm Prosperity Depended on Industrialization

Long-run economic growth depended on the contributions of both agriculture and industry, with farmers providing a ready market for farm inputs and consumer goods during cyclical upswings. The clear distinction between agriculture and non-agriculture labour found in the population censuses were much less apparent in real life, as farmers frequently spent part of their time working in non-farming activities, while the growth of cooperatives allowed farmers to extend their economic interests along the food chain, and into the manufacturing and distribution sectors.

Contemporaries were correct in seeing farming as a very different type of business organization to those of the new industrial and commercial enterprises appearing in the period. Most farms were family concerns, and their owners responded quite differently to changes in supply and demand. Outside North-Western Europe especially, the farm guaranteed employment and food for the family, while village networks offered social stability. Labour was usually allocated according to consumption needs rather than its marginal-return, encouraging families to work longer hours than would have been profitable using paid labour. Family farmers were also quick to respond to new commercial opportunities although these were generally few given the difficult market conditions of the period.

While the contribution of both industry and agriculture were crucial for long-run economic development, the business cycle was driven primarily by the industrial sector. As farm prices fell and businesses closed their doors in the early thirties, many farmers reduced market operations to protect their farms. The rural equivalent of urban Europe's long dole queues was self-sufficiency, and the attempts by farmers to grow wheat on marginal plots of land. It was hardly surprising therefore that so many contemporaries spoke negatively about 'surplus' labour and persistence of 'backward' farm technologies in the period. Agricultural recovery was also dependent on industrial growth and export demand, so that rearmament in Nazi Germany after 1935 saw the rural exodus renewing while in France, as domestic farm workers became scarce, migrant workers quickly reappeared.[1] By contrast, export demand for agricultural products from Eastern Europe remained weak during most of the 1930s.

11.2 Farmers and Technological Change

Economists see creative destruction as an important source of economic growth, with new technologies and business models continually replacing older, less productive ones as firms go bankrupt. These changes were especially rapid in the interwar years as new general-purpose technologies, such as the internal combustion engine and electricity made older machinery, work skills, and traditional factory organizations obsolete. By contrast, few European farmers even in industrial economies went bankrupt. The fact that many farmers inherited their farms also limited the pool of innovative ideas associated with generational change.

Yet family farmers unquestionably did show interest in change, particularly as mechanization promised to reduce the physical work needed in traditional farming, and biological technologies allowed them to increase output with no extra effort. Farmers did not need 'experts' to show them the attractions of not having to work hundreds of hours a year to collect water from a distant well; or being able to use electric lighting in the winter; or saving massive amounts of physical labour in the transport of goods from the field to the farm, or the farm to the consumer.

An important constraint to change were the small, and often fragmented farms, a problem made worse by land reform. The supply of capital for farm investment was limited, in part because farmers with insufficient land had to use it for consumption needs, rather than productive uses (Chapter 6). Even so, the heavy seasonal fluctuations in demand for agricultural labour and the limited time available to carry out essential tasks, implied that many small farmers *overinvested* in capital goods. Work animals were frequently poorly fed as they were underutilized during the year while the capital costs of a plough had to be spread over two, rather than twenty hectares. One solution was to amalgamate the large numbers of plots to form larger fields, which indeed was the logic behind the Soviet Union's large mechanized collective farms. In Western Europe land consolidation was beginning to be seriously considered in countries such as Belgium and France in the 1920s but in general it only became important following the rapid rural exodus after 1945, allowing farm size to increase sufficiently for the new mechanical technologies to be profitable.

Nevertheless, it would be wrong to suggest that the only solution to low productivity in European agriculture was the creation of Soviet-style collectives. As this book has emphasized, the high labour monitoring costs in farming favoured the family farm, and farmers were quick to work the land intensely to produce a whole range of cash crops, including wine, milk, oranges, and tobacco. The constraining factor in interwar Europe was not so much a lack of skills but the low and volatile prices; the weakness of the family farm in the lengthening commodity chains; and governments closing their markets to protect domestic farmers.

11.3 Land Reform and Inequality

For Scheidel (2017), there is a historical tendency for inequality to grow in societies until it is reversed by a sudden major catastrophe. The years of devastating wars between 1912 and 1923 was one such period. As Europe's frontiers were radically redrawn, the landed elites in some countries were left as 'foreigners' and politically vulnerable. Eastern European land reforms redistributed a fifth of farmland and were especially important where the large estates were in the hand of ethnic minorities, including the Baltic States, Czechoslovakia, and 'to some extent' in the Balkans (Mazower 1999: 12).

Land reform reduced the economic resources of potential opponents to the new governments and ended the communism threat in rural Europe. Land ownership provided families with work and helped them survive at times of economic distress, of special importance given the limited capacity of many governments to intervene effectively in the 1930s. Diets in much of Eastern Europe remained monotonous, but individuals continued to consume over 2,700 calories a day even during the worst of the downturn (Zagoroff et al. 1955: ch.4).[2] Alongside land reform, the new governments encouraged schooling in an attempt at nation-building, resulting in a significant increase in literacy, albeit often only in the language of the new majorities.

An interesting counterfactual of what might have happened if land reform had not taken place in Eastern Europe is provided by Spain in the early 1930s. Spain's land reform failed because of the high costs of compensating landowners, their ability to use the courts to delay expropriation, and weak state capacity. The demand for reform was geographically restricted to the South, and while living standards for the landless were often desperate, many family farmers opposed it, seeing well-organized socialist and anarchist groups as a major threat to social stability. The failure to carry out an effective land reform not only condemned several hundred thousand families to extreme poverty during the Great Depression, but it polarized the countryside and, following the failed military coup, led to mass killings during, and after, the Civil War.

Eastern Europe's land reforms were less successful when considered in the long-run. Farmers were given too little land, making it difficult for them to respond to market incentives when growth eventually returned. Too much land was kept under cereals because of natural resource endowments and weak markets for alternative crops, requiring farmers to work long hours and delaying the introduction of the mechanical technologies. Farm size did matter if sufficient food was to be sold to urban consumers at reasonable prices. Land reform delayed the rural exodus, rather than making it unnecessary.

11.4 When Did Farmers Form Effective Voluntary Associations?

It was perhaps in areas of political empowerment that land reform failed most to live up to expectations. The creation of vibrant voluntary associations is often considered by social scientists as being crucial if new democracies are going to have any chance of prospering. The fact that most voters lived in rural societies in the period under discussion gave village-level organizations considerable importance. Cooperatives were considered the most effective means of both strengthening the family farm in the lengthening commodity chains and helping to integrate villagers into national politics. Yet, despite their considerable success in Denmark and a few other places, it was the absence of cooperatives which was the most notable feature in interwar Europe.

Village cooperatives were most effective in areas of specialized farming, explaining their concentration in the industrial economies of North-Western Europe. Success was also more likely in dairy farming and viticulture, where farmers had traditionally processed the milk and grapes themselves, than in cereals or olives, where farmers met opposition from private flour mills and olive oil producers. Many farmers, especially in Eastern Europe, were marginal producers and marketed far too little for them to contemplate risky commercial ventures with their neighbours such as a cooperative.

The market power and political influence of village cooperatives was considerably strengthened when they were integrated into regional or national networks, something made difficult because, unlike village organizations, individual members no longer knew each other. In North-Western Europe, hierarchical groups involving the landed elites and the Church before 1914 had enjoyed incentives to dedicate the necessary resources to resolve the collective action problems among family farmers to help build cooperative networks and, after 1918, some of the new political parties also assisted. These gave farmers greater negotiating powers and assisted them in controlling product quality and problems of mislabelling at the different stages of the food chain, particularly when governments delegated them the necessary powers. The export success of Danish butter and pork lay not just in strict village-level quality controls, but also to the fact that British retailers could identify the origin of an individual item. Networks, without government support, usually remained weak, making it difficult for farmers to control the quality and origin of 'Spanish oranges' or 'Corinth raisins' sold in Liverpool or Dublin, or to influence government farm policy. Instead, governments in agrarian economies especially saw the possibility of using cooperatives as a means to extend their own economic and political influence in village society, the very opposite of how the successful voluntary societies in countries such as Denmark operated.

11.5 Why Did Agrarian Parties Fail?

Farmers may have been the largest constituents in many countries, but they faced significant difficulties to organize into political parties. In addition to the free-rider problem, which rewarded individuals regardless of whether they contributed to the costs of party building, governments in countries including Hungary and Romania frequently repressed political opposition. When farmers found it difficult to organize to influence government policy, they resorted to private solutions by retreating from an inhospitable marketplace, and allocated their resources to defend the family farm (Bates 1981: 87). When governments were unable to offer farmers practical solutions to their economic problems, they sought their support by appealing to issues of social identity, especially nationalism.

By contrast, agrarian parties in countries such as Denmark or Sweden were successful because farming was relatively homogenous, reducing collective action costs to form lobbies, and governments enjoyed strong incentives to assist them because of the foreign exchange generated by agricultural exports. Indeed, self-sufficiency for a farmer with a dairy herd of 15 cows producing 3,000 litres of milk a year was hardly feasible, as it implied that the family had to consume around 125 litres each day. Governments helped farm groups create monopsonies to support prices, which avoided free-riding problems by legally obliging all producers to join, with the monitoring and enforcing being carried out by the farm organizations themselves. Surplus production was removed from the market and destroyed, and the cost divided among all producers, benefitting farmers financially, and strengthening democracy.

Several distinct scenarios therefore existed in European agriculture by the 1930s. Those countries where a significant number of farmers had incentives to organize, and their governments enjoyed economic and political advantages from cooperating with them; those cases were farmers organized, but governments saw few benefits in helping them; and finally, those cases where farmers failed to organize, and governments largely ignored the sector. It was only in parts of North-West Europe that family farmers successfully created producer cooperatives and family farmers were integrated into political parties.

11.6 When Did Conservative Farmers Become Fascists?

European farmers were frequently conservative, but rarely attracted to fascism. Not only did most find the fascist notion of a strong state, and hence an interfering one, unattractive, but fascist ideology was decidedly modern, appealing to the young urban middle classes.[3] A brief discussion of the experience of two pairs of countries, Italy and Spain, and Germany and France, suggests that farmers generally preferred traditional, hierarchical conservatism and it was only when this failed to protect their interests did a political space open for fascists to organize in the countryside.

In Italy, rural conflicts played a major part in bringing Mussolini to power. The demands of farm workers for better work conditions and land reform challenged the traditional patronage systems of the landed elites as well as the profitability of the modern commercial farming sector. Fascist groups successfully exploited class cleavages in the countryside and the fear of 'Bolshevism', but landowners and farmers only supported them because the government failed to protect their interests by ending strikes. Armed fascist groups, enjoyed the passive support of the police and judiciary, attacked trade unionists, and destroyed their property and meeting places.[4] Once Mussolini seized power, landowners and farmers benefitted from the repression of trade unions, while his followers used the patronage systems to allocate scarce land and work to their supporters.

In Spain there were also frequent harvest strikes and land occupations in the early 1930s but complaints about government enforcement of law and order were over its excesses, so came from trade unionists, rather than farmers. Few farmers supported fascist candidates in the elections of February 1936, although the failed coup a few months later gave them a simple choice of supporting either a Catholic backed military promising the repression of labour organizations, or an anticlerical government enjoying the support from groups that actively supported land invasions.

The fact that the class cleavage divided rural society in both Italy and Spain helped the landed elites to attract considerable support from small farmers in the defence of property rights. By contrast in Ireland, where the traditional landed elite also attempted to preserve their political influence and opposed land reform, the nationalist cleavage dominated, and explains why the Anglo-Irish lost their landed estates and saw their country houses being burnt down. Ireland, in this respect, reflects better the examples of Eastern Europe than those of Southern Europe.

Mann has suggested that France and Germany were both 'swing' countries, with the growth in fascism in France being halted only by the outbreak of war, while 'an advanced democracy … might have survived' in the Weimar Republic (Mann 2004: 40). Yet in the countryside the political space for fascism was always greater in Germany. German farm organizations were deeply divided along commodity and religious cleavages, but even the traditional conservative farm lobby, the Reichs-Landbund, supported Hitler in the presidential elections in March 1932, rather than Hindenburg, 'a Junker and symbol of conservative rural Germany' (Corni 1990: 31). The Nazi NSDAP had successfully infiltrated voluntary organizations, promising measures to restore farm prosperity and the self-respect of being a family farmer, helping the NSDAP to increase its vote from 2.6% in 1928 to 37.3% in July 1932. The government established the Reichsnährstand (RNS) to protect farm incomes and guarantee a supply of cheap food for urban consumers. However, priorities changed with rearmament and industrialization, while the abolition of political parties and elections made the farm vote unnecessary. The price mechanism, backed by state coercion, was now used to squeeze agriculture.

Angry farmers were also numerous in France, and Henry Dorgères claimed that his Green Shirts numbered around half a million by 1939, making it 'by far the strongest (peasant) organisation in the country' (in Paxton, 1997: 6). Nevertheless, its support was highly regional, failing to expand outside northern and western France, as most farmers elsewhere were already represented in specialized associations for commodities such as wheat and wine. Unlike Italy, the French government guaranteed law and order even during the conflictive years of the Popular Front. Dorgères failed to widen his support beyond the 'paysan', while his policy of making the family farm the centre of an authoritarian, corporatist, paternalistic, and autarkic regime made it similar, but no more successful, than the agrarian parties of Eastern Europe (Paxton 1997: 62; 66).

Before 1914, Western Europe had depended on Eastern Europe for part of its food needs. The Great War interrupted these flows, and Western governments were required to intervene in domestic agriculture to generate the necessary food to feed their civil populations and armed forces. Within a decade of hostilities ending, governments everywhere faced the very different problem of having to support domestic farm prices in the face of global gluts. In North-West Europe especially, the significant short-term difficulties that farmers experienced during the Great Depression were resolved with the institutionalization of government support which would help guarantee the long-term future of farming. By contrast, governments in Eastern Europe found it harder to help their farmers, forcing them instead to withdraw from the market to protect their farms.

This book has placed the family farm at the centre of economic and political change during the interwar period. It has argued that farmers were highly responsive to economic incentives, experimenting and expanding production when prices rose, but being equally quick to limit market transactions in periods of high volatility, or low farm prices. This was as true on the commercial farms in industrial societies, as it was for the small, fragmented holdings in the agrarian societies across large areas of Eastern and Southern Europe. Yet the hegemony of the family farm would be brief. In Western Europe, the post-1945 industrial growth rapidly depleted the countryside, even in the most backward regions, while farmers finally resolved the problem of how to produce large quantities of cheap food profitably. As labour left the land, larger farms were created to permit mechanization, while the growing use of farm inputs, such as fertilizers and diesel, were heavily subsidized by governments.

Large areas of Eastern Europe would be devastated once more between 1939 and 1945, and the region witnessed the massive movement of population in the wake of ethnic cleansing and boundary changes. Industrialization after 1945 helped reduce the numbers of family farmers, but the new communist governments looked to large mechanized collectives as the solution to supplying urban consumers with cheap food. These were not established with the same brutality as in Stalin's Russia, but they proved equally unsuccessful in creating the necessary work incentives to be efficient. As a result, it was Western European governments that by the early 1950s were beginning to have to come to terms with overproduction, while Eastern European countries were importing food.

Notes

1. Schultz (1945: 113) noted for the United States in 1945 that 'the failure of industrial output to expand during the thirties was the basic factor in the worsening of the agricultural situation. The main cause of the unproductive employment and low earnings in agriculture was unemployment in industry'.
2. Tomasevich (1955: table 40) gives a figure of 3366 calories for 1934–8 in Yugoslavia.
3. Mann (2004:79) notes that most fascist movements appealed 'disproportionately to the well educated—to students in high school and universities and to the most educated middle-class strata'.
4. Socialists were twice as likely to be killed as fascists, but between two and four times more likely to be arrested (Mann 2004: 121).

References

Bates, Robert H. 1981. *Markets and States in Tropical Africa. The Political Basis of Agricultural Policies*. Berkeley: University of California.

Corni, Gustavo. 1990. *Hitler's Peasants*. Oxford: Berg.

Mann, Michael. 2004. *Fascists*. Cambridge: Cambridge University Press.

Mazower, Mark. 1999. *Dark Continent. Europe's Twentieth Century*. London: Penguin.

Paxton, Robert O. 1997. *French Peasant Fascism*. Oxford: Oxford University Press.

Scheidel, Walter. 2017. *The Great Leveler: Violence and the History of Inequality from the Stone Age to the Twenty-First Century*. Princeton: Princeton.
Schultz, Theodore W. 1945. *Agriculture in an Unstable Economy*. New York and London: McGraw-Hill.
Tomasevich, Jozo. 1955. *Peasant, Politics, and Economic Change in Yugoslavia*. Stanford: Stanford University Press.
Zagoroff, S.D, Jeno Végh, and Alexander Bilimovich. 1955. *The Agricultural Economy of the Danubian Countries, 1935–45*. Edited by Food Research Institute. Stanford: Stanford University Press.

Index

J. Simpson, *Family Farmers, Land Reforms and Political Action*, Palgrave Studies in Economic History,
https://doi.org/10.1007/978-3-031-67281-1

The manufacturer's authorised representative in the EU is Springer Nature Customer Service Centre GmbH, Europaplatz 3, 69115 Heidelberg, Germany. If you have any concerns regarding our products, please contact ProductSafety@springernature.com

Printed and bound by CPI Group (UK) Ltd, Croydon, CR0 4YY
30/09/2026
02225595-0006